HICKMAN & ROSE
144 LIVERPOOL ROAD
LONDON N1 1LA

HICKMAN & ROSE
144 LIVERPOOL ROAD
LONDON N1 1LA

HICKMAN & ROSE
144 LIVERPOOL ROAD
LONDON N1 1LA

Active Defence

ACTIVE DEFENCE

A Lawyer's Guide to Police and Defence Investigation and
Prosecution and Defence Disclosure in Criminal Cases

2nd Edition

Roger Ede
*Solicitor, Secretary of the Law Society's
Criminal Law Committee*

and

Dr Eric Shepherd
*Chartered Forensic Psychologist
Investigative Science*

law society publishing

© The Law Society 2000

First published 1997
Revised first edition 1998
Second edition 2000

ISBN 1–85328–681–8

The material in Appendices 10 and 11 is Crown Copyright

Published by the Law Society
113 Chancery Lane, London WC2A 1PL

Typeset by Type Generation, London
Printed and bound by TJ International Ltd, Padstow, Cornwall

Contents

APPENDICES   493

Foreword

It is a pleasure to welcome the second edition of what surely must now be seen as an essential working tool for the practising solicitor and, one would hope, for barristers in criminal practice as well.

This is not an abstract treatise on the law: it is a guide to how to prepare a criminal defence and it appears at a time when law and practice are becoming increasingly complex. Its aim is to equip defence solicitors with the analytical and information-processing skills needed to challenge the prosecution case. The authors aim to provide a sound understanding of how police investigations are conducted and what information and evidence should be made available to the defence.

The interaction of law and practice is of the first importance. The practitioner needs to know how investigations are mounted, how information is collected and secured, and what matters must be disclosed to the defence. Our system is not one of trial by ambush but police officers are not always the best guide to what disclosure the defence requires. And non-disclosure can readily lead to injustice.

It is apparent, furthermore, that the uses, strengths and limitations of scientific evidence need to be at the forefront of the defence lawyer's mind. Again, these matters are not static: the advent of DNA testing has had a profound effect upon investigation and proof. But scientific evidence is not immune from challenge and one of the virtues of this book is that it provides a guide to the assessment of such evidence.

And of course we all have a deep interest in the integrity of the system of criminal justice. Miscarriages of justice arise as much from flawed defence work as from police malpractice, and they usually arise because fundamental shortcomings are not addressed at the earliest stages of proceedings. Close attention to this book should ensure that defence solicitors will avoid such shortcomings. I should not be surprised to find that copies of this book adorn shelves in chambers as well. I wish it every success.

Professor Leonard Leigh

Commission Member, Criminal Cases Review Commission

March 2000

Acknowledgements

In memory of John Dundon, a criminal defence solicitor who left no stone unturned.

Our thanks to Dr Richard Shepherd (Head of the Forensic Medicine Unit, St George's Hospital Medical School) for compiling the forensic glossary; Michael Hayden and a number of serving police officers for their comments upon the police investigation; Russell Stockdale and Dr Angela Gallop (founders of Forensic Access) for a defence view of prosecution forensic investigation and examination; Peter Swan (fingerprint analyst) and Dr Peter Green (forensic medical examiner) for their advice on their particular areas of forensic expertise; Andrew Macfarlane (barrister, formerly a solicitor) for his advice on a staged, systematic, focused and managed response by solicitors to prosecution disclosure; Professor Graham Davies (forensic psychologist) for his advice on particular aspects of witnessing; and Anthony Edwards (solicitor) for his comments on the text.

Abbreviations

ACCESS	assess; collect; collate; evaluate; survey; summarise
ACPO	Association of Chief Police Officers
ADVOKATE	amount of time under observation; distance; visibility; obstruction; known or seen before; any reason to remember; time lapse; error or material discrepancy
APS	Association of Police Surgeons
ASU	Adminstration Support Unit
BADMAN	Behavioural Analysis, Data Management, Auto indexing, Networking
BAFS	British Academy of Forensic Sciences
BCU	Basic Command Unit; Beat Crime Unit
CAD	computer-aided despatch
CATCHEM	Collating Homicide Expertise and Management
CID	Criminal Investigation Department
CIS	crime information system criminal intelligence system
CIT	case investigation team
CJA	Criminal Justice Act 1967
CJPOA	Criminal Justice and Public Order Act 1994
CM	Command Paper
CPA	crime pattern analysis
CPIA	Criminal Procedure and Investigations Act 1996
CPS	Crown Prosecution Service
CROP	covert rural observation post
CRS	crime reporting system
CSC	crime scene co-ordinator
CSM	crime scene manager
CSU	Crime Scene Unit

CTM	contact trace material
DCW	designated caseworker
DO	disclosure officer
DOB	date of birth
DoH	Department of Health
DNA	deoxyribonucleic acid
DSS	Department of Social Security
EAH	early adminstrative hearing
EFH	early first hearing
ESDA	electrostatic deposition analysis
FIB	Force Intelligence Bureau
FID	force intelligence developer
FIO	field intelligence officer
FIS	Force Intelligence System
FMT	forensic management team
FOA	first officer attending
FS	forensic scientist
FSS	Forensic Science Service
HMI	Her Majesty's Inspector
HMIC	Her Majesty's Inspectorate of Constabulary
HOLMES	Home Office Large and Major Enquiry System
IC	intelligence cell
INT	interrupt
IO	investigating officer
IRB	incident record book
IU	intelligence unit
IVRI	index of video-recorded interview
LIO	local intelligence officer
MCA	Magistrates' Court Act 1980
MCU	Major Crime Unit
ME	medical examiner
MIR	major incident room
MO	*modus operandi*
NCF	National Crime Faculty

NCS	National Crime Squad
NCIS	National Criminal Intelligence Service
NFA	no further action
NTCSSCI	National Training Centre for Scientific Support to Crime Investigation
OCR	optical character recognition
OIC	officer in charge
OIS	operational information management system
OT	overtalk
PACE	Police and Criminal Evidence Act 1984
PB	pocketbook
PCA	Police Complaints Authority
PDF	personal descriptive form
PDH	plea and directions hearing
PEACE	planning and preparation; engage and explain; account; close; evaluate
PHU	prisoner-handling unit
PII	public interest immunity
PIMS	police informant management system
PNC	Police National Computer
POLSA	police search adviser
PTI	pre-trial issues
RCS	Regional Crime Squad
RCCJ	Royal Commission on Criminal Justice
ROTI	record of tape-recorded interview
RTA	Road Traffic Act
SA	specialist adviser
SB	Special Branch
SCU	Serious Crime Unit
SDN	short descriptive note
SE3R	survey, extract, read, review, recall
SIO	senior investigating officer
SIU	Special Investigation Unit
SOCO	scene of crime officer

SSM	scientific support manager
SSO	scientific support officer
SSU	scientific support unit
THEMA	thematic emergence of anomaly
TIC	taken into consideration
TIE	trace, interview, eliminate
USG	uniform support group
VFM	value for money

CHAPTER 1

The CPIA in practice: the experience of the legal profession and the need for active defence

> *'The objective of the criminal justice system is the control of crime. But in a civilized society that objective cannot be pursued in disregard of other values. That everybody who comes before our courts is entitled to a fair trial is axiomatic...In our adversarial system, in which the police and the prosecution control the investigatory process, an accused's right to fair disclosure is an inseparable part of his right to a fair trial.'*

Lord Justice Steyn (1995)[1]

THE ILLUSION OF QUALITY INVESTIGATION

In the first edition of *Active Defence* we drew attention to the fact that the community and the courts are led to believe that the evidence presented in cases by the prosecution, and upon which they rely, is the product of a quality investigative service rendered by police officers, civilian support staff and forensic scientists:

- who are professionally trained;
- who are subject to supervision and quality controls;
- who have open minds;
- who are committed to exposing to the prosecution and the defence, the gaps and anomalies in:
  - the police investigation;
  - the police representation of the case; and
  - the prosecution evidence.

We asserted that the reality does not support the belief. What is presented to the court in all too many cases is a complex, collaborative illusion.

The evidence of the illusion was widespread at the time of the first edition of *Active Defence*. It was to be found in many cases that had come before the courts and had prompted adverse judicial commentary. A wide spectrum of research findings and policy documents[2-11] had shown that judicial disquiet had been, and continued to be, well founded. The truth of the matter was that:

- many police officers, scientific support staff, medical examiners, and even forensic scientists, were untrained for their investigative tasks;

- there was no real supervision;

- there were no real quality controls;

- there were strong group pressures on police officers, civilian staff and external personnel:
  - to attach criminality to an individual within the frame rather than to investigate objectively;
  - to ignore shortcomings in the conduct and outcome of their decision-making and actions, and those of others, involved in the investigative process.

We argued that the only prospect of demonstrating the illusion to the court was to allow the defence relatively free access to unused material held by the police in the case and to make the court the only arbiter of what sensitive material should be disclosed.

The changes introduced by the Criminal Procedure and Investigations Act 1996 (CPIA) are summarised in Appendix 1. As a result of these, the judgement of the *investigating officer* (IO) and the *disclosure officer* (DO) has largely replaced that of the prosecutor.

Before the passage of the Bill through Parliament, the government had explained that in the future there would be a heavy reliance on the police service to identify material that ought to be disclosed, given that the material itself would not necessarily be scrutinised by the prosecutor.[12] The IO decides what material is relevant to the investigation and what must be recorded and retained. The IO and the DO, who in the majority of cases may be one and the same person, are effectively responsible for deciding what material fits the tests for disclosure and for categorising certain material as sensitive.

As the prosecutor's duty to disclose is limited to material that the prosecutor has obtained or inspected, the initial decisions made by police officers are critical in determining what information comes before the prosecutor and is available to the defence. It is the police who decide what material undermines their own case and, relying upon the defence's written statement, what unused material is helpful to the defence case. The CPS has acknowledged that substantial responsibility and trust are now placed upon the police.[13-14]

THE LIGHT OF EXPERIENCE

One year on from the implementation of the CPIA, at a seminar organised by the Association of Chief Police Officers (ACPO) and the National Crime Faculty in spring 1998, it was apparent that the Act was not being applied properly.[15] The results were presented of a national survey[16] of police forces on disclosure. One of the key problems in practice was identified as items regularly being left off the MG6 series of forms.[17]

The results of a national review of disclosure by the CPS[18] were also presented. Police completion of schedules was identified as being consistently poor. The following shortcomings were extremely common:

• inadequate, incomplete or missing schedules;

• poor police descriptions on schedules;

• relevant materials not copied;

• difficulty in contacting the disclosure officer.

Later that year, an *ad hoc* survey of disclosure by the Chairman of the Bar Council[19] produced an appalling catalogue of non-disclosure.

In 1999 the Criminal Bar Association[20] and the Law Society[21] conducted surveys concerning the operation of the CPIA. Salient detail from each survey is presented below.

Salient detail from the Law Society survey

Defence solicitors were invited either to express their satisfaction with the disclosure provisions or to raise concerns about their operation and provide examples of particular difficulties in practice. Respondents were typically partners in their firms, with an average of 15 years experience of criminal defence work.

Over nine out of 10 respondents said that they had not identified any reliable way for defence lawyers or the courts to establish the comprehensiveness and specificity of police non-sensitive schedules.

Eight out of 10 respondents said that:

- schedules of non-sensitive unused material are either *unlikely* or *highly unlikely to be comprehensive and reliable*;

- the information listed on the non-sensitive unused material schedule is either *insufficiently* or *highly insufficiently described,* thus rendering the prosecutor and the defence unable to consider the disclosure officer's assessment as to disclosability;

- disclosure officers' analyses as to whether items listed on non-sensitive unused material schedules undermine the prosecution case or assist the defence case are either *unreliable* or *highly unreliable*;

- the CPS and other prosecuting authorities do not usually inspect the items listed on the unused material schedule before making primary or secondary disclosure decisions, i.e. they do not usually call for sight of items listed on unused material schedules, relying instead upon disclosure officers' judgement;

- prosecuting authorities' decisions on secondary disclosure are either *unreliable* or *highly unreliable*;

- disclosure officers' and prosecuting authorities' endeavours to ensure that the continuing duty to consider disclosure is complied with, e.g. by providing the prosecuting trial advocate with copies of items of unused material, are either *inadequate* or *highly inadequate*;

- the disclosure provisions of the CPIA are 'not working well' or 'working badly' in practice.

Seven out of 10 respondents said that the disclosure provisions of the CPIA are unworkable in the interests of justice.

Six out of 10 respondents said that when requesting disclosure of unused material, the prosecution response was either non-compliant or highly non-compliant.

Examples of documents that were not listed in schedules of unused material included:

- records of telephone calls to the police from members of the public reporting a crime;

- records of messages between the police control room and individual officers, describing the offence and the offender;

- statements made by witnesses whom the police were not calling;

- previous drafts of witnesses' statements and notes of interviews with witnesses;

- previous convictions of prosecution witnesses;

- details of people who were spoken to by the police but from whom statements were not taken;

- crime reports;

- incident logs;

- records of taped interviews with suspects who were not charged;

- incident report books;

- video films of incidents.

Examples of documents that were listed but inadequately described in schedules of unused material included:

- the contents of police officers' notebooks;

- the contents of statements of witnesses who were not being called;

- the content of telephone calls to the police from members of the public reporting a crime;

- the content of messages between the police control room and individual officers;

- documents which were identified by a police reference number instead of a title;

- documents which were described only as 'a bundle of documents';

- references to 'fingerprints' without saying whether they had been identified and, if so, whose fingerprints they matched;

- references to 'witness statements' without saying to whom they related;

- references to 'videos' without giving any further information about their content or where or when the films were taken.

Examples of non-disclosure included:

- the statements of witnesses helpful to the defence;

- the addresses of witnesses helpful to the defence;

- a complainant's criminal record;

- the first description of an offender that did not match the accused;

- a forensic report supporting the accused's version of events;

- a medical report supporting the accused's version of events;

- a 999 call from a member of the public supporting the accused's version of events;

- the fact that the complainant had made similar allegations against other people in the past;

- the fact that a person arrested but not charged had accused someone other than the defendant;

- the fact that the complainant and a prosecution witness were initially arrested and interviewed as suspects;

- a video interview in which a child witness had given a contradictory account of the alleged offence;

- a statement by a complainant that her original statement was not accurate;

- CCTV tapes.

One respondent reported a case in which a police officer, who was the subject of a formal complaint of assault by the accused and was the alleged victim of an assault by the accused, was also the disclosure officer responsible for deciding what information should be released to the defence. In this case, the police withheld a record of a telephone call to the police station by a member of the public stating that at the time of the alleged incident members of the public were in fact being assaulted by the police.

Typical comments as to why the disclosure provisions of the CPIA are unworkable, were:

- It is not possible for a police officer to know what documents might assist the defence.

- It is difficult for an officer closely connected with a case to disclose information that undermines the case.

- Police officers are not qualified or properly trained to make disclosure decisions about the defence case.

- You cannot expect a police disclosure officer involved in a case to be non-partisan.

- The whole system is very 'hit and miss'.

The following observations exemplify adverse views concerning the conduct of the CPS:

- 'my experience of the [CPS] lawyer with conduct of that case is that disclosure is an issue for the disclosure officer and not her and that she is not prepared to give any independent consideration to whether items are appropriate for disclosure beyond reiterating the officer's view [that they are not]' (a consultant with 10 years' experience).

- 'requests to CPS caseworkers go unanswered or unmet up to and including trial dates. We often have to obtain an order from the trial judge before we can obtain satisfactory disclosure' (a senior partner with 25 years' experience).

- 'CPS are unable or unwilling to challenge those (police) decisions [that material is not disclosable]' (a partner with 10 years' experience).

- 'the CPS say that they will keep their disclosure obligations under continuing review, but the prosecution advocate does not have any documents other than those relied upon in evidence' (a partner with 19 years' experience).

6

- 'in everyday cases, the CPS do not ever see the documents in the schedule before deciding that the prosecution case is not undermined. How can they possibly make this decision without assessing the papers? (a sole practitioner with 14 years' experience).

Examples of non-disclosure from the Criminal Bar Association's survey

The following examples were reported by barristers who were prosecuting as well as defending.

- *Grievous bodily harm*. Failure to disclose a statement of a witness who said that the defendant was acting in self-defence because the defence was alibi.

- *Actual bodily harm*. Failure to disclose a call to the police station from the complainant's wife (who was not a witness) in which she said that a man was attacking her husband but no weapon was involved. The complainant alleged that he had been hit with a bottle.

- *Attempted murder*. Failure to disclose that the initial description of the assailant was of a person of mixed race and that a Caucasian hair had been found in the balaclava. The defendant was black.

- *Robbery*. Failure to disclose that the complainant had picked out someone other than the defendant when shown a photo album. The complainant's statement had given the impression that the defendant had been arrested after the complainant had been shown the album. In fact, the arrest was as a result of information given to the police.

- *Indecency with a child*. Failure to disclose that a video with the child complainant had been edited to remove material that would undermine the complainant's credibility.

- *Armed robbery*. Failure to disclose that a prosecution witness had been shown the defendant a half-hour after the robbery and had said that he was not involved.

- *Malicious wounding*. Failure to disclose an earlier statement by an eyewitness that he had not actually seen the alleged attack as he had looked away, but was relating what the complainant had told him afterwards.

- *Robbery with firearms*. Failure to disclose that a witness had been taken to a location containing the defendant and had failed to identify him.

- *Rape*. Notes taken by the police when interviewing the complainant shortly after the alleged rape were described in the schedule to appear as notes taken during a video interview of the complainant. The complainant's version of events in the notes was inconsistent with that given in the video.

- *Robbery*. Failure to disclose a security video which provided the defendant with an alibi.

- **Robbery**. Failure to disclose a crime report entry showing a description of the offence by two prosecution witnesses, which did not agree with their formal statements.

- **Malicious wounding**. Failure to disclose a crime report entry that the assault was by 'persons unknown'. In a formal statement, the complainant accused the defendant who was known to him.

- **Rape of children; indecent assault**. Failure to disclose a video interview with a child witness who said that she was present in the room but did not see the event alleged take place.

- **Attempted rape of a young child**. Failure to disclose a video recording of the complainant's evidence, which was inconsistent with (disputed) admissions on which the prosecution case was based.

- **Robbery**. Failure to disclose a call to the police station from the complainant in which he indicated that three youths were responsible for robbing him. In his formal statement he only referred to the defendant.

- **Theft**. Failure to disclose a shop security video tape which showed that the defendant was not present with two prosecution witnesses when they said that he was.

- **Affray/ABH**. Failure to disclose a police interview with a co-suspect (who was not charged and who was unknown to the defendant), which supported the defendant's account.

- **Aggravated burglary**. Failure to disclose a police message, a description in an officer's notebook and an entry in a crime report, which all gave a different description from that in the complainant's statement. The issue in the case was identity.

- **Murder**. Failure to disclose the statements of three eyewitnesses who gave statements that the defendant was present, but a mere bystander, because the defence asserted in interview was alibi.

- **Malicious wounding**. Failure to disclose an incident log, which showed that police officers at the scene (who did not make statements), had observed that the complainant was drunk. The issue in the case was did the complainant fall downstairs or was he pushed?

- **Grievous bodily harm**. Failure to disclose a crime report entry that two witnesses at the scene (who had not made statements) had said that the offender was white. The defendant was black.

- **Actual bodily harm**. Failure to disclose a police message that a witness at the scene had said that the complainant was the aggressor. In a formal statement, the witness said that the defendant was the aggressor.

We will return to these survey findings throughout this text. Taken together the two surveys have produced examples, staggering in their numbers, in their breadth and in their implications, of serious and fundamental failures of the police service and the CPS to operate the Act's provisions properly. In particular, the following should be noted:

- disclosure officer omissions;

- lack of sufficient detail about unused material in schedules;

- disclosure officers having an insufficient grasp of the nature of their role and the gravity of not performing it properly;

- CPS lawyers failing to ensure that they receive sufficient schedules;

- CPS lawyers failing to apply the primary disclosure test properly;

- the police and the CPS failing to deal properly with secondary disclosure.

Vital documents continue to be missed out of schedules. When they are included, all too often the lists of material in the schedules are not in sufficient detail, rendering the information meaningless. The extent to which the CPS take things at face value at the primary disclosure stage, rather than making proper enquiries of the disclosure officer, is a matter of enduring alarm.

Practitioners are left with the impression that the police and the CPS approach disclosure in the wrong spirit – determined to disclose as little as possible instead of considering what, in fairness and justice, should be disclosed. The whole procedure under the Act depends upon comprehensive disclosure schedules.

IDENTIFIED RISKS AND PROPOSED REMEDIES

The Crown Prosecution Service

In early 1999, David Calvert-Smith QC, the Director of Public Prosecutions, told a conference[22] that the CPS was committed to scrupulously complying with the duty of disclosure. He went on to say: 'I am concerned, and have been for some time, that at present there is a significant number of cases in which the prosecution are not so complying.' Commenting upon the consequences of non-compliance he observed:

> 'innocent people will be convicted because the prosecution has failed to disclose material which would have enabled him to show his innocence...guilty people will be acquitted, because the late disclosure of material will poison the minds of the judge and jury against the prosecution.'

The CPS Inspectorate found it necessary to make recommendations about improvements in dealing with unused material in 18 of the 29 branches it had inspected by March 1999.[23] Out of 41 reasons for recommendations, this area of improvement was the third most frequent.

The police service

There has been no response by the police service to the research findings of the Law Society and the Criminal Bar Association. There has been no fundamental research to examine police performance concerning disclosure (or indeed retention of information) from a quality control or quality assurance perspective.

The service has yet to recognise the extent to which the cumulative failure of officers to fulfil their duties under CPIA is damaging, and will increasingly damage, its good name. As the service does not perceive there to be a significant problem in the conduct of police officers, no immediate remedies have been proposed to put the service's house in order.

The legal profession

The Law Society has called for urgent action to deal with these disclosure failures:[24]

> 'To avoid the criminal justice system falling into disrepute. The status of the disclosure officer must be enhanced. He must receive proper training and should never be a witness in the case or involved in the investigation. Certain key documents should always be copied to the prosecutor and the defence, such as the crime report and the previous convictions of prosecution witnesses. Prosecutors must be much more rigorous in their examination of police schedules and unused material and much more generous in their response to requests for non-sensitive unused material from the defence. Prosecuting advocates should always look at all the unused material at as early a stage as possible. These measures should reassure defendants who are being tried currently. In the longer term, a safer system must be found.'

A barrister, responding to the CBA survey, spoke for all those who seek to protect the integrity of the criminal justice system in suggesting that the prosecutor should disclose *as a matter of course*:

- copy notebook entries of each officer;

- the defendant's custody record;

- the custody record of any co-accused or person arrested but not charged;

- the interview (tape or summary) of any person arrested but not charged;

- the crime report;

- the command and control log.

The government's response

Arguably, it was inevitable that the government would have to take notice of the problems that have been revealed concerning the operation of the CPIA:[25]

> 'The Government is aware of concerns about the operation of the disclosure provisions following changes to the law, which were implemented in April 1997...the Home Secretary has asked Home Office officials to consider what further needs to be done.'

The Home Office has now set up a steering group to commission and oversee research on the operation of the Act.[26] A report is unlikely before April 2001. This will come four years after the Act's implementation. During this period, over a quarter of a million people will have been prosecuted and convicted, after pleading not guilty, in the magistrates' courts and Crown Courts. We cannot guarantee that the process by which they were convicted was fair.

At the time of writing, concerns about the operation of the Act had led the Attorney General to issue draft guidelines on disclosure, for consultation. These are referred to later in the text in relation to the provisions which they bear upon.[27]

ACTIVE DEFENCE

In respect of the defence role a distinguished legal observer wrote:[28]

> 'the role of the defence lawyer acting within the rules in the best interests of his clients is not a negotiable part of the system. It is a vital safeguard of the innocent citizen from false accusation and of the guilty that, if he is to be convicted, it should be done according to due process and according to law on the basis of proof beyond a reasonable doubt.'

In the first edition of this book we posed the question: how does the police service regard the defence role, which it necessarily has to adopt when making disclosure decisions? We reported upon our experience of this matter, now reinforced by the experience since the enactment of the CPIA and which we have reported above. Too many police officers either fail to understand the defence solicitor's role or regard it in a negative way as an unnecessary barrier to the process of convicting the 'plainly guilty' rather than as an essential safeguard.

The fundamental position that we stated in the first edition remains unchanged.

It is ironic that the police service, which exercises little or no quality control over the way in which it tackles investigations, has been given this vital quality control task: to reveal to its opponents the weaknesses in its investigative system.

The police service can hardly be expected to reveal its own shortcomings. With current restrictions on expenditure, prosecutors are often hard pressed to carry out a full review of a file before trial, let alone to take on new work.[29] Hence it falls squarely on the defence to bring the realities described above to the court's attention.

Paradoxically, defence solicitors, who are denied access to the fruits of police investigation, have been criticised for not being sufficiently proactive. They have been accused of relying instead upon the manifest inadequacies in the prosecution case as the route to an acquittal. This reactive approach by defence solicitors is due in part to the fact that the defence solicitor can never become an investigator to the same extent as the police officer. The time scale between the commission of an offence and identifying a suspect often prohibits an investigation of the sort mounted by the police. The police officer has powers of entry, seizure and interrogation, which the defence does not. As the Devlin Committee observed: 'In criminal cases, the state has, in the police, an agency for the discovery of evidence superior to anything which even the wealthiest defendant could employ.'[30] Furthermore, there is the battle to be fought to obtain criminal legal aid to resource a comprehensive analysis of a case, let alone investigation by a solicitor.

However, by taking a systematic approach to analysing the evidence and investigating the case from the moment that the first instructions are received and thereafter through all the stages of disclosure, the active defender is able to take the prosecution case apart to examine the processes by which the evidence came into existence. This book arms you with the required analytical and information-processing skills. It provides you with a sound knowledge of how police investigations are conducted and what information and evidence should have been collected and should have been made available to the defence. It provides you with a clear understanding of how evidence presented by the prosecution may be invalid and unreliable. With these skills and with this knowledge and understanding, you will be able to challenge the limits that are otherwise placed on your defender role.

Lawyers' experience of the CPIA since its enactment has provided ample evidence that the concerns we expressed in the first edition were well founded and that there is a continuing need for active defence.

HUMAN RIGHTS ACT 1998

Will the CPIA survive the introduction of the Human Rights Act 1998 on 2 October 2000? Lawyers will be able to make challenges based upon the shortcomings of the Act. Structural challenges may be made to the CPIA because of the absence of independent safeguards in relation to decisions about disclosure and the need for the service of a defence case statement before secondary disclosure is given. These challenges may be argued before the higher courts on a judicial review of the CPS or an appeal against conviction. The higher courts would then have power to grant a declaration of incompatibility.[31]

Notes

1. R. v. *Brown* [1995] 1 Cr. App. R. 191 C.A.

2. Ryan, P. (1993) *The Future of Police Training*. Bramshill: Police Staff College.

3. Audit Commission. (1993) *Helping with Enquiries: Tackling Crime Effectively*. London: HMSO.

4. Association of Chief Police Officers/Forensic Science Service. (1996) *Using Forensic Science Effectively*. Birmingham: Forensic Science Service.

5. Tilley, N. and Ford, A. (1996) *Forensic Science and Crime Investigation. Crime Detection and Prevention Series: Paper 73*. London: Home Office Research Group.

6. Robertson, G. (1992) *The Role of Police Surgeons. RCCJ Research Study No. 6*. London: HMSO.

7. Baldwin, J. and Maloney, T. (1992) *Supervision of Police Investigations in Serious Criminal Cases. RCCJ Research Study No. 4*. London: HMSO.

8. Maguire, M. and Norris, C. (1992) *The Conduct and Supervision of Criminal Investigations. RCCJ Research Study No. 5*. London: HMSO.

9. Irving, B. and Dunningham, C. (1993) *Human Factors in the Quality Control of CID Investigation. RCCJ Research Study No. 21*. London: HMSO.

10. Stockdale, J. (1993) *Management and Supervision of Police Interviews. Police Research Series: Paper No. 5*. London: Home Office Police Department.

11. Shepherd, E. (1996) *Becoming Skilled*. London: Law Society Publishing.

12. Mortimer, A. (1994) 'Asking the right questions'. *Policing*, 10, 111–24.

13. Disclosure. (1995) CM 2864 Home Office Consultation Paper. London: HMSO.

14. Mills, B. (1996) 'Disclosure: the role of the CPS'. Paper delivered at the British Academy of Forensic Sciences seminar on the future of disclosure. Zander, M. (1994) 'Every which way'. *Police Review*, 18 February, 24–5.

15. Association of Chief Police Officers and National Crime Faculty seminar 'Disclosure and the CPIA: implementation in practice', Police Staff College, Bramshill, 12 May 1998.

16. South Wales Police. (1998) 'Criminal Procedure and Investigations Act 1996 disclosure review'. Presented at Association of Chief Police Officers and National Crime Faculty seminar 'Disclosure and the CPIA: implementation in practice', Police Staff College, Bramshill, 12 May 1998.

17. The MG6 forms are used by the police to reveal unused material to the prosecutor. The MG6C also discloses a list of unused material to the defence.

18. Crown Prosecution Service. (1998), 'Disclosure, the CPS experience'. Presented at Association of Chief Police Officers and National Crime Faculty seminar 'Disclosure and the CPIA: implementation in practice', Police Staff College, Bramshill, 12 May 1998.

19. Hallett H. (1998) 'Chairman's column'. *Counsel*, December.

20. Criminal Bar Association. (1999) CPIA 1996 Disclosure Provisions Survey.

21. Law Society. (1999) CPIA 1996 Disclosure Provisions Survey.

22. Calvert-Smith, D. (1999) 'Problems and solutions'. Address to Crown Prosecution Service Disclosure Seminar, 18 May.

23. Chief Inspector of the Crown Prosecution Service. (1999) Annual Report of the Crown Prosecution Service 1998–9.

24. The Criminal Practitioners Newsletter, July 1999.

25. Lord Burlison, written Parliamentary answer 6th May 1999.

26. Home Office Justice and Victims Unit, Disclosure Evaluation Steering Group.

27. Attorney General. Draft Guidelines on Disclosure: A Consultation Document. 14 February 2000.

28. Zander, M. (1994) 'Every which way'. *Police Review*, 18 February, 24–5.

29. Edwards, A. (1996) 'The defence perspective'. Paper delivered at the British Academy of Forensic Sciences seminar on the future of disclosure.

30. Lord Devlin. (1976) *Report on Evidence of Identification in Criminal Cases.* London: HMSO.

31. Emmerson, B. (1999) 'The CPIA and the Human Rights Act – Compatibility'. Address to the British Academy of Forensic Sciences. 1 December 1999.

CHAPTER 2

The framework of investigation: from offence to evidence

THE POLICE CASE, THE PROSECUTION EVIDENCE AND THE POLICE INVESTIGATION

Police investigation is triggered when the police decide to respond to information that an offence has been committed or is likely to be committed. A complex infrastructure of units, teams, and specialists is mobilised, with police and civilian support staff, and, where necessary, external specialists gathering, recording and exchanging information, and making decisions in the light of these activities. Their investigative efforts provide the basis for identifying the actual, or intended offence, and create the *police case*. This is a representation of reality: a constructed narrative of events and outcomes, which the police believe to be, literally, the case as to what happened prior to, during and after an offence.

This effort also produces *prosecution evidence*. This is oral and written testimony and, perhaps, exhibit material with a potential to assist the identification and interviewing of a possible suspect, and subsequent charging of that individual as the first step towards possible prosecution. The police case, the prosecution evidence and the police investigation are thus interdependent (Figure 2.1).

The CPS, the defence and the courts are therefore wholly dependent on the objectivity and integrity of the police image of 'what happened' – who did what to whom, when, how, why and to what effect – in terms of:

- the actions of suspects, victims and witnesses;
- the actions of investigators: police officers, civilian support staff and external providers of specialist services.

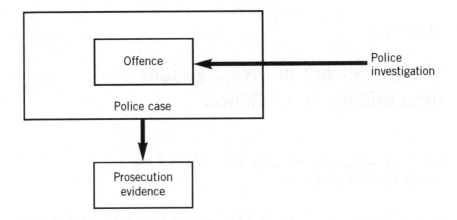

Figure 2.1 The police investigation, police case and prosecution evidence

THE FUNDAMENTALS OF INVESTIGATION

The aim of investigation

Investigation is the process of testing whether a report of an offence – an actual or intended illegal act or omission and its accompanying mental state – is able to be supported by evidence.[1]

The aim is straightforward: to reconstruct the actual or intended offence assisted by the evidence. This offers the prospect of identifying and apprehending a suspect, if not already apprehended, and putting that individual before the courts.

Investigative actions and outcomes: accountability and integrity

Investigation involves decision-making and, specifically, actions. The term 'action' has a discrete connotation in the police context. An 'action' is a specific activity directed at: identifying sources of information and potential evidence – individuals, entities, physical circumstances; collecting, collating, evaluating and responding to derived information and potential evidence.

'Actions' may be specified by a police manager, supervisor or generated by the individual police officer or civilian. An action may be a matter of routine, speculative effort, or a response to an earlier action or to changing circumstances. Actions have to be recorded, be this in manuscript on a form, in a book or log, as an entry in a computer document, or electronically. The logic for this is simple and critical: the requirement for accountability of actions. Fellow police and civilian colleagues, managers, supervisors, the CPS, the defence, the courts, and, where necessary, any external authority, body or institution, are all able to know from the record 'what happened' – 'warts and all'. This enables assessment of performance: the effectiveness and probity – the ethics – of investigative effort expended (or withheld). Records of 'actions' are the fundamental basis for quality control of decisions, actions and deployment of resource by those directing and those being directed in an investigation.

The CPS, the courts, the defence and the public presume that in any police investigation the service will act with integrity in that:

- the search is lawful for people, information and exhibit material to enable:
  - the reconstruction of the offence (reactive investigation); or
  - the pre-emption of, or the timely arrest of those engaged in, crime having identified and monitored the criminal (proactive investigation);
- decision-making and actions, and the reporting of the results of these, are directed by an unqualified commitment to fidelity, accuracy and probity.

INVESTIGATION AND THE DIFFERENT MODES OF POLICING

Reactive policing

The traditional mode of policing has been *reactive*, i.e. investigation has been *demand-led*.

If a crime comes to police attention, response decisions have to be made. Reactive investigation involves conducting *post factum* inquiries, i.e. a backward search following the commission of an identifiable offence in order to identify likely suspects, if a suspect has not already been apprehended.

Despite very wide differences in offences and the investigative demands involved, every reactive investigation follows a basic sequence (Table 2.1).

Reactive investigation involves:

- *the search for witnesses*: at or near the scene or in the vicinity, who are able to give an account of the movements, attributes and routines of the victim and the offender, whether or not a suspect has been identified or arrested;

1.	Crime reported, discovered or detected.
2.	Police officers respond.
3.	Investigation, i.e. the search for, and if successful the arrest of, the suspected offender, the search for sources of evidence, and collection of evidence (testimonial and forensic): • **preliminary investigation**: initial and early commitment of investigative resource (police officers, scientific support staff, medical examiners and other forensic specialists) at the scene and in the vicinity of the incident leading to a decision to continue or discontinue investigation; • **continuing investigation**: further commitment of investigative resource including the analysis of forensic evidence in force and by external providers.

Table 2.1 The reactive investigation sequence

- *the search for physical evidence*: the systematic examination of the material location and the vicinity for marks, imprints, impressions and trace evidence, including actual items, with a potential evidential value;

- *the search for crime-solving information*: the consultation of material collated in information systems, interviewing of witnesses and suspects, and analysis and 'reality-testing' of their descriptions and accounts.[2]

In effect, reactive investigation subsumes the search along two parallel, interdependent paths to translate the circumstances of the offence into evidence enabling a suspect to be put before the courts:

- *the path of testimonial investigation*: obtaining descriptions and accounts from victims, witnesses, onlookers, people who live in the vicinity (*house-to-house enquiries*), from the public (*questionnaire enquiries*), suspects, sources of alibi, police officers, and others with knowledge that has a potential bearing upon the material circumstances of the police case, the emerging evidence and the police investigation;

- *the path of forensic investigation*: obtaining physical material derived from key individuals in the case, key locations, and key objects (including vehicles), and submitting these to scientific examination and analysis informed by contextual information about ambient conditions, contact and potential contamination.[3-4]

The community and the courts require proper reactive investigation since this is the only guarantee that victims and suspects are justly served, rightful prosecution and conviction occur, and miscarriages of justice are minimised. It is therefore incumbent on investigators to conduct, or to commission, whatever inquiries the circumstances dictate to fulfil effectiveness, ethical and integrity criteria. This has obvious cost implications.

The police service now has to think in terms of resource, ultimately expressed in terms of budgets and the cost of every aspect of investigative effort. Two allied factors – cost and likelihood of a detection – have required an evolution in the police approach to reactive investigation.

- Proper investigation of commonly occurring offences, which may be serious but are deemed to be of 'lesser' seriousness, can be costly. The cost of investigating a murder or a complex crime, e.g. fraud, is inherently open-ended. The circumstances are necessarily unique.

- Deploying officers to investigate crimes which occur with high frequency (volume crime), e.g. burglary, is particularly expensive.

The nature of reactive investigation is fundamentally determined by cost considerations, specifically cost–benefit, or value for money (VFM).[5-6] This is achieved in two ways.

- All police managers and supervisors are now required:
  - to predict what resource – manpower, time, specialist and forensic – is needed ahead of the circumstances which generate the demand to react;
  - to limit expenditure of resource – directing investigative effort that is selective rather than comprehensive, in order to keep costs down: the aim being to deploy the minimum resource to get a 'positive' outcome.
- Forces employ screening systems, matching the speed of response, and nature of reactive investigation, to the reported circumstances.[7-8] Within all screening systems a major cost–benefit factor is the likelihood of achieving a 'result': a detection.

Proactive policing

In 1993 the Audit Commission[9] exhorted the service to 'target the criminal and not the crime', and to engage in *proactive policing* 'which targets prolific and serious criminals'. The concept of proactivity was by no means new. For years it had been the guiding principle behind the work of specialist police units, e.g. squads at various levels within the force tasked with investigating particular types of crime, and the national structure of Regional Crime Squads, (RCSs).

The Audit Commission, however, saw widespread commitment to proactive policing as the rational, economically driven response to rising workload and pressure on resources. Proactive policing was offered as providing VFM in dealing with:

- *volume crime* (high-frequency offending), e.g. burglary, a substantial proportion of which is committed by a relatively small number of people, a 'hard core';

- *serious organised crime* e.g. large-scale drugs importation and supply, planned and executed by 'professional' criminals operating across borders;

- *serial crime* – a series of similar offences committed by the same individual;

- *'hot spot' crime* – crimes occurring in particular locations but not necessarily committed by the same people.

The aim is to target the criminal who:

- is unidentified but known to operate in a specific location; or

- is identified and is monitored in the processes of organisation and planning 'ahead of the offence', i.e. before the offence if possible, or just as the criminal seeks to effect the offence.

At the heart of proactive policing lies intelligence – the critical assessment of a recurrent crime situation, the systematic collection, collation, evaluation, analysis and integration of information to identify patterns and key persons. *Information* is collected, particularly through maximum use of covert methods: surveillance, informants and undercover operations. It becomes *intelligence* through the systematic processes of collation, evaluation (in terms of the reliability of its source and the status of information) and analysis conducted by intelligence staff. Complex matching and analysis of patterns and concentration of linkages in relation to offending enable further targeting and use of covert methods, and so the cycle continues.[10] For this reason, proactive policing is deemed to be *intelligence-led*.

> *'Intelligence-led policing may rely upon traditional paperwork but it implies that the police have access to computerised systems for storing, searching, and analysing information. Indeed the availability of such systems underlies the increased use of intelligence-led approaches. It signals a quantum leap forward in the development of them and allows the police to interface with similar systems held by other agencies such as telecommunications companies, Customs and Excise or the Department of Social Security (DSS). In that sense intelligence-led policing is increasingly associated with an IT-based approach.'*[11]

20

The Audit Commission acknowledged that commitment to proactive, intelligence-led policing required wholesale institutional change. It involves fundamental reorganisation, implementing management models, installing systems and redeploying resources, for a force to engage effectively and ethically in proactive investigation.[12-15]

The common pattern has been for a force to carry out a 'force intelligence review' and to institute:

• A *Force Intelligence System* (FIS) for the processing and storage of intelligence derived from all sources and informants.

• A *Force Intelligence Bureau* (FIB) that is located centrally and is organised:

  – to support the development of the FIS and the collection, input and analysis of information force-wide, channelled through intelligence cells (ICs) throughout the force area within Basic Command Units (BCUs), i.e. local 'divisions', and the IC of the Major Crime Unit (MCU) (or each MCU where the force has more than one);

  – to provide a central point for authorising electronic surveillance and the collection of information from a variety of external sources and agencies;

  – to provide a source registry for all informants, operating a police informant management system (PIMS) and processing all requests for informant registration;

  – to operate crime desks, where considered appropriate, dedicated to the analysis of intelligence aimed at target operations, e.g. burglary, drugs, robbery, firearms;

  – to provide a strategic IC to support MCU work.

• Training of all officers to enable them to understand, and thus equip them to contribute to, the operation of the *intelligence cycle*: a continuous loop of activity – direction, collection, evaluation, analysis, development, dissemination, direction, and so on.[16] The steps in practice should be as follows:

  – Force and area plans direct the development of priorities for information collection.

  – Information is collected from a variety of sources: interviewing of victims and witnesses, informants, 'Crimestoppers', surveillance in its many forms, observations, stop searches, analysis of crime patterns, repeat victimisation, other agencies and institutions.

  – The reliability of the source and the accuracy of the information is assessed at a number of levels. The officer obtaining the information applies the 4 x 4 criteria for reliability and accuracy (see Table 2.2). These assessments are screened and intelligence, once on the FIS, is subject to 'weeding'.

- Intelligence is evaluated and analysed within ICs by Intelligence Co-ordinators and Crime Prevention Officers (CPOs). Using the FIS and *crime pattern analysis* (CPA) information is linked and further developed as intelligence.
- Target packages containing details of identified targets, or information relating to crime and incident 'hot spots' are disseminated to particular functional sub-units within the BCU.
- Registered informants and sub-units are tasked, and the proactive cycle continues.

Source reliability	Information validity
A. Reliable	**1. Accurate**
Where there is no doubt of the authenticity, trustworthiness and competence of the source; or If the information is supplied by an individual who, in the past, has proved to be *reliable in all instances*.	When the information is known **without reservation to be true.**
B. Usually reliable	**2. Believed accurate**
A source from whom information in the past has, in *the majority of instances, proved to be reliable.*	When the information is **known personally to the source** but is not known personally to the reporting officer.
C. Not usually reliable	**3. Probably accurate**
A source from whom information in the past has, in *the majority of instances, proved to be <u>un</u>reliable.*	When the information is **not known personally to the source** but is **corroborated** by information already recorded.
X. Reliability unknown	**4. Accuracy cannot be judged**
An *untried* source where there is doubt about the source's authenticity, trustworthiness or competence.	When the information is **not known personally to the source and cannot be corroborated in any way.**

Table 2.2 The police 4 x 4 system for grading reliability of source and validity of information

Again, despite very wide differences in offences and the investigative demands involved, every proactive investigation follows a basic sequence (Table 2.3).

1.	Crimes of a particular type occur.
2.	Intelligence gathered on specific offenders – through systematic examination of crime details (crime pattern analysis; *modus operandi*; forensic patterns), interviewing of suspects and witnesses, tasking of informants, surveillance, monitoring (including interception of mail and telecommunications, and proactive collection of forensic evidence).
3.	Pre-emptive action – planned and prepared operation to effect an arrest prior to or during the commission of the offence.

Table 2.3 The proactive investigation sequence

Proactive investigation involves a location-centred or offender-centred approach.

Location-centred approach

Here, the offender is unknown and cannot be identified through reactive investigation.

Where there is information and intelligence collated on volume, serial and 'hot' spot crime, CPA enables identification of common features, e.g. time of day, methods used, words spoken, gestures used, objects or property involved, types of victim, characteristic circumstances or venues, descriptions of the offender.

CPA enables use of appropriate covert techniques, particularly informants and static surveillance, as additional means to assist in the targeting of potential high-risk locations frequented by victims, and where there is a strong likelihood that another offence will occur. Operations can then be planned, with surveillance leading up to the moment of arrest.

Offender-centred approach

Here, the police possess intelligence that connects a specific individual to a number of offences but the evidence to prove this connection is not available. As the targeted package, the individual becomes the subject of a co-ordinated proactive investigation using covert techniques deemed to be appropriate. The derived intelligence enables the planning of undercover operations against the package, with officers on hand to effect an arrest, if necessary after effecting a forced entry or creating a trap into which the suspect enters.

COVERT POLICING METHODS

Covert policing methods are a predominant feature of proactive investigations. They are called upon in reactive investigations where the circumstances indicate a benefit. ACPO and HM Customs and Excise have issued a Public Statement on Standards in Covert Law Enforcement Techniques[17] and Codes of Practice in respect of informants,[18] surveillance,[19] undercover operations,[20] interception of communication and accessing communications data,[21] and the dissemination of intelligence between agencies with law enforcement responsibilities.[22]

Informants

We devote some attention to the issue of informants since:

- The ACPO, HMIC and the Audit Commission declared that informers are good VFM and that extra money would be spent by police on paying informers;

- despite the fact that the police service has been encouraged to make greater use of informants, and they are the central plank of intelligence-led policing, the subject is completely unregulated by statute: the only form of regulation is a Code of Practice issued by ACPO and HM Customs and Excise;

- HMIC[23] has observed that:

  'In the context of a potential lack of integrity, the use of informants is possibly the highest-risk area in the work of the modern police service.'

The main categories of informer are as follows.

- *confidential source*: a person who gives information to the police but who does not want to be registered as an informant or who may not seem worthy of registration.[24]

- *informant*: a person who gives information to the police about the crime or about persons associated with criminal activity or public disorder. Such an individual will typically have a criminal history, habits or associates, and gives the information freely whether or not in the expectation of a reward, financial or otherwise.[25]

- *participating informant*: an informant who is, with the approval of a designated authorising officer, permitted to participate in a crime which others already intend to commit.[26]

- *tasked informant*: a person who is actively managed by the police to gather specific information on suspected criminals for an extended time period. This may involve participating in the planning and commission of offences.[27–8]

- *supergrass*: a person who agrees to testify in court on the activities of his or her former criminal associates in the expectation of some form of advantage, normally a substantial sentence discount.[28]

Each informant has a *handler*, an officer who has day-to-day responsibility for contact with an informant and for the initial evaluation of the information supplied by the informant. Such an officer should be trained. Each informant handler is under the aegis of an *informant controller*, a supervisory officer who has responsibility for the control and supervision of the conduct of the informant handler, the maintenance of legal and ethical standards in informant operations and the assessment of suitable rewards. This officer should be trained. An *authorising officer* is an officer designated to approve the use of informants – a superintendent in a force, on the National Crime Service (NCS) or, in the case of the National Criminal Intelligence Squad (NCIS) a designated officer of equivalent rank.[29]

An informant *reward* is defined as:

> '*a consideration in cash, goods or other benefits, whether from official or other sources, given to an informant or another on behalf of the informant in connection with the supply of information by the informant. A 'benefit' may include the supply to the Court of information which may lead to a mitigated sentence for such an informant who has been convicted of an offence.*'[30]

Information supplied to the court as a benefit is commonly referred to as a 'text'.

The Code specifies, among other things, that:

- a register be kept of all informants;

- before authorising registration and use of an informant (which must be given in writing) the authorising officer in the police context must be satisfied that the following criteria apply:
  - the informant's use is likely to be of value in the prevention or detection of crime or in the maintenance of public order or community safety;
  - the desired result of the use of the informant cannot reasonably be achieved by other means;
  - the risks of collateral intrusion have been properly assessed;

25

- before giving authorisation to the handler to direct the activity of an informant, the controller must be satisfied of the applicability of the same criteria applied by the authorising officer;

- a confidential record will be maintained of:

  - applications for authorisations to register and authorisations given;
  - at registration, an assessment of perceived risks in the use of the informant together with rewards sought or offered to the informant;
  - subsequent controller tasking and further rewards sought or offered;
  - contacts between the informant handler and the informant;
  - information passed to the handler by the informant;
  - arrests or other law enforcement benefits gained from the use of the informant;
  - the outcome of reviews;
  - the grounds for withdrawal of, or refusal to renew, authorisations.

In the case of participating informants, the confidential record will show additionally:

- authorisations given and the extent of criminal participation authorised;

- oral authorisations and the reasons for urgency;

- rewards or other benefits received by the informant and expenses directly incurred in using the informant.

In respect of the use of juvenile informants the Code:[31]

- recognises this carries particular risks.

  'Authorising officers will give close attention to the issue of proportionality in the use of juvenile informants. As a general rule the younger a juvenile the more compelling a case for his/her use needs to be established. The use of a juvenile informant to give information about members of his/her immediate family requires the most careful consideration of the question of proportionality. Such use of a juvenile will be exceptional.

  Authorising officers will weigh the seriousness of the criminality which is being investigated against the risks to the informant, given that informant's age and awareness. In every case involving the use of juvenile informants, the authorising officer must satisfy himself that the risks have been properly explained and are understood by the informant.'

- designates the authorising officer should be an assistant chief constable.

In respect of retention of material, the Code give the following directions.

- Where there is a reasonable belief that material relating to any informant activity could be relevant to pending or future criminal proceedings, it should be preserved in accordance with the requirements of CPIA and other relevant legislation.

- Where the use of an informant has been cancelled, or where the investigation involving the informant has concluded but there is no belief that the material will be required in pending or future criminal proceedings, the material will be destroyed except where its retention is justified on the grounds set out in the Code of Practice for Recording and Dissemination of Intelligence Material.

Surveillance

In this section we summarise issues in respect of surveillance by officers watching and listening, and interception of communications and technological surveillance.

ACPO and HM Customs and Excise[32] define surveillance as:

'the ability to monitor the movements of active criminals by watching or listening in person and electronically in order to provide the best available evidence of their participation in crime.'

In respect of the technological surveillance, i.e. the interception of communications and accessing of communications data they say[33] this is:

'the ability to monitor criminals' use of communications systems, as a means to uncovering their associations, movements and criminal behaviour.'

In respect of the justification for using these techniques, the Codes say:

'Surveillance will only be used by law enforcement agencies where they judge such use to be proportionate to the seriousness of the crime being investigated, and the history and character of the individual(s) concerned.'[34]

'The interception of communications and accessing of communications data will only be used to achieve what cannot be reasonably achieved by other means.'[35]

HMIC[36] has observed that:

> *'Surveillance remains amongst the most useful intelligence gathering tools in the law enforcement armoury.'*

Surveillance can be one, or a combination of, the following options:

- foot surveillance;

- mobile surveillance;

- static observation points;

- covert rural observation posts (CROPs);

- technological surveillance.

Officers watching and listening

In 1994, ACPO recommended surveillance should fall into two tiers:

- *Level one*: static and mobile surveillance using vehicles and technical support where necessary.

- *Level two*: static observations only.

In respect of mobile surveillance:[37]

- The majority of forces have one or more dedicated (full-time, specialist, trained) mobile teams or have the capacity to set up teams on an *ad hoc* basis. Teams are made up of police officers, or civilian surveillance officers (with a title such as force intelligence developers (FIDs).

- Teams are typically based at force HQ or in a large division. Their services have to be requested, in the form of properly researched and formally presented 'target packages'. The two main kinds of task which teams are asked to do are:
  - to gather further intelligence about particular targets, e.g. to follow them to see where they are living or with whom they are associating;
  - less often, to watch targets in the hope of 'catching them in the act', or at least, producing photographic or other hard evidence of their involvement in a particular crime.

- As far as possible, specialist surveillance teams avoid becoming directly involved in arrests, as this could compromise their cover and reveal their methods. Where arrests are expected, other officers will normally be available to effect these.

- In addition, given the rapid growth in demand for proactive policing, surveillance is carried by officers who fulfil other duties, and who may not be formally trained.

In respect of static surveillance, officers locate themselves in a location chosen because it has an overview of the target location.

Equipment commonly used in both mobile and static surveillance includes binoculars, night-vision equipment, telescopes, cameras and video recorders.

The ACPO Codes on Surveillance give direction on:

- authorisation criteria, temporary unforeseen surveillance, authorisation procedures, duration of authorisations in respect of surveillance in, or into, private and public places;

- maintenance of photographic intelligence records;

- retention of material – the provisions being the same as for material relating to informant activity.

Interception of communications and technological surveillance

This subsumes:

- the interception of mail;

- the interception of telecommunications: telephone, facsimile and telex communications on public and private telephone networks;

- the interception of electronic communications: mainly the interception of e-mail and other Internet-based forms of communication;

- the interception of wireless telegraphy;

- the use of listening devices ('bugs'): a range of equipment and methods from hidden microphones to the use of laser beams;

- the use of video surveillance devices including the use of CCTV systems for criminal investigation purposes;

- the use of tracking and tracing devices such as bleepers that transmit a radio signal.

The ACPO Codes on Interception of Communications and Accessing Communications Data[38] give direction on authorisation criteria, authorisation procedures, duration of authorisations, and records of material in respect of:

- interception of communications conveyed on a public telecommunication system and interception of mail;

- interception of communications conveyed by wireless telegraphy;

- consensual interception of communications conveyed on a public telecommunications system;

- interception of communications conveyed on a private telecommunications system;

- accessing communications data.

Undercover operations

According to the ACPO and HM Customs and Excise Code[39] the term 'undercover operations' includes the activity of undercover officers, test purchasers and decoys in order to:

- gather intelligence in support of the prevention of crime;

- to secure evidence to bring offenders before the courts.

There are three types of operator involved in different types of operation. For each type of deployment, the Code specifies authorisation criteria, authorisation procedures, duration of authorisations, and records. In addition, it gives direction on the retention of material, i.e. being exactly the same provisions as for informant material.[40]

Undercover officers

These are specially trained officers who work under the direction of an authorised investigation, using an alias and false identity to conceal their identity from third parties in order to:

- infiltrate an existing criminal conspiracy;

- arrest a suspected criminal or criminals;

- counter a threat to national security, or a significant threat to community safety or the public interest.

Test purchasers

These are appropriately trained officers who seek, by means of authorised activity, to establish the nature and/or availability of a commodity or service, the possession, supply or use of which involves an offence. Test purchasers would be involved in 'sting' or a 'buy and bust' operation.

Decoys

A decoy is an appropriately trained officer who places himself or herself passively in a position where he or she seeks to become the intended victim of a crime for the purpose of securing the arrest of the offender. An example of a decoy is a female police officer who befriends a targeted individual, e.g. *R.* v. *Stagg* [1994] Central Criminal Court, September 14.

Covert gathering of forensic material

Where necessary, officers will covertly gather material for forensic analysis (see next section) in order to generate intelligence, e.g. footmarks, the contents of waste disposal; evidence traps, e.g. marking fluids; paints.[41]

FORENSIC INVESTIGATION

The term 'forensic' means 'legal'. Forensic science is a term that refers to any application of scientific knowledge and method – systematic data collection and analysis – to inform the criminal justice process. Traditionally, the focus has been almost exclusively on the examination of physical evidence using knowledge and techniques from the physical sciences – principally chemistry, biology, physiology, anatomy and medicine.

Increasingly, those professions involved in the scientific study of behaviour, particularly psychologists and psychiatrists, are becoming involved in the process of forensic investigation. They and police officers and civilian staff trained in behavioural science and its statistical methods are able to assist in reactive and proactive investigation to identify patterns in offending behaviour.

Physical forensic science

Forensic science with the traditional, physical evidence focus has the potential:

- to eliminate suspects;

- to inform enquiries, e.g. by reducing the range of possible suspects or by clarifying circumstances;

- to link incidents;

- to corroborate suspicions by linking suspects to scenes;

- more rarely, to identify directly an 'unknown' suspect.

It does this by the systematic examination and analysis of *contact trace material* (CTM)[42] found in, or in the vicinity of, a material location or discovered through the process of investigation, i.e.

- *marks, imprints and impressions* – comprising *damage-based evidence*, e.g. a mark or impression made by a tool, instrument, shoe, tyre or glove; *non-damage-based evidence*, e.g. a fingerprint, thumbprint, palmprint;

- *trace evidence*, e.g. fibres, particles of metal, wood, glass and other materials; implements (including weapons), clothing, personal effects, dropped stolen property; potentially informative items such as a crumpled cigarette packet or a cigarette end; hair, body tissue and body fluids, e.g. blood, secretions and excretions.

Forensic science is also applied in:

- the analysis of body fluids – blood, semen, saliva – and DNA (deoxyribonucleic acid);

- the analysis of drugs of abuse, e.g. hallucinogens (such as cannabis, LSD, cocaine), narcotic analgesics, barbiturates (sleep-inducing drugs), and benzodiazepines (sedatives and sleep-inducing drugs);

- forensic toxicology – analysing specimens, e.g. blood and urine, for the presence of poison;

- alcohol analysis;

- fire investigation;

- explosions;

- firearms;

- the forensic examination of documents;

- the forensic linguistic analysis of speech.

The above list is illustrative. The spectrum of physical forensic science is extremely wide.

Forensic science has been, and continues to be, used predominantly in reactive investigations to support existing evidence or to link scenes after the event. This is because, although results of forensic testing may conclusively eliminate suspects, most forensic science techniques provide *associative* evidence short of conclusive proof. However, with increasing emphasis on proactive investigation there will be more requests for the forensic analysis of covertly obtained CTM as part of the intelligence-gathering process.

Underlying the approach to any scene examination and the subsequent analysis of CTM is Locard's *theory of interchange at the scene*, i.e. that the person or persons at the scene when a crime is committed will almost always leave something and take away something. This doctrine of *exchange* or *transfer* is based upon observations that:

- the perpetrator will take away traces of the victim and the scene;

- the victim or scene will retain traces of the perpetrator or leave traces on the perpetrator;

- the perpetrator will leave behind traces of him or herself at the scene.

The principal aim of the forensic investigation is:

- to find, properly collect and preserve any traces left at the scene;

- to locate matching materials on a suspect in order to provide objective evidence that he or she was present at the scene at the material time.

The definition of the crime scene

The *crime scene* has been traditionally perceived as a physical location, e.g. a piece of land, an area within a street, a vehicle, a building or a specific room within a building. In a wider forensic sense, the scene includes:

- those physical changes to a victim's body or clothing arising from the commission of the offence;

- all material places of contact between the offender and victim.

In an even wider definition advanced by the ACPO and the Forensic Science Service (FSS), the scene includes the location, the victim, the suspect, any witness to be interviewed or eliminated from the investigation, and the homes of suspects, victims and witnesses.[43]

Classifications of physical evidence

Forensic evidence can be classified as:

- *inceptive*: pointing directly to an 'unknown' suspect, e.g. fingerprints, DNA database, physical databases;

- *corroborative*: tending to confirm an existing hypothesis – the predominant use at present in respect of volume crime;

- *mandatory*: necessary to satisfy a specific legal requirement, e.g. drugs, RTA alcohol.

The collection and analysis of physical evidence

Table 2.4 shows how the path of forensic investigation is trodden at various stages by police officers, *scenes of crime officers* (SOCOs) (also called crime scene examiners), scientific support officers (SSOs) from the force Scientific Support Department, *medical examiners* (MEs), and external *forensic scientists* (FSs).

Stage	Location of activity	Investigators
Collection	physical location of the offence ('scene')	Police; SOCO; FS
	Victim (at 'scene'; in another location, e.g. hospital, medical room in police station)	Police; SOCO; ME; FS
	Suspect (at 'scene'; in another location, e.g. in medical room at police station, hospital)	Police; ME
In-force examination	Scientific Support Unit Fingerprint bureau	SSO
External analysis	External forensic supplier	FS

Table 2.4 Investigators at stages in the path of forensic investigation

Collecting, recording, and handling physical evidence: fundamental principles

All those involved in the process of investigation – police officers and civilian support staff, SOCOs, SSOs, MEs, and FSs – must observe a number of fundamental principles in respect of forensic evidence.

1. ***The evidence must be obtained legally.***

2. ***The evidence must be documented fully.*** This is a basic, commonsensical duty of all investigators.

3. ***The evidence must be properly marked.*** This should be in a manner that does not destroy the evidential value of the item and should include the initials of the investigator, the item number and the date.

4. ***The evidence must be correctly and separately packaged.*** Items should be wrapped where necessary, placed in appropriate bags or containers (e.g. in the case of liquids and small items), sealed to avoid contamination, and appropriately stored to prevent damage and degrading. All containers and seals should be marked with the initials of the person collecting the evidence.

5. ***Proper controls and standards must be maintained if the evidence is to be subject to comparison and rigorous analysis.*** In most cases it is necessary to obtain the standards for comparison, typically taking a control sample, e.g. from an adjacent unaffected area.

6. ***The chain of custody (continuity) must be maintained and accounted for.*** Investigators must be able to document every person who has had custody of the evidence from the time it was found at the scene until it is presented in court. The police service and forensic suppliers should have procedures to document the chain of custody, but it is the individual investigator's duty to make sure these are followed.

Continuity is fundamental to ensuring the *integrity* of an item of collected CTM. Integrity means the expectation by the forensic scientist who conducts the analyses that there has been no change, loss or addition, such that the item received is in precisely the same state as when it was collected at the scene (accepting the occurrence of natural physical changes such as desiccation, i.e. that blood dries and semen cracks and powders).

The police, civilian staff, external providers of services and the prosecution have to demonstrate to the defence and the courts integrity in the process of collecting, recording and handling of physical evidence: that nobody, or nothing, affected, or was allowed to affect, the character of the item from the time of collection to the time of analysis, e.g.

- nobody shook or otherwise disturbed an item of clothing;
- no finger was poked through a stab or bullet hole in a given item or surface;
- there was no scraping of a body part, clothing or item across a blood stain;
- no debris was removed;
- there was no contamination (addition of traces) in the process of:
  - collecting the evidence (at the scene or elsewhere);
  - packaging, e.g. blood or semen being inadvertently transferred to other surfaces of an item; more than one item being placed in one bag;
  - packaging being opened by investigators, wishing to examine the item or to show it to a suspect in interview as 'persuasive evidence'.

Integrity relies upon:

- all those responsible for collecting, recording and handling of physical evidence are fully aware, through training and specific instructions, of the fundamental principles;
- individuals actually observing these principles,
- the existence of real, as opposed to notional, supervision and monitoring to ensure observance.

Assessing the value of physical evidence

Forensic evidence must be assessed by reference to all the circumstances of the case and the other available evidence. The discriminating power of tests varies from absolute, e.g. in the case of a physical fit, to poor, e.g. in the case of mass-produced items such as window glass. Transferred material can only assist in proving contact between one individual and another, or between an individual and a location, or, in some cases, that a crime has been committed.

In all cases, the significance, or meaning, of the result depends upon the context in which the evidence was found. This is why it is essential for everyone involved along the path of forensic investigation to have the fullest understanding of the case, the issues raised and the circumstances in which they are operating. This is especially so for the forensic scientist commissioned to answer specific questions.

Protocol for the supply of forensic science services to the police and the CPS

Issued in June 1999, this protocol has the following objectives:

- to raise awareness within each agency – the FSS, the police and the CPS – of the need for quality and timely information between the three;
- to improve efficiency by harmonising the method of submission of exhibits to the FSS by the police;
- to improve the efficient processing and examination of exhibits submitted by the police to the FSS;
- to establish systems for prioritisation of examinations by the FSS against agreed timescales;
- to improve the efficiency of the flow of information between the police, the FSS and the CPS.

To effect the local implementation of the protocol, there is a service level agreement attached as s schedule to the protocol, which specifies the parties who sign up to the agreement.

Key elements of the protocol are as follows:

- The police provide the laboratory, as early as possible, with advance notice (using form MG FSS) of their intention to submit an item for examination.
- The decision to send a particular item for examination rests solely with the police and should be made as soon as possible. The item should then be sent as soon as possible.
- Where there is doubt whether a proposed examination is capable of providing the information required, before any examination is commenced, the officer in the case should seek advice and receive assistance from contacts in the force Scientific Support Department or the FSS.
- When submitting an item for examination to the laboratory the police should use form MG FSS containing details of surrounding circumstances affecting the case.
- The FSS should be given information concerning a custody or other statutory time limit/court direction.
- The police should provide the laboratory with any further information, which might be relevant to the examination, which subsequently, comes to light. Documents and information should be dispatched to

37

the laboratory either with form MG FSS or as soon as possible afterwards.

- The police will decide on the priority of any work submitted for examination and mark the form accordingly.

- Not all work in one case requires the same degree of priority: the police should indicate when the results are required for each subset of work.

- Jobs will be classified as *urgent*, *critical* or *standard*. It is recognised that the classification of a submitted item of work can change at any time.

  - **Urgent jobs**. These are specific items of work the results of which the police require to assist in their investigations. Results will be delivered to the police as soon as practicably possible. The FSS and the police, following a locally identified procedure, should agree on the date and time of delivery of results for urgent jobs. Urgent work should always be pre-ordered using agreed means in accordance with local provisions which identify how this will be done and those responsible.

  - **Critical jobs**. These are cases where it is essential that results be delivered in advance of specified court date – usually a custody or statutory time limit. This category includes work on cases involving youth offenders, adults remanded (or likely to be remanded) in custody, sexual abuse/violence towards children, child witnesses, and any other case where there is a risk of the case being stayed by the court if forensic results are not given by a specified date. Delivery of the results should always be at an agreed earlier date to enable the CPS to process and to serve the evidence on the defence and the court as soon as possible and within the relevant time limit.

  - **Standard jobs**. This classification covers all non-urgent or non-critical jobs within a case. Results are provided on the basis of default delivery dates reflecting current FSS turnaround times. The FSS provides the police and the CPS with a list of default delivery times, which are regularly updated. The FSS does not guarantee delivery to these dates: they constitute 'best endeavours'.

The MG FSS form

The form provides information on:

- officer-in-case or day-to-day contact of another officer in respect of the case;

- proposed offence charged;

- for urgent and critical submissions only, the category of justification, i.e. young, offender, adult in custody, PACE requirement, child victim of sexual abuse/violence, child witness or other (at the request of the CPS);

- appropriate forms and documents submitted at the same time, e.g.
    - glass/fibre form;
    - sexual offences form;
    - firearms safety form;
    - toxicology form;
    - drugs/drive form MG DD/E;
    - technical defence form MG DD/D;
    - plans;
    - victim's statement;
    - voluntary statement, i.e. by suspect;
    - photographs;
    - scene examiner's (i.e. SOCO's) report;
    - relevant additional documentation;

- subjects – for each subject: surname, forename(s), sex, DOB, ethnic code, occupation, status (i.e. deceased, victim, suspect, subject for elimination), date and time of arrest;

- circumstances of incident;

- what needs to be established, stating the priority: 1 – urgent; 2 – critical; 3 – standard;

- listed items for scientific examination: for each item specifying:
    - item no.;
    - exhibit no.;
    - exhibit bag no.;
    - description of items;
    - subject or location from which recovered;
    - date/time found/taken;
    - name of person seizing the item.

Note: there is a very significant difference between the information now required on the MG FSS form and that which was required on the form it supersedes, the HOLAB3 form. The MG FSS only requires listing of those *items submitted for analysis*. In contrast, the HOLAB3 required the police to list **all** appropriate items collected or seized by the police – not just those submitted for analysis – and to *give reasons why certain items were not being submitted for analysis.*

Forensic behavioural science

Behavioural science and techniques used by behavioural scientists are able to assist in the process of deducing a description – a *profile* – of an unknown offender based upon evaluating minute details about the crime scene, in the widest definition of this term, and other available evidence.

> *'Profiling is a term of convenience which is applied to a range of approaches to criminal investigation in which the behaviour exhibited at the crime, or a series of similar crimes, is studied and inferences are drawn about the offender.*
>
> *In the first instance, the inferences drawn from such a study of a criminal's behaviour may focus on predicted characteristics of the offender, such as domestic and social circumstances, domestic and criminal histories, and education and employment records. They may go further, for example, postulating mental health or sexual preferences and dysfunctions. This inferred picture of the offender can then be used as a basis for a range of observations, predictions, and recommendations.'*[44]

Profilers are typically psychologists or psychiatrists, and other individuals working inside the police service, i.e. police officers and civilian staff in crime analysis. The common denominator is the ability to offer advice to a police investigation based upon having collected data on past crimes, on relevant professional expertise or a combination of these.

There are essentially two approaches to profiling: *clinical* and *statistical*.

• The clinical approach attempts to determine aspects of the offender's personality from the offender's choice of action before, during and after the criminal act. This information is combined with other pertinent details and physical evidence and is then compared with the characteristics of known personality types and mental abnormalities. From this, a working description of the offender is drawn up. This can be compared with databases of known offences and known offenders.

• The statistical approach focuses upon using the 'signature' of the offender, i.e. the objective properties identifiable from actions before, during and after the offence, and identifying as many ecological (contextual, situational, systemic) variables as possible. A working description (a statistically derived profile) is drawn up, which can be compared with known offences and offenders.

The ACPO Crime Sub-Committee on Behavioural Sciences had defined police policy on profiling. This is based upon:

- *Articles of faith*: offender profiling advice:
  - should be considered essentially viable, even though it has not yet been properly scientifically validated;
  - should be 'owned' by the service.
- *Articles of purpose*: offender-profiling advice:
  - must be understood not to amount to probative evidence;
  - should be understood to be about informing investigators to help them in decisions concerned with the management of investigative options and resources in the pursuit of evidence.

It is essential for all those involved in the criminal justice system to understand the limitations of profiling.

'Offender profiling does not solve crimes and, despite a handful of quite exceptional cases, is does not identify criminals directly. Almost any objective reference you might read will tell you so. In a criminal trial, an offender profile which fits the defendant, however exactly, can no more be proof of guilt than one which is wildly inaccurate can be proof of innocence.'[45]

POLICE ORGANISATION OF INVESTIGATIVE RESOURCES

Offences against the person and property, their gravity, their complexity, and the circumstances under which they come to notice, vary greatly. This implies that the investigation of a given type of offence will vary greatly in terms of its conduct – actions to be taken and tasks to be completed. For this reason, there will be wide variations in the demand for time, human resources, expertise and supporting services to ensure that the process and outcome of the investigation is lawful, effective, exact and ethical.

The Audit Commission exhortation to the service to commit itself wholeheartedly to proactive policing, as a means to increasing VFM, has confronted each force with the requirement to organise itself to engage in operations which are intelligence-led, while still being demand-led – engaging in reactive investigations, following the occurrence of a crime.

Individual forces have implemented similar crime management models to respond to this demand. However, there is no standard model and titles containing such terms as 'area' and 'tactical' can have different meanings even within the same force. This means that it is only possible to give a general description of police organisation of investigative resources.

Each force is divided into a number of geographical areas each policed by a Basic Command Unit (BCU). It is commanded by a superintendent, called the Area Commander. He or she has a management team comprising uniform, CID and civilian managers, responsible for directing and working together to co-ordinate the deployment of resource – functional units in the BCU – to achieve proactive and reactive objectives. An illustrative organisational model of a BCU is at Figure 2.2.[46] However, the organisation of BCUs can differ widely even within a given police force.

Basic Command Unit resources

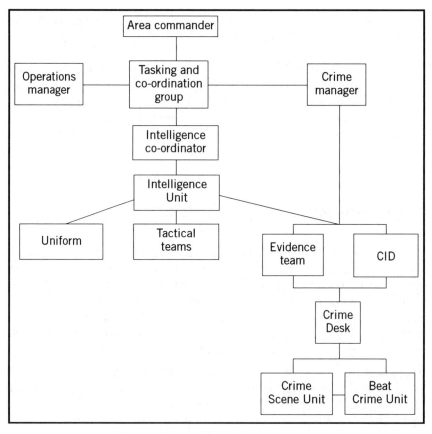

Figure 2.2 An organisational model integrating reactive and proactive investigation

Intelligence Unit

The Intelligence Unit (IU) is central to the working of the BCU.

All intelligence is routed through the IU. Led by the intelligence co-ordinator, it typically comprises a number of *field intelligence officers* (FIOs), a *source co-ordinator* and a number of *intelligence* and *crime analysts*. The IU produces strategic objectives and provides the intelligence necessary for targeting of individuals, locations and types of crime, for the process of tasking, and then to give and receive intelligence once an operation is underway.

The IU may be a separate entity or, together with the Crime Desk, make up a Crime Management Unit.

Crime Desk

The Crime Desk is responsible for screening demands for reactive investigation and deciding what resource will be deployed. Crimes are recorded and tracked on the computer. The ideal is to deal with the majority of demands with little or no likelihood of producing a 'result' through a telephone investigation or a single visit to the location by a member of the Crime Scene Unit (CSU).

This enables resource to be directed to detectable cases, which might yield a 'positive outcome', i.e. a 'clear up' by the particular grouping to which the Crime Desk refers the request: the Beat Crime Unit, Uniform Patrol or Area CID.

Crime Scene Unit

Officers in this unit are called *crime scene attenders/assessors.* Though their title may differ across the country, their job is the same: to examine the scenes of volume crime, e.g. burglary. They are uniform officers trained to conduct a detailed search, identifying key features of the offence particularly bearing upon method and other potentially 'signature' characteristics.

Although they interview victims and witnesses, they do not investigate the case as such. Theirs is an intelligence role. They are not SOCOs. Where they consider it worthwhile, they can initiate the deployment of a SOCO.

Members of this unit typically assist in the operation of the Crime Desk.

Beat Crime Unit

Also called the Uniform Crime Unit, this is staffed by uniform officers, with a CID manager if not supervisor. This unit investigates less serious 'street crimes', classed as detectable by the Crime Desk and allocated to the unit. Typical crimes include street robbery, deception and cheque frauds. They complete a crime report (see p. 52) supported by other material, (e.g. witness statements, exhibit evidence), interview the suspect, and, following charge, are responsible for preparation and submission of files to the CPS.

Although essentially reactive, in many forces these units have always directed some of their effort towards proactive policing, e.g. carrying out observations of crime 'hot spots'.

Tactical teams

These may be uniform, CID ('tactical CID') or a mixture.

They are tasked by the IU to obtain further intelligence, to carry out observations and surveillance (principally static) of targets and to mount operations to arrest targeted individuals.

Such operations commonly occur in uncongenial circumstances, e.g. with resistance, obstruction, potential confrontation, physical contact, the use of force, and the risk of assault and injury. Tactical teams therefore often operate in protective clothing and headwear, equipped to switch to public order mode.

Tactical teams do not investigate since this diverts them from their proactive role. Having arrested a suspect, they prepare a crime report and other material, and hand over the case (and the suspect in detention) to others tasked with continuing the investigation, such as the evidence team.

Uniform patrol

Working mostly on three shifts: day (6 am–2 pm); late (2 pm–10 pm); night (10 pm–6 am), uniform patrol officers act as the 'fire brigade'. When an offence occurs, if they are not at or near the scene, they are assigned at short notice to attend when there is an urgent request for police assistance. In addition to foot patrols, uniform officers are deployed in vehicles, e.g. area vehicles (for general duties) and rapid response vehicles.

The change in emphasis towards proactive policing has meant that more and more uniform officers are required for intelligence support duties and deployment on tactical teams. This has meant a significant depletion in numbers available for uniform patrol duties and a resulting reduction in experience and expertise. Typically, the limited manpower of a shift will comprise a disproportionately large element of probationers (trainees) and officers still junior in service. The remainder will include officers more senior in service who are unwilling or unsuited to be assigned to proactive policing duties.

Although forces vary on this matter, it is increasingly the case that uniform officers have limited investigative responsibilities due to limited numbers; lack of time, knowledge, expertise and experience; lack of overtime; and the shift system. If the incident to which the officer has responded spontaneously, or been assigned by the Operations Room, proves not to be serious or is serious enough to merit investigation by CID, the uniform officer is responsible for the preliminary investigation. The officer prepares a crime report and other material, and hands over the case (and any suspect in detention) to the evidence team.

Evidence team

Not all forces have evidence teams in their BCUs. The actual nomenclature of an evidence team differs widely, e.g. case investigation team (CIT) or prisoner-handling unit (PHU). Working mostly on two shifts, days and lates, the team is tasked with:

- interviewing prisoners arrested by tactical teams and uniform patrols and gathering further evidence;
- obtaining potential intelligence through a suspect's disclosures within interview and 'off tape';
- recruiting informants;
- preparing and submitting material to:
  - the Administration Support Unit (ASU), which is responsible for liaising with, and submitting files and copies of evidence (e.g. audio and video recordings) to, the CPS;
  - where no ASU facility is available, the CPS directly.

The team therefore is usually very busy, confronted with large numbers of crime reports to be processed and individuals in cells to be interviewed.

For ease of reference, and because the title accurately captures the essential role of the unit, throughout this text we use the term CIT to refer to the evidence team.

Area CID

This unit conducts reactive investigation crimes (routed through the Crime Desk), which are serious but not so serious as to merit the commitment of the Major Crime Unit (see next section). Area CID attend the scene, summon and task SOCO and other support staff, e.g. the medical examiner or an external forensic science provider.

Typically, Area CID will also engage in proactive work: gathering intelligence, recruiting and handling informants, conducting observations and surveillance.

The Major Crime Unit

Force numbers, size of force area, the types of community to be policed, and the amount and types of extremely serious crime to be investigated dictate whether a force has one or more Major Crime Units (MCUs). A large force may decide to have just one unit and deploy this as a number of 'syndicates'. Another may decide to deploy particular types of unit, e.g. Murder and Drugs Unit.

The national trend in forming MCUs is to dispense with the specialisation and separation of resource as 'squads' or units tasked with investigating particular types of crime, e.g. the Murder Squad, the Drugs Squad, the Serious Crime Squad (or Unit), the Fraud Squad (also called the Commercial Branch). This enables MCU officers to be deployed to investigate on a case-by-case basis. Hence, its members will be grouped, organised and resourced to investigate: murders and other extremely serious and serial crimes against the person, individuals who do not necessarily confine themselves to particular crimes but instead are active in various types of serious criminal activity, drugs, firearms, money laundering and extremely high-value fraud.

Officers are able to conduct their investigations across the force area and also to work collaboratively with the *National Crime Squad (NCS)* – the former Regional Crime Squads – and the *National Criminal Intelligence Service (NCIS)*, Customs and Excise investigation units, the Inland Revenue Department, the DSS, the Department of Transport, the Department of Trade and Industry, the Serious Fraud Office, the Security Service and other institutions in the public and private sectors.

The MCU has its own Intelligence Unit, supported by specialist desk officers in the Force Intelligence Bureau (FIB).

Each investigation is directed by a *senior investigating officer* (SIO).

Special investigation units

Titles for these units vary greatly across the country and the range of duties can also vary. Typically, the SIU is responsible for the investigation of abuse (sexual and otherwise) of children, domestic violence and sexual offences against females. SIU officers are specially trained to carry out their specialist duties, e.g. attending courses in joint investigation (child protection) and sexual offence investigation.

The unit services a geographical area (subsuming one or more BCU areas). The number of units within a force is necessarily finite. It follows that officers in the SIU and area CID work in close collaboration.

Special Branch

The Special Branch (SB) is tasked with monitoring and operations in respect of subversive individuals and organisations, anti-terrorism and other threats to security. It has close functional links with the Security Service and other agencies.

Specialist support

Uniform support group

Although it may not have this name and may be either located centrally or dispersed throughout the force area, this group includes authorised firearms officers, divers and, of particular use to the MCU, *POLSA* (police search adviser) officers.

POLSA officers are trained to a high level in the processes of searching. Some have attended a long formal course conducted by external agencies. These officers train other officers on slightly shorter courses within their forces.

POLSA teams are deemed to be the experts in searching, i.e.

*   they keep full records of their searching (documentary, illustrations, and, as necessary, video recordings or photographs);

*   they survey the scene, noting its dimensions and adjoining entry and exit areas;

*   they adopt searching methods suited to the scene, e.g.

    –   *point-to-point* – following a chain of objects that are obviously evidence;

— *an ever widening circle* – starting at a focal point of the scene or the centre of an area and working outwards, circling in a clockwise or counter-clockwise direction until the edge of the secured area is reached. The spiral is then reversed, working towards the centre or focal point (NB: although applicable to outside and inside, within a room, account must necessarily be taken of size and contents);

— *a sector search* – the scene is subdivided into a chequer board of segments with the victim or the building in the centre sector; each sector is searched as an individual unit;

— *a strip search or grid search* – applied to outside areas. First, the area is searched up and down (in strips), then the area is searched back and forth (completing a grid coverage).

Scientific Support Department

The force's Scientific Support Department (or Unit) is able to provide, on requests, specific forensic expertise in an investigation. Headed by a **scientific support manager** (SSM), it is staffed by SOCOs and **scientific support officers** (SSOs), comprising fingerprint bureau officers, technical staff and specialist photographers. Originally, these roles were performed by police officers but are now largely occupied by civilian staff.

SCENES OF CRIME OFFICERS

Also called crime scene examiners, SOCOs fulfil the following investigative functions:[47]

• to examine systematically, assess and interpret the crime scene;

• to identify the location of, and to assess the quality of, physical evidence, specifically any form of CTM:

— keeping a record of his or her searching;

— noting ambient conditions, i.e. source and level of any illumination, the weather, temperature;

— recording the scene – in note form and graphically – identifying the location of physical evidence, i.e.

(a) taking photographs, video recording, making suitable drawings of, and notes concerning the layout of, and any specific locations within, the scene and the vicinity – noting North and useful dimensions, whether inside a room, a building or outside – and, in the case of premises, any structural features such as doors, windows, and, in the case of an outside location, features, e.g. trees, undergrowth, paths, gates, roads, alleys, walls, hedges, watercourses, rivers, bridges, areas of grass and gravel;

(b) taking photographs, video recording, making sketches of, and notes (with appropriate indication of measurements) concerning the locations of: the victim, marks, imprints and impressions, trace evidence, items;

(c) making a record of each item of evidence identified – a description, including a note of measurements and markings; who found it, where, when;

– being alert to, and making a record of, any form of *negative evidence*, i.e. detail which bears upon what was *not* the case, e.g. something was missing which should have been, or could have been reasonably expected to be, present;

• to collect and control exhibits – marks, imprints, impressions trace evidence, samples, and items – and conduct other forms of recording, with a view:

– to subsequent in-force forensic analysis and checking against records and databases;

– to assessing which items of CTM should be submitted for analysis by an external forensic science provider;

• to liaise with all involved in the case;

• to complete necessary forms and to prepare reports and statements;

• to advise investigators and their supervisors on forensic scientific matters – particular appropriate testing;

• to provide intelligence – linking scenes or crimes together.

FINGERPRINT BUREAU STAFF

Bureau staff compare fingerprints, thumbprints and other handprints, collected at the scene and other material locations and from material items, with those taken at the police station and with those held on indexes – within the force and nationally. In particular, this involves the examination and interpretation of ridge characteristics, which may be distorted for some reason. Hence conclusions by fingerprint bureau staff have the status of an expert witness report, and they should be ready to give oral evidence in court concerning their opinions.

Eliminatory testing

Unidentified prints recovered from the scene must be subject to *eliminatory testing* (elimination). In addition to suspects, fingerprints should be taken from all those who have had contact with the scene, e.g. other occupants of the location, those discovering the offence, police officers, civilian support staff including external staff, personnel from other services.

Classification of marks

Marks are classified in a number of ways.

- *A match*. In the past, a 16-point standard has been applied. Since 1983, however, matches of less than 16 point have been allowed with the court being made aware of the lower number involved. On 3 April 2000 there will no longer be a numerical standard. Bureau staff will be free to exercise their own particular judgement as to what constitutes a match.

- *Outstanding*. This is a mark which is not identified or eliminated to specific 'donor', i.e. the suspect or those with access to the scene or material location/item. Such marks are often classified, and referred to, as being of *'No value'* or having *'Insufficient detail for comparison purposes'*. This is an interpretation and, like all interpretations, is open to challenge.

TECHNICAL STAFF

Technical staff carry out in-force forensic testing in laboratory conditions. They typically fulfil the following tasks:

- testing of CTM – the range of testing varies greatly and includes:
  - presumptive testing, e.g. of blood or of drugs, where a positive result indicates the necessity to refer for further analysis by a forensic supplier;
  - restoration of serial numbers;
  - examining shoe and toolmarks;
  - examining altered and forged documents;
  - examining documents for indented writing e.g. conditioning ESDA;

- maintenance of indexes of particular items, e.g. tyre and footwear prints.

SPECIALIST PHOTOGRAPHERS

Not found in all forces, these are essentially 'professional' photographers, producing high-quality photography and video images, where necessary using non-routine techniques and specialist equipment.

INFORMATION AND INTELLIGENCE SYSTEMS

Force operational information management system

Forces differ in the name they give to their system for capturing, processing and creating a retrievable record of *operational information.* Titles include *operational information management system* (OIS) or the *computer-aided despatch* (CAD) system.

Irrespective of its name, the purpose of the system is the same: to record chronologically information arising from requests for a police response and deployment of police officers – including all requests and reports from deploying and deployed officers. It is the medium for the subsequent:

- immediate tasking of officers;

- immediate referral to the Crime Desk for screening;

- communication and circulation of reports and descriptions by officers.

Each transaction is a *message* and has a discrete serial reference. There is maximal use of abbreviation and coding, e.g. codes for source and type of request, incident, venue of incident, complainant (ethnic origin), action; identification codes/call-signs for stations, units, vehicles and personnel. In addition it is important to know that:

- the cumulative contents (with sequential serials) of a day/shift are printed out, circulated and collated in information systems, e.g. shift logs;

- the particular serials relating to a given offence are printed out and placed on the *crime file* (see p. 53);

- the hard disk is routinely backed up onto floppy disks and cleared on a regular basis;

- floppy disks are held for a specified time, cleared and re-used.

The crime reporting system

This is a cumulative database of information on all crimes reported, each crime having a discrete *crime number*. Information is abstracted from every *crime report* (see next section) onto a CRS form. Typical details abstracted include:

- *offence details*: information on reporting officer, department, offence, reporting person, complainant, witness, how reported, injuries, who interviewed, when (with brief details), modus operandi (free text), property, drugs, vehicles, officers involved;

- *investigation details*: a checklist of key descriptors to which the officer should record 'yes' or 'no'. Table 2.5 shows typical descriptors.

Scene visited	Scene searched	House-to-house enquiries
Photographs taken	Fingerprints found	SOCO requested
Racial motive	Victim support	Photofit made
Photographs shown	Dealers visited	Other evidence
Liaison with LIO	Liaison with IU/FIB	Liason with NCS/ NCIS/other agencies
Local informants	Liaison with another force	Scene re-visited
Crime prevention officer requested	Complainant agrees TIC	Enquiries complete

Table 2.5 Typical list of investigation descriptors (illustrative)

This information is another source of data for the Force Intelligence System (FIS) described earlier. (See p. 21.)

The crime report

The *crime report* is a standardised form, the design of which varies greatly between forces. It is cumulatively completed by both police officers and civilian staff.

Despite differences in design, the content is common, is cross-referenced to the OIS, and contains data fields in respect of:

- *crime number*;

- *offence*: finally recorded, legal description;

- *disposal*: undetected, no crime, detected, detected no further action (NFA), TIC (taken into consideration);
- *complaint details*: time and date, whether discovered by police, reporting officer, investigating officer;
- *complainant details*: sex, ethnic origin, name, DOB, address, occupation, contact numbers, victim care given;
- *details of the offence*: time, date, location;
- *description of suspect*;
- *vehicles seen*;
- *modus operandi*: using codes to describe:
  - type of premises/scene of crime, point of entry;
  - method of weapon use, burglary, deception, theft;
  - additional specific features, e.g. method of gaining entry, actions within, use of incendiary devices and accelerants, objects, marks and other CTM, victim attributes;
- *vehicle offence details*: e.g. relating to theft of/from or criminal damage to a vehicle;
- *property – stolen and damaged*: description, value, whether recovered;
- *details of offenders*;
- *details of SOCO:* attending scene;
- *details of enquiries*:
  - enquiries at the scene, in the vicinity, potential outlets for stolen items, potential locations visited by suspect;
  - actions: in serial number order, time and date, details of action including all persons involved (e.g. victim, witnesses, informants, officers, civilian staff), signature of person directing or effecting action.

Although the form is completed manually, the data fields constitute detail for inputting into the crime reporting system.

The crime file

This is opened to house:

- documentation (including: the crime report and enclosures; copies of forms, including the IRB; copies of print-out from the OIS; witness statements; photocopies of pocket book or desk diary extracts; notes);

- a record of exchanges and correspondence with key individuals within the force, e.g. scientific support department, and external to the force, e.g. CPS, medical examiner, forensic scientists.

Force Intelligence System

This has been described in detail earlier: see p. 21.

The Police National Computer

The *Police National Computer* (PNC) is a computer database located at Hendon, linked to terminals within each force HQ and force police stations, which provides access to, and ability to contribute to, information on all individuals who have been arrested, convicted, cautioned or who have otherwise come to attention. It is linked to other government databases, e.g. Driver Vehicle and Licensing Centre, DSS. Entries can be annotated or flagged with markers giving intelligence on the individual, e.g. movements, associates. It now has a powerful search capability. Entering partial information about a suspect, such as description or *modus operandi* (MO) can produce within seconds a list of known offenders satisfying these criteria.

National Criminal Intelligence Service systems

Forces have access to, and contribute to, the systems operated by the *National Criminal Intelligence Service* (NCIS). The functions of NCIS are:

- to gather, store and analyse information in order to provide criminal intelligence;
- to provide criminal intelligence to police forces in Great Britain, the Royal Ulster Constabulary, the NCS and to other law enforcement agencies;
- to act in support of such bodies when carrying out their criminal intelligence activities.

The NCIS has a number of branches and units, including the Strategic and Specialist Intelligence Branch, which itself includes:

- the *Organised Crime Unit*, which provides intelligence on organised crime trends, threats and activities;
- the *Drugs Unit*, which provides intelligence on drugs, including trends in drugs supply and the location of drugs laboratories;

- the *Economic Crimes Unit*, which provides intelligence on business crime, money laundering, gaming and lotteries;

- the *Football Unit*;

- the *Specialist Crimes Unit*, which deals with crimes such as kidnapping, extortion, counterfeit currency, organised vehicle crime and paedophiles.

National DNA database

The Forensic Science Service (FSS) inputs, updates and manages this database of chromosomal DNA (inherited from both mother and father) and mitochondrial DNA (inherited only from the mother). Using mouth swab kits, DNA samples are now routinely taken from suspects in volume crimes, e.g. burglary, vehicle crime, criminal damage, as well as suspects in serious and serial crimes against the person.

The DNA database holds DNA samples from suspects charged, cautioned or convicted for recordable offences. It also holds DNA profiles from stains found at scenes of crime. The database is able to make matches between suspects and crime scenes, or one crime scene to another.

Other databases

There are forensic collation systems maintained within forces and accessible upon request from other forces, e.g. fingerprint indexes, DNA databases, footwear marks and tyre marks.

In addition there are a number of databases in respect of offender profiling. (See section on investigations by the Major Crime Unit, p. 88.)

THE DECISION TO DEPLOY INVESTIGATIVE RESOURCE

The occurrence of an offence may come to immediate attention in those situations where a police officer is at or near the scene and either attends of his or her own accord or receives an urgent face-to-face summons, e.g. from the victim or witness, to attend. The officer becomes the *first officer attending* (FOA).

The majority of requests for police attendance, i.e. incoming reports of crime, are received and processed by personnel in the *force control room*, which assesses all calls, and by the crime desk of the BCU (i.e. in whose area the request originates), which accepts calls routed from the control room or direct incoming calls from police officers on the ground.

Both the control room and the crime desk screen requests, determining the response, deciding what priority should be given, whether an officer should attend and, if so, who should attend.

The decision whether to deploy, whom, and what priority to assign to the request, are guided by a number of factors:

* the fundamental duty of any police officer to protect and to preserve the life, well-being and property of members of the public, i.e. to attend:
  - where a crime is in progress;
  - to the needs of victims;
* force investigation policy, i.e. which categories of crime will be investigated, how, when and by which kind of investigator, dictated by:
  - crime seriousness;
  - crime solvability;
  - level of requisite investigative expertise;
  - availability of resource (manpower, expertise, time and cost).

The aim is greater selectivity in deploying officers, a decision in some cases not to send an officer where this is neither necessary to further the investigation nor required by the victim.[48]

All information, decisions, and actions are logged onto the OIS.

The control room response

Typically, the control room will send officers to scenes with the following attributes:

* where there is a traumatised victim;

* where the crime is in progress or offenders are at or near the scene;

* where there are known leads at the scene to follow up;

* where the crime is of a serious nature.

The FOA will almost inevitably be a uniform officer.

Serious crimes requiring immediate attention

In the case of a report of a crime of obvious seriousness against a person, e.g. murder or violent rape, or involving property, e.g. a major fire, the requirement for specialist investigation is clear. The control room will despatch uniform to attend and will inform the appropriate HQ or area CID unit.

The uniform FOA's tasks are to secure the scene and to ensure the integrity of potential evidence. Typical tasks are:

* to attend to the needs of the victim;

* to exclude the public from the scene and to prevent key individuals leaving the scene;

* to arrest the suspected offender;

* to prevent the contamination or removal of physical evidence;

* to prevent victim and witnesses communicating in a way that influences or contaminates their testimonial evidence (descriptions and accounts).

Other crimes requiring immediate attention

In the case of a report of a crime which requires immediate attention but in which decisions cannot be made as to investigative implications, the control room will despatch uniform to attend.

All incoming communications to the control room and the response to these requests are recorded. Incoming calls are recorded on tape. Detail (date and time of the report, its originator, the offence, its location and other detail, including the identity of officers despatched, when and how) is entered into the OIS.

Incident forms are also manually completed. In the case of serious crimes (e.g. murder, sexual offences) the specialist team or unit is informed and a log is opened, commencing the record of actions taken by the team. If the report occurs during the late or night shift and there is no duty officer coverage this first action will occur when the team commences work with the next day shift.

The crime desk response

The crime desk officer screens cases referred by the control room or by FOAs. Screening involves a *telephone investigation or crime evaluation/ assessment* and a decision as to the appropriate response.[49-50]

Calls are usually classified into one of four grades:

*   Immediate response.

*   Delayed response (usually within two or three hours).

*   By appointment (usually within seven days).

*   Advice only.

Seriousness, solvability and resource availability (expertise and manpower) are all factors taken into account when making a decision that:

*   no further investigation should take place – with the victim given, or pointed towards sources of, advice and counselling;

*   the merit of further investigation is questionable but there may be information and evidence that has intelligence potential, hence a crime scene attender/assessor should be deployed from the Crime Scenes Unit in due course;

*   there is merit in a SOCO attending in due course to identify, to record and to remove items of potential forensic value;

*   there is merit in referring the case to officers whose specific duty is to investigate this category of offence, e.g. the BCU.

A summary of deployment options

Table 2.6 summarises the range of investigative resources deployed according to type of offence. It is illustrative and should not be taken to be definitive or exclusive.

Investigative resource	Major Crime Unit (MCU)[1]	Area CID	Special Investigation Unit (SIU)	Beat Crimes Unit (BCU)	Uniform patrol[2]
Offences investigated	All extremely serious, serial and series offences, e.g. murder; serial rape; organised crime; extremely high monetary-value fraud and other financial crimes	Serious assault, suspicious death, large-scale theft, fraud (other than very large-scale), arson/ suspicious fire, robbery, aggravated burglary, rape, indecent assault, other sexual offences	Physical and sexual abuse of children; domestic violence; rape	Street crimes, e.g. street robbery deception, cheque fraud, possession/ supply of drugs	Small-scale theft, theft from/of motor vehicle, public disorder offences, assault, burglary, possession/ supply of drugs

Notes
1   In some forces, particular types of offence are investigated by specialist units, e.g. Serious Crime Unit, Fraud Squad.
2   Uniform patrol and tactical teams hand over cases to the evidence team (CIT) to continue investigation.

Table 2.6 The range of investigative resources deployed according to offence type

To illustrate similarities and differences in investigative expectations and procedures, the following sections will detail the investigative response of:

•   a uniform FOA at the scene or deployed by the control room;

•   the Evidence Team;

•   area CID;

•   the Special Investigation Unit;

•   the Major Crime Unit.

INVESTIGATION BY A UNIFORM FOA

The uniform FOA's fundamental task is to assess the circumstances, to act immediately as required to take charge of the situation and to decide how the crime can best be investigated:

•   by the officer himself or herself – bringing to bear his or her generic (non-specialist) investigative knowledge, skill and experience;

- by calling out CID – either area or MCU;

- by referring the matter to the Crime Desk for a decision.

It was pointed out earlier that, although forces differ, uniform officers have limited investigative responsibilities due to limited numbers, lack of time, knowledge, expertise and experience, lack of overtime and the shift system. If the case is not of an order of seriousness or of a category requiring investigation by area CID, the MCU or the SIU (in the case of alleged rape), the uniform officer is responsible for the preliminary investigation and preparing a crime report and other material as the medium of handing over:

- the case (and any suspect in detention) to the CIT (evidence team);

- the case to the SIU (e.g. following the FOA taking a complaint from a parent concerning suspected abuse of a child; following initial response to a 'domestic', the case being referred to officers who are specialists in dealing with domestic violence).

Initial crime-scene processing

Good practice and common sense mean that the officer should be mentally prepared for arrival at the scene, ready to ask questions appropriate to the type of crime and, in the case of crimes such as robbery and public order offences, scanning the vicinity as he or she approaches the scene.

On arrival, the FOA should engage in initial crime-scene processing. The officer must gain a visual picture, making a quick survey of the scene and its surrounding context to determine:

- who is present, their relative location and condition – being potential victims, witnesses and suspects;

- the physical setting and objects within this – in terms of condition and relative location;

- the presence of security devices, e.g. video surveillance equipment;

- what seems to have happened.

The FOA's initial processing of the crime scene is vital not least because it forms the initial start point for the subsequent search for physical evidence.

Hence an officer's fundamental information-processing skills and ability as a professional eyewitness and earwitness are on the line: to observe in detail and in the round, to note what is before his or her eyes and ears, to register and to hold this vital detail in working memory, and to store it in longer-term memory.

Immediate actions

Caring for the victim is the priority task. However, differences in crimes and the circumstances within which they occur mean there is no sequential checklist that covers every offence. Having attended to any individual requiring assistance, administering urgent first aid or summoning medical back-up, investigation must take place.

The FOA must search for the suspected offender, sources of evidence and evidence itself. This search focuses on *leads* (*solvability factors*). Typical leads are:

- witnesses to the crime – usually the most important source of information;
- knowledge of the suspect's name;
- knowledge of the suspect's location;
- knowledge of the suspect's description – arising from witnesses, video recordings, or still photographs;
- knowledge of the suspect's vehicle (where applicable) – the more specific the better;
- identification of the suspect;
- traceable items, i.e. with identifiable characteristics, marks or numbers;
- significant physical evidence – objects, marks and traces;
- a significant *modus operandi* – akin to a 'signature' in respect of the approach to effecting the crime, idiosyncratic patterns of behaviour and communication, weapon usage, style of dress and so on.

In his or her search for leads, an FOA applies a mental framework of investigative tasks, which need to be conducted at the scene – the 'hot' investigation – or in the vicinity of the scene – the 'warm' investigation. The actual sequence of tasks is a matter of personal and professional judgement, based upon the officer's assessment of the situation: the nature of the offence, the circumstances in which it occurred and the circumstances currently confronting the officer.

Whatever task the FOA decides to engage in, or in whatever order, it constitutes an investigative action.

Identification, management and interviewing of key witnesses

Having verified the actual occurrence, time and place of an offence and cared for the victim, the identification, management and initial interviewing of key witnesses as soon after the offence occurred, is the single most important aspect of the preliminary investigation. The FOA must necessarily obtain a suitably detailed description and account from every available witness. In general terms, only witnesses (including the victim) provide information leading to a suspect, with the officer seeking evidence which is:

- *positive* – stating something that was the case;

- *negative* – stating something that was not the case;

- *confirmatory* – converges with something asserted by another;

- *disconfirmatory* – counters something asserted by another.

As pointed out earlier, physical evidence seldom establishes the identity of a suspect. It can assist in proving guilt once a suspect has been identified.

The FOA must not be satisfied with one witness, even if the individual gives a very large amount of information. It is essential to search for additional witnesses. The widest possible range of witnesses is necessary because each one is a potential source of extra evidence to that asserted by the first and subsequent witnesses, enabling balanced and objective assessment of each account and the relationship between accounts.

The FOA must therefore be systematic in identifying and dealing with particular categories of witness or potential witness. These will include the following.

All people present at the scene during the commission of the offence and other persons currently at, or known to have entered, the scene

Appropriate contact with this group is essential to the subsequent investigation and sorting of fingerprints and other clues at the scene.

Witnesses and others at the scene must be:

- told to remain at the scene – bearing in mind a witness may well be the offender;

- told not to discuss the events – given the risk of contaminating their descriptions or accounts, or collaborating in constructing these;

- kept separate from the suspect wherever possible – if they are allowed to talk this may interfere with later questioning;

- told to remove nothing from the scene and to leave the scene untouched.

If the suspect has not been detained, any information on the suspect – identification and address (if known) or description – should be circulated urgently by radio to the operational information system.

Descriptions should be as full as possible. Typical contents are:

- physical description – including ethnic appearance using the classifications in Table 2.7;

- stance;

- build;

- clothing – colour and type.

IC1	White-skinned European
IC2	Dark-skinned European
IC3	Negroid
IC4	Indian or Pakistani (Asian)
IC5	Chinese or Japanese (Oriental)
IC6	Arabian or Egyptian (Arab)

Table 2.7 Ethnic classifications

Additional details should be obtained wherever possible, e.g.

- any outstanding physical features or behaviour, e.g. mannerisms, gait;

- 'way of speaking' – vocal features, regional accent, indicators to background/education, noteworthy vocabulary or phrasing.

Where a motor vehicle was involved, the make, model, colour and registration number should be ascertained if possible.

Witnesses need to be asked for detail that will guide the further course of the investigation, e.g.

- the manner of the attack;

- the means of entry;

- tools or weapons used;

- the purpose, intent or object of the offender;

- any objects known, or believed, to have been touched, handled or moved by the offender;

- peculiarities of the offender – actions, gestures, mannerisms and other pointers, e.g. words used or way of talking constituting a possible pattern, 'trademark' or modus operandi;

- any vehicle used;

- identification of any property stolen or damage done.

Whenever a witness gives a description of a location, object, person or arrangement of objects or persons, he or she should be invited to make a sketch or drawing of whatever he or she is describing. The officer should endorse any sketch or drawing to make clear its provenance to the court, i.e.

- ensure the drawing bears:
  - the details and signature of the witness;
  - the officer's details and signature;
  - date, time and place of production;

- assign a reference to the drawing, which is in effect an exhibit, using the officer's initials and a number (referring to its place in the sequence of exhibits collected by the officer);

- ensure there is an appropriate entry, including the exhibit reference, in the officer's pocket book concerning the production and collection of the sketch or drawing.

Those with a view of the scene of crime and the suspect's arrival and departure route.

The FOA must inspect the scene and the vicinity to identify and assess:

- actual or potential approach and exit routes taken by the offender;

- size of aperture at point of entry and exit;

- vantage points, fields of vision, obstacles;

- illumination, shadow, dead ground;

- visibility and audibility;

- distances and dimensions.

Adopting this essentially 'outsider looking in' perspective, the officer is able to assess potential witnesses with a view of the scene of the crime and the suspect's point of arrival and departure route. The officer can then speak to these potential witnesses who might have had an opportunity to see the offender.

The FOA should not accept assertions that an individual is, or would not have been, at home. The person may have been at home due to sickness or away on holiday.

Others who may have been in the vicinity at the material time

This includes anyone near the scene immediately prior to, during or following the offence, e.g. Royal Mail personnel, gas and electricity meter readers, newspaper deliverers, roundsmen.

A comprehensive search for witnesses is hard work. It particularly puts on the line the officer's ability in respect of:

* interviewing skills – to elicit descriptions and accounts in a manner that generates as much detail as possible, without the officer influencing the content of these by prior knowledge of what another individual has said or the officer's knowledge of the description and account of the suspect;

* note-taking skills – to record accurately and in appropriate level of detail all material information, including key verbatim utterances, in an *incident record book* (IRB) or, in forces that do not have IRBs, a notepad or the officer's *pocket book* (PB).

Some forces are experimenting with equipping FOAs with information technology, i.e. laptop computers linked to the OIS, CRS and the PNC.

In some instances, the FOA may judge it appropriate to conduct a full interview at this stage with a view to obtaining an immediate statement. More commonly, witnesses may:

* be advised that they will be interviewed later at their home address (or other location of their choosing);

* be invited or taken to the police station to be interviewed or for a medical examination followed by an interview.

Such 'second stage' or 'follow up' interviewing is necessarily part of the process of continuing investigation. In some forces, uniform patrol officers may be called upon to conduct such follow-up interviewing. However, uniform patrol officers are a limited resource. The capacity to deploy officers to emergency calls is already stretched, particularly with the increasing emphasis on proactive policing, which requires uniform officers to be deployed to tactical teams and other intelligence-gathering tasks. Thus, a patrol officer engaging in follow-up investigation reduces immediate response capacity even further.

In forces which have evidence teams (CITs), it is more likely that these follow-up interviews, which may ultimately produce witness statements, are conducted by officers in these units or, where available, available officers selectively tasked by CIT officers.

Detention of the suspect

On some occasions the suspect will be, or have been, detained at or near the scene. The FOA should arrest the suspect if the information from witnesses (including the victim) justifies this. The officer must mentally note, if not immediately writing down, the content of any utterances by the suspect or any exchanges between:

- the suspect and the FOA or another police officer – with particular reference to significant statements and silences;

- the suspect and others, i.e. witnesses.

If the FOA is with the victim when the suspect is detained at or near the scene, or as a result of a circulated description, the officer must ensure that the victim does not see the person detained until a formal identification parade is arranged.

The FOA must then arrange for transportation of the suspect to the police station. Typically, this involves calling for back-up in the form of other officers with a vehicle.

When a police vehicle arrives, the FOA may decide to hold the suspect in the vehicle while the officer conducts the form of searching appropriate to the circumstances, e.g. where incriminating evidence such as a weapon or bunch of keys would appear to have been thrown away.

There is an obvious risk of:

- the FOA who comes into contact with both the victim and the suspect cross-contaminating the two, e.g. attending to the victim then arresting the suspect; arresting the suspect and then attending to the victim;

- the FOA failing to ensure that the same vehicle does not transport the victim and the suspect at different times.

Conducting searches for physical evidence

A search for physical evidence is particularly necessary in offences against property, particularly burglary. A search can:

- establish whether the crime was committed;
- establish the *modus operandi* of the offender;
- assist in proving guilt once a suspect has been identified, but is seldom able to establish the identity of a suspect.

The FOA is in charge of the crime scene and is responsible for:

- seeing that all necessary action is taken to protect it and any physical evidence therein;
- keeping a record of others who attended the scene, e.g. a medical examiner, paramedics, fire officers, their time of arrival and departure and what they did at the scene.

There is always the risk of:

- the FOA destroying evidence by a vague and unprofessional approach to searching;
- the victim or others unwittingly interfering with evidence, e.g. following an initial desire to sort through the mess to find out what is missing, to engage in cleansing.

Forces differ as to the circumstances under which an FOA is expected to conduct a search for physical evidence.

- An FOA may have to carry out a 'holding exercise' in the case of crime requiring the attendance of MCU officers, e.g. a murder, or area CID, e.g. a serious sexual assault, wounding.
- The officer secures the scene and makes every effort to preserve evidence as necessary and waits for the arrival of officers from the specialist team who will have summoned SOCOs on a priority basis. A boundary around the scene must be marked off wherever possible, signalling to passers-by and those stopping to look that they must keep away and not enter the bounded area.
- The FOA may be required to contact the Crime Desk, which will use information provided by the officer to make a screening decision, i.e. whether it merits the deployment of a trained crime scene attender/analyst who will decide whether a SOCO should attend.

- In other forces, the FOA is expected to conduct a more than basic crime scene search in order to assess whether a SOCO should be requested to attend.

- In at least one small force in which SOCOs are a scarce resource and the force area is large, uniform patrol officers are trained to carry out SOCO duties, as opposed to crime scene attender/analyst duties, at the time of initial search of the crime scene.

Where an FOA is expected, or is directed, to search this must be:

- systematic to ensure it covers all the 'ground' to be examined;
- painstakingly recorded – what was searched, how and to what effect – in order to cope with the demands of accountability and disclosure, i.e.
  - scrupulous notes must be taken;
  - sketching is essential;
  - where equipment is available, photographs should be taken and video recordings made.

Where the FOA makes a sketch or drawing of his or her pattern or approach to searching and of locations or objects, he or she must follow the standard procedure for proving its provenance:

- ensure the drawing bears:
  - the officer's details and signature;
  - date, time and place of production;
- assign a reference to the drawing, which is in effect an exhibit, using the officer's initials and a number (referring to its place in the sequence of exhibits collected by the officer);
- ensure there is an appropriate entry, including the exhibit reference, in the officer's pocket book concerning the production and collection of the sketch or drawing.

The FOA should be properly equipped to conduct the search, to record this and to take appropriate action in respect of identified physical evidence. A police magazine advised probationer constables to equip themselves to do a professional job of searching, i.e. with a torch, a magnifying glass, a clipboard, a sketch pad, graph paper, compass, steel tape, chalk, sealable polythene bags, and simple tools including a multi-purpose penknife with a screwdriver and tweezers.[51]

The FOA must have the requisite knowledge, skills, awareness and motivation:

- to conduct and to record a search;

- to note ambient conditions;

- to draw the scene, annotating sketches with the location of physical evidence;

- to take appropriate measures to preserve physical evidence, i.e.

  - marking off any marks, imprints, impressions and trace evidence noted within a location or outside;
  - during rain or snow conditions diverting water and covering tyre, shoe and other impressions with available boxes or cardboard (but preferably not polythene);
  - drawing the attention of those remaining at the scene and others who will either be recommended to attend or will attend as a matter of course (e.g. the crime scene attender/analyst or SOCO) to physical evidence that has been marked off and protected;
  - extending the secured area if searching has led to the discovery of potentially more physical evidence;

- to remove 'at risk' physical evidence to a safe place, i.e. removing:

  - entire items of evidential value that are liable to inadvertent removal or destruction, or are of immediate investigative value, e.g. a cassette containing a video recording by a security camera; a weapon or tool; trace material that should be removed with tweezers and placed in a polythene bag;
  - material, or an object, liable to irreversible change, e.g. in hot weather, a sample of putty containing marks; an item bearing a mark, such as a container of spread.

Actions and reporting that complete the preliminary investigation

Processing the suspect

If a suspect has been arrested, the FOA presents the suspect to the custody officer, giving the circumstances and the grounds for arrest, details of actions taken by the officer and evidence, including witnesses and any recovered items. A custody record is opened and a custody number allocated. The suspect is searched, items are recorded in the custody record (and in any additional property registers), and sealed in bags with unique reference numbers.

Preserving evidence and making records

The FOA is required:

- *to preserve evidence*: bagging up, sealing and assigning reference numbers to physical evidence recovered from the scene or removed from the suspect;

- *to complete entries in his or her IRB or pocket book*: taking in particular a record of actions and the detailed content of verbal exchanges between the officer and the victim, witnesses and the suspect – including in the latter's case significant responses, including silence;

- *to open a crime report form (allocated a unique crime number)*: making entries in respect of:
  - complaint details;
  - complainant details;
  - details of the offence;
  - description of suspect;
  - vehicles seen;
  - *modus operandi*;
  - vehicle offence details, e.g. relating to theft of/from or criminal damage to a vehicle;
  - property – stolen and damaged: description, value, whether recovered;
  - details of offenders;
  - details of enquiries:

    (a) request for a SOCO with reasons;
    (b) enquiries at the scene and in the vicinity;
    (c) actions: in sequential order, time and date, giving details of all persons involved and actions taken, requests made and directions received.

- *to enclose/attach essential additional items in the crime report*: e.g. photocopies of pocketbook entries, drawings made at the scene, copies of statements taken, notes or any reports made by the police surgeon (forensic medical examiner) or a social worker if one has been called to attend, notes from hospital casualty staff and notes made by other agencies – such as the fire service.

Checking records

All FOAs should carry out appropriate checks, e.g. PNC, accessing the FIS, and contacting the local intelligence officer (LIO) at his or her station in order to access and to task the intelligence system.

Follow-up witness interviewing

If the officer has sufficient time left on shift and, as pointed out earlier, if it is the particular force policy for FOAs to engage in follow-up interviewing witnesses, the FOA conducts witness interviews (including the victim) with a view to obtaining statements.

All officers – uniform and CID – should be trained in the national PEACE model of investigative interviewing. PEACE is an acronym that stands for the stages for which there are guidelines to best practice: *planning and preparation; engage and explain; account; close; evaluate*.

The model has evolved since its introduction in 1992, reflected in three texts.[52–54]

Originally, officers were made aware[55] of two approaches to interviewing:

- *the management of conversation approach*: obtaining the fullest possible first account, and asking for second and subsequent accounts, which are systematically probed and summarised;

- *the cognitive approach*: a memory-enhancing method applicable to willing and vulnerable witnesses in which the individual is helped to envisage mentally the context, then to give the fullest account leaving out nothing, however seemingly inconsequential, then asked to recount key parts in reverse order or to adopt a different perspective, i.e. that of someone else observing the offence, and then offered some memory-jogging aids.

The officer had to decide which approach was most suited to the interviewee. Conversation management was considered appropriate for those who were resistant, whereas cognitive interviewing was suitable for interviewees who were vulnerable in some way, particularly in the manner spelled out in PACE Code C. The revised model[56–57] has dispensed with the two different interviewing approaches. It incorporates the conversational techniques and elements of cognitive interviewing within a management of conversation approach.

However, in all three versions, PEACE says officers must apply *R. v. Turnbull* criteria to accounts given by witnesses and provides them with a checklist mnemonic ADVOKATE (Table 2.8).

A	Amount of time under observation	How long did the witness have the suspect in view?
D	Distance	What was the distance between the witness and the suspect?
V	Visibility	What was visibility like at the time?
O	Obstruction	Were there any obstructions to the view of the witness?
K	Known or seen before	Had the witness ever seen the suspect before? If so, where and when?
A	Any reason to remember	Did the witness have any special reason for remembering the suspect?
T	Time lapse	How long has elapsed since the witness saw the suspect?
E	Error or material discrepancy	Are there any errors or material discrepancies between descriptions given in the first and subsequent accounts of the witness?

Table 2.8 ADVOKATE: the *R.* v. *Turnbull* checks that officers should apply to witness statements

In the case of discrepancies between a witness's first and any subsequent accounts, PEACE guidelines say an officer should:

• account for these discrepancies if possible;

• include these discrepancies in the witness's statement, i.e. not clean up the witness's account by omitting them.

In respect of translating what has been said to the officer in the interview (or others prior to the interview) very few witnesses write their own statement. In the vast majority of cases, the officer will use his or her memory, aided by notes taken of the witness's responses, to draft a statement for the witness to sign.[58]

Handing over

The FOA has to hand over to other officers to continue the investigation:

• in those forces where there are evidence teams – which typically operate day and late, but not night, shifts;

• where it requires this to be done by specialists in investigating cases involving child abuse or domestic violence.

Hand over is effected by preparing a 'package' for the officer assigned to be the investigating officer (IO). This package should contain:

- The crime report, with any enclosures.

- Key texts: photocopies of relevant pocket book entries; IRB; original or copy of notes taken at the scene; notes arising from conversations/ interviewing of the victim, witnesses, other significant individuals and the suspect, with particular reference to significant statements and silence.

- Draft and final-version statements.

- Exhibits and items found at the scene, or in the possession of the suspect, and taken by the FOA.

- Written handover notes, i.e. a document giving a briefing. These notes may be informal (on notepaper or a statement form) or entered on a locally devised form. (Note: such forms are the exception rather than the rule. There is no standard format.) The notes should provide IO with:
  - a fuller account of the FOA's preliminary investigation and subsequent actions by the FOA and others, e.g. police officers involved in the investigation, requests for, and attendance by, SOCO;
  - fuller details concerning witnesses, their accounts, instructions given to them by the FOA, and their availability;
  - details of FOA's availability to give the officer a verbal briefing or to answer any queries.

This last item on availability underlines the recognised usefulness of the FOA briefing the IO – shift patterns permitting. Furthermore, an aware and professional FOA will include illustrations and drawings with the crime report and with his or her handover notes.

At this point, we conclude the response by the FOA. In those forces where FOAs are tasked with continuing the investigation, their actions will closely correspond to those described in the next section.

INVESTIGATION BY THE EVIDENCE TEAM

It will be recalled that the evidence team (CIT) is responsible for continuing the investigation, gathering evidence in cases handed over by uniform patrol officers or by tactical team officers – typically producing one or more arrested suspects.

The CIT officer taking over as IO in the case inherits:

- a handover 'package' from the FOA (or the arresting officer in the tactical team);

- potential witnesses to be interviewed;

- where a suspect has been arrested, one or more individuals in cells requiring interview and for whom a custody record exists.

The officer should:

- if possible, obtain a verbal briefing from the FOA or arresting officer;

- examine the custody record and speak to the custody officer and civilian custody staff about factors such as the suspect's behaviour in custody, any requests made, and the attendance of the medical examiner (police surgeon).

The IO's first task is to integrate this material and then to assess the preliminary investigation, the nature of the police case as reported, and the status, strength and sufficiency of evidence gathered thus far. Whether or not there is a suspect awaiting interview, the officer must decide whether it is appropriate to commit further resources to investigating the offence and, if so, how to progress the investigation.

We describe below an illustrative, not exhaustive, list of actions by an IO where investigation should continue. The actual circumstances will dictate that some occur earlier or later in the sequence – one key factor being the point at which the suspect is arrested. Throughout the entire process, however, the IO must keep a full record:

- of actions: taken or directions given to others, entering these in the crime report, making pocket book entries, or keeping a manual or computerised action log ('book');

- of items likely to be offered as evidence.

It will be clear that in the main these activities – which are essentially the systematic gathering and processing of information and checking out sources of information – constitute a process of logical progression leading up to, and in preparation for, interviewing the suspect. PEACE acknowledges that the detention clock might limit the officer's time to engage in some or many of these activities.

Consulting information and intelligence systems

The IO should access information and intelligence systems – searching for information or intelligence on the suspect, associates of the suspect, the victim, witnesses, the location, the *modus operandi,* vehicles, weapons, and so on.

Visiting the scene

Lay people assume that it is a matter of course, indeed, common sense for investigators to go to look at the scene of an offence. However, resource constraints (staffing and time constraints, workload, absence of vehicles and a long distance between the CIT location and the scene) are often the reason for a scene not being visited.

Conducting searches

Searches may be necessary, conducted by the IO and colleagues, or others tasked by the IO. Whoever carries out searches to seize items deemed to be of evidential value found in locations and in vehicles must make full records of searching. These should be supported by sketches and diagrams, using the standard method of proving their provenance.

Witness-focused actions

These include:

*   liaising with the witnesses (which includes the victim) who gave accounts and descriptions during the preliminary investigation – making arrangements for interviews at appropriate locations;

*   identifying new witnesses, e.g. through 'house-to-house' inquiries, whose questionnaire responses indicate a potential to provide evidence;

*   conducting formal initial, or further, interviews to obtain statements.

Like the FOA, the IO must apply *R.* v. *Turnbull* criteria to accounts given by witnesses, applying the ADVOKATE checklist and, if there are discrepancies between a witness's first and any subsequent accounts, the IO should:

*   account for these discrepancies if possible;

*   include these discrepancies in the witness's statement, i.e. not clean up the witness's account by omitting them.

Common sense and professionalism require the IO to request a witness to make a sketch when the witness verbally describes a location, object, person or arrangement of objects or persons. The IO may also ask:

- witnesses to assist in the creation of a photo-fit/E-fit.

- the victim to complete standardised 'checklist' questionnaires, e.g. sexual offence forms.

Communicating with the medical examiner

Where the suspect is in custody, the IO may liaise with the medical examiner in order:

- to obtain an assessment of whether the suspect is fit to be interviewed, requires an appropriate adult, is suffering from a particular physical complaint, is mentally ill or has a psychological disorder;

- to ask about treatment given;

- to learn the outcome of any relevant communication between the medical examiner and another or institution, where the suspect gave the doctor permission for contact to be made;

- to request an immediate written report (for inclusion in the crime file) of the conduct and outcome of, and opinion upon, any examination of:
  - the body – which he or she certified as dead;
  - the victim;
  - witnesses – in order to exclude these as suspects;
  - the suspect;

- to request a list of samples taken;

- to take charge of samples taken – signing the doctor's notes to such effect.

Communicating with any relevant medical practitioner or institution

If it appears relevant, following conversation with the medical examiner, and where the suspect has signed an authorisation granting permission for information to be disclosed to the police, the IO may decide to contact a doctor or institution which might provide the necessary information.

Communicating with the SOCO

The IO will need to exploit forensic aspects further by speaking with the SOCO, the forensic 'expert', to establish:

- if, or when, the SOCO had attended or intends to attend the scene;
- the results of any attendance:
    - description and assessment of the scene;
    - the outcome of his or her search for forensic evidence, i.e. a list of CTM recovered;
- the location (at the scene) of any CTM recovered – preferably assisted by an explanatory drawing;
- the SOCO's assessment of recovered CTM;
- if the SOCO has not handed over the CTM to the IO, its present whereabouts.

Selecting and making a case for submission for forensic testing of items collected by the FOA, the IO, the medical examiner or the SOCO

The IO may have a wide range of material available for forensic testing. In each case, the IO must answer the following questions:

- Is the probative value of the evidence already available to the investigation sufficient to implicate or eliminate? Is it anticipated to be so for charging, proceeding, or court purposes?
- If the answer to the previous questions is no, and should a forensic examination be positive, will the total amount of evidence then be sufficient, or justify further enquiries?
- Are the costs involved justified in the light of the circumstances and force priorities?

The IO considering submission of case material for external forensic analysis by the FSS or other provider:

- should always seek the advice of the SOCO, or the FSS or other provider, on the scientific potential of the material in question;
- will need to consult with a supervisor or manager, who will decide whether the proposed analysis, or analyses, of an item is VFM.

In the case of fingerprints, the IO must bear in mind:

- the force policy on the number of points deemed to constitute a match worthy of progressing the case, since as of 3 April 2000 there will be no national standard;
- that the discovery of unidentified prints at the scene imply eliminator tests, i.e. the prints of officers who attended must be checked, as well as those of individuals who live at or have had access to the scene, in addition to the suspect.

In the case of submissions for analysis by an external forensic provider, the MG FSS form must be submitted (see section on forensic investigation, pp. 38–9). In sum, the form covers:

- contact details of the officer in the case or other officer with responsibility for the case;
- proposed offence charge;
- for urgent and critical submissions only, the particular category of justification;
- specification of forms, documentation, photography and other relevant case material enclosed with the submission;
- method of delivery to the laboratory;
- details of subjects, including their status – deceased, victim, suspect, subject for elimination;
- the circumstances of the incident – including any explanation given by the suspect in relation to the CTM;
- what is required to be established – stating priority (urgent, critical, standard);
- a list of found or seized items submitted for scientific examination.

We draw attention again to the fact that the MG FSS only requires the police to list items *being submitted for analysis*. The predecessor to the MG FSS, the HOLAB3, required the police to inform the forensic scientist of *all* items collected or seized by the police, giving reasons why certain items were not being submitted for analysis.

Planning and preparing for the interview of the suspect

PEACE in its latest version[59] guides officers:

- to understand how this interview might contribute to the investigation;

- to review what is known or what further needs to be established about the suspect, details likely to assist the development of a constructive relationship, e.g. age, gender, domestic circumstances, cultural background, physical and mental health, previous contact with police, traumatic experiences;

- to know the legal requirements:

  - PACE Code C, with particular reference to legal advice, vulnerable persons, communication difficulties significant statements and silences and relevant comments;
  - CJPOA provisions on special warnings;
  - offences and points to prove;

- to identify practical issues in addition to visiting the scene and searching of premises, i.e. location of the interview, number of interviewers and their respective roles, timing of the interview, equipment, and exhibits and property;

- to consider pre-interview disclosure of evidence and the management of active defence by the legal adviser.

  'In some cases you may feel it appropriate to disclose information to the defence prior to the interview. There is, however, no requirement for you to do this. Police still retain the right to decide how much information they will disclose prior to interview.'[60]

The important points the IO must consider are:

- What to disclose?
- When to disclose?
- How the officer is going to disclose – verbally or in written format?
- What not to disclose?
- Why the IO is not disclosing this information?
- How to handle non-disclosure if challenged?

Disclosure is a very thorny issue. To assist officers in the making of these decisions, the new guidelines:

- Provide extensive advice and directions.

- Include a copy of the relevant checklists for legal advisers in *A Pocket Reference*, observing that these 'are a valuable tool when deciding such issues'.[61]

- A written record of these decisions must be kept. In some forces, there is a form or a section in a pro forma booklet, for noting this detail.

Finally, the PEACE model recommends two methods to assist officers in analysing and using information at the preparation and planning phase:

- an *interview plan* – a pro forma method for sorting out points to prove, available evidence, evidence to be obtained and possible sources;

- a *planning sheet* – a sequence of topics, each able to be expanded into focused areas for questioning.

In a number of forces, particularly those which conduct advanced investigative-interviewing courses, officers are taught methods for collating information, which facilitate analysis, highlight anomalies and assist preparation and planning for interviews and briefings of fellow officers and legal adviser. These methods include:

- *SE3R (S – E – three – R)*. This represents narrative detail graphically and in a form that is easily committed to memory. It is applicable to written or recorded text from one or more individuals. SE3R is a mnemonic, specifying the steps involved: skim, extract, read, review and recall.

- *Tabulation of detail (grids)*. This is a simple method for collating and representing detail from one or more texts.

- *THEMA*. This is a particular application of grids to aid the analysis of recordings and transcripts to identify consistency and oddities. THEMA is an acronym: *the*matic *e*mergence of *a*nomaly.

These methods are referred to again in this text and are described in Appendix 7.

Briefing the appropriate adult and interpreter

Where there is a requirement for an appropriate adult or interpreter, this individual needs to be briefed by the IO.

Briefing the legal adviser

In some forces, officers make a note both of what the legal adviser requests and of the officer's replies. In others, the officer tape-records the exchange. Most forces accept that the exchange may be tape-recorded by the legal adviser.

Interviewing the suspect

The IO will apply the latest version of the PEACE model[62] for interviewing suspects, including in the Account Phase the three stages:

- *the suspect's agenda*: giving the suspect the opportunity to say what he or she wants or to raise issues that he or she wishes to cover;
- *the police agenda*: informing and questioning the suspect about matters considered by the IO to be material issues;
- *challenge*: confronting the suspect with anomalies, and apparent deception, identified by the IO within the interviewee's disclosures and responses in the previous stages.

The IO may decide to break the interview between stages or, after the police agenda, in order to analyse what the suspect has said and to prepare for the next phase.

Some forces have adopted a three-step approach to interviewing suspects:

- *Step 1*: there is no disclosure to the suspect or the suspect's legal adviser prior to interviewing. There is a relatively brief interview in which the suspect is invited to give his or her account, e.g. in response to a trigger such as, 'Give us your side of things?' The interview is then ended.
- *Step 2*: evidence is disclosed, particularly guided by what the suspect has said.
- *Step 3*: the suspect is then interviewed, with the officers following the standard PEACE model in respect of the account phase.

When following the PEACE guidelines officers are directed:

- to keep an open mind;

- to not assume the suspect's guilt;

- to be vigilant for negative information and for information that is disconfirmatory as well as confirmatory of the suspect's guilt;

- that they must not tell lies: R. v. Mason [1988] W.L.R. 139; [1987] Crim. L.R. 757, CA.

Identification procedures

At an appropriate time, either before or after interviewing or charging, the IO may:

- take fingerprints – when done after charging: this is a very common point when overtures will be made to invite the suspect to become an informant;

- make arrangement for identity procedures.

Action after charging

There are many tasks to be fulfilled after charging:

- seeking to recruit the individual to be an informant – typically done at the stage of taking fingerprints, taking defendant details (i.e. completing the MG3), escorting back to the cell, or where the individual is bailed and has accepted a lift home en route in the police vehicle;

- completing and forwarding to the CPS files containing the range of material specified in the *Manual of Guidance for the Preparation, Processing and Submission of Files*,[63] and subsequently liaising with the CPS;

- preparing records of tape-recorded interviews (ROTIs);

- producing copies of the working tapes of PACE interviews for the suspect's solicitor;

- arranging for copying of any video recording to be forwarded to the CPS;

- obtaining formal statements from witnesses, the police surgeon and individuals in other institutions involved with the case, e.g. hospital doctors, specialists, fire officers;

- liaising with the SSU in respect of:

    - in-force testing of items;

- submission of items for analysis by external forensic science providers;

• liaising with the external forensic scientist prior to and following requested analyses.

In some forces, where the workload on the CIT is recognised to be heavy, the tasks of file completion and submission and liaison with the CPS, are performed by an Administration Support Unit (ASU).

INVESTIGATIONS BY AREA CID

When a serious offence against the person or property occurs, this becomes the responsibility of the area CID unit. Officers work flexible hours, but typically cover extends across the day shift and part of the late shift, with an 'out of hours' duty officer on call.

When a serious offence occurs, uniform officers attend rapidly to secure the scene and to await the arrival of officers from the area CID unit and the priority attendance of SOCOs.

Depending upon the investigative demands of the case, the detective inspector assigns one or more detectives (constables, sergeants or a combination). Detective sergeants are deemed to fulfil a supervisory role, but, in effect, constables and sergeants work as relative equals.

Area CID staff carry out both the preliminary and the continuing investigation, i.e.

• commencing an actions log (see next section);

• initial crime-scene processing;

• identifying solvability factors;

• identifying key witnesses:
  - those who may have been, or claim to have been, an eyewitness or witness to the immediate event in some other way;
  - those who stand in a particular relationship to the victim;
  - someone having a central position in the enquiry;

• identifying other witnesses, extending the potential range of these by using different avenues of enquiry, e.g.
  - immediate, limited house-to-house enquiries, particularly focusing on those areas within line of sight and earshot of the crime scene;
  - passers-by;

- CCTV of public places;
- persons having legitimate access to the scene;
- relatives;
- video security systems – in commercial and private premises;
- local tradesmen and businesses;

- arranging systematic house-to-house enquiries, including the administration of questionnaires;

- interviewing and taking formal statements from witnesses (see below);

- asking witnesses to assist in the creation of a photo-fit/E-fit;

- asking victims to complete standardised 'checklist' questionnaires;

- conducting searches for physical evidence – assisted by uniform shift officers, with the possible assistance of a POLSA officer;

- where applicable, liaising with the SOCO – in respect of assessment;

- of the crime scene, identification of actual and potential marks and other CTM;

- making pocket book entries;

- opening a crime report form;

- accessing, interrogating and studying the content of information and intelligence systems, e.g. identifying local informants of potential value, suspects in the vicinity with records for similar offences, crime patterns similar to the one in this case;

- tasking informants;

- if not already arrested, arresting and initially processing the suspect into custody;

- where applicable, tasking the police surgeon or hospital staff to conduct an examination of the victim or the suspect;

- contacting external medical practitioners and other relevant professionals able to provide information, subject to caveats, on the victim and the suspect;

- fingerprinting and taking samples from the suspect;

- briefing the legal adviser, the appropriate adult and interpreter;

- interviewing the suspect (see below);

- selecting and making a case for submission of items for forensic testing;

The above list is illustrative not exhaustive.

The actions log

Area CID is not excepted from the requirement to keep records of its actions and items likely to be offered as evidence. Given the larger scale of its enquiries, actions are recorded in an actions log, which may be a manuscript or computer record.

Interviewing key witnesses

Key witnesses – also called significant witnesses – are those whose evidence is perceived to be of significant evidential value. Often they are identified early on in an investigation.

When the individual is, or claims to be, an eyewitness his or her account and especially descriptions can become a matter of dispute, particularly at trial. In the case of other key witnesses, the fine-grain detail of their disclosures is of great potential in assisting further lines of enquiry and also because they may later emerge as a potential suspect.

The service is coming increasingly to recognise that the accounts of such key witnesses should not be left to the vagaries of standard interviewing of witnesses. Typically, interviewing officers in pursuit of a statement, wittingly and unwittingly, influence what the witness says, edit, delete, amend and otherwise distort detail contained in spontaneous disclosures and responses to questions.[64]

There is a growing trend to recording the initial interviewing of such witnesses. There is a declared preference for video recording, but it is acknowledged that for a number of reasons this is not possible and that audio recording is the more practical method.

Interviewing the suspect

CID officers are obliged, like all officers, to follow the PEACE guidelines. As we pointed out earlier, these now require officers to engage in a three-stage approach to the account phase:

- *the suspect's agenda*: giving the suspect the opportunity to say what he or she wants or to raise issues that he or she wishes to cover;

- *the police agenda*: informing and questioning the suspect about matters considered by the IO to be material issues;

- *challenge*: confronting the suspect with anomalies, and apparent deception, identified by the investigating officer within the interviewee's disclosures and responses in the previous stages.

The IO may decide to break the interview between stages or, after the police agenda, in order to analyse what the suspect has said and to prepare for the next phase.

Some forces have adopted a three-step approach to interviewing suspects:

- *Step 1*: there is no disclosure. In a relatively brief interview, the suspect is invited to give his or her account, e.g. in response to a trigger such as, 'Give us your side of things?'.

- *Step 2*: evidence is disclosed, particularly guided by what the suspect has said.

- *Step 3*: the officers follow the standard PEACE model in respect of the account phase.

Action after charging

Area CID is responsible for the range of post-charge tasks:

- completing and forwarding file to the CPS files, and subsequently liaising with the CPS;

- preparing records of tape-recorded interviews (ROTIs);

- producing copies of the working tapes of PACE interviews;

- arranging for copying of any video recording to be forwarded to the CPS;

- obtaining formal statements from witnesses, the police surgeon and individuals in other institutions involved with the case, e.g. hospital doctors, specialists, fire officers;

- liaising with the SSU in respect of:
  - in-force testing of items;
  - submission of items for analysis by external forensic science providers;

- liaising with the external forensic scientist prior to and following requested analyses.

In some forces, the tasks of file completion and submission, and liaison with the CPS, are assisted or performed by an Administration Support Unit (ASU).

INVESTIGATION BY THE SPECIAL INVESTIGATION UNIT (SIU)

SIU officers are deployed in cases of child abuse, domestic violence and rape.

Child abuse

Abuse comes to light in many ways. A common way is its occurrence, or the suspicion of this, being brought to attention by a mother, a teacher or other third party contacting social services or the police.

Forces have explicit guidelines for the investigation of reported abuse. These are closely linked to central (DoH and Home Office) and local government (social service department) guidelines. The emphasis is upon *joint agency* working. In practice, SIU officers tend to take a lead role in terms of the direction of the investigation.

Once a report is received, this is logged on the OIS. Since numbers of SIU officers are limited, and certainly insufficient to provide 24-hour coverage, typically a uniform officer is deployed to attend as FOA to take the complaint. Akin to the CIT, the SIU takes over the continuing investigation.

With obvious adjustments, the FOA should carry out a preliminary investigation with the same basic elements as described earlier. The FOA should brief the SIU officer verbally wherever possible, but always provide comprehensive handover notes.

The SIU then takes over the case, arranging for the child to be medically examined and to attend the *video interview suite*, accompanied by a parent or suitable adult, for video-recorded interviewing to take place. In those instances where video recorded interviewing is considered inappropriate, or will not be countenanced by the child or adult, the interview will be tape recorded. Although joint-agency working notionally allows for a social worker to interview the child, in the greater proportion of cases, SIU officers fulfil this task. The planning, preparation and conduct of interviews is subject to DoH/Home Office guidelines.[65]

On completion of this interview, and either prior to or some time after witness interviewing, the suspect is typically arrested and interviewed under PACE. If legal advice is requested, the adviser is briefed. Whether legally advised or not, it is very common for suspects to be shown the video recording of the interview of the child.

SIU officers are again not excepted from the requirement to keep records of their actions and items likely to be offered as evidence. Typically, these include telephone logs, diaries, pro formas, records of case conferences, planning and preparation notes, and an *actions book*, which may be a manuscript or computer record.

After charging

Like CIT officers, SIU officers are responsible for progressing the preparation of files for the CPS. The major differences are that in addition to producing ROTIs and tapes of the PACE interviews of the suspect:

- indexes of video-recorded interviews (IVRIs) must be prepared – akin to ROTIs, these seek to summarise aspects of the interview where disclosures are deemed to have evidential significance;

- copies of video recording to be forwarded to the CPS;

- statements are required from medical examiners and social workers involved in the case.

Domestic violence and rape

When these offences occur, the SIU and the area CID unit work closely together. The area CID will take a lead role, with the SIU officers bringing to bear their experience and expertise in 'special care' interviewing.

There is a requirement to keep full records as with any other crime investigation.

INVESTIGATION BY THE MAJOR CRIME UNIT (MCU)

As explained earlier, the range of investigation conducted by the MCU is now very wide. In this section we will briefly describe what characteristically happens in the investigation of one type of major incident, murder.

The management of a murder investigation now involves:

- appointing key police and support personnel, and additional supporting personnel;

- establishing a Major Incident Room (MIR) and maintaining an incident log;

- implementing the HOLMES system for creating a database of information both on the management of the investigation and information generated;

- creating an intelligence capability;

- the appointing of analysts/investigative researchers;

- the implementation of the ACPO 'best practice' model of murder investigation.[66]

Appointment of police and support personnel

Initially, a *senior investigating officer* (SIO) is appointed to head the investigation. The SIO must create a management team. The ACPO model suggests the following composition:

- *Permanent members* – SIO, investigative team leaders, *crime scene co-ordinator* (CSC), *scientific support manager* (SSM), house-to-house team leader, forensic specialist adviser, pathologist;

- *Co-opted members* – Deputy SIO, office manager, analyst, press officer, search advisers, offender profiler, community awareness specialist, other specialists.

The CSC and SSM are senior SOCOs. The SSM is the SIO's main source of advice on, and interpretation of, physical evidence or *contact trace material* (CTM). Together, the two are responsible for directing and co-ordinating the collection of forensic information (photographs, drawings, video recordings) and CTM.

Additional supporting personnel

Additional support to the MCU includes:

- the medical examiner summoned to the scene;
- officers assigned from the uniform support group – particularly POLSA (police search adviser) officers;
- uniform officers to assist in the conduct of:
  - house-to-house enquiries, completing questionnaires of occupants' responses;
  - administering questionnaires to the public;
  - systematic and, where necessary, large-scale searches, as directed by the POLSA team.

The major incident room (MIR) and the incident log

An MIR is set up in a suitable locations.

An incident *log* (manuscript and computer-based) is opened, recording all actions taken.

HOLMES

Any major enquiry quickly generates and accumulates very large amounts of information, particularly in the early stages. HOLMES (Home Office Large and Major Enquiry System) enables the systematic processing, compilation and analysis of this growing database.

All information coming to the attention of the police regarding the case is entered into a computer using a nationally standardised format, allowing this to be collated and integrated, and selected material and combinations of detail, to be retrieved as requested.

There are key roles in the implementation of the HOLMES system:

- the *receiver*, who examines all information coming into the incident room, who indicates what actions are required, and whose comments are found on most incident documentation;

- the *statement reader*, who examines particular aspects of document-ation, especially statements, and indicates what requires specific action and indexing;

- the *office manager*, who examines every document before it is filed to ensure that all necessary work has been done;

- *indexers*, who index in detail information (in order to enable it to be later worked upon, combined and retrieved), creating a range of indexes:

  - document indexes:

    (a) *statements*: all statements taken within the course of an enquiry should be served on the defence;

    (b) *actions*: in any investigation when an officer is given or carries out a task this is called an *action*, but in the HOLMES context this involves:

      (i) a written instruction to perform a particular activity;
      (ii) the officer endorsing the action with his or her findings;
      (iii) the officer passing the action to the receiver for attention;

    (c) *messages*: messages are the source of a large amount of information coming into an enquiry, e.g. telephone calls from members of the public, all of which are written down, entered into the computer and passed to the receiver for decisions as to action;

    (d) *officers' reports*: whenever an officer submits a report on any aspect of the enquiry this should be recorded as an officer's report;

(e) *other documents*: any other documentary information is stored under this heading, with subsequent print-outs giving a one-line résumé indicating the contents of the document to assist in subsequent decisions as to the worth of full retrieval. (Note: only a selected number of other key documents will be entered in full into the computer, the majority will be one-line references indicating where the original document is located and can be examined);

(f) *property*: this is a record of all exhibits;

(g) *telex*: this is a list of all outgoing and incoming telexes that are dealt with in the same way as other documents;

(h) in addition, according to the nature of the case and the enquiry, other types of documentation are used, e.g.

  (i) *personal descriptive forms (PDFs)*: these are completed for all individuals who may be suspects or who were at or near the scene of the offence at the material time, with details being extracted from the form and entered under appropriate indexes;

  (ii) *questionnaires*: where questionnaires are administered, e.g. to the public, their contents are indexed where applicable;

  (iii) *house-to-house enquiries*: officers conducting house-to-house enquiries complete forms, the content of which is indexed and actioned in the event of positive information;

– information category indexes:

(a) *nominals*: this is the names index, containing the personal details of the individual plus all documentary references, and which enables an alphabetical print-out annotated with documentary references;

(b) *vehicles*: this a record of all vehicles of note coming to the attention of the enquiry, with the vehicle details along with any nominal cross-references, and which also enables a print-out;

(c) *streets*: this is a record of streets/locations which have come to the attention of the enquiry, e.g. home and business addresses, and which are cross-referenced as necessary, e.g. nominals of people who frequent the street; vehicles seen; reference of (documentary) source;

(d) *houses*: this is a list of all locations of particular interest to the enquiry – usually because they are a key individual's home address, workplace or business address, or a location frequented by a given individual or group of individuals – with each entry cross-referenced in a similar manner to streets;

(e) *categories*: these are any specific categories of information considered to be of likely value, which are deemed worthy of collation, and which can be interrogated or printed out;

(f) *telephones*: this is a list of telephone numbers of individuals and businesses, as well as telephone boxes where these are an aspect of the case;

(g) *sequence of events*: movements of an individual or events in respect of a particular location or item, e.g. a letter, are collated and enable the construction and print-out of a chronology, with each entry annotated with the number of the document containing a given piece of information and a short résumé, together with times and dates.

Indexing lies at the core of HOLMES. The accuracy of inputting text is vital given that errors of omission and commission corrupt the database.

Another vital function is the storage of documents themselves – these being cross-referenced to the indexes. This is the most vital information in terms of disclosure.

HOLMES II

HOLMES permits the creation of a growing database. While it has a 'search engine' to enable specified searches, e.g. to retrieve, cross-reference, cross-check and combine stored material on one or more items, there has never been a capability for what computing science terms 'intelligent' analyses. These kinds of analysis require dynamic reasoning, where the computer suggests areas to search if requested searches are of limited success or are unsuccessful. To construct this kind of 'search engine' requires very high-level computing: software applications able to manipulate intelligently a suitably constructed database and appropriately formatted material.

This development has been completed and is termed HOLMES II. It reduces the need for manual indexing by doing this automatically, thus reducing the number of human errors introduced in the indexing process. The 'search engine' is extremely powerful being able to engage to very great effect in dynamic reasoning.

The intelligence capability

Optimally, an intelligence cell (IC) should be sited within, or very close to, the MIR and have ready access to all information which comes into the MIR. Like all ICs within the force, it will have direct links to the Force Intelligence Bureau (FIB) and the FIS.

As an alternative to establishing an IC, intelligence officers may be seconded to the investigation.

Investigative analysts/researchers

Investigative analysts/researchers are assigned to the investigation. They work either as an integral aspect of, or alongside colleagues, within the MIR and the IC.

Analysts are able to identify information gaps an items of information that require corroboration. Their contribution enables:

- assessment of information;

- structuring of information;

- assessment of the progress of lines of enquiry;

- identification of new lines of enquiry;

- research into specific aspects of the investigation, e.g. descriptions of persons present at the time of the offence.

Analysts/researchers have typically undergone what is termed *ANACAPA* training.[67] This training enables officers to produce, manually, representations of text and images based upon information retrieved from HOLMES and derived from other sources. In addition, they use IT, particularly analytical software that enables patterns to be identified within a large database.

The application of analytical software and manual methods enable the generation of graphic representations:

- victim association charts – including networks, addresses, background and history;

- sequence-of-events charts – victim, suspect, parallel events;

- time lines on suspects – including milestone events and offences;

- case comparison, e.g. in a series of cases;

- mapping – of the scene, routes, search zones, scene features;

- scene assessment – linking of predictive/supportive crime scene findings with the current case;

- house-to-house focus analysis;

- significant evidential links;

- lines of enquiry charts;

- database searching;

- statement analysis – identifying important missing links, omissions or associations;

- telephone calls.

The 'best practice' model for investigation

The service now has an excellent 'best practice' model for murder investigations, specified in a manual commissioned by the ACPO Crime Committee.[68] It is understood that it is intended to produce similar manuals to assist SIOs in investigations into other types of serious crime.

The model gives explicit advice on 'best practice' from the discovery of the murder up to investigation following the charging of the suspect.

- *Initial stages*: the application of five fundamental 'building block' principles:

  - preservation of life;
  - preserve scene(s) (including opening up a crime scene log (see next section);
  - secure evidence (through focused questioning at the scene to identify witnesses, obtaining details of all persons at the scene, and noting index numbers of all vehicles in the vicinity);
  - identify the victim (questioning those present; making a record of the victim's physical description and clothing) – a critical step to triggering fast-track actions (see below, p. 95);
  - identify suspects – including early arrest of suspects (to avoid contamination, wherever possible, the arrest should be by officers who have not attended the scene).

The Crime Scene Log

This is used to account for the presence and movements of personnel within a designated crime scene area, to provide continuity of exhibits and to prevent contamination. The log should be started immediately and kept by a designated officer.

The officer keeping the log must sign, date and time the log both at the commencement and conclusion of the task. The log should show:

- the name of the officer keeping the record;
- the name of the person entering or leaving the scene;
- date and time of each entry/exit;
- reason for entry.

Fast-track actions

These are defined as:

> *'Any investigative actions which, if pursued immediately, are likely to establish important facts, preserve evidence or lead to the early resolution of the investigation.'*[69]

The manual specifies a fast-track menu that includes the following.

- ***Identification of suspects*** – taking into consideration: offender at the scene, information from the scene, following escape routes, and vehicle enquiries.
- ***Exploitation of intelligence*** – including identification and, where applicable, tasking of local informants, crime pattern analyses.
- ***Scene forensics*** – applying a ***significant murder scenes model***, i.e. last seen alive, initial 'contact', attack site, murder site, body deposition site to assist: the search for, and retrieval of, exhibit material, scene interpretation (aided by intelligence), systematic photography and video recording of scenes; calling upon the assistance of the medical examiner and, only when initial crime scene examination is completed, the pathologist.
- ***Crime scene assessment*** – systematically considering every possible aspect of the three factors common to every murder enquiry: location, victim, offender.
- ***Witness search*** – including passers-by, CCTV, persons with legitimate access to the scene, relatives, private security videos, tradesmen and businesses, clubs and public houses; limited house-to-house enquiries may also be of benefit, confining these to areas within line of sight and earshot of each of the significant murder scenes: last seen alive, initial 'contact', attack site, murder site, body deposition site.

- *Victim enquiries* – including identification, associations, lifestyle, victimology (focusing on the selection of the victim, the significance of the location, the significance of the time of death), behaviour patterns (an area likely to benefit from an input by an offender profiler, either from within the service or a psychologist or psychiatrist employed on a consultancy basis).
- *Possible motives.*
- *Post mortems.*
- *Significant witnesses.*
- *Other critical actions*, e.g. preliminary house-to-house enquiries, locating CCTV sites and securing tapes.

- *Planned method of investigation*: a sequence of strategies developed by the SIO, assisted by the management team, in respect of:

  - forensic issues;
  - searching;
  - arrest of the suspect;
  - interviewing of the suspect;
  - suspect identification;
  - communications;
  - family liaison;
  - continuity;
  - retention and handling of exhibits;
  - reconstructions.

- *Suspect enquiries*: a range of investigative options including:

  - researching the *modus operandi* of offences committed by potential suspects;
  - completion of personal descriptive forms (PDFs) for individuals fulfilling target criteria;
  - *TIE actions* – tracing, interviewing and eliminating potential suspects;
  - accessing suspect and profile specific databases (see next section);
  - alibi enquiries;
  - forensic elimination;
  - surveillance.

- *Post-charge activities* – preparing and submitting case files to the CPS; conducting further investigations, including offender analysis in order to:

  - obtain further evidence to strengthen any existing charges against the suspect;
  - obtain further intelligence about the suspect;

- establish the suspect's links to similar offences in a series of offences;
- establish the suspect's links to other offences.

At every stage of the investigation, it will be seen that the 'best practice' model relies heavily upon the use of intelligence, structured research and analysis to assist the assessment of information.

Specific databases of assistance in suspect enquiries

A number of databases are available, which are able to assist in profiling the suspect.

BADMAN murder database

BADMAN is an acronym for: behavioural analysis, data management, auto-indexing, networking. It holds a very wide range of data in respect of several hundred cases. It can assist in:

- identifying, and providing background details on, offenders who have committed similar offences to the one being investigated;
- identifying similar offences for a link analysis;
- the compilation of 'similar fact' evidence.

CATCHEM database

CATCHEM is an acronym for: collating homicide expertise and management. Administered by Derbyshire Police, this database holds details on all child murders committed in England, Wales and Scotland since 1 January 1960.

NIMROD

This is a database on sex offenders and offences throughout the West Midlands area, and is maintained by the West Midlands Police.

SO11 Metropolitan Police Rape Database

This is a database of solved 'stranger' rapes and includes information on offenders and victim statements.

Interviewing significant witnesses

It was pointed out earlier, under area CID investigation, that there is a growing trend to recording the initial interviewing of significant, or key, witnesses.

The 'best practice' model guides SIOs to authorise the recording of the initial interviewing of significant witnesses. This should be preferably on video, but tape recorded where this is the only practical or possible option. However, it stresses that under no circumstances should recording be authorised of witnesses who are suspected of involvement in the case under investigation.

Interviewing the suspect

The SIO has the task of selecting officers with the appropriate experience and expertise 'set', i.e. the requisite training, skills, awareness and capacity to relate to the suspect to be interviewed.

The 'best practice' model gives a key role to a nominated *interview co-ordinator*, who is tasked with:

- selecting and briefing interviewers;
- co-ordinating interviewing teams;
- strategies for dealing with particular behaviours, or responding, by the suspect;
- debriefing and giving feedback to interviewers;
- the SIO may also consider it appropriate to call upon the services of an offender profiler or a psychologist to advise on the suspect's reaction to particular lines of questioning.

The interviewing may be conducted in an interview room with remote video-recording facilities linked to a monitoring room:

- enabling disclosures and responses to be concurrently checked out during the course of the interview;
- facilitating monitoring, debriefing, feedback, and briefing for subsequent interviews.

Officers tasked with interviewing the suspect in a murder enquiry are obliged to follow the PEACE guidelines, incorporating the three-stage approach to the account phase described earlier.

The 'best practice' model does not make reference to the 'three-step' approach to interviewing suspects used by some forces, also described earlier.

ADVICE FROM THE CROWN PROSECUTION SERVICE (CPS)

The CPS may become involved in the case at any stage of the investigation. The national guidelines[70] give examples of when the police are likely to seek advice, e.g.

- when difficult questions of evidence occur, such as hearsay, similar fact, corroboration;
- where there is contested identification or possible breaches of PACE;
- when foreseeable defences are likely to cause difficulty;
- where the defendant was acting in self-defence or defending another or property;
- where there are a large number of suspects and possible offences;
- where there has been a use of surveillance, an informant or an *agent provocateur*;
- where there are complex disclosure issues, such as evidence in the hands of third parties.

If advice is required, the police will send an advice file to the CPS, prepared in accordance with the criteria and guidelines set out in the manual.[71]

Advice on the investigation

The manual outlines the advice that the CPS may give to the police on the investigation, e.g.

- which lines of further investigation are likely to be useful;
- whether an operational procedure is legal;
- whether the evidence obtained from an operational procedure is admissible;
- what further evidence is needed.

The manual cautions that the CPS:

• will not become involved in the investigation itself;

• will not advise on the propriety or effectiveness of any proposed police operational procedures;

• will not give advice in circumstances where a member of CPS staff is at risk of being called as a witness as a result of giving advice.

Advice on the evidence

The manual also outlines the advice that the CPS may give on evidence, already obtained or not, as to its sufficiency, reliability, admissibility and probativeness.

CPS lawyers in police stations

During a pilot period between 1 October 1998 and 31 March 1999 in six areas of England and Wales, legal advice concerning matters of law, evidence and procedure was made available from the CPS to the police out of normal office hours. During this period, only 12 calls for out-of-hours advice were made.

This low take-up of CPS advice mirrored research findings in October 1996.[72] This examined the extent to which police officers sought advice from Crown Prosecutors prior to charge during the operation of the LAPS – Lawyers at Police Stations Scheme. The scheme had involved the placement of Crown Prosecutors in police stations for certain hours in the week to offer advice on the spot to officers about charging decisions. The research indicated that seeking pre-charge advice was a rare event, occurring in only 1.8 per cent of 600 cases examined. In one of the six CPS areas studied, no pre-charge advice was sought.

It is possible, following the introduction of the Narey provisions, for the police to obtain legal advice within office hours from CPS lawyers at ASUs, with the agreement of a senior officer or ASU manager. A CPS lawyer requested to give legal advice should give priority to preparing files for early first hearings (EFHs) and early administrative hearings (EAHs). If legal advice cannot be given at the time, it should be given as soon as possible thereafter.

Notes

1. Weston, P. and Wells, K. (1996) *Criminal Investigation: Basic Perspectives.* Upper Saddle River, NJ: Prentice-Hall.

2. *Ibid.*

3. *Ibid.*

4. Association of Chief Police Officers/Forensic Science Service. (1996) *Using Forensic Science Effectively.* Birmingham: Forensic Science Service.

5. Audit Commission. (1993) *Helping with Enquiries: Tackling Crime Effectively.* London: HMSO.

6. Association of Chief Police Officers/Her Majesty's Inspectorate of Constabulary/Audit Commission. (1996) *Tackling Crime Effectively: Management Handbook.* London: Audit Commission.

7. Jolowicz, C. and Read, T. (1994) *Managing Demand on the Police: An Evaluation of a Crime Line.* Police Research Series, Paper 8. London: Home Office Police Department.

8. Diez, L. (1995) *The Use of Call Grading: How Calls to the Police are Graded and Resourced.* Police Research Series, Paper 13. London: Home Office Police Department.

9. Audit Commission. (1993) *Helping with Enquiries: Tackling Crime Effectively.* London: HMSO.

10. Amey, P., Hale, C. and Uglow, S. (1996) *Development and Evaluation of a Crime Management Model.* Police Research Series, Paper 18. London: Home Office Police Department.

11. Barton, A. and Evans, R. (1999) *Proactive Policing in Merseyside.* Police Research Series, Paper 105. London: Home Office Police Department.

12. Audit Commission. (1993) *Helping with Enquiries: Tackling Crime Effectively.* London: HMSO.

13. Association of Chief Police Officers/Her Majesty's Inspectorate of Constabulary/Audit Commission. (1996) *Tackling Crime Effectively: Management Handbook.* London: Audit Commission.

14. Amey, P., Hale, C. and Uglow, S. (1996) *Development and Evaluation of a Crime Management Model.* Police Research Series, Paper 18. London: Home Office Police Department.

15. Barton, A. and Evans, R. (1999) *Proactive Policing in Merseyside.* Police Research Series, Paper 105. London: Home Office Police Department.

16. *Ibid.*

17. Association of Chief Police Officers and HM Customs and Excise. (1999) *Public Statement on Standards in Covert Law Enforcement Techniques.*

18. Association of Chief Police Officers and HM Customs and Excise. (1999) *Use of Informants: Code of Practice.*

19. Association of Chief Police Officers and HM Customs and Excise. (1999) *Surveillance: Code of Practice.*

20. Association of Chief Police Officers and HM Customs and Excise. (1999) *Undercover Operations: Code of Practice.*

21. Association of Chief Police Officers and HM Customs and Excise. (1999) *Interception of Communications and Accessing Communications Data: Code of Practice.*

22. Association of Chief Police Officers and HM Customs and Excise. (1999) *Recording and Dissemination of Intelligence Material: Code of Practice.*

23. HM Inspectorate of Constabulary. (1999) *Police Integrity: Securing and Maintaining Public Confidence.* London: Home Office Communication Directorate.

24. *Ibid.*

25. Association of Chief Police Officers and HM Customs and Excise. (1999) *Use of Informants: Code of Practice.*

26. *Ibid.*

27. Colvin, M. (1999) *Under Surveillance: Covert Policing and Human Rights Standards.* London: JUSTICE.

28. *Ibid.*

29. Association of Chief Police Officers and HM Customs and Excise. (1999) *Use of Informants: Code of Practice.*

30. *Ibid.*

31. *Ibid.*

32. Association of Chief Police Officers and HM Customs and Excise. (1999) *Recording and Dissemination of Intelligence Material: Code of Practice.*

33. Association of Chief Police Officers and HM Customs and Excise. (1999) *Surveillance: Code of Practice.*

34. Association of Chief Police Officers and HM Customs and Excise. (1999) *Interception of Communications and Accessing Communications Data: Code of Practice.*

35. *Ibid.*

36. HM Inspectorate of Constabulary. (1998) *Thematic Report on Good Practice 1997/98. Policing with Intelligence: Criminal Intelligence.* London: Home Office Communication Directorate.

37. Maguire, M. and John, T. (1995) *Intelligence, Surveillance and Informants: Integrated Approaches. Police Research Group: Crime Detection and Prevention Series: Paper No. 64.* London: Home Office.

38. Association of Chief Police Officers and HM Customs and Excise. (1999) *Interception of Communications and Accessing Communications Data: Code of Practice.*

39. Association of Chief Police Officers and HM Customs and Excise. (1999) *Undercover Operations: Code of Practice.*

40. *Ibid.*

41. Association of Chief Police Officers/Forensic Science Service. (1996) *Using Forensic Science Effectively.* Birmingham: Forensic Science Service.

42. White, P. (ed.) (1999) *Crime Scene to Court: The Essentials of Forensic Science.* London: Royal Society of Chemistry.

43. Association of Chief Police Officers/Forensic Science Service. (1996) *Using Forensic Science Effectively.* Birmingham: Forensic Science Service.

44. Copson, G. and Marshall, N. (1999) 'Mind over matter'. *Police Review*, 11 June, 16–7.

45. *Ibid.*

46. Maguire, M. and John, T. (1995) *Intelligence, Surveillance and Informants: Integrated Approaches. Police Research Group: Crime Detection and Prevention Series: Paper No. 64.* London: Home Office.

47. Weston, N. (1999) 'The crime scene'. In P. White (ed.), *Crime Scene to Court: The Essentials of Forensic Science.* London: Royal Society of Chemistry.

48. Association of Chief Police Officers/Her Majesty's Inspectorate of Constabulary/Audit Commission. (1996) *Tackling Crime Effectively: Management Handbook.* London: Audit Commission.

49. Jolowicz, C. and Read, T. (1994) *Managing Demand on the Police: An Evaluation of a Crime Line.* Police Research Series, Paper 8. London: Home Office Police Department.

50. Diez, L. (1995) *The Use of Call Grading: How Calls to the Police are Graded and Resourced.* Police Research Series, Paper 13. London: Home Office Police Department.

51. Leadbetter, M. (1996) 'Probationers' skills shop: week 33: preserving evidence at crime scenes'. *Police Review*, 16 August, 30–1.

52. *A Guide to Interviewing.* (1992) Harrogate: Central Planning and Training Unit.

53. *Investigative Interviewing: A Practical Guide.* (1996) Bramshill: Police Staff College.

54. *A Practical Guide to Investigative Interviewing.* (1998) Bramshill: National Crime Faculty.

55. Shepherd, E. and Milne, B. (1999) 'Full and faithful: ensuring quality practice and integrity of outcome in witness interviews.' In A. Heaton-Armstrong, E. Shepherd and D. Wolchover (eds), *Analysing Witness Testimony: A Guide for Legal Practitioners and Other Professionals.* London: Blackstone.

56. *Investigative Interviewing: A Practical Guide.* (1996) Bramshill: Police Staff College.

57. *A Practical Guide to Investigative Interviewing.* (1998) Bramshill: National Crime Faculty.

58. *A Guide to Interviewing.* (1992) Harrogate: Central Planning and Training Unit.

59. *A Practical Guide to Investigative Interviewing.* (1998) Bramshill: National Crime Faculty.

60. *Ibid.*

61. *Ibid.*

62. *Ibid.*

63. *Manual of Guidance for the Preparation, Processing and Submission of Files.* Produced by ACPO and the CPS for internal distribution. First edition 1 April 1992 (updated periodically).

64. *A Guide to Interviewing.* (1992) Harrogate: Central Planning and Training Unit.

65. Home Office. (1992) Memorandum of Good Practice on Video-Recorded Interviews with Child Witnesses for Criminal Proceedings. London: HMSO.

66. ACPO Crime Committee. (1999) *Murder Investigation Manual.*

67. Anacapa Sciences. (1989) *Criminal Intelligence Analysis.* Santa Barbara, CA: Anacapa Sciences.

68. ACPO Crime Committee. (1999) *Murder Investigation Manual.*

69. *Ibid.*

70. *Manual of Guidance for the Preparation, Processing and Submission of Files.* Produced by ACPO and the CPS for internal distribution. First edition 1 April 1992 (updated periodically).

71. *Ibid.*

72. Baldwin, J. and Hunt, A. (1989) 'Prosecutors advising in police stations.' C.L.R. 521.

CHAPTER 3

Process corruption: the threat to effective police investigation

'the task of the police is not only to seek the truth but to tell the truth...
a deliberate breach of investigative procedure may be as serious a crime
as the crime under investigation ... the integrity of the way in which
police investigate crime is at least as important as the success of the
investigation.'

Sir John Woodcock, Chief HMI (1992)

THE EMERGENCE OF PROFESSIONAL INVESTIGATION

The view that all officers should play an active part in the investigation of crime is a very recent development. Until some 20 years ago, the generality of police officers had nothing to do with investigation. This was done by the investigative specialists, officers in the Criminal Investigation Department (CID).

Investigative effort was fundamentally directed to one aim: to secure the suspect's voluntary confession of guilt. To this end the investigative specialists operated autonomously. They were accountable to no one, particularly in their unmonitored use of techniques to persuade the suspect to confess.

We would argue that the pursuit of the voluntary confession has represented the single greatest block on the service emerging as a professional investigative body. In this chapter, we first describe this traditional approach, which became increasingly unacceptable on the grounds of its ineffectiveness and absence of ethics. We summarise a new approach to investigation that has since been advocated, in which officers engaged in investigation fulfil forensic criteria akin to forensic scientists.

We then review the range of widespread, existing and potentially enduring obstacles to officers fulfilling these forensic criteria. These obstacles constitute a continuing threat of *process corruption*: aspects of the police service which distort, undermine and render inferior the investigative process and, through this, its effectiveness and integrity.

THE TRADITIONAL INVESTIGATORS

To become one of the specialists in the CID an officer had first to demonstrate prowess at being a good 'thief taker'. It was not just a matter of being prolific in arresting people for offences. The evidence adduced had to make the allegation 'stick'. Principal was the officer's oral account of activity observed, the suspect's behaviour and the content of the critical verbal exchange with the arrested individual, particularly any incriminatory utterances he or she made. This gave rise to the practice of 'verballing', in which the officer would give an untruthful account of what the individual had said. The officer's account, truthful or otherwise, was necessarily enhanced if there was any exhibit evidence found in a search of the scene, the suspect, or a location or vehicle associated with the suspect. This evidence served to add to the process of 'attaching criminality' to the suspect.

Success at 'thief taking' set the uniformed officer apart from the rest who were content with fulfilling the historically predominant policing role, protecting property, particularly that of the middle class. A good 'thief taker' was not content with checking locks and door handles. He (she did not come along until much later) showed initiative, autonomy of action, a desire and an ability to generate 'self-directed' work without resort to supervising and senior officers. In order to 'feel collars' he kept his ear to the ground and developed an eye for the 'signs of crime'. These were attitudes and actions constituting the basis for the development of CID craft.

CID CRAFT

CID officers were expected to know their 'patch': those engaged or suspected of being engaged in crime, those with convictions, and those whose culpability of an offence or offending was a matter of local gossip or local knowledge. CID officers had to create a web of relationships, cultivating individuals as potential sources of information and inducing some to act as 'snouts' (tasked informants). If necessary, relationships were forged with those actually engaged in crime. Establishing and maintaining this web was viewed as an important part of a CID officer's 'craft', making conversation and forming it principally through social drinking and socialising. Not unsurprisingly, many considered there was no clear dividing line between 'craft' and the individual's 'personality'. Being in CID was a matter of charisma: the 'skills' were essentially innate, something that the individual had, and others did not, and which could not be taught, only given the opportunity to develop by doing the 'job'.

The CID has historically operated as a verbal culture created and passed on by an oral tradition. Information was held in the heads of individual CID officers. Hence the 'snout' was the property of the officer. What went on between the officer and the informant was not written down. The absence of any record allowed the unfettered use of initiative, guile, cunning, and, where necessary, appropriate persuasion, to secure this information from the informant.

The traditional functional unit has been a duo of detective constables acting autonomously and democratically. There was no such thing as supervision. One would be the officer in charge of the case (OIC), but this was the 'name' on the file. In effect, the two would discuss ideas and proposals as to what they should do next, consensus would be achieved and they would carry out the agreed actions. Certainly, notions of supervision, monitoring and checking did not enter into it. There would be no means or purpose. Who would do it? Why? Hence, historically, there was until relatively recently no functional distinction between detective constables and detective sergeants. Formal management only entered into it in more complex crimes, which demanded a team. Then a senior officer (inspector and above) would manage. Optimally, he would be the charismatic leader, determining which actions should be done and directing the team from the front.

Until relatively recently, forensic science played little part in the investigation of the majority of cases. It was the complete range of CID 'craft' that solved crimes.

'Craft' involved bringing to bear cumulative experience gained by observing and assisting and, in due course, being the lead investigator (i.e. the OIC), in similar investigations. The 'right' conduct was defined by a 'means–ends' relationship. It was right if, either explicitly or tacitly, it was advocated, required, or endorsed (or at least not disapproved or discouraged) by those with significant views, particularly peers and seniors. If the conduct produced the aspired for 'result' – the suspect's confession – this endowed personal and professional kudos and status.

A CID officer acquired a mental framework of criminal patterns or stereotypes: forms of offence, committed in characteristic ways, to particular categories of person by particular categories of perpetrator. This knowledge enabled sense to be made of a crime scene and the formation of a 'case theory' – a combination of observation, known and presumed fact, intuition, hunch and conjecture – linking the *modus operandi*, the victim, and likely motive, and even pointing to a notional suspect.

A 'case theory' acted as a powerful guide to the investigation. Essential was the early identification and arrest of a suspect deemed to 'fit' the 'case theory'. It is a historical fact that most crimes have been (and continue to be) solved if members of the public supply information to the police about the identity of the offender. Investigation involved the assembling of a prosecution case against an identified suspect in order to satisfy relevant authorities that prosecution and conviction are justified. This required the application of yet more 'craft' in the task of interviewing witnesses and the identified suspect.

THE 'INTERVIEW AND CONFESS' MODEL

It is not hard to understand why interviewing has always been viewed as the core skill, which CID officers were traditionally assumed to have. The skill was necessary to conduct early, focused interviews of witnesses. The information these generated could be placed in the context of the officers' local knowledge of likely perpetrators, and to guide the questioning and tasking of sources. Above all, however, interviewing skill was at the defining requirement of the 'interview and confess' model applied in all investigations.

Once identified, the suspect would either be arrested and taken to, or be invited to attend, the police station, where he or she was deemed to be 'helping the police with their enquiries'. Being held incommunicado, being isolated, being unable to control events and circumstances, and being outnumbered, all progressively created the 'climate for confession'. They 'softened up' the suspect, and made him or her increasingly receptive to persuasive communication and robust questioning in the interview room, in the cell, anywhere the CID officer chose, at any time (particularly late at night and into the early morning), for however long it took.

More CID 'craft' was necessary to draft the confession statement to be signed by the suspect. Further 'craft' would, in many cases, be necessary to get the suspect to confess to other offences to be taken into consideration (TICs). TIC were of enormous benefit, because they enabled a large amount of crime to be solved at the stroke of a pen: they were 'written off'.

The 'interview and confess' model took place behind the closed door of the interview room or the cell. It was not subject to any scrutiny. If they belittled, hectored, insulted, bullied, or threatened in any way, particularly with physical ill-treatment, or were actually violent towards the suspect, it was a matter of the word of the police officers against that of the suspect. The only official record was the CID officers written account of who said what to whom, when. Inevitably, this was in the form of written notes, created after the interview by an act of joint remembrance deemed to have been assisted by 'trigger' notes made during the interview.

After years of claiming that officers assiduously wrote up interview notes immediately after the interview, it was eventually admitted that this was all a fiction.[1] Officers would write their notes some several hours after interviewing had finished. It would have required superhuman memory, therefore, to remember verbatim the exact detail (placed in quotation marks) of each utterance of each individual, across a period of interviewing, which may have lasted many hours and into the early morning.

To 'attach criminality' to the suspect required the interviewing of witnesses in a way that generated responses – evidence – pointing to the suspect's guilt. Where necessary, the witness would be revisited, perhaps more than once, in order to obtain statements that supported the prevailing 'case theory' or converged with the accounts of other witnesses indicating the suspect's guilt. Often a key witness would be interviewed, or rein-terviewed, after the suspect had made an admission to obtain a statement to accord with the admission.

THE DEMISE OF THE 'INTERVIEW AND CONFESS' MODEL

Inappropriate conduct in the gathering of evidence, particularly in the Maxwell Confait case,[2] led ultimately to PACE and the requirement to tape-record suspect interviews. There was a sustained rearguard action by the police service to prevent this. Although this was not successful, it was still not until the late 1980s that recording equipment was to be found in most designated police stations. Inevitably, as more and more tapes were being subjected to scrutiny by the prosecutors, defending lawyers and the courts were confronted with the reality of what had gone on behind closed doors before tape recording. The courts reacted strongly to transparent evidence of the unethical persuasive questioning techniques, as well as the occurrence of 'off-tape' interviewing and 'welfare visits' to cells.

Tape recording of PACE interviews led to a sharp decline in forceful interviewing and revealed the widespread ineptitude of police officers in the interviewing role. The rise in crime, particularly volume crime, required the creation of teams, such as beat crime units, deploying more and more uniform officers to take on the traditional CID role of investigation. The frequently inept performance of uniform officers was indistinguishable from that of their CID colleagues, who had been held out, and held themselves out, to be experts for so long.

PACE accountability, the transparency of taping and the reaction of the judiciary, and the public, to revealed improprieties rendered it increasingly difficult to create the 'climate for confession'. There was no longer continuous access to the suspect, no more wearing down by protracted interviewing and interviewing into the early hours, no more pressuring communication and questioning. The long-established 'interview and confess' could no longer be applied. There was a dramatic decline in admissions, not least in respect of TICs.

To professionalise investigative interviewing, the service introduced PEACE,[3] which accorded with Home Office principles of investigative interviewing.[4] PEACE seeks to increase the effectiveness and to ensure the integrity of one aspect of the investigative endeavour. It was quickly recognised that the model made it even harder to secure a confession and to induce the suspect to admit to TICs. Tape recording and PEACE have cast the 'interview and confess' model into terminal decline. Alternative ways of securing 'results' have had to be found:

- proactive policing, with particular reference to the use of covert techniques against identified targets;

- the growth in the use of forensic science techniques, most especially DNA profiling;

- the gradual lowering and now abolition of the numerical standard for fingerprints.

THE 'FORENSIC INVESTIGATOR' MODEL

A leading ACPO figure, David Phillips, has accurately described the situation in respect of the CPIA and active defence:[5]

'The essence of a successful defence now often lies in attacking the provenance of the evidence. Disclosure provides the ammunition for that assault.

Traditionally forensic evidence has always relied upon proving continuity to rebut any possible argument or contamination or interference. In a very real way this regime is now an imperative for all evidence. The

Criminal Procedure and Investigations Act 1996, in formulating the present position, recognises the logical consequences of a disclosure regime and in effect makes the conduct of the investigation accountable to the trial. If you are obliged to capture all possible evidence of value to prosecution or defence, and preserve it for possible disclosure, and if you can be tested upon your observance of this rule, then effectively the policy decisions of the investigation and the methods of evidence procurement themselves become an issue.

The signal lesson for policing, and indeed prosecutors, is that we must take the forensic model as a paradigm for investigation in general. Given the sheer complexity and confusion of many enquiries at the outset, if we are not to reduce the investigator to a neurotic state fearing some minor fragment might not have been captured, we have to bring order to the febrile and confused circumstances which often occur at the early stages of an investigation. This means formulating the investigative method and buttressing it with an accountable regime.'

He describes how the ACPO Murder Investigation Manual[6] provides investigators with a logical system and teaches them to move away from a 'craft' model, and, it is hoped, in a more scientific direction. He advocates strongly the adoption of a 'forensic detective' model, in which 'the investigation and the collection of evidence by the police is an activity akin to the forensic search of a crime scene'.[7]

As more and more officers become involved in proactive and reactive investigation, the traditional term detective is becoming less and less relevant. Numerically speaking, as forces change their policing emphases, increasing numbers of officers are engaged in detective work who do not have the descriptive title 'detective' before their rank. They outnumber those with the title 'detective' and who also do detective work. To add more confusion, many individuals with the title 'detective' are not engaged in recognisably detective tasks! Whether a uniform officer or CID officer has the title 'detective', common sense argues that, if an officer is engaged in investigative activity, he or she is to all intents and purposes an investigator. It is clear that, in using the term 'forensic detective', David Phillips is referring to 'forensic investigator'.

Adopting many of the principles of scientific method, the forensic investigator can:

- calculate probabilities;
- create hypotheses;
- test these hypotheses;
- search for incongruities;

111

- locate fragments of evidence within a logical scheme.

In his view, 'To be "scientific" all must be recorded and accountable' and he concludes:[8]

> *'The real test for policing will be our ability to provide investigators of such credibility that they resemble in every respect the best forensic scientists.'*

He has spelled out an excellent model that could serve the criminal justice system well and, vital for all, protect the good name of the service. It is necessary, however, to review what is implied by the model.

Forensic investigators must fulfil the same professional criteria as forensic scientists.

- The forensic investigator must have the knowledge to do the job competently. Like a forensic scientist who does not know the particular field in which he or she is expected to operate, or lays claim to knowledge he or she does not have, the ignorant forensic investigator:
  - is inherently engaged in self-deception and deception of others;
  - is a danger, whose lack of awareness is liable to produce blunders, which lead to the conviction of the innocent and enable the guilty to remain at liberty.

- The forensic investigator must have the requisite technical skills, methods and techniques to collect, assemble, analyse and evaluate evidence – and to record fully and faithfully these processes and their outcomes. Like a forensic scientist unable to fulfil these basic competency criteria, the investigator cannot do the job correctly.

- The forensic investigator must adopt a rigorous 'warts and all' scientific approach. It is not about setting out to confirm what an individual believes to be the case. This is easy. Intellectual rigour – and integrity – requires spelling out the 'null hypothesis', i.e. the opposite of what the individual might believe, then setting out to test this counter-proposition. The forensic investigator is obliged to hypothesise the suspected person to be innocent, not guilty, and to gather and examine a suitably wide spectrum of information to test this hypothesis.

- The forensic investigator must be open-minded. Like scientists, they have to resist becoming partisan, getting emotionally involved in a game that must be won. Should this happen, the real and growing risk is of the individual:
  - rejecting all semblance of the required disconfirmatory stance;

- selectively attending to evidence that buttresses the 'case theory' and attaches criminality to the suspect, at the expense of counter, i.e. contradictory, or equivocal evidence.

- It follows that the forensic investigator must be prepared to gather and to record honestly all emergent evidence irrespective of its status, whether pointing to the suspect's innocence (i.e. is disconfirmatory), to his or her guilt, or which is ambiguous. A scientist should be emotionally neutral as to the character and content of emergent data.

- The forensic investigator must adopt a 'hands off' approach to information and evidence arising from the investigation. In the same way, scientific integrity means that the forensic scientist cannot choose to ignore the occurrence of contrary or equivocal data. Nor can he or she influence its collection, content or continued existence. Nothing must be altered, deleted or added. Nothing is destroyed. Everything is open to objective assessment by another scientist.

- The forensic investigator must be prepared to present findings that point away from the suspect as the offender, or are equivocal on the matter, as well as findings that indicate the suspect is the offender. Like the forensic scientist, integrity requires the reporting of all findings: disconfirmatory, ambiguous and confirmatory.

- The forensic investigator's performance in all aspects of investigation must be subject to real, as opposed to nominal, quality control and quality assurance checks. Similarly, the forensic investigator whose personal performance is not monitored, is not checked, is not given feedback on errors of omission and commission, and is subject to no sanctions for an unprofessional performance is, in effect, told that quality does not matter. Even if poor quality is revealed in the court process, it does not matter: nothing will change.

PROCESS CORRUPTION IN POLICE INVESTIGATION

Investigators and forensic scientists are in a position of power. We entrust them not to misuse or abuse this power by conducting an investigation and recording its outcomes in order to fulfil their personal intentions. Irrespective of any justification that might be offered for using power in this manner it necessarily distorts, undermines or renders inferior the investigation. It corrupts, i.e. distorts, undermines and renders inferior, a process that the criminal justice system entrusts to the police service and assumes the service will conduct effectively and with integrity.

In the following sections, we review aspects of the police service with potential to bring about *process corruption* in police investigations.

CORRUPTING MODES OF THINKING

The single-minded pursuit of a prosecution

Historically, police investigation has always been directed towards a single investigative aim: the prosecution (and conviction) of suspects. As we explained earlier, the traditional approach to investigation has been directed at identifying a suspect, and then providing the court with the evidence to convict: a voluntary confession, and, particularly if one did not emerge, evidence attaching criminality to the suspect, i.e. incriminating testimony from one or more witnesses, including the police officer's account of critical utterances by the suspect at the time of arrest.

A former Chief HMI argued[9] that the police service:

> '*must cease to believe that they are solely the agents of the prosecution and become, what...they were originally designed to be, the gatherers of evidence. The police have taken on too great a burden in the body politic: they have assumed that it is their job to find evidence to convict. There is a need for bipartisan investigations, seeking the truth about those matters which indicate innocence as well as guilt.*'

To change this long-established, ingrained mindset, from single-minded pursuit of a prosecution to bipartisan investigation, will be difficult. PEACE constitutes a first, widely disseminated step towards bringing about a change in the mindset of the majority of officers. It invites them to keep an open mind when collating information and to separate facts from preconceptions and opinions.[10]

> '*It is important to consider that some of the information and evidence that you obtain may be to the suspect's advantage. Do not just dismiss it because it does not point towards the suspect's guilt. Witnesses can be wrong and it is part of your duty to keep and open and enquiring mind.*'

In the forensic endeavour, neither forensic investigators nor forensic scientists have a choice. They have to be bipartisan. They must collect the evidence dispassionately and must allow it to speak for itself.

Prejudging and perceptual bias

There are two common psychological barriers that hinder effective problem-solving and decision-making in any context. In the case of the police service, however, they assume even greater significance, not least because they are intrinsic to the traditional approach to investigation.

- **Premature closure**. The desire to make sense and to make connections leads the officer to 'rush to get it wrong', i.e.

  - to read the situation, circumstances and available information inappropriately – making invalid links and excluding or ignoring potentially relevant detail;
  - to arrive at a single explanation – leading the officer to believe, or convince himself or herself, that he or she 'knows' what happened;

- **Confirmatory bias**. This is the tendency to seek out or selectively attend to information that confirms what one believes or 'knows' to be the case. This may even impel the individual to ignore or to dispose of information that does not fit. (The disconfirmatory stance of the scientist is the conscious counter to this bias.) Confirmatory bias is endemic in the police service. The situation is made all the worse by:

  - many officers being unaware of it;
  - when made aware of it, many arguing that it is a sensible and natural way to solve problems, in particular to conduct investigations.

It is no surprise that confirmatory bias lies at the heart of the traditional approach to police investigation, the single-minded pursuit of the prosecution of a suspect, i.e.

- information is sought that supports the officer's case theory;
- information that does not support the theory is ignored, discarded or not disclosed to the rest of the criminal justice system;
- it is thought illogical – a waste of effort and precious resource – to engage in activity that disconfirms or undermines the theory.

Corner-cutting

For the service to emerge as a professional investigative body, every officer must be committed to think in terms of detail: detailed observance of procedures and the totality of detail derived through investigation. However, the former chief HMI observed:[11]

'I believe that an everyday proximity to the effects of violence and an everyday experience of competing moral imperatives have a corrosive effect on policing culture, which tends to make most police officers uninterested in the fine details of procedure...

The police working environment is one in which some procedures compete with others – the impetus of investigation versus the rights of suspects – so that crime control is in conflict with due process. And from the very beginning of a police officer's career, he or she finds that the demands of the tasks in front of him or her tend to overwhelm the procedures laid down to deal with them. There is a constant sense of urgency in the police world, which often leads to corner-cutting... the working culture of the police service is shot through with corner-cutting and with expediency...

The police process hundreds of thousands of cases a year and I believe that a considerable number of them would, upon the closest possible examination, be found to be affected by some degree of expedient action.'

Expedient action may produce the outcome desired by the officer (who is merely thinking in terms of the 'little picture'). It is very likely to be ineffective if, should it be detected, it brings the service for that moment into disrepute. Expedient actions cause the public to lose confidence in the police whom they entrust to apply the law and to act lawfully and properly. The officer would, in effect, have given no thought to the 'big picture'.

One thing about which there is no doubt: expedient action is inherently unethical.[12]

Defensive avoidance

Most groups are usually incapable of handling overt disagreement among members. The working group exerts pressure upon its members towards uniformity of beliefs and attitudes This social reality is very apparent when a probationer officer joins his or her first shift. The clear message is sent: 'Forget what you were told at training school, we'll show you how things really are.'[13] Thereafter, across the officer's career span, each group will communicate and confront the officer with its own particular reality.

Officers become dependent on, and compliant to, their peer group who defines the 'job' and satisfies their need for acceptance and status. The group creates and sustains an 'informal code':[14] norms for decision-making and actions to be observed by its members, e.g.

• take care of your partner first, then other officers;

• don't inform on other officers – be secretive about what they do;

116

- don't interfere with another officer's area of work;

- if you get caught making a mistake, don't implicate anybody else;

- don't 'make waves' – don't make problems for the system or managers;

- don't 'suck up' to supervisors;

- don't trust managers, they may not look out for your interests.

Under conditions of stress, individuals are particularly sensitive to issues of membership, self-image and relationships to others. Coping involves increased emphasis upon identification with the group and upon unity.[15] The officer seeks to behave in a manner that places him or her at one with the group. Under stress, officers do not 'rock the boat' – they strive to stay on board.

Solving a crime is an inherently stressful task. In a large proportion of cases, police officers know there is no realistic prospect of resolving manifest shortcomings in the police case and the prosecution evidence. An IO in a CIT (evidence team) is particularly vulnerable since he or she inherits the decision-making and actions of the FOA and any others involved, who may have acted in a blundering or even improper manner in respect of:

- initial investigation at the crime scene;

- questioning of victims or witnesses;

- the discovery and scanning of evidence;

- the arrest and questioning of the suspect:
    - at or near the scene;
    - *en route* to the police station.

- completing the crime report;

- completing basic documentary records, e.g. pocket book entries, handover notes.

The result is that the police case and the prosecution evidence in many cases contain manifest gaps, inconsistencies, contradictions and ambiguities.

The IO's problem is that in all too many cases the advice of PEACE cannot be followed:

- the crime scene cannot be visited since there is neither the means nor the time to do this;

117

- the FOA and other officers have gone off shift so no briefing can take place to resolve:
  - lack of detail;
  - inconsistencies within the crime report;
  - absence of copies of relevant documentation, e.g. pocket book entries, handover notes;
- witness statements cannot be gathered because there is neither the means nor the time to see the individuals in question;
- fingerprints have yet to be examined and reported upon in terms of quality and identification;
- photography taken at the scene has yet to be processed;
- the crime is cash-capped, i.e. of insufficient seriousness to merit expenditure on expensive forensic analyses;
- even where approved, forensic analyses normally take a long time – far greater than that encompassed by the limits of PACE upon the detention of the suspect.

In such circumstances, the influence of the code is particularly great, i.e. there are real pressures not to 'rock the boat', not to question the quality or propriety of other officers' conduct, decision-making, actions and attitudes.

Whereas PEACE assumes officers are ready, willing and able to identify, confront and act upon shortcomings in the police case and the prosecution evidence, many officers confronted with dilemmas of investigation act in a different manner. They engage in what has been termed 'defensive avoidance', a form of unconscious expediency.[16] They survive against the odds, and defend themselves against organisational criticism, counter-productive working arrangements and poor practices by:

- not registering much of the detail in the crime report and other case material;
- ironing out gaps, inconsistencies and contradictions by not noticing or ignoring them.

The officer copes by gaining a 'near enough' – as opposed to a detailed – grasp of the police case and the prosecution evidence.

The perceived necessity to lie and to correct and adjust fact

The former chief HMI who brought to public attention the pervasiveness of corner-cutting and expediency also indicated[17] that:

> 'Among police officers there is a widespread distrust of the current system, the mechanisms of which are seen broadly and unnecessarily to favour the accused at the expense of the rights of victims. As a result, some parts of the working culture of the police service have become distorted by a concern to get round the effects of such mechanisms.'

He described how officers, who believe they 'know' the truth of what has happened in a particular case, who know who is the offender, and believe due process will prevent the conviction of the offender, are prepared to engage in 'noble cause corruption', to lie or do whatever is necessary to increase the likelihood of conviction.

A chief constable wrote some time later[18] about the police service's criticisms:

> 'the flaws in an adversarial system that does little to inspire confidence in its ability to deal with crime – contrary to what the public want and have a right to expect. Its obsession with rules, complexity and the ritual has masked a lack of moral principle that stems from the trial's failure to find the truth.
>
> In the pre-PACE era some police officers frustrated by this inability to get at the truth, may have felt tempted to circumvent the rules – and indeed the whole trial system quietly accepted as much.'

Officers are prepared also to lie to pre-empt stressful, searching cross-examination. The former chief HMI argued[19] that the adversarial system, with advocates increasingly attacking police evidence, has had the effect of:

> 'making police officers fully aware of the disastrous effect of an apparent error: for some, it makes them determined to cover up by correcting and adjusting fact.'

PEACE is categorical in its assertion that officers must not lie or deliberately mislead: R. v. Mason [1987] Crim. L.R. 757. Hence it is unlikely that an officer would seek to lie or to cover up for a shortcoming in a tape-recorded interview. However, if an officer is minded, any investigation offers many opportunities to deceive or to modify facts, e.g. when interviewing witnesses (which is not recorded except for key witnesses in serious cases); when briefing appropriate adults; recording an action that did not take place, or not recording one which did.

The HMIC has reported[20] that:

> *'Whilst the Inspection Team concluded that any bending of the rules is largely an activity of the past, broadly it is seen by those still guilty of it as not being for personal gain but to protect society, and therefore not at the worst end of corruption. This is sometimes referred to as "noble cause corruption", which like the term "joyriding", somehow seems to lend a sense of legitimacy to unlawful activity. Her Majesty's Inspector totally rejects this view and repeats the requirement for investigations to be carried out entirely within the rules, otherwise the credibility of the whole Service is devalued – the police do not administer justice but enforce the law with justice.'*

The position of the HMIC is clear and that is as it should be. However, the HMIC has no evidence upon which to base the claim that 'bending the rules is largely an activity of the past'. This is because 'front line' supervision all too often is nominal rather than real, and the service still lacks systems, mechanisms or sanctions (or the will to put these in place) to ensure quality control and quality assurance of individual officers' performances.

Rather than concentrating on quality of decision-making and actions, police managers have become obsessed with counting particular activities, and in doing this have created a 'performance culture' based on statistics rather than standards.

THE PERFORMANCE CULTURE

Historically, police performance has always been measured in terms of 'numbers' or statistics. However, as senior police managers have been required to think in terms of cost–benefit and VFM this has created an increasingly aggressive and demonstrable 'performance culture' in the police service.[21] It affects everything. Number of arrests is a performance indicator that affects every uniform patrol officer from the youngest probationer to the most senior constable on the shift. Indeed, it is an aspect of probationer performance that he or she must make a particular number of arrests for a given category of offence.

Management's (and the system's) demand for numbers has the effect of forcing officers to effect more and more increasingly speculative arrests. This alienates officers who know that what they are being required to do is to harass the public in order to produce statistics for the public that the police are doing their job. The officers realise, even if management does not, that this cumulatively alienates the public.

The HMIC observed that the performance culture in the police service has emerged as a major factor affecting integrity.[22] For some years there has been an apparent tendency for some forces to 'trawl the margins' for detections and generally to use every means to portray their performance in a good light. Chief constables, in reply to questionnaires, highlighted the performance culture as a cause for 'lapses' in integrity. A CID trainer cited in the report commented that: 'The performance culture forces you to operate at the edge of the ethical envelope.'[23]

One increasing example of officers being required to operate at the edge of the ethical envelope is managerial and supervisory pressure to produce rapid, expeditious, expedient 'positive' outcomes to investigations. The pressure is particularly great upon officers tasked with 'clearing up' volume crime and offences deemed to be less serious. The resource to conduct a thorough investigation is limited and there are frequently shortcomings in the evidence, often due to other officers' being under pressure, their lack of knowledge and skills, incompetence, lack of motivation, or any combination of these.

A decision to charge the suspect following the investigative-interviewing stage, irrespective of the strength or the sufficiency of evidence, or the existence of anomalies within the evidence, creates a 'positive' outcome – a detection – whereas a decision to release to police bail pending further investigation is not. Furthermore, the decision to bail implies continuing the investigation, adding to the amount of resource absorbed by this problematic case.

Within this mentality, in which charging equates to detection as a key performance indicator, a high level of charging following a measured amount of effort is considered VFM and evidence of the efficiency of the individual officer, team or unit. Where this pressure exists to charge irrespective of the circumstances, investigating and custody officers are in a wholly invidious position. It corrupts the investigative process because:

• it perpetuates the view that the police are agents of the prosecution;

• it robs the officer of any opportunity to engage in bipartisan investigation and to follow the PEACE guidelines:[24]

'In relation to suspect interviews, you should also consider speaking to all witnesses, complainants and victims first. The detention clock, however, might limit your time. Consideration can always be given to bail, either before the suspect interview, or after a preliminary interview to establish certain facts.

If you believe that the information is likely to be worthwhile or relevant to the investigation, and there is a realistic chance of it being available, then obtain it prior to the suspect interview.'

- it pressures officers to act expediently, to cut corners, to correct and to adjust facts or to ignore shortcomings in the crime report, the crime file and its contents – either consciously, or through 'defensive avoidance'.

Custody officers should not charge if the evidence is lacking. However, an already stressed group (approximately 23 per cent of whom are carrying out their duties without specialist training) custody officers are heavily dependent upon the integrity of the investigating officer and the officer's account concerning the police case and the prosecution evidence.[25] Where there is pressure for 'positive' outcomes, a custody officer is under even greater pressure not to 'rock the boat' by questioning the investigating officer's account.

Charging irrespective of the status of the evidence is blatant corruption. However, it is a very clever corrupt device.

- It enables the force to get away with inadequate investigations (known to be so by all involved – managers, supervisors, investigators and custody officers). The subsequent unethical act of charging on the illusion of 'sufficient evidence' enables the presentation to the public of an illusion of effective performance in detecting crimes but also tangible evidence of the offenders being placed on the first step of the path to prosecution.

- When the CPS decide to discontinue, as they do in an extraordinary number of cases, because there is insufficient evidence to proceed, absence of essential elements to prove the offence and manifest inadequacy of investigation, the police can protest to the public (who never know the truth) that:

    - they did their job as investigators;
    - it was the civil servant 'administrators' and 'pen pushers' who obstructed the path to prosecution, failed the victim and let the 'guilty' person go free.

DEFICITS IN PROFESSIONAL KNOWLEDGE AND SKILLS

Knowledge of the law

The House of Commons Home Affairs Select Committee observed that many police officers have a poor knowledge of the law because of inadequate and patchy training.[26] The Police Federation in its evidence stated that 'training and development are in a parlous state. The majority of officers simply do not feel adequately trained in basic law and operational procedures to do the job.' According to the CPS, who have to deal with officers on a daily basis, a change in police priorities has led to a switch in police training away from legal, evidential and procedural issues.

Police officers learn basic law, procedure and how to handle interpersonal situations through 'classroom' teaching and practicals, i.e. formal training at the probationer training centre. Thereafter they extend this knowledge and the skills through 'on the job' training, in the workplace: the police station, the streets, and specifically the scenes of crime.

Up to the early 1980s, law and procedure constituted the major part of formal probationer training. Following the riots there was a fundamental change in probationer training, with a heavy emphasis on interpersonal skills. This has led to a persistent complaint that probationers are in very great measure ignorant when it comes to law and procedure.

Police officers have always picked up the *what* and *how* by a combination of 'learning by doing' (solving problems, making decisions and taking actions for the greater part out of the view of any other officer, experienced or otherwise), 'sitting by Nellie' (observing others solve problems, make decisions and take actions), or 'listening to Nellie' (particularly noting what are deemed to be acceptable, and therefore required, ways of thinking, feeling and acting). Such 'on the job' training is predominantly practical. It is not an effective medium for increasing an officer's knowledge of law and procedure.

Once an officer has finished probationer training across the remainder of his or her career, specialist training may involve further instruction in the law and procedure, e.g. CID courses, which until a matter of years ago were essentially law 'crammers'. However, there is no formal process for ensuring the continuous professional development of those who do not proceed to a specialist role. Now BCU superintendents have, as cost centres, to 'buy' training. To send officers on constables' development (or refresher) courses has major resource implications, and takes all important numbers away from the workplace.

Unlike other professions involved in the criminal justice system, the service does not make it the officer's responsibility to engage in continuous professional development, e.g. to read case law reports. It is telling, however, that the *Police Review* (read by a proportion of the total service) acts as a low-key medium for 'updating', in the form of regular features for probationers and those aspiring for promotion.

The outcome is entirely predictable. While those attending a recent PEACE course or a specialist course may have a reasonable awareness of relevant law in respect of investigation, many officers – across the rank, role and seniority spectrum – are likely to have an inadequate grasp of the law, particularly case law. Such ignorance of the law risks corrupting the investigative process at any point. This was well demonstrated in a much publicised murder case in the 1990s, where the senior police officers interviewing misrepresented evidence but subsequently claimed they were unaware of rulings concerning the unacceptability of such conduct.

In Chapter 6, we report on the extraordinary level of shortcoming detected by the CPS in files submitted by the police. Paradoxically, even when there is help on hand in respect of legal advice, the police have signally chosen not to use this. As we pointed out in Chapter 2, during a six-month pilot period in six areas in England and Wales, when the CPS made available legal advice concerning matters of law, evidence and procedure only 12 calls for advice were made.[27] Similarly the LAPS – Lawyers at Police Stations Scheme – was resoundingly shunned. In only 1.8 per cent of 600 cases examined was pre-charge advice sought.[28]

The researchers of the LAPS concluded that those officers who needed advice most were the ones least likely to seek it. For the scheme to work, officers themselves had to be able to identify appropriate cases in which advice was needed. Many police officers did not have the training or the understanding of the law necessary to recognise the circumstances in which they needed advice.

There is another possible explanation for police reticence to talk to the CPS prior to charging decisions. Rather than being the result of ignorance it may well be a reflection of the 'performance culture' we described earlier. Were the CPS to be consulted, this might produce advice indicating insufficient grounds for charging and no charge would take place. This might be getting it right in terms of the law, but it would be getting it wrong in terms of losing an opportunity to charge, to 'clear up' the offences in question, and to add to the 'statistics'.

Whether it is ignorance or lack of motivation, the CPS reported 40 per cent of those cases that were discontinued lacked sufficient evidence to proceed.[29] The most common reason for the CPS discontinuing a case is the absence of essential legal elements.

Knowledge of forensic science

Common sense would argue that, since all police officers are liable to be confronted with the task of investigation, the training of officers across the rank, role and seniority spectrum must make them aware of the forensic issues:

- the potential of physical evidence;

- forms of physical evidence;

- the protection and collection of physical evidence;

- the imperative for contamination to be avoided at every link in the chain;

- the assessment and analysis of physical evidence.

Furthermore, common sense would also argue that supervisors and managers, particularly those in investigations conducted or led by CID, who are routinely called upon to make critical usage and authorisation decisions about forensic evidence – must be particularly informed in respect of forensic issues.

The logic for this common sense requirement is all too clear. As we pointed out in Chapter 2, whatever the officer's particular role in the path of investigation he or she must have the professional ability to fulfil basic professional criteria, i.e.

- to apply basic forensic knowledge competently;

- to apply consistently force procedures and policy concerning forensic evidence;

- to achieve investigative integrity by observing, and ensuring that others observe, the fundamental principles in respect of forensic evidence, i.e.
  - the evidence must be obtained legally;
  - the evidence must be documented fully;
  - the evidence must be properly marked;
  - the evidence must be correctly and separately packaged;
  - proper controls and standards must be maintained if the evidence is to be subject to comparison and rigorous analysis;
  - the chain of custody (continuity) must be maintained and accounted for;

- to ensure that they, and others (most particularly every police officer involved in the case, in whatever role), do not bring about contamination of collected or seized materials.

Research[30] has shown that there is a disturbing lack of understanding of the forensic process, i.e. the solution of investigative problems by scientific means. The majority of police officers have received no training in forensic issues. There is an almost complete absence of forensic science content in probationer and refresher training.[31]

Ignorance is widespread, even among those charged with administering the forensic process. A test with a maximum score of 15 points was taken by a range of officers. On a scale of 'most unaware to least unaware', the order was: detective sergeants, uniform constables, uniform sergeants, detective constables, SOCOs, SIOs and senior SOCOs. The detective sergeants scored marginally better than that which could be achieved by pure chance. Uniform officers were only slightly better.

It is acknowledged[32] that:

- few officers realise how little they know or understand;
- in respect of FOAs, there is a lack of:
  - competence to apply basic forensic knowledge;
  - knowledge of force procedures and policy;
  - consistency in applying force procedures and policy;
- those dealing with crime routinely are not currently well placed to assess the potential value of various forms of forensic analysis.

ACPO and the FSS jointly recommended that, for all officers, physical evidence procedures should be part of their basic skills and their knowledge should be tested and recorded at regular intervals.[33] This has not happened. Given the size of the training, the task is enormous and the service's acknowledged inability to engage in 'catching up' training for those officers outside probationer training, across the career spectrum, the likelihood of regular knowledge testing and recording is remote.

A reflection that there is an urgent requirement to educate even senior officers is the ACPO *Murder Investigation Manual*.[34] This contains a complete chapter on forensic awareness, providing SIOs with a complete introduction to forensic science including how it can be used and best explained, how evidence can be recovered, types of evidence and its analysis. However, for the generality of officers, the service has still to take even the most fundamental of steps to ensure a basic common denominator in respect of forensic knowledge. Whereas following the introduction of PEACE, all officers were issued with two pamphlets[35-6] spelling out guidelines, core issues and 'good practice', no such pamphlet on forensic matters has emerged despite the acknowledged widespread ignorance in the service on such matters.

It is telling, therefore, that the only educational material on forensics potentially accessible to large numbers of officers was in two series of articles[37-8] in 1997 in the *Police Review*, a commercially produced weekly magazine. However, the majority of police officers do not subscribe to the *Police Review*.

All too many officers remain woefully unaware of the absolute imperative of forensic principles. Awareness of the dangers of contamination is particularly poor among police officers. We gave examples of contamination in Chapter 2. Here is another example drawn from a case concerning an armed robbery of a sub-post office.

> *Textile fibres linked clothing found abandoned nearby with the postmaster and his wife, and one fibre also provided a link to the defendant's sweatshirt. The prosecution case rested its case on the basis of this one fibre and some rather dodgy eyewitness testimony. There was only one fibre when it could have been expected to be many more if the clothing and the sweatshirt had been worn together. It was subsequently discovered that, at some stage, a police officer had both items out on her desk, one after the other. This provided an opportunity for contamination of the second item by fibres from the first – a fatal weakness that the prosecution eventually acknowledged.[39]*

Against this background of general ignorance on forensic matters, the service has been made increasingly aware by ACPO and the FSS of the potential of forensic science to inform decisions as to whether a crime has been committed and informing the investigation. This has led to more than a doubling of the number of cases between 1991 and 1997 in which forensic science has been involved.[40]

There has been an exponential growth in the demand for DNA testing, particularly in the light of the creation of the National DNA database and awareness of the potential to conduct DNA analysis on minute, even single-cell, samples. This mentality is set to become even more widespread following the discovery of the ability to create profiles from DNA collected from surfaces merely touched by an offender.[41]

There has been a steady growth of a 'swab everything' mentality – swabbing of any surface and anyone who was touched. This has paralleled the taking of DNA samples as a matter of routine from suspects, particularly by the use of mouth swab kits. This raises very important issues.

•   As the sensitivity of DNA techniques has increased and with it police expectations, there has not been a concomitant understanding of the constraints in respect of DNA. The swabbing of a complete surface, such as a steering wheel, can produce a mixed profile and a situation where material is mixed with other material, the interpretation of which is extremely fraught: begging the question in such circumstances when is a profile a profile?

- This constraint is particularly salient in respect of contamination of minute amounts of DNA. It is entirely possible for minute amounts of DNA to be transferred quite innocently:

  - from an individual to one or more people, e.g. by a sneeze, and for any one of these to transfer this DNA to a crime scene surface, be that an inanimate object or person;
  - from a suspect to a crime scene surface if measures have not been taken to ensure that contamination by the suspect does not occur *after the offence*;

- The risk of innocent or post-event contamination is a major consideration, among others, in the interpretation of DNA on objects or surfaces that are merely touched. The FSS has indicated that it is alert to the necessity for all the scientific checks, balances and quality controls to be in place before this latest application of DNA techniques becomes available to the police.[42]

Lack of fundamental awareness among IOs is compounded by their experience of cases where particular kinds of material submitted for testing produced, or did not produce, a 'positive outcome'. Where particular testing, e.g. glass, has not produced the desired outcome this increases the likelihood among some officers to discount such testing in future cases as an inherent waste of valuable resource.

Taken together, widespread lack of knowledge, lack of adherence to fundamental principles, ignorance of the most basic kind concerning contamination, overvalued notions of what forensic science can do, and the overarching pressure to secure VFM and 'positive outcomes' all present factors able to bring about process corruption in respect of the path of forensic investigation.

Investigative interviewing

The basic PEACE 'package'

Probationers receive the PEACE 'package' as part of their training at the training centre. All other officers should attend a course as part of the 'catching up' process within their own forces. However, in evidence to the Select Committee, the HMIC indicated[43] that: 'Over the past five years some forces have let it slip, changed the programme or taken a day off what is a nationally agreed programme. We are chasing some to complete that training who are four years behind.'

Taking PEACE forwards

It was always accepted that the basic 'package' or course was not sufficient on its own. The PEACE course can only raise awareness and provide limited opportunity to practise that which officers are guided to do. To ensure what is termed 'transfer of learning', i.e. that officers actually put the material and methods into practice in the workplace, they require the support of supervisors. It is regrettable that, rather than train supervisors first, then the generality of officers, the reverse happened. Hence, very many officers have found themselves in the position of returning to the workplace and receiving no sensible feedback (or no feedback at all) because the supervisor had not been on the course.

Although a supervisor's self-teaching package, with video cassette and a feedback template, was produced very early on there were fundamental problems with its acceptance and implementation, with one of the largest forces in the country rejecting it out of hand. Hence it is still the case that a significant number of supervisors have not been on a PEACE course at all and a very large proportion of supervisors have received no training in how to monitor and to give feedback. We shall return to this issue later.

While some forces have allowed PEACE training to lapse, and the majority have yet to implement the supervisory means to ensure PEACE is applied and standards achieved, in contrast a few forces have adopted a wholly responsible approach to the development of investigative-interviewing skills. They recognise that basic skills need to be honed on 'development' courses and have created Level 1 and Level II PEACE courses and 'advanced' courses for officers assigned to appointments where they are to deal with particularly challenging interviewees, e.g. in particularly serious and especially sensitive investigations. Very few forces have adopted this career span perspective.

In respect of witness interviewing, although this was an integral part of the original PEACE package, the subsequent developments of PEACE have led to an increasing, and now predominant focus, on suspect interviewing. In all too many forces this has led to progressively less and less course time being devoted to developing witness interviewing. This has necessarily contributed to the now critical shortcomings in witness interviewing (see below, p. 137).

Overall, the service as a whole is unable to guarantee consistency of training, or even any training at all, given to officers responsible for interviewing witnesses or suspects. The risk of process corruption through ineffective and unethical interviewing is all too obvious.

Investigative skills

The service has never sought formally to impart the skills of investigation to officers. 'How to investigate' was yet something else to be picked up as a probationer or when seconded to a plain clothes or CID unit. Up until recently, this was not a matter of concern for the service as a whole, for as we pointed out earlier 'uniform' was not seen as responsible for investigating, or indeed interviewing: both being specialist, i.e. CID work.

Now the service expects officers – all officers – to be able to deliver a professional investigative performance characterised by effectiveness and integrity.

Reactive investigative skills

To gain some idea of the scope of activity expected, we invite you to reread the section 'Investigation by a uniform FOA' in Chapter 2, p. 59. This spells out decisions and actions that presume not only awareness of forensic science but fundamental investigative skills.

There is a problem. The former Director of National Police Training reported to the service[44] that which PEACE courses since 1993 have consistently revealed. The community and the police service have paid a heavy price for a tradition of the service not providing officers with relevant training: a widespread and fundamental deficit in investigative skills among uniform officers and CID. Beyond the very basic procedural training received in probationer training, the vast majority of officers have received no subsequent training to enable them to render a professional performance as an investigator.

Proactive investigative skills

The increasing demand for proactive policing necessarily calls upon increasing numbers of officers to engage in covert techniques. Shortage of personnel, suitably qualified staff and time, continue to ensure that most officers have received little or no training to prepare them:

- to engage in surveillance;
- to recruit and to handle informants, and to control informant handlers.

Training to recruit and to handle informants and to control handlers

Traditionally, most officers have not cultivated informants, preferring to approach a particular person, e.g. a publican, for specific information.

Research[45-6] shows that prior to the Audit Commission endorsement of informants, very few officers made the effort to recruit informants. The investigative specialists – CID officers – received no training in recruiting and handling informants. Similarly untrained were those tasked in controlling the activities of handlers.

It is acknowledged that all officers who handle informants must be trained. Given the press for informants, this constitutes an enormous training demand – in addition to other pressing demands for essential training in law, procedure, forensic awareness, fundamental investigative skills, PEACE interviewing and post-PEACE, advanced and specialist interviewing. It is understandable, therefore, why in many forces there is insufficient or no training of handlers and controllers. About a quarter of all forces in England and Wales conduct such training but there is a lack of consistency across courses. Following the implementation of National Standards for Covert Policing and the production of a manual of guidance and a Code of Practice in respect of informants,[47] the National Crime Faculty has been tasked to produce accredited courses.

We return to the issue of informants later in this chapter.

THE BALANCE BETWEEN REACTIVE AND PROACTIVE POLICING

Increasingly, forces are rationalising resources and organising the division of work, other than specialist reactive crime teams, to allow substantial emphasis upon intelligence-led policing. Whether someone will be sent in response to a call, and the likely quality of investigation that takes place, will necessarily reflect force policy decisions as to what level of manpower and investigative competence will be devoted to reactive policing and how much to proactive policing. Large numbers of officers are being shifted from reactive to proactive policing, such that those left to fulfil the uniform role find it difficult to cope.[48]

Although assurances may be given that various plain clothes team members will be assigned to reactive tasks when the situation dictates, inevitably this will not apply to incidents that require an immediate response by uniform police officers at or near the crime scene or despatched by the control room. These officers, in reduced numbers, constitute the service's immediate response team, responsible for the vital initial stages of investigation or securing the scene of the crime for others to attend. It will be a continuing fact of life that:

- within this reduced group there will be an over-representation of inexperienced officers (probationers in training and those very junior in service) or officers out of training of varying seniority who lack the necessary disposition, awareness and ability to be assigned to proactive teams;

- actual performance will continue to confirm the observations of PEACE trainers and government research, that uniform officers are forensically unaware and lack the most basic skills of investigation and crime scene management.

The next link in the reactive chain – the CIT (evidence team) – fulfils crucial functions:

- taking over the investigation of cases, with suspects in cells left by:
  - uniform personnel deployed on reactive run-of-the-mill cases;
  - tactical teams who have arrested individuals – identified by proactive policing – often doing so without informing the evidence team members about the operation and thus confronting them with alienated, angry, disorientated, disaffected suspects arrested in raids effected at extremely unsocial hours and involving breaking in, distress to family members, and physical contact and force;
- preparation of crime files, paperwork and exhibits and conducting transactions with the CPS.

The shift in focus towards intelligence-led policing, involving fundamental changes in organisation, working practices and resourcing necessarily sends powerful messages to officers, affecting their perceptions, attitudes and behaviour. Intelligence-led policing is viewed as both cost-effective and fighting crime 'for real' by taking the initiative, committing resources and energy to target criminals and to take them out of circulation. A 'package' (criminal) is identified, targeted, and followed through to the commission, or attempted commission, of an offence, interviewing, charging and beyond. Officers assigned to proactive teams feel valued for their prowess and potential to perform policing tasks which provide a real sense of coherence, achievement and job satisfaction.

In contrast, lower-priority, lesser-resourced, reactive policing implies lower status. This is not simply a reflection on the fact that many officers fulfilling this role are in training or otherwise lack the wherewithal to be selected for proactive duties. Assignment to a reactive policing role has a great potential to demotivate. This is even greater for the otherwise able officer. It is difficult to remain motivated when:

- officers are essentially 'fire-fighting', being despatched from one incident to another, rendering it difficult to investigate systematically;

- it is deemed that there is little or no prospect of identifying the suspect and the officers know they are going through the motions;

- there is a prospect of identifying a suspect or a suspect has been detained but little time or effort can be devoted to the processes of hot and warm investigation;

- there is no sense of ownership, i.e. however well or indifferently handled the case, witnesses and suspects are, 'evidence'-gathering teams assume responsibility for investigation and beyond.

Evidence-gathering teams, being an extension of the process of reactive policing, have somewhat higher status but still less than teams engaged in proactive work. Evidence gathering is essentially a response to a continuous conveyor belt of inherited cases. This becomes cumulatively demotivating and stressful. They are confronted with circumstances over which they have no real control: the sheer number of cases, time pressure, limited resources and, perhaps most significantly, too many cases that do not withstand close scrutiny in terms of the quality of the case, the evidence and the investigation thus far.

The pressures increase the likelihood of defensive avoidance and a resort to traditional investigative aims – attaching criminality in the most expedient manner, i.e. by seeking to induce the suspect to confess, a solution that overcomes evidential shortcomings.

A CIT officer who struggles against the odds to investigate effectively and ethically still faces further barriers:

- the backlog of cases and lack of resources may preclude efforts to check out a suspect's confession;

- the pressure for more admissions – TICs – not for testing admissions;

- the pressure for 'positive outcomes', i.e. to charge the suspect irrespective of the insufficiency of the evidence

Increasing emphasis upon proactive policing is dramatically reducing the resources available to engage in reactive policing. Having hard-pressed 'fire fighters' and 'front end' investigators passing on subsequent investigation to evidence teams undermines the ability (and cumulatively the argument) to ensure all officers have a common core of investigative knowledge, awareness and skills, i.e. basic forensic awareness, crime scene management, searching, physical evidence protection and identification, collation, analysis and evaluation of information, and investigative interviewing beyond the basic level. Paradoxically, it risks deskilling not only officers engaged in reactive policing but also officers in proactive teams for whom tasks outside their own specialist context are increasingly viewed as someone else's specialist job.

Intelligence-led policing is demanding on resources, increasing demands for results to justify this in VFM terms. This increases the pressure upon an officer:

- to bend the rules;

- to be economical with the truth;

- to assert that:
    - things were said or happened that in fact did not;
    - things were not said or did not happen that in fact did.

POOR MANAGEMENT OF INFORMATION

Analysing the available evidence is but one part of the continuous investigative task, which demands a professional performance in managing and processing the entire range of information arising across the course of the investigation. It is essential that an officer be able to work substantial amounts of fine-grain detail.

In recommending that officers analyse the available evidence, PEACE presumes officers are good enough, if not good, at these fundamental activities. Research for the RCCJ and the Home Office has shown that they are not – a fact recognised by supervisors and managers.[49-51]

Information management is all too often haphazard and inefficient. There is heavy reliance upon individual wit, motivation and method.

PEACE training has only served to confirm the underlying message from the research: that lack of training, supervision and systems has created within the service a very low level of information-handling skills in the basic processes of:

- *planning*, i.e. identifying and prioritising what to investigate, how, where, when and in what time frame;

- *collating* and *integrating* the information obtained;

- *evaluating* the information;

- *analysing* the information;

- *using the information to plan further investigation* – including the interviewing of witnesses and the suspect.

SHORTCOMINGS IN CRIME SCENE MANAGEMENT AND SEARCHING

As we pointed out earlier, the majority of officers, both uniform and CID, lack basic awareness and knowledge of forensic issues. They are unaware of the details of physical evidence and lack the skills (having never been trained) in crime scene management, recording and searching the crime scene and vicinity, and securing, preserving or taking other appropriate action in respect of, physical evidence.

The absence of such essential knowledge skills will continue to be a fundamental source of process corruption, across the entire course of an investigation but especially in the very early stages from the time the first officer arrives. Widespread ignorance and ineptitude will mean for the foreseeable future that in many investigations officers will:

- perform poorly in managing and searching the crime scene;

- perform poorly in recording the scene, the management of the scene and any searching;

- contaminate the scene, inadvertently bring about the contamination of victim and suspect, and contaminate evidence collected or seized from the suspect.

PROBLEMS ACHIEVING COMPREHENSIVE INVESTIGATION PRIOR TO INTERVIEWING THE SUSPECT

The previous chapter indicated that PEACE guides officers prior to interviewing the suspect:

- to analyse what evidence is available;

- in the light of this analysis to assess what evidence is needed and where it can be obtained.

It is better to exhaust other possible sources of information rather than rely upon interviewing the suspect. PEACE recommends actions that any lay person and any court would consider obvious, common sense and essential steps before embarking upon an interview of a suspect about an offence, alleged to have taken place in a particular location, in a particular way and in a particular set of circumstances:

- speaking to the reporting officer, i.e. obtaining a briefing;

- speaking to all witnesses, complainants and victims;

- visiting the scene of the crime or incident;

- examining exhibits and property found at the scene or in possession of the suspect;

- making use of information and intelligence systems.

The performance culture, the lack of resource, and the pressure for VFM combine to create a working environment that discourages, and actually prevents, officers from engaging in the full common-sense range of investigation.

SHORTCOMINGS IN THE BRIEFING PROCESS

Accurate briefing is essential as one officer hands over a case to another, e.g. the FOA to a member of the CIT or the SIU. Assuming the handing-over officer is ready, willing and able to give a briefing, unlike other investigative agencies, e.g. the intelligence and security services, the police service does not have a standardised approach to, or system for, briefing:

- verbally;

- in written form.

In the case of a briefing, what gets covered, in what sequence and in what detail is a matter of chance and the two officers' individual dispositions. In the case of an officer writing down a note or an official statement:

- the same criteria for 'good' witness statements (as described below) apply;

- the same processes to achieve these are likely to apply.

The CPS, the defence and the court cannot assume that these activities – systematic processing of information and checking out sources of information – have taken place or, if they took place, that they fulfilled basic criteria of effectiveness and ethical criteria.

CRITICAL SHORTCOMINGS IN THE INTERVIEWING OF WITNESSES

Descriptions

Witnesses are the major source of information in identifying the suspect. Their descriptions, particularly the initial description, are vital.

Failing to take a full, accurate description

The police should systematically question witnesses to obtain the fullest possible descriptions of people. Frequently they do not.

Most people are not good at describing other people. Recognition is always better than description. This applies to our descriptions of those whom we know very well, including our nearest and dearest and people we meet and work with every day. Most people are not very observant and have an impression rather than a mental image of the person in question.

Describing someone is a difficult task since:

- it involves expressing verbally a visual image that the person has in mind;

- there is no vocabulary to describe faces adequately.

It is therefore no surprise that victims and witnesses experience difficulties when asked to give a verbal description of someone involved in the commission of a crime:

- their descriptions tend to be short and relatively incomplete, becoming even shorter and less useful when there is a time delay between the event and giving the description;

- the description is harder to give and more fragmentary if their visual image is vague and incomplete;

- those who have little or no recall may give a stereotype description.

Lay people have limitations when it comes to descriptions. However, they assume that those who are deemed to deal daily with descriptions – police officers – are expert. They assume the police service has appropriate systems and skills for the acquisition and communication of information about how people look and behave.

Although the service has systems for specialist officers to construct images and categorical systems for computer databases there is an astonishing paradox. Officers on the beat, in CID and special task units, e.g. street crime, have no standard system for obtaining descriptions in everyday cases.

This lack of a standardised system necessarily creates and sustains another anomaly: the basic training of officers does not include the development of skilled, systematic obtaining and communication of descriptions. Officers are left to their own devices. Supervising officers and those responsible for inputting and working upon data in collation systems repeatedly bemoan the shortcomings of descriptions sent over the OIS, recorded in crime reports, pocket books and statements. Despite the known deficiencies, little or no real effort is applied to foster and maintain systematic and consistent standards of description taking.

The result is that inaccurate and inadequate descriptions are endemic. Lack of a basic system and lack of skill and systematic behaviour compound:

- problems of distortion created by officers using inappropriate, suggestive questioning, particularly when the officer has prior knowledge of the suspect in the form of a visual image or another witness description;

- problems with witnesses:

  - the compliant, those who want to appear helpful, and those who are 'second guessing' the description sought by the officer, can give a description fitting what they think will satisfy the officer;
  - the suggestible or those who distrust their memory are particularly susceptible to suggestive questioning and negative feedback about their performance.

The 'first' and subsequent descriptions

Typically, the description contained in formal statement from the witness has been presented by the police, and accepted by the CPS, the defence and the court, as the witness's only description, i.e. singular and consistent in its detail. In reality, it is only the latest in a sequence of descriptions in exchanges with the witness stretching back to the original version given at the time of the initial report received by the control room and passed over the OIS or received by the FOA.

Given the fallibility of people's descriptions, compounded by all too many police officers' lack of skill or system in obtaining descriptions, it is the case that in many instances a description goes through a process of evolution with additions, subtractions and alterations to the first description. This process is obscured by the disinclination of officers to apply the final element of the ADVOKATE checks, i.e. rather than confront contradiction and anomaly in the evolving description, they make no mention of this, fail to bring the changes to the court's attention and offer the description in the statement as the only description.

Missing witnesses

Officers have always been able to decide not to make a record of questioning, or not to obtain a statement from, an individual:

- who generated *negative* evidence when questioned;
- who gave detail which did not accord with:
  - that of the victim or other witnesses;
  - the officer's case theory.

These individuals constitute missing witnesses.

Statement taking

Most witnesses allow the police officer to write the statement and, having read the statement or had it read to them, sign it as true. The general assumption is that a statement constitutes the witness's own words. There is no audio recording of the course and the content of the interview, which gave rise to the statement. A court has no means of knowing:

- what influence the officer exerted over what was disclosed or what manner of editing took place;
- whether the statement is the complete and accurate record of what the witness said.

Cumulatively, the PEACE model of investigative interviewing and trainers, particularly those prepared to confront realities:

- warn that witnesses can be wrong, requiring the officer to keep an open and enquiring mind;
- stress the requirement for a full record of the interview and the statement-taking process (as opposed to the statement):
  - minimally this should be a written record (not just notes);
  - tape recording is preferable – particularly:

    (a) in more serious cases;
    (b) when the officer conducts a cognitive (memory-enhancement) interview in which the interviewee is instructed to 'leave nothing out' and a range of techniques is applied to increase the amount of detail disclosed;

- stress the requirement to apply the ADVOKATE (the *R.* v. *Turnbull* criteria checklist) when questioning and taking a statement, with particular reference to the need to confront contradictions or anomalies and, where these cannot be resolved, to include these in the document – not to edit them out.

Despite an extremely large expenditure of time and money on PEACE training in basic investigative interviewing, witness interviewing remains the Achilles' heel of police investigations. The evidence is that PEACE training is not impacting upon officers' actual daily behaviour. Research, particularly that based upon recordings of officers interviewing witnesses, shows that witness interviewing and its product – witness statements – leave a lot to be desired.[52]

For a comprehensive explanation of the factors, which prevent the emergence of full and faithful testimony from witness interviews, see *Analysing Witness Testimony*.[53] It is of value to draw your attention to factors that corrupt the investigative process.

The disinclination to record

Very large numbers of officers:

- do not make full notes;
- reject the idea of tape recording.

The absence of a record obscures those instances where:

- the witness gave an account characterised by inconsistency and anomaly;
- the officer did not follow best-practice guidelines and failed to implement techniques properly and to observe safeguards, particularly when conducting a cognitive interview.

The reasons are straightforward: the risk of a request for disclosure and subsequent discovery that the statement obscures:

- contradiction and anomaly in what the witness actually said;
- the influence of the officer's management of the interview and statement-production practices in pursuit of a 'good' statement.

The pursuit of a 'good' statement

Three common approaches to interviewing in order to obtain a statement are:

- to ask the witness to give an account, listen to this without interruption while taking notes, then cross-examine what can be remembered and what is written in the notes;

- to ask the witness to give an account and interrupt throughout with cross-examinatory questions, noting down the answers;

- to ask a series of focused questions to generate information that will lead to a 'good' account.

The officer then composes a statement based upon what he or she can recall, original notes and notes of answers to questions. Quality of listening and note-taking skills, linked to attention and memory, impose limitations on what is actually recalled and retrieved from notes.

Whatever the approach, some information is likely to generate a statement that is not 'good'.

Common notions of a 'good' statement have it that a witness account should:

- sound plausible, i.e. implying exclusion of material that seems improbable or impossible;

- be chronological, i.e. implying credibility is enhanced by the reordering of events into a sequence;

- have no detail that is contradictory, vague, ambiguous, or negative, i.e. something that was not the case;

- be consistent with, or provide confirmation of, prior information, particularly:
  - the officer's case theory;
  - what other witnesses have said;
  - what the officer knows or believes;

- address specific points to prove, preferably:
  - not raising possible defences for the suspect;
  - negating possible defences.

The most effective and rapid route to a 'good' statement is editing: across the course of the interview and in the compilation of the statement.

This brings to the fore the operation of the officer's case theory, premature closure, confirmatory bias and, where there are manifest gaps and anomalies within the prior investigation of others, defensive avoidance. Editing across the course of the interview occurs by exercising very strong control over what gets talked about and in what level of detail. Leaving aside whether it occurs consciously or unconsciously, editing is extremely common. This is common knowledge throughout the police service, confirmed by research.[54]

Very often officers conduct interviews that excessively shape what the witness says,[55] i.e.

- the officer talking more than the witness;

- the officer posing predominantly suggestive questions, i.e. leading, option (either/or) and closed yes/no (confirmatory) questions, influencing the witness to go along with what is being asserted or implied by the officer;

- the officer overtalks and interrupts;

- the officer ignores responses;

- the officer rapidly changes the topic, leaving the matter unprobed.

In addition, there is widespread inattention to:

- the unreliability of eyewitness testimony and the need to question, mindful of the guidelines laid down in *R. v. Turnbull*. In all too many interviews leading to statements, no attention is paid to applying ADVOKATE criteria, particularly the requirement to face up to, and if unresolved, include contradiction and anomaly;

- the common-sense necessity to assess the assertion and the person making the assertion in terms of:
    - the *validity* of the information, e.g. does it agree with objective reality? Could the detail have been manifest or physically detectable in the manner described?;
    - the *reliability* of the witness, e.g. what limitations does he or she have? Does he or she wear spectacles? Were these worn at the time?

Finally, all too many officers fundamentally change the content of what the witness actually said by altering or substituting words, phraseology and verbal constructions.

These inappropriate practices in pursuit of a good statement, indicate the triumph of 'facts of life' over PEACE 'best practice' guidelines and

142

underline yet again the effect of minimal or non-existent supervision and quality controls.

Cognitive interviewing

Cognitive interviewing, which PEACE terms the *cognitive approach*, is an extremely effective method of getting maximum disclosure of detail. It involves a number of specific techniques, including *context reinstatement*, all of which are applied in a manner that ensures the interviewer has minimal influence over the disclosure process. Cognitive interviewing is a particularly demanding form of interviewing and requires:

* proper training from instructors who themselves have, and can pass on, the necessary fundamental grasp of psychological issues, practical realities, and the skills in question;
* continuous and supervised practice.

Only with these can an officer develop basic skills and, in time, the requisite expertise.

All too many PEACE trainers have lacked the wherewithal in terms of knowledge, and any experience of doing it, to train officers how to conduct proper cognitive interviewing. It was very much a case of the unaware requiring other to 'do as I tell you'. Once back from their basic PEACE course, very few officers have been encouraged, or felt competent, to conduct cognitive interviews. Those that are conducted are not subject to quality controls and supervision, which is infrequent, and in all too many cases involve officers who are enthusiastic and little else.

Research is now showing the outcome. The vast majority of police officers have failed to put their training into practice. In the majority of cases where officers reported they were using cognitive interviewing, their responses indicated that in fact all they are doing is:

* exercising better listening skills;
* asking more open-ended questions;
* deluding themselves into thinking that they are applying memory-enhancing techniques when in reality they are not.

These results were entirely predictable, given that the psychologists who developed cognitive interviewing have been quite explicit as to what kind of programme of training and supervised practice is necessary to develop the basic skills of cognitive interviewing.[56]

Cognitive interviewing demands a sound grasp of concept and time developing actual skill. It is not something that can be imparted in the form of a simple instruction 'do it this way'. It is not surprising therefore that in two subsequent developments of PEACE the distinction between 'conversation management' and the 'cognitive approach' has been lost. Officers attending courses are no longer taught the 'cognitive approach'. While some forces are seeking, against the odds, to continue training officers in cognitive interviewing, it is likely that this very valuable method for interviewing victims and eyewitnesses (when done properly) will become less and less commonly applied as progressively fewer officers are trained and apply it.

The statement takers

One method of ensuring VFM and maximising the number of operational officers able to be deployed on proactive policing is to give the task of statement taking to a civilian 'statement taker', e.g. retired police officers re-employed to fulfil this role.

Such appointments are based upon the assumption that years of service have endowed the individual with the skills to perform this role. We have described above the characteristic manner of approaching the task of obtaining witness statements and there is no reason to believe that re-employed officers would be any different in their approach.

Furthermore, it would appear that, in respect of civilian statement takers:

- there is no check upon the actual quality of their performance prior to appointment, i.e. in terms of monitoring and assessing the individual's interviewing and relating this to its outcome;

- there are no provisions for their training, particularly continuation training;

- there are no provisions for quality control and quality assurance of their performance once they are appointed.

LACK OF KNOWLEDGE OF THE SCENE

The public and the courts would be astonished to learn that in many instances an IO, e.g. in a CIT (evidence-gathering team), will not visit the scene before embarking upon an interview of a suspect.[57] A number of reasons may lead to this decision including:

- lack of time, e.g. the detention clock;
- lack of resource, e.g. no transport available;
- too many additional cases to be processed;
- the offence being relatively low in seriousness compared to others to be investigated.

The Audit Commission argued that sending an officer to the scene of every crime is not an effective use of limited resources, particularly in the case of volume crime and where there is a low likelihood of the crime being solved.[58-9] However, where there is a suspect in custody, failure to visit the scene becomes a critical source of ignorance. This is especially so if the IO:

- has received no briefing from the FOA or arresting officer;
- has a poorly completed crime report;
- has inadequate handover notes;
- has not spoken to the SOCO;
- has no sketches or diagrams to assist in visualising the scene, approach routes, points of entry and exit, and locations where CTM was found;
- has to rely upon statements and descriptions:
  - that are characterised by gaps and anomalies;
  - in which ADVOKATE criteria were not applied.

In these circumstances, an IO is functionally blind to the realities of the location about which he or she intends to question the suspect. He or she is completely unable to judge the validity of the suspect's responses. The IO, particularly one who has engaged in defensive avoidance in respect of gaps and anomalies in the police case, the evidence and the investigation, is under some pressure to bluff it out – asserting that he or she knows something when this is in fact not the case.

CRITICAL SHORTCOMINGS IN THE INTERVIEWING OF SUSPECTS

The PEACE model is based upon an ethical philosophy: interviewers should be open-minded and be prepared to disclose evidence, albeit exercising professional judgement as to what, when, and to what degree. It points out that, before conducting an interview, an officer should be able to answer the question: why do I need to interview this person?

In respect of a suspect, if neither of the following aims apply no interview should take place:

- to obtain evidence to prove or disprove the suspect's involvement in the allegation;

- where evidence is available to prove a suspect's involvement in an alleged offence, to provide him or her with the opportunity to explain or to test that evidence.

In many instances, the factors described above in this chapter create a situation in which there are substantial shortcomings in the prosecution evidence, linked to problems in the police case and the conduct and outcome of the police investigation.

All that is left to the IO, particularly one who is engaged in defensive avoidance, who has not been briefed, and who has not visited the scene, is:

- to terminate the interview;

- to bluff it out, to go onto the offensive and to attempt to get a confession to a representation of reality offered by the officer.

Actual cases, particularly those where the interviewing is excluded under sections 76 and 78 of PACE, and research show that going onto the offensive is a very common pattern[60-1] in which:

- the officer presents a synthesis of selected details from the material he or she has, i.e. what is presented is not reflective of any one account and its selection obscures the existence of gaps and anomalies;

- in the face of resistance – the exercise of the right to silence or assertions, which counter the officer's synthetic representation of reality – the officer engages in dominant, constraining and coercive questioning, i.e.

   - switching very early on in the interview from obtaining a narrative to direct questioning, with the synthetic representation in mind;
   - hindering the suspect by disruptively interrupting and overtalking;
   - restricting the suspect's latitude of response content by engaging in a high frequency of suggestive questioning, i.e. confirmatory yes/no, leading and option questions; interrogative assertions, e.g. reading from a statement details as though these are statements of fact, which, in the absence of a response, are taken as confirmation;

- upgrading the suspect's responses, i.e. the officer believes he or she knows the answer, progressively reframes (shapes) the responses of the suspect and incorporates these in the officer's questions:

  (a) to arrive at a final response which confirms the officer's beliefs;
  (b) to achieve legal closure, i.e. leading the suspect to give a legally significant response when the officer has yet to establish the foundational elements of the offence;

- misrepresenting what the suspect or others said during the interview or earlier;
- misrepresenting something that is not a fact as a fact.

Intelligence-led policing places IOs tasked with interviewing the suspect in a dilemma:

- officers involved in the proactive investigation prior to the offence, or attempted offence, will consider they know or strongly believe that the targeted individual is incontrovertibly guilty;

- there will be substantial pressures on the officers to engage in defensive avoidance, i.e. choosing to turn a blind eye to shortcomings in the police case, prosecution evidence and the police investigation, ignoring gaps, vagaries, ambiguities, contradictions and anomalies in information and evidence obtained proactively;

- officers will not be ready, willing or able to disclose source, content and status of proactively obtained information to suspects or their legal advisers in consultations prior to the interview and even in the interview. Furthermore, they will be unwilling to disclose at any time certain sources of information, e.g. from informants; from electronic or mail intercept.

Firm in the knowledge or belief that the individual is guilty, whether or not turning a blind eye to shortcomings in the evidence, intelligence-led policing is destined:

- to run counter to PEACE guidance to present the evidence;

- to induce officers to engage in dominant questioning in pursuit of a confession.

The 'confession culture', which PEACE has sought to counter, is rendered precarious by increasing numbers of officers for whom the aim of the interview is to get a 'cough' (admission), since:

- confessions are tangible, best evidence, 'results' – justifying the cost of proactive effort;

- confessions conserve resources – once obtained, further investigation is rendered unnecessary;

- confessions enable the police to keep the suspect in the dark as to the nature of the intelligence-derived prosecution evidence, and as to police inability or unwillingness to disclose such evidence, i.e. that which gave rise to, and emerged during, an 'operation' (informant detail and information; conduct and content of surveillance, particularly technological).

In the face of resistance there will be an increased likelihood of:

- questioning in a manner that pressurises the suspect in order to obtain a confession, particularly in the challenge phase of interviews;

- conversation 'off tape' to pressure or to persuade the suspect to confess:
  - in interview rooms;
  - in visits to cells;
  - outside the confines of the cell, e.g. in the exercise yard, in a police vehicle ostensibly to take the suspect to a particular location.

Given their knowledge or firm belief that the individual is guilty, officers will be motivated to adopt the traditional perspective that legal advisers obstruct the course of justice,[62] particularly those who:

- actively defend, pressing for detail on the police case, the prosecution evidence and the police investigation;

- advise their clients to exercise the right to silence, when the adviser's questions prior to or during the interview have revealed that the investigating officer lacks the readiness, willingness or ability to give information about the source or the detail of the evidence;

- closely monitor and intervene appropriately during the interview.

Intelligence-led policing has added to the pressure for TICs, since these reflect extra value for proactive effort and are likely to be yet another performance indicator. The pursuit of TICs will have a number of effects:

- to encourage officers to blur the distinction between questioning and interviewing, such that exchanges outside the interview room will be deemed to be the former and not the latter;

- to increase the advantage, and therefore the likelihood, of increased frequency of questioning 'off tape' in interview rooms and during visits to cells;

- to encourage officers to make minimal records of their 'off tape' exchanges with suspects;

- to render officers less disposed to spend time and effort checking TICs, i.e. to establish whether they are valid and reliable, and whether the admitted offences could have been carried out by the individual.

In addition, intelligence-led policing has added the further pressure to recruit informants. This is typically done after the interview and before charging, e.g. when taking fingerprints or completing the MG3, or, when the suspect has been bailed, while being taken home in a police vehicle.

SURVEILLANCE STANDARDS

All surveillance is a highly skilled, resource demanding activity. There is widespread acknowledgement that:

- officers should be trained. However, this is extremely expensive and formal training is restricted, e.g. to SCU officers. Forces are obliged to use surveillance-trained officers to conduct 'local' training of officers, e.g. those fulfilling tactical CID and beat crime unit duties. Even this is often too expensive or resource demanding, such that a large proportion of investigations have untrained officers carrying out surveillance tasks;

- it is not solely a matter of individual skill. Surveillance should be done by dedicated teams, for whom this is their primary task, to ensure professional standards through the maintenance and development of professional skills. Most forces can only assign a finite number of officers in full-time teams or part-time teams – the latter being recognised as less effective than the former;

- *ad hoc* surveillance is the least effective.

The deployment of officers on part-time or *ad hoc* surveillance risks:

- with static (fixed-point) surveillance – the officers being unwilling or unable to keep detailed, contemporaneous, comprehensive records;

- with mobile surveillance – the officers stating that they kept the individual under constant surveillance when in fact it was interrupted.

THE THREAT POSED BY INFORMANTS

The Audit Commission declared that informers are good value for money.[63] Increasing amounts of money are being spent, as forces seek to maximise the use of informants and more and more reliance is being placed upon informants. There is enormous pressure on officers to recruit informants:

> 'One of the unfortunate by-products of the intelligence-led approach is that in some areas officers are being urged to recruit informants with little regard for their quality. In one force, staff were told that to get onto and to remain on CID they would need to have at least five registered informants.'[64]

The use of informants has been identified as possibly the highest area of risk to the integrity of police work in terms of susceptibility to corruption.[65] This is because officers are exposed to close contact with criminals in contexts where controls are minimal or completely absent.

A retired senior detective observed[66] that:

> 'In my early days we used to say the three most dangerous things were what we called the three Ps: prisoners, prostitutes and property. But the one I, the I for informant, can make the three Ps pale into insignificance. They tend to be untrustworthy, unbalanced, greedy and treacherous and, yes, dangerous.'

Research and the HMIC[67] report on integrity provide ample evidence of the problems and the risks created by transactions between police officers and informants. It is worth summarising key points from this material.

The information given by informants and the typical informant

The police recognise that informants are devious and untrustworthy. Information received is often unreliable or incomplete. Most officers are apprehensive that they will be set up by the informant. The police 'con' them and are 'conned' by them.

The typical registered informer is an unemployed male with a long history of criminality.[68]

There are increasing calls to extend the use of juveniles as informants – particularly in return for money rather than gifts – in the proactive policing of volume crimes, e.g. domestic burglaries, vehicle theft, street theft, and drug use and trafficking.[69] The Code of Practice recognises the particular problems necessarily raised by the use of this vulnerable group, e.g.

- should the parents be told;

- asking for information about, and therefore exposing the individual to, an area of crime in which he or she is not involved;

- asking for, and using, information about relatives and close family;

- using juveniles in an *agent provocateur* role to trap offenders.

The most effective informers are those who are actively involved in the crime they are informing about: in the research, 36 per cent were participating informers.[70] In some instances they operate as an *agent provocateur*. During the passage of the Bill before Parliament, the government acknowledged that 'at times, it is difficult for the police to run informers properly and within the law without crossing the line and becoming *agents provocateurs*'.[71]

Once registered, informants tend to have short careers, often because payments are low, suspicion falls upon the informant because it is noted that cumulatively many of the informant's acquaintances are arrested, or the informant's handler transfers to other duties or another area.[72–3]

Recruiting and handling informants

Most informers are under arrest or subject to police enquiries when they are recruited. Recruitment is achieved by a process of inducement, psychological coercion, deception and manipulation.

Without any supervisory oversight, officers arrange for no charging or charges to be reduced or dropped, detention to be shortened, bail to be expedited, to arrange for a 'text' (a mitigating letter to the court), and undertake to do favours, e.g. with the housing department.

Circumstances arise where informants recruit themselves to become registered informants:

- in exchange for a 'text' or for bail, less so for money;

- as an 'insurance policy', when arrested again;

- in order to remove the 'competition', particularly so with drug dealers;

- in order to gain revenge on the persons being informed upon.

Insidiously, officers undertake not to investigate, or arrange for no investigation, of crimes committed or being committed by the informer.

Hence many informants continue to commit crime in the knowledge that the police will turn a 'blind eye'.

Increasing amounts of money are being allocated to paying informants.[74] This parallels decisions to extend the circumstances under which payments will be made:

- payments in advance for informants who perform well;

- payments for those whose information allows preventative action so a crime does not occur;

- payments in the absence of results – as regular retainers to secure the services:

  - over a longer period of high performers;
  - of individuals deemed to have a potential or prospective value.

Two processes – inability to cope with close monitoring of large-scale increases in the number of informants and hiking of payments (inflation) – risk undermining the integrity of the intelligence base by the widespread generation of unreliable or spurious information by unevaluated informants.

Supervision and accountability

The declared aim of the service is to have informants who will be more effectively registered, monitored and controlled. However, although the service recognises that there needs to be effective mechanisms for registration, monitoring and control of informants, in many forces such systems either do not exist at all, or are ignored.[75]

Some individuals who give information to the police do not want to become registered informants. An alternative is to call them 'confidential sources' who are not subject to whatever controls that do exist within the force for managing informants. The risk here is that informants and their handlers use this alternative status to avoid their relationship being subject to scrutiny.

Police handlers have a track record of bypassing the supervisory system.

- They have no faith in controllers whom they consider to be out of touch, from whom they would not receive support if the 'wheel comes off' in handling the informant. Their concerns are not without foundation. The HMIC reported that, in the main, the quality of supervision given to informant handlers is seriously inadequate. Controllers are remote, untrained and, in general, trying to control too many informants. While the Inspectorate consider it unreasonable for an individual to manage more than 20–25 informants, it found that detective inspectors are often expected to control 100 or more.[76]

- Handlers resort to secrecy, keeping controllers in the dark and exercising tight control over what information is passed back to the force.

- They flout guidelines on the use of participating informers.

- They flout the rules governing disclosure. In none of 31 cases examined by researchers,[77] and where the informer had been paid, had the fact of the informer's involvement been revealed to the CPS. This breaches the Code of Practice under CPIA.

Police officers already have problems of accountability in their dealings with witnesses, i.e. keeping a detailed record of the exchange. As the traditional perspective has been that the informant belongs to the officer not the service, officers have decided what, if anything, would be recorded concerning meetings with the informant. Explicit instructions have in the past been lacking for the completion of comprehensive and regular records of meetings. With the advent of explicit instructions and rules to ensure accountability, large number of officers, whether experienced or inexperienced in recruiting and working with informants, will be unwilling or unable to observe these.

In a similar vein, controllers will also experience difficulty following explicit instructions and rules given long-established shortcomings in, and widespread avoidance of, controlling, monitoring and supervising of handlers and their informants.

The relationship between the police officer and the informant

Whenever an officer is handling the informant there is an ever present risk of the officer getting out of his or her depth and ending up being manipulated by the informant. Allied to this is a very great risk indeed: the relationship that develops between the two individuals.

Officers become increasingly protective of the informant and less and less objective in their assessments: of the informant, the informant's way of life, what the informant does, and what constitutes the boundary between acceptable and unacceptable in terms of their relationship and their respective conduct towards each other. Research revealed that one-third of officers were prepared to lie in court to protect their informers.[78]

With continuity of contact, growing knowledge about the informant as an individual, officers are at risk of 'bonding' with the informant, becoming over-involved with the informant's personal circumstances. As the

153

boundary between them becomes progressively blurred, a handler may come to perceive the informant as a friend or even confidant. The ultimate evolution is when the officer identifies totally with the informant: viewing their interests as synonymous, both united against the 'system' which they have no qualms exploiting to mutual benefit.

The longer the relationship between an informant and the informant's handler lasts, the greater the risk of the police officer progressively losing sight of the original basis of the relationship. The HMIC was disturbed to note many instances where officers had run informants for very many years, noting in one case how the two individuals moved up through the criminal and police hierarchy simultaneously.[79]

One approach to guarding the generality of officers from this risk is the use of 'source units'. These are staffed by specialist informant handlers – hand-picked detectives of proven ability and integrity. Once recruited, an informant is passed over to the unit. However, to protect even these specialists it will be necessary to limit the officer's tenure, i.e. the time he or she fulfils these duties. As additional protection against corruption, when the officer's tenure ends he or she should have no influence over the appointment of successor.

Even with these protective devices, it is recognised that risks may still exist in the processes of recruiting and maintaining a relationship with an informant. The HMIC recommends forces consider using an 'overseer' system. Officers independent of an investigation or department using an informant and with full access to all information are tasked to inspect randomly the integrity of the case and the use of the informant.[80]

Recognising and responding to the risks

We argue that the criminal justice system has every justification to be apprehensive in every respect about informants: the individual's motivation to inform, the individual's history of information given, the validity and reliability of that information, and the history of the relationship between informant and handler. In not one of these areas has the police service had, or exercised, effective quality control. Informants have always been recognised to be a risk. The growth in numbers of informants, fuelled by the pressure on officers to perform, and the increasing numbers of investigations and prosecutions involving informant information, will necessarily increase the size of the risk, and with it the scope for process corruption.

The sheer numbers involved challenge the service's ability to implement measures to manage and to control an ever-growing threat to police integrity in the form of process corruption. The example of PEACE is telling. Millions of pounds have been spent, but still not everyone is trained in a 'national' package, which has been progressively changed by individual forces. And supervision, as we shall see in the next section, still remains an undelivered necessity.

ENSURING QUALITY: THE ENDEMIC, ENDURING PROBLEM

Poor management practices

Police officers are individual decision-makers. From probationer days onwards, they learn to value, and be valued, for independent decision-making and action. It is, of course, difficult to manage a workforce made up of individual decision-makers. It demands a particular form of management: one which manifests 'caring to care'.

This implies genuine interest in men and women as individuals, and commitment to provide direction and to foster, maintain and extend awareness of quality – effectiveness and integrity of conduct – in individuals' performances. Police officers need managers who help them to develop new competencies, to cope with change and to commit themselves to sincere two-way communication.[81] Everything rests upon:

- *continuity of monitoring* – of the individual and of his or her needs as demonstrated by how he or she does the job;

- *continuity of contact and communication* – creating a constructive context of coaching (having identified the officer's needs), counselling (finding out 'why' if the officer observably underperforms) and, only when attempts at counselling have manifestly failed on more than one occasion, correcting in the sense of bringing to bear sanctions.

The police service has accepted that the answer is to make quality a core issue: quality of conversation (the way officers talk to each other) and quality of working life (caring about the line officer) – such that all officers, managers, supervisors and line officers have a sense of shared responsibility for the quality of service.[82] Forces have been urged to introduce a range of common-sense, obvious and well-known methods to ensure the necessary upward communication and 'worker involvement'.[83] However, the essential rigidity of the service makes it difficult to introduce such concepts based upon the conditions of open-mindedness, openness to feedback and ethical conduct towards fellow officers.

155

It continues to be the case that, despite expenditure on training courses –
at the Police Staff College and within forces – and policy initiatives, to a
large extent recommended managerial practices fail to translate into actual
performance. Line managers and middle managers – who impact most
upon the lives of officers trying to do a good job – are felt by supervisors
and line officers to manage in a style and to communicate in a manner that
is traditional:[84] intermittent contact, a disposition to respond negatively,
unwillingness to put themselves in the officer's shoes, a wish to be brought
solutions not problems, e.g. not wanting to hear that the system is not
working and that proper investigation cannot take place.

Furthermore, police management is stressful to those whom they
manage.[85-6] Indeed, in an extensive study of stress and burn-out in the
police service[87] management style and management communication far
exceeded that occasioned by the traumatic nature of policing. Indeed, the
quotation by a constable introduces the report's description of the
managerial burdens that the service heaps upon willing workers: 'There's
more stress inside the nick than there is out on the streets.'

In the HMIC report on integrity[88] one chief constable said:

> 'Junior managers do not perceive themselves to be involved in day-to-day
> policing. Everyone wants to be a strategist...No-one is 'hands on'
> anymore, managing the day-to-day business.'

The stress induced by police management has increased apace as the
'performance culture' has grown, with each layer of management seeking
to demonstrate managerial prowess by squeezing out more and more
numerical evidence of achieving VFM. According to the HMIC:[89]

> 'There is perhaps a misunderstanding over what constitutes good
> management. There are many plans and policies, much chasing of targets
> and publishing of statistics, but the leadership of staff and management
> of day-to-day operations seems increasingly to be neglected.'

Stress is induced in officers because they struggle to cope with 'mixed'
messages. On the one hand there are 'top landing' and 'national' messages
exhorting them to be honest and to act with integrity. These messages are
to be found:

• in the display notices on police station walls spelling out the chief
  officer's annual statement of goals, which always includes an explicit
  statement concerning the fundamental police duty of ethical conduct;

- in PEACE training, which offers practical guidance to enable an officer to manifest ethical conduct, through effective, open-minded, comprehensive 'warts and all' investigation and investigative practices.

On the other hand there are the messages of front-line managers, requiring results achieved by conduct, which runs completely counter to effective and ethical investigation, exemplified by the 'positive outcome' policy. There are many others.

The HMIC defined[90] the core imperative for the service:

> 'There can be no more important qualities for members of the police service than that they are honest and act with integrity. Without these basic attributes the public can never be expected to trust the police and have the confidence in them that is necessary for a system of "policing by consent".'

By analogy, there can be no more important qualities for police managers than that they are honest and act with integrity. Without these basic attributes police officers can never be expected to trust in management and have the confidence in them that is necessary for a system of policing by effective and ethical conduct. We reiterate the point we have made more than once in this chapter, shortcomings in police management actually create the conditions for process corruption. Their behaviour sustains the 'informal code' view of management: it is not to be trusted since it does not look after your interests.

Lack of supervision

Where there is uncaring management sending 'mixed' messages, attitudes towards supervision are destined to be wholly ambivalent. Historically, the distinction between constables and sergeants in uniform was always much more marked than these ranks in the CID. Uniform sergeants have always tended to spend the greater part of their time in the police station engaged in administrative tasks, leaving officers to do their job as they consider appropriate out on the streets. As we pointed out earlier, in the CID, the typical working unit investigating quite serious crimes has been the duo – normally two detective constables with one acting as the designated OIC. In a larger enquiry, more officers might be involved, including a detective sergeant fulfilling the role of the OIC. In larger enquiries, a detective inspector, or higher, directs the case as SIO.[91]

Supervision of investigations

Research[92] into the supervision of police investigation into serious cases found two distinct models of supervision. There was effectively no supervision in investigations involving small numbers of officers.

> 'The word "supervision"', was not much liked, then, by the officers to whom we spoke, and it is a concept that is very much in the eye of the beholder... it is a rather nominal activity. Most officers in charge of enquiries do not view it as their business to direct operations, to tell others what to do or to criticise them. They tend to see it not only as unnecessary but even demeaning to peers or subordinates for them to be concerned to any extent in their activities, let alone comment on them...
>
> Supervision itself was viewed as so minor and routine an activity that it was looked on as an abstraction without any real operational significance...
>
> Whilst senior officers often claim to cast a supervisory eye over the detective constables who are responsible for leading enquiries so that they can intervene if any problems arise, this is in truth a thoroughly nominal and indirect form of supervision.'

In contrast, major enquiries led by senior officers were supervised in the sense that the OIC directed operations and assumed a full managerial role in the enquiry.

This situation still obtains. The HMIC saw[93] it as due to motivation:

> 'Her Majesty's Inspector is firmly convinced supervisory officers of EVERY rank have the time to provide support and guidance to their service deliverers outside the stations IF they have the inclination.'

This is recent evidence of the 'informal code' still operating. A critical mass of supervisors and the notionally supervised view supervision:

- as intrusive to the individual decision-making of the officer, i.e. interfering;

- as synonymous with fault-finding – traditionally, something only gets said by management if things go wrong;

- as something required by the inexperienced or those unable to perform without being checked;

- as something that should not be sought – a belief expressed within the group code, which says officers should not 'suck up' to supervisors, e.g. be seen to communicate with them about how the job could, should or might be done.

Ambivalence is compounded by anxiety and doubts:

- about the supervisor's inherent ability, i.e. he or she lacks the skills to do the job, and copes by:
  - talking in general, global terms about what is required;
  - not pressing, and not expecting to be pressed, in any detail about the practicalities of decision-making and action;
- about where the supervisor's loyalties would lie if push came to shove, i.e. when confronted with the likelihood of management criticism or a requirement to account for an officer's decisions and actions.

For many supervisors there is a pragmatic logic for *avoidant supervision*, i.e. keeping stress at bay by adopting an *laissez-faire* uninvolved style, by not bothering to find out, or by not bothering with detail. This affords the potential protection of ignorance:

- the supervisor cannot worry about that which he or she does not scan for, i.e. shortcomings within the conduct of the investigation, the nature of the police case and the status of the prosecution evidence;
- like management, supervision is rarely blamed. Courts are confronted by individual officers. There is a natural tendency for any inadequacy or impropriety to be attributed to an officer's critical, faulty decision or action, to a deficiency in the officer's character, to lack of training, or to expediency occasioned by operational pressures. Courts hardly ever make reference to the absence, or inadequacy, of quality controls and those who are responsible for this: supervisors;
- where blame is attached to supervision, very rarely does anything happen to the avoidant supervisor, or indeed the uncaring manager who should have been monitoring the quality of supervision.

Official research provides extensive proof of the pervasiveness of avoidant supervision.[94-6]

Supervision of investigative interviews

Many supervisors are reluctant, or claim limited opportunity, to devote time and effort to this crucial task. Research into supervision of investigative interviewing illustrated this point.[97] Lack of direct supervision was seen to be a matter of management expediency rather than an explicit management decision. Reasons given for lack of supervision included:

- lack of time or poor time management;
- conflicts between operational demands and organisational objectives;
- pressures and priorities;
- lack of the necessary supervisory training;
- the possibility of being called as a witness;
- officers were regarded as trained and expected to do their job without supervision.

It was not surprising that:

- the research found that quality only becomes an issue when the 'wheel falls off';
- in a significant number of forces, training of supervisors to monitor officers following the PEACE guidelines in their everyday interviewing behaviour has either never been implemented, only partially implemented, or suspended.

The fundamental necessity to monitor

It is paradoxical that both PEACE and police managers seeking to implement ACPO, HMIC and the Audit Commission's recommendations assign supervisors with a crucial quality control function to ensure effective and ethical investigation and investigative interviewing takes place. Put simply, they have to monitor and check the decision-making and actions of officers for whose quality of work they are ultimately responsible. Monitoring and checking should be detailed and not cursory.

To measure up to this key quality control role implies that the supervisor has:

- the knowledge and skills that he or she is seeking to monitor in the officer, i.e. you can hardly assess that which you do not have yourself;
- the necessary knowledge and skills to foster disclosure, engage in feedback and correct erroneous and inappropriate decisions and actions;
- time management skills – to monitor and to communicate;
- an active commitment to share his or her knowledge and skills.

Negative attitudes to supervision and the absence of close supervision place a question mark over fundamental issues of accountability, quality control and quality assurance in respect of decisions and actions at each and every stage of an investigation. This applies as much to the performance of the FOA as it does to members of the CIT, area CID or the SIU, as much to those operating the various intelligence systems as it does to those inputting data into a HOLMES database. There is little or no actual monitoring, thus creating the conditions for the emergence of process corruption in the many forms we have described.

Lack of sanctions

A chief constable argued that PACE was introduced to prevent corner-cutting and 'noble cause corruption'. He asserted[98] that the systems are now in place to root it out:

> *'It is now well accepted that the slightest "corner cutting" is unacceptable to the public and courts and will be severely dealt with through police discipline and the criminal law.'*

This presumes that there are effective quality control and quality assurance measures in place, most particularly in the form of real, as opposed to nominal, supervision ready, willing and able to monitor, to check and to detect even the slightest corner cutting in investigations. There are not.

Cicero commented that "…extremely few people will refrain from doing a wrong action if they have the assurance that this will be both undiscovered and unpunished." Lack of supervision, lack of monitoring and lack of checks, mean that at present within the police service there is very little likelihood of detecting investigative decisions and actions which are ineffective and lack integrity.

However, even when ineffective investigation and lack of integrity are inadvertently exposed, nothing happens to the officers involved. They are not subject to any real corrective response by police managers and supervisors. This sends a powerful message to those who are prepared to cut corners and who, in order to enhance the chances of a conviction, are prepared to lie and to correct and adjust fact. The 'system' says to these individuals that it does not matter. If detected, nothing will happen to them. They can continue with the 'wrong' behaviour. The lack of corrective sanction only serves to confirm to these officers, and those looking on, that such behaviour is policing 'for real' and that it is not *really* wrong.

A distinguished legal observer highlighted[99] how the lack of sanctions condones unethical conduct:

> *'...there have been virtually no disciplinary charges even for serious breaches of PACE. A striking case is Canale (Royal Commission Report, pp. 46–8), where, in quashing the conviction, the Lord Chief Justice said that the court found that there had been "flagrant, deliberate and cynical" breaches of the rules of PACE Code C. Yet there were no disciplinary proceedings. I find this inexplicable.*
>
> *In my view, in any case where a conviction is quashed by the Court of Appeal because of police misconduct, the officers concerned should automatically face formal disciplinary charges. The same rule should perhaps apply equally whenever a trial judge has excluded evidence on account of police misconduct. Certainly, it should follow where under the new procedure the presiding judge reports the conduct to the force concerned. Such rules, rigorously enforced, would send a much needed message both to the force and to the general public that serious misconduct in the course of criminal investigation will not be brushed under the carpet or treated as a matter simply for informal "advice".'*

Lack of sanction is, and is destined to remain, the ultimate factor that fosters, maintains and extends process corruption within police investigation.

Notes

1. Woodcock, J. (1992) 'Why we need a revolution'. *Police Review*, 16 October, 1929–32.

2. Fisher, H. (1977) *Report of an Inquiry by the Hon. Sir Henry Fisher into the Circumstances Leading to the Trial of Three Persons on Charges Arising out of the Death of Maxwell Confait and the Fire at 27 Doggett Road, London, SE6.* London: HMSO.

3. *A Guide to Interviewing.* (1992) Harrogate: Central Planning and Training Unit.

4. Home Office Circular 22/1992. *Principles of Investigative Interviewing.*

5. Phillips, D. (1999) 'Editorial: the forensic detective'. *Medicine, Science and the Law*, 39, 185–7.

6. Association of Chief Police Officers. (1998) *Murder Investigation Manual.*

7. Phillips, D. (1999) 'Editorial: the forensic detective'. *Medicine, Science and the Law*, 39, 185–7.

8. *Ibid.*

9. Woodcock, J. (1992) 'Why we need a revolution'. *Police Review*, 16 October, 1929–32.

10. *A Guide to Interviewing.* (1992) Harrogate: Central Planning and Training Unit.

11. Woodcock, J. (1992) 'Why we need a revolution'. *Police Review*, 16 October, 1929–32.

12. Shepherd, E. (1993) 'Ethical interviewing'. In E. Shepherd (ed.), *Aspects of Police Interviewing. Issues in Criminological and Legal Psychology. No. 18*. Leicester: British Psychological Society.

13. Roberg, R. and Kuykendall, J. (1990) *Police Organisation and Management Behaviour: Theory and Processes*. Pacific Grove, CA: Brooks-Cole.

14. Reuss-Ianni, E. (1983) *Two Cultures of Policing: Street Cops and Management Cops*. New Brunswick, CONN: Transaction Books.

15. Horowitz, M. (1983) 'Psychological response to serious life events'. In S. Breznitz (ed,), *The Denial of Stress*. New York: International Universities Press.

16. Mortimer, A. (1994) 'Asking the right question'. *Policing*, 10, 111–25.

17. Woodcock, J. (1992) 'Why we need a revolution'. *Police Review*, 16 October, 1929–32.

18. Pollard, C. (1994) 'A law unto themselves'. *Police Review*, 11 February, 20–1.

19. Woodcock, J. (1992) 'Why we need a revolution'. *Police Review*, 16 October, 1929–32.

20. HM Inspectorate of Constabulary. (1999) *Police Integrity: Securing and Maintaining Public Confidence*. London: Home Office Communications Directorate.

21. *Ibid.*

22. *Ibid.*

23. *Ibid.*

24. *A Guide to Interviewing*. (1992) Harrogate: Central Planning and Training Unit.

25. House of Commons Home Affairs Committee. (1999) *Police Training and Recruitment. Volume II. Minutes of Evidence and Appendices*. London: Stationery Office.

26. *Ibid.*

27. Baldwin, J. and Hunt, A. (1989) 'Prosecutors advising in police stations'. C.L.R. 521.

28. *Ibid.*

29. Crown Prosecution Service. (1994) *Discontinuance Survey*. November.

30. Tilley, N. and Ford, A. (1996) *Forensic Science and Crime Investigation. Crime Detection and Prevention Series: Paper 73*. London: Home Office Research Group.

31. Association of Chief Police Officers/Forensic Science Service. (1996) *Using Forensic Science Effectively*. Birmingham: Forensic Science Service.

32. *Ibid.*

33. *Ibid.*

34. Association of Chief Police Officers. (1998) *Murder Investigation Manual*.

35. *A Guide to Interviewing*. (1992) Harrogate: Central Planning and Training Unit.

36. *The Interviewer's Rule Book*. (1992) Harrogate: Central Planning and Training Unit.

37. Benham, A. (1997) 'Setting the scene'. *Police Review*, 18 July, 22–3. (Initial article in a series on scenes of crime investigations over the succeeding months.)

38. Forensic Science Service. (1997) 'Probationers skill shop: 1: cracking the code'. *Police Review*, 28 November, 30–1 November. (Initial article in a series on forensic science matters over the succeeding weeks.)

39. Taken from 'Law and disorder' by A. Gallop (1998), in *Chemistry in Britain* (London: Royal Society of Chemistry). Reprinted in *Forensic Science Society Newsletter*, January 1999, 6–7.

40. Thompson, J. and Gunn, B. (1998) 'Tomorrow's world'. *Policing Today*, March. 12–13.

41. Adams, D. (1999) 'Prints among thieves'. *Police Review*, 16 April, 26–7.

42. *Ibid.*

43. House of Commons Home Affairs Committee. (1999) *Police Training and Recruitment. Volume II. Minutes of Evidence and Appendices*. London: Stationery Office.

44. Ryan, P. (1993) *The Future of Police Training*. Bramshill: Police Staff College.

45. Maguire, M. and John, T. (1995) *Intelligence, Surveillance and Informants: Integrated Approaches. Police Research Group: Crime Detection and Prevention Series: Paper No. 64*. London: Home Office.

46. Dunninghan, C. and Norris, C. (1996) 'The nark's game'. *New Law Journal*, 22 March, 402–4; 29 March, 456–7.

47. Association of Chief Police Officers and HM Customs and Excise. (1999) *Use of Informants: Code of Practice*.

48. Potter, K. (1996) 'Patrol officers "under pressure"'. *Police Review*, 13 December, 10.

49. Maguire, M. and Norris, C. (1992) *The Conduct and Supervision of Criminal Investigations. RCCJ Research Study No. 5*. London: HMSO.

50. Irving, B. and Dunninghan, C. (1993) *Human Factors in the Quality Control of CID Investigations. RCCJ Research Study No. 21*. London: HMSO.

51. Stockdale, J. (1993) *Management and Supervision of Police Interviews. Police Research Series: Paper No. 5*. London: Home Office Police Department.

52. McLean, M. (1995) 'Quality investigation? Police interviewing of witnesses'. *Medicine, Science and the Law*, 35, 116–22.

53. Shepherd, E. and Milne, B. (1999) 'Full and faithful: ensuring quality practice and integrity of outcome in witness interviews'. In A. Heaton-Armstrong, E. Shepherd and D. Wolchover (eds), *Analysing Witness Testimony: A Guide for Legal Practitioners and Other Professionals*. London: Blackstone.

54. *Ibid.*

55. *Ibid.*

56. Fisher, R. and Geiselman, R. (1992) *Memory-enhancing Techniques for Investigative Interviewing: the Cognitive Interview*. Springfield, ILL: Thomas.

57. Shepherd, E. (1996) 'The trouble with PEACE'. *Police Review*, 26 July, 14–16.

58. Audit Commission. (1993) *Helping with Enquiries: Tackling Crime Effectively*. London: HMSO.

59. Johnson, C. (1996) 'Defending PEACE'. *Police Review*, 13 September, 24–5.

60. Mortimer, A. (1994) 'Asking the right question'. *Policing*, 10, 111–25.

61. McConville, M. and Hodgson, J. (1993) *Custodial Legal Advice and the Right to Silence. RCCJ Research Study No. 16*. London: HMSO.

62. Shepherd, E. (1996) *Becoming Skilled*. London: Law Society Publishing.

63. Association of Chief Police Officers/Her Majesty's Inspectorate of Constabulary/Audit Commission. (1996) *Tackling Crime Effectively: Management Handbook*. London: Audit Commission.

64. HM Inspectorate of Constabulary. (1999) *Police Integrity: Securing and Maintaining Public Confidence*. London: Home Office Communications Directorate.

65. *Ibid.*

66. Jones, J. (1995) 'It's good to talk'. *Police Review*, 29 September.

67. HM Inspectorate of Constabulary. (1999) *Police Integrity: Securing and Maintaining Public Confidence*. London: Home Office Communications Directorate.

68. Dunningham, C. and Norris, C. (1996) *The Role of the Informer in the Criminal Justice System*. London: Economic and Social Research Council.

69. Potter, K. (1996) 'Teenage sources'. *Police Review*, 8 November, 22–3.

70. Dunningham, C. and Norris, C. (1996) *The Role of the Informer in the Criminal Justice System*. London: Economic and Social Research Council.

71 David Maclean, House of Commons Committee, 30 April 1996 col. 20.

72. Maguire, M. and John, T. (1995) *Intelligence, Surveillance and Informants: Integrated Approaches. Police Research Group: Crime Detection and Prevention Series: Paper No. 64*. London: Home Office.

73. Dunninghan, C. and Norris, C. (1996) 'The nark's game'. *New Law Journal*, 22 March, 402–4; 29 March, 456–7.

74. Gibbons, S. (1996) 'Squad gets more cash for informants'. *Police Review*, 6 September, 7.

75. HM Inspectorate of Constabulary. (1999) *Police Integrity: Securing and Maintaining Public Confidence*. London: Home Office Communications Directorate.

76. *Ibid.*

77. Dunningham, C. and Norris, C. (1996) *The Role of the Informer in the Criminal Justice System*. London: Economic and Social Research Council.

78. *Ibid.*

79. HM Inspectorate of Constabulary. (1999) *Police Integrity: Securing and Maintaining Public Confidence.* London: Home Office Communications Directorate.

80. *Ibid.*

81. Roberg, R. and Kuykendall, J. (1990) *Police Organisation and Management Behaviour: Theory and Processes.* Pacific Grove, CA: Brooks–Cole.

82. Association of Chief Police Officers Quality of Service Committee. (1993) *The Police Service Statement of Ethical Principles.* London: ACPO.

83. Association of Chief Police Officers Quality of Service Committee. *(1993) Getting Things Right: A Licence For Change.*

84. Smith, D. and Gray, J. (1983) *Police and People in London.* London: Policy Studies Institute.

85. Manolias, M. (1983) *A Preliminary Study of Stress in the Police Service. Conclusions and Recommendations as submitted to the Association of Chief Police Officers Working Party on Police Stress.* London: Home Office.

86. Brown, J. and Campbell, L. (1993) *Stress and Policing.* Chichester: Wiley.

87. Manolias, M. (1983) *A Preliminary Study of Stress in the Police Service. Conclusions and Recommendations as submitted to the Association of Chief Police Officers Working Party on Police Stress.* London: Home Office.

88. HM Inspectorate of Constabulary. (1999) *Police Integrity: Securing and Maintaining Public Confidence.* London: Home Office Communications Directorate.

89. *Ibid.*

90. *Ibid.*

91. Baldwin, J. and Maloney, T. (1992) *Supervision of Police Investigations in Serious Criminal Cases. RCCJ Research Study No. 2.* London: HMSO.

92. *Ibid.*

93. HM Inspectorate of Constabulary. (1999) *Police Integrity: Securing and Maintaining Public Confidence.* London: Home Office Communications Directorate.

94. Baldwin, J. and Maloney, T. (1992) *Supervision of Police Investigations in Serious Criminal Cases. RCCJ Research Study No. 2.* London: HMSO.

95. Maguire, M. and Norris, C. (1992) *The Conduct and Supervision of Criminal Investigations. RCCJ Research Study No. 5.* London: HMSO.

96. Irving, B. and Dunninghan, C. (1993) *Human Factors in the Quality Control of CID Investigations. RCCJ Research Study No. 21.* London: HMSO.

97. Stockdale, J. (1993) *Management and Supervision of Police Interviews. Police Research Series: Paper No. 5.* London: Home Office Police Department.

98. Pollard, C. (1994) 'A law unto themselves'. *Police Review*, 11 February, 20–1.

99. Zander, M. (1994) 'Ethics and crime investigation by the police', *Policing*, 10, 39–47.

CHAPTER 4

The path of forensic scientific investigation: theory and practice

Chapter 3 indicated the very low level of forensic knowledge, awareness and skills among police officers, a situation that applies across the rank, role and seniority spectrum. This chapter further examines the problems and the pressures within the police service and institutions providing external forensic services that place a question mark over the path of forensic investigation.

Official research,[1-4] commissioned consultancy work,[5] parliamentary examination,[6-7] inter-departmental and inter-agency studies and policy working groups[8] and contributions to the literature by practitioners have enabled identification of:

- the theory – what common sense if not the law suggests should be the case and what the CPS, the defence, the courts and the community have to date assumed to be the case;

- the practice – what actually occurs.

The deployment of forensic resource varies according to the type of case – seriousness, complexity, and management's strategic objectives (e.g. the aim to focus on particular offences) are critical defining factors. Space does not allow us to differentiate forensic investigation in different types of case. Like much of policy and research material on forensic matters, our descriptions of theory and practice give an 'across the board' understanding of the issues. However, we conclude with a brief overview of forensic investigation reflected within the ACPO 'best practice' guidelines for murder investigation.

AWARENESS AND COMPETENCE OF SOCOs AND SCIENTIFIC SUPPORT OFFICERS IN RESPECT OF FORENSIC ISSUES

The theory

SOCOs and scientific support officers are the key element in the physical evidence process. Their skills are crucial to the whole system of advising IOs and SIOs upon, gathering, collecting and analysing, physical evidence.[9] They must have a grasp of basic concepts in order to perform these roles – based upon a clear definition of their role and supported by appropriate training and performance assessment.[10]

The practice

Research[11] found that even in the case of experienced SOCOs, serious weaknesses were to be found in their grasp of basic concepts.

It has been recommended that there should be a realignment of national training to further emphasise basic principles.

SOCOs and scientific support officers now attend formal courses of training, e.g. at the National Training Centre for Scientific Support to Crime Investigation (NTCSSCI) in Durham and the Metropolitan Police Scientific Support College at Hendon. In addition to initial training, there is development and refresher training, and courses designed to impart higher-level skills associated with crime scene management, scientific support co-ordination, fingerprint enhancement, fire scene investigation and bloodstain evidence. The increasing range of 'higher level' training is a direct reflection of the need for the service to keep costs down, more readily achieved by having in-force scientific support officers who become experts able to give opinions upon issues, which in the past would have been automatically referred for analysis by external forensic scientists.

There is also a Forensic Science Society Diploma in Crime Scene Investigation, where candidates must provide evidence of at least three years in crime scene investigation.

The experience of forensic scientists working for the defence has indicated a number of problems.

• The increasing scope of analysis being undertaken in-force by SOCOs and scientific support officers deemed to have 'higher level' expertise, formally the province of forensic scientists, brings great risks. An independent forensic scientist is much more likely than a support officer to identify the boundary of his or her expertise and, consistent with his or her professional code, act accordingly, i.e. to call upon the requisite academic applied knowledge, discrete experience and specialist expertise to assist in the process of evaluation and interpretation. For example, the proper analysis of blood traces is increasingly requiring the contribution of physicists and mathematicians in respect of issues such as momentum, gravity and droplet size. The momentum to keep costs down, to conduct as much analysis as possible in-force, risks officers for whatever reason not recognising, or wishing to disclose, the limitations of their expertise. Hence proper analysis is obstructed.

- SOCOs and scientific support officers may be well trained to an advanced level but, unless they are able to keep abreast of developments in the scientific world the status of their knowledge, and therefore their expertise and ability to give fully informed expert opinion, is necessarily limited.

- The expertise of SOCOs and scientific support officers is limited by the actual content of courses that they attend and when these were attended. If these courses are not up to date in respect of being informed by the latest scientific research and developments, in the absence of any means for ensuring that in-force staff are kept continuously abreast of what is happening in the field in question, then the potential of these staff to give balanced, fully informed expert evidence is necessarily constrained.

- There would appear to be a lack of consistency between what is being taught formally by different providers and even the same type of course from a given provider.

These factors create another facet to the problem of process corruption. This is bound to occur if IOs and SIOs are liable to be given for whatever reason completely different assessments, advice and recommendations by SOCOs and scientific support staff, concerning the necessity for, or relative potential value of, submitting a given type of material for external forensic analysis.

PRESERVATION OF THE SCENE

The theory

The scene is well preserved by the caller (the victim or the reporter of the incident) and the FOA.[12-13]

Advice is routinely given to the caller in terms of do's and don'ts. Official policy texts[14-15] list the following do's and don'ts.

These do's and don'ts are equally applicable to police officers and other personnel attending the scene, either as initially deployed FOAs or in some other investigative role. We replicate the lists with a couple of modifications, and adding another do and another don't as critical, prime considerations.

DO'S

- Make a record of:
    - any accidental or unavoidable contamination of the scene (widely defined, i.e. including the victim, the suspect, any witness), e.g. by touching first one person and then another;
    - any accidental or unavoidable disturbance of the scene.
- Preserve the scene for forensic examination, disturbing as little fingerprint or forensic evidence as possible.
- Protect items where these are open to the elements, e.g. covering with some protective layer.
- Protect blood and other bodily fluids – resisting wherever possible the pressure to clean these away from the location or from one's body.
- Protect potential footmark impressions – particularly at the point of entry or on hard surfaces.

DON'TS

- Cross-contaminate victims and suspects: touching one and then the other; touching first one, then the other, and returning to touch the first; continuously touching the two.
- Leave items outside to be spoilt by the elements, particularly rain and snow.
- Expose oneself to a health risk.
- Handle items.
- Touch windows, doors, items and other surfaces likely to have been touched by the offender.
- Walk on evidence, e.g. broken glass, footprints.

Scene protection is vital and therefore a fundamental responsibility of an FOA and IOs. As investigative professionals they are fully aware of the do's and don'ts.

The practice

With the exception of callers in direct contact with a crime desk, in a large proportion of cases no advice is given at the time of receiving the request to attend. Evidence is therefore frequently disturbed, contaminated, rendered uncollectable or washed away.

In the list above we have slightly modified the guidance contained in the official policy document:[16] items open to the elements should not be picked up or otherwise handled. As we indicated, they should be covered, preferably with something like a cardboard box. Wherever possible, plastic sheeting should be avoided because of the risks of condensation and channelling of water.

Given the widespread lack of forensic awareness in the service, particularly but not only among uniform officers, it is a commonplace complaint by SOCOs and forensic scientists that a very large number of FOAs – and IOs who should know better – do not think and act 'protection', failing to protect and to preserve, disturbing, touching, contaminating or destroying evidence. Again, this demonstrates the widespread ignorance and indifference among officers concerning matters forensic. Because they do not have physical evidence to the fore of their minds, they cannot connect their 'normal' actions – walking over surfaces, picking up and touching items – with the acts of contamination and destruction.

Such lack of awareness in respect of transfer and disturbance of contact trace material (CTM) is crucial, e.g.

- the FOA attends to – touching – the victim, then leaves to apprehend and to arrest – touching – the suspect, then returns to – touching – the victim;

- the FOA attends the scene, coming into contact with CTM, separately apprehends two suspects, takes suspects in the same vehicle to the station – meaning extensive likelihood of transfer of CTM between suspects;

- the FOA attends the scene, takes the opportunity to have a cigarette, a cup of tea, and a general poke about;

- the FOA attends the scene of a fire, unthinkingly picks up an upturned heater – away from the seat of the fire – and puts the heater upright in the seat of the fire.

It also accounts for officers attending the scene and fundamentally changing its character, e.g.

- altering the position of light switches such that it is not known later whether the scene was fully or partially illuminated;
- closed curtains are opened to bring in light; open curtains are closed to prevent prying eyes.

SCENE ASSESSMENT

The theory

The FOA or IO assesses the scene accurately to identify the most effective direction of SOCO and forensic scientist effort in the identification and collection of case relevant and useful CTM.[17]

The practice

In Chapter 3, we pointed out that lack of training means a large proportion of FOAs and all too many IOs make faulty decisions because:

- they are ignorant about the forensic science and its potentially discriminative powers;
- they have insufficient understanding of the potential contribution of SOCOs and forensic scientists;
- they do not realise how little they understand about, and how incapable they are of, assessing a crime scene;
- they are subject to pressures to achieve VFM. Although the service states that it is concerned about quality, timeliness and costs, it is the latter, relative to the perceived likelihood of securing a 'positive outcome', which has increasingly become the decisive factor in decisions concerning the submission of items and materials for forensic analysis.

The outcome of such faulty decision-making is that, in all too many cases ignorance and the desire to keep costs down combine to prevent effective and ethical investigation. With the advance of the 'swab everything' mentality significant financial resource is being directed to DNA testing, which necessarily impacts upon the overall resource – the budget for a given case and, indeed, the entire force budget, available for forensic testing.

BRIEFING OF SOCOs

The theory

Briefing is recognised as essential by police officers and SOCOs alike.[18–20]

Every effort is made by police officers to brief SOCOs adequately in order to ensure an effective examination of the scene for CTM, which confirms, disconfirms and adds to the initial line of investigation.

Wherever possible, the briefing of the SOCO should be verbal. They should always be informed of the arrest of a suspect.[21]

The practice

Research[22] has shown that SOCOs believe a briefing prior to the scene visit is either essential or useful, with verbal briefings being the most effective.

Briefing of SOCOs by police officers is commonplace in major crimes. The SOCO typically arrives with the CID or when officers are still at the scene. The SOCO will discuss possible pieces of evidence and the uses to which they might be put. If the SOCO attends alone, he or she will be fully briefed before doing so.

In cases investigated by uniform officers, e.g. volume crimes:

- the officer has departed;
- SOCOs most commonly attend the scene 'blind':
  - with no background information;
  - at best with only sketchy information, e.g. some details available on the CRS (crime reporting system).

Lack of briefing results in the SOCO conducting a 'routine' examination without specific focus on the details of the case, which are unknown to the SOCO.

This situation of non-communication and SOCOs and IOs working independently of each other underlines the extent to which the two paths of investigation are not interactive except in the most major crimes.

THE APPROACH OF SOCOs TO SEARCHING

The theory

Scene examination by SOCOs should be as comprehensive as possible.[23-5]

What gets examined is guided by a yardstick: what is the reasonable expectation of what would be found at the scene – or away from the scene – given the circumstances of the case?

What gets collected will not be influenced by cost nor by a pressure to convict.

The practice

Research reflects a recognition that almost all scene examination is less than fully comprehensive. Exhaustive combing of a scene is resource demanding and therefore impracticable in all but exceptional circumstances, e.g. terrorist offences, high-profile murders.

The approach to searching is directly linked to the issue of briefing. In serious cases where the SOCO typically attends with the IO or SIO, there will be discussion as to the approach to be adopted. However, it must be borne in mind that for many SOCOs where the case is not serious in the sense of the involvement of area CID or the Major Crime Unit, this will have been the umpteenth 'routine' scene visited on a given day. No detailed briefing is likely to have been given or sought, with the SOCO being deployed in response to routine tasking through the crime reporting system.

Research[26-7] indicates that:

- in a sample of forces, SOCOs were deployed in about one in five cases;

- in the case of burglaries, with large numbers of scenes to be attended, scene examination focuses on a small number of evidence types. There is not enough time to collect forensic in every case. If there is a suspect, then SOCOs will respond to a request for other forensic;

- some forces have a limited search policy, i.e. SOCOs are required to collect tangible CTM – fingerprints, footwear marks, blood/DNA if the offender bled – and to ignore other evidence such as particles, e.g. glass, fibres;

- increasingly, forces are unwilling to expend time and money on collecting a wide range of CTM, which yields a series of negative results, since this does not support the police case (though it is important to the defence), e.g. a car is stolen to effect an armed robbery and is then abandoned; a suspect is arrested on foot nearby;

the police take his clothing; the SOCO takes tapings from the car seats (sellotape strips to lift textile fibres and debris); clothing should be taken from all those who have legitimately used the vehicle, not just from the suspect; the decision is made not to take tapings from anyone other than the suspect. It is not VFM to find out – by examining large numbers of garments belonging to legitimate users – that the match with fibres on the suspect is fortuitous;

- limited searches, i.e. those adopting a narrow focus concerning CTM, are generally thought to be undesirable by SOCOs who are worried that restricted scene examination practices or policies create the possibility of missing evidence which might either implicate or eliminate suspects;

SOCOs' prioritisation in scene examination is generally *ad hoc*;

- on average, SOCOs spend 70 per cent of their time searching for fingerprints and 30 per cent searching for other forensic evidence;

- in a sample of forces, less than 2 per cent reported lifting footwear marks in a lot of cases; in no force were they lifted in all cases – this raises the question of the extent to which, unless the mark is staring them in the face, as it were, SOCOs routinely consider using enhancement techniques, e.g. special lighting;

- SOCOs are jealous of their professional autonomy as to what should be examined and collected – an understandable sentiment given the research indicating widespread police ignorance of forensic issues.

THE RECORDING OF SOCO SCENE EXAMINATIONS AND FINDINGS

The theory

Given the widespread reliance upon the SOCO as a key contributor to the process of forensic investigation, the IO or SIO, external forensic providers, the CPS, the defence and the courts require a comprehensive and fully detailed account of:

- the search conducted by the SOCO;

- the ambient conditions, i.e. source and level of any illumination the weather, temperature;

- a graphic representation of the scene, identifying the location of physical evidence, i.e.

  - drawings of the layout of, and any specific locations within, the scene – noting north and useful dimensions, whether inside a room or a building or outside – and, in the case of premises, any structural features such as doors and windows, and, in the case of an outside location, features, e.g. trees, undergrowth, paths, gates, roads, alleys, walls, hedges, watercourses, rivers, bridges, areas of grass and gravel;

  - annotated sketches, with appropriate indication of measurements, showing the locations of:

    (a) the victim;
    (b) marks, imprints and impressions, e.g. a fingerprint, thumb-print, palmprint or a print made by a tool, instrument, shoe, tyre or glove;
    (c) trace evidence, e.g. particles of metal, wood, glass and other materials; implements including weapons, clothing, personal effects, dropped stolen property; potentially informative items, e.g. a crumpled cigarette packet or a cigarette end; body fluids, e.g. blood, secretions and excretions;

- a record of each item of evidence identified – a description, including a note of measurements and markings;

- a record of impressions and samples collected;

- any form of *negative evidence*, i.e. detail that bears upon what was not the case, e.g. something was missing that should have been, or could have been reasonably expected to be, present;

- a record of any photographs and/or video recording of:

  - the scene and the vicinity, and key locations within these;
  - marks, traces and other material;

- a standardised form, indicating which forms of searching or examination were not carried out.

To ensure consistency of standards in communication a standardised format should be used.[28] This has been produced by the Home Office.[29]

The practice

Despite recommendations from Home Office commissioned consultants,[30] forces still differ in the way SOCOs record the results of their scene examinations[31-2] – ranging:

- from forces where there is no scene examination form, the results being recorded in a pocket book;

- to forces where SOCOs complete a very comprehensive pro forma, which requires the officer to indicate which forms of searching/examination were not carried out.

Most forces use broadly similar scene examination forms. Comprehensive and fully detailed accounts are a relative rarity.

Because of this, ACPO and the FSS have recommended a national template with information that can be fed into the force's crime recording system (CRS) and the crime intelligence system (CIS).

QUALITY CONTROL OF SOCO SCENE EXAMINATIONS AND FINDINGS

The theory

Given the significant potential contribution of forensic to confirm, disconfirm and to add to a line of enquiry, the quality of SOCO performance must be controlled and assured.[33-6]

SOCOs, as the 'sharp end' of the forensic science process, must, like others in the forensic investigative process, be subject to scrutiny and accountability criteria.

SOCOs can be called upon to give evidence of fact, i.e. he or she found the scene in a particular state, collected a range of specified samples. Much more rarely, a court may decide that it wishes the SOCO to give opinion evidence, in the same way as a forensic scientist.

The practice

Despite recommendations from Home Office consultants,[37] the House of Lords Select Committee[38] and the RCCJ,[39] there is very little in-force quality control or quality assurance of scene visits.

Research[40] has shown disturbing, ill-conceived attitudes to the work of SOCOs, i.e.

- it is based, and taken, on trust and logistics;

- SOCO evidence is fact: no quality assurance is needed;

- a SOCO attending a scene and collecting evidence is different from a forensic scientist who will be called upon as an expert witness to give an opinion – therefore only the expert witness needs to be checked for quality.

There is a closed loop which renders the issue of quality problematic:

- the autonomy of SOCOs arises from their limited numbers and their specialist role;

- they are rarely briefed before they attend a crime scene;

- they consider they know – with justification – more than most police officers about forensic issues. There would be some reticence about having police officers (other than in serious cases) direct what should be sought;

- SOCOs consider searches to be inadequate: they are generally ad hoc, and, in the absence of case related information, are necessarily routine and limited in focus;

- SOCO records are rarely comprehensive or fully detailed, with little or no mention of tasks not carried out and of negative evidence. What is found is considered fact and not amenable to question. To do so undermines their autonomy...and so on.

Paradoxically, the closed loop and the absence of urgently required quality control ultimately undermines confidence in the evidential reliability of 'sharp end' forensics.

COMMUNICATION OF SOCO FINDINGS

The theory

IOs should receive timely and full feedback from SOCOs on the crime scene examination and useful findings.[41–2]

The practice

Research[43-4] shows that:

- in major crimes there is immediate and direct feedback;

- in volume crimes there is very little feedback, i.e. the IO may believe or know particular evidence may have been collected but is in the dark as to its worth in terms of disconfirming, confirming or adding to the officer's line of investigation.

This situation of continuing non-communication and SOCOs and IOs working independently of each other underlines yet again the extent to which the two paths of investigation are not interactive except in major crimes.

QUALITY CONTROL OF THE MEDICAL EXAMINER'S PERFORMANCE

The theory

Research for the RCCJ[45] indicated a consensus that medical examiners must 'be thorough – observe, measure, record'. This particularly applies in the forensic aspect of their role:

- the examination of suspects – particularly in respect of:
  - fitness to be detained;
  - fitness to be interviewed;
  - the requirement for an appropriate adult;
  - physical examination and the taking of samples, e.g. in sexual offences;
  - mental examination to identify the presence of psychiatric illness or psychological disorder;
- the examination of victims – particularly for physical examination and the taking of samples, e.g. in a case of alleged rape;
- the taking of blood samples from people suspected of driving whilst intoxicated and other Road Traffic Act examinations.

Given the significant potential contribution of the findings of a medical examination to confirm, disconfirm and add to a line of enquiry, on common-sense and professional grounds:

- any medical examiner should have the appropriate undergraduate and postgraduate experience, training and qualification in physical medicine and psychological medicine to fulfil the fundamental tasks of physical and mental examination;

- a medical examiner's performance must be subject to quality control.

The practice

The RCCJ research[46] showed that using the narrow sense of the term forensic – examination for specific evidential purposes – some 19 per cent of medical examiners' work fell into this category. Table 4.1 shows the proportion of particular types of examination.

Type of examination	Proportion of all forensic work (%)
Body (certification of death)	9
Victim	28
Witness (for the purposes of exclusion as suspect)	2
Suspect	7
Alleged police assault	14
RTA/blood	40

Table 4.1 Forensic examinations conducted by medical examiners

Increasingly, the opinions of medical examiners are being challenged at court.

The police service has become increasingly concerned that cases are being lost due to inadequate forensic medical evidence from medical examiners.

The only qualification necessary to be appointed a medical examiner is to be a registered medical practitioner. The undergraduate training of doctors includes a block of psychiatric study. Although a large proportion of the workload in general practice involves psychological problems, methods of assessment employed are rarely beyond those taught in medical school.

For most appointees, the only forensic skills and experience they bring (if any) were acquired at undergraduate level. It is up to individual police forces to decide if it demands postgraduate qualifications of any kind.

Now, there are courses that newly appointed medical examiners can attend, if they so wish. Forces are able to make attendance a condition of employment with the period before attendance regarded as probationary.

The Association of Police Surgeons has sought to make membership a condition of employment as a medical examiner. ACPO has rejected this. Research[47] found that forces in large rural areas are unwilling to risk losing medical examiners.

Across the country, only a disturbing minority of medical examiners has sought to take a professional postgraduate qualification, the Diploma in Medical Jurisprudence.

There is no quality control or quality assurance of an individual medical examiner's performance. In respect of physical or psychological examination, a medical examiner is akin to a SOCO in that:

- his or her actions and conclusions are based, and taken, on 'trust';

- his or her evidence is accepted as fact: no quality assurance is needed.

MEDICAL EXAMINATION OF THE VICTIM

The theory

The examining doctor should be:

- comprehensively briefed as to the allegation;

- appropriately briefed as to the police case, the other prosecution evidence, and the investigation thus far.

This should occur especially in cases of sexual assault. Such briefing allows the examining doctor:

- to place the victim's account in the context of the detailed police briefing;

- to take the samples appropriate to the alleged offence;

- to provide the IO or SIO with a fuller, more timely, written report, supported by a list of samples taken:

181

- – that informs the investigation at a crucial early stage;
- – that should be included in the crime file;

- to provide a comprehensive statement in due course – aided by the examiner's personal notes made during the examination.

The practice

In all too many cases, examining doctors are not comprehensively briefed. This necessarily risks giving rise to:

- a failure to take appropriate samples, e.g. a buccal (mouth) sample is not taken from an individual where oral sex took place but neither the police nor the individual tell the doctor;

- a partial picture upon which the IO or SIO bases further investigation – particularly:

  - – interviewing of the suspect;
  - – further interviewing of, and statement taking from, the victim.

In all too many cases, a copy of the medical examiner's report is not placed in the crime file.

TAKING OF SAMPLES FROM THE SUSPECT AND SUBMISSION FOR ANALYSIS

The theory

Samples are taken by police officers and medical examiners to eliminate the suspect or to corroborate suspicions by linking the suspect to scenes. The whole purpose is to gather samples with the express purpose of submitting these to analysis, thus clarifying the situation for the prosecution and the defence.

Samples should be taken:

- judiciously – related to the nature of the case and the investigation;

- with the clear intention of submission for analysis;

- correctly.

The practice

There is a frequently a blunderbuss approach, i.e. a lot of samples are taken by police officers and medical examiners that are passed to the IO. In the case of a medical examiner, the IO should sign the doctor's notes that he or she has taken charge of the samples.

There is no requirement for an IO to submit samples immediately for analysis. This creates situations where samples are left in a refrigerator for so long that meaningful analysis cannot be, and is not, performed.

The inappropriate application of a blunderbuss approach to collecting samples and the failure to submit samples for analysis, either within an appropriate time or at all, highlights yet again the fundamental lack of forensic awareness by police officers.

Instances occur where the medical examiner has not taken the sample correctly.

SELECTION OF ITEMS COLLECTED BY SOCO FOR ANALYSIS

The theory

Items are selected for submission for in-force testing or analysis by an external forensic supplier where there are prospects of evidence informing the direction of the enquiry and the incurred cost is warranted.[48–50]

IOs should be advised by SOCOs on this matter.[51]

The practice

In major crimes, a core function of the CSM/SSM (a senior SOCO) is to advise the SIO on CTM. The situation is more problematic in other offences.

Although SOCOs in general have a better understanding than police officers of the potential benefits from forensic testing, the research has shown that in some forces their understanding is weak.

The absence of sound advice, or any advice, to the IO is crucial. Budgetary constraints are a major source of tension, particularly since decisions are devolved in the majority of forces. IOs have to make (or to ask a superior officer to make) cost–benefit decisions as to what will, or will not, be subjected to forensic testing.

Decisions made by IOs indicate that:

- the seriousness of the case is often more significant than the prospects of useful investigative results;

- there is little use of analysis for inceptive purposes, i.e. identifying an 'unknown';

- there is an orientation towards testing for corroboration rather than elimination.

This creates the real risk of a decision not to submit for in-force testing or external analysis CTM, which may well have eliminated a suspect or failed to corroborate suspicions that linked the suspect with the scene.

TESTING FINGERPRINTS

The standard applied

The purpose of fingerprint evidence is to establish identity. Any fingerprints must be considered in the context of all the other available evidence and may assist in establishing either guilt, or equally as important, innocence. Print identification is more than simply counting ridge characteristics. It is a matter of expert judgement, involving interpretation of detail, an awareness of possible movement, distortion and other factors in a crime scene mark. Fingerprint experts should be capable of expressing their expert opinions, otherwise there is no point in them being experts.

In the past, a 16-point standard has been applied when presenting fingerprint evidence at court. Since 1983, however, matches of less than 16 points, known as *partial prints*, have been allowed in serious cases. However, when this has happened, the court has been made aware that the evidence did not meet the 16-point standard.

ACPO has decided to abolish this 'numerical standard' but guidelines produced are no more than general recommendations within which the fingerprint bureau member, as expert, has the freedom to exercise his or her own professional skills.

Cases will now proceed on the basis of there being no required number of matching characteristics, the logic being that fingerprint evidence is opinion evidence like any other and as such there is no legal justification for a national standard. Fingerprint evidence should be contested at court. Fingerprint bureaux are producing highly skilled staff who are knowledgeable and well versed in court presentation skills.

The practice

Only one in five of fingerprint bureau heads have endorsed the change.[52]

Those who oppose the change believe it will:

- increase the demand for independent expert witnesses to question finger-print evidence;

- mean an increase in challenges to fingerprint evidence – from the relatively few where the 16-point standard is applied;

- create a situation where, in the absence of a common standard, one laboratory will be willing to make an identification and another is unable to do so;

- have an adverse effect upon juries – in the words of one bureau head:

  'What the word fingerprint means is absolute identity to judges, barristers, juries and the public. If we get into the realm of "maybes" we run the very grave danger of losing cases, particularly serious ones.'

Fingerprint bureaux staff are indeed knowledgeable and well versed in court presentation skills, but only in giving evidence to the 16-point standard.

A move from the 16-point standard must be preceded by the retraining and testing of experts.

Unidentified prints

The theory

When unidentified prints are found at the scene, there should be a process of eliminatory testing, i.e. in addition to the suspect, fingerprints should be taken from all officers, civilian support staff and all external forensic providers who attended as well as those who live at, or have had occasion to visit the scene.

The practice

Elimination is a time-consuming and expensive process. In all too many cases it is not carried out. The fact that it has not is withheld by simply failing to report on the matter.

Outstanding marks

The theory

In Chapter 2, we explained that marks not identified or eliminated to specific donors, i.e. the accused person or persons with access from a crime scene, are classified as *'Outstanding'*.

The practice

'Outstanding' are further classified as being either of *'No value'* or of *'Insufficient detail for comparison purposes'*. 'No value' means that there are no ridge characteristics present to assist in any comparison process. On the other hand, 'insufficient detail' means that there are characteristics present, but in the opinion of the examiner there are not enough for him or her to arrive at any conclusion.

This is one opinion. Another examiner may see sufficient detail to justify a positive result. A situation summed up in the words 'One person's "insufficient detail" is another person's "identification".' A situation destined to become all the more common with the abolition of a 'numerical standard' and reliance on individual judgement as to number and significance of characteristics.

It is important to understand that elimination can take place on far fewer characteristics than are needed to make a positive identification. If as few as only one or two characteristics are present in a particular mark, which are found not to be present on a suspect's prints, then he or she can be eliminated as being the donor of that mark. This is particularly important if the position of a mark, or marks, at the crime scene take on a similar degree of importance, i.e. marks on a murder weapon or at a point of entry.

It was pointed out above that eliminatory testing is in many cases not carried out because of time and resource constraints. In these instances, marks found, other than those of the suspect and victim, are classified as *'Not useful for classification purposes'*. In effect, this classification, as is the misuse of the terms *'No value'* or *'Insufficient detail for comparison purposes'*, is a disingenuous device. The court is deceived and is in no position to know that there were fingerprints that are able to be compared and classified with integrity, but no effort has been made to do this because they did not match either the victim but, most significantly, the suspect.

These terms must always be challenged.

TESTING OF MATERIALS IN-FORCE

The theory

The Home Office recommended that forces should take on more testing in-force in order:

- to reduce the workload of forensic laboratories;

- to extend the scientific support officer's role;

- to obtain quick results for the police;

- to sift cases in-force so that only essential items are submitted to laboratories for analysis.

The range of testing should include presumptive testing of blood and of drugs.

The RCCJ endorsed this recommendation with the proviso that there must be adequate, specified arrangements for quality and performance control.

Official policy[53] is clear. In respect of devolved in-force testing, this should be subject to the same quality control procedures that should apply to an external forensic supplier:

- routine testing of operators and equipment, with records kept;

- specific checks by team leaders on the interpretation and quality of reporting;

- each operator and assistant should have a personal competence record, based on assessment, authorising them to undertake work activities;

- there should be a clear record of actions requested of, and supervision of, assistants;

- reports should deal with the manner in which tests were conducted;

- a disclosable schedule should be kept indicating the name of the person who conducted each test in the report and whether these were conducted independently or under supervision;

- any database used for the interpretation of results, e.g. library of tyre or footwear marks, should be subject to the same quality control procedures as other instruments and procedures;

- here should be a formal system of quality assurance, i.e. the testing of the whole system by blind and declared trials.

The practice

It was pointed out in Chapter 2 that the range of scientific processes carried out in-force by scientific support staff varies greatly. Among police officers there is widespread ignorance of what testing is done in-force, and to what end.

Table 4.2 summarises research[54] in respect of the proportion of forces sampled who carry out in-force forensic testing in all or many cases.

Scientific testing	Proportion % of sample forces testing in all or many cases
Presumptive testing of blood	92
Restoration of serial numbers	75
Examine altered/forged documents	75
Presumptive testing of drugs	58
Examine documents for indented writing (ESDA)	33
Examine tyres	33

Table 4.2 Proportion of sampled forces who carry out in-force forensic testing in all or many cases

Research[55-6] has shown that the commitment to in-force testing has not been matched by quality and performance controls:

- there is little or no quality control and quality assurance of in-force scientific work;

- some forces are planning to introduce quality checks;

- research has found the prevailing attitude to be that where the expertise of the SOCO/scientist is not going to be put to the test as expert evidence, no quality check is necessary.

If a presumptive test produces a positive result, the item should be sent to an external forensic scientist for secondary testing to confirm or disconfirm the result, e.g. a positive presumptive test for blood may subsequently emerge as not being blood at all.

In a number of forces, there is a tendency to take a positive presumptive test as fact and not to send it for external testing. This can lead to a case being founded upon wholly spurious evidence, e.g. a schoolboy was charged with supplying a controlled substance, in-force testing having obtained a positive result with the material, which was subsequently found to be sherbet.

ACPO and the FSS have acknowledged[57] that, in addition to the inadequacy or absence of quality control in in-force testing, there were disadvantages to in-force examination that are not readily identified:

- it emerges as more expensive when the full economic costs are analysed;

- it provides evidence that may be subject to attack in court due to lack of impartiality and deficiencies in scientific standards;

- when done incautiously, particularly for blood, it has the potential to destroy evidence.

In-force examination may well, therefore, not be cost-effective. In monetary terms, as the demand for in-force testing grows, there will be unanticipated cost factors such as time lost by SOCOs and scientific support officers giving evidence more often, in more and more courts. The pursuit of such illusory cost savings could be at tremendous cost to the credibility of the police when systematic cross-examination of the individual reveals a lack of substantive, up-to-the-minute knowledge of the subject, lack of scientific rigour, poor procedures, partiality, and a view – individual, institutional, or both – that the in-force experts are the 'last word' in all senses. Despite these risks, there continues to be over-whelming pressure upon IOs to achieve VFM by restricting forensic analysis as much as possible to in-force testing rather than submitting material to external suppliers.

TASKING AND COMMUNICATING WITH THE EXTERNAL FORENSIC SUPPLIER

The theory

Common sense argues that the police should provide external forensic suppliers with:

- full background information on the case – particularly witness statements providing accounts of what happened, when and how;

189

- items selected for analysis by the supplier – with a view to throwing light on the case;
- a list of all other items collected which might be analysed;
- questions that, it is hoped, forensic analysis will resolve.

The logic for such full communication is that the value of any item of CTM depends upon the individual circumstances of the case. It enables the forensic scientist to choose and to plan the analyses appropriately and to consider alternative possible explanations for the findings. Hence open disclosure enables the forensic scientist to make objective judgements about specific questions in terms of:

- their intelligibility;
- their answerability.

The practice

Typically, forces provide forensic suppliers with:

- a summary of the case;
- a sample of the items collected;
- the questions, which, it is hoped, examination will resolve.

Research[58] has identified the following criticisms by forensic suppliers:

- inappropriately formulated questions – some that cannot be answered by forensic examination;
- bare minimum information;
- inappropriate or inadequate range or form of items for examination;
- the absence of a full list of items retrieved – which would provide information to allow advice on further tests of items that have not been submitted.

Given that there is insufficient understanding of what reasonably can be expected from various scientific procedures, it is not surprising that:

- police users are often not in a position to determine in advance the usefulness of analyses conducted by a forensic scientist;
- they ask inappropriate questions.

In respect of information provision, the more serious the case, the more information is typically provided to the supplier. Much less information is given in commonplace or volume crimes.

Hence a research comparison of the same number of serious crimes as volume crimes found that witness statements were supplied in 37 per cent and 5 per cent of cases respectively. The researchers failed to stress the disturbing fact that in two-thirds of the serious cases sampled, forensic scientists were completely in the dark concerning the content of key witness accounts.

Policy research[59] indicates there is a persistent myth, particularly among the minority of SIOs, that forensic scientists should not be told the full facts of a case:

- in order to ensure the scientists are demonstrably unbiased;
- in the (false) hope that the confirmation of facts unknown to the scientist may appear stronger to the courts.

Other research[60] offers an alternative logic for this gatekeeping of information, i.e. keeping the scientist in the dark as to the full list of items retrieved. It is a logic that is known to the force and the forensic provider: forces do not trust suppliers. The force believes that providing more information will lead suppliers to advise further testing, adding to the cost incurred. This is deemed to be a poor investment if the consequence is a series of negative results.

THE ANALYSES UNDERTAKEN BY THE EXTERNAL FORENSIC SUPPLIER

The theory

The forensic scientist should examine items that are likely to throw light on:

- the questions posed by the police;
- other issues relevant to the case and the investigation.

The forensic scientist must be intellectually independent and scientifically objective.

191

The practice

Some suppliers examine almost all, if not all, materials submitted for analysis.

Some fail to assess or to indicate whether additional forensic analyses might be useful or are essential to the enquiry.

Independent (formerly Home Office) forensic scientists have consistently argued that forensic scientists commissioned by the prosecution are inevitably unable to be all things to all men.[61-5] Key factors are:

- in the early stages of a serious crime enquiry, the forensic scientist may be called upon to be the scientific adviser to the IO or SIO;[66-7]

- it is psychologically difficult, if not impossible, having tested the items collected and selected for analysis and been intimately involved in the case to then destroy the analyses, their outcome and the scientist's opinion. This is effectively 'expecting the hound who has just caught the hare to set to with a will to give it the kiss of life'.[68-9]

The reality was aptly described by Glidewell LJ giving the judgment of the Court of Appeal in *R. v. Ward* (1993) 96 Cr. App. R. at p. 51:

> 'For lawyers, jurors and judges a forensic scientist conjures up the image of a man in a white coat working in a laboratory, approaching his task with cold neutrality, and dedicated only to the pursuit of scientific truth. It is a sombre thought that the reality is sometimes different. Forensic scientists may become partisan. The very fact that the police seek their assistance may create a relationship between the police and the forensic scientists. And the adversarial nature of the proceedings tends to promote this process. Forensic scientists employed by the government may come to see their function as helping the police. They may lose their objectivity.'

COMMUNICATION BETWEEN THE FORENSIC SCIENTIST AND THE INVESTIGATING OFFICER

The theory

The forensic scientist should communicate verbally with the IO in respect of the detail, the outcome and the implications of requested analyses.[70] Such conversations should take place both prior to and following the production of the scientist's statement (see next section).

The forensic scientist and the IO should make a record of the exchange – in the case of the officer this should be as a formal note, e.g. in a pocket book or a formal report.

The practice

The research[71] showed that in a comparison of samples of serious and volume crime cases, the forensic scientists had direct contact with the investigating officer in 44 per cent of the serious cases and 37 per cent of the volume cases. In other words, in over half the serious cases there was no dialogue between the forensic scientist and the officer in the case.

Cumulatively, this lack of feedback and contact keeps police officers in the dark as to the potential of forensic examination: not only in the case in question but with prospective case investigations by the officer.

A request to the police officer and the forensic scientist to disclose the content of their record of communication could well be expected to present individuals with some difficulties.

THE FORENSIC SCIENTIST'S REPORT

The theory

A forensic scientist should produce a witness statement that:

- outlines the background of the case – as reported to the scientist;

- notes the questions posed by those commissioning the analyses;

- gives an explanation of the tests undertaken;

- gives the results of the tests – frequently referring to the probability of matches examined in the light of statistical data and reported norms/ tabulated data;

- gives an opinion in the context of the circumstances as presented to the scientist as to:

  - the meaning of the results in terms of the questions posed;
  - the strength of the evidence – particularly that a given individual was somewhere or did something because of the co-presence of trace materials (with known distributions) and other circumstantial evidence.

The copy served upon the defence must be accurate, i.e. a photocopy of the original or an error-free print-out from HOLMES.

The practice

No witness statement should be assumed to be incontrovertible fact, beyond challenge or question, and totally accurate because:

- it emanates from a laboratory;

- it has been produced by a scientist;

- it creates the impression of precision and impregnability by virtue of the use of numbers, probability values and confident assertions.

There is a wealth of evidence arising from subsequent examination by independent forensic scientists, which indicate that:

- no forensic analysis should be accepted without appropriate inspection and the conduct of independent analyses;

- the quality of work of individual scientists cannot be assured and must be subject to challenge (see next section).

Common problems[72–7] are:

- Assertions as to the unassailability of a method and its outcome, e.g.
  - DNA analysis definitively identifying the guilty party, is without foundation;
  - technology, scientific procedures, statistics and assertions concerning probability are meaningless if the scientist loses sight of the cardinal role of context, e.g. dried semen on bedclothes of a man's bed where an alleged rape took place was indeed his, but he had been sleeping regularly in the bed and had not changed the bedclothes for a matter of weeks, giving rise to extensive semen staining;

- inappropriate methodology;

- erroneous data handling and reporting;

- unfounded opinions, e.g.
  - *opinion*: controlled substance; *reality*: substance available over the counter in a chemists;
  - *opinion*: incriminating marks on victim's skull; *reality*: a completely innocent cause;

- *opinion*: instrument was used to make 40 cuts in a plastic-covered wire fence; *reality*: there was no match between the instrument and the cuts and there was no transferred plastic material from the wire onto the cutter as would have been expected;
- *opinion*: blood distribution pattern on carpet indicated sustained assault nearby; *reality*: the scientist was inexperienced and did not recognise the blood distribution pattern for what it was, i.e. indicative of something else;
- *opinion*: 'the presence of semen on a vaginal swab is evidence of rape'; *reality*: if this were so then the incidence of rape must be a good deal higher than any would ever have imagined;
- *opinion*: semen detected on the slide of a high vaginal swab taken from a child – insufficient to create a DNA profile, but deemed to be incriminating for the suspect; *reality*: the cells were not spermatozoa heads – furthermore, when the FSS scientist was recommended to invite fellow FSS colleagues to examine the slide, not one was able to identify semen;
- *opinion*: hair sample found at the scene of a robbery came from the suspect; *reality*: it was dog hair;
- *opinion*: a woman had killed her baby by dosing it with barbiturates; *reality*: the scientist had put the decimal point in the wrong place, thus multiplying the amount of the drug supposedly in the child's body by a factor of ten – the dose was too low to be lethal: it was a cot death;
- *opinion*: glass fragments found on suspect matched those at the scene of an earlier burglary; *reality*: the officer who arrested the suspect was also the FOA at the scene and could thus have transferred the fragments via his hands or clothing;
- *opinion*: fibres on a rape suspect matched those on the victim; *reality*: the suspect had been put into the same car and sat on the same seat that the victim had been sitting on a few hours earlier – hence fibres could have been transferred from victim to the car seat and from the car seat to the suspect;

• a failure to note the significant absence of forensic evidence, e.g. a woman alleged that she had been raped by a taxi driver. He admitted getting into the back of the taxi cab with her and kissing her. There were no semen traces and she said that he had not ejaculated. The defence forensic scientist was able to satisfy the court that it was inconceivable that he could have behaved in the way she alleged without fibres being transferred from her woolly skirt to his underclothes.

Instances occur where the report has been entered into the HOLMES database and errors have been introduced by the indexer inputting the data. Hence the print-out provided to the defence gives a false picture in respect of the erroneous detail.

QUALITY CONTROL OF THE FORENSIC SCIENTIST'S PERFORMANCE

The theory

All external forensic suppliers must have:

- the necessary level of expertise and experience to undertake the requested analyses;

- quality control and quality assurance procedures for the forensic analyses and the reporting of their scientists.

The laboratory must be regulated and accredited in respect of its fulfilment of quality criteria.

Specified good practices[78] for the examination of items within the supplier's laboratory are:

- quality control procedures should be implemented, which include the routine testing of operators and equipment, with records kept;

- specific checks should be made by team leaders of the interpretation and quality of the statement;

- critical observations, i.e. unrepeatable or qualitative observations, should be confirmed in writing;

- there should be a handbook of authorised procedures and authorised operators, to be revised periodically;

- each research officer and assistant should have a personal competence record, based on assessment, authorising them to undertake work activities;

- there should be a clear record of actions requested of, and supervision of, assistants;

- the research officer's statement should deal with the manner in which tests were conducted and the use of assistants;

- a disclosable schedule should be kept, which should include the name of the person who conducted each test referred to in the statement and whether an assistant performed some or all of the tests under the research officer's supervision;

- the databases and research necessary to allow interpretations of results should be subject to the same quality control procedures as other instruments and procedures;

- there should be a formal system of quality assurance, i.e. the testing of the whole system by blind and declared trials.

The practice

Traditionally, the FSS has been the major external supplier. A number of factors have created a problematic situation for the FSS: a major exit of experienced forensic scientists from the FSS; the deployment of experienced scientists to fulfil the role of FSS scientific adviser to individual forces; the rapid recruitment of a large cohort of young scientists who must necessarily take time building up the requisite expertise and experience to fulfil a very demanding task; competition from other independent suppliers, able to deliver analyses by experienced scientists within tight timescales.

Some forces commission analyses by other suppliers. A major independent supplier is Forensic Alliance, which, for all of the reasons outlined above, places emphasis on.

- quality control and quality assurance procedures;

- calling upon very advanced (e.g. nuclear) technology;

- recognising the need for, and calling upon, expertise outside the confines of the institution, i.e. actively resisting the view that once in-house procedures have been exhausted that is the 'last word'.

However, there are other independent suppliers among whom:

- not all have quality control or quality assurance procedures;

- some claim competencies that they do not have.

It is crucial to recognise that laboratories are accredited as institutions, declaring a standard they wish to achieve. Accreditation is given if this proposed standard is met. Declared quality standards do not apply to individual scientists within the laboratory.[79]

The RCCJ[80] recommended that there should be a forensic science advisory council, enabling the statutory accreditation and registration of forensic scientists. The Council for the Registration of Forensic Practitioners has recently been established as a step towards this goal.

Until these goals are achieved this means that, even in accredited laboratories, there is no way of determining the competence of individual scientists to draw correct inferences and to pass a professional opinion.

PACKAGING AND HANDLING OF ITEMS

The theory

It is fundamental to the legal, investigative and scientific integrity of physical evidence that:

- it should be correctly and securely packaged, i.e. in a sealed, referenced container appropriate to the character and properties of the item;

- where applicable, it has been stored in appropriate ambient conditions;

- continuity is absolutely assured, i.e. that from the moment of initial packing until removal by the scientific support officer or forensic scientist:

  - the item has been held under secure circumstances;
  - no individual has unsealed, removed to inspect or handle, or occasioned others to remove or handle (particularly the suspect) the item in question.

Official policy[81] indicates that good practice within forces will be to ensure that:

- there are appropriate and adequate containers, packages and equipment for packaging samples;

- there are adequate procedures for continuity, storage and preservation (including drying) of items;

- there is separation of victim and offender samples.

The practice

Research[82] has indicated that there is 'some evidence of packaging problems'. This applies to all involved in the collection of physical evidence, including instances where the medical examiner has not appropriately packaged or sealed a sample.

Anecdotal evidence from medical examiners and forensic scientists indicates a disturbing occurrence of:

- improper storage, e.g. clothing from a number of suspects not being individually packaged but placed in one large paper sack;

- improper handling (destroying the continuity principle), e.g.

  - the item of clothing recovered at the scene being properly bagged and sealed – with a statement to this effect – but an IO removing the item and offering it to the suspect to hold and to comment about;
  - the IO opens packages of CTM in a case in order to gauge whether it is worthwhile sending the particular item in for forensic analysis.

FORENSIC INVESTIGATION IN A MURDER CASE

SIOs in murder cases are guided in the ACPO 'best practice' manual[83] to consider constructing a forensic management team (FMT) to assist and to advise on forensic issues. In addition to the SIO and deputy SIO, the team should consist of the scientific support manager, the crime scenes co-ordinator, the crime scenes manager and the exhibit officer. SIOs should also consider involving the FSS scientific adviser, the Home Office pathologist and other experts.

We briefly summarise the roles of key members of the team and others who are on hand to assist.

SCIENTIFIC SUPPORT MANAGER

The scientific support manager (SSM) has the following responsibilities:

- management of scientific support resources;

- provision of scene management, co-ordination and operational advice;

- strategic and tactical management of scientific support services to meet investigative needs;

- consultant/adviser on forensic science matters to the force.

CRIME SCENE MANAGER

The crime scene manager (CSM), who should normally be a senior SOCO:

- advises the Team about the requirement for specialist services;

- manages all aspects of the scene examination – ensuring the agreed strategy is delivered.

CRIME SCENE CO-ORDINATOR

The crime scene co-ordinator (CSC) is a police officer, but may be a civilian. Depending upon the scale of the investigation, the CSM may also fulfil the responsibilities of the CSC:

- ensuring that all staff attending a crime scene are briefed and debriefed;

- chairing meetings at which forensic exhibits and issues are discussed. These should be attended by either the scientist attending the scene or the specialist adviser (see next section);

- ensuring that any forensic information is communicated to the interview co-ordinator and officers interviewing suspects – since this will necessarily affect the overall interviewing strategy (see Chapter 2).

FORENSIC SCIENCE SERVICE SPECIALIST ADVISER

The FSS deploys specialist advisers to forces. The specialist adviser (SA) has a broad knowledge of forensic science, enabling him or her to fulfil what is in effect a public relations, maintaining awareness in the force of the FSS and its capability to deliver external scientific support services and, where these are being delivered in a particular case, acting as a communication and liaison link between the police involved in the case and the scientist 'on the bench'.

In keeping with this intermediary role delivered by a generalist, as opposed to that of the 'hands on' scientist conducting the specialist examination, the prime role of the SA is communication. He or she may be requested:

- to work with the SIO to ensure the FSS provides cost-effective and timely service to meet the requirements of the investigation;

- to provide advice and co-ordinate the FSS response.

However, where the SA has a particular scientific specialism, experience and expertise applicable to the case in hand, he or she may be requested to go beyond this communication role and to bring this specialism to bear.

Because forensic science is most likely to make major contributions when all the available options have been assessed, early forensic advice is considered essential. While this comes from the SSM who makes arrangements for handling and processing the scene, it will often be desirable for the SIO to obtain early advice from the SA deployed to the force who is able to speak as a generalist forensic scientist.

NATIONAL CRIME FACULTY LIAISON OFFICER

National Crime Faculty (NCF) liaison officers are deployed to facilitate SIOs in their strategic and tactical management of the murder investigation. They maintain close liaison with SAs, NCF consultant scientists and offender profilers. This ensures timely response to emergent forensic issues, including second opinions, advice on procedures, devising or revising strategy and tactics. Where the requirement emerges for unusual expertise to assist the investigation, the NCF researches potential candidates and identifies those whom it considers to be creditable.

Notes

1. Ramsay, M. (1987) *The Effectiveness of the Forensic Science Service. Home Office Research Study 92*. London: Home Office.

2. Saulsbury, B., Hibberd, M. and Irving, B. (1994) *Using Physical Evidence*. London: Police Foundation.

3. McCulloch, H. (1996) *Police Use of Forensic Science. Police Research Series: Paper 19*. London: Home Office Research Group.

4. Tilley, N. and Ford, A. (1996) *Forensic Science and Crime Investigation. Crime Detection and Prevention Series: Paper 73*. London: Home Office Research Group.

5. Touche Ross. (1987) *Review of Scientific Support for the Police*. London: Home Office.

6. Home Affairs Committee. (1989) *Report on the Forensic Science Service*. London: HMSO.

7. House of Lords Select Committee on Science and Technology. (1993) *Forensic Science: Report (Chaired by Lord Dainton), HL Paper 24*. London: HMSO.

8. Association of Chief Police Officers/Forensic Science Service. (1996) *Using Forensic Science Effectively*. Birmingham: Forensic Science Service.

9. Association of Chief Police Officers/Her Majesty's Inspectorate of Constabulary/Audit Commission. (1996) *Tackling Crime Effectively: Management Handbook*. London: Audit Commission.

10. Association of Chief Police Officers/Forensic Science Service. (1996) *Using Forensic Science Effectively*. Birmingham: Forensic Science Service.

11. *Ibid.*

12. *Ibid.*

13. Association of Chief Police Officers/Her Majesty's Inspectorate of Constabulary/Audit Commission. (1996) *Tackling Crime Effectively: Management Handbook*. London: Audit Commission.

14. Association of Chief Police Officers/Forensic Science Service. (1996) *Using Forensic Science Effectively*. Birmingham: Forensic Science Service.

15. Association of Chief Police Officers/Her Majesty's Inspectorate of Constabulary/Audit Commission. (1996) *Tackling Crime Effectively: Management Handbook*. London: Audit Commission.

16. Association of Chief Police Officers/Forensic Science Service. (1996) *Using Forensic Science Effectively*. Birmingham: Forensic Science Service.

17. Association of Chief Police Officers/Her Majesty's Inspectorate of Constabulary/Audit Commission. (1996) *Tackling Crime Effectively: Management Handbook*. London: Audit Commission.

18. Tilley, N. and Ford, A. (1996) *Forensic Science and Crime Investigation. Crime Detection and Prevention Series: Paper 73*. London: Home Office Research Group.

19. Association of Chief Police Officers/Forensic Science Service. (1996) *Using Forensic Science Effectively*. Birmingham: Forensic Science Service.

20. Association of Chief Police Officers/Her Majesty's Inspectorate of Constabulary/Audit Commission. (1996) *Tackling Crime Effectively: Management Handbook*. London: Audit Commission.

21. *Ibid.*

22. Tilley, N. and Ford, A. (1996) *Forensic Science and Crime Investigation. Crime Detection and Prevention Series: Paper 73*. London: Home Office Research Group.

23. *Ibid.*

24. Association of Chief Police Officers/Forensic Science Service. (1996) *Using Forensic Science Effectively*. Birmingham: Forensic Science Service.

25. Association of Chief Police Officers/Her Majesty's Inspectorate of Constabulary/Audit Commission. (1996) *Tackling Crime Effectively: Management Handbook*. London: Audit Commission.

26. Tilley, N. and Ford, A. (1996) *Forensic Science and Crime Investigation. Crime Detection and Prevention Series: Paper 73*. London: Home Office Research Group.

27. Association of Chief Police Officers/Forensic Science Service. (1996) *Using Forensic Science Effectively*. Birmingham: Forensic Science Service.

28. Touche Ross. (1987) *Review of Scientific Support for the Police*. London: Home Office.

29. Tilley, N. and Ford, A. (1996) *Forensic Science and Crime Investigation. Crime Detection and Prevention Series: Paper 73*. London: Home Office Research Group.

30. Touche Ross. (1987) *Review of Scientific Support for the Police*. London: Home Office.

31. Tilley, N. and Ford, A. (1996) *Forensic Science and Crime Investigation. Crime Detection and Prevention Series: Paper 73*. London: Home Office Research Group.

32. Association of Chief Police Officers/Forensic Science Service. (1996) *Using Forensic Science Effectively*. Birmingham: Forensic Science Service.

33. Touche Ross. (1987) *Review of Scientific Support for the Police*. London: Home Office.

34. Home Affairs Committee. (1989) *Report on the Forensic Science Service*. London: HMSO.

35. House of Lords Select Committee on Science and Technology. (1993) *Forensic Science: Report (Chaired by Lord Dainton), HL Paper 24*. London: HMSO.

36. Association of Chief Police Officers/Forensic Science Service. (1996) *Using Forensic Science Effectively*. Birmingham: Forensic Science Service.

37. Touche Ross. (1987) *Review of Scientific Support for the Police*. London: Home Office.

38. Home Affairs Committee. (1989) *Report on the Forensic Science Service*. London: HMSO.

39. Royal Commission on Criminal Justice. (1993) *Report (Chairman Viscount Runciman), Cm 2263*. London: HMSO.

40. Tilley, N. and Ford, A. (1996) *Forensic Science and Crime Investigation. Crime Detection and Prevention Series: Paper 73*. London: Home Office Research Group.

41. Association of Chief Police Officers/Forensic Science Service. (1996) *Using Forensic Science Effectively*. Birmingham: Forensic Science Service.

42. Association of Chief Police Officers/Her Majesty's Inspectorate of Constabulary/Audit Commission. (1996) *Tackling Crime Effectively: Management Handbook*. London: Audit Commission.

43. Tilley, N. and Ford, A. (1996) *Forensic Science and Crime Investigation. Crime Detection and Prevention Series: Paper 73*. London: Home Office Research Group.

44. Association of Chief Police Officers/Forensic Science Service. (1996) *Using Forensic Science Effectively*. Birmingham: Forensic Science Service.

45. Robertson, G. (1992) *The Role of Police Surgeons. RCCJ Research Study No. 6*. London: HMSO.

46. *Ibid.*

47. *Ibid.*

48. McCulloch, H. (1996) *Police Use of Forensic Science. Police Research Series: Paper 19*. London: Home Office Research Group.

49. Association of Chief Police Officers/Forensic Science Service. (1996) *Using Forensic Science Effectively*. Birmingham: Forensic Science Service.

50. Association of Chief Police Officers/Her Majesty's Inspectorate of Constabulary/Audit Commission. (1996) *Tackling Crime Effectively: Management Handbook*. London: Audit Commission.

51. Tilley, N. and Ford, A. (1996) *Forensic Science and Crime Investigation. Crime Detection and Prevention Series: Paper 73*. London: Home Office Research Group.

52. Graham, V. (1996) 'Points to prove'. *Police Review*, 9 August, 16–18.

53. Association of Chief Police Officers/Forensic Science Service. (1996) *Using Forensic Science Effectively*. Birmingham: Forensic Science Service.

54. Tilley, N. and Ford, A. (1996) *Forensic Science and Crime Investigation. Crime Detection and Prevention Series: Paper 73*. London: Home Office Research Group.

55. *Ibid.*

56. Association of Chief Police Officers/Forensic Science Service. (1996) *Using Forensic Science Effectively*. Birmingham: Forensic Science Service.

57. *Ibid.*

58. *Ibid.*

59. *Ibid.*

60. Tilley, N. and Ford, A. (1996) *Forensic Science and Crime Investigation. Crime Detection and Prevention Series: Paper 73*. London: Home Office Research Group.

61. Stockdale, R. (1991) 'Running with the hounds'. *New Law Journal*, 7 June, 772–5.

62. Gallop, A. (1992) 'Points of view'. *Journal of the Forensic Science Society*, 32, 59–67.

63. Gallop, A. (1993) 'Blinded with science'. *Legal Aid News*, May/June, 8–9.

64. Stockdale, R. and Walker, C. (1993) 'Forensic evidence'. In C. Walker and K. Starmer (eds), *Justice in Error*. London: Blackstone.

65. Gallop, A. (1994) 'Market forensics'. *Journal of the Forensic Science Society*, 34, 121–6.

66. Association of Chief Police Officers/Forensic Science Service. (1996) *Using Forensic Science* Effectively. Birmingham: Forensic Science Service.

67. Association of Chief Police Officers/Her Majesty's Inspectorate of Constabulary/Audit Commission. (1996) *Tackling Crime Effectively: Management Handbook*. London: Audit Commission.

68. Stockdale, R. (1991) 'Running with the hounds'. *New Law Journal*, 7 June, 772–5.

69. Stockdale, R. and Walker, C. (1993) 'Forensic evidence'. In C. Walker and K. Starmer (eds), *Justice in Error*. London: Blackstone.

70. Association of Chief Police Officers/Forensic Science Service. (1996) *Using Forensic Science Effectively*. Birmingham: Forensic Science Service.

71. Tilley, N. and Ford, A. (1996) *Forensic Science and Crime Investigation. Crime Detection and Prevention Series: Paper 73*. London: Home Office Research Group.

72. Stockdale, R. (1991) 'Running with the hounds'. *New Law Journal*, 7 June, 772–5.

73. Gallop, A. (1992) 'Points of view'. *Journal of the Forensic Science Society*, 32, 59–67.

74. Gallop, A. (1993) 'Blinded with science'. *Legal Aid News*, May/June, 8–9.

75. Stockdale, R. and Walker, C. (1993) 'Forensic evidence'. In C. Walker and K. Starmer (eds), *Justice in Error*. London: Blackstone.

76. Gallop, A. (1994) 'Market forensics'. *Journal of the Forensic Science Society*, 34, 121–6.

77. Bawdon, F. (1996) 'Who checks forensics?'. *The Times*, 28 May, 31.

78. Association of Chief Police Officers/Forensic Science Service. (1996) *Using Forensic Science Effectively*. Birmingham: Forensic Science Service.

79. Stockdale, R. and Walker, C. (1993) 'Forensic evidence'. In C. Walker and K. Starmer (eds), *Justice in Error*. London: Blackstone.

80. Royal Commission on Criminal Justice. (1993) *Report (Chairman Viscount Runciman), Cm 2263*. London: HMSO.

81. Association of Chief Police Officers/Her Majesty's Inspectorate of Constabulary/Audit Commission. (1996) *Tackling Crime Effectively: Management Handbook*. London: Audit Commission.

82. Tilley, N. and Ford, A. (1996) *Forensic Science and Crime Investigation. Crime Detection and Prevention Series: Paper 73*. London: Home Office Research Group.

83. Association of Chief Police Officers. (1998) *Murder Investigation Manual*.

CHAPTER 5

Retracing the police investigation: how it should be recorded

POLICE RESPONSIBILITIES UNDER THE CPIA

Chapter 2 provided a detailed review of what takes place by way of investigation and the recording of the processes and outcomes of reactive and proactive investigation. The CPIA spells out the responsibilities of the police to record, retain and reveal to the prosecutor relevant information obtained during an investigation. These responsibilities are laid out in a Code of Practice under section 23 of the Act. The Code is reproduced in Appendix 3.

DATE OF OPERATION

The Code was brought into operation on 1 April 1997. The Code applies in relation to the same suspected or alleged offences as the provisions of the Act, i.e. those into which no criminal investigation was begun before 1 April 1997: section 25(3).

FORCE OF THE CODE

The Act requires the court to take into account, when determining any question arising in the proceedings, a failure by a police officer to comply with, or a failure of any other person charged with the duty of conducting an investigation to have regard to, the Code: section 26(4).

OTHER INVESTIGATORS

The Code is written only for police officers because the Home Secretary, who prepared the Code, is only responsible for the police. Also, some authorities investigate and prosecute so that it is not practical for the Code, which also sets out the responsibilities of the police to reveal material to the prosecutor, to require someone to reveal material to himself. 'The aim is that investigators other than the police should follow the principles of the Code.'[1] They are required to take them into account in applying their own operating procedures: para. 1.1.

Other investigators are required to have regard to any relevant provisions of the Code: section 26(1). This is based on the precedent in section 67 of the Police and Criminal Evidence Act 1984 (PACE), which requires persons other than police officers who are charged with a duty of investigating offences to have regard to the relevant provisions of the Codes of Practice issued under PACE. The effect of case law is to apply the PACE provisions to other diverse groups, such as Customs and Excise. Examples of other investigators are serious fraud officers and local authority trading standards officers.

RECORDING INFORMATION AND THE RETENTION OF RECORDS

The Code refers to the duties of the police to record information and retain records of information and other material.

Material is defined as material of any kind, including information (oral or written) and objects, which is obtained in the course of a criminal investigation and which may be relevant to an investigation.

The term 'relevant' means that it appears to an investigator, or to the officer in charge of an investigation, or to the disclosure officer, that the material has some bearing on any offence under investigation or any person being investigated, or to the surrounding circumstances of the case, unless it is incapable of having any impact on the case: para. 2.1.

THE INVESTIGATOR, DISCLOSURE OFFICER AND OFFICER IN CHARGE OF THE CASE

The Code of Practice gives specific responsibilities to the *investigator*, *the disclosure officer* and the *officer in charge of the case*. These may be one, two or more people.

207

Chapters 2 and 3 show that it is not always clear who is the officer in charge:

- in major investigations, it is an SIO;

- in other investigations, e.g. conducted by area CID, there may be a designated IO;

- in other investigations, the IO and the officer in charge are the same person.

There is no requirement for the disclosure officer to sign and date the schedule.

The identity of the officer in charge of the investigation and the disclosure officer will be separately recorded: para. 3.2, 3.6.

Paradoxically, there is no requirement to record the identity of any person acting as a deputy for either of them.

The Code assigns different duties:

- the investigator is responsible for the recording and retaining of information;

- the disclosure officer is responsible for revealing material to the prosecutor and disclosing material to the defence.

DUTIES OF THE INVESTIGATOR

According to the Code, the investigator is any officer involved in the conduct of the investigation. The investigator must:

- record relevant information at the time it is obtained or as soon as practicable thereafter. This includes, for example, information obtained in house-to-house enquiries, although the requirement to record information promptly does not require an investigator to take a statement from a potential witness where it would not otherwise be taken: para. 4.4;

- put the information into durable or retrievable form, such as writing or tape: para. 4.1:

    'He (an investigator) should not have to take statements when they would not ordinarily be taken, although he should make a note of any potential witnesses.' [2]

- record negative information that may be relevant to an investigation, e.g. a series of persons present in a particular place at a particular time who state that they saw nothing unusual: para. 4.3. The relevance of this to the investigation may be that if the offence had occurred as alleged, they would be expected to have noticed something;

- retain relevant material obtained by him, including material coming into his possession (such as documents seized in the course of a search) and material generated by him (such as interview records). Material may be retained in the form of a copy or photograph rather than the original if the original is to be returned to its owner or is perishable: para. 5.1:

  'Where papers are obtained from a company, it makes sense for the police to take a copy and return the originals to the company so that it can continue its work.'[3]

DUTIES OF THE OFFICER IN CHARGE OF THE CASE

The officer in charge of investigation is the officer responsible for directing the investigation and ensuring that proper procedures are in place:

- if relevant information is not recorded in any form, he or she must ensure it is recorded in a durable or retrievable form (whether in writing, on video or audio tape or on computer disk): para. 4.1,

- where it is not practicable to retain the initial record of information because it forms part of a larger record that is to be destroyed, its contents should be transferred as a true record to a durable and more easily stored form before that happens: para. 4.2;

- if he or she becomes aware as a result of developments in the case that material previously examined but not retained, because it was not thought to be relevant, may now be relevant to the investigation, he or she should take steps to obtain it wherever practicable: para. 5.3.

209

MATERIAL THAT MUST BE RETAINED

The Code of Practice lists in para. 5.4 the categories of material which there is a particular duty to retain if they may be relevant to the investigation. This is the material that the disclosure officer will list on the non-sensitive and sensitive schedules:

- crime reports;

- crime report forms;

- custody records;

- relevant parts of incident report books (IRBs);

- relevant parts of police officer notebooks;

- records that are derived from tapes of telephone messages (e.g. 999 calls) containing descriptions of an alleged offence or offender;

- final versions of witness statements;

- draft versions of witness statements where they differ from the final version (except for draft statements of opinion prepared by expert witnesses);

- exhibits (unless they have been returned to their owner on the understanding that they will be produced in court if necessary);

- interview records (written, audio or video tapes) with potential witnesses;

- interview records (written, audio or video tapes) with suspects;

- communications between the police and experts such as forensic scientists;

- reports of work carried out by experts, such as forensic scientists;

- schedules of scientific material prepared by the expert for the investigator;

- material casting doubt on the reliability of a confession;

- material casting doubt on the reliability of a witness;

- material falling within the test for primary disclosure.

The Code gives licence to police officers to dispose of information with immunity for their decision if at the time they had doubts about its status:

- the investigator is not required to retain material if he or she is doubtful about its likely relevance;

- the Code excludes from the duty of retention items such as routine exchanges of information or other material that is purely ancillary to the material in these categories: para. 5.5.

At the time of writing, the Attorney General had issued draft guidelines on disclosure for consultation which stated that investigators should always err on the side of recording and retaining material where they have any doubt as to whether it may be relevant.[4]

PERIODS OF RETENTION

The material must be retained until:

- a decision is taken whether to institute proceedings against a person for an offence: para. 5.6;

- if proceedings are instituted: para. 5.7, until at least:

> the prosecutor decides not to proceed with the case;
> - the case results in an acquittal;
> - the case results in a conviction following a guilty plea;
> - where the accused pleads not guilty and is convicted: para. 5.8:
>
>   (a) at a summary trial – one year after;
>   (b) at a trial on indictment – three years after;

- if there is an appeal against conviction in progress at the end of the one- or three-year periods, when the appeal is determined: para. 5.9.

Material need not be retained by the police for these periods if: para. 5.10:

- it was seized and is to be returned to its owner;

- it is not durable;

- another criminal justice agency agrees in writing to retain copies for these periods.

The police officer will retain reports of work by expert witnesses and, if necessary, the material which is the basis of the report will be available for inspection. Earlier versions of statements of opinion prepared by expert witnesses will not be available for inspection as these:

> *'tend to evolve as further information comes to light and additional expert contributions are obtained. Earlier versions of such statements tend to be based on incomplete information and could be misleading.'* [5]

Notes

1. Mr Kirkhope, House of Commons Committee. 21 May 1996, col. 100.
2. Baroness Blatch, House of Lords Report Stage. 5 February 1996, col. 24.
3. Baroness Blatch, House of Lords Report Stage. 5 February 1996, col. 27.
4. Attorney General. Draft Guidelines on Disclosure: A Consultation Document. 14 February 2000.
5. Baroness Blatch, House of Lords Report Stage. 5 February 1996, col. 28.

CHAPTER 6

The police duty to reveal information to the prosecutor

HOW INFORMATION REACHES THE PROSECUTOR

Prosecution evidence (used material) and other information about the case, which may be relevant to the defence comes to you through the CPS, either directly, or from the police following a request to them from the CPS.

In order to understand your possible interaction with the CPS in relation to disclosure, it is necessary to know about the process by which the information is revealed by the police to the CPS in the first place.

Chapter 2 explained how the police investigation gives rise to the police case. This is a narrative that gives the CPS, and, in turn, the defence and the courts, a representation of reality as to what happened prior to, during and after an offence.

As the police investigate, information and evidence is likely to emerge that is equivocal, supports some but not all, or actually runs counter to:

- investigators' notions of what happened (their 'case theories');

- what they choose to believe to be 'true' or 'facts of the matter' in respect of:
    - accounts given by particular individuals, deemed by the police to be 'reliable';
    - specific critical detail contained in these accounts or in the form of images, recordings, objects, materials, marks, impressions and CTM.

Such information and evidence is out of step with the police case being constructed against the suspect. In varying degree, it questions critical aspects of the police case and, because of this, the strength of this case. We wish to stress that such out-of-step information is patently obvious. Officers are only too well aware when the detail of what someone says, or if something, does not 'fit', whether partially or totally with what they would prefer to be the case.

Recognition of the obvious is not the difficulty. It is the ethical stance adopted by the officer towards information and evidence that does not 'fit'. The original PEACE guidelines[1] for investigating officers are categorical as to what constitutes professional, ethical conduct in relation to information and evidence:

> *'Once this evidence has been obtained, analyse it and compare it with the points to prove to identify any further gaps, inconsistencies or ambiguities in the information.*
>
> *Keep an open mind when collating information. Try to separate facts from preconceptions and opinions.*
>
> *It is also important to consider that some of the information and evidence that you obtain may be to the suspect's advantage. Do not just dismiss it because it does not point towards the suspect's guilt. Witnesses can be wrong and it is part of your duty to keep an open and enquiring mind.'*

It is fundamental that the CPS, the defence and the courts know what PEACE requires and that all police officers are patently aware of what is their duty when something does not 'fit' the police case. This is because the entire criminal justice system relies upon police officers acting, and continuing to act, ethically at all stages of their involvement in the process of progressing the police case through the prosecutory system. This requirement is critical at the stage of reviewing and deciding which information should be revealed to the CPS, i.e.

- When, in the majority of cases, the investigating officer is also the disclosure officer, tasked with examining and evaluating objectively the police case, 'warts and all', in terms of information and evidence to be sent to the CPS:
  - that supports the police case;
  - that does not 'fit' the police case to whatever degree.
- When there is a designated disclosure officer (appointed in more complex, larger serious and serial cases), providing that officer with all the information, 'warts and all', on the police case, the investigation and its outcomes, to enable that officer to examine and evaluate objectively information and evidence to be sent to the CPS:
  - that supports the police case;
  - that does not 'fit' the police case to whatever degree.

Information is sent to the CPS:

- on forms and statements in files;
- listed on non-sensitive and sensitive schedules;
- by word of mouth (if the material is particularly sensitive); or
- specifically as information that may undermine the prosecution case or assist the disclosed defence case.

The term *undermine* is of central importance. During the passage of the Bill through Parliament, there was a lengthy debate on this matter. The government explained that it was intended to mean:

> *'Material which, generally speaking, has an adverse effect on the strength of the prosecution case ... (for example): a witness statement containing a description of the alleged offender, which is different from the description of the accused ... a psychiatric report showing that the main prosecution witness has a history of psychiatric disorder with a tendency to fantasise.'*[2]

Examples of undermining material are given in the government White Paper, 'Disclosure' CM 2864 at para. 42:

- if part of the prosecution case is a statement by a witness that he or she saw the accused near the scene of the crime shortly after it was committed, it will be necessary to disclose a statement by another witness that he or she saw a person of a different description from the accused at the same time and place;
- if the defendant has told the police in an interview that he or she was acting in self-defence, it will be necessary to disclose the statement of any witness who supports this but whom the prosecution does not regard as truthful;
- if the prosecution is aware that its main witness has a previous conviction, it must disclose it to the defence, since it may affect the weight to be placed on his testimony;
- if previous versions of witness statements are inconsistent with the final version served on the defence, they must be disclosed.

In the light of what we have said above about the obviousness of information and evidence that does not 'fit' the police case, we argue that the notion of undermining is therefore extremely clear and simple. There is no ambiguity: that which does not 'fit' in with the police case *to whatever degree* must undermine the strength of that case.

The responsibility of the police to reveal information to the CPS covers all relevant material. In contrast, under CPIA, the responsibility of the CPS to disclose information to the defence is limited to material that is either in the possession of the CPS or which the prosecutor has inspected, unless the court orders otherwise. This underlines the extent to which the CPS fundamentally relies on the police to be open-minded, and open, about information bearing upon the police case, the police investigation, and information and evidence, which supports the police case and undermines the strength of the police case.

To provide you with a clear understanding of the issues this chapter examines:

- police files;
- the duty of the police to examine the records created during the investigation and reveal material to the prosecutor;
- the role of the CPS.

POLICE FILES

The police case is submitted to the prosecution in a file that is prepared in accordance with the national *Manual of Guidance*.[3] The manual sets out:

- the standard content of police files;
- the time guidelines within which they are to be prepared and presented to the CPS.

Original statements and exhibits are retained by the police. Every file is given a unique reference number.

The amount of information that the CPS receives in the file depends upon the anticipated outcome of the case: whether, on the one hand, it is anticipated that it will result in a guilty plea in the magistrates' court or, on the other hand, a not-guilty plea in the magistrates' court, or a committal, transfer or sending to the Crown court.

On receipt of the file the CPS:

- conducts an independent review, deciding whether it is appropriate to proceed with the prosecution and on the level of charges;
- for an either-way case, prepares advance information for service on the defence.

TYPES OF POLICE FILE

Expedited files

In a straightforward guilty-plea case, the defendant appears at the next available court at an early first hearing (EFH) and an *expedited file* will be prepared.

Straightforward guilty-plea cases

These are cases:

- in which a guilty plea is anticipated, i.e. the defendant admits all the elements of the offence or the offence was witnessed by a police officer and the defendant has given no indication of an intention to deny the matter;

- that are considered to be straightforward – no complicated or contentious issues of fact or law involved, and no aggravating public interest issues involved that require in-depth consideration;

- that have, generally, a maximum of two defendants;

- that have, generally, a maximum of three *key witness statements* (see next section);

- that are capable of being dealt with at the first hearing. (Note: some cases may require an adjournment to resolve straightforward issues in relation to sentencing – for example for a pre-sentence report, compensation or for previous criminal history issues to be resolved. Such cases may be proceeded with under the straightforward guilty-plea procedures.)

Witness statements

Key witness statements are those that prove the elements of the offence(s). Where the evidence of one witness simply duplicates that of another, only one statement need be taken.

Where additional statements have been taken, these should be submitted to the CPS with the file.

Interview evidence

Where more than one police officer is present during an interview it is only necessary for one officer to make a statement producing the record of interview. A statement that only corroborates the interview is not required. If, however, the second officer is required to make a statement to provide key evidence, presence during the interview must be included.

A short descriptive note (SDN) may be submitted instead of a record of a tape-recorded interview (ROTI) for interviews of the suspect, provided that:

- there is a full admission of the prosecution version of events; and
- that any dispute relates only to peripheral circumstances and does not go to the heart of the prosecution case.

Police action to ensure appropriate expedited file completion

As a result of the need to include key witness statements in an expedited file at an EFH, police officers are routinely taking these statements earlier than before. In some areas, custody sergeants are reviewing files at the time of charge to ensure that at least three key witness statements and an SDN are included in the file.

You can expect the witness statements and short descriptive note (SDN) of police interviews of the suspect to be handwritten rather than typed.

Remand files

In all other cases, a *remand file* is prepared for the first hearing, which may be an early administrative hearing (EAH).

Full files

Where a remand file was prepared for the first hearing, a *full file* will be prepared for subsequent hearings in the following types of cases:

- indictable-only offences;
- either-way offences where the magistrates have directed that it be heard at the Crown Court or the defendant has elected trial;
- special-category cases, where the defendant has been charged with a racially motivated or child abuse offence;
- cases in which the defendant has pleaded not guilty in the magistrates' court.

Advice files

The police may submit an *advice file* about the conduct of the investigation or decisions relating to charging. In 1997–8, the CPS advised the police before a prosecution had begun in 3.8 per cent of cases.[4]

CONTENTS OF POLICE FILES

The contents of expedited, remand and full files are given in Appendix 5. It will be seen that there are core items that a file must contain, while other items are included only if they are applicable and available.

There is no settled list of contents for an advice file.

TIMESCALES FOR THE SUBMISSION OF FILES

The period between receipt of an advice file by the CPS and the giving of advice should be two weeks. This target was met in 64.4 per cent of cases in 1998–9.[5]

Following the introduction of the Narey provisions, an expedited and remand file for the EFH and EAH respectively are normally available within 24 hours of charge. A beneficial result of this is that police officers are required to take statements from witnesses much earlier than before.

If a not-guilty plea is entered in the magistrates' court, the full file should be sent to the CPS within seven days in a custody case, 14 days in a simple or urgent bail case and 21 days in other bail cases.

If the offence is either way, and there has been an election or direction for trial by jury, the committal file should be sent to the CPS within 21 days of the defendant's first appearance or mode of trial, if he or she is in custody, and 28 days if he or she is on bail.

THE SCHEDULES AND UNDERMINING MATERIAL: REVEALING MATERIAL TO THE PROSECUTOR

The responsibility of the police to reveal information to the CPS covers all relevant material: section 23(1)(b) and (e); paras. 5.1, 6.1.

As explained in Chapter 5, the Code of Practice creates the role of disclosure officer. Most of the duties in relation to disclosure fall upon this person.

The Code points out that the disclosure officer is not necessarily the officer in charge (OIC) of the investigation or the investigator. As pointed out earlier, however, in the main, the investigating officer (IO) in the case acts as the disclosure officer in respect of that case.

The prosecutor has access to all the material obtained by the police during an investigation: section 24(4); para. 7.4.

THE RESPONSIBILITIES OF THE INVESTIGATOR

Specific responsibilities

The Code says in respect of the investigator that:

- he or she is to draw the attention of the disclosure officer to material he or she has retained, which may undermine the prosecution case and state why he or she has come to that view: para. 7.2;

- if he or she considers that material is so sensitive that it should not be included in the sensitive schedule, he or she is responsible for telling the prosecutor of the existence of this material and arranging for its inspection. Examples are where, if the material was compromised, that would be likely to lead directly to the loss of life, or directly threaten national security: paras. 6.13, 6.14;

- he or she may seek advice from the prosecutor about whether a particular item of material may be relevant to the investigation: para. 6.1 (such as the fact that a police officer who has made a statement in connection with an investigation has disciplinary matters or convictions and cautions for criminal offences, including spent convictions, recorded against him, which may cast doubt upon his reliability).

Equipping officers to fulfil their investigating officer responsibilities

All forces have sought to train officers in the provisions of CPIA. Typically, officers have been exposed to around a day's instruction.

No officer should therefore be in a position to claim ignorance of the duties of an investigating officer as specified in the Code. Most particularly, officers cannot claim ignorance as to what constitutes undermining material. As pointed out earlier, undermining material comprises anything that does not 'fit' with, and hence adversely affects the strength of the police case. Since they know what does not 'fit' they know what is undermining.

Furthermore, all officers should have attended not only training in CPIA but also PEACE, which as pointed out earlier, defines their duty as investigating officers to have an open mind in respect of information and evidence.

The potential for unacceptable performance by investigating officers

At the time the government was presenting the Bill before Parliament, ample evidence existed in the form of HMIC reporting, commissioned research, PCA (Police Complaints Authority) and other inquiries, and publicised miscarriages of justice, about the widespread existence of barriers to effective and ethical investigation by the police. Chapter 3 summarises these: an endemic lack of requisite knowledge and skills, 'noble cause corruption', the pressures of the performance culture, poor management, supervision, which is inadequate or completely absent, and the 'informal' code of conduct.

The government chose to ignore these factors that create the conditions for process corruption of police investigation. It was never conceived that police performance in respect of disclosure would be anything other than wholly proper: an extension of the same proper behaviour exhibited in the investigative process.

It was taken as axiomatic that, having investigated and gathered evidence effectively and ethically, producing the legal basis to charge the suspect, police officers would have no difficulty adopting an open, 'warts and all' stance towards *all* information generated, in existence, and bearing upon the investigation and its outcomes. It was assumed that there would be no problem, motivationally, in dealing even-handedly with information and evidence that did not 'fit' the police case, which undermined the strength of that case and would assist the suspect's defence. An observer suggested that the government had cast police officers in the role of a foxhunter who, having caught the fox, was then obliged to give it the 'kiss of life'.

Investigating officers who believe that the public interest, justice, the organisation, management, and colleagues are best served by corrupting the disclosure process are able to do this.

• Information concerning the investigation and information and evidence generated by the processes of investigation, and which are recognised to undermine the police case (and therefore the potential for a prosecution to succeed) or would assist any future defence, can be 'lost'.

221

- Rather than actively 'losing' information and evidence, investigating officers can be economical with the truth. They can deceive by simply not telling the disclosure officer: selectively disclosing only that which supports the police case and failing to mention that which undermines the police case and could be of potential future assistance to the defence.

This raises therefore the question: what legal and police organisational protection exists against such conduct, which, like all corruption, as it is cumulatively exposed, erodes public confidence in the integrity of police handling of information and evidence? The answer is, at the time of writing, none.

When it emerges, in the event of a subsequent request by the CPS, on their own part or on behalf of the defence or the court, that:

- Critical undermining information or evidence does exist but has been withheld, officers merely need to say they did not realise it was undermining. Nothing happens.

- Critical undermining information or evidence did exist but now no longer exists having been disposed of or destroyed, officers can offer the same excuse: they were unaware at the time of disposal or destruction that the material was significant, that it undermined the police case or that it would be of likely assistance to the suspect's defence. Nothing happens. There are no sanctions in the CPIA.

Chapter 3 highlighted the organisational barriers to effective and ethical investigation. In particular, we described the absence of basic quality control mechanisms able to prevent process corruption:

- managers and supervisors ready, willing and able to set standards, to monitor and to reward integrity of decision-making and action;

- the existence of, and willingness to apply, real sanctions when an investigating officer acts unethically.

There are no monitoring mechanism or supervisory systems, procedures or processes to make investigating officers accountable for their actions in respect of information and evidence, which is undermining. The police service is unable to demonstrate to a court the existence of effective checks upon the conduct of investigating officers in all cases, and, in particular, the case currently before the court.

- There are no checks, on a routine or random basis, directed at identifying officers withholding, removing or disposing of patently undermining material.

- There are no sanctions to encourage officers to behave differently when it comes to light that they have withheld, removed or disposed of patently undermining material. This contrasts with investigators in the private sector, whose improper conduct risk damaging the institution's good name and prejudicing costly court proceedings. They receive appropriate feedback and guidance, have their performance closely monitored, and, in the event of repeated misconduct, are subject to disciplinary procedures - formal, written warnings, and, ultimately, face dismissal.

Training in CPIA provisions is essential, but not enough. To protect its good name, the service must implement the real (as opposed to illusory) means to ensure integrity: to reveal, and to deal positively with, those instances of process corruption when officers 'lose' information and evidence, deceive disclosure officers, or claim, fatuously, that they did not realise that material was undermining when it patently was undermining. Only thus will the service show it is active and effective in discouraging unacceptable performance by investigating officers and thus secure and maintain public confidence.

THE RESPONSIBILITIES OF THE DISCLOSURE OFFICER

The role of disclosure officer

As we indicated earlier, in the majority of cases, the investigating officer assumes the role of disclosure officer. Individual force policy specifies which types of case require a designated officer to fulfil these duties. Typically, a disclosure officer, who is not an investigating officer, will be appointed in serious and complex cases.

Specific responsibilities

The tasks, which the Code requires a designated disclosure officer, or an investigating officer doubling up as a disclosure officer, to fulfil, are extremely demanding. The law requires them in the public interest:

- to conduct an objective examination of material bearing upon the investigation and its outcomes, *both in the round and in fine-grain detail*;

- to evaluate the material they examine objectively from a dual perspective: from the position of the prosecution and the defence;

- to ensure absolute fairness in the process of identifying and dealing with material, particularly that which undermines the prosecution case;

- to communicate in the manner specified and in sufficient detail to allow the CPS its reviewing and own disclosure duties.

The Code says in respect of the disclosure officer that:

- he or she must examine the material retained by the police during the investigation: para. 2.1;

- he or she must prepare a schedule: paras. 6.2, 6.3, listing material retained that may be relevant to the investigation and which he or she believes will not form part of the prosecution case against the accused if (paras. 6.6, 6.8):
  - he or she believes the accused is likely to plead not guilty at a summary trial; or
  - he or she believes the case will be tried in the Crown Court; or
  - there is an unexpected election/direction for Crown Court trial or the accused pleads not guilty and the case proceeds to summary trial, a guilty plea having been expected; or
  - the accused is charged with an indictable-only offence;

- after the prosecutor has determined what material will form the case against the accused, the disclosure officer must give the prosecutor an amended schedule listing material which is not sensitive and is not already listed on the schedule: para. 8.1;

- he or she may decide that it is not in the public interest to disclose certain material and that it should be on a sensitive schedule: para. 6.4.

In respect of sensitive schedule material:

  - each item must be listed separately on the schedule, and each item numbered consecutively;

- the description of each item should make clear the nature of the item and contain sufficient detail to enable the prosecutor to decide whether he or she needs to inspect the material before deciding whether or not it should be disclosed: para. 6.9;
- items of a similar or repetitive nature that meet the test for primary disclosure must be listed and described individually: para. 6.11;
- material must be listed in a separate schedule showing reasons for its sensitivity. This will be material that the disclosure officer or the officer in charge of the investigation believes it is not in the public interest to disclose. Examples of these are (para. 6.12):

(a) material relating to national security; received from the intelligence and security agencies; or relating to intelligence from foreign sources that reveals sensitive intelligence-gathering methods;

(b) material relating to the use of a telephone system and which is supplied to an investigator for intelligence purposes only;

(c) material given in confidence;

(d) material relating to the identity or activities of informants, or undercover police officers, or other persons supplying information to the police who may be in danger if their identities are revealed;

(e) material relating to the location of any premises or other places used for police surveillance, or the identity of any person allowing a police officer to use them for surveillance;

(f) material revealing, either directly or indirectly, techniques and methods relied upon by a police officer in the course of a criminal investigation, for example covert surveillance techniques, or other methods of detecting crime;

(g) material the disclosure of which might facilitate the commission of other offences or hinder the prevention and detection of crime;

(h) internal police communications such as management minutes;

(i) material upon the strength of which search warrants were obtained;

(j) material containing details of persons taking part in identification parades;

(k) material supplied to an investigator during a criminal investigation, which has been generated by an official of a body concerned with the regulation or supervision of bodies corporate or of persons engaged in financial activities;

(l) material supplied to an investigator during a criminal investigation, which relates to a child or young person and has been generated by a local authority social services department, an Area Child Protection Committee or other party contacted by the investigator during the investigation;

- – he or she may (having consulted the officer in charge of the investigation) decide that the material is too sensitive to be copied and must be inspected: para. 7.4;

- • he or she must give the prosecutor, at the same time as he or she gives him the schedule, a copy of any material that falls into the following categories (unless such material has already been given to the prosecutor as part of the file containing the material for the prosecution case): para. 7.3:

  - – records of the first description of a suspect given to the police by a potential witness, whether or not the description differs from that of the alleged offender;
  - – information provided by an accused person, which indicates an explanation for an offence with which he or she has been charged;
  - – any material casting doubt on the reliability of a confession;
  - – any material casting doubt upon the reliability of a witness;
  - – any other material that the investigator believes may fall within the test for primary disclosure in the Act;

- • he or she must draw the attention of the prosecutor to any material that the investigator believes may undermine the case for the prosecution, and explain why the investigator came to that view: para. 7.2;

- • he or she may seek the advice of the prosecutor about whether a particular item of material may be relevant to the investigation: para. 6.1 (such as previous convictions and cautions for criminal offences, including spent convictions, which are recorded against prosecution witnesses);

- • he or she must send the schedule to the prosecutor together with the file containing material for the prosecution case or after an election or direction for Crown Court trial or a not-guilty plea in the magistrates' court when a guilty plea had been expected: para. 7.1;

- • he or she must allow the prosecutor to inspect any material, which the prosecutor requests and which has not been copied to him, or give him a copy unless the officer in charge of the investigation or the disclosure officer (having consulted the officer in charge of the investigation) believes that it is too sensitive and must be inspected instead: para. 7.4;

- • after a defence statement has been given, he or she must look at the retained material and draw the attention of the prosecutor to any material that might assist the defence case and reveal it to the prosecutor if requested: para. 8.2;

- he or she must certify to the prosecutor that to the best of his or her knowledge and belief all material that has been retained and made available to him or her has been revealed to the prosecutor in accordance with the Code: para. 9.1:

  - when the schedules and accompanying material was submitted; or
  - when retained material has been reconsidered after a defence statement.

At the time of writing, the Attorney General had issued draft guidelines on disclosure,[6] for consultation, which stated that when the disclosure officer is in doubt about whether material might undermine the prosecution case, he or she should draw the material to the attention of the prosecutor and should seek the advice and assistance of the prosecutor when in doubt about his or her responsibility.

The range of material retained and processed

It will be seen that the disclosure officer's duty to examine 'material retained' (para: 2.1) and his or her certification requirement (para. 9.1) is limited to material that is 'made available to' the disclosure officer. It does not necessarily include all material that has been retained and may be relevant to an investigation.

The wording is consistent with disclosure officers, who are designated as such, being passive in the task of collating and reviewing procedurally generated information concerning the investigation and recipients of information that investigating officers and others choose to tell them. Designated disclosure officers will naturally differ in their approach to their role. This creates variation in terms of the range and amount of material retained and which they ensure is made available to them. However all designated disclosure officers are to some degree or other hostage to the ethical stance of investigating officers, as well as senior investigating officers.

In the case of investigating officers cast in the role of disclosure officer for their own cases, it follows that they will have decided what needs to be retained and what will be processed.

The description of items

The Code of Practice specifically requires the disclosure officer to describe each item sufficiently to enable the prosecutor (there is no reference to the accused) to form a judgement as to whether the material needs to be disclosed.

Equipping officers to fulfil their disclosure officer responsibilities

As part of forces' training in the provisions of CPIA, officers were made aware of the responsibilities of the disclosure officer.

The performance of officers in the disclosure officer role

Research conducted by the CPS has led it to complain[7] about poorly completed police schedules of unused material. Items were regularly left off schedules, copies of material were not sent to the CPS and disclosure officers were difficult to contact. Research carried out in 1999 by the Criminal Bar Association and the Law Society provides telling, disturbing confirmatory evidence.

Eight out of 10 respondents to the Law Society research said schedules of non-sensitive unused material are either 'unlikely' or 'highly unlikely' to be comprehensive and reliable. The same proportion considered disclosure-officers' analyses, as to whether items listed on non-sensitive unused material schedules undermine the prosecution case or assist the defence case, to be either 'unreliable' or 'highly unreliable'.

Table 6.1 gives examples provided by solicitors of material that was not listed in police schedules or, if listed, was not disclosed.

Eight out of 10 respondents described the information listed on the non-sensitive unused material schedule as being either 'insufficiently' or 'highly insufficiently' described to enable the disclosure-officer's assessment as to disclosability to be independently considered by the prosecutor and the defence. Examples of inadequate description of material included:

- The contents of police officers' notebooks.
- The contents of statements of witnesses who were not being called.
- The content of telephone calls to the police from members of the public reporting a crime.
- The content of messages between the police control room and individual officers.
- Documents being identified by a police reference number instead of a title.
- Documents being described only as 'a bundle of documents'.
- References to 'fingerprints' without saying whether they had been identified and, if so, whose fingerprints they matched.
- References to 'witness statements' without saying to whom they related.
- References to 'videos' without giving any further information about their content or where or when the recordings were taken.

Not listed in police schedules	Listed but not disclosed
Telephone calls to the police from members of the public reporting a crime.	A 999 call from a member of the public supporting the accused's version of events.
Messages between the police control room and individual officers, describing the offence and the offender.	CCTV tapes.
	The first description of an offender which did not match the accused.
Video films of incidents.	A statement by a complainant that her original statement was not accurate.
Incident report books.	
Crime reports.	The fact that the complainant had made similar allegations against
Incident logs.	other people in the past.
Previous convictions of prosecution witnesses.	A video interview in which a child witness had given a contradictory account of the alleged offence.
Details of people who were spoken to by the police but from whom statements were not taken.	A complainant's criminal record.
	The fact that the complainant and a prosecution witness were initially arrested and interviewed as suspects.
Previous drafts of witnesses' statements and notes of interviews with witnesses.	The statements of witnesses helpful to the defence.
Taped interviews with suspects who were not charged.	The addresses of witnesses helpful to the defence.
Statements made by witnesses whom the police were not calling.	The fact that a person arrested but not charged had accused someone other than the defendant.
	A forensic report supporting the accused's version of events.
	A medical report supporting the accused's version of events.

Table 6.1 Examples of material not listed or listed but not disclosed

This inadequate performance by police officers necessarily creates a domino effect. It constrains the performance of the CPS. The experience of eight out of 10 respondents in the Law Society research was that prosecuting authorities do not usually call for sight of items listed on unused material schedules but they rely on disclosure-officers' judgements. Unquestioning CPS acceptance of the correctness of police decision-making and action is endemic.

> *'my experience of the (CPS) lawyer with conduct of that case is that disclosure is an issue for the disclosure officer and not her and that she is not prepared to give any independent consideration to whether items are appropriate for disclosure beyond reiterating the officer's view.'*

(A consultant with 10 years' experience)

> *'CPS are unable or unwilling to challenge those (police) decisions.'*

(A partner with 10 years' experience)

This behaviour and mindset by the CPS in respect of what the police give them, in turn, affect primary disclosure and responses to requests for disclosure from the defence and the courts. The statement in the Attorney General's draft guidelines on disclosure[8] that 'prosecutors must not take schedules prepared by disclosure officers at face value' is unlikely to change this situation on its own.

The standard response of the police service is to diagnose performance shortcomings as a training problem and to prescribe more training. To be fair, the amount of training officers have received can be argued to be insufficient to equip them to fulfil the duties of the disclosure officer. But training alone will not solve the problem.

Lack of knowledge, skills, experience and expertise cannot account for the breadth of inappropriate performance of officers occupying the role of disclosure officer. There are clearly disclosure officers who are prepared to corrupt the disclosure process. Where they perceive there is material that undermines the strength of the prosecution case or might assist the defence, this material is withheld.

For whatever reason, whether incompetence or a desire to improve the likelihood of successful conviction, in all too many instances, the CPS are kept in the dark. For example, it is a widespread practice not to disclose responses to particular inquiries, whether taken down on a pro forma, notes, in pocket books or as formal statements, which give divergent accounts or descriptions. Effectively, such undermining material does not exist.

When the Bill was being debated, the government held out the crime report as a fundamental means of identifying the potential existence of undermining material. This is indeed the case. The report, with enclosures and attachments, provides an insight into the management of the investigation, a record of investigative efforts and the outcomes of these. Prior to the introduction of CPIA, it was routine for the full crime report to be forwarded and subsequently disclosed to the defence. Now it is widespread police practice to forward only the first page, and the research showed that the report may not be forwarded at all! Lack of training cannot account for this change in police behaviour. Unless the CPS have a copy of the full crime report and listed actions, they cannot know of the full range of inquiry. They cannot carry out the most basic series of quality control checks.

THE ROLE OF THE CPS

Initial and full review

The CPS review of a file commences when it is received from the police and before the first hearing. An initial review is carried out in accordance with the 3rd edition of the Code for Crown Prosecutors published in 1994 (set out in Appendix 6), issued under section 10 of the Prosecution of Offences Act 1985. The review includes consideration of:

•   whether there is sufficient admissible, substantial and reliable evidence to give a realistic prospect of conviction;

•   whether it is in the public interest to prosecute;

•   whether the number and level of charges are appropriate;

•   the mode of trial representations in respect of either-way offences.

A non-lawyer – a designated caseworker (DCW) – may review a straight-forward guilty-plea case.

Request for additional information

A second, full review by a lawyer takes place after mode of trial in an either-way case when the full file has been received from the police (usually three to four weeks later). Crown Court case preparation may have been undertaken by the caseworker at that stage.

The CPS may identify additional information that the police could obtain. Lack of effective investigation by the police may leave points to prove and statements, which fail to deal with the issues. If the CPS advises the police about this, it is up to the police whether they follow this advice.

Problems of delay are caused by the absence of the police officer responsible for progressing the case, e.g. on rest days, leave or patrol. Occasionally, the work required is not actioned at all.

231

A late review by the CPS – the prosecutor may be at court or on leave – leads to late requests for further statements.

In *R.* v. *Fergus* (Ivan) (1994) 98 Cr. App. R. 313, Ivan Fergus was arrested for attempted robbery. The prosecution case depended solely on the visual identification of the defendant by the victim. There was no evidence that supported the identification. On the day of his arrest, he named four alibi witnesses. They were readily traceable. Giving the judgment of the Court of Appeal that 'the truth is that Ivan was wholly innocent of the offence', Lord Justice Steyn criticised the police for their failure to investigate the case properly or follow the advice of the CPS:

> '*On 14 May 1991 the Crown Prosecution Service asked the Lewisham Police to take statements from the four alibi witnesses. They did nothing.*
>
> *On 24 May 1991 the CPS sent a reminder to the Lewisham Police to the same effect. They did nothing.*
>
> *On 23 October the CPS sent a memorandum to the Lewisham Police, with the names and addresses of the four alibi witnesses. They were requested to take statements. They did not do so.*
>
> *On 8 November the CPS sent a reminder to the Lewisham Police. They did nothing.*
>
> *On 20 November an officer of the Lewisham Police attended a conference with counsel. He was instructed to take statements. He said that he was doubtful whether he would be able to do so.*
>
> *On 22 November the same officer was asked by telephone to take statements. He said it was unlikely he would be able to do so in time.*
>
> *On 26 November, the first day of the trial, the officer was instructed to take statements if the alibi witnesses attended. Two attended. The officer did not try to take statements from them.*'

Lord Justice Steyn concluded:

> '*We readily accept that the CPS and counsel for the Crown did all they could to ensure that statements from these witnesses were taken. Yet in a serious case against a 13-year-old schoolboy the Lewisham Police blandly ignored repeated instructions about important investigations.*'

Following the introduction of the Narey provisions, face-to-face talking between police officers and Crown Prosecutors and DCWs at ASUs, when the first file review takes place, is more likely to identify shortcomings in files and agreement about remedial action before the first hearing.

The obligation on the CPS to review a file continues during the lifetime of a case.

However, the Law Society research points to shortcomings in the CPS fulfilment of their role from the point of initial review on. As pointed out earlier, the experience of eight out of 10 respondents was that items listed on the unused material schedule are not inspected before primary- or secondary-disclosure decisions are made. Prosecuting authorities do not usually call for sight of items listed on unused material schedules but they rely on disclosure-officers' judgements, whose decision-making and actions are accepted without question.

POLICE AWARENESS OF THE CODE FOR CROWN PROSECUTORS

In 1996, the CPS carried out a research project to assess police awareness of the new Code issued in June 1994. More than half the officers surveyed had not seen the new Code. The Code for Crown Prosecutors, although aimed at prosecutors, contains general guidance for the police on the right charge.

CHARGING STANDARDS

The CPS and police have agreed detailed guidance for certain offences, called *charging standards*. Charging standards on assaults and other violent crimes were introduced in 1994. Charging standards on driving offences and public order offences and a revised charging standard on assaults (containing new guidance on self-defence) were introduced in 1996. In 1998–9, the CPS discontinued 11.9 per cent of cases, 27.9 per cent of these before the first hearing.[8]

TIMELINESS AND QUALITY OF POLICE FILES

In 1996–7, just under a half of police files were not submitted to the CPS within agreed timescales, with performance in CPS areas ranging between 16 and 84 per cent. Almost half of the files received failed to meet quality standards. Taking timeliness and quality together, only one-third of files met the agreed standard for both.[9]

REASONS FOR DISCONTINUANCE

The most common reason why the CPS discontinued a case was the absence of an essential legal element, particularly in theft, handling stolen goods and motoring offences. Unreliable witnesses, victims or witnesses refusing to give evidence, or the victim refusing to attend court accounted for 20 per cent of discontinuances. The majority of these offences were for violence against the person. Not proceeding because the CPS thought that the most likely outcome was very small or minimal penalties was most common in offences of theft, handling and motoring offences. Motoring was the most common offence for which discontinuance was due to unreliable identification.

In 1994, a CPS survey[10] identified the reasons for discontinuing magistrates' court cases. Salient findings of the survey were as follows.

* Insufficient evidence to proceed:

    – essential legal element missing: 13 per cent;
    – doubts concerning identification evidence: 11 per cent;
    – doubts concerning other evidence: 19 per cent.

* Not in the public interest to proceed:

    – very small or nominal penalty likely: 14 per cent;
    – caution considered to be more suitable: 6 per cent;
    – other public interest grounds: 8 per cent.

It will be seen that in over 40 per cent of cases perceived shortcomings led to the decision to discontinue.

Notes

1. *A Guide to Interviewing.* (1992) Harrogate: Central Planning and Training Unit.

2. Baroness Blatch, House of Lords 3rd Reading. 19 February, 1996, col. 866.

3. *The Manual of Guidance for the Preparation, Processing and Submission of Files.* Produced by ACPO and the CPS for internal distribution. First edition 1 April 1992 (updated periodically).

4. Crown Prosecution Service. (1998) *Annual Report 1997–8.* London: The Stationery Office.

5. Crown Prosecution Service. (1999) *Annual Report 1998–9.* London: The Stationery Office.

6. Attorney General. Draft Guidelines on Disclosure: A Consultation Document. 14 February 2000.

7. 'Disclosure and the CPIA: implementation and practice'. Conference organised by ACPO in conjunction with the National Crime Faculty, Police Staff College, Bramshill, 1998.

8. Attorney General. Draft Guidelines on Disclosure: A Consultation Document. 14 February 2000.

9. Crown Prosecution Service. (1999) *Annual Report 1998–9*. London: The Stationery Office.

10. Crown Prosecution Service. (1997) *Report to the Audit Commission*. London: The Stationery Office.

11. Crown Prosecution Service. (1994) *Discontinuance Survey*. November.

CHAPTER 7

Disclosure to the defence: the unfolding picture

DISCLOSURE AND ITS IMPLICATIONS

This chapter focuses upon disclosure of material to the defence and the implications for the active defence of your client. It describes:

- the information you should receive;
- when you should receive it;
- the significant stages in responding to disclosure and non-disclosure;
- the management of information in your client's case;
- the activities that are involved in systematic investigation.

THE INFORMATION YOU SHOULD RECEIVE

The police and then the prosecutor will progressively disclose to you:

- first, material that forms part of the case against your client;
- then selected unused material.

The disclosure of material is a staged process.

Disclosure at the police station

At the police station, information is potentially available to a legal adviser about the police investigation, the police representation of events (the police case) and the prosecution evidence.

Apart from showing a legal adviser the custody record, police officers still retain the right to decide how much information they shall give and are advised to disclose voluntarily the minimum necessary. In many cases, it is likely that the IO will not allow a legal adviser sight of statements, choosing to read selected extracts from these either during the consultation prior to interview, or during the interview, or both.

It may be that your firm did not represent the suspect at the police station stage. This represents a degree of disadvantage:

- there may be some delay while material is obtained from the solicitor who advised, or whose representative advised, your client; and

- you will be hostage to fortune as to the extent to which the individual who advised your client was skilful in negotiating disclosure of information.

Disclosure of tape recordings of police interviews of your client

See pp. 239 below.

Disclosure at the bail hearing at court

At a bail hearing, the prosecutor will decide how much information to release from the expedited or remand file.

Disclosure of advance information

Rule 4 of the Magistrates' Courts (Advance Information) Rules 1985 requires the prosecutor on request before mode of trial to provide the accused with either:

- a copy of those parts of every written statement that contain information as to the facts and matters of which the prosecutor proposes to adduce evidence in the proceedings; or

- a summary of the facts and matters of which the prosecutor proposes to adduce evidence in the proceedings.

Internal guidance to CPS staff states that, when available, statements (or parts of statements) should be served instead of a summary for advance information purposes.

In Chapter 5, we described expedited and remand files. Instead of a summary of the evidence, expedited and remand files contain key witness statements. A summary of the evidence is no longer required in full files either. This means that the CPS has no choice but to supply copies of the key statements instead.

The Manual of Guidance[1] lists key witness statements as required in the remand file. The *Manual* advises their inclusion to enable a proper remand application to be made and for a decision to be taken by the CPS to accept a plea where appropriate. We stress that at this stage, the police and CPS acceptance of this advice is essential. *Only* key witness statements are acceptable.

Disclosure of prosecution witness statements in summary cases

In summary-trial cases where there is a pre-trial review, the Working Group on Pre-Trial Issues (PTI)[2] recommended that the CPS serve all the evidence on the defence. The CPS implemented this by internal guidance to staff, which states that a copy of all the evidence should be served before pre-trial review.

In cases where pre-trial reviews are not held, the guidance given to CPS staff concentrates on the proper use of section 9 of the Criminal Justice Act 1967 (CJA). Statements are served in order to spare inconvenience to witnesses, present evidence more clearly and shorten the trial.

The CPS has told the Law Society that:

- requests for statements will be treated sympathetically and reasonably;

- there will be cases where statements, which are unlikely to be agreed, will be served before trial;

- a routine request for statements for a minor offence, such as drunk and disorderly, may not be met.

Perhaps anticipating the implementation of the Human Rights Act 1998, at the time of writing, the Attorney General had issued draft guidelines on disclosure, for consultation, which stated that the prosecutor should provide the defence with all the evidence upon which the Crown proposes to rely in a summary trial in sufficient time to allow the defence lawyer to consider the evidence properly before it is called.[3]

Disclosure of the committal bundle

Before your client can be committed for trial, the prosecutor must serve the evidence for the prosecution in the form of written statements that comply with section 5A of the Magistrates' Court Act 1980 (MCA) (conditions similar to those in section 102 of MCA, repealed).

Disclosure of the prosecution case: indictable-only cases under s.51 Crime and Disorder Act 1998

Following the sending of the case, the prosecution evidence will be served, either as one bundle or, in a complex case, as it becomes available.

Prosecution primary disclosure: unused undermining material and schedule

Juries necessarily reach their verdicts according to the evidence that the prosecution and defence present before them. Most of the evidence in a case comes from the prosecution, which has the significant advantage of being able to choose the evidence from the police investigation that suits its case.

The first time that you are entitled to a glimpse of the bigger picture is at *primary disclosure*, when the prosecutor should disclose:

- material that in his or her opinion may undermine the prosecution case;

- a schedule of the other non-sensitive unused material.

Prosecution secondary disclosure: disclosure of material that may assist the defence case

If your client gives a defence statement, you may be allowed to see more information in the form of prosecution secondary disclosure of any relevant material that may reasonably be expected to assist the defence disclosed in the written statement.

WHEN YOU SHOULD RECEIVE INFORMATION

Tape recording of the police interview

If you were present at the police interview with your client, it is important that you ask for copies of tape recordings before you leave the police station. The police are required to supply a copy of the tape as soon as practicable if the person is charged: para. 4.16, PACE Code of Practice E. All designated police stations have rapid-recording facilities, i.e. a machine that takes less than a couple of minutes to produce a copy of the working copy of the tape. We stress the importance of: requesting the investigating officer to give a little of his or her time to make fast copies; listening to, and considering the content of, tape recordings as soon as possible after the interview. This enables early reflection on the officer's observance of PEACE guidelines and very often reveals detail that was missed, misheard or misunderstood in the interview by you, your client or the police officer.

If you leave the police station before your client is charged, you should request that the tape is sent to you. There is no excuse for the police not doing so and there is no justification for their waiting for a further request from you.

If your client was unrepresented, the tape may have been given to him or her. The custody record should show whether the tape was handed to your client.

You may to have to recover the tape from your client or a solicitor who was only instructed for the police station stage of the case. Solicitors who are present during the interview should keep their notes and any tapes supplied in a place where they can be easily located and supply these promptly to any solicitor who is instructed subsequently.

If your client cannot provide you with a copy of the tape or the police were unable to copy it there and then, if it is appropriate to listen to it, you should apply to the police immediately for a copy.

Advance information

Following the receipt and review of a file involving an either-way offence, the CPS will automatically prepare *advance information*.

Once prepared, the advance information documents will be sent to the defence solicitor if:

• they are requested by the defence solicitor;

• the CPS knows the name of the solicitor who represents the accused;

• the magistrates' court informs the CPS of the firm of solicitors to whom legal aid has been granted.

In 1997–8, in 82.3 per cent of cases, advance information was sent to the defence within seven days of the CPS being aware of the name of the defence solicitor and being in possession of a file.[4]

As a result of the introduction of the Narey provisions, the advance information documents should normally be handed over at court before the first hearing.

Uncontentious prosecution witness statements in summary cases

The Law Society, as a member of the Trials Issues Group, has agreed to national standards of witness care with the CPS, the Court Service, the Police Service and the Bar. They require the prosecutor, at the time of the first review of the full file or when undertaking the review of the full file following a not-guilty plea:

- to decide which statements can appropriately be tendered in evidence under section 9 of CJA;

- to serve copies of these statements on the defence within seven working days of the relevant review date: para. 6.2.

The prosecutor should serve any additional witness statements, which can appropriately be tendered in evidence under section 9, on the defence within seven days of coming into possession of them: para. 6.3.

Committal bundle

All the criminal justice agencies aim to prepare most cases within the national time guidelines recommended by PTI:

- where a defendant is remanded in custody, a national guideline of six weeks has been set between mode of trial in an either-way case and committal;

- within that six-week period, the police should provide a full file to the CPS within 21 days and the CPS should prepare the committal papers and the indictment within 10 days of receipt. This should leave the defence with a minimum of 10 days to consider the papers;

- where the defendant is remanded on bail, the national guideline for committals has been set at eight weeks. Within that eight-week period the police should provide a full file within 28 days and the CPS should prepare the committal papers and the draft indictment within 14 days of receipt. This should leave the defence with a minimum of 14 days to consider the papers.

There is an unacceptable degree of non-compliance with these time guidelines, resulting in committal papers often being served on the defence at the committal hearing. A Home Office Study[5] found that many of the guidelines were being exceeded by around half the sample:

- for charge cases in the magistrates' court with a not-guilty plea, nearly 60 per cent of custody cases and 50 per cent of bail cases exceeded the guidelines;

- of all the cases dealt with summarily, 75 per cent of not-guilty pleas cases exceeded the guidelines. The lowest levels of compliance were for the period from not-guilty plea to summary trial;

- for indictable-only custody cases, 83 per cent exceeded the overall guidelines, the lowest compliance being for the period between first appearance and committal;

- in either-way offences, the guidelines for the period between mode of trial and committal were exceeded in 40 to 45 per cent of cases.

We acknowledge that the CPS is striving to ensure that committal papers are served in advance of the committal hearing. They recognise that they do not always achieve this and are working to improve the timeliness of file submission by the police so that they, in turn, can improve CPS performance. In 1998–9, the CPS sent committal papers to the defence within the agreed timescales in 51.9 per cent of cases.[6]

However, the inescapable fact is that existing PTI time guidelines, particularly in summary not-guilty cases where the accused gives a defence statement, do not allow sufficient time for the disclosure procedure to be gone through adequately before trial.

Indictable-only cases sent under s.51 Crime and Disorder Act 1998

At the preliminary hearing in the Crown Court, a date will be set for service of the prosecution case.

MILESTONES: SIGNIFICANT STAGES IN RESPONDING TO DISCLOSURE AND NON-DISCLOSURE

The review of police investigations in Chapter 2 looked at the path of testimonial investigation and the path of forensic investigation. You also are committed to an investigative path – a path of actively defending your client. This path is characterised by significant milestones, each of which tests your ability:

- to manage the growing mass of information on your client's case;

- to investigate the prosecution evidence, the police case and the police investigation;

- to analyse the information disclosed so that you can both respond and think and act proactively, particularly through further investigation.

At each milestone you will need to bring to bear your knowledge of what should happen in a police investigation (Chapter 2) and of the multiple barriers to effective performance by police officers and individuals tasked with forensic investigation (Chapters 3 and 4).

Each milestone is an occasion:

- to analyse and to take stock of the information obtained so far;
- to consider the implications of this for the prosecution and defence cases;
- to make decisions about the actions to be taken as a consequence, particularly defence investigation.

At each milestone you should:

- consider what could undermine the prosecution and defence cases;
- assess the relative strengths and weaknesses of the prosecution and defence cases;
- have in mind not only the defence that the client wishes to pursue but also any others that may be available.

Cases fall into different categories, depending upon their seriousness and complexity. There are some simple pleas of not guilty where there is only one issue and no other material will assist. However, to ensure quality and consistency in the defence of your clients, the systems you use in all cases should be the same. Only the degree to which they are used will reflect the difference in approach that results from personal and professional judgement in identifying the category into which a particular case falls.

A. Police station

This is the first milestone. Chapter 9 gives clear advice on this stage, in particular:

- the information that the police should have, but may not reveal;
- the information that you should attempt to obtain from the police;
- how to negotiate disclosure of information.

243

At this stage of the investigation, the prosecution evidence and the police case will be at their most vulnerable to systematic examination. For example, in many instances, formal statements will not have been taken and interviewing will be based upon first accounts contained, or derived from, notes, pocket book entries and handover documentation. In many instances, investigating officers will not have been to the scene and will lack any form of visual representation to assist them. They may possess object or forensic evidence the existence of which they will not refer to, and will therefore not become an issue, unless you specifically ask if a given type of evidence exists.

Furthermore, that which is 'held up the sleeve', while the officer may believe it to be conclusive, may be very far from this, e.g.

- In the case of fingerprints, these are cast into doubt:
  - with the removal of a numerical standard – the opinion of the fingerprint bureau officer is open to question, particularly for matches;
  - if eliminatory testing has not taken place.
- In the case of video recordings, there are many factors liable to provide distorted images, e.g. the positioning of the camera (height and distance from what it trained upon), its operation, the quality of the equipment, illumination and ambient conditions.

We are unequivocal in our assertion that actively defending your client means at this stage:

- you must obtain the fullest possible *case narrative* – a briefing containing as much detail as possible on the facts of the matter concerning, the police case, the prosecution evidence, and the police investigation – making the fullest possible notes of this and, optimally, simultaneously tape-recording;
- you must be wholly systematic – methodically working through, and probing about, *every* conceivable form of information and evidence, again recording responses as fully as possible and electronically.

It is imperative, therefore, that you follow the detailed checklists given in the *Pocket Reference*.[7]

> *The police are under no obligation to tell you what they are doing by way of investigation and what information or evidence they have to hand and upon which they may rely. You must therefore ask. Officers are not allowed to lie. Therefore if you ask about something, e.g. whether the evidence to hand includes video recordings, they either have to address*

244

the issue or to avoid telling a lie by using a 'blocking' ploy, ignoring your question and asserting something to the effect that there has been sufficient disclosure and that you should now consider advising your client. Such ploys serve to confirm that the subject of your inquiry is indeed a material issue.

Throughout this stage you must consider the relevance and significance of:

• what has, or has not, been revealed by the police;

• what has been disclosed by your client.

One among many issues may be that of alibi and what needs to be done to establish it.

Subsequent actions to be taken will in many instances include steps:

• to obtain information that has not been revealed;

• to undertake investigations that the police did not carry out.

B. Tape recordings of police interviews

Chapter 3 indicated the factors that sustain the predominance of the confession as a prime investigative aim. What goes on in the interview room, and admissions by your client, have a fundamental bearing upon the prosecution case and the defence case. The records of these significant changes contain vital evidence. The only indisputably authentic record is the tape recording. All too often, however, the ROTI and the SDN are offered by the prosecution and accepted by the defence as accurate written records of the interview. Their contents go unchallenged by those who accept that the record fulfils guidelines[8] providing:

'a balanced, accurate and reliable summary of what has been said which contains sufficient information to enable the Crown prosecutor to decide whether a criminal prosecution should proceed, whether the proposed charges are appropriate, what lines of defence to anticipate and what mode of trial is appropriate.'

The logic for this acceptance is not difficult to explain:

• the criminal justice system is predominantly a 'paper' system: everyone working within it has greater facility working with the word on the page since this can be read anywhere, annotated, and particular points, utterances and exchanges can be readily located, discussed and disputed;

- the intonation of an utterance – which provides clues to difference in emphasis and nuance in meaning – can be a matter of dispute with parties suggesting the words were said in a particular way (when in fact the only true record is the tape);

- tape recordings are not user-friendly: for most people it is difficult if not impossible to locate accurately a particular point, utterance or segment in a tape recording – most playback machines have trip-meters unlike machines in the police service and in courts (but not all courts), which have minute and second timers;

- you cannot mark a tape – a full transcript is still required, which needs to be prepared from the tape recording and its accuracy verified.

All the research evidence indicates that a high price is paid for the convenience of written records and avoiding the inconvenience of working with tape recordings. In Chapter 3 we indicated that police officers are particularly poor at preparing written records of interviews. Research for the RCCJ found that police officers 'because of their temperament, aptitude, educational background, tradition and training are unlikely to be predisposed to summarise complex materials in a way that can safely be relied upon by other parties.'[9]

Other official research[10] found that in four out of 10 cases, a ROTI prepared by a police officer is inaccurate. Civilians are markedly better at preparing ROTIs than the police. A higher proportion of ROTIs prepared by the police compared to civilians in complex cases contained prosecution bias – 45 per cent compared to 29 per cent – and were judged to be inadequate – 42 per cent compared to 18 per cent.

Up until now, the Law Society has advised solicitors who doubt the reliability of a written record of an interview – the ROTI or the SDN – that it is necessary to listen to the tape recording in the following circumstances.

- When the client:
  - instructs the solicitor to do so;
  - is unable to confirm the accuracy of the contents of the summary; or
  - is a juvenile or a mentally disordered or mentally handicapped person.

- If the client is uncertain about how to plead or intends to plead not guilty:
  - where the written record is materially disputed and resolution of the dispute is relevant to the conduct of the case;

- where the client complains of oppression or circumstances tending to create unreliability in the confession made by the client;
- where the solicitor is informed by the client, or the solicitor present at the interview, that the 'tone', timing, phrasing or intonation in the interview, as would be disclosed by the tape recording, is relevant to the conduct of the defence and is not apparent from the written record;
- where the CPS and/or prosecuting counsel has listened to the tape in the course of preparing the prosecution case.

The Legal Aid Board agreed that it is reasonable in principle for solicitors to listen to tape recordings of police interviews where the client cannot confirm that the summary is correct.[11]

The Lord Chancellor's Department was consulted about and gave its approval to the Law Society's guidance.

We argue that it is not just a case of doubt as to accuracy, of putting the onus on the client to recall what happened and to judge the written record, of manifest client vulnerability, or indecision about which way to plead. It is the solicitor's professional duty to defend actively his or her client by analysing the content of the tape recording, bringing to bear professional awareness of:

- problematic interviewing behaviours exhibited by interviewers and interviewees;
- questioning with a potential for the interview to be ruled inadmissible under PACE, ss. 76 and 78;
- clues to 'off-tape' interviewing.

We are unequivocal in our argument that actively defending your client means:

- you must listen to the tape recordings of interviews of your client – Chapter 8 spells out what you need to look for as you listen;
- you must never accept a ROTI or an SDN as an authentic (summary) record of an interview until such time as it has been checked for accuracy with the tape recording.

If, after listening to the tape recording, you consider the interview forms a substantive issue in the defence of your client:

- you will need to prepare or obtain a transcript of part or all of the interview. Application may be made to the appropriate area committee for prior authority to incur the cost of bespeaking a transcript. If the transcription is undertaken in-house, this work will be an overhead of your practice and not recoverable from the legal aid fund;

- you will need to instruct an expert in the analysis of the interviewing behaviour of your client and those who questioned him or her – with particular reference to any confession made during the interview.

If you cannot agree a record of interview or transcript, you must notify the prosecution.[12]

C. Bail hearing at court

Chapter 6 explained:

- how the prosecutor will have received a case file from the police and may also have been briefed verbally;

- the type of file that the prosecutor will have: details of their contents are given in Appendix 5.

The file can be a valuable source of information. Notwithstanding the time constraints, using the techniques explained later in this chapter and analysing the material in the manner described in Chapter 8, you need:

- to identify shortcomings in the material;

- to take appropriate corrective action.

D. Advance information

In many cases, this will be your first sight of the available prosecution evidence. *Only witness statements are acceptable.*

Only witness statements are acceptable because of the inevitable outcome of summarising by police officers. Their task is to edit and compress in order to present a brief account with contents inherently supportive to the prosecution. The risks are obvious: the deletion of essential contextual detail, including reported utterances, disclosed by witnesses as well as the many forms of anomaly to be found in testimony: detail and anomaly with a potential to undermine the prosecution case.

You must make yourself fully conversant with the forms of anomaly to be found in testimony. These are described in detail in *Analysing Witness Testimony*.[13]

You must examine the material closely:

- to consider:
    - whether there is a prima facie case;
    - the strength of the prosecution case (including the admissibility and availability of the evidence);
    - the merit of putting the prosecution to proof;
    - the advantage of claiming a sentence discount for a plea of guilty;
    - plea; and when the plea should be entered;
    - mode of trial;
    - type of committal;
    - the likelihood of obtaining bail;

- to identify shortcomings in the evidence and missing evidence – taking the appropriate action to correct these.

E. Prosecution witness statements in summary cases

These should be available following a plea of not guilty.

Chapter 8 gives detailed advice on how to analyse statements to identify both shortcomings and missing statements.

Such fine-grain analysis will enable you:

- to request the prosecutor to supply the statements of all prosecution witnesses who are to be called at the trial;

- to bring to his or her attention statements that would appear not to have been included.

At this stage you will need to obtain further instructions from your client and to consider:

- which witnesses need to give oral evidence;

- whether expert evidence is required;

- to instruct suitable experts to provide reports, subject to the availability of legal aid. Chapter 14 provides advice on these matters.

F.   Committal bundle/service of prosecution case following sending or transfer

Chapter 8 gives detailed advice on how to analyse statements and other forms of evidence in order to identify shortcomings and missing material.

Your fine-grain analysis will enable you:

*   to bring shortcomings and missing material to the prosecutor's attention;

*   to request the disclosure of:

    –   material able to resolve the shortcomings in the material in question;
    –   the missing material you have identified.

At this stage, you will need to obtain further instructions from your client and to consider:

*   which witnesses need to give oral evidence;

*   the likelihood of expert evidence to counter the prosecution case or assist the defence;

*   the availability of legal aid to enable the instruction of an expert: see Chapter 14;

*   preparing a brief for the trial advocate;

*   drafting the defence statement.

G.   Prosecution primary disclosure: unused undermining material and schedule

By this stage, your fine-grain analyses of the evidence may have brought to the attention of the prosecutor manifest indications of shortcomings, questioning already the status of the police case.

This stage provides an opportunity to gain a bigger picture of the police investigation and its outcome when the prosecutor should disclose:

*   material that in his or her opinion may undermine the prosecution case;

*   a schedule of the other non-sensitive unused material.

Using the same, proven methods that you have applied earlier, you need to analyse this latest material:

- to establish whether there is further unused material that should have been disclosed at this stage: see Chapter 10;

- to provide you with the basis to request disclosure of this material from the prosecutor by reference to the defence statement: see Chapter 12.

H. Prosecution secondary disclosure: disclosure of material that may assist the defence case

At this stage, the aim is to secure disclosure of information that may reasonably be expected to assist the defence disclosed in the defence written statement.

Chapter 11 gives advice on the giving of a defence statement aimed at obtaining secondary disclosure.

You will need:

- to conduct an exhaustive review of the material disclosed thus far;

- where appropriate, to consult with instructed expert witnesses for advice on further material of potential to assist your client's defence;

- to secure unused material which should have been disclosed by this stage.

Annex 1 at the end of this chapter (p. 272) summarises the milestones and indicates where in this book you can find the necessary information on the issues involved in respect of each milestone.

CASE MANAGEMENT SYSTEMS

It goes without saying that you will need to have systems for ensuring the effective and efficient management of your client's case.

Files

How you organise case files will be a matter of personal preference. We can only recommend that you keep separate distinct types of material.

251

1. Material concerning the management of the case – in a large or complex case, you should keep a case management file. You will find it useful:

    - to number sequentially each folio that is placed on the file;
    - to have a *'state of case'* pro forma, an *actions management sheet* and the *case chronology* (see Figure 7.1 p. 253). You may find it convenient to place these in Nyrex, see-through folders, attached to the file as the top folio and/or inside the file cover.

2. Material concerning disclosed information should be kept separate. In a large or complex case, you should keep this in *case information files* – one or more Lever-Arch files, subdivided into sections, each containing the information released at successive milestones.

3. You will find it useful:

    - to reference sequentially each item on the file in each section, e.g. 'PS 4', the fourth item of material obtained (disclosed or discovered) during attendance at the police station;
    - to produce a cumulative index of the material in each section, i.e. reference number, details of item.

4. Material of an exhibit or collated nature should be kept separate. In a large or complex case, you should keep this in *exhibit/master collation files* – Lever-Arch files containing the product of your collation effort, and any appropriate exhibits.

'State of case' pro forma

This is a simple pro forma that shows at a glance the present stage the case has reached. The range of detail included will be a matter of personal preference. An example is given in *Criminal Defence: The Good Practice Guide*.[14]

Case chronology

As indicated above, the case chronology is a useful means of sorting and keeping track of information across the course of your client's case. It is a diary of key events: arising before the offence, during the commission of the offence and during the police investigation. Figure 7.1 gives an illustration of a case chronology.

Appendix 7 gives some advice on how to compile a chronology, either manually or using IT.

CASE CHRONOLOGY: Defendant .... ; **Court**.................... ; **URN**.................... **Date opened**....................
Date updated....................

Date/Time		Item/Event	Reference/Source	Comments/Action
Pre-offence				
Offence				
Police investigation				

Notes:
1. This format can be created manually or using any word-processing package with a 'table' or 'spreadsheet' option.
2. The number of rows is necessarily dictated by the number of *pre-offence, offence* or *investigation* events in the case.
3. The date of update = when events in the chronology are added.
4. The source of the information is entered in the *Reference* column, e.g. committal bundle (CB) page numbers; unused material (UM) page numbers (as paginated by firm); proof of evidence (PE) page numbers.
5. URN = unique reference number.

Figure 7.1 A case chronology

253

ACTIONS MANAGEMENT SHEET: Defendant.................; Court................; URN.................. Sheet number ....

Action number	Action	Who to action	By when	Date initiated	Date completed	Number(s) of further action(s) generated

Notes:
1. A template can be created by using any word-processing package with a 'table' or 'spreadsheet' option.
2. The template serves as a 'master' for photocopying.
3. Entries are made in manuscript.
4. *Number(s) of further action(s) generated*. This column enables you to keep track of a sequence of actions on a given issue or topic.

Figure 7.2 An actions management sheet

254

Actions management sheet

With an actions management sheet you can translate action planning into reality. It provides the means to keep track of the assignment of actions, the progress of actions and the outcome of actions by you and others. As such, it is an essential means for ensuring continuity and monitoring progress. The latter is essential. The actions management sheet enables you to enter an action and to specify 'by when', making an entry for the point when to chase up the absence of a response or apparent inaction.

Figure 7.2 on page 254 gives an illustration of an actions management sheet.

A MODEL OF SYSTEMATIC INVESTIGATION

Your ability to engage in active defence, to respond appropriately at each of the significant milestones, rests fundamentally on your ability to investigate exhaustively and effectively. What is on the line is your capacity to manage and to respond to information arising across the course of your client's case.

The process of investigation is a continuous cycle of decision-making and action. It enables you:

•   to gain access to information by methodical processes of planning and actions;

•   to gain a systematic understanding of the information, particularly features and characteristics about the information which under other circumstances would be far from obvious.

You can remember the processes involved in gaining this very special access to information by the letters of the acronym *ACCESS*:

•   **a**ssess;

•   **c**ollect;

•   **c**ollate;

•   **e**valuate;

•   **s**urvey;

•   **s**ummarise.

The way in which these processes relate to each other is shown in Figure 7.3. You will be engaging in these processes throughout your active defence of your client. These processes are common to every step, to every milestone, to every occasion when you have:

- to consider the situation that confronts you, the information you have, the information you need, how you are going to get it;

- to go out and get it;

- to record or store what you have gathered;

- to work upon the information you have (your information base);

- to reappraise the situation.

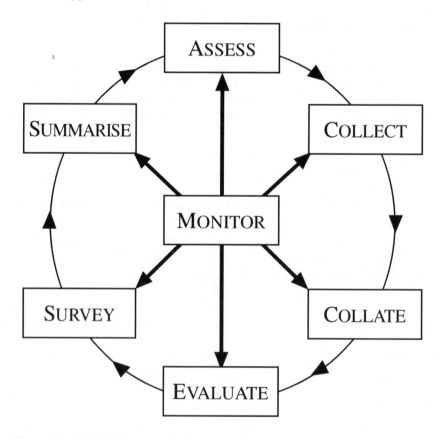

Figure 7.3 ACCESS'M: the processes of systematic investigation

It is noteworthy that the ACCESS model is now taught to officers attending advanced investigative interviewing as an easily learned and implemented way to approach the process of investigation. In the following sections we describe the typical activities involved in each process.

Assessing the situation confronting you

The police service is devoting substantial effort in seeking to convince its officers through PEACE and other guidelines[15-19] that professional investigation rests squarely upon the investigator being aware of the key issues and assessing the situation that confronts the officer. Since investigation lies at the heart of active defence, a solicitor faces a similar imperative.

In simple terms you need:

- to know what information you have concerning the police case, the prosecution evidence and the police investigation;
- to establish what further information you need to obtain, from where, in what time frame, and how. This implies a conscious plan of action and a detailed 'wants' list, i.e. specific questions that need answering or a checklist of areas to be covered.

You need to keep track of your assessment and its outcome by:

- entering details in the case management file;
- making appropriate entries in the action management sheet, i.e. the key facts in respect of your plan of action, 'wants' list, who is to do what, how, and when or in what time frame.

Some practitioners might baulk at such considered thought and specificity. They believe they can cope on the basis of 'having done it umpteen times before'. The risks attendant upon this strategy are high. The practitioner is unaware of many of the issues and is liable to respond inappropriately in the face of obstruction, surprise tactics (unexpected and unwanted conduct) and lack of disclosure. Furthermore, since there is no shared, clear understanding and no record of what needs to be done by way of investigation, by whom and when, the danger is that valuable time is lost and the defence of the client is irreparably damaged.

This book spells out the issues involved. *A Pocket Reference*[20] and *Becoming Skilled*[21] describe issues at each stage of defending in the police station but provide wider insight into police attitudes and conduct, the construction of the police case, the derivation and disclosure of the prosecution evidence and the nature of the police investigation.

We cannot stress enough that you must have a clear idea of what you want to do and what you want to find out at whatever stage you are at in defending your client. It is not an accident that in the armed services all those who aspire to conduct and to win battles observe unswervingly a basic principle: time spent in reconnaissance is never wasted.

Collecting the information you require

The process of collection implies communication. In the vast majority of cases, to achieve your specified aims and objectives, this will be through managed conversations with key individuals, e.g. at the police station, at court, on the telephone to the CPS or the police.

Your management of these conversations will demonstrate the benefit of considered assessment of the situation. Your requests, questions and responses will be guided, and rendered more confident, by you having a clear plan of action, a 'wants' list and checklists.

In the police station

In the police station there will be a heavy emphasis upon collecting information in face-to-face encounters. Your access to documentary material is likely to be restricted to what you are entitled to, e.g. sight of the custody record, pocket book entries and other material officers are prepared to disclose. Other disclosure will be severely regulated. When defending in the police station, you must have a crystal-clear idea of what must be asked for given that you cannot count on being told.

Legal advisers who are not qualified solicitors must go through the process of accreditation and are obliged to be aware of the issues and to engage in systematic practices, particularly in the process of implementing checklists[21] and negotiating disclosure. Qualified solicitors are not subject to an accreditation process. This has created a paradox, noted by police officers who inevitably make assessments of the relative performances of those advising in the police station. They cannot fail to note when the performance of some solicitors contrasts markedly with the methodical practice exhibited by unqualified legal advisers, who are either probationary or who have achieved accreditation.

It is still the case that all too many practitioners do not use comprehensive checklists, do not assert themselves in the face of inappropriate behaviour, and do not seek to engage in principled negotiation. In so doing they do their clients a disservice since the likelihood of disclosure is paradoxically greater at this stage than at any other: not least because the police case, the prosecution evidence and the police investigation are likely to be at their most vulnerable to focused questioning. Furthermore, such questioning to negotiate disclosure is fundamental to the skilful defence of the client since it is upon police response to detailed probing that advice will be given as to the exercise of the right to silence.

In this we are unequivocal. In the police station, follow best practice for skilful, active defence of your client: use the checklists and use focused questioning and negotiation to secure as comprehensive disclosure as possible of the police case, the prosecution evidence and the police investigation.

Using checklists, probing, commenting, observing and summarising in the light of what has been disclosed – or not disclosed – potentially generates a wealth of detail. It is crucial that you obtain copies of material which police have produced or acquired in a collated form, i.e. information contained in event lines, tables, diagrams, charts and sketches.

Stages beyond the police station

After the police station stage, the traditional perspective upon collection has been predominantly passive: the defence being issued with, and being expected to put up with, documentary and exhibit material in measured doses. Active defence runs counter to this perspective. The fact that measured information is handed over does not mean that the recipient is not already thinking and acting ahead of this happening – being proactive – and is not ready to switch into active mode in respect of the current material.

At later stages, you must systematically scan and make a timely response to the material you are given.

1. Do not rush to get it wrong. Tell the person handing over the material that you need to absorb what is there and that you will want to get back to him or her in the light of what you have received.

2. Consult the contents pages.

3. Make a written note of anything that you consider to be inappropriate, inadequate or missing.

4. Switch immediately into response mode – communicate:

   - tell the individual in question – CPS or police – what is inappropriate, inadequate or missing;
   - give (or confirm you will send) to the person a copy of what you have noted;
   - question the individual closely, making a written record, as to:

- the reason for the inappropriate, inadequate or absent material;
- what action is being taken, or instructions have been given, by the individual (or others) to correct the situation;
- who the responsible person is – his or her appointment, name and contact details;
- what the time frame is.

- In effect, you need to secure disclosure of the CPS's or police's action plan.

You must not forget:

- to enter details of the problems in the disclosed material and the substance of your exchange in the case management file;
- to make appropriate entries in the action management sheet, particularly identifying when you or another must chase up matters.

It is imperative that, having acted responsibly and immediately, you do not let matters slip. Act upon what you were told and the entries in the action management sheet.

The logic for doing so is all too clear. Letting the CPS and the police off the hook by not following up the problem actually harms the defence of your client, because you do not have the necessary material to work upon in terms of appropriate collation and analysis.

Verbal exchanges, whether in the police station or at later stages in defending your client, have a drawback. You are exposed to a wealth of detail as the individual responds:

- initially to your focused questioning, i.e. as you work through your 'wants' list or checklist;

- as you probe, comment, observe and summarise, in the light of what has been disclosed – or not disclosed.

The risk here is of being overwhelmed by the detail, missing gaps and anomalies in the individual's responses. You have be methodical in collating – capturing and representing – the detail so that you can work upon it.

Collating the information you have

The problem here is that the majority of information is distributed, i.e. most typically it is not in one place but several. This makes it difficult to access and to represent detail contained within any number of statements, reports, notes, completed forms, tape recordings and exhibits.

You need methods that enable you to gain a rapid and yet detailed grasp of information. People tend to think one is achieved at the expense of the other. It is possible to do both if you use appropriate methods:

- to capture emergent detail from a single source, i.e. an individual's verbal disclosures or detail within a document, and to represent these in a simple, easy-to-grasp form;

- to combine detail from a number of sources – enabling rapid evaluation.

Manual collation methods

You need to employ the collation methods appropriate to the context (e.g. police station; courtroom; your offices) and the content of the disclosure.

Effective collation is really an extension of effective study skills. The effective student knows when to use notes, when to create a graphic representation, to construct a diagram or chart, or to draw a sketch.

Established practitioners vary greatly in their approach to collating material. All too many resemble the student who lacks effective study skills. They lack practice in, and therefore commitment to, notionally more mentally demanding but more effective approaches to capturing and representing information that is being, or has been, disclosed. However, methodical collation is essential to provide you with a valid and reliable information base for subsequent systematic evaluation.

Notes

Solicitors are well used to taking notes from what they are listening to or are reading.

Notes are risky in that:

- you commit yourself to a process of screening – you edit or compress detail, typically into 'gist' understanding, bullet points, keywords, ideas and, occasionally, note key verbatim utterances;

261

- you will differ from others – often markedly so – as to what is deemed to be important or significant;

- your attention will fluctuate as you screen what is being said or has been written – running the risk of not detecting critical detail.

To overcome these problems you need to acquire and use more appropriate methods – which enable rapid, systematic extraction of detail and comprehensive grasp. We are not saying that you should not take notes. We are recommending that you know when an alternative method will capture detail more effectively and efficiently than notes.

We briefly describe below and in Appendix 7 alternative methods of collation, which are adjuncts to conventional notes. They may seem odd and they require more effort (and somewhat more time) than applying your long-established method of note-taking. You may find them irksome or overly demanding, but perseverance will pay handsome rewards. This is because:

- they very quickly reveal shortcomings in the police case, the prosecution evidence and the police investigation;

- they give you at the same time a sound overall and detailed grasp, and memory, of what you are listening to or reading;

- they facilitate the management of information of the active defence of your client through the creation and application of:

  - a *case chronology* – a comprehensive record of key events occurring before the offence, during the offence and after the offence up to the current time;
  - an *actions management sheet* – enabling you to chart and to specify actions taken, or to be taken, by you and others, including the actions planned as a result of your assessment.

With this greater awareness of and ability to manage information, you can communicate quickly, confidently and effectively with members of your staff, your client, counsel, instructed experts, witnesses, the police, the CPS and the court.

Graphic representations

It will be recalled from Chapter 2 that the police, e.g. investigating officers, analysts and researchers, now use graphic methods to represent detail. Graphic methods facilitate analysis, highlight anomalies and assist preparation and planning.

The methods you require should be:

- applicable to written or recorded text from one or more individuals;
- enable collation of detail from one or more texts.

We briefly describe some methods below and return to these in later chapters.

- **SE3R (S – E – three – R)**. This is a graphic method for representing narrative detail. This represents narrative detail graphically and in a form that is easily committed to memory. A sequence of events is translated into a horizontal line going across the page (= the passage of time) and short vertical lines cutting the horizontal, each representing a key event or episode. Date, time and location of the event is written above the vertical line; who was involved and what happened is written below the vertical. Figure 7.4 shows an extract from an event line.

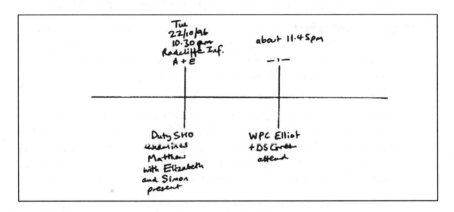

Figure 7.4 An extract from an event line

The amount of detail entered above and below the vertical lines in Figure 7.4 varies according to the objective you are seeking to achieve. Appendix 7 briefly explains SE3R, to enable you to extract fine-grain detail of episodes and identities (people, places, objects) and in so doing detect gaps and anomalies.

- **Software**. There is now computer software entitled **RealSense** that enables you:
  - to perform rapid SE3R analyses on disclosed material;
  - to capture immediately in SE3R format what a person is saying, e.g. the investigating officer giving you disclosure, particularly a

case narrative, in the police station; your client giving you a proof of evidence; a witness whom you have decided to interview, either face-to-face or over the telephone.

RealSense is able to be run on a laptop as well as desktop computers. Further details can be obtained from *Forensic Solutions Limited* (01235 821205; fax 01235 821547).

- *Tabulation of detail*. Tables (or grids) are the best method for collating key detail for the purpose of comparison. Tabulation highlights gaps, ambiguities, vagueness, contradiction and contrasting versions occurring:

  – within the detail of one account or description;
  – between a number of accounts or descriptions.

  Appendix 7 explains how to tabulate events and descriptions to enable fine-grain analysis.

- *THEMA.* This is a particular application of grids to aid the analysis of recordings and transcripts to identify consistency and oddities.

- *Diagrams and charts.* When detail is contained within words, particularly when distributed across a number of documents or recordings, it is difficult to build up a mental image of links, connections and other relationships. The simplest solution is to draw a diagram or chart mapping the details.

  When the detail involves identities and relationships this is called a genogram. It is a method that is widely used in the police service (particularly in SIUs and by officers who have attended advanced interviewing courses), social services and other helping professions. Appendix 7 explains how to construct a genogram.

- *Sketches.* This is simply applying the adage that a picture speaks a thousand words.

  Spoken or written words invite you to conjure in your mind's eye a description of a location, an object, a person, or an arrangement of objects or people. The problem here is that people vary as to the image they construct from the words. The same words can give rise to incorrect or dramatically different representation.

  As a rule of thumb, whenever someone uses words to describe what is really an image, take the effort to draw what is being said.

  When you or someone instructed by you visits a location it is essential that you obtain a visual record. Photographs or video recordings are useful but nothing can replace a sketch:

- for capturing essential detail, e.g. dimensions, directions of movement, fine-grain information;
- for its potential to be annotated.

Appendix 7 explains how to draw and annotate sketches with fine-grain, forensic detail.

Further information on these methods is to be found in *Analysing Witness Testimony*.[23] If you are wedded to bullet or gist notes:

- experiment with translating detail into event lines, tabulating, making diagrams and charts;
- learn how your experiments can:

  - give you a firmer grasp and memory of the fine-grain detail;
  - reveal gaps and anomalies in the police case, the prosecution evidence and the police investigation.

Evaluating the information

Once collected and collated you need to evaluate the information. This involves two processes:

1. *Integration*. All too often practitioners do not pull material together. Instead they move from one consultation to another in the police station or read through the material provided, one document at time. There is little or no effort devoted to extracting information that is distributed across the available aggregation of oral or written testimony. Because of this, many fail to detect multiple versions, gaps, mismatches, contradiction and other anomalies.[24]

   It is essential that you get into the habit of pulling together particular aspects of the base of information you have available to you. Integration requires taking the (minimal) effort to draw up a table or to place two or more event lines, diagrams, charts or sketches beside each other.

   The key activities are selecting, organising and mapping against one another:

   - different accounts or description from the same or different sources;
   - different pieces of information with a potential bearing upon a specific issue, topic or question.

Unless you do this you have little or no prospect of conducting a systematic analysis of detail bearing upon the police case, the prosecution evidence and the police investigation.

2. *Analysis.* Whether you have integrated a number of accounts, descriptions or pieces of information, or you are working on just one selected item, analysis (pulling apart) is the core evaluative activity. Analysis enables you:

   – to examine, highlight, identify and understand features, characteristics and attributes of the detail before you, its source, or indeed the entire case, e.g. match/mismatch, the presence and degree of gap, ambiguity, vagueness, contradiction, contrast and variation – in breadth and amount of detail, at one point in time and across a time span;

   – to test the status of specific detail, its source, or the case, e.g. in terms of validity, coherence, plausibility, credibility;

   – to do something about it, i.e. to plan further investigation, e.g. to resolve gaps and anomalies in the case, in the evidence or in particular accounts and descriptions.

All analysis involves going one step further, going 'beyond the facts'. This is particularly the case in identifying the significance of anything that is not contained within the police case, the prosecution evidence and the police investigation – as represented by the police and the CPS and as represented in your fine-grain collation of detail.

Chapter 3 gave examples of 'curious, non-barking dogs': the existence of missing witnesses, crime reports with no continuation pages, and decisions and actions by police officers made conspicuous by the lack of any record of a decision or action. Chapter 4 gave examples of similar anomalies in the path of forensic evidence.

Your capacity to analyse is greatly enhanced if you know what should, or must, be the case in terms of the journey from offence to evidence.

The timing of evaluation

- *During face-to-face encounters.* During an interview, while collecting and collating detail, you have to be able to identify where further account or further detail, or probing questions, are required.

- *Post hoc evaluation.* After you have collected (or have been provided with) material, and collated this, you need to evaluate this systematically.

Assessing validity and reliability

In Chapter 2, it was explained that police officers should assess the status of information and its source. When you are evaluating detail you must also assess:

* the *validity* of what is being asserted in an account or description;

* the *reliability* of the information.

Validity refers to the extent to which that which is asserted passes muster in terms of:

* logical status and psychological facts of life – most particularly the yardsticks of reasonableness, common sense, or shared understanding of how the world operates and human experience;

* correspondence to physical reality and objective facts, e.g. concerning the scene, its attributes and condition.

Reliability involves a judgement about trustworthiness:

* the *individual's character* – does his or her usual pattern of communication lead one to conclude he or she is trustworthy by disposition?

* the *individual's testimony in the circumstances of the case* – does his or her account lead one to conclude that one can rely upon – have confidence in – what he or she is saying in this matter?

You should be on the look-out for the presence or absence, and degree of:

* *internal consistency* – repetition of particular detail originating from one source, e.g. responses across a single interview; material within a written statement made by, or written down for, an individual;

* *external consistency* – repetition or coming together of particular detail originating from two or more sources, e.g. responses from the same individual in two or more statements or interviews; responses from more than one individual in separate statements or interviews.

Computer analysis of aggregated data

There is software that enables you to collate, query, visualise and analyse aggregated information. Material, e.g. the entire committal bundle, is entered manually or optically scanned into a computer and the software operates on the database in any number of ways. Further information can be obtained from *i2 Limited* (01223 844032).

The outcome of evaluation

The activities of analysis described above ensures that:

- you maintain professional objectivity;

- you are provided with objective, fact-based arguments for further disclosure;

- you are able to withstand attempts at rebuttal by the CPS, the police and the court because you are able to back up your arguments with representations – event lines, tables, diagrams, charts, sketches, which provide the court with an insight into shortcomings that were otherwise far from manifest in the police case, the prosecution evidence and the police investigation.

Survey

Surveying means conducting a methodical, broad, general or comprehensive appraisal of the situation that has emerged from your analysis of the information. It enables you:

- to draw conclusions – particularly in terms of the need to revise your perspective on a given matter;

- to think in terms of the implications and to predict and estimate, e.g. risk, likely actions by key players;

- to identify alternatives, e.g. other lines of enquiry or courses of action.

Summarise

The process of surveying should lead to a straightforward summary of the situation. Optimally, this should be a simple document that spells out the key issues, i.e. where you now stand in respect of the case at this moment.

Thus the summary constitutes a position document, enabling you to assess the situation that confronts you. Thus the investigative cycle begins again.

Notes

1. *The Manual of Guidance for the Preparation, Processing and Submission of Files.* Produced by ACPO and the CPS for internal distribution. First edition 1 April 1992 (updated periodically).

2. *Report of The Working Group on Pre-Trial Issues.* (November 1990), para. 199. The group was chaired by the Lord Chancellor's Department and comprised representatives of the CPS, Home Office, Justices' Clerks' Society, the Legal Secretariat to the Law Officers and the police. It is now named the Trials Issues Group and its membership includes the Law Society.

3. Attorney General. Draft Guidelines on Disclosure: A Consultation Document, 14 February 2000.

4. Crown Prosecution Service. (1999) *Annual Report 1998–9.* London: The Stationery Office.

5. Unpublished.

6. Crown Prosecution Service. (1999) *Annual Report 1998–9.* London: The Stationery Office.

7. Shepherd, E. (1996) *A Pocket Reference.* London: Law Society Publishing.

8. *Police and Criminal Evidence Act 1984: Record of Tape-Recorded Interview.* Home Office Circular 26/1995.

9. Baldwin, J. (1992) *Preparing the Record of Taped Interview. RCCJ Research Study No. 2.* London: HMSO.

10. Hooke, A. and Knox, J. (1995) *Preparing Records of Taped Interviews. Research Findings No. 22.* London: Home Office Research and Statistics Department.

11. Legal Aid Board ref. CRIMLA 35.

12. See Practice Direction (Crime: Tape Recording of Police Interviews: Preparation for Proceedings in the Crown Court), para. 15-246 Archbold (1997), for the solicitor's duties concerning the preparation of tape-recorded interviews for court.

13. Shepherd, E. and Mortimer. A. (1999) 'Identifying anomaly in evidential text'. In A. Heaton-Armstrong, E. Shepherd and D. Wolchover (eds), *Analysing Witness Testimony.* London: Blackstone.

14. Ede, R. and Edwards, A. (1999) *Criminal Defence: The Good Practice Guide.* London: Law Society Publishing.

15. *A Guide to Interviewing.* (1992) Harrogate: Central Planning and Training Unit.

16. *A Guide to Interviewing.* (1996) Bramshill: Police Staff College.

17. *A Practical Guide to Investigative Interviewing.* (1998) Bramshill: National Crime Faculty.

18. Home Office. (1992) *Memorandum of Good Practice on Video-Recorded Interviews with Child Witnesses for Criminal Proceedings.* London: HMSO.

19. ACPO Crime Committee. (1998) *Murder Investigation Manual.*

20. Shepherd, E. (1996) *A Pocket Reference.* London: Law Society Publishing.

21. Shepherd, E. (1996) *Becoming Skilled.* London: Law Society Publishing.

22. Shepherd, E. (1996) *A Pocket Reference.* London: Law Society Publishing.

23. Shepherd, E. and Mortimer. A. (1999) Identifying anomaly in evidential text. In A. Heaton-Armstrong, E. Shepherd and D. Wolchover (eds), *Analysing Witness Testimony.* London: Blackstone.

24. *Ibid.*

ANNEX 1

MILESTONES: WHERE TO FIND RELEVANT INFORMATION

Advice on
The scope for police investigation: what information the police should have obtained and may be available to you.
Possible shortcomings in the police investigation: how you can challenge it and what investigations you may have to carry out.
Prosecution scientific material: its shortcomings and how you can challenge it.
Information you can obtain at the police station: this may not be available later.
Information which the prosecutor has been given in police files and which is potentially available to you from the prosecutor.
Unused material which is revealed to the prosecutor by the police and which is potentially available to you through the prosecutor.
An analysis of prosecution testimony: looking for gaps and anomalies and assessing whether it is a true representation of the person's account.
Unused undermining material and the schedule you should obtain at the primary stage: the material you are entitled to be given.
Unused material which you should obtain at the secondary stage: the unused material which assists the defence disclosed and which you are entitled to.
Providing the justification for the prosecutor to give you unused material.
Sensitive and third-party material: finding out if it exists and getting to see it.
Expert evidence: obtaining legal aid, choosing and instructing an expert.
Other defence investigations which can be carried out: interviewing prosecution witnesses, reconstructing the crime, photographs, plans, sketches, instructing an investigator.

Legend of milestones

A = Police station

B = Tape recording of police interview

C = Bail hearing at court

D = Advance information

A	B	C	D	E	F	G	H	See chapter
●								2, 5, 9
●								3, 9
				●	●			2, 4
●								9
		●	●					6
						●	●	6, 12
	●		●	●	●			8
						●		10
							●	11
							●	11
						●	●	13
				●	●			14
				●	●			14

E = Prosecution witness statements in summary cases

F = Committal bundle

G = Prosecution primary disclosure: undermining material and schedule

H = Prosecution secondary disclosure: disclosure of material which may assist the defence case disclosed

CHAPTER 8

The analysis of disclosed material

DIFFERENT CONTEXTS AND CONTENT – SAME DEMAND TO ANALYSE

Chapter 7 summarises the sequence of disclosure across the course of your client's case and describes milestones, the significant stages in responding to disclosure and non-disclosure. In the course of defending your client, the context and the content of disclosure differ greatly. If you are defending your client at the police station you will be under a wide range of practical constraints, not least because:

- there is very little that the police are obliged to disclose – putting to the test your skills at negotiating disclosure;

- you are working against the clock in a rapidly evolving situation;

- there are substantial and increasing pressures upon you, your client and the police.

When tape recordings are disclosed, time again will be at a premium – taken up with listening to tape recordings, comparing these with ROTIs or the SDN and, where necessary, making arrangements to have a full transcript prepared – involving contact with the Legal Aid Board in respect of resourcing this.

At the bail hearing at court, time will again be precious and the psychological pressures will be different, but still there. Advance information brings its own problems: having to make assessments on 'key' witness statements (or just one statement). The widespread, unacceptable degree of non-compliance with PTI guidelines means that in all too many cases the committal bundle will arrive so late that you will have very little time to assess and to respond to its contents before your client is committed for trial. Given the problems with the timely despatch of committal bundles, it is likely that similar problems will emerge in respect of primary disclosure, putting you under time pressure yet again. Further problems can be expected with secondary disclosure.

The important issue is that at each stage there is the same demand: to analyse the nature of the police case, the prosecution evidence and the police investigation.

THE AIMS AND OBJECTIVES OF ANALYSIS

Your aims in analysing disclosed material are:

- to establish anything that is problematic or missing, leading to questions about the probity and status of the prosecution evidence, the police case and the police investigation that gave rise to these;

- to bring to the attention of the CPS, the court and the police anything that is problematic or missing;

- to use the demonstrably problematic as a prima facie case for the disclosure of what we term their *antecedents*:

  - information recorded in manuscript, computer, pro forma, graphic and audio-visual formats – forms, manuscript notes, computer notes, entries in pocket books, IRBs, diaries, logs, drawings, sketches, illustrations, tape recordings, video recordings, photographs;
  - requests, responses, actions, decisions, verbal exchanges, all forms of questioning and interviewing, briefings, reporting, meetings, preparation and planning, forensic evidence collection, handling, transmission, decision-making, testing and analyses;

- to use anything that is demonstrably missing as a prima facie case for:

  - an explanation of its absence;
  - the disclosure of what has been omitted and its antecedents;

- to plan further investigations of the prosecution evidence, the police case and the police investigation.

THE TOOLS TO ENGAGE IN ANALYSIS

Analysis means minute examination of the constitution of something. To do this in respect of disclosed material you need the requisite knowledge concerning that which is to be analysed and to apply appropriate methods for detecting anomalies, i.e. incongruities within a given process, item of information or evidence, or aggregation of material.

Requisite knowledge

The police investigative process

Fundamental is a sound grasp of what police officers must, should or could, do when deployed to conduct an investigation (Chapter 2) and a clear recognition of the multiple ways in which these shades of imperative are not observed (Chapter 3). Knowing the chronology of actions, which ought to have taken place to achieve effective and ethical investigation, is the starting point. Your contact with the police at the police station and with the prosecutor thereafter, specifically disclosed material and verbal and written exchanges about this, and with others whom you consult, e.g. your client, witnesses in the case, expert witnesses, enable you to identify shortcomings, gaps, the absence of reasonably expected detail, behaviour counter to reasonable expectations, and blatant departures from what the law, directives and guidelines to the police and the CPS specify.

For a basic introduction to issues to do with the gathering of evidence we recommend: Heaton-Armstrong, A., Shepherd, E. and Wolchover, D. (1999) *Analysing Witness Testimony: A Guide for Legal Practitioners and Other Professionals*. London: Blackstone. (Part 2: Investigative Perspectives.)

Basic forensic knowledge

The contribution of forensic science is growing in its application and, commensurately, the requirement to challenge every aspect of purported forensic finding and opinion.

As we pointed out in Chapter 4, there is a disturbing lack of understanding among police officers of the forensic process, i.e. the solution of investigative problems by scientific means. The majority of police officers have received no training in forensic issues. There are no pamphlets or guidelines. The nearest to this is a series of articles in the *Police Review*, which is not subscribed to by all officers. This creates a situation in which many of those responsible for the continuity of forensic evidence and, even those making decisions about what to submit for analysis, are fundamentally ignorant.

In contrast, you must be aware. You cannot afford not to have a background knowledge of forensic science. We recommend the following texts as an introduction: White, P. (1999) *Crime Scene to Court: The Essentials of Forensic Science*. London: Royal Society of Chemistry; Horswell, J. (2000) *The Practice of Crime Scene Investigation*. London: Taylor & Francis.

Annex 1 at the end of Chapter 14 gives further recommended introductory reading on specific aspect of forensic science.

Appropriate methods for detecting anomaly

In Chapter 7 we pointed out that the police, e.g. investigating officers, analysts and researchers, now rely upon graphic methods to collate detail in a manner that enables rapid, comprehensive analysis and highlights anomalies. When conducting active defence, you will need to use similar methods, as well as others, to enable you to analyse rapidly and reliably material that is disclosed and which you gather by your own efforts, or by others at your direction.

We recommend the following as an introduction to the detection of anomaly and appropriate methods to achieve this: Shepherd, E. and Mortimer, A. (1999) 'Identifying anomaly in evidential text', in Heaton-Armstrong, A., Shepherd, E. and Wolchover, D. (eds) *Analysing Witness Testimony: A Guide for Legal Practitioners and Other Professionals*. London: Blackstone.

Table 8.1 summarises a range of methods for detecting anomaly.

Method	Applications	Details
SE3R	Visual representation of verbal narrative detail e.g. written statement; account given in any form of interview or focused conversation (recorded; live face-to-face/telephone). Converts detail into episodes on an event line, and sorts large amounts of descriptive detail, in formats that allow convenient, rapid analysis.	See Appendix 7 and 'Identifying anomaly in evidential text' (Shepherd and Mortimer). Training available from Forensic Solutions Ltd (01235 821205, fax 01235 821547).
***RealSense* (Software version of SE3R)**	Rapid SE3R representation of narrative detail on laptop or desktop computer. Able to be linked with existing databases of evidence.	See Appendix 7. Software and training available from Forensic Solutions Ltd (01235 821205, fax 01235 821547).

Table 8.1 Methods for detecting anomaly

275

Method	Applications	Details
Tabulation (grids)	Highlights gaps, ambiguities, vagueness, contradiction and contrasting versions occurring: • within the detail of one account or description; • between a number of accounts or descriptions.	See Appendix 7 and 'Identifying anomaly in evidential text' (Shepherd and Mortimer).
THEMA	Particular form of grid method that highlights emergent anomaly (gaps, ambiguities, vagueness, contradiction and contrasting versions) in recordings of any kind.	See 'Identifying anomaly in evidential text' (Shepherd and Mortimer).
Imaging and creating images (sketches)	Identification of critical gaps and what is unstated in text of any kind, i.e. by revealing: when so much detail is missing that it is impossible to create mentally or to draw an image; when imagination is necessary to fill in the gaps and the unstated.	See 'Identifying anomaly in evidential text' (Shepherd and Mortimer).
Diagrams and charts	Brings together detail distributed across a number of documents or recordings, enabling rapid grasp and identification of connections and other relationships.	See Appendix 7 (example of genograms) and 'Identifying anomaly in evidential text' (Shepherd and Mortimer).
Crime reconstruction (experiment; enactment, i.e. role-play)	Testing the validity of asserted detail by recreating that which is asserted.	See Chapter 14 and 'Identifying anomaly in evidential text' (Shepherd and Mortimer).

Table 8.1 *(continued)* Methods for detecting anomaly

Method	Applications	Details
Drawing the crime scene	Best method for capturing the total reality (including measurements) of the scene, the vicinity and entry/exit routes (in contrast to the inherently selective, limited representations of photography and video recordings created by the police and others).	See Appendix 7 and Chapter 14.
Photography	Provides permanent, demonstrable, still record of: • any experiment or enactment revealing assertions to be invalid; • the actual crime scene including vicinity, entry/exit routes, lines of sight, angles, arcs of vision (but not shown in police photography) • Aerial photography (now very inexpensive) provides particularly useful 'overview' images.	

Table 8.1 *(continued)* Methods for detecting anomaly

Method	Applications	Details
Video and audio recordings	Provides permanent, demonstrable dynamic record of: • any experiment or enactment revealing assertions to be invalid; • the actual crime scene including vicinity, entry/exit routes, lines of sight, angles, arcs of vision (but not shown in police photography). Aerial photography provides particularly useful 'overview' images, e.g. demonstrating the impossibility of dragging an individual over the ground and obstacles shown.	

Table 8.1 *(continued)* Methods for detecting anomaly

ANALYSING THE PROSECUTION EVIDENCE, THE POLICE CASE AND THE POLICE INVESTIGATION

The range of prosecution evidence that may be disclosed is extremely wide:

- *statements* – by the victim, witnesses, key police officers, e.g. the FOA, the arresting officer, the IO, the custody officer; police and civilian support staff, e.g. SOCO, technician; specialist investigators, e.g. fire investigation officers; forensic scientists and their assistants, forensic pathologists, medical examiners, other clinicians, e.g. who attended to the victim or the suspect;

- *exhibits* – the custody record, audio recordings of PACE and other interviews, video recordings, e.g. of victim and suspect interviews; of activity in the custody suite; photographs, maps, sketches;

- *antecedents* – arising as:

  - a result of your feedback concerning shortcomings in what has already been disclosed;
  - part of primary disclosure;
  - part of secondary disclosure.

278

Before the introduction of the CPIA, the defence was able to construct a chronological account – albeit partial – of the police investigation by extracting information from the content of statements, the custody record, unused disclosed material and requested additional material, e.g. copies of the crime report (usually only the front page), IRBs, pocket book entries, OIS print-out, medical examiner's notes, sexual offence questionnaires and the like.

Chapter 6 describes how the disclosure officer, in most cases the officer who carried out the investigation, selects and discloses to the CPS – for onward disclosure to the defence and the court – a representation which is deemed:

• to support the police version of events (the police case);

• to be the product of a search for evidence (the police investigation), which was subjected to quality control to ensure its effectiveness and ethical criteria.

What he or she discloses will only reflect the latest stages in a sequence of actions by police officers and others. The CPS, the defence and the court are left in the dark as to:

• the antecedents to the material which the officer chooses to disclose;

• what the officer has chosen not to disclose.

Crucially, it is within the antecedents to the disclosed evidence and what is omitted that proof lies as to:

• the achievement of effectiveness and ethical criteria;

• the observance of legal requirements, official guidelines, best practice and common sense;

• the operation of quality control and supervision.

Chapter 3 describes the problems and pressures in police investigation. Chapter 4 highlights the gap between theory and practice in forensic investigation. There is a wealth of evidence, much of it originating from official research and working groups, that the service comprehensively lacks the resources to engage in, and to ensure, quality investigation. Given this, it would be foolish:

• to assume that the disclosure officer – in most cases the IO – will be ready, willing or able:

- to adopt an impartial perspective upon the probity and status of the prosecution evidence, the police case and the police investigation;
- to conduct a fine-grain examination and quality checks upon the evidence and the processes of investigation – in effect, carrying out a supervisory function that should have been fulfilled by others;
- to bring to the attention of fellow police officers, and the CPS, shortcomings and omissions in the form and content of the evidence or in the conduct of the investigation that generated the evidence;

• not to assume that the disclosure officer will be disposed:

- to engage – or to continue engaging – in defensive avoidance, i.e. ignoring the manifest shortcomings in the police evidence and the police investigation;
- to restrict disclosed evidence to a minimum – reducing the potential for the defence to identify areas of concern;
- to withhold as a matter of course the antecedents to disclosed evidence – since this would reveal shortcomings, which the officer has sought, or been obliged, to ignore;
- to withhold any material that records the conduct of the police investigation – since disclosure would reveal:

  (a) shortcomings in the performance of other officers, if not the officer himself or herself;
  (b) all those individuals to whom the police had spoken, allowing the defence to request disclosure of those not included in the disclosed material; and in those instances where the police chose not to take a statement, to ask why the police did not do so.

DISCLOSURE CONCERNING THE POLICE INVESTIGATION

Common sense argues that the defence and the court should have knowledge of the conduct of the police investigation – not least because of the extensive evidence of the inability of the service to fulfil supervisory and quality controls to ensure effective and ethical performance.

There will be many circumstances where material on the police investigation – minimally crime reports, action books, HOLMES action indexes, entries in pocket books, copies of IRBs, OIS messages and crime desk records, but also manual and computer notes – is not disclosed and should be requested.

However, it is likely that a justification will have to be provided for any request for material on the police investigation. This will rest squarely upon your analysis of the disclosed evidence, which will form the basis for disclosure:

- of antecedents to evidence that is problematic because it has manifest shortcomings;

- of missing evidence and its antecedents.

Active defence therefore involves rigorous analysis of every item of disclosed evidence.

ANALYSING DISCLOSED EVIDENCE

Identifying problematic evidence

Problematic evidence is that which has shortcomings. These come in many forms, either alone or in combination:

- invalid representation – contrary to reality or objective facts;

- ambiguity and equivocal representation – with a double, doubtful or uncertain meaning or nature;

- vagueness, e.g. acting upon information received;

- mismatch – absence of correspondence;

- contradiction – conflicting versions or details;

- gaps – an unaccountable absence of detail where detail could be reasonably expected, e.g. accounts of contact between the victim and the suspect which are apparently wordless or are 'one-sided' in terms of reported speech; missing detail concerning crucial actions constituting a break in narrative continuity;

- omissions.

Some examples of omissions are listed below.

- *Sketches or drawings.* The statement alludes to a sketch or drawing of a significant location, individual, or object but there is no sketch or drawing included in the disclosed material;

- *Absence of material indicative of ADVOKATE checks.* There should be material on:

–   the time the suspect was observed;
–   the distance between the witness and the suspect;
–   issues to do with visibility, including whether the witness wears spectacles or contact lenses and if these were worn at the time of witnessing;
–   obstructions to the witness's ability to see;
–   whether the suspect was known or seen before by the witness;
–   the time delay between seeing the suspect and giving the description.

It is important to check whether the officer taking the statement fulfilled the final criterion, i.e. ensuring that any errors or material discrepancies within and between the witness's earlier versions and the current version are accounted for.

The PEACE model[1] says all of the ADVOKATE checks should be included in the written statement. *This is rarely done completely and very often not done at all.*

•   *Omissions in respect of forensic detail.* The statement of a police officer, member of scientific support staff, medical examiner or an external forensic provider should contain full and specific detail as to his or her involvement in forensic evidence collection, handling, transmission, decision-making and analysis. In all too many cases:

–   statements by police officers make no mention at all of their involvement in these processes;
–   statements by medical examiners and forensic scientists are far from complete;
–   statements do not list items and CTM collected, selected *and NOT selected* for testing and analysis, consultations concerning selection, and the reasons for decisions taken (particularly not to submit specific items or material for testing);
–   statements by forensic bureau officers do not give a detailed description of marks they classify as 'outstanding', of 'no value', or having 'insufficient detail for comparison purposes' and do not justify these classification (an essential requirement now that there is no numerical standard).

•   *Procedural anomalies.* E.g.

–   absence of sketches or diagrams by a witness, e.g. of a location, relative positions, descriptions – or by a police officer, e.g. of the scene, of the vicinity;
–   absence of signatures and details of the person witnessing a statement.

- *Language anomalies*. The vocabulary and verbal constructions are unlikely to have been the actual words of the witness, e.g. polysyllabic words; words that rarely occur in the vernacular (such as the verb *to alight*).

It will be clear that many of these anomalies are the product of inadequate or inappropriate investigative performances and practices described in Chapters 3 and 4.

Missing evidence

Missing evidence comprises the many instances of 'non-barking dogs': material that you could reasonably expect to be there but is absent, e.g.

- individuals referred to in disclosed statements but for whom no statements are to be found in the disclosed material;

- individuals of whom it can be inferred were involved in contact with the police but to whom there is no direct reference in the disclosed material, e.g. people spoken to by an FOA searching the vicinity or in house-to-house enquiries; those witnesses whose accounts are deemed to duplicate the single 'key' statement submitted in an abbreviated file;

- individuals involved in the police investigation for whom there are no statements, e.g. SOCO or scientific support staff conducting in-force tests.

'Non-barking dogs' can only be detected if:

- you examine evidence in fine-grain detail such that you spot silent identities and instances when a natural, reasonable response or action did not take place;

- you know what happens in the search for testimonial and forensic evidence.

ANALYSING STATEMENTS

Chapter 2 explains that testimonial evidence forms the substantive basis for the prosecution case, with forensic playing in most cases a much smaller part. You must therefore become an expert at analysing statements in order to identify anomaly.

The identification of anomaly – incongruity – in evidential text is comprehensively covered in *Analysing Witness Testimony*. It summarises some of the many forms of incongruity.

- *Deficiencies in detail.*
  - Deficient descriptions.
  - Failure to identify key individuals: the use of the passive voice obscuring identification, e.g. *The knife was handed to me.*
  - Conversational deficits, e.g. an account of an encounter but without mention of words exchanged; an account that describes a one-sided conversation – what one said but with no reference to what the other said.
  - Discontinuity: the narrative 'jumps' or there is a missing link in reasoning.
  - Empty accounts: a superficial account, lacking detail throughout.
  - Missing statements: there is a reference or allusion to one or more individuals for whom there are no disclosed statements.

- *Anomalous contrast.*
  - Incongruous use of language: language in key parts of the account does not match the remainder, suggesting the words came from someone other than the giver of the statement.
  - Narrative contrast: different stages of the narrative are characterised by varying degrees of detail, with overdetailed and underdetailed episodes being potentially significant.
  - Extraordinary detail, e.g. *A white, plastic bag with draw string handles, measuring about 40 centimetres by 40 centimetres,* suggests the words came from someone other than the statement giver.
  - Invalid descriptions: counter to psychological and physical reality (the 'laws of nature') or what can be observed to be the case, e.g. mismatch between the description of an aspect of the scene, *he pushed the shed door in,* and the actuality 'on the ground' – the shed door swings out; disparity between asserted height and actual height).
  - Incongruous variation and contradiction.

- *Inconsistency.*
  - Evolving descriptions: the description changes gradually across two or more accounts from an individual.
  - Differing versions: incompatible versions of an incident or a description.
  - Migrating detail: significant detail disclosed in the statement of one witness crops up in an account subsequently obtained from one or more other witnesses.
  - Ratcheting: in a sequence of alternate interviewing of two witnesses giving rise to a run of statements, each modifies what is said in the light of knowing beforehand (or being told in interview) what the other one said.

The detection of such anomalies rests heavily upon systematic collation.

Collating information from statements

Clearly, this involves reading the statement. Wherever possible, get into the habit of *double-pass reading*, i.e.

* *Skim-read the statement in its entirety*. Read at slightly faster than normal speed. Do not stop to go back. The aim is to gain an overall picture, or grasp, of the informativeness of the individual's assertions, i.e. the range of information given and the level of detail.

* *Reread the statement*. This time read a chunk at a time, extracting information systematically. You will find that your skim-reading will make the material more familiar, easier to absorb, to picture in your mind's eye, to hold in memory and to examine in detail.

The methods you use to collate as you reread the document will vary according to context.

In the police station

On those occasions when you are allowed to read statements, we strongly recommend that you use graphic approaches since these are the most reliable means of capturing a breadth of detail for subsequent analysis. Use any of the following as appropriate:

* *SE3R* – applied manually and/or its software version *RealSense* on a laptop computer;

* *sketches* – of verbally described detail, where no sketch or diagram has been obtained from the statement giver;

* *tabulation (grids)* – enabling the detail of two or more statements to be compared.

The more you practice graphic methods, the more adept you will become at them, such that you will be able to produce these quickly.

At court

Although you may have little time when served with information at court, again we recommend graphic approaches wherever possible. The time spent systematically collating information using these methods at court will be amply repaid in those instances – of which there will be many – in which you are able to demonstrate visibly to the CPS and the court fundamental shortcomings within a statement. This is particularly important when you are confronted with 'key' statements, or a single 'key' statement, as a central element of an expedited file.

At later stages in the defence of your client

When you are served with statements or similar text, we recommend that you use, as many of the methods as possible listed in Table 8.1 (see p. 275).

We stress that you must be prepared to check out the assertions within the detail by visiting the scene and conducting other investigations as described in Chapter 14.

Technical statements

Statements by fire officers, medical examiners, clinicians, forensic scientists, pathologists and other specialists tend to be technical. The recommended reading will assist you in making sense of their approach, their methods and basic technical terminology.

Appendix 9 contains a glossary of common forensic terms.

You need to instruct an appropriate expert to analyse specialist statements (see also Chapter 14). He or she will be able:

• to translate the technicalities into lay language;

• to tell you if the analyses, the results and the specialist's conclusions and opinions are open to question;

• to give you the basis of an argument for the disclosure of antecedents to the specialist's statement.

Problematic statements with no forensic content

Statements with forensic content are those made by police officers and others involved with forensic evidence collection, handling, transmission, decision-making and analysis. These are dealt with in the next section.

In some instances, you will have more than one linked statement. This is another reason why you need to adopt the double-pass method of reading statements. The first skim-read is an aid to identifying linked statements. Obvious examples of linked statements are:

• a number of statements made by a complainant;

• eyewitnesses to the offence.

Action

You must carry out a systematic analysis:

- if there are linked statements arrange these in chronological order;
- take the statement (or the first occurring in a sequence) and make a note when you detect any shortcomings – you will most easily detect these by inspecting the detailed content of the event line and identity bins;
- where there are linked statements open up a table;
- proceed to the next statement and repeat the collation process;
- when you have completed all linked statements:
  - compare the event lines and identity bins derived from the statements;
  - make a note of any anomalies revealed by your comparison;
  - read across the rows of your table;
  - make a note of any anomalies revealed.

The shortcomings and anomalies you have identified provide you with the basis:

- to question the status and the origin of the statement or statements you have analysed and found wanting;
- to request police disclosure of antecedents to the statement or statements in question;
- in the case of a single 'key' statement, to require statements from all witnesses and antecedents to these statements.

Tracking antecedents to problematic statements with no forensic content

Table 8.2 summarises common antecedents to a statement with no forensic content. It enables you to track and to identify the antecedents to the statement in question, i.e. the material:

- that the CPS, the court and the defence have a right to know about;
- for which the identified shortcomings in the statement(s) constitute a prima facie case for police disclosure.

When tracking which antecedents will need to be disclosed, bear in mind that:

- the chain of recorded actions differs slightly according to the type of offence: control room (offences requiring immediate response), crime desk (screened crimes, e.g. volume offences), crime report (all offences), actions book (in larger cases where the crime report is insufficient to record a very large number of actions), HOLMES action index (in major or serious series crime), crime information system forms (all offences), pocket books (all offences), manual and computer notes (either or both);

- some offences involve actions by, and witness and suspect contact with, specialists, e.g. sexual offences imply contact with SIU personnel and a medical examiner or clinician; offences against property imply contact with the crime desk and a SOCO;

- in the case of shortcomings and anomalies within second or subsequent statements by the same individual, for each additional statement it will be necessary to request antecedents occurring in the final column of Table 8.2.

Problematic statements with forensic content

Statements with forensic content are those made by police officers and others involved with forensic evidence collection, handling, transmission, decision-making and analysis.

In some instances you will have more than one linked statement, e.g the statements by the SOCO, a member of the fingerprint bureau, and the external forensic scientist; statements by a general practitioner who examined a complainant and a consultant paediatrician; statements by a fire investigation officer from the local fire brigade and the external forensic scientist.

It does not require technical or scientific knowledge or expertise to detect shortcomings is such statements. Chapters 2 to 4 provide enough knowledge to enable you to carry out a non-technical analysis. You should be able to identify:

- statements by police officers and others involved in the path of forensic investigation, which make little or no mention of:
  - the processes of forensic evidence collection, handling and decision-making;
  - their involvement or the involvement of others in these processes;
  - advice and warnings given to individuals;
  - the nature of the scene, its condition and the location of objects, items and CTM;
  - ambient conditions;

- items and CTM protected, collected, selected or not selected for testing and analysis and the logic behind these decisions;
- the presence of unidentified fingerprints found at the scene of the crime and the result of eliminator tests;
- mutual contact with, or between, the victim and the suspect constituting the basis for contamination;
- the continuity of evidence;
- the occurrence and content of briefings, discussions, requests, consultations and other communication in respect of CTM submitted or not submitted for testing or analysis;

- the absence of statements by the SOCO and by scientific support technical staff conducting in-force tests or examining fingerprints (see next section).

The services of an expert are necessary to analyse any forensic statement from a technical standpoint.

Action

You must carry out a non-technical analysis:

- if there are linked statements arrange these in chronological order;

- take the statement (or the first occurring in a sequence) and make a note when you detect any of the shortcomings listed above – you will most easily detect these by inspecting the detailed content of the event line and identity bins;

- where there are linked statements open up a table;

- proceed to the next statement and repeat the collation process;

- when you have completed all linked statements:

    - compare the event lines and identity bins derived from the statements;
    - make a note of any anomalies revealed by your comparison;
    - read across the rows of your table;
    - make a note of any anomalies revealed.

You need to be particularly alert to:

- any statement made by a fingerprint bureau member – with particular reference to:

    - what standard of agreement was applied – the number of matches should be stated explicitly;

Antecedents to a single/initial statement		
Contact with others prior to police contact	**Contact with police, scientific support staff and external providers of services**	
Actions by witness and others	*Request for police response*	*Initial actions*
Verbal exchanges between witness and one or more other individuals, e.g. relative, neighbour, social worker, GP, teacher = significant utterances/conversation: • notes made by witness; • notes made by other person; • sketches by witness; • sketches by other person	Control room record: • logged/recorded telephone call = significant utterances/conversation; • manual log; • completed pro formas; • OIS entries Crime desk record: • logged/recorded telephone call = significant utterances/conversation; • manual log; • completed pro formas; • computer entries SIU, e.g. child protection team, record: • logged telephone call = significant utterances/conversation; • manual log; • completed pro formas; • diary entry; • computer entries	Control room tasking/assignment of response: • messages = significant utterances/conversation; • OIS entries Crime desk tasking/assignment of response: • calls made = significant utterances/conversation; • manual log; • completed pro formas; • computer entries SIU tasking/assignment of response: • calls made = significant utterances/conversation; • manual log; • completed pro formas; • diary entry; • computer entries FOA: • calls made to/contact with witness = significant utterances/conversation; • urgent radio messages – including first description; • actions at scene; • pocket book entries; • notes; • sketches by officer; • sketches by witness; • diary entries; • computer entries SOCO: • significant utterances/conversation with witness/others present at scene during SOCO visit; • notes taken at scene; • notes made after visit to scene; FOA handover to IO: • verbal briefing = significant utterances/conversation; • pro formas; • notes of FOA/arresting officer; • notes of IO; • computer entries Crime report: • manual entries; • computer entries; • actions requested, directed and taken CRS (crime reporting system): • manual entries; • computer entries Actions book: • manual entries; • computer entries; • actions requested, directed and taken HOLMES: • entries; • actions requested, directed and taken; • manual notes; • computer notes

Table 8.2 Antecedents to a statement with no forensic content

Antecedents to a single/initial statement	
Contact with police, scientific support staff and external providers of services	
Secondary (follow-up) actions	*Interview leading to witness making the statement*
Interviewing by FOA/IO: • preparation and planning notes; • notes of interview; • audio/video recording of interview; • sketches made by witness; • sketches made by officer Witness visits to scene with IO: • preparation and planning notes; • notes; • audio/video recording; • sketches made by witness; • sketches made by officer Briefing of ME (medical examiner) = significant utterances/conversation: • notes of briefing officer; • notes of ME Disclosures made by individual during examination by ME = significant utterances/conversation: • ME's notes; • notes made by other person present during examination (where applicable); • ME's report Disclosures made by individual during examination by clinician (other than ME) = significant utterances/conversation: • clinician's notes; • notes made by other person present during examination (where applicable); • clinician's report to police (police officer's notes; clinician's notes) Sexual offence questionnaire Disclosures during construction of photo fit/E-fit = significant utterances/ conversation: • officer's notes; • officer's pocket book entries Disclosures during identification procedures = significant utterances/conversation: • notes of officer i/c ID procedure Crime report: • manual entries; • computer entries; • actions requested, directed and taken CRS: • manual entries; • computer entries Actions book: • manual entries; • computer entries; • actions requested, directed and taken HOLMES: • entries; • actions requested, directed and taken; • manual notes; • computer notes	Briefing of officer obtaining statement = significant utterances/conversation: • pro formas; • notes of briefing officer; • notes of officer briefed Interviewing by officer = significant utterances/conversation: preparation and planning notes; • notes of interview; • audio/video recording of interview; • sketches made by witness; • sketches made by officer Draft statement Sexual offence questionnaire (if not completed earlier) Crime report: • manual entries; • computer entries; • actions requested, directed and taken; CRS (manual entries – on forms; computer entries) Actions book: • manual entries; • computer entries; • actions requested, directed and taken HOLMES: • entries; • actions requested, directed and taken; • manual notes; • computer notes

Table 8.2 *(continued)* Antecedents to a statement with no forensic content

- whether eliminatory tests were conducted, i.e. in addition to checking your client's prints, the police should have taken prints from all officers, civilian support staff and all external forensic providers who attended as well as those who live at, or have had occasion to visit the scene;

• any statement made by a medical examiner in the police station.

Instruct an expert, e.g. a forensic scientist, medical examiner or fire expert, to examine statements – briefing him or her comprehensively, aided by the outcome of your non-technical analysis.

The shortcomings and anomalies you and the expert identify provide you with the basis:

• to question the status and the origin of the statement or statements you have analysed and found wanting;

• to request police disclosure of antecedents to the statement or statements in question;

• in the case of a single 'key' statement, to require statements from all witnesses and antecedents to these statements.

Tracking and requesting antecedents to statements with forensic content

Where you detect, or have been advised of, shortcomings in a statement by an individual involved with forensic evidence collection, handling, transmission, decision-making and analysis, you have the basis to request the antecedents of the problematic statement.

Table 8.3 summarises antecedents to a forensic statement. As with Table 8.2, it must be viewed in the context of the type of case.

In the case of a statement by a medical examiner you must always, as a matter of course, ask for:

• a copy of his or her notes made at or immediately following the examination;

• a copy of the medical examiner's report that he or she will have given to the IO after the examination.

We stress that you need the notes. These contain vital details that will not be reflected in the pro forma format of the report. You must not be fobbed off simply with a copy of the medical examiner's report. Ensure you provide your expert with a copy of the notes and the report.

Antecedents to a statement with forensic content

Request for police response	Initial actions	

Control room record:
- logged/recorded telephone call = significant utterances/conversation;
- manual log;
- completed pro formas;
- OIS entries

Crime desk record:
- logged/recorded telephone call = significant utterances/conversation;
- manual log;
- completed pro formas;
- computer entries

SIU, e.g. child protection team, record:
- logged telephone call = significant utterances/conversation;
- manual log;
- completed pro formas;
- diary entry;
- computer entries

Control room tasking/assignment of response:
- messages = significant utterances/conversation;
- OIS entries

Crime desk tasking/assignment of response:
- calls made = significant utterances/conversation;
- manual log;
- completed pro formas;
- computer entries

SIU tasking/assignment of response:
- calls made = significant utterances/conversation;
- manual log;
- completed pro formas;
- diary entry;
- computer entries

FOA:
- securing of scene;
- instructions given to those present at scene in respect of protection of evidence;
- searching – identification of significant items and CTM and their location;
- protection of forensic evidence;
- removal/collection and packaging of CTM;
- pocket book entries;
- notes;
- list of items and CTM identified, protected, removed;
- sketches by officer;
- diary entries;
- physical contact/transportation of witness and suspect at different points in time = risk of contamination;
- computer entries;
- continuity of evidence, i.e. handover and storage of collected items (identity of person receiving and storage location)

Briefing of SOCO = significant utterances/conversation:
- notes of SOCO;
- notes of briefing officer

SOCO response:
- significant utterances/conversation with those at scene;
- searching – identification of significant items and CTM and their location;
- notes taken at scene;
- crime scene examination form;
- list of items and CTM collected;
- photographs;
- video recording;
- sketches;
- notes made after visit to scene;
- continuity of evidence, i.e. handover and storage of collected items (identity of person receiving and storage location)

FOA/arresting officer handover to IO:
- detail bearing upon actions at scene with particular reference to forensic evidence;
- list of items and CTM removed/collected;
- continuity of evidence

Briefing of ME/forensic scientist = significant utterances/conversation:
- notes of briefed person;
- notes of briefing officer

ME response:
- significant utterances/conversation with those present at scene;
- notes taken at scene;
- scene examination form;
- list of items collected;
- sketches;
- notes made after visit to scene;
- continuity of evidence: handover and storage of collected items (identity of person receiving and storage location)

Forensic scientist response:
- significant utterances/conversation with those present at scene;
- notes taken at scene;
- crime scene examination form;
- list of items collected;
- photographs;
- video recording;
- sketches;
- notes made after visit to scene;
- continuity of evidence: handover and storage of collected items

Fire investigation officer response:
- significant utterances/conversation with those present at scene;
- notes taken at scene;
- scene examination form;
- list of items collected;
- photographs;
- video recording;
- sketches;
- notes made after visit to scene;
- continuity of evidence: handover and storage of collected items

Crime report:
- manual entries;
- computer entries;
- actions requested, directed and taken

CRS:
- manual entries;
- computer entries

Actions book:
- manual entries;
- computer entries;
- actions requested, directed and taken

HOLMES:
- entries;
- actions requested, directed and taken;
- manual notes;
- computer notes

Table 8.3 Antecedents to a statement with forensic content

Antecedents to a statement with forensic content	
Secondary actions	
Briefing of IO by SOCO: • notes of SOCO; • notes of IO; • computer notes Briefing of IO by ME: • notes of ME; • notes of IO; • computer notes Briefing of IO by forensic scientist: • notes of forensic scientist; • notes of IO; • computer notes Briefing of IO by fire investigation officer: • notes of fire investigation officer; • notes of IO; • computer notes Briefing of ME by IO (prior to examination of witness/suspect): • notes of briefing officer; • notes of ME ME examination of witness/suspect: • examination pro forma; • list of samples taken; • packaging of samples; • ME's telephone contact with clinician with knowledge of witness/suspect; • ME's notes; • notes made by other person present during examination (where applicable); • ME's verbal briefing to IO; • ME's report; • continuity of evidence, i.e. handover and storage of collected items (identity of person receiving and storage location) Examination of witness/suspect by clinician (other than ME): • clinician's notes; • notes made by other person present during examination (where applicable); • clinician's briefing of police; • clinician's report to police Samples removed by police officers: • list of samples taken; • notes; • pocket book entries; • continuity of evidence, i.e. handover and storage of collected items (identity of person receiving and storage location) IO consultation with SOCO concerning submission of items/CTM for testing/analysis: • notes of IO; • notes of SOCO; • list of items/CTM submitted for in-force testing; • list of items/CTM submitted for analysis by external forensic provider; • list of items not selected for testing/analysis; • pro formas completed; • HOLAB3 and full details of supporting items submitted;	• continuity of evidence, i.e. handover and storage of collected items (identity of person receiving and storage location) Crime report: • manual entries; • computer entries; • actions requested, directed and taken CRS: • manual entries; • computer entries Actions book: • manual entries; • computer entries; • actions requested, directed and taken HOLMES: • entries; • actions requested, directed and taken; • manual notes; • computer notes

Table 8.3 *(continued)* Antecedents to a statement with forensic content

Antecedents to a statement with forensic content	
In-force testing	*External forensic provider*
Tasking of scientific support technical staff: • briefing given; • questions posed; • tests requested; • notes of briefing officer; • notes of member of technical staff; • computer entries; • continuity of evidence, i.e. handover and storage of items submitted for testing (identity of person receiving and storage location) Testing by scientific support staff: • tests conducted – including eliminator tests in respect of fingerprints; • identity of the individual conducting each test; • results; • conclusions; • recommendations; • communication with IO; • continuity of evidence, i.e. handover and storage of items (identity of person receiving and storage location) Crime report: • manual entries; • computer entries; • actions requested, directed and taken CRS: • manual entries; • computer entries Actions book: • manual entries; • computer entries; • actions requested, directed and taken HOLMES: • entries; • actions requested, directed and taken; • manual notes; • computer notes	Tasking of forensic scientist: • briefing given; • questions posed; • list of items/CTM provided; • list of items/CTM not provided (with reasons); • statements provided; • other background information provided, e.g. photographs, sketches; • tests requested; • conversation with IO; • notes of scientist; • notes of IO Testing by forensic scientist: • tests conducted; • identity of the individual conducting each test; • results; • conclusions; • opinion; • communication with IO; • continuity of evidence, i.e. handover and storage of items (identity of person receiving and storage location); • notes of forensic scientist; • notes of IO Examination by pathologist: • results; • conclusions; • opinion; • communication with IO; • notes of forensic scientist; • notes of IO Crime report: • manual entries; • computer entries; • actions requested, directed and taken CRS: • manual entries; • computer entries Actions book: • manual entries; • computer entries; • actions requested, directed and taken HOLMES: • entries; • actions requested, directed and taken; • manual notes; • computer notes

Table 8.3 *(continued)* Antecedents to a statement with forensic content

Missing statements

The detection of missing statements results from painstaking analysis of the material that has been made available to you.

Action

When you have processed all the disclosed statements:

- take each statement one at a time;
- consult the identity bins, i.e. the details you extracted on all people mentioned in the statement;
- note which people are likely to be a potential source of testimonial evidence with a bearing upon the offence and the conduct of the police investigation;
- check the list of disclosed statements to establish whether these people have made statements which have been disclosed;
- if the individual has made a statement, annotate the identity bin to this effect – cross-referencing it to the statement;
- if there is no statement – place the individual's identity on a list of missing statements.

In respect of statements by police officers, note:

- any reference to speaking to unidentified individuals at the scene or in the vicinity;
- any reference to house-to-house enquiries – which will have involved contact with unidentified individuals;
- any – or paradoxically no – reference to:
  - a request for, attendance by, briefing of, response by, and consultation with the SOCO – but for whom there is no statement;
  - in-force testing by scientific support technical staff – but for whom there is no statement.

Add the unidentified individuals, the SOCO and scientific support staff to your missing statements list.

At this stage:

- assume that the missing statements have been withheld rather than that no statements exist;

296

- use Tables 8.2 and 8.3 to track the antecedents to the statements in question.

Having identified the missing statements and their antecedents you are able:

- to inform the CPS and the court of named individuals, unidentified individuals and police support staff:
  - with a potential to contribute material evidence to the case;
  - for whom there has been no police disclosure of testimonial evidence;
- to provide the CPS and the court with the basis:
  - to ask whether statements have been made;
  - if statements have not been made, to ask why not;
  - if statements have been made, to ask why they were not disclosed; and to direct disclosure of the missing statements and their antecedents.

Analysing missing statements that are subsequently disclosed

These should be analysed in the same way as any statement.

Analysing antecedents to statements

When you receive antecedents of statements as a result of bringing shortcomings and omissions to the prosecutor's attention, or as part of primary or secondary disclosure, the content of antecedents must be compared with the problematic statement or the missing statement.

Action

You must follow a systematic sequence of analysis.

1. Arrange antecedents in chronological order.
2. Analyse the content of the earliest occurring antecedent. If it is a document, treat it as though it were a statement. If it is a recording, follow the procedure described in the next and subsequent sections.
3. Prepare a grid – see Appendix 7 – entering key detail from the antecedent.
4. Process each subsequent antecedent in the same way as the first.

5. Enter key detail from the statement the content of which you, or your expert, found to be problematic or from the missing statement.

6. Examine the grid for anomalies.

ANALYSING TAPE RECORDINGS OF PACE INTERVIEWS

In the vast majority of cases, PACE interviews will be audio-recorded or video-recorded. These PACE recordings are a vital source of material in the active defence of your client.

Chapters 3 and 7 highlight the widespread shortcomings in the preparation of ROTIs. SDNs have similar shortcomings. These will be discussed in a later section on the analysis of these two types of document.

Action

You must check that:

• you have been issued with copies of all PACE recordings;

• there is a ROTI or short descriptive note (SDN) for each recording;

• the recording is of an acceptable quality.

Remember the following vital basic rules concerning tape recordings:

1. You must **ALWAYS** listen to tape-recordings.
2. If a PACE recording is missing, you must insist on having a copy of the tape-recording.
3. If a PACE recording is missing, **NEVER** accept the content of a ROTI purporting to be a summary of the missing tape.

Processing PACE interview recordings

Each recording must be processed systematically. This involves very much more than just listening to the recording.

When processing the recording you need:

• to be aware of the police case, the prosecution evidence and the police investigation at the time of interviewing;

- to be aware of situational pressures;
- to be aware of your client's particular vulnerabilities;
- to be aware of antecedents to the interviewing of your client;
- to examine the conduct of the IO and any others involved in questioning your client;
- to examine the conduct of your client;
- to examine the interaction between the IO and your client;
- to examine for clues to 'off-tape' interviewing;
- to assess the quality of the recording.

The nature of the police case, the prosecution evidence and the police investigation at the time of interviewing

Awareness of the nature of the police case, the prosecution evidence and the police investigation at the time of interviewing constitutes the context for understanding:

- the circumstances of the interview;
- the pressures upon the police;
- the pressures upon your client;
- the police representation of 'facts' during the interview.

Action

The court must be told that the CPS, the court and the defence cannot properly assess the probity and the quality of the evidence on the tape without documentation that provides a clear narrative of the police investigation, i.e.

- OIS entries;
- the crime report;
- the actions book;
- HOLMES actions index.

The production of this documentation presents no difficulty for the police since:

- the amount of paperwork is relatively minimal;

- production merely requires:
  - the photocopying of a simple form;
  - a command to the computer to print out the material in question.

Antecedents to the interviewing of your client

In addition to having a clear narrative of the police investigation, you need disclosure of the antecedents to the interviewing of your client. Only then will you and the court know from the police perspective:

- the IO's aims and objectives;
- the logic for the timing and duration of the interview;
- the conduct of the IO;
- the IO's representation during the interview of the police case and in particular 'facts' and evidence.

Action

You must treat the recording as though it were a statement. Ask for all antecedents with a bearing upon the interview:

- pocket book entries;
- computer notes;
- notes of meetings and consultations, e.g. with other officers (particularly supervisors and managers), SOCOs, forensic scientists, MEs, social workers, clinicians;
- briefings – of fellow officers, the appropriate adult, the interpreter;
- preparation and planning notes and pro formas – including detail on aims, objectives and information to be sought;
- SE3R sheets since SE3R is increasingly used by the police service;
- diagrams, sketches, maps and other exhibits referred to in the interview.

The production of this documentation presents no difficulty for the police since:

- the amount of paperwork is relatively minimal;
- production merely requires:
  - the photocopying of a simple form;
  - a command to the computer to print out the material in question.

Situational pressures

The Law Society text *Becoming Skilled*[2] describes the psychological factors involved when an individual is in custody and confronted with questioning. Individuals experience a compressed-stress response such that in a very short space of time they start acting in a manner that those who have not been in custody consider to be wholly illogical. Commonly, people lose their ability to absorb information, they think and act irrationally, principally to bring the experience of custody and questioning to an end.

Fatigue is a major compounding factor. Examination of the custody record will enable you to note the presence, and particularly combinations, of the following:

- your client did not rest when detained overnight – examine the entries in the custody record where regular checks will indicate if he or she was awake;

- interviewing late at night, into the early hours and very early in the morning – times at which the body clock of the individual affects behaviour – the individual has a strong desire to sleep and has difficulty concentrating, listening, keeping track, remembering what has been said earlier, and coping with those who are much more alert;

- protracted interviewing, i.e. extending beyond the duration of two interview tapes. Even though your client may have agreed to continue being interviewed, both PACE and PEACE provide common-sense guidance to officers to ensure the fairness of interviewing, i.e. the suspect should not be fatigued;

- visits to cells, i.e. extending questioning beyond the confines of the interview room.

Action

You must be in a position to draw to the court's attention the significance of situational pressures. This can be done by:

- producing a suitable document – an event line or table – which shows clearly and graphically the build-up of pressure;

- instructing a forensic psychologist who specialises in the field of investigative interviewing, with particular reference to stress factors.

Particular vulnerabilities

Becoming Skilled[3] describes the range of particular vulnerabilities with a potential bearing upon your client's conduct within, and capacity to cope with, custody and questioning:

- there were internal pressures to confess, e.g. your client wished to protect another person; your client wished to be punished or take the blame even though he or she did not commit the offence;
- your client was suffering at the time, or continues to suffer, from psychological problems, e.g. depression, anxiety, paranoia, claustrophobia, which affect thought processes, mood, behaviour and ability to control behaviour;
- your client was on medication at the time, e.g. anti-depressants or anxiety suppressants, but detention and questioning had disrupted the taking of prescribed drugs;
- your client was in withdrawal at the time – planned or imposed by detention;
- your client has a personality that renders him or her vulnerable:
  - to suggestive questioning – particularly if he or she has (or had at the time) problems with recall;
  - to compliance due to extreme respect for authority figures, submissiveness, problems with assertion, low self-esteem, or strong desire to please;
  - to acquiesce, i.e. to agree unreflectively to questions that are mutually contradictory;
  - by virtue of intellectual disadvantage, particularly in terms of verbal intelligence (limitations in ability to understand or to reason verbally) – a background of special schooling is frequently a clue to this;
  - by virtue of communicative disadvantage, e.g. speech or hearing disorder, inability to speak or to understand English at the required level.

Action

You must be in a position to draw to the court's attention the significance of particular vulnerabilities of your client at the time of the interview. This can be done by:

- interviewing your client on these matters;
- contacting those who were treating your client at the time;

- instructing a suitable expert, e.g. forensic psychologist, who specialises in the field of investigative interviewing, with particular reference to psychological vulnerability.

The conduct of the IO and the content of his or her utterances

It is essential that you know what to look for in terms of the conduct of the IO and the content of what he or she says. *Becoming Skilled*[4] provides an extensive insight into all aspects of police-interviewing behaviour. A *Pocket Reference*[5] summarises some of these. You need to look for:

1. **The officer's observance of PEACE guidelines in the management of the interview**, particularly:

   - checking your client's comprehension of the caution – especially the content of any explanation given to your client, given that research has shown that very large numbers of the general population do not understand the caution even when it is broken down;[6]
   - giving a reason for the interview;
   - use of special warnings;
   - reference to significant statements and silences;
   - obtaining an uninterrupted first account from your client before proceeding to focused (direct) questioning upon specific issues or areas of information;
   - acting appropriately in situations of extreme emotion, i.e.

     - suspending the interview if the suspect becomes very distressed, e.g. breaks down;
     - suspending the interview if the interaction between the officer and the suspect leads to both becoming aroused;
     - considering a change of interviewing officer if it is clear that there is a personality clash between the IO and the suspect.

2. **Inappropriate and improper questioning**:

   - the use of confusing words or verbal constructions;
   - improper lines of questioning;
   - inappropriate parameter questions;
   - suggestive questioning;
   - multiple questions;
   - hypothetical questions;
   - invalid trailers;
   - marathon questions.

3. **Inappropriate or improper presentation and management of information**:

   • misrepresentations of the law;
   • telling your client 'facts' rather than asking questions;
   • asserting 'facts' that were, in effect, police beliefs or assumptions;
   • asserting that your client is guilty;
   • overstatement;
   • understatement;
   • disingenuous generalisations;
   • upgrading your client's responses;
   • misinterpreting key items of information;
   • inaccurate summarising.

4. **Pressurising forms of talking and questioning**:

   • dominant talk – interrupting, overtalking, rapid topic changing, not listening to your client's replies;
   • raising of voice;
   • abuse and swearing;
   • demeaning and degrading observations;
   • direct or implied threats;
   • rapid-fire questioning;
   • two officers talking at once;
   • protracted silence;
   • demanding or commanding your client do or say something;
   • pressurising commentary about the offence, your client, your client's motivation, your client's response, i.e. negative feedback;
   • engaging your client in protracted accusation/denial sequences;
   • assuming your client's guilt and questioning his or her motivation for committing the offence;
   • continued questioning in the face of your client's continued denial;
   • rejecting your client's requests for the introduction of evidence supportive of your client.

Action

You must be in a position to draw to the court's attention the significance of particular conduct or utterances by the IO, particularly in the light of the potential applicability of PACE, s.76 or s.78. This can be done by:

• producing a suitable document – an event line or table, combined with tallies (counts) of particular types of behaviour – showing clearly and graphically:

  – failure to observe guidelines;
  – the frequency and duration of inappropriate, improper and pressurising behaviours;

- preparing or obtaining a transcript of the entire interview or relevant sections of the interview;

- instructing a suitable expert, e.g. forensic psychologist, who specialises in the field of investigative interviewing, with particular reference to the instruction and training of police officers in best practice guidelines.

The conduct of your client and his or her utterances

It is essential that you know what to look for in terms of the conduct of your client and the content of what he or she says. *Becoming Skilled*[7] gives a detailed description of the factors that give rise to false confessions and types of false confession. A *Pocket Reference*[8] provides a comprehensive summary of clues that something is wrong. You need to look for:

1. **Signs of fatigue**, e.g. excessive yawning, periods of inattention, problems following the IO's communications, drawn-out speech.

2. **Signs of vulnerability in the way your client was talking**. These include:

   - signs of problems with comprehension;
   - signs of problems with reasoning;
   - signs of intellectual immaturity;
   - signs of problems with expression and emotion;
   - treatment clues to psychiatric disorder;
   - signs of extreme arousal, loss of control, overcontrol;
   - speech impediments

3. **Signs of vulnerability in the content of your client's responses**. Any of the following, particularly if repeated:

   - acceptance of the content of suggestive questioning – especially when coupled with declared problems in remembering;
   - compliance;
   - acquiescence;
   - direct requests and indirect requests, e.g. 'pardon', for the question to be asked again;
   - assertions of not understanding.

4. **Signs of confusion**, e.g. your client clearly misses the point or is talking at odds to the content of the officer's question.

5. **Repeated assertions of innocence** – particularly across the course of the interview or several interviews.

6. **Full or partial admissions**. Particularly in the light of factors described above concerning the IO's conduct and utterances, i.e. potentially indicative of your client making:

- a *coerced compliant false confession* – in order to stop the interviewing and to be allowed to leave police custody;
- a *coerced internalised confession* – he or she has come to believe what the officer is asserting.

Action

You must be in a position to draw to the court's attention the significance of your client's conduct during the interview. This can be done by:

- interviewing your client on these matters;
- producing a suitable document – an event line or table, combined with tallies (counts) of particular types of behaviour – showing these clearly and graphically;
- preparing or obtaining a transcript of the entire interview or relevant sections of the interview;
- instructing a suitable expert, e.g. forensic psychologist, who specialises in the field of psychological vulnerability in the interrogative context, particularly by:
  - conducting a wide range of psychological assessments of a suspect, e.g. suggestibility, compliance, acquiescence, anxiety, self-esteem, intellectual functioning, language ability, memory, developmental and social functioning;
  - analysing the form and content of a suspect's behaviour in interview;
  - placing these findings in the context of situational pressures and other areas of vulnerability.

Clues to 'off-tape' interviewing

Your client may fail to mention or to recall accurately details of 'off-tape' interviewing. Clues that this has taken place are to be found:

- in the content of utterances in the recording, e.g. 'As we said earlier', when there is no reference to the detail in question being mentioned earlier in this or any previous interview;

- in inordinate periods of elapsed time:
    - in the custody record, e.g. between your client being collected from his or her cell and the start of interviewing and between the end of interviewing and the return of your client to cells;
    - between the end of one tape and the start of another when in the interview room.

Action

You must be in a position to draw to the court's attention the potential clues to 'off-tape' interviewing by:

- producing a suitable document;
- producing a tape with the extracts which are indicative of 'off-tape' interviewing.

The quality of the recording

You must not accept a recording of inadequate quality.

Action

You must:

- immediately request another copy of the tape;
- not accept excuses for not producing a copy within a very short time frame;
- bring this matter, and the attendant delay, to the court's attention.

As pointed out in Chapter 7, all designated police stations have rapid-recording facilities, i.e. a machine that takes less than a couple of minutes to produce a copy of the working copy of the tape.

Missing PACE recordings of interviews with your client

All too often PACE recordings are missing when other material is disclosed.

Action

Remember the two basic rules:

---

1. **You must never accept the accuracy of a ROTI. It must always be compared with the tape-recording.**

2. **If a PACE recording is missing, NEVER accept the content of a ROTI purporting to be a summary of the missing tape.**

Always respond immediately:

- request a copy of the missing recording;

- do not accept excuses for not producing a copy within a very short time frame. As pointed out above, there is no excuse since all designated police stations have rapid-recording facilities;

- point out that until such time as the recording is produced it is impossible to examine the status of the ROTI;

- these matters, and the attendant delay, must be brought to the court's attention.

Missing PACE recordings of witnesses who were originally suspects

Very often the police will not:

- disclose that a current witness was originally interviewed as a suspect;

- provide PACE recordings of the interviews of this witness.

Action

Always respond immediately:

- request a copy of the missing recording;

- do not accept excuses for not producing a copy within a very short time frame;

- point out that until such time as the recording is produced it is impossible to examine the status of the witness's statement;

- these matters, and the attendant delay, must be brought to the court's attention.

ANALYSING RECORDINGS OF WITNESS INTERVIEWS

Interviewing of a witness may be recorded in the following circumstances:

- when the witness is a juvenile or a child, i.e a video recording is made of the interview conducted by a police officer, social worker or other professional within the framework of the *Memorandum of Good Practice* (for the sake of brevity we term these Memorandum interviews);[9]

- when the witness is a juvenile or a child who refuses, or whose parent or guardian refuses, to have an interview video-recorded;

- when the individual is a key or significant witness in a case involving serious offences and the CID officer in the case, or SIO, has decided that the guidance of PEACE and/or the *Murder Investigation Manual* will be followed, i.e. initial interviewing will be recorded – optimally on video but otherwise tape-recorded;

- when it has been decided to record an interview of a complainant or key eyewitness, applying the cognitive (memory-enhancing) approach – which has the potential to generate a large amount of detail.

Memorandum interviews

The CPS will endeavour to offer the contents of the recorded interview as testimonial evidence equating to evidence-in-chief. This form of witness statement can have great impact.

As with any statement, it must be examined systematically. It involves very much more than just viewing the recording.

When processing the recording of a Memorandum interview you need:

- to be aware of the police case, the prosecution evidence and the police investigation at the time of interviewing;

- to be aware of situational pressures;

- to examine the conduct and contribution of the interviewer and any others involved in questioning the witness;

- to examine the conduct and contribution of the witness;

- to examine for clues to 'off-tape' interviewing;

- to assess the quality of the recording;

- to be alert to missing interviews.

The nature of the police case, the prosecution evidence and the police investigation at the time of interviewing

Awareness of the nature of the police case, the prosecution evidence and the police investigation at the time of interviewing constitutes the context for understanding:

- the circumstances of the interview, e.g. where a 15-year-old girl alleges rape took place shortly before the end of the summer term but waits until the autumn term to disclose this to a friend, who sets in train a series of disclosure exchanges resulting ultimately in a police response;
- the pressures upon the police – all too often there is a rush to interview, despite the sound advice of the Memorandum that there should be due consideration, reflection and appropriate prior action, e.g. medical examination, resolution of gaps and anomalies within the accounts of key individuals involved in receiving the witness's complaint;
- the pressures upon the witness, e.g. the 'dynamics' of the family and the witness within the family, which occasioned the witness to disclose to a particular person at a particular time in a particular way;
- the police representation of 'facts' during the interview, e.g. the interviewing officer has inadequately or inaccurately represented or noted down the facts obtained and briefed by the FOA.

Action

You need to piece together the police case, the prosecution evidence and the police investigation at the time of interviewing. To do this you need:

- statements of others materially involved, e.g. police officers, parents, teachers, social workers, clinicians;
- the antecedents to these statements;
- the antecedents to the interview of the witness, i.e. all forms of record – documentary and visual – bearing upon requests, responses, actions, decisions, briefings, meetings, interview planning and preparation, in respect of police, social workers, other professionals and other involved persons;
- a clear narrative of the police investigation, i.e. crime report, logs, diaries;
- material on the interviewing of your client, i.e. PACE recordings and ROTI, particularly if this interviewing takes place ahead of or within a very short time of the interview of the witness;

- the antecedents to the interviewing of your client.

Again, the production of this documentation presents no difficulty for the police since:

- the amount of paperwork is relatively minimal;
- production merely requires:
    - photocopying of material that will already be in the possession of the disclosure officer;
    - a command to the computer to print out the material in question.

You must process statements and their antecedents, the antecedents to the interview, the narrative of the police case, the interviewing and antecedents to interviewing of your client. Only then will you have a sound grasp of:

- problematic aspects of the police case, prosecution evidence and the police investigation that should have been detected and acted upon prior to the interviewing of the witness;
- missing material that should have been detected and obtained prior to the interviewing of the witness.

Analysing the content of the tape

Analysing video recordings is not easy. A transcript assists the process enormously. We strongly recommend you to bear in mind the following:

- All transcripts provided by the Crown must be checked against the actual video. Very often transcripts are inaccurate, e.g. the transcriber mishears, or does not hear at all, utterances that are in fact quite audible, or can be disambiguated by a number of replays of the video segment.
- Very few Crown transcripts indicate pauses or silence. When these are shown they are often unhelpful, e.g. a series of full stops, arbitrary in their occurrence and, when duration is indicated, this is usually also arbitrary and inaccurate in terms of description, e.g. the annotation (*long pause*) turns out to be momentary; very long pauses are not registered.
- Hardly any transcripts give an indication of non-verbal behaviour, e.g. a clear look of confusion; stammering, stuttering, tears, anger.
- Few indicate incomplete or unfinished utterances with any degree of consistency or accuracy.

	Purpose	Approach
Phase I **Rapport**	To settle the child and relieve anxiety. To supplement the interviewer's knowledge of the child. To explain the reason for interviewing. To admonish the child to speak the truth.	Any topic which relaxes the child. Play may be needed.
Phase II **Free narrative** **account**	To enable the child to give an account in his or her own words.	Provide opportunities to talk about the alleged offence at the child's pace. Use a form of 'active listening'.
Phase III **Questioning**	To find out more about the alleged offence.	Questions graduating from general to more specific.
Stage A **Open-ended** **questions**	To enable the child to provide more information without presssure.	Use focused but non-leading questions.
Stage B **Specific yet non-** **leading questions**	To extend and clarify information. To remind the child of the purpose of the interview.	Use specific questions which may inevitably refer to disputed facts. Probe factual and linguistic inconsistencies gently.
Stage C **Closed questions**	To encourage a reticent child to speak.	Questions which allow a limited number of responses.
Stage D **Leading questions**	To encourage a reticent child to speak.	Questions can be used which imply answer or assume disputed facts.
Phase IV **Closing the interview**	To ensure the child has understood the interview and is not distressed.	Go over relevant evidence in the child's language. Revert to rapport topics. Thank the child and allow him or her to ask questions.

Table 8.4 Summary of the recommended phased approach to interviewing

	To be avoided	Additional comments
Phase I **Rapport**	Any mention of the alleged offence. Staring at or touching the child at any time.	This phase may need to be repeated at several points in the interview. Never start without it.
Phase II **Free narrative** **account**	Questions directed to events not mentioned by the child. Speaking as soon as the child appears to stop.	Be patient. If nothing related to the alleged offence is mentioned, consider moving to phase IV.
Phase III **Questioning**	Interrupting the child even to clarify language. Repeating a question too soon. Using difficult grammar/sentence construction. Asking more than one question at a time.	Consider at each stage of questioning whether it is in the interests of the child and justice to proceed further.
Stage A **Open-ended** **questions**		
Stage B **Specific yet non-** **leading questions**	Questions which require a 'yes' or a 'no' answer or allow only one of a possible two responses.	
Stage C **Closed questions**		Consult with other interviewer before questioning further.
Stage D **Leading questions**	Questions which invariably require the same answer.	Avoid all directly leading questions. Revert to 'neutral' mode as soon as possible, and in all cases in which an answer seems evidentially relevant.
Phase IV **Closing the interview**	Summarising in adult language.	Never stop without it. Give the child or accompanying adult contact name and number.

Table 8.4 *(continued)* Summary of the recommended phased approach to interviewing

You should therefore always commission a full transcript of any video recording. Ask the transcriber to provide you with the transcript in hard copy and as a file on a computer disk. You will then be able to load the disk onto a computer and, watching the video, drop into the text the additional detail you require:

- within parentheses, pauses and their duration, and (using suitable abbreviations) the occurrence of non-verbal behaviours and when an individual interrupts the person talking;

- by underlining and using appropriate annotation – OT for overtalking – indicating when two people are talking at once.

You are now ready to start analysing the recording. Having gone through the tape to ensure accuracy and to annotate the computer file, you will find that you have a very good remembrance for the entire interview and the detail of the exchanges within it.

You have a number of options:

- you can either continue with your analyses using the file you have created;

- you can conduct a THEMA analysis (see Shepherd and Mortimer 'Identifying anomaly in evidential text'). This is a grid approach in which you progressively cut and paste sections from the computer file into a growing table, created using the 'Tables' facility of the word-processing package on your computer or a program such as EXCEL.

Either way, you can proceed to analyse the recording to identify the conduct and contribution of the interviewer, the child and others.

The conduct and contribution of the interviewer

The Memorandum (p. 15) indicates that:

> *'The basic aim of the interview is to obtain a truthful account from the child, in a way which is fair and in the child's interests and acceptable to the courts...the recommended protocol for interviewing based on a phased approach...treats the interview as a process in which a variety of interviewing techniques are deployed in relatively discrete phases, proceeding from general and open to specific and closed forms of questions.'*

A summary of the recommended phased approach is shown in Table 8.4.

Each phase has a definite purpose achieved by:

- adopting an explicit approach to managing the course and the content of the exchange;

- avoiding particular counter-productive and risky forms of conversation, questioning and information management.

The Memorandum points out that the phased approach is not a checklist to be rigidly worked through. However, the sound legal framework it provides should not be departed from by investigators unless they have fully discussed and agreed the reasons for doing so and have consulted with their senior managers.

Despite these explicit guidelines and substantial attention to training in vulnerable-witness interviewing and joint-agency working, SIU officers and social workers in all too many instances:

- fail to create the appropriate rapport with the child, creating an 'authority adult who already knows'/'anxious to please child seeking to give the "right" answers' relationship;

- fail to communicate at the level of the child;

- fail to explain the reason for the interview;

- fail to set up circumstances to obtain the fullest, uninterrupted first account;

- resort prematurely to direct questioning;

- engage in closed and leading questioning without prior consultation and consideration;

- effectively shape the responses of the child towards the interviewer's antecedent notions or understanding of 'what happened' by:
  - talking more than the child;
  - posing predominantly suggestive questions, i.e. leading, option (either/or), and closed yes/no (confirmatory) questions, influencing the child to go along with what is being asserted or implied by the officer;
  - overtalking and interrupting the child;
  - ignoring the child's responses;
  - rapidly changing the topic, leaving the matter unprobed.

Action

You must be in a position to draw to the court's attention the significance of particular conduct or contributions by the IO. This can be done by:

- producing a suitable document – an event line or table, combined with tallies (counts) of particular types of behaviour – showing clearly and graphically:
    - failure to observe the Memorandum guidelines;
    - the frequency and duration of inappropriate and improper behaviours, including those that shape the witness's responses;
- instructing a suitable expert, e.g. a psychologist, who specialises in the interviewing of vulnerable witnesses, with particular reference to the instruction and training of police officers and other professionals in best-practice guidelines.

The conduct and contribution of the child

You need to look for both verbal and non-verbal clues. Common important clues include:

- signs of distractibility, e.g. inattention, problems following the interview, involving the interviewer in activities other than the focus of the interview;
- signs of problems with comprehension;
- signs of problems with language and reasoning – frequently compounded by the interviewer conducting the interview at the wrong pitch;
- signs of extreme arousal, loss of control, over-control;
- signs of acceptance of the content of suggestive questioning – particularly when coupled with declared problems in remembering;
- signs of compliance;
- signs of acquiescence;
- signs of confusion, e.g. missing the point or talking at odds to the content of the question;
- accounts, descriptions and responses that are anomalous by virtue of:
    - invalid representations, e.g. stating that he or she was asleep and did not wake up, but able to describe what was happening;
    - vague, ambiguous and equivocal descriptions;
    - two or more versions of 'what happened';

- contradiction and mismatch;
- gaps, e.g. lack of dialogue in the account; lack of narrative continuity within or between particular episodes creating an effect like a 'jump' in an edited film;
- narrative contrast, e.g. a large degree of detail concerning episodes prior to or after the incident but little detail concerning the incident.

In all too many instances:

• interviewers fail to detect these clues during the interview;

• there is a lack of critical evaluation after the interview, not least when preparing the IVRI, such that officers ignore such basic anomalies as invalid representations and multiple, contradictory versions of 'what happened'.[10]

Action

You must be in a position to draw to the court's attention the significance of the child's conduct and contributions during the interview. This can be done by:

• producing a suitable document – an event line or table, combined with tallies (counts) of particular types of behaviour – showing clearly and graphically the occurrence, frequency and duration of problematic behaviours;

• instructing a suitable expert, e.g. a psychologist, who specialises in the interviewing of vulnerable witnesses and assessing interviewee responses.

The conduct and contribution of the other person present

In many interviews, there is another person present tasked with:

• supporting the child;

• facilitating disclosure by the child;

• assisting in the interviewing process.

Action

Analyse the other person's conduct and contribution in the same way as you would an interviewer.

Clues to 'off-tape' interviewing

Clues that this has taken place are to be found in the content of utterances, by the interviewer, the child or the other person present, e.g. 'when we spoke earlier', when there is no reference to the detail in question being mentioned earlier in the interview.

Action

You must be in a position to draw to the court's attention the potential clues to 'off-tape' interviewing by:

• producing a suitable document;

• producing a tape with the extracts which are indicative of 'off-tape' interviewing.

The quality of the recording

You must not accept a recording of inadequate quality.

Action

You must:

• immediately request another copy of the tape;

• not accept excuses for not producing a copy within a very short time frame;

• bring this matter, and the attendant delay, to the court's attention.

If the original recording is of inadequate quality, you must instruct a forensic linguist.

Missing recordings

Instances still occur where a Memorandum recording is missing when other material is disclosed, so always remember the following rule:

> **If a Memorandum recording is missing NEVER accept the content of an IVRI purporting to be a summary of the missing tape.**

Action

Always respond immediately:

- request a copy of the missing recording;
- do not accept excuses for not producing a copy within a very short time frame;
- point out that until such time as the recording is produced, it is impossible to examine the status of the IVRI;
- these matters, and the attendant delay, must be brought to the court's attention.

There is no excuse for this since all forces have cross-recording facilities. Any failure to produce a copy is therefore the product of obstructiveness, indifference, sloth or a combination of these.

Audio recording of a Memorandum interview

Refusal by the child or parent or guardian for a video-recorded interview is potentially indicative of a cause for concern. The audio recording must be examined as closely as any video recording.

Although audio recording should be disclosed as a matter of course, it may not be – the police preferring to disclose written notes of the interview.

Only close examination of the recording in the same manner as any Memorandum interview will establish whether:

- there was a cause for concern – as indicated by the conduct of the child;
- the officer followed the Memorandum and did not interview inappropriately or improperly.

Action

Even though contemporaneous notes are disclosed, you must establish:

- whether the interview was audio recorded;
- why the child, the parent or guardian refused a video recording.

When the audio recording is disclosed, treat it in the same manner as a video recording.

Recordings of adult complainants and key witnesses

As pointed out earlier, there will be instances when the police:

- have decided to record the interviewing of the witness, particularly the exchange leading up to the production of a witness statement;
- have decided to record an interview involving the cognitive (memory-enhancing) approach – which has the potential to generate a large amount of detail.

Chapter 3 explains why there is a reluctance to record the interviewing of witnesses. It is likely that where a recording has taken place, its occurrence and the existence of tapes will not be volunteered to the CPS, the defence and the court. This is because the recording allows the court to ascertain:

- what influence the officer exerted over what was disclosed or what manner of editing took place;
- whether the witness's statement is the complete and accurate record of what the witness said;
- the extent to which the officer applied the ADVOKATE criteria, with particular reference to the need to confront contradictions or anomalies.

Recording of a witness interview should be noted in the officer's pocket book, the crime sheet, action book or on the HOLMES actions index.

The same considerations apply to the examination of a recording of an adult witness interview as to that of a child. When processing the recording, you need:

- to be aware of the police case, the prosecution evidence and the police investigation at the time of interviewing;
- to be aware of situational pressures;
- to examine the conduct and contribution of the interviewer and any others involved in questioning the witness;
- to examine the conduct and contribution of the witness;
- to examine for clues to 'off-tape' interviewing;
- to assess the quality of the recording.

Obtain a transcript – hard copy and computer file – and, loading the file and watching the video, annotate the transcript in the manner described earlier.

If you use the same methods and follow the same format as for a Memorandum interview, you will be able to identify when:

- the witness gave an account characterised by inconsistency and anomaly;
- the officer did not follow 'best practice' guidelines and failed to implement techniques properly and to observe safeguards, particularly when conducting a cognitive interview;
- the officer shaped what the witness said by:
  - talking more than the witness;
  - posing predominantly suggestive questions, i.e. leading, option (either/or), and closed yes/no (confirmatory) questions, influencing the witness to go along with what was being asserted or implied by the officer;
  - overtalking and interrupting the witness;
  - ignoring the witness's responses;
  - rapidly changing the topic, leaving the matter unprobed.

By comparison with the witness's eventual statement, you will be able to identify where the officer fundamentally changed the content of what the witness actually said by altering or substituting words, phraseology and verbal constructions.

Action

You must establish whether the interviewing of a witness has been recorded. Once it has been established that audio recording has taken place, draw to the court's attention the significance of:

- particular conduct of the IO;
- particular conduct of the witness and the content of his or account or descriptions.

This can be done by:

- producing suitable documents to demonstrate areas of concern:
  - an event line or table, combined with tallies (counts) of particular types of significant behaviour displayed by the IO and the witness;
  - a table showing anomalies in the witness's utterances;
- instructing a suitable expert, e.g. a psychologist, who specialises in the interviewing of vulnerable witnesses, with particular reference to the

instruction and training of police officers and other professionals in best-practice guidelines.

Analysing missing recordings that are subsequently disclosed

These should be analysed in the same way as any recording.

Analysing antecedents to recordings

When you receive antecedents of recordings as a result of bringing shortcomings and omissions to the prosecutor's attention, the content of antecedents must be compared with the problematic recording or the missing recording.

Action

You must follow a systematic sequence of analysis.

1. Arrange antecedents in chronological order.

2. Analyse the content of the earliest occurring antecedent. If it is a document, treat it as though it were a statement. If it is a recording follow the same procedures as for any recording.

3. Prepare a grid – see Appendix 7 – entering key detail from the antecedent.

4. Process each subsequent antecedent in the same way as the first.

5. Enter key detail from the recording whose content you, or your expert, found to be problematic or from the missing recording.

6. Examine the grid for anomalies.

ANALYSING CONTEMPORANEOUS NOTES

Instances of contemporaneous notes are likely to be more common with the introduction of the Criminal Justice and Public Order Act 1994 (CJPOA), which has:

- brought to the fore the evidential potential of the significant statement or silence;

- led more police managers to encourage interviewing outside the interview room at the point of, and immediately after, arrest.

There are significant issues concerning contemporaneous notes:

- people speak on average between 120 and 180 words per minute – more when emotionally aroused;

- the speed of the spoken word exceeds the ability of police officers to write utterances down;

- unless the officer is able to regulate the exchange – instructing the individual to pause while the officer writes and pausing after the officer has spoken to write down what the officer has just said – most contemporaneous notes taken at or after arrest are likely to be bullet points expanded by the later recall of the officer;

- most officers will experience problems recalling verbatim what was said given that research has shown that memory for verbatim utterances is extremely limited – only one or two sentences since subsequent sentences interfere with the material of previous sentences;

- if the officer engages in other activities and other verbal exchanges before writing the utterances down, the product:
  - will not be contemporaneous;
  - is more likely to be inaccurate, given the effects of post-event interference with the officer's recall.

Even extremely swift and adept note-takers make a high proportion of mistakes – a combination of mishearing, problems holding the material in memory, and the effects of internal and external disruptions.

Given the police disposition to 'clean up' utterances there is also a likelihood that the vocabulary and verbal constructions are not those of the suspect or witness but witting or unwitting substitutions by the officer.

Prior to the introduction of PACE recordings, there were two common patterns to be found in purportedly contemporaneous notes:

- some contained many more words than could be physically uttered within the time frame of the purported exchange or interview;

- some contained very few words, e.g. sufficient to account for a slow five-minute exchange leaving the remainder of the purported time spent in the exchange or interview unaccounted for.

Action

You must examine the form and content of contemporaneous notes very closely, treating them as though they were a statement.

323

If you have any cause for concern you need:

- to instruct appropriate expert witnesses – forensic psychologists or forensic linguists – who specialise in such issues as memory for speech, discourse, characteristic speech patterns and note-taking;
- to obtain copies of antecedents – analysing these in the same way as antecedents to statements.

ANALYSING RECORDS OF TAPE-RECORDED INTERVIEWS (ROTIs)

Chapter 7 points out how research has shown the standard of ROTI preparation to be extremely poor, particularly where these have been prepared by police officers as opposed to civilian staff.

Even where a full transcript is prepared, this cannot be accepted as an accurate record. It must first be checked and appropriately annotated and amended since:

- there are no conventions as to the representation of:
  - parallel talk (when an officer and the interviewee, or two officers, are talking at the same time);
  - interruption and overtalking;
  - pause, silence, or the duration of pause and silence;
  - instances of audible vocal non-verbal behaviour, e.g. crying, shouting, whispering;
- what is often annotated as being indistinct frequently is audible;
- instances of mishearing give rise to errors in transcription.

Action

Remember the two basic rules.

> 1. You must never accept the accuracy of a ROTI. It must always be compared with the tape recording.
> 2. If a PACE recording is missing, NEVER accept the content of a ROTI purporting to be a summary of the missing tape.

You must be in a position to draw the court's attention to shortcomings in the ROTI. As you process the recording in the manner described earlier, compare its content to the ROTI:

- where there are instances where the ROTI makes no mention of utterances by the interviewing officer or your client, which you consider to be significant – make a note and annotate the ROTI with the significant omission;

- where there are anomalies in the tape recording that you wish to bring to the court's attention and where these are not mentioned in the ROTI – make a note and annotate the ROTI with the omission;

- where the ROTI accurately reflects the content of the tape, highlight the correspondence using a green fluorescent marker pen or underlining in pencil or biro;

- where the ROTI does not accurately reflect the content of the tape, highlight the mismatch by using a red fluorescent marker pen;

- where the ROTI gives a disingenuous account of the content of the tape, i.e. brings together as an apparently continuous utterance shreds of responses to questions across a period of time in the interview, draw double lines // to signify the separate utterances.

Where you instruct an expert to analyse the interview, always provide him or her with the ROTI.

Where a full transcript has been prepared, it is necessary to compare this with the tape recording:

- making appropriate annotations to indicate what is not immediately obvious from the text:
  - parallel talk – underlining those parts of the utterances of the two speakers which are simultaneous;
  - overtalking – underlining the simultaneous utterances and marking the overtalker's text with the letters OT;
  - interruption – marking the interrupter's utterance with the letters INT;
  - pauses and silence – inserting the elapsed time in brackets, e.g. (20 secs);
  - indicating vocal non-verbal behaviour – inserting the type of behaviour in brackets, e.g. (crying);
- substituting audible text for the purportedly inaudible;
- amending transcription errors.

Where the ROTI is so inaccurate as to require extensive amendment and annotation, you should commission a full transcript. Ask the transcriber to provide you with the transcript in hard copy and as a file on a computer disk. You will then be able to load the disk onto a computer and, listening to the tape, drop into the text the additional detail and annotations required.

Having gone through the tape to ensure accuracy and to annotate, the original or a transcript in the form of a computer file, you will find that you have a very good remembrance for the entire interview and the detail of the exchanges within it.

ANALYSING SHORT DESCRIPTIVE NOTES (SDNs)

An SDN is a short summary of an interview submitted with an abbreviated file. Being even shorter than the conventional ROTI, their status as a valid and reliable record is even more questionable.

They should be treated in the same manner as a conventional ROTI. The same two basic rules apply to SDNs as to ROTIs.

ANALYSING INDEXES OF VIDEO-RECORDED INTERVIEWS (IVRIs)

IVRIs fulfil the same function as a ROTIs, but in respect of video-recorded interviews of witnesses, particularly Memorandum-style interviews:

- they suffer from the same shortcomings as ROTIs;

- they should be treated in the same manner as a ROTI.

ANALYSING THE CUSTODY RECORD

You must be provided with a copy of the custody record. There is no excuse for it not being provided:

- in the case of a manuscript record, it can be readily photocopied on the machine, which is to be found in, or in an office close to, the custody suite;

- in the case of a computerised record, all the custody officer has to do is press a button to produce a computerised print-out of previous and current pages.

Action

Insist on a copy of the custody record. Do not be fobbed off with excuses.

Your client's account provides a useful check on entries in the custody record. Therefore, obtain from your client an account, in as much detail as he or she can give, of what he or she can remember happened from the time he or she was arrested and for the whole of the time he or she has been, or was, in custody. *Becoming Skilled*[11] and *A Pocket Reference*[12] give advice on how to consult with your client on these and other matters.

Examine the record for information concerning:

- the police investigation;
- police conduct towards, and care of, your client;
- examination by the medical examiner – on all too many occasions this is not recorded;
- clues to:
  - your client's increasing vulnerability, e.g. checks finding him or her awake throughout the night;
  - 'off-tape' interviewing, e.g. 'welfare' visits to your client's cell; an inordinate delay between being collected from the cell and a PACE interview commencing or between the end of interviewing and return to the cell.

Where the custody record has been maintained in manuscript, i.e. is not computerised, examine for signs of tampering with entries, e.g.

- spaced out or compressed writing and wording – indicative of an officer trying to fill in the space on a substituted page;
- text continuing below the bottom line of the form instead of running on to the first line of the next page.

If you have any concerns, instruct a forensic document examiner to analyse the record.

ANALYSING VIDEO RECORDINGS OF CUSTODY SUITE

Increasingly, activity in the custody suite desk area is monitored by video. Video recordings are not released as a matter of course.

Action

You must establish whether the custody suite is monitored by CCTV.

Examine the custody record and request a copy of the tape recordings covering those times when your client was in the custody suite.

Examine the video recordings for detail in respect of:

- the interaction between the custody officer, police officers and others and your client;

- your client's demeanour, behaviour and utterances – all manifest indicators of vulnerability, comprehension, state of mind and physical state, e.g. when being presented, searched, informed of his or her rights, being asked to consent to the taking of samples.

If you have any concerns, instruct a forensic psychologist to carry out requisite analyses.

ANALYSING VIDEO RECORDINGS OF SECURITY SYSTEMS

Increasingly, video recordings made by CCTV systems are offered as evidence. It is not widely known that a range of factors renders such video recordings problematic as evidence. Technical factors include variable quality of equipment, positioning of the camera, form and level of illumination, resolution, distortion, the presence and accuracy of superimposed data strips (time/date), differential effects of contrast, lighting, black-and-white and colour pictures.

Psychological factors include:

- difficulties people have in identifying individuals on the basis of a videoscreen image;

- individuals are often able to recognise people they know from even very poor video images;

- individuals are often unable to recognise strangers even from high-quality video images.

Action

After examining the video recording and noting any causes for concern from a lay perspective, it is wise to instruct appropriate experts, i.e. in the field of video recording and visual identification from both technical, e.g. enhancement, and psychological perspectives, e.g. eyewitness limitations.

ANALYSING EXPERT REPORTS

Reports, as opposed to statements, by medical examiners, clinicians, forensic scientists, pathologists and other specialists, should be treated as though they are statements.

Action

Read the report even though its contents will be technical. Reading the introductory texts we have recommended will greatly assist in comprehending the report. The glossary of common forensic terms in Appendix 9 will assist in respect of some of the terminology.

You will need to instruct an appropriate expert to analyse specialist reports. He or she will be able:

- to translate the technicalities into lay language;

- to tell you if the analyses, the results and the specialist's conclusions and opinions are open to question;

- to give you the basis of an argument for the disclosure of antecedents to the specialist's report.

Notes

1. *A Guide to Interviewing*. (1996) Bramshill: Police Staff College.

2. Shepherd, E. (1996) *Becoming Skilled*. London: Law Society Publishing.

3. *Ibid.*

4. *Ibid.*

5. Shepherd, E. (1996) *A Pocket Reference*. London: Law Society Publishing.

6. Shepherd, E., Mortimer, A. and Mobasheri, R. (1995) 'The police caution: comprehension and perceptions in the general population'. *Expert Evidence*, 4, 60–7.

7. Shepherd, E. (1996) *Becoming Skilled*. London: Law Society Publishing.

8. Shepherd, E. (1996) *A Pocket Reference*. London: Law Society Publishing.

9. Home Office. (1992) *Memorandum of Good Practice on Video-Recorded Interviews with Child Witnesses for Criminal Proceedings*. London: HMSO.

10. Shepherd, E. and Mortimer, A. (1995) 'Putting testimony to the test'. *Practitioners' Child Law Bulletin*, 8, 44–6.

11. Shepherd, E. (1996) *Becoming Skilled*. London: Law Society Publishing.

12. Shepherd, E. (1996) *A Pocket Reference*. London: Law Society Publishing.

CHAPTER 9

Active defence in the police station

DEFENDING BY SECURING DISCLOSURE IN THE POLICE STATION

When a suspect is in the police station, the police case is almost invariably at its most tenuous. Lack of resource and pressure of work mean that in many instances an IO cannot visit the scene: hence they will not have any real idea of, or feel for, the scene. Many IOs, particularly in a CIT (evidence team), will be functionally ignorant of critical detail, particularly if they have not received a briefing from the FOA or the arresting officer. Statements will be few, many still remain to be taken or are in the process of being taken. If forensic evidence has been collected, either a decision will still have to be taken concerning the testing or analysis, or it will have been sent for testing and analysis and things are out of the IO's hands for the moment.

If there are manifest shortcomings in the police case, in the evidence that has been gathered thus far and in the investigation, the IO may well be engaged in defensive avoidance in the manner described in Chapter 3.

Whether or not they are engaged in defensive avoidance, given the continuing pre-eminence of the confession, all too many IOs:

- decide to question the suspect with the aim of securing an admission of guilt – a solution that overcomes shortcomings in the police case, the evidence and the investigation, produces an instant result, enhances kudos and is seen as a mark of prowess;

- construe a legal adviser engaged in active defence as an obstacle to this solution to police problems and to a quick result.

The necessity for active defence in the police station cannot be overemphasised. Both *Becoming Skilled*[1] and *A Pocket Reference*[2] spell out the issues. Skilfully effected, your defence at this stage will contribute greatly to negating the injurious effects of the CPIA should your client be charged. This is because you will have sought exhaustively and systematically to investigate every aspect of the police case, the prosecution evidence and the police investigation at the point when these are far from clear or complete – not least in the mind of the IO. Any information you gain at this stage is vital since it can be compared with the later version of reality, which the police provide to the CPS.

Without knowledge of the early stages and circumstances of the investigation when the police wished to interview your client – particularly to obtain a confession – the future defence of your client is placed in jeopardy.

THE PROCESS OF ACTIVELY DEFENDING

Becoming Skilled[3] and *A Pocket Reference*[4] spell out the issues involved and guidelines for skilful defence from the initial request to attend the police station to the final police decision concerning the case against your client.

You must think ahead, from the moment you receive the telephone call requesting you to attend, and prepare for the potential scenario of your client being charged and the defence experiencing problems with prosecution disclosure. With this prospect in mind, you must engage in active defence – using every opportunity to achieve the primary aim of investigating the nature of the police case, prosecution evidence and the police investigation.

You must be prepared to interview each officer with whom you consult in order to:

- test the police case – particularly their reconstruction of the offence and your client's role within this reconstruction;

- identify gaps, shortcomings and selectivity within the prosecution evidence and the police investigation.

What the client and the appropriate adult disclose must also be noted in the context of police disclosures. Finally, attempts by the IO to use disclosure of the police case and prosecution evidence tactically in the interview room should be met with a consistent response from the legal adviser: the interview of the client ceases and the interview of the officer commences.

You need to be systematic throughout in your approach to the investigation in the manner described in Chapters 7 and 8:

- continually assess the situation before you;

- be focused in your collection of information using checklists;

- use appropriate methods for collating information – particularly those statements, recordings, documents and exhibits that the police choose to disclose to you;

- take every opportunity to evaluate what you already have and what is currently being disclosed;

- pull the information you have together and analyse it – to spot the shortcomings, the problematic and the missing;

- survey the totality of what you have;

- summarise, to clarify your thinking and to help to reassess the situation.

WHAT YOU NEED IN ORDER TO CAPTURE THE INFORMATION

Take with you to the police station the full range of material (including blank SE3R pro formas – see Appendix 7), and equipment you need to capture information.

In respect of equipment:

- We strongly recommend you take a handheld tape recorder, to record the consultations you have with the custody officer and, particularly, with the IO, and the appropriate adult. The police should have no qualms about you recording. In many forces now the consultations are recorded: by the custody suite CCTV and by IOs who, in accordance with force policy, tape-record exchanges with legal advisers and use official forms (booklets) with sections in which they have itemised information to be disclosed to the legal adviser, and may even ask the legal adviser to sign as confirmation of having received the information listed on the form.

- Now that SE3R exists in software form (*RealSense*) you are able to use a laptop/notepad computer and the power of computing to capture and to work upon the detail that is disclosed.

SOURCES OF INFORMATION

The main sources of information concerning the police case, prosecution evidence and the police investigation will be your consultations with the IO, the police interview and, to a lesser extent, the custody officer.

Other sources are necessarily those who have had contact with the police through the process of police investigation: your client and, where applicable, the appropriate adult.

GOOD PRACTICE FOR INVESTIGATING THE POLICE CASE, THE PROSECUTION EVIDENCE AND THE POLICE INVESTIGATION

There is very little that the police are obliged to disclose or do to help you fulfil your active defence aim. They have wide powers of discretion in giving you information and in making time and themselves available to speak with you.

You must assume that police officers will disclose voluntarily the minimum considered necessary for you to advise your client as to his or her legal position. They will be reluctant to disclose more, lest this reveal shortcomings in the police case, the prosecution evidence and their investigation. A situation will inevitably arise when a police officer:

• will refuse to provide information you need;

• will deny knowledge of information you need;

• will procrastinate;

• will respond pre-emptively, e.g. says: 'I'm not prepared to give any more information'.

You need to persuade or to influence the officer to adopt a course of action that recognises your perspective. You need to engage in *principled negotiation*. This requires:

• a clear understanding of your position and the officer's position;

• a positive attitude;

• a clear idea of what you want to achieve;

• empathy – putting yourself in the police officer's position despite unreasonableness, intransigence and even impropriety on his or her behalf;

• a simple five-step process (see Table 9.1).

Probe	e.g. *Could you let me know why not?*
Write down the reply verbatim	
Ask reality-testing questions	e.g. *What position does that put me in?* *What would you do in my position?* *What do you expect me to do?*
Warn if your questions have no effect	e.g. *Your refusal to help on this matter forces me to draw conclusions which will affect the advice I give my client.*
Spell out your 'bottom line' if your warning has no effect	e.g. *If you are unwilling to tell me then I must inform my client that no evidence has been disclosed and advise him accordingly.*

Table 9.1 The five steps of principled negotiation

CONSULTATIONS WITH THE CUSTODY OFFICER

Your consultations with the custody officer will be on the telephone and, later, face to face at the police station (by which time it may be a different officer).

A Pocket Reference[5] gives detailed coverage of the issues involved in these consultations and provides simple objectives and checklists to achieve these (see Sections 6, 8, 9, 16 and 17 of that book).

In your telephone consultation, you should assume that the officer will not be ready, willing or able to tell you more than the most basic information. Do not expect the officer to volunteer the range or depth of detail you require. You have to ask.

At this early stage, Table 9.2 shows that some information is essential, other information is desirable.

Essential information	Desirable information
1. Full details of your client 2. Custody record number 3. Offence details 4. Circumstances leading up to arrest 5. Details of arrest 6. Events following arrest up to the present 7. Critical timings – arrest, detention, charge 8. Details of police officers involved – arresting officer and IO 9. Interviewing of your client – to date, in progress and intended 10. Details of any examination, advice and reporting by a medical examiner 11. Details of any first aid or medical treatment given 12. Taking of samples – to date, in progress and intended 13. Identification procedures – to date, in progress and intended	1. Other persons involved 2. Section 18 searches

Table 9.2 Essential and desirable information required from the custody officer

When you arrive at the police station, you will need to examine the custody record. PACE Code C, para. 2.4 states:

> *'A solicitor or appropriate adult must be permitted to consult the custody record of a person detained as soon as practicable after their arrival at the police station.'*

You must examine it closely since it provides crucial information concerning:

- decision-making and behaviour by the police, by your client and third parties from the time your client was initially brought to the police station;

- circumstances leading up to your client's arrest and police investigation, since it records interviewing, identification procedures and other statutory procedures, e.g. taking of samples.

You must ensure that you obtain a copy of the custody record before you leave the police station.

Custody officers, custody records and evidence

The custody officer and the custody record are unlikely to be a source of information concerning prosecution evidence. Custody officers and custody suite staff are instructed not to enter such information in the custody record. Furthermore, custody officers are now required to enter in their pocket books evidence given by officers presenting suspects for a detention decision. A request for details of evidence – as opposed to details of circumstances leading up to the arrest and the arrest itself – will be met with a refusal or a recommendation to ask the IO.

CONSULTATIONS WITH THE IO

In all your consultations with the IO, your task is to assess:

- the integrity of the police case;
- the nature, strength and sufficiency of the prosecution evidence;
- the adequacy of the police investigation.

You achieve this by interviewing the officer to establish:

- the purported facts of the matter and the officer's grasp of these;
- the extent to which sound investigative practices, particularly those covered by guidelines, have been observed and the officer's awareness of these matters.

Disclosure by IOs

The police service accepts that to cope with the prospect of being systematically interviewed by a legal adviser, an IO must:

- think and act in terms of quality investigation;
- have a sound grasp of the facts of the matter;
- have considered the matter of disclosure.

There is no obligation on the police to disclose the whole of the evidence against the suspect prior to interview: *R.* v. *Imran and Hussain* [1997] Crim. L.R. 754.

PEACE[6-8] advises officers to plan ahead for the police interview and for being interviewed by the legal adviser. The PEACE guidelines say they must not lie when briefing legal advisers. In the face of systematic, exhaustive and tenacious interviewing by a legal adviser an officer must respond flexibly, judging whether:

- to disclose the requested detail; or

- to refuse to say anything else on the issue in question; or

- to attempt to bring an end to questioning completely – giving a pre-emptive evasive response, e.g.

  'We have given what we consider to be the fullest appropriate information at this stage and now wish to give your client the opportunity of giving his account of this incident.'

Disclosure by the IO prior to the police interview of your client

Your first consultations with the IO may be on the telephone but certainly later, will be face to face, at the police station. Again, *A Pocket Reference*[9] gives detailed coverage of the issues involved in these consultations and provides simple objectives and checklists to achieve these (see Sections 10, 11, 19 and 20 of that book).

When you telephone the police station and are referred to the IO, it is again best to assume that he or she is neither ready, willing, nor able to tell you more than the basic information. As with the custody officer, do not expect the officer to volunteer the range or depth of detail you require.

Your attendance at the police station in person is a completely different matter. Here your task of active defence focuses upon:

- what the IO discloses;

- how he or she copes with:
  - being asked to give the fullest possible briefing on the police case, the prosecution evidence and the police investigation (i.e. a *case narrative*);
  - being systematically questioned concerning missing material, anomalous detail and the officers' observance of good practice and guidelines.

Responding to an attempt by the police to engage in the 'three-step' approach

In Chapter 2 we indicated that some forces have adopted a three-step approach to interviewing suspects:

- *Step 1*. There is no disclosure to the suspect or the suspect's legal adviser prior to interviewing. There is a relatively brief interview in which the suspect is invited to give his or her account, e.g. in response to a trigger such as, 'Everyone saw you attack him, what's your side of the story?' After the suspect has had his or her say the interview ends.

- *Step 2*. Evidence is disclosed, particularly guided by what the suspect has said.

- *Step 3*. The standard PEACE model is followed in respect of the three stages of the account phase:
  - *The suspect's agenda*: giving the suspect the opportunity to say what he or she wants or to raise issues he or she wishes to cover;
  - *The police agenda*: informing and questioning the suspect about matters considered by the IO to be material issues;
  - *Challenge*: confronting the suspect with anomalies, and apparent deception, identified by the IO within the interviewee's disclosures and responses in the previous stages.

The three stages of the PEACE model are entirely proper. The 'three-step' approach is wholly improper. *Under no circumstance whatsoever should you allow the police to engage in the 'three-step' approach*.

You must *never* allow your client to be interviewed until such time as disclosure has been made, a process which requires you to interview the IO systematically as an integral part of engaging in active defence of your client. If the police refuse to allow you to address the issue of disclosure and insist on interviewing your client first to get his or her 'version' or 'side of the story' (i.e. to implement step 1 of the 'three-step' approach), you must:

- state this is unacceptable;

- insist on advising your client in private;

- inform the police that you will be advising your client to remain silent in the intended interview and that at the outset of the interview you will be stating this and the reason for this, i.e. that there has been no disclosure of evidence;

- when alone with your client, advise him or her accordingly, i.e.
  - to remain silent throughout the interview;
  - that at the beginning of the interview you will advise him or her to remain silent because there has been no disclosure of evidence;
  - if there is any attempt by the police to get your client to answer questions you will intervene;

- if the police proceed to interview, at the outset of the interview when you are invited to introduce yourself, make a statement:
  - that you are advising your client to remain silent;
  - explaining why you give this advice;
  - indicating that your client will remain silent;
  - indicating that you will intervene if any attempt is made to influence your client to answer questions.

It is to be hoped that the police see sense and do not attempt to go further in implementing the 'three-step' approach.

Investigating the police case, the prosecution evidence and the police investigation

Investigate systematically, exhaustively and tenaciously.

Your investigation of the police case, the prosecution evidence and the police investigation will be systematic, exhaustive and tenacious if you consistently observe 'best practice' behaviours.

1. **Ask the question in the first place**. If you do not ask for information the officer does not have to worry about disclosure: you keep yourself in the dark.

2. **Omit nothing from your checklist**. This the only way you will establish whether the officer is withholding information.

3. **Record what the officer discloses as accurately and fully as possible**. You must not discard detail at this critical first stage of active defence. This means *do not* mentally edit, delete and compress what the IO tells you:

   - always, wherever possible, create a visual representation entering detail onto SE3R sheets or into *RealSense* on your laptop;
   - always, where appropriate, create grids;
   - always, where appropriate, draw diagrams;
   - do not make bullet notes;
   - do not summarise;
   - do not write down 'gist'.

If the officer goes too fast, break in, and ask him or her to slow down, or to stop, in order for you to keep up. If necessary, remind the officer that people speak at around 180–200 words a minute but can only write or type in tens of words a minute.

4. **Make no assumptions**. Resist the urge to fill in gaps on the basis of your knowledge or imagination:

   - this prevents you from spotting 'non barking dogs', i.e. actions and responses that could be reasonably expected to have happened;
   - assists an IO who wants to keep disclosure to a minimum or to withhold particular information to gain a tactical advantage:

     – hoping that your client might mention in interview something that is inconsistent with something that he police know or have;
     – hoping to surprise you and your client by producing an unanticipated piece of information or exhibit.

5. **Do not be seduced into solely processing the stated – always listen and look out for the unstated**. This is vital. Simply not saying something is the most common form of deception through avoidance, i.e. evasion.

6. **Look out for any lack of specificity**. *Lack of specificity* is the second most common way of deceiving, i.e. the recipient of the non-specific information jumps to conclusions and makes assumptions, a classic example of this being the response of the lawyer on the receiving end of information in *R.* v. *Mason* [1987] Crim. L.R. 757: assuming the police were alluding to his client's fingerprints

   You can expect lack of specificity to be very common in police disclosure so you must be extremely alert to its occurrence. Look out for vague and ambiguous verbs (action words). When you spot lack of specificity, stop the officer as quickly as possible, note the actual word or phrase and be prepared to probe it, either immediately or once the officer has finished talking on the topic in question.

   This scanning for lack of specificity applies to *all* aspects of the officer's disclosures. It is particularly significant in special warning conditions where *explicit detail* is necessary concerning:

   - the object, mark or substance (CJPOA, s.36);
   - your client's presence at a place at or about the time that the offence was committed (CJPOA, s.37).

   Be prepared to press immediately for the explicit detail.

7. **Always get IOs to produce visual representations**. You must explicitly ask the officer if he or she has:

- diagrams, sketches, illustrations or photographs of critical locations, relative positions, approach and exit routes, events and discovered items, marks and impressions in locations;
- any video recordings:

  - made at the scene by the FAO, crime scene attender/analyst or the SOCO;
  - made by CCTV surveillance cameras;
  - made by personal or commercial security cameras.

When the officer indicates the existence of any of these you must ask to view them. If the officer says they are not to hand:

- You must ask where they are.
- You must ask the officer to suspend your conversation in order to obtain them given the potential significance of these.

If the officer refuses, explain that:

- you will need to see the item(s) in question before advising your client, and will be questioning the officer about it then;
- since this is the case it will be of immediate benefit to both the officer and you to have the item(s) to hand to inform and to assist what you are talking about now;
- you can only urge the officer to get the item(s) at this point rather than to have further delay later, when you will be questioning the officer.

It is to be hoped that the officer sees the wisdom of getting and inspecting the items immediately.

Asking to view such material enables you:

- to find out whether the officers conducting the preliminary investigation or briefing produced a visual representation;
- to find out whether the IO has visited the scene of the crime or has liaised with the FAO, crime scene attender/analyst or the SOCO;
- in the case of an IO who has not been to the scene and has no visual representation in the crime file, to get the officer to represent graphically his or her understanding of spoken and written descriptions, e.g. briefings, handover notes, statements;
- to copy the representation, which later:

  - can be used to test the validity of further assertions by the IO – particularly in interview;
  - is likely to have evidential value should your client be charged and go to trial.

8. **Get the officer to state his or her line of reasoning**. Do not do the work of the police for them. It is down to the IO to explain:

   - how your client came to be associated in the arresting officer's mind with the offence in question;
   - why the police choose to believe the assertions of particular individuals;
   - the nature of the police case against your client and the underpinning evidence, which has emerged and exists (or potentially exists) that supports this case.

9. **Look at the officer's behaviour for non-verbal clues of stress**. Table 9.3 shows BASELINES – an acronym that conveniently summarises the major categories of behaviour that change when an individual is under stress. Look out for changes in the IO's BASELINES that can be expected to occur if the officer:

   - knows there are shortcomings in:

     - the police case, the prosecution evidence and the police investigation;
     - his or her grasp of these matters;

   - is seeking to avoid disclosing evidence.

Obtaining a case narrative

You must request the fullest possible case narrative from the officer. This is a briefing on the facts of the matter as he or she sees these concerning the police case, the police investigation and the prosecution evidence.

Typical police narrative content with a bearing upon disclosure is shown in Table 9.4 on page 345.

It is unlikely that the officer's narrative will include all the topics or the breadth of detail shown in Table 9.4.

Capture the officer's narrative, such as it is – in notes, on SE3R sheets or in *RealSense* on your computer, and in grids.

B	Blink rate	Increase
	Blood vessels (neck)	Swelling; pulsating
	Blushing	
	Breathing rate	Increase
	Brow	Creasing (perplexity)
A	Adaptors (grooming, manipulating)	Increase in most people; decrease in some
S	Shakling (hands; body) Sniffing Swallowing Sweating (hands; nostril; armpits)	
E	Eyes *Gaze:* Upwards; sideways Downwards *Pupils* *Eyebrows* ('flashes')	Thinking; memory recall Emotion; 'inner dialogue' Dilation Surprise; alarm
L	Lips Lower trunk 'Leakage'	Biting; licking Fidgeting Limb movements
I	Illustrators (demonstrative/emphatic hand movements	Decrease in most peoeple; increase in some people
N	Nods	Change in amount
E	Expressiveness: *Words* *Tone of voice*	Change in amount RSVP (rhythm; speed, volume; pitch) changes
S	Space Silence	Turning away, pushing backwards in the chair Long pauses; rejecting the talking turn

The acronym BASELINES helps you:

- to remember what changes are consistent with changes in an individual's 'base music' indicative of changes in arousal (stress);
- to monitor systematically – by knowing what momentary changes to look out for.

(From E. Shepherd, *A Pocket Reference.* Law Society Publishing, 1996).

Table 9.3 BASELINES: a checklist for stress indicators in behaviour

Topic	Examples of detail
Circumstances leading up to the offence	• Police acting on information received • Police surveillance
The occurrence of the offence	• Offence • Your client's involvement • Other persons involved
How the offence came to police attention	
Initial police response to the offence	

Initial police actions at the crime scene	• Identification of, and contact with:
	  • victims
	  • witnesses

Immediate police contact with other officers and police locations via radio	• Content of situation report • Circulated description of the offender or offenders (NB: This is the first description)
Subsequent police actions at the crime scene	• Interviewing of victims and witnesses • Recording of scene and vicinity (sketches; photographs; video recording) • Physical searches of scene and vicinity • Identification of material locations • Discovery of material items, marks, traces, etc • Securing the scene • Identification of further witnesses (by house-to-house enquiries)
Police contact with your client – prior to, at the time of and after the offence	• Questioning and arrest of your client (or the request to attend the police station) • During the journey to the police station • Whilst being booked into custody
Interviewing of your client	• At or near the scene of the offence • At another location, e.g. your client's home • *En route* to the police station • Following arrival at the police station
Identification procedures	• Type of procedure • Modality examined (visual; auditory)
Taking of fingerprints, photographs, body samples, swabs and impressions	
Physical examination of your client by a medical examiner (police surgeon)	
Subsequent police investigation	• Interviewing of the victim or witnesses • Taking, or making, of formal statements • Attendance by crime scene attender/SOCO • Searches of locations and vehicles • Submission of items for forensic analysis;
Other contact between your client and police officers since detention	• Requests by your client to talk with an officer • Taking your client to the scene

Table 9.4 Typical case narrative topics

As pointed out in Chapter 7, SE3R (described in detail in Appendix 7) is widely used throughout police forces, as well as being used in other agencies and by investigators in the private sector. If you see that the officer is briefing you from an SE3R sheet it is sensible to:

- ask if you can have a copy;

- if the officer refuses, use his or her briefing from the SE3R to enable you to construct your own SE3R sheets or enter the detail into *RealSense* on your computer. This will be extremely simple, and rapid, since he or she will be giving you the detail for each event, which you merely have to replicate on your own event line and abstract into identity bins.

Where the IO mentions two or more individuals involved in a process or action, or two or more sources of information, e.g. witnesses to the offence, quickly construct a grid for each action or scenario. If it is just two individuals, create two columns, and for more than two however many columns are required. Then you can draw rows across, thus creating cells in which to put corresponding information. This method will highlight what was, and, what was not done or said by a particular individual.

The result of these kinds of representation is a base of information for both analysis and probing purposes.

Reacting to disclosure

You must ask the officer for time to review your notes and to take stock. You need this to get a firm grasp of the material and to identify those areas which require probing. Resist being stampeded into responding quickiy to the officer's disclosures. The fact that the officer has disclosed material is not the end to it. You have to take the time to make sense of the material. *You must not 'rush to get it wrong'.*

Most particularly when you are reviewing what has been disclosed, you must be alert to:

- what the officer has not said;

- what the officer has said with particular reference to:
  - vague or ambiguous detail, i.e. lack of specificity;
  - anomalies, particularly deficiencies in detail, e.g. 'non barking dogs', absence of reasonably expected detail (e.g. the first description – and when and how this was relayed), jumps, gaps, partial descriptions, to name but a few.

Use the advice in Chapters 7 and 8 to guide your approach to collation and your search for these properties.

When you are ready, and only then, probe systematically and exhaustively information:

- that the officer has disclosed;

- that he or she has disclosed non-specifically; and

- that he or she has not disclosed.

Table 9.5 summaries:

- areas that commonly require probing;

- the detail to be questioned;

- recording requirements additional to that of taking detailed notes.

It follows that wherever possible you should add emergent information to your SE3R sheets or *RealSense* screens, as well as any grids you have created.

Reacting to blocking responses by the IO

If the IO seeks to block you when you are following a particular line of questioning, you should be persistent in negotiating disclosure. If the officer is obdurate in his or her refusal, you can be relatively sure that the topic of your questioning, and unsuccessful negotiation, is likely to be a material issue in terms of evidence. Conclude your questioning by asking the officer directly a suitably phrased question to establish whether that which you are asking about is a material issue in the case, e.g. 'Is finger-print evidence linking my client to the scene material evidence against my client?'

Note the officer's reply and move on, making a note that this form of evidence must be covered in your consultation with your client.

CONSULTATION WITH THE APPROPRIATE ADULT

A Pocket Reference[10] covers in detail the issues involved in, and objectives and checklists for, your consultations with the appropriate adult (see Sections 21 and 22 of that book).

347

Area	Detail to be questioned	Additional recording requirements
Covert information on your client	• If police acted upon information received, ask for details of: – source of information; – circumstances which led informant to provide information – including the motivation/inducement involved; – involvement of informant in the offence in question. • If your client was subject to surveillance, ask for details of: – duration of surveillance; – type of surveillance; – results of surveillance.	
Crime scene	• Ask for details of individuals who have attended the crime scene – FOA, crime scene attender, SOCO. • Ask to see copies of written records of actions prepared by each of these individuals. • Ask to see copies of visual records (sketches; video recordings) made by each of these individuals: – of the scene; – of the vicinity; – of searches conducted of the scene and the vicinity.	Reproduce any sketches.
Key visual representations (scene; other material locations, e.g. of your client's arrest if purportedly near to scene)	• Ask if there are key visual representations in the crime file. • If none, ask why not. • Ask if the IO has visited key locations – the crime scene or any other material location in the case: – if yes, ask him or her to draw a visual representation; – if no, ask him or her to draw a visual representation based upon his or her understanding of the material in the crime file.	Reproduce any sketches.
Searches of locations and vehicles associated with your client	• Ask for details – where, what, when, who authorised, grounds. • Ask for outcome – what was found.	
Circulated description of offender	• Ask if the FOA circulated a description of the offender. • Ask for details of the description (from force operational information system). • Ask to see the description (print-out from system).	

Table 9.5 Areas that commonly require probing

Area	Detail to be questioned	Additional recording requirements

Witness accounts, descriptions and formal statements (NB: victim = witness)	• Ask if accounts, descriptions and formal statements have been obtained from all witnesses at the scene, in the vicinity or associated in any way with the offence and circumstances leading up the offence.
	• If not, why not.
	• If not disclosed, ask if any witnesses gave accounts, descriptions or statements which constituted negative evidence.
	
	For each witness:
	• ask how many accounts/statements has he or she given;
	• ask if the witness:
	  – was at the scene;
	  – was subsequently contacted – if so, why and how;
	  – contacted the police – if so, why and how;
	• ask if the witness had, or would have had, the opportunity to:
	  – hear any other witness give an account or description;
	  – talk with other people or hear other people talking, before speaking to the police;
	• for each account/statement, ask about:
	  – its form (verbal/written; audio/video taped);
	  – its provenance (where, when and to whom given);
	• ask for details of:
	  – the first description given;
	  – every subsequent description given.
	• ask if the PEACE ADVOKATE (*R.* v. *Turnbull*) checks have been applied (see Annex to this chapter);
	• where applicable, ask why the final element of ADVOKATE (action with discrepancies) has not been implemented;
	• if the ADVOKATE checks have not been applied, ask:
	  – why not;
	  – when they will be applied;
	• ask to see each statement;
	• if statement interview was audio/video recorded, ask to listen to/view interview;
	• if refused, ask for the salient points in each statement to be read to you.
		• Note all instances of negative evidence.
		• Prepare a grid with a separate column per account, description or statement:
		  – put detail as key points in the first column (= first description);
		  – put detail from the account, description or statement in corresponding positions in next column;
		  – repeat process for next statement, and so on.
		
		• Inspect the grid:
		  – examine entries across (rows) and down (columns);
		  – identify consistencies, gaps, vagaries, anomalies and inconsistencies.

Table 9.5 *(continued)* Areas that commonly require probing

Area	Detail to be questioned	Additional recording requirements

House-to-house enquiries	• Ask if these have been conducted.
	• If yes, ask for details of:
	  – location canvassed;
	  – number of enquiries;
	  – questionnaire (request sight of this);
	  – results.
	• If negative evidence is not mentioned, ask if any respondents gave such evidence.
	• If yes, ask for details.
		Note:
		• wording of questionnaire;
		• all instances of negative evidence.

Specialist opinion and testimony	• Where applicable, ask if specialist opinion has been sought or provided, e.g. fire service IO; force scientific support staff; medical examiner; forensic scientist. • If yes, ask for results and sight of reporting. • If not, ask why no report has been requested or provided.	Reproduce any visual representations.

Object evidence	• Ask systematically about every possible kind of object evidence – recovered or discovered through searching/examining locations, vehicles and people:
	  – material items of any kind;
	  – marks and traces of any kind – including fingerprints, impressions, fibres, etc;
	  – substances of any kind – including human body fluids;
	  – recordings of any kind – audio, video, e.g. security CCTV.
	• Ask for current location of item.
	• Where applicable, ask if item sent for forensic analysis or any other form of analysis.
	• If yes, ask for results.
	• If no, ask why not.
	• Where applicable, ask to see item (or listen to/view recording) (NB: do not accept a partial viewing/hearing).
		Make sketches where appropriate.

Significant statements by, or silence from, your client (NB: statements include admissions)	• If not mentioned, ask if there has been any statement or silence deemed to be significant.
	• If mentioned, ask for details:
	  – ask if, and when, your client has been requested to sign notes;
	  – ask to see notes.	

Table 9.5 *(continued)* Areas that commonly require probing

Area	Detail to be questioned	Additional recording requirements
Identification by witnesses	• Ask for details – what kind of procedure, where, when, what modality tested. • Ask for results. • If no mention of someone other than your client being identified, ask if such an identification occurred. • If yes, ask for details – including descriptions of the individual identified.	
Interviewing of your client to date	• If interviewed outside the police station: – ask if, and when, your client has been requested to sign notes; – ask to see the notes. • If interviewed on tape ask to listen to the working copy: – either a 'fast' copy made by the officer; – or the actual working copy with an officer present.	
Accounts or statements by co-accused	• Ask if there is a co-accused. • Ask if the co-accused has given an account or a statement (given in interview or under other circumstances) to which the officer will be referring. • If yes, ask for the details to which the officer will be referring. • Ask for sight of the document or to listen to the recording (NB: do not accept a partial viewing/hearing).	

Table 9.5 *(continued)* Areas that commonly require probing

351

CONSULTATION WITH YOUR CLIENT

A Pocket Reference[11] covers in detail the issues involved in, and objectives and checklists for, your consultations with your client (see Sections 25 and 26 of that book). You must continuously assess your client in terms of his or her vulnerability.

Your client's narrative

You must compare what the IO has disclosed with what your client and the appropriate adult disclose in relation to the police case, the prosecution evidence and the police investigation. You need to note instances of match and mismatch, probing where appropriate to explore manifest anomalies, as well as revealed omissions or inconsistencies in the police account.

Defending by giving disclosure in the police station

Becoming Skilled[12] (Chapter 8) explains in detail the issues in respect of advising your client about whether he or she should give disclosure in interview (Section 8.3). *A Pocket Reference*[13] presents these in succinct form. If you advise your client to give disclosure, you should consider how this should best be done and the extent of the facts that should be disclosed.

By this point you will have done the following.

- Obtained as much information as you can about the police case and the prosecution evidence.

- Made a judgement concerning the degree to which the police have disclosed detail on the police case and the prosecution evidence, mindful that:

  – there is no obligation on the police to disclose the whole of the evidence against a suspect prior to interview: *R.* v. *Imran and Hussain* [1997] Crim. L.R. 754;

  – blocking responses to your systematic requests for disclosure, and to your focused questions on particular types of evidence, point to the likelihood that evidence is being withheld;

  – non-disclosure by the police may be a good reason for persuading the court not to draw an adverse inference from your client's corresponding non-disclosure.

  In *R.* v. *Roble* [1977] Crim. L.R. 449 the Court of Appeal stated that the fact that the police have disclosed to the solicitor little or nothing of the nature of the case against the suspect, so that the solicitor cannot usefully advise the suspect, is a matter which might be relevant when a court is considering whether it is reasonable to expect a suspect to mention a fact when questioned under CJPOA, s.34.

- non-disclosure by the police in relation to any aspect of the police case or prosecution evidence may not be a good reason for non-disclosure by your client about another aspect in relation to which there has been disclosure.

  In *R.* v. *Kavanagh* 1997 (unreported) the Court of Appeal approved the trial judge's summing-up, that a failure by the police to disclose the location of fingerprints, while it might make a failure by the accused to mention facts in relation to fingerprints reasonable, did not make it reasonable for the accused to fail to give detail of his alibi or earlier visits to the victim's house.

• Assessed the strengths and weaknesses of the prosecution evidence and police case – applying the following questions:

- What is the evidence?
- How strong is the evidence?
- Is it admissible?
- Will it be available at trial?
- Are there admissions already made in a signed pocket book entry or in an earlier interview?

• Obtained sufficient instructions from your client about his or her version of events.

A written statement taken from your client to be used if necessary as an alternative to your client answering questions in interview and to rebut an inference of recent fabrication at trial, should contain as many of the facts as possible to be used at trial. Otherwise there is a risk that the court will infer that the missing facts were fabricated subsequently or were not sufficiently robust to withstand police investigation.

The statement should be taken before the police interview, timed, dated and signed by you and your client.

• Assessed your client's potential vulnerability when called upon to give reliable disclosure in interview in terms of his or her:

- age – with particular reference to maturity;
- experience of contact with the police, of being in custody and of being questioned in interview rooms;
- mental state – in terms of cause for concern.

In *R.* v. *Argent* [1997] Crim. L.R. 346, the Court of Appeal stated that matters such as the following may all be relevant when a court is considering whether it is reasonable to expect the accused to have mentioned a fact when questioned under CJPOA, s.34:

- the time of day;
- the suspect's:

    (a) age;
    (b) experience;
    (c) mental capacity;
    (d) state of health;
    (e) sobriety;
    (f) tiredness;
    (g) personality.

The Court of Appeal clarified the term 'accused'. This refers to the actual accused with such qualities, apprehensions, knowledge and advice as he or she is shown to have at the time 'not to some hypothetical, reasonable accused of ordinary phlegm and fortitude'.

You will find that monitoring your client's BASELINES is a useful guide to identifying your client's level of stress. Detailed advice on assessing a suspect's vulnerability, including mental state, intellectual disadvantage and problems with comprehension, is given in *A Pocket Reference*.[14]

Adverse inferences

Of fundamental importance is your judgement as to what advice to give in respect of the safest option – mindful of the issue of a potential adverse inference being drawn from a failure to give relevant facts in answer to police questions. The adverse inference that may be drawn from silence and which you will wish to negate may be:

- that your client did not have a defence at the time of the interview;

- that key elements of your client's false defence were lacking, or had not been fully thought through, at the time of the interview;

- that your client's false defence would not stand up to critical scrutiny through police questioning;

- that non-co-operation with the police is indicative of your client's guilt, because it is believed that innocent people co-operate with the police and answer questions.

R. v. Daniel [1998] Crim. L.R. 819; *R. v. Randall* CA 3 April 1998 6 Archbold News [1998]; *R. v. Taylor* [1999] Crim. L.R. 77; *R. v. Beckles and Montague* [1999] Crim. L.R. 148.

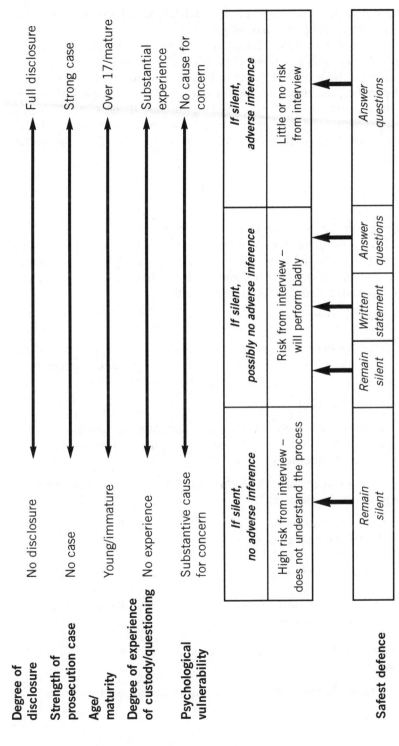

Figure 9.1 The safest option: a decision-making template

If a suspect is refused access to legal advice before the interview, the prosecutor may not attach any weight to the suspect's failure to answer questions in that interview. The interviewing officer should make written notes of those questions that the suspect failed, or refused, to answer. Once the suspect has been offered access to legal advice, the interviewing officer should put the previously unanswered questions to the suspect again and ask if the suspect wishes to add anything further. If the suspect remains silent when reinterviewed, an inference may be drawn: Home Office Circular 53/1998 *Inferences from Silence where Access to Legal Advice has been Delayed.*

The advice given

The advice you give and the decision your client makes at this stage have vital implications for the later conduct of active defence on behalf of your client – particularly in terms of the prosecutor's disclosure of unused material and the inference that could be drawn from a failure to make a defence statement, and the ramifications of these.

The alternatives open to you are:

- to delay the interview because you consider your client to be unfit to be interviewed, by virtue of the effects of drink, drugs or degree of distress;
- to advise your client:
  - to answer no questions and make no written statement;
  - to answer no questions but to give a written statement;
  - to answer questions;
- if you advise your client to give a written statement, to recommend the stage at which this is given:
  - before the interview;
  - during the interview;
  - at the close of the interview;
  - after the interview.

You have the difficult task of coming to an overall decision based upon five dimensions of assessment:

- degree of police disclosure of information: from no disclosure to full disclosure;
- strength of the prosecution case: from no case to strong case;

- your client's maturity as indicated, albeit approximately, by his or her age: from young to 17 and over;

- your client's degree of experience of being questioned by the police: from no experience to very experienced;

- your client's mental state: from a clear cause for concern to no cause for concern.

Figure 9.1 on page 355 provides a decision-making template, which enables you:

- to map your assessments of these five dimensions upon the likelihood of an adverse inference being drawn from silence;

- to identify the degree of risk posed by the interviewing process;

- to identify the appropriate advice to give to your client.

PRESENTING REASONS FOR NON-COOPERATION

If non-cooperation is based on legal advice, it is particularly important that you present the reasons for this and in a way that does not waive legal privilege, e.g. the advice and the reasons for it are given to the suspect at the beginning of, and during, the taped interview. (Note: if at *voire dire*, privilege is waived when evidence is being given of the advice to remain silent, privilege is waived in front of the jury later even if the evidence of the advice to remain silent is not repeated to the jury: *R.* v. *Bowden* [1999] 1 W.L.R. 823.)

DISCLOSURE TO THE POLICE OF AN ALIBI

You must be extremely wary when disclosing to the police an alibi and naming alibi witnesses. You must be mindful of the wider implications of *R.* v. *Seymour* [1996] Crim. L.R. 512, where the defence:

- served an alibi notice before it had taken proof from the alibi witness;

- imposed no requirement in its notification that the prosecution should take its statement from the witness in the presence of the defence.

As a result, the police interviewed the alibi witness in the absence of the defence solicitors and obtained a statement which:

- was not disclosed to the defence;
- was used to destroy the credibility of the alibi witness at trial.

The defence appealed that the statement should have been disclosed to them. The Court of Appeal did not agree.

You can avoid this problem by:

- bearing in mind that you must be present in any interview conducted by the police, i.e. of witnesses whom you intend to call for the defence but whom the police will seek to interview in order to obtain a statement;
- serving notice on the police that if they wish to interview a (named) alibi witness:
  - you must be informed;
  - you will wish to attend;
- advising the witness to refuse to be interviewed if you are not present.

DISCLOSURES BY THE IO IN THE POLICE INTERVIEW

It is crucial that you monitor and intervene in a timely and appropriate manner in the police interview. This is because it is in the interview room that the majority of officers disclose most information on the nature of the police case, the prosecution evidence and the police investigation. *A Pocket Reference*[15] describes the issues involved and gives simple objectives and a checklist of actions (see Sections 29 and 30 of that book).

In many instances, the IO will produce information or evidence that he or she did not allude to, or refused to disclose, in your earlier consultation. For example, the officer may:

- attempt to read from an account, description or statement attributed to a unnamed or named individual or a co-accused;
- refer to photographs, electronic recordings, and other forms of technologically derived data, e.g. video recordings (including security CCTV, overt recordings and covert – surveillance – recordings), audio recordings (including PACE recordings), intercepted telecommunications, and information gathered from various forms of information technology used by, or accessible to, your client.

If this happens, simply follow the advice in *A Pocket Reference*.[16] This guides you:

• to stop the interview;

• to request, and where necessary negotiate, full disclosure of the information or evidence;

• to probe for detail;

• to request, where applicable, sight of, a viewing or a hearing of the material;

• to request time to advise your client in private before interviewing recommences.

IDENTIFICATION PROCEDURES

Identification procedures are a minefield. However, if you follow the advice given in *A Pocket Reference*,[17] and have a firm grasp of the issues explained in *Becoming Skilled*,[18] you will find that the conduct of an identification parade can be a vital source of information in the subsequent defence of your client, e.g.

• the content of the briefings given to you and to witnesses;

• the behaviour and utterances of the officer in charge of the parade;

• the behaviour and utterances of witnesses.

OBTAINING DETAIL FROM WITNESS STATEMENTS AT THE TIME OF CHARGING

In a number of forces, custody officers are requiring officers to have copies of key witness statements prepared at the time of charging.

At the time your client is being charged:

• Establish whether key witness statements are ready.

• If the key witness statements are ready, then immediately request sight of the statements – this request should be granted since it is the defence's right to see key witness statements.

- If the officer refuses sight but is prepared to disclose the detail, take this down verbatim, simultaneously recording this on your handheld tape-recorder.

TAPE RECORDINGS

You must request copies of tape recordings of interviewing of your client before you leave the station. As pointed out in Chapters 7 and 8, there is no reason why they cannot be produced immediately given that designated police stations have fast tape-copying machines that take a couple of minutes to reproduce a tape.

ACTIONS ONCE YOU HAVE LEFT THE POLICE STATION

Briefing alibi witnesses

You must immediately contact any alibi witness in order:

- to take a statement from him or her;
- to give him or her your 24-hour contact details;
- to brief him or her that:
  - your client has nominated him or her as an alibi witness;
  - the police may seek to interview him or her;
  - you have told the police that they are not to interview him or her without informing you and enabling you to be present during the interview;
  - you will contact him or her when the police inform you that they wish to interview him or her;
  - should the police attempt to contact him or her:

    (a) he or she should politely say that he or she will not agree to be interviewed until the police have told you and made sure that you will be present;

    (b) he or she is to contact you immediately the conversation with the police ends.

Processing the information you have collected and collated

You must make full notes. If you will continue to represent the client after charge, you must:

- open up a case file and start a case chronology (assisted by your systematic interviewing of the IO and the IO's disclosures in the interview) and a case information file: see Chapter 7;

- analyse the material you have accumulated: see Chapter 8.

Notes

1. Shepherd, E. (1996) *Becoming Skilled.* London: Law Society Publishing.
2. Shepherd, E. (1996) *A Pocket Reference.* London: Law Society Publishing.
3. Shepherd, E. (1996) *Becoming Skilled.* London: Law Society Publishing.
4. Shepherd, E. (1996) *A Pocket Reference.* London: Law Society Publishing.
5. *Ibid.*
6. *A Guide to Interviewing.* (1992) Harrogate: Central Planning and Training Unit.
7. *A Guide to Interviewing.* (1996) Bramshill: Police Staff College.
8. *A Practical Guide to Investigative Interviewing.* (1998) Bramshill: National Crime Faculty.
9. Shepherd, E. (1996) *A Pocket Reference.* London: Law Society Publishing.
10. *Ibid.*
11. *Ibid.*
12. Shepherd, E. (1996) *Becoming Skilled.* London: Law Society Publishing.
13. Shepherd, E. (1996) *A Pocket Reference.* London: Law Society Publishing.
14. *Ibid.*
15. *Ibid.*
16. *Ibid.*
17. *Ibid.*
18. Shepherd, E. (1996) *Becoming Skilled.* London: Law Society Publishing.

ANNEX 1

THE ADVOKATE CHECKS

The PEACE guidelines say that officers must apply *R.* v. *Turnbull* guidelines when:

- questioning an eyewitness or victim to obtain information;
- compiling a witness statement from the eyewitness or victim.

The PEACE model provides officers with a mnemonic – ADVOKATE – to enable them to apply the *R.* v. *Turnbull* guidelines as a series of systematic checks.

A	Amount of time under observation	How long did the witness have the suspect in view?
D	Distance	What was the distance between the witness and the suspect?
V	Visibility	What was the visibility like at the time?
O	Obstruction	Were there any obstructions to the view of the witness?
K	Known or seen before	Had the witness ever seen the suspect before? If so, where and when?
A	Any reason to remember	Did the witness have any special reason for remembering the suspect?
T	Time lapse	How long has elapsed since the witness saw the suspect?
E	Error or material discrepancy	Are there any errors or material discrepancies between descriptions given in the first and subsequent accounts of the witness?

Accounting for discrepancies

In the case of discrepancies between a witness's first and any subsequent accounts PEACE guidelines say an officer should:

- account for these discrepancies if possible;
- include these discrepancies in the statement, i.e. not clean up the account by omitting them.

CHAPTER 10

Primary disclosure: the prosecutor's duty to disclose unused material to the defence

This chapter considers the responsibility of the prosecutor to make primary disclosure to the accused. In our explanation, we will draw attention to the debate that surrounded the Criminal Procedure and Investigations Bill prior to its enactment as the CPIA – in particular to the issue of what constitutes undermining material.

THE PROSECUTOR SHOULD CONSIDER DISCLOSURE BEFORE THE ACT'S PROVISIONS APPLY

The CPS must consider from the initial stage of a case whether unused material should be disclosed to the defence before the time when CPIA applies. This was the decision of the Divisional Court on 18 March 1999, which went on to indicate how the common law obligations in relation to the pre-committal period should be 'radically recast'.

Giving judgment in *R. v. DPP ex parte Lee* (1999) 2 All E.R. 737, Kennedy LJ said:

> *'The 1996 Act does not specifically address the period between arrest and committal, and whereas in most cases prosecution disclosure can wait until after committal without jeopardising the defendant's right to a fair trial, the prosecutor must always be alive to the need to make advance disclosure of material of which he is aware (either from his own consideration of the papers or because his attention has been drawn to it by the defence) and which he, as a responsible prosecutor, recognises should be disclosed at an earlier stage. Examples canvassed before us were:*
>
> *(a) Previous convictions of a complainant or deceased if that information could reasonably be expected to assist the defence when applying for bail;*

(b) Material which might enable a defendant to make a pre-committal application to stay the proceedings as an abuse of process;

(c) Material which will enable the defendant to submit that he should only be committed for trial on a lesser charge, or perhaps that he should not be committed for trial at all;

(d) Material which will enable the defendant and his legal advisers to make preparations for trial which may be significantly less effective if disclosure is delayed (e.g. names of eye-witnesses who the prosecution do not intend to use).

Even before committal a responsible prosecutor should be asking himself what, if any, immediate disclosure justice and fairness requires him to make in the particular circumstances of the case. Very often the answer will be none, and rarely if at all should the prosecutor's answer to that continuing piece of self-examination be the subject of dispute in this court.'

THE REQUIREMENT TO DISCLOSE UNDERMINING MATERIAL

Under CPIA, the prosecutor is required to disclose to the accused previously undisclosed prosecution material, which, in the opinion of the prosecutor, might undermine the prosecution case, or else to give the accused a written statement that there is no such material: section 3(1).

WHEN THE PROSECUTOR MUST GIVE PRIMARY DISCLOSURE

This applies where a person pleads not guilty to a summary or indictable offence in a magistrates' court or youth court (section 1(1)), or where a person is sent for trial for an indictable offence: section 1(2).

It does not apply to a person who is charged with an indictable offence and has indicated an intention at mode of trial to plead guilty (section 41), and has as a result been convicted by a magistrates' court or sentenced by that court or committed to the Crown Court for sentence. The government wishes to spare the police the task of preparing and the CPS the work involved in reading papers where the accused is likely to plead guilty anyway.

Although it does not require the prosecutor to disclose any unused material if the accused pleads guilty in the magistrates' court, the *Manual of Guidance*[1] requires the police, if it is available and applicable, to submit form MG6 to the prosecutor with all files. In this form, the investigator is asked to comment on the strengths and weaknesses of the witnesses and give information about 'others arrested and not charged', relevant previous convictions of witnesses and anything with a bearing on the offence or decision to prosecute.

Timescale

Under the Act, the prosecutor must give primary disclosure during a period beginning and ending with such days as the Secretary of State prescribes by regulations under section 3(8). The period fixed by regulations can be extended, on application, by the court: section 12(3).

The government has not set time limits for prosecution disclosure. The timing of disclosure is governed by the transitional provisions in section 13 of the Act: the prosecutor must act as soon as is reasonably practicable after the accused pleads not guilty or is committed or sent for trial or the proceedings are transferred.

If time limits are set, a failure to make prosecution disclosure within a time limit will not of itself constitute grounds for staying proceedings for abuse of process (section 10(2)), but the protection does not apply if delay by the prosecution is such as to prevent the accused from receiving a fair trial: section 10(3).

It applies in relation to alleged offences into which no criminal investigation had begun before the day on which the provisions were brought into force: section 1(3). The Secretary of State appointed the date 1 April 1997 for this purpose. The existing common law rules on disclosure continue to apply to offences where the investigation began before the appointed day. The 'old' and the 'new' schemes operate at the same time.

Different disclosure provisions may apply to individual co-accused or to separate offences alleged against one accused.

At what point does a criminal investigation begin? A criminal investigation is defined as an investigation that police officers or others have a duty to conduct with a view to it being ascertained whether a person should be charged with an offence or whether a person who has been charged with an offence is guilty of it: section 1(4); CPIA Code of Practice, para. 2.1.

The CPIA disclosure provisions apply to an alleged offence committed before 1 April 1997 where a criminal investigation had not begun until on or after that day, e.g. which was not reported to the police until on or after 1 April 1997. It also includes investigations the purpose of which is to ascertain whether a crime has been committed, with a view to the possible institution of criminal proceedings: Code of Practice, para. 2.1. However, an investigation that begins before 1 April 1997 in the belief that a crime may be committed, for example when the police keep premises or individuals under observation for a period of time, again with a view to the possible institution of criminal proceedings, only becomes an investigation into the alleged offence once the alleged offence has been committed. This means that if the investigation began before 1 April 1997, but the alleged offence was committed on or after that date the CPIA will apply: *R.* v. *Norwich Stipendary Magistrate ex parte Keable (and other appeals)* [1998] The Times 5 February. The CPS and the court will rely upon the police to inform them when an investigation began for the purpose of determining whether the 'old' or 'new' disclosure provisions apply.

MATERIAL

Material is defined as material of all kinds, including information and objects of all descriptions: section 2(4). The prosecutor's duty of disclosure is limited to material that is in the prosecutor's possession, or which he or she has been allowed to inspect in pursuance of the Code of Practice: section 3(2). The Code is reproduced at Appendix 3.

The Code provides that the prosecutor may inspect any material obtained in the course of a criminal investigation and recorded in accordance with the provisions of the Code: section 23(1)(e). The definition of prosecution material is case specific, so that the duties of disclosure relate only to material obtained in the present case: section 3(2).

METHOD OF DISCLOSURE

If the material is information that has been recorded, the prosecutor discloses it to the accused either by giving him or her a copy or, if the prosecutor thinks that it is not practicable or desirable (or under section 3(5), if it is not recorded because it is an object of some kind) by allowing the accused to inspect it at a reasonable time and place or by taking steps to secure that he or she is allowed to do so: section 3(4).

MATERIAL THAT UNDERMINES THE DEFENCE CASE

There is no duty on the prosecutor to disclose material that undermines the defence case. The prosecution's duty of disclosure does not extend to material that is only relevant to the credibility of a defence witness: *R.* v. *Brown* [1994] 1 W.L.R. 1599.

SANCTION FOR FAILURE

If the prosecutor does not make primary disclosure, an adverse inference cannot be drawn if the accused does not make a written statement of his or her defence.

THE MEANING OF UNDERMINING MATERIAL

We pointed out in Chapter 6 that during the passage of the Bill through Parliament, there was a lengthy debate about the meaning of undermining material. We reiterate here the government explanation of what it intended the term to mean:

> *'Material which, generally speaking, has an **adverse effect on the strength of the prosecution case**... (for example): a witness statement containing a description of the alleged offender, which is different from the description of the accused... a psychiatric report showing that the main prosecution witness has a history of psychiatric disorder with a tendency to fantasise.'*[2]

The government White Paper, 'Disclosure' CM 2864 at para. 42 gave examples of undermining material:

• if part of the prosecution case is a statement by a witness that he or she saw the accused near the scene of the crime shortly after it was committed, it will be necessary to disclose a statement by another witness that he or she saw a person of a different description from the accused at the same time and place;

• if the defendant has told the police in an interview that he or she was acting in self-defence, it will be necessary to disclose the statement of any witness who supports this but whom the prosecution does not regard as truthful;

• if the prosecution is aware that its main witness has a previous conviction, it must disclose it to the defence, since it may affect the weight to be placed on his testimony;

• if previous versions of witness statements are inconsistent with the final version served on the defence, they must be disclosed.

What is the responsibility of the prosecutor if the accused discloses a defence to the police during the initial investigation? The prosecutor should

367

clearly respond by disclosing, as undermining material, any material that assists that defence. Self-defence was an example given in the list above.

The government in Parliament gave this example of an early disclosure of alibi:

> 'Let us suppose that the accused has given to a police officer an explanation for the offence with which he or she has been charged. That will be passed on to the prosecutor and will tell him or her something about what the defence case might be ... If ... material points away from the accused, it is very likely to undermine the prosecution case and fall within the ... disclosure test.'[3]

In addition, the Code of Practice, para. 7.3, makes specific provision for this by requiring the disclosure officer, at the same time as he or she gives the prosecutor the schedule, to copy to the prosecutor 'information provided by an accused person which indicates an explanation for an offence with which he or she has been charged'.

It has always been accepted that, if the accused discloses a defence to the police during the investigation, the prosecutor should clearly respond by giving any material that assists that defence on primary disclosure.

What has taken longer to be recognised is that the prosecution case may be undermined as a result of a particular defence that the defendant may or may not run: the mere fact that there is material in the possession of the prosecution that raises a new issue in the case, which may assist the defence, is sufficient to fulfil the test 'might undermine'.[4]

It is now widely acknowledged that the statutory test for primary disclosure is the same as the test of relevance confirmed by the Court of Appeal in R. v. Keane (1994) 1 W.L.R. 746; (1994) 2 All E.R. 478; (1994) 99 Cr. App. R. 1; (1995) Crim. L.R. 224. Documents are material, and therefore ordinarily felt to be disclosed, if they can be seen on a sensible appraisal by the prosecution:

1. to be relevant to an issue in the case;

2. to raise or possibly raise a new issue the existence of which is not apparent from the evidence the prosecution proposes to use;

3. to hold a real (as opposed to a fanciful) prospect of providing a lead on evidence that goes to either of the above two.

This means that, generally speaking, any material that goes to an essential element of the offence(s) charged and which points away from the accused having committed the alleged offence(s) with the required intent, will have an adverse effect on the strength of the prosecution case and so ought to be disclosed to the defence at the primary stage.[5]

At the time of writing, the Attorney General had issued draft guidelines, for consultation, on disclosure[6] which adopted this approach. They stated that primary disclosure will include anything that tends to show a fact inconsistent with the case that must be proved by the prosecution and required the prosecutor also to pay particular attention to material that may weaken the prosecution case such as material which may point to another person having involvement in the commission of the offence. They required such material to be given as primary disclosure even though it suggests a defence inconsistent with or alternative to one already advanced by the accused or his solicitor.

The prosecutor should disclose anything which might:

- assist the defence to cross-examine prosecution witnesses;

- enable the defence to call evidence;

- enable the defence to advance a line of enquiry/argument;

- explain or mitigate the defendant's actions.

In most cases, it should be possible for the prosecutor to disclose all necessary material in primary disclosure. The defence is usually known and material, which might assist a different defence than that, falls to be disclosed then anyway. A prosecutor should resist any temptation to wait until he knows the defence before carrying out the disclosure exercise. Secondary disclosure should be a backstop only: for material that the prosecutor could not be expected to identify for himself as disclosable.

The CPS on 8 September 1999 issued instructions to staff that the previous convictions of all prosecution witnesses must be disclosed to the defence at the same time that primary disclosure is dealt with. These instructions reflected advice from Senior Treasury Counsel as to the effect of the decision of the Court of Appeal in *Guney* [1998] Cr. App. R. 242; [1999] Crim. L.R. 485.

PROSECUTION WITNESS'S PREVIOUS CONVICTIONS

The courts have concluded that when deciding whether to disclose a prosecution witness's previous conviction, 'the test must be whether a reasonable jury or other tribunal of fact could regard it as tending to shake confidence in the reliability of the witness': *Wilson* v. *Police* [1992] 2 N.Z.L.R. 523. The presumption must be that a previous conviction would have that effect and should always be disclosed.

A POLICE OFFICER'S DISCIPLINARY OR CRIMINAL CONVICTIONS

The credibility of a police officer's evidence may be of great importance. Internal disciplinary findings may reflect significantly upon the officer's honesty. That officer's evidence in later court proceedings should be treated with caution.

A police officer's disciplinary record will be disclosed to the CPS on confidential information form MG6B. The form will report the following kinds of information:

- disciplinary finding;

- criminal convictions/cautions;

- the officer is charged with a disciplinary offence or a criminal offence.

The disclosability of a police officer's criminal convictions, disciplinary charges found proved and the fabrication of evidence in other cases by an officer who is alleged to have fabricated evidence in the present case has been established. But an officer should not be cross-examined about a criminal offence in respect of which he or she has been charged but not yet tried, complaints to the Police Complaints Authority upon which there has been no adjudication, an acquittal in a previous case, which did not necessarily indicate that the jury disbelieved the officer, or the alleged discreditable conduct of the officer's colleagues: *R.* v. *Edwards* [1991] 2 All E.R. 266.

The fact that a jury returns a verdict of not guilty does not go to prove that an important witness for the prosecution, albeit the sole witness, is a liar: *R.* v. *Thorne and Others* (1978) 66 Cr. App. R. 6.

The common law decisions referred to in this chapter remain persuasive as the judicial reasoning behind them still holds good.

SUBJECTIVE TEST

What the prosecutor should disclose is a subjective test at the primary disclosure stage and this decision is not open to review, as the prosecutor assesses whether there is any material that, in his or her opinion, may undermine the case against the accused.

The government explained that:

> *'The prosecutor lays a case against the accused by charging him or her*
> *... If evidence Y undermines the prosecutor's case, it is perfectly right*
> *that the prosecutor's opinion should be the judge of that ... The*
> *prosecutor must bring his best judgement to bear, bound by his*
> *professional ethics and the Code for Crown Prosecutors.'[7]*

THE SCHEDULE

At the same time as he or she discloses any material that may undermine
the prosecution case, the prosecutor is required to provide the accused with
a schedule of non-sensitive unused prosecution material. The government
told Parliament that the main function of the schedule is to notify the
prosecutor of material retained by the investigator, which does not form
part of the case against the accused and which the prosecution will not
previously have seen, so that the prosecution can make informed decisions
on disclosure.[8]

This is reflected in the Code of Practice, which specifically requires the
disclosure officer to describe each item sufficiently to enable the prosecutor
(there is no reference to the accused) to form a judgement on whether the
material needs to be disclosed.

What the government never envisaged was the situation that now obtains.
Chapter 3 described the interplay of cultural, operational, psychological,
managerial and supervisory realities, which act as continuing barriers to
effective and ethical investigation. These same realities now, following the
manner in which the CPIA assigns an all-powerful role to disclosure
officers, militate to corrupt the process of disclosure at the vital initial
stage. Disclosure officers whose performance, reasoning, decisions and
actions, essentially unmonitored and unregulated, are able, for whatever
cause, reason or motivation, to deny prosecutors the information they
need. Without this information, prosecutors are unable to bring to bear
best judgement, guided by professional ethics.

The evidence for our assertion is incontrovertible. In Chapter 6 we referred
to research conducted by the CPS,[8] which has led it to complain[9] about
poorly completed police schedules of unused material. Items were regularly
left off schedules, copies of material were not sent to the CPS and
disclosure officers were difficult to contact. We referred to other research
carried out in 1999 by the Criminal Bar Association and the Law Society,
which provides telling and disturbing confirmatory evidence of the
existence of process corruption by disclosure officers and the 'knock on'
effect this necessarily has upon the decision-making and actions by the CPS.

371

It is now all to clear that there are disclosure officers who, whether through incompetence or a desire to increase the likelihood of a prosecution and conviction, withhold undermining material. In effect, prosecutors are potentially hostage to the conduct of disclosure officers whose detailed work is not subject to fine-grain, in-force monitoring and spot checks: both essential requisites to ensure quality assurance and integrity of functioning of individuals, the system and the operation of the law itself.

The extent to which the prosecutor will have to look through the retained material for him or herself will depend upon the quality of performance of the disclosure officer in describing it in the schedules MG6C (non-sensitive unused material) and MG6D (sensitive material). Each prosecutor will have to judge for him or herself how far he or she can depend upon the work and the advice of the disclosure officer and how proactive he or she needs to be. The fact that the prosecutor can refer to form MG6E will allow the disclosure officer to minimise the information in form MG6C.

Lord Runciman was concerned that the defence should be able to judge whether the schedule contains something that might show that the prosecution case was not as well founded as it appears.[10] Recognised as a critical document, the schedule is a safeguard against inadvertent non-disclosure and the defence may be better able than the prosecutor to appreciate the relevance to the defence of piece of information or document.

The defence have to justify an application for such material to be disclosed by showing that it might reasonably be expected to assist the defence disclosed by the defence statement. This becomes an impossible task if the schedule merely lists documents and categories of information without any reference to show how they may bear upon the case. Everyday experience, reinforced by research findings, has provided ample evidence of how schedules listing documents and categories of information are now commonplace means of denying the fair disclosure, which Lord Justice Steyn stated to be the inseparable part of an individual's right to a fair trial: *R. v. Brown* [1995] 1 Cr. App. R. 191 CA.

The prosecutor, on the other hand, has the benefit of additional information from the police – not given to the defence – contained in the Disclosure Officer's Report (MG6E). Using this confidential information form, the disclosure officer reports to the prosecutor about items listed on the schedule(s) for the case, which may undermine the prosecution case and the following items that must be supplied to the prosecutor:

- information containing a description of the alleged offender, which does not conform to the description of the person charged with an offence;

- material casting doubt on the reliability of a confession;

- material casting doubt upon the reliability of a witness.

The prosecutor will be able to use form MG6E in conjunction with the schedule(s), and forms MG6C and 6D when deciding whether a listed item is likely to fit the tests for disclosure. The situation is even more grave if, as sometimes happens, a schedule lacking detail is not accompanied by a form MG6E to the prosecutor. In a big case, the prosecutor will look at all the documents, but, in a smaller case, decisions are made entirely on the schedules. If the schedules are inadequate, the prosecutor cannot disclose fairly.

Chapter 5 lists the categories of material that the investigator is under a particular duty to retain: para. 5.4. The disclosure officer is required to list that material in the schedule, providing that it does not form part of the case against the accused: para. 6.2.

The defence solicitor will have to write to the prosecutor asking for more information about specific entries in the non-sensitive schedule. The CPS has stated that:

> 'Defence practitioners will not routinely be given access to unused material which does not meet either of the two tests. But the defence can request that the prosecutor will identify any information in that (unused) material which will be of assistance to the defendant's defence.'[11]

The prosecutor is not required to disclose any of the actual material in the schedule that does not come within the test of primary disclosure until the accused has disclosed a defence, and has justified requests for material in the schedule by reference to that defence.

It was pointed out in Chapter 6 that during the Parliamentary passage of the Bill it was suggested that inspection of the crime report is a route to identifying the existence of potentially undermining material. Clearly, the assumption was that, following the enactment of the CPIA, the police would continue as a matter of course to forward the entire crime report to the CPS. This was not an unreasonable assumption since prior to the enactment of the CPIA the crime report was disclosed as a matter of routine, being an easily photocopied insight into a case, its management and its outcomes.

This has proved to be a significant and problematic assumption. It was pointed out in Chapter 6 that there has been a widespread practice in the police service of submitting to the CPS (and thus to the defence) only the covering page of crime reports. Other pages have been withheld, particularly those showing police actions with their potential to reveal material that questions the police case, the evidence and the nature of the police investigation. Through this effortless tactic of withholding the actual contents of a document able to inform on these realities, disclosure officers ensure all others involved in the justice system – the CPS and therefore the defence, the magistracy, the judiciary and juries – are kept in the dark.

It will now be apparent why it is imperative to analyse material in the manner described in Chapter 8 in order to identify problematic material, i.e. that with manifest shortcomings, and missing material. As pointed out, fine-grain analysis gives you the prima facie case to request missing material and the antecedents of problematic and missing material. The very existence of material that has shortcomings and material that has either been withheld or not collected in the first place points to their potential to undermine the strength of the prosecution case. It will even more apparent why we stressed in Chapter 9 that active defence begins in the police station. It is here that systematic, comprehensive, exhaustive questioning of the IO in the manner spelled out in *A Pocket Reference*[12] offers the prospect of revealing shortcomings in the police case, the evidence and the police investigation which the subsequent disclosure process is able to remove from objective scrutiny.

SENSITIVE MATERIAL

The officer in charge of the case or the disclosure officer will initially categorise material as sensitive or non-sensitive.

Examples of the kinds of material that should be regarded as sensitive, such as details of informants and covert surveillance techniques, are given in para. 6.12 of the Code and listed in Chapter 6. The disclosure officer must list sensitive material on a separate schedule, giving reasons for its sensitivity.

This means that the police will decide what the defence will not be told about, by including the material in the sensitive schedule. If the prosecutor considers that material has been incorrectly categorised, he or she is not required to amend the schedules accordingly. Instead, the prosecutor's duty is to assess whether the material listed on the sensitive schedule meets the test for disclosure in the Act, and if so, whether he or she should apply to the court for a ruling to protect it if it is so sensitive that it is not in the public interest to disclose it.

The government argued that the prosecutor should not be required to satisfy him or herself that the material had been correctly categorised because a police officer who knew that the prosecutor would be going over the same ground would not be inclined to be scrupulous and the prosecutor would have to consider all the material, to see if anything not on the sensitive schedule ought to be.[13] If the disclosure officer has put material on the sensitive schedule that is disclosable and the prosecutor considers it is not sensitive, the prosecutor is likely only to request the disclosure officer to disclose it.

The court rules on whether it is in the public interest to disclose sensitive material.

However, a prosecutor need not bring such material before the court unless he or she thinks it undermines the prosecution case or might reasonably assist the defence disclosed by the accused. Neither the defence solicitor nor the court will know anything about sensitive material that the prosecutor decides is not disclosable, and the defence will not be in a position to challenge this decision unless it finds out about the material through its own investigations. Undermining material may not be disclosed if the court decides that it is not in the public interest to do so and orders accordingly: section 3(6).

The government explained to Parliament that:

> *'Where sensitive information might undermine the prosecution case or help the defence, it should not be automatically and unquestionably withheld. Neither ... is it in the interests of justice to provide that such sensitive information should always be disclosed. There needs to be a balance between the public interest in protecting sensitive information from disclosure and that of enabling the accused to put his or her case in the best light. The disclosable material the prosecution has identified as being subject to PII is put in front of the judge if the prosecutor wants to go ahead with the case.*

> *The judge carries out the balancing exercise, balancing the competing public interest considerations ... There is a public interest in not disclosing the identity of police informants, to encourage people to come forward and report crimes. There is also a public interest in not disclosing the location of police observation sites.'* [14]

PROSECUTOR PERFORMANCE IN RESPECT OF PRIMARY DISCLOSURE AND CONTINUING DUTY TO DISCLOSE

We return to the Law Society research responses on this matter. The experience of eight out of 10 respondents was that items listed on the unused material schedule are not inspected before primary- (or secondary-) disclosure decisions are made. Prosecuting authorities do not usually call for sight of items listed on unused material schedules but they rely on disclosure officers' judgements, whose decision-making and actions are accepted without question. As one respondent observed:

'in everyday cases, the CPS do not ever see the documents in the schedule before deciding that the prosecution case is not undermined. How can they possibly make this decision without assessing the papers?
(A sole practitioner with 14 years' experience)

Eight out of 10 respondents considered that the endeavours of prosecuting authorities (and police disclosure officers) to ensure that the continuing duty to consider disclosure is complied with, e.g. by providing the prosecuting trial advocate with copies of items of unused material, to be either 'inadequate' or 'highly inadequate'.

Notes

1. *Manual of Guidance for the Preparation, Processing and Submission of Files.* Produced by ACPO and the CPS for internal distribution. First edition 1 April 1992 (updated periodically).

2. Baroness Blatch, House of Lords 3rd Reading. 19 February 1996, col. 866.

3. David Maclean, House of Commons Committee. 14 May 1996, col. 36.

4. Sprack, John. 'The Criminal Procedure and Investigations Act 1996: (1) the duty of disclosure [1997]' Crim. L.R. 308.

5. *CPIA 1996 – Joint CPS/Police Training – A Guide to the Disclosure of Unused Material.*

6. Attorney General. Draft Guidelines on Disclosure: A Consultation Document. 14 February 2000.

7. David Maclean, House of Commons Committee. 14 May 1996, col. 34.

8. Baroness Blatch, Report Stage. 5 February 1996, col. 34.

9. 'Disclosure and the CPIA: implementation and practice'. Conference organised by ACPO in conjunction with the National Crime Faculty, Police Staff College, Bramshill, 1998.

10. Lord Runciman, House of Lords 2nd Reading. 27 November 1995, col. 487.

11. 'Director of Public Prosecutions sets out new rules on disclosure of unused evidence', press release issued by the CPS on 10 December 1996.

12. Shepherd, E. (1996) *A Pocket Reference.* London: Law Society Publishing.

13. Lord Mackay of Drumadoon, House of Lords 3rd Reading. 19 February 1996, col. 874.

14. The Solicitor General, House of Commons Committee. 14 May 1996, col 48.

CHAPTER 11

Making defence disclosure

WHY THE LAW WAS CHANGED

Lord Taylor gave the following reasons for requiring defence disclosure:[1]

- it enables early identification of the issues;
- it enables the weeding out of cases that should never have come to trial because the defendant has a good answer to the charges against him;
- it enables genuine alibis to be confirmed by the police as soon as possible;
- it deprives guilty defendants of the opportunity to use ambush defences that cannot be properly tested in court.

Baroness Mallalieu mentioned additional benefits arising from defence disclosure:[2]

- it is likely to mean cases are prepared better, and earlier, by the defence;
- openness may result in the prosecution being stopped by the Crown;
- clarification of the issues can and does sometimes lead to an additional or alternative charge being added so that the case results in a plea of guilty;
- it will enable the jury to see from the outset what the issues in a trial are and what the case is about and therefore enable the court more readily to come to a correct verdict;
- the length of trial could be more readily estimated.

DEFENCE DISCLOSURE: THE LAW

The magistrates' court – voluntary disclosure

If the case is to be tried summarily and the accused pleads not guilty:

- the prosecutor makes primary prosecution disclosure under section 3 CPIA;
- the accused may give a defence statement to the prosecutor and the court, which must satisfy the conditions set out in section 5(6): section 6(2).

The effect of voluntary disclosure by the accused is to place a requirement on the prosecutor to make secondary disclosure to the accused: section 7.

If the defence gives a defence statement, it will be particularly difficult to complete all the disclosure requirements within the PTI national time guidelines, particularly if the accused is in custody.

Expert evidence

Under section 81 PACE and the Crown Court (Advance Notice of Expert Evidence) Rules 1987, the defence must give advance notice of any expert evidence it proposes to lead.

The magistrates' courts (Advance Notice of Expert Evidence) Rules 1997 extend the requirement to give advance notice of expert evidence to the magistrates' court: section 20(3).

The Crown Court – compulsory disclosure

The disclosure of certain information by the accused to the prosecutor, in cases that are to be tried in the Crown Court, is compulsory: section 5(5). This is where the case has been committed to the Crown Court, or a serious and complex fraud or a case involving a sexual or violent offence against a child has been transferred, or a voluntary bill of indictment has been preferred and the prosecutor has made primary prosecution disclosure under section 3 and the conditions in section 5(2)–(4) have been complied with.

There is no obligation to serve the defence statement on a co-accused, but there is nothing to prevent voluntary service.

The specification in the Act

The Act specifies the contents of the defence statement in section 5(6). The statement should indicate:

- in general terms the nature of the accused's defence;

- the matters on which he takes issue with the prosecution;

- in respect of each matter the reason why he takes issue with the prosecution.

It is only if there is a preparatory hearing (section 29) and the prosecution gives a case statement that the accused can be ordered by the court to give written notice of any point of law (including any point at to the admissibility of evidence) that he wishes to take and any authority on which he intends to rely: section 31(6).

Format of defence disclosure

The statement must be in writing.

The nature of defence disclosure

When the Bill went before Parliament, the government said in respect of defence disclosure:

> 'We intend that...
>
> (a) only the general terms of the nature of the defence [needs] to be disclosed: self-defence, accident ... alibi ... whatever...
>
> (b) [the defendant] will indicate the matters on which he takes issue with the prosecution, e.g. if he is alleged to have picked up a chair in an assault case when he had in fact picked up an umbrella, he will say so...
>
> (c) [the third part of the defence statement] deals with a much narrower issue ... (it) requires him to set out the reasons why he takes issue with the prosecution ... in a shoplifting case, where a witness for the Crown alleges that he saw a particular event and the defence pleads not guilty, a reason falling within paragraph (c) would be that the witness could not have seen what he said he saw because he was somewhere else...

There is no suggestion that in giving the reason, detail of the evidence to support that reason should be given. So the fear ... that this might require the defence to set out its oral cross-examination is not well founded. This is not intended at all...

In providing a defence statement it is not intended that the accused should have to provide every last detail of the defence, such as the name and addresses of witnesses and so on...

If (c) is properly set down in sufficient detail it will help the prosecutor to fulfil his obligation on secondary disclosure. It will result in more information potentially helpful to the defendant being given...'[3]

Drawing of inferences from the defence statement

A court or jury may draw inferences from certain faults in relation to disclosure by the accused in deciding whether he or she is guilty: section 11(3). This is where the accused is required to give the prosecutor a defence statement under section 5, the case having been committed or transferred to the Crown Court (section 11(1)), or where the accused voluntarily gives a defence statement under section 6 in a case to be tried summarily: section 11(2).

Inferences can be drawn under CPIA if (section 11(1), (2)):

- the accused fails to give the prosecutor a defence statement;
- the accused gives the prosecutor a defence statement but after the end of the period mentioned in section 5(9) or 6(4);
- the accused gives the prosecutor a defence statement that sets out inconsistent defences;
- the accused at trial puts forward a defence that differs from any defence set out in the statement given under section 5 or 6;
- the accused at trial adduces evidence of an alibi without having given particulars of it in the defence statement;
- the accused at trial causes a witness to give evidence in support of an alibi without having given details of that witness as required in section 5(7).

If there is a failure in the disclosure made by the accused in accordance with section 11(1) or (2), then the court, or with leave of any other party, may make such comment as appears appropriate and the court or jury may draw such inferences as appear proper in deciding whether the accused is guilty: section 11(3).

If the accused puts forward a defence at trial that differs from any defence set out in the defence statement given under section 5 or 6, the court, when applying section 11(3), is to have regard to the extent of the differences in the defence and whether there is any justification for it: section 11(4). This is to cater for circumstances where, for example, the prosecution case develops or changes after the prosecutor has complied with the disclosure requirements imposed on him or her, and the accused's defence develops or changes in response to that. Lord Mackay of Drumadoon, the Lord Advocate commented that:

> '*If the change is a consequence of something done by the prosecution, I think it unlikely that the court would allow such an (adverse) inference to be drawn.*'[4]

A person cannot be convicted solely on an inference drawn under section 11(3): section 10(5).

The following information about the prosecution case must have been given to the accused before disclosure by the accused is compulsory: section 5(2)–(4):

- details of the charges against the accused and a set of documents containing the evidence on which the charges are based; or

- in cases of serious and complex fraud, a copy of the notice of transfer and documents containing the evidence; or

- in certain cases involving children, where the offence is a sexual or violent offence, a copy of the notice of transfer and documents containing the evidence; or

- where a voluntary bill of indictment is preferred, the service of a copy of the bill together with the set of documents containing the evidence on which the charge is based.

When the defence statement must be given

Where these conditions have been complied with, the accused must, under section 5, or may under section 6, give a defence statement to the prosecutor. The accused must give the defence statement to the prosecutor within 14 days from the day when the prosecutor gives, or purports to give, primary disclosure: regulation 2 of the Criminal Procedure and Investigations Act 1996 (Defence Disclosure Time Limits) Regulations 1997, reproduced in Appendix 11.

A notice that was drafted by the Home Office and is sent out by the CPS to each accused with primary disclosure, states that the 14-day period for giving a defence statement begins on the day when the prosecutor writes to you, not on the day when you receive primary disclosure. The Law Society, CPS Headquarters and some Crown Court judges who have had to determine the issue take the view that the 14 days begins instead on the day when the defence receives primary disclosure. This period cannot begin until committal or the entry of a not-guilty plea in the magistrates' court.

The application for an extension must:

- be made in writing;

- be served at the same time on the court and the prosecutor;

- state that the accused believes, on reasonable grounds, that it is not possible for him or her to give a defence statement under section 5 or 6 within the prescribed period;

- specify the grounds for so believing;

- specify the number of days by which he or she wishes the period to be extended.

Representations by the prosecutor

The prosecutor may make written representations about the application to the court within 14 days of the service of the defence statement.

The court's decision

On receipt of written representations from the prosecutor or the expiry of the 14-day period, the judge may determine the application, without a hearing.

If there is a hearing, it will be *inter partes,* with the prosecutor and accused able to make representations.

A copy of an order made by the court will be served on the prosecutor and the applicant.

The procedure is set out in the Magistrates' Courts (Criminal Procedure and Investigations Act 1996) (Disclosure) Rules 1997 and the Crown Court (Criminal Procedure and Investigations Act 1996) (Disclosure) Rules 1997, reproduced in Appendix 11.

ALIBI

If the defence is alibi, the accused must include particulars of the alibi in the statement.

Section 5 of the CPIA replaces section 11 of CJA. A separate notice of alibi is not required. The definition of evidence in support of an alibi reproduces the definition from section 11(8) of CJA: 'Evidence tending to show that by reason of the presence of the accused at a particular place or a particular area at a particular time he was not, or was unlikely to have been, at the place where the offence is alleged to have been committed at the time of its alleged commission': section 5(8). There is no longer a requirement to obtain the leave of the court to call alibi evidence when prior notice has not been given. Instead, an adverse inference may be drawn when the evidence is called in these circumstances.

You need to consider whether the charge allows a defence of alibi to be raised. The time and place of the offence may not be specifically defined. Evidence in support of an alibi envisages an offence that necessarily involves the defendant being in a particular place at a particular time, rather than evidence to counter some other allegation, such as that the defendant fled from his home when the police went to arrest him: *R.* v. *Hassan* [1970] 1 Q.B. 423.

A true alibi is one where the accused can give evidence that he was 'miles away' at the time when the offence is alleged to have been committed. What if the accused's instructions are that he or she was nearby at the time, but not actually present, or present at times but absent at others during the period when the crime is alleged to have taken place? Or that the accused cannot remember where he or she was at the time but that the accused's usual routine would not have taken him or her to the place of the crime then? Section 5(8) requires evidence which tends to show that the accused was unlikely to have been there. Evidence of the accused's whereabouts at a time earlier than the time of the commission of the offence, which was intended to discredit the evidence of a witness who claimed to have seen the defendant both taking part in the offence and in the vicinity a few hours earlier, is evidence of alibi: *R.* v. *Fields and Adams* [1991] Crim. L.R. 38 CA.

The details that must be given include the name and address of any witness the accused believes is able to give evidence in support of the alibi (if the name and address of the witness is known to the accused at the time). If the accused does not know the name and address of the witness, the particulars must include any information in the accused's possession that might be of material assistance in finding any such witness: section 5(7).

CPIA does not incorporate section 11(2)(b)-(d) of CJA. This means that there is no ongoing duty on the defence to secure the name and address of the alibi witness and give this information to the court and the prosecutor.

As we pointed out in Chapter 9, you must be extremely wary when you disclose details on alibi witnesses. You must be mindful of *R.* v. *Seymour* [1996] Crim. L.R. 512, CA, where the defence:

- served an alibi notice before it had taken proof from the alibi witness;

- imposed no requirement in its notification that the prosecution should take its statement from the witness in the presence of the defence.

As a result, the police interviewed the alibi witness in the absence of the defence solicitors and obtained a statement, which:

- was not disclosed to the defence;

- was used to destroy the credibility of the alibi witness at trial.

The defence appealed that the statement should have been disclosed to it. The Court of Appeal did not agree. The lesson here is that you must:

- take statements from alibi witnesses before the point of defence disclosure;

- give them your 24-hour contact details;

- brief every alibi witness that:

  - your client has nominated him or her as an alibi witness;
  - the police may seek to interview him or her;
  - you have told the police that they are not to interview him or her without informing you and enabling you to be present during the interview;
  - you will contact him or her when the police inform you that they wish to interview him or her;
  - should the police attempt to contact him or her:

    (a) he or she should politely say that he or she will not agree to be interviewed until the police have told you and made sure that you will be present;

    (b) he or she is to contact you immediately the conversation with the police ends.

THE USE OF THE DEFENCE STATEMENT BY THE PROSECUTION AT TRIAL

There is debate about whether the defence statement can be referred to by the prosecutor in an opening speech without the consent of the defence and proved as part of the prosecution case. The CPS has stated that the defence statement will not be used by the CPS as part of the prosecution case as led. Only in the case of alibi defences may the defence statement (as in the old days of the alibi notice) form part of the prosecution case.[5] This will enable the Crown to introduce comprehensible evidence rebutting an alibi as part of its case, having made the jury aware of the alibi claimed in the defence's statement.

No other prosecution agency has made such a policy statement, however at the time of writing the Attorney General had issued draft guidelines, for consultation, which adopted the CPS approach. They stated that prosecutors should not adduce evidence of the contents of a defence statement other than in the circumstances envisaged by section 11 of the Act or to rebut alibi evidence.[6]

The point is of importance, since the prosecution could then use what is disclosed by the defence to strengthen its case. We are not dealing here with the ability of the court to draw an inference. A defendant may be charged with assault and in the written statement disclose a defence of self-defence, but wish to challenge the reliability of the complainant's identification of him or her as the person who struck the blow. If the identification evidence given was weak, a defence submission of no case to answer may be precluded by the prosecutor being able to refer to the fact that the defence statement indicates that the defendant had admitted that he or she had struck the complainant.

The RCCJ[7] recommended that any defence disclosed in advance of the trial should never be disclosed to the jury until the defence, or an alternative, is advanced at trial. That would ensure that the defendant was not prejudiced by disclosure before the trial and that the evidence led by the prosecutor could not include anything disclosed by the defence. That approach, it concluded, is more consistent with the principle that the burden of proof should lie upon the prosecution. The Act only prohibits the disclosure of a defence statement in the trial without the consent of the accused (unless the defence departs from the statement) if it is given as a result of a judge's order at a preparatory hearing: section 34(4). During the Parliamentary debates, Lord Ackner commented:

> 'That would debar the prosecution from submitting, "you say that there is no case to answer, but you have provided a statement which accepted that there was a case to answer and have put forward a substantive defence".'[8]

It can be argued that in the absence of evidence that the defence written statement is made with the client's authority, the statement is not the client's statement and cannot be used as part of the prosecution case to fill a gap left by the prosecution evidence or add to the strength of the prosecution case. At common law, to make a defendant responsible for his solicitor's letters they must be shown to have been written in pursuance of specific instructions from the client and not merely the consequence of interviews with or general instructions from him: *R.* v. *Downer* (1880) 14 Cox 486. Until the CPIA, any alibi notice given on behalf of a client, unless the contrary was proved, was deemed to have been given with the authority of the defendant: section 11(5) of CJA. Section 11(5) created an exception to the common law principle that a solicitor did not have implied authority in criminal cases to affect his client by admissions of fact incidentally made. In view of subsection (5), the position as to an alibi notice was the same as that of any other relevant statement made by the defendant to the police. The prosecution was always entitled to put such a statement in as part of their case: *R.* v. *Rossborough* (1985) 81 Cr. App. R. 372.

CPIA repealed section 11 of CJA 1967 and replaces it with subsections 5(7) and (8), which do not contain a 'deeming' provision. According to this argument, if a prosecution witness at trial fails to come up to proof on an essential element of the prosecution case, a defence statement, which concedes that point, cannot be used to prevent a submission being made after the close of the prosecution case.

Those who argue that it can be proved as part of the prosecution case, point out that where section 11 of CJA only required the defence to give a notice to the examining magistrate or the solicitor for the prosecution, section 5 of CPIA requires the accused (not his legal representative) to give a defence statement to the court and the prosecutor. The notion that for one purpose it is a statement of the accused, but for another purpose it is not to be attributed to him or her if filed by his or her solicitor is not correct, they say. If it is the defendant's own statement, then it should be capable of being used against him or her if it contains an admission. As the accused cannot be compelled to comply, it is a voluntary statement and potentially admissible evidence.

But during the Parliamentary debates on the Bill, the government gave '*an important assurance*' that:

> '*It is implicit that things that may be done by the accused may also be done through his legal representative or an expert acting on their instructions. Where the legislation mentions the accused, both the accused and his legal representative are automatically included in the term.*'

A statement given by the defence solicitor would appear to fulfil the requirements of section 5(5) and at the same time provide the required information to satisfy all Parliament's reasons for defence disclosure: early identification of issues; weeding out of cases which should never have come to trial because the defendant has a good answer to the charges; allowing the police to check alibis; and preventing guilty defendants from using ambush defences which cannot be tested in court.

We will consider an example. Your client's defence to an assault charge is self-defence and he or she has not raised this defence yet. You consider the identification evidence against your client to be poor and you wish to cross-examine the complainant about his or her identification of your client, not to claim that he or she was mistaken when he or she identified your client but to raise a doubt about whether this evidence should be relied upon. If the defence statement cannot be proved as part of the prosecution case and you give the defence of self-defence in the statement and your submission of 'no case to answer' at the close of the prosecution evidence (on the basis of the unreliable identification evidence) fails, the court should not be able to make an adverse comment or draw an adverse inference when you later run the defence of self-defence. This is because you have not put forward a defence at trial that is different from the defence given in your statement. When you challenged the identification evidence you were not putting forward a defence, but merely putting the prosecution to proof.

If the defence statement can be proved as part of the prosecution case, and the prosecution is likely to introduce it as an admission by the accused, you may choose not to give a defence statement. That way, you will still be able to put the prosecution to proof of the accused's presence. The disadvantage is that you will not receive secondary disclosure. Although you will put forward a defence at trial if a submission of 'no case to answer' fails, you could assert that the justification for not giving a defence statement was that the prosecutor would otherwise have been able, unfairly, to rely upon your defence statement to prove a fact that he or she would otherwise have been unable to.

Section 11(4) of the Act provides that, where the accused puts forward a defence that is different from any defence set out in a defence statement given under section 5 or 6, before making any comment or drawing any inference the court must consider whether there is any justification for the differences in the defence. A court should also consider your justification for not giving a defence statement.

What will happen if a defence statement is given that is expressed to be conditional upon the prosecutor being able to discharge the burden of proof before relying upon the defence set out in it? Will a court accept that the statement has only been given when the prosecutor has proved a prima facie case? If a court accepts that the statement has not been given until the condition is satisfied, but a submission of 'no case to answer' fails, technically, the statement has not been given in time: section 11(1)(b). But what adverse comment or inference could be drawn as a result? The prosecutor and the court have been informed about the defence that will be run if the prosecutor is able to discharge the burden of proof. Another approach may be to state that the general nature of the defence is that 'he was not the aggressor'. That is not inconsistent with self-defence, nor is it inconsistent with the offender being someone other than your client.

If these approaches are shown to fail, the defence may always apply to the court to exercise its discretion under sections 78 and/or 82(3) of PACE and exclude any evidence of the defence statement for the purpose of proving a fact that the prosecutor would otherwise be unable to prove. A section 78 PACE submission may succeed not only because the defence statement is capable of fulfilling the purposes of CPIA without becoming part of the prosecution case, but also because the giving of such a statement may be discouraged (and so would have an adverse effect on the fairness of the proceedings) if it was used to strengthen the prosecution case.

DEFENCE DISCLOSURE: PRACTICE

Drafting the defence statement to avoid an adverse inference: key considerations

The nature of a defence statement

A defence statement is not:

- a précis or statement of the defence case that will be presented at court;

- a copy of or extracts from your client's proof of evidence;

- a list of the challenges which you intend to put to the prosecution witnesses.

It does not:

- set out the defence case;

- give details of the defence evidence that will support the reasons for taking issue with the prosecution case;

- deal in 'facts' in the way in which section 34 CJPOA 1994 does.

Although called a defence statement, its focus is on the prosecuti\
A defence statement is a document in which the accused:

- answers the three questions posed in section 5(6) CPIA 1996;

- gives particulars of an alibi.

The three questions

There is only one direct question about the defence case:

> *section 5(6)(a)* 'What, in general terms, is the nature of the accused's defence?'

Significantly, this first question does **not** ask about the 'facts' that will be presented as part of the defence case. It asks about the type of defence that will be presented.

The other two questions focus on the prosecution case not the defence case:

> *section 5(6)(b)* 'What are the matters on which he takes issue with the prosecution (case)?'

This second question asks the accused to identify those allegations with which he or she disagrees. The matters at issue having been identified, the third question asks the accused to explain the basis for his or her disagreement:

> *section 5(6)(c)* 'In respect of each matter, what is the reason for taking issue (with the prosecution case)?'

It is important to recognise that there is no obligation upon the accused:

- to raise any legal issues that the defence intend to raise at the trial, e.g. issue of inadmissibility of evidence;

- to identify or deal with any factual issue that does not form part of the defence being put forward, e.g. insufficient evidence – this is merely putting the prosecution to proof;

- to state facts that are admitted, e.g. possession of drugs in cases alleging possession with intent to supply. It is for the prosecution to prove possession.

Annex 1 at the end of this chapter gives an example of a letter to assist with the processes of drafting. It will be seen that it gives the defence statement, gives responses to the three fundamental questions and gives evidence of alibi.

When a defence statement must be given

Just as there is no obligation to answer police questions, there is no obligation to give a defence statement. But, if the accused fails to give a defence statement, or gives it late, he or she risks an adverse inference being drawn.

- In a summary trial, an adverse inference **cannot** be drawn if a defence statement is not submitted.

- In a Crown Court trial, unless the accused gives a defence statement in time, which answers the three questions, an adverse inference could be drawn.

The risks arising from the submission of a defence statement before a Crown Court trial

During the Second Reading of the Bill, Sir Ivan Lawrence commented that:

> 'There is no point in the defence revealing the details of its case if the police are not able to check up and follow through the information that they have been given ... Between committal and the trial the police should consider whether there is an answer to the allegation in the defence case.'[9]

At the time of writing, the Attorney General had issued guidelines on disclosure, for consultation, which stated that there may be occasions when a defence statement points the prosecution to other lines of inquiry. Evidence obtained as a result of this may be adduced as part of the prosecution case.[10]

In simple terms, defence disclosure allows the police to investigate the substance of the defence and will, in many cases, lead to the reinterviewing of prosecution witnesses. The risks are obvious. Chapters 3 and 4 presented a wealth of evidence concerning pressures and problems, and gaps between theory and practice, in respect of the police investigation that gave rise to your client being charged. It is fair to expect that in all too many cases police investigation subsequent to defence disclosure will not be open-minded and objective. Rather it will be instrumental in its aims:

- to undermine if not to negate wholly the defence case;

- to attend to shortcomings in the police evidence in order to buttress the prosecution case.

The risks of an adverse inference being drawn if the defence statement is not submitted before a Crown Court trial

The prosecutor will seek to draw an adverse inference from a failure to give a defence statement, i.e. that the line of defence, or parts of it that contradict the prosecution allegations, were fabricated after disclosure was due. However, this inference may be rebutted if the accused shows that:

- the defence was communicated to you before, or at the time, when the defence statement was due (note: any rebuttal statement should be signed by the accused and the legal adviser who took it and contain the time and date when it was made);

- he or she disclosed the defence to the police in the police station, or to the police or the prosecutor at another stage in the proceedings.

The Court of Appeal has said that what is significant, for consideration by the jury, is whether and when, in the sequence of events, as between arrest and charge and trial, the defendant mentions, if he does mention, matters relevant to his defence. It is for the judge to tailor his summing up to the circumstances of the particular case, in order to deal with these matters: *R.* v. *Kavanagh* [1997] 7 February (unreported).

The government gave examples of circumstances in which the failure to give a defence written statement at all should not result in an adverse inference being drawn: 'If there is a good reason for the failure to provide a defence statement – and I have heard some good reasons during the course of discussions on the amendment – the court would decide that the only proper inference to be drawn is that the accused was justified in not providing a defence statement.'[11] Examples given by Baroness Mallalieu[12] during the course of the debate included:

- where no purpose will be served because the issues are abundantly clear;

- the defendant suffers from serious mental illness, the issue is fitness to plead, the defendant is incapable of giving lucid instructions;

- an unrepresented defendant who is semi-literate.

In the following circumstances, it would be unfair to infer recent fabrication:

- The accused may already have made disclosure – in the ways described above.

- You may have a statement from the client to rebut an inference.

- The delay in submitting the defence statement may not be due to late instructions about the defence given by the accused, or it may not have been possible for the accused to have given the instructions earlier. There is a range of work that may be delayed by late service of the committal papers and/or late or inadequate primary disclosure, which may in turn delay the giving of the defence statement:

- considering the prosecution evidence;
- considering the primary disclosure of unused material;
- taking the accused's instructions on these (the accused may be in custody);
- discussing the contents of the defence statement with the defence trial advocate;
- drafting the defence statement;
- obtaining the accused's agreement to the draft;
- submitting it.

- You may have made an application to the court to extend the period for submission of the statement and have given details of why it was not possible to give disclosure within the time allowed.

How much information must the defence statement contain to avoid an adverse inference being drawn

It is necessary to distinguish in your mind between the information required to comply with section 5(6) (the defence statement) and the information required to support a request for unused material. This approach will help you to remain clear about the two distinct purposes of the document:

- to satisfy section 5(6);

- to obtain secondary disclosure.

To avoid an adverse inference being drawn, you need to give just sufficient information to answer the three fundamental questions. You must avoid including material that may allow:

- the prosecution witnesses to be rehearsed for cross-examination;

- the prosecution witnesses to be reinterviewed by the police to cover gaps in the prosecution case;

- the police/prosecutor to build a case around the defence statement;

- the defence statement to be used as evidence to form part of the prosecution case.

It is important to achieve balance. The more detail you go into in respect of one matter, the more you risk an adverse comment because of something that you failed to refer to in respect of another matter.

You should not set out a defence that may be different from that presented at trial. If you do, the prosecutor, with the court's leave, may comment on this and the court or jury may draw an adverse inference about the defence being presented at trial.

Formulating the request for secondary disclosure of unused material

In order to decide which unused material you want to obtain, you need to pose the question: what do I wish to establish?

You may wish to establish that:

- the prosecution have made a mistake about the need to disclose evidence;
- a witness is mistaken;
- a witness is unreliable;
- a witness is lying;
- a witness has a motive to falsely accuse your client;
- a description is mistaken;
- the accused does not match the description that was given;
- the crime was committed by someone else;
- relevant evidence has been withheld;
- the accused was not there at the time;
- an identification is unsafe;
- the crime was not committed in the manner alleged;
- the factual evidence is open to a different, innocent explanation;
- the forensic evidence is capable of a different interpretation;
- the accused has an alibi;
- a confession is inadmissible or should be excluded.

You must therefore consider the range of unused material that you think:

- may exist;
- may help in establishing that which you wish to establish;

- may show that a witness's evidence to be presented to the court is contradicted by:
  - earlier information from that witness;
  - information given by another witness;
- the prosecutor will give you, or the court will order the prosecutor to give you.

When considering the range or potential unused material, you need to look for pointers from:

- what you found out from your investigations in the police station;

- what you have already received as primary disclosure;

- what you have received as used material;

- what you found out through your other investigations;

- the contents of the non-sensitive schedule;

- what information you would expect to exist from experience;

- what an expert advises you to request.

Refining the defence statement to support the request for unused material: relevant factors

The unused material which should be disclosed, whether or not you give a defence statement

If the accused explains his or her defence in the police station, the disclosure officer is obliged to copy it to the prosecutor, who should then disclose any material that supports this explanation as primary disclosure.

In addition, joint CPS/police training guidelines state that, generally speaking, any material that goes to an essential element of the offence charged and points away from the accused having committed the alleged offence with the required intent, will have an adverse effect on the strength of the prosecution case and so ought to be disclosed to the defence.

The CPS has stated that the vast majority of material which might reasonably assist the defence might also undermine the prosecution and that the circumstances in which disclosure takes place after the defence case statement should be limited.[13]

What the prosecutor must do on receipt of the defence statement

The disclosure officer is obliged to look again at the material that has been retained and draw the attention of the prosecutor to any material that might reasonably be expected to assist the defence disclosed by the accused (paragraph 5.2, Code of Practice).

The prosecutor's knowledge of the accused's defence beyond what is in the defence statement

The accused may already have made disclosure, e.g. disclosing information about his or her defence in the police station.

When additional information should be given in the defence statement

You should not confuse the requirement to comply with the limited defence disclosure specified in section 5(6) with the additional information that the accused may be advised to volunteer to support a request to the prosecution or an application to the court for outstanding unused material.

If, in your judgement, there is no outstanding unused material that may help the defence case, it will be in the accused's interests to restrict the defence statement to the information required by the three fundamental questions.

What information should the defence statement contain in order to obtain the requisite secondary disclosure

You need to ensure that the draft defence statement supports the request for unused material.

It follows that, if there is a specific aspect of the defence for which you require unused material, and which is not already supported by the draft defence statement, it must be referred to in the defence statement.

Drafting the request for unused material: key considerations

A prosecutor who may be unconvinced by requests for disclosure, may nonetheless sooner copy the material to you than go to the trouble and expense of defending an application to the court for its disclosure.

The court will have a copy of your defence statement when considering an application for disclosure by you or an application for a non-disclosure order by the prosecutor.

Simon Brown LJ said in *R.* v. *Bromley JJ ex p. Smith and Wilkins* [1995] 2 Cr. App. R. 285 DC that:

> *'The prosecutor should always be prepared to review the question of materiality. Generally, no doubt, even if they are still unconvinced of the materiality of the document, they (the prosecution) would presumably prefer to disclose it rather than go to the lengths of seeking a ruling on the point.'*

Three ways of requesting unused material

There are three ways of requesting unused material.

First. General reference – in effect a blanket request for material.

> *e.g.* 'any material which may support the defence set out in the defence statement.'

Second. Specific reference – linking the request to specific content of the defence statement.

> *e.g. 'in the defence statement reference is made to the fact that*
>
> . . . .
>
> . . . .
>
> *Disclosure is requested of any material which is capable of supporting this'.*

A checklist can be used. Annex 2 at the end of this chapter gives an illustrative example of a checklist.

> *'The following material (ticked below) is likely to contain such information and should be disclosed'.*

Third. An invitation to the prosecutor to inspect a specific item – again using a checklist.

> *e.g. 'If the prosecutor has not inspected an item ticked below, the prosecutor is asked to do so before making a decision about disclosure of it'.*

Using a checklist of critical unused material produces practical and psychological benefits.

- A checklist helps you to be systematic in reflecting upon and examining step by step, in fine-grain detail the entire narrative of events in respect of your client's case: from initial police deployment (either reactively or proactively) and subsequent deployment of further police, civilian support staff, and expertise from external providers through to the point of primary disclosure.

- It is an invaluable aid to keeping track of, and evaluating, a bewildering, almost overwhelming combination and sequence of processes, decision points, actions and outcomes of police and others engaged in multiple forms of communication aimed at directing (or withholding) resource to gather and generate information and evidence (testimonial, physical and expert in their many various forms) in antecedent and final versions.

- Your step-by-step, fine-grain reflection, examination and evaluation enables you to identify fundamental shortcomings in the breadth, as well as the quality, of prosecution disclosure – from what was disclosed in the police station through to primary disclosure. This helps you in your task of spelling out the matters on which you take issue with the prosecution and your reasoning.

- Presenting the prosecutor with a checklist constitutes a potent means of demonstrating that the defence has conducted a thorough chronological, evaluative review of material processes, decision points, actions and outcomes with reference to the police case, the evidence and the police investigation.

The prosecutor should inspect the requested material

The CPS Inspectorate recommends that when the prosecutor cannot inspect all the material that the defence can show may be reasonably relevant to the case and may assist them, the requested documents should be disclosed upon receipt of a clear defence statement.[14]

Annex 1 at the end of this chapter shows where the request is located in the letter forwarding the defence statement.

Drafting the defence statement: a summary

Figure 11.1 summarises the stages involved in drafting the defence statement.

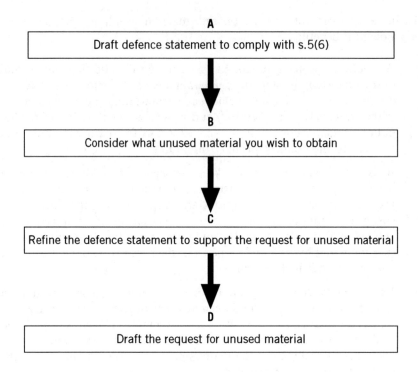

Figure 11.1 Drafting the defence statement

DEFENCE DISCLOSURE: OTHER ISSUES

Sensitive material

It is important to know whether sensitive material exists, which the prosecutor does not feel obliged to disclose or about which the court makes an *ex parte* non-disclosure order. This may help you to decide whether to carry out your own investigation in relation to it and make an application to the court for its disclosure. You need to know:

- what sensitive material there is;

- whether it can help to establish a defence to the charge.

If the defence statement is sufficiently focused on the possibility of the existence of sensitive material:

- the information contained in the material in question may force the prosecutor to apply to the court for non-disclosure of the material;
- it may provide the court with a sufficient understanding of the defence case to cause the court to order disclosure.

You must therefore systematically investigate the issue of sensitive material. You must ask the prosecutor:

- whether a sensitive schedule has been prepared;
- whether the prosecutor has been informed separately of the existence of material deemed to be too sensitive to include in a schedule;
- whether the prosecutor has been informed separately of information about:
  - any prosecution witness's previous convictions (including spent convictions); or
  - disciplinary matters relating to a police officer;
- if the answer to any of the above questions is 'yes', whether the prosecutor has decided that he or she is not under a duty to disclose any of it;
- if the prosecutor has decided that he or she is under a duty to disclose it, whether the court has been or will be asked to order its non-disclosure.

The example letter at Annex 1 at the end of this chapter asks these questions.

The prosecutor, of course, does not have to reply to the questions you ask about sensitive material.

Respect your client's instructions

You need to bear in mind a number of issues here:

- beware of preventing your client from running a viable line of defence;
- listen to and respect your client's instructions;
- don't close off the opportunity to run a defence based upon your client's instructions just because, for tactical reasons, you think that another and different defence is more likely to succeed, e.g. running provocation instead of self-defence in a murder case;

- by not referring to the original defence in the written statement you may exclude the possibility of receiving information from the prosecution which will enable you to build it into a viable defence.

Obtaining your client's consent

Disclosing your client's defence involves disclosing your client's confidential communications with you. Before a defence written statement can be given, your client must give his or her consent.

You must:

- ensure that you have correctly recorded your client's instructions to you;
- decide what advice you will give your client about making a statement and its contents;
- explain to your client:
  - the reasons for your advice;
  - the likely consequences of not taking that advice;
- ask your client to check and agree the defence written statement and to sign a copy of it (for you to retain) to that effect.

This means you must pay particular attention to the explanation you give to your client. An example of an appropriate explanation is as follows:

'You must give a defence statement in writing to the prosecutor and the court. In the statement you must in general terms:

(a) say what type your defence is;

(b) say what you disagree with in the prosecution case;

(c) for each area of disagreement, say why you disagree;

(d) give details of an alibi and any alibi witnesses.

The prosecutor may be holding back information which could help your defence. If you do not tell him about your defence in this statement, he may be less likely to give you this information.

If you do not give this statement, or give it late or give it but use a different defence at trial, the fact that you have done so may count against you.

I advise you to give a statement. I have prepared a statement for you from what you have told me. Please read it through and tell me whether it is correct. Do you agree to my sending it to the prosecutor and the court on your behalf?'

The responsibility for drafting the defence statement

Should the defence statement be drafted by the litigator or the trial advocate? Factors indicating that the trial advocate should draft it are:

- the case is complex;

- the litigator cannot be sure what defence will be run at trial.

When describing a much simpler 'tick box' scheme limited to disclosing the substance of the defence such as accident, self-defence, consent, no dishonest intent, no appropriation, abandoned goods, claim of right and mistaken identification, the RCCJ[15] commented that:

'In most cases disclosure of the defence should be a matter capable of being handled by the defendant's solicitor (in the same way that alibi notices are usually dealt with at present) ... There will be complex cases which may require the assistance of counsel in formulating the defence.'

Once the defence has been committed to paper, there is not only a danger that the accused may change his instructions. A change of trial advocate could bring about a different approach to how the defence case should be run. The RCCJ[16] recommended that:

'Where counsel are involved, they should if practicable stay with the case until the end of the trial: where this is impracticable, the barrister who has been involved with the pre-trial work should pass on his or her preparation to the barrister who is to present the case at trial.'

The Bar Council has issued guidance to counsel about the circumstances that should exist before counsel agrees to draft a defence statement. This is reproduced in Appendix 12.

Access to the defence statement

You must restrict access to the defence statement.

There is a particular risk should you give a copy of your defence statement to a co-accused. A co-accused who has not yet given his or her defence statement may well seek to construct his or her defence around that of your client.

Flow chart

A flow chart showing a recommended approach by the defence solicitor to defence disclosure is set out in Appendix 2.

Notes

1. Lord Taylor, House of Lords 2nd Reading. 27 November 1995, col. 477.

2. Baroness Mallalieu, House of Lords 2nd Reading. 27 November 1995, col. 483.

3. The Solicitor-General, House of Commons Committee. 16 May 1996, cols. 66–9.

4. Lord Mackay of Drumadoon, House of Lords Report Stage. 1 February 1996, col. 1589.

5. Calvert-Smith, D. (1999) Address to the British Academy of Forensic Sciences. 1 December 1999.

6. Attorney General. Draft Guidelines on Disclosure: A Consultation Document. 14 February 2000.

7. *The Report of the Royal Commission on Criminal Justice.* (1993) CM 2263, Chapter 6, para. 72.

8. Lord Ackner, House of Lords Committee. 19 December 1995, col. 1568.

9. Sir Ivan Lawrence, House of Commons 2nd Reading. 27 February 1996, col. 762.

10. Attorney General. Draft Guidelines on Disclosure: A Consultation Document. 14 February 2000.

11. Baroness Blatch, House of Lords Report Stage. 1 February 1996, col. 1568.

12. Baroness Mallalieu, House of Lords Report Stage. 1 February 1996, cols. 1592, 1593.

13. Calvert-Smith, D. (1999) Address to the British Academy of Forensic Sciences. 1 December 1999.

14. Crown Prosecution Service. The Inspectorate's Report on the Thematic Review of the Disclosure of Unused Material. March 2000.

15. *The Report of the Royal Commission on Criminal Justice.* (1993) CM 2263, Chapter 6, para. 68.

16. *Ibid.*

ANNEX 1

DEFENCE STATEMENT

(CPIA 1996, section 5(5))

To the prosecutor:

To the court:

Name of accused: URN:

Charge: Date of next hearing:

Name and address of solicitors for the accused:

Date:

1. The nature of the accused's defence is:

2. The accused takes issue with the prosecution in relation to the following matters:

3. The accused takes issue with the prosecution about these matters for the following reasons:

4. The accused will give the following evidence of alibi:

5. The accused requests the disclosure of the following material as it might undermine the prosecution case or might be reasonably expected to assist the defence disclosed by this written statement.

6. (a) Has a sensitive schedule been prepared?

   (b) Has the prosecutor been informed separately of the existence of material deemed to be too sensitive to include in the schedule?

   (c) Has the prosecutor been informed separately of information about any prosecution witness's previous convictions (including spent convictions) or disciplinary matters relating to a police officer?

   (d) If the answer to (a), (b) or (c) above is 'yes', has the prosecutor decided that he is not under a duty to disclose:

      (i)   any material in (a) above?

      (ii)   any material in (b) above?

      (iii) any material in (c) above?

   (e) If the answer to (a), (b) or (c) above is 'yes', is an application to be made or has an application been made to the court to order the non-disclosure of any material:

      (i)   in (a) above?

      (ii)   in (b) above?

      (iii) in (c) above?

ANNEX 2

CHECKLIST OF TYPES OF UNUSED MATERIAL

The checklist given below is an illustrative example. It will be seen that it focuses on key aspects of police activity, investigation by police officers, civilian support staff and external supporting personnel such as forensic scientists and medical examiners, and the antecedent and final forms of a wide range of information and evidence.

Word-processing packages allow the creation of 'stationery' files which are, in effect, templates. These can be reproduced and then amended and edited to fit a particular set of circumstances. It will be of use to create a 'stationery' file of all types of unused material, or even a number of files focusing upon particular types of offence.

The actual content of the checklist template can be compiled by incorporating material from the illustrative checklist below, material in the checklist in *A Pocket Reference* covering the consultation with the IO, material in Chapters 2, 4, 8 and 9 in this volume, and your own experience of working with particular cases and types of offence.

Thus, when a particular case arises, you can create a copy of the checklist template and then add, amend or delete to fit your requirements.

TYPES OF UNUSED MATERIAL	✓	MG6C NO. (Where referred to in police schedule)	INSPECTED BY PROSECUTOR (Prosecutor please indicate yes/no)
Operational Information (Note: includes print-out of operational information system, computer-aided despatch system, or this force's equivalent.)			
Request for a police response			
Deployment of police officers			
Requests, instructions, briefings and reports from deploying and deployed officers			
Circulations of reports and descriptions by officers			
Tasking of officers – identifying those tasking and those tasked			

TYPES OF UNUSED MATERIAL	✓	MG6C NO. (Where referred to in police schedule)	INSPECTED BY PROSECUTOR (Prosecutor please indicate yes/no)
Crime Report information			
Offence:			
Finally recorded Legal description			
Complaint details: Time Date Whether discovered by police Reporting office Investigating officer			
Complainant details			
Details of the offence: time, date, location			
Description of suspect: First description Subsequent descriptions			
Vehicles seen			
Modus operandi			
Property – stolen and damaged			
Details of offenders Details of enquiries:			
At the scene In the vicinity (e.g. house-to-house questionnaires) Actions Details of action, including all persons involved			

TYPES OF UNUSED MATERIAL	✓	MG6C NO. (Where referred to in police schedule)	INSPECTED BY PROSECUTOR (Prosecutor please indicate yes/no)
Identity of all people spoken to by the police and the outcome, including: All individuals who made a witness statement All individuals who did not make a witness statement			
Key documentary material generated by police officers and, where applicable, civilian support staff			
Handwritten notes, with particular reference to content covering: Verbal exchanges with complainant/other witnesses Actions taken Suspect description Sketches made			
Entries in pocket notebook(s), including content covering: Verbal exchanges with complainant/other witnesses Actions taken Suspect description Sketches made			
Incident Report Book(s), including content covering: Verbal exchanges with complainant/other witnesses Actions taken Suspect description Sketches made			

TYPES OF UNUSED MATERIAL	✓	MG6C NO. (Where referred to in police schedule)	INSPECTED BY PROSECUTOR (Prosecutor please indicate yes/no)
All handover, briefing and tasking notes (including those from FOA to IO, and between IOs and civilian support staff), including content covering: Verbal exchanges with complainant/other witnesses Actions taken Suspect description Sketches made			
Custody record(s)			
Witness statements			
For each witness Antecedents to each statement: Notes and, where made, tape recording(s) of disclosures – including description of offender(s) – made on initial and each subsequent contact with police Notes and, where made, tape recording(s) of disclosures during each statement-taking interview			
Forensic scientist / SOCO			
Crime scene examination form All marks, including fingerprints, and impressions found at scene and taken, all items, materials and CTM found at scene and removed (including swabbing) All marks (including fingerprints), impressions, items, materials and CTM submitted for in-force analysis, including eliminatory testing – with records of tasking, reporting at all stages and results;			

TYPES OF UNUSED MATERIAL	✓	MG6C NO. (Where referred to in police schedule)	INSPECTED BY PROSECUTOR (Prosecutor please indicate yes/no)
All marks (including fingerprints), impressions, items, materials and CTM submitted for external scientific analysis, including eliminatory testing – with records of tasking, reporting at all stages and results;			
All marks (including fingerprints), impressions, items, materials and CTM not submitted for in-force analysis – with reasoning			
All marks (including fingerprints), impressions, items, materials and CTM not submitted for external scientific analysis – with reasoning			
Medical examiner/police surgeon			
All records, notes, official forms, other documentation and reporting in relation to:			
All physical examinations conducted, findings, recommendations and actions taken			
All mental assessments conducted, findings, recommendations and actions taken			
Samples taken			
Samples submitted for testing and results			
Samples not submitted for testing – with reasoning			
CCTV film			

409

CHAPTER 12

Prosecution secondary disclosure

'The prosecution has at its disposal the machinery of the police with their considerable and necessary resources and a necessary coercive power. The prosecution also has access to specialist services such as those of forensic scientists. The defence has none of these resources and is heavily reliant on the material which the prosecution discloses to it. The principle of equality of arms requires that both sides have equal access to all the evidence.'

Lord Lester of Herne Hill, during the second reading of the Criminal Procedure and Investigations Bill in the House of Lords

THE RESPONSIBILITIES OF THE PROSECUTOR AND THE DISCLOSURE OFFICER

Under section 7 of the CPIA, the prosecutor is required to make further disclosure of unused material to the accused – secondary prosecution disclosure – after the accused has given a defence statement disclosing aspects of the defence to the prosecutor:

- compulsorily under section 5; or

- voluntarily under section 6.

The further disclosure is limited to prosecution material:

- that has not previously been disclosed;

- that might reasonably be expected to assist the accused's defence as disclosed by the defence statement: section 7(2).

410

There is no obligation under CPIA on the prosecutor to disclose material that might assist another defence. At the time of writing, the Attorney General had issued guidelines on disclosure, for consultation, which made it clear that material which might undermine the prosecution case should be disclosed even though it suggests a defence inconsistent with or alternative to one already advanced by the accused or his solicitor.[1]

As pointed out in Chapter 11, after a defence statement has been given, the disclosure officer is obliged:

- to look again at the material which has been retained;

- to draw the attention of the prosecutor to any material that might reasonably be expected to assist the defence disclosed by the accused: Code of Practice, para. 8.2.

An obvious example of secondary disclosure was given by the Home Secretary:

> 'If, at the second stage of prosecution disclosure, the defence team had identified its defence as an alibi defence ... it would certainly be part of the prosecution's duty to disclose any material available to it that supported that alibi defence.'[2]

Otherwise, the prosecutor must give the accused a written statement that there is no such material.

Secondary disclosure and primary disclosure are the same in respect of:

- the definition of prosecution material: section 7(3);

- the treatment of sensitive material;

- the circumstances in which material must not be disclosed to the accused if the court so orders.

THE TIME FRAME FOR SECONDARY DISCLOSURE

Under the CPIA, the prosecutor must give primary and secondary disclosure during a period beginning and ending with such days as the Secretary of State prescribes by regulations under section 12: section 7(7). The period fixed by regulations is capable of extension by the court, on application: section 12(3).

The government has not set time limits for prosecution disclosure. These are governed instead by the transitional provisions in section 13. The prosecutor must act as soon as is reasonably practicable after the accused gives a defence statement under section 5 or 6.

If time limits are set, a failure to make prosecution disclosure within a time limit will not of itself constitute grounds for staying proceedings for abuse of process: section 10(3). This protection does not apply if delay by the prosecution is such as to prevent the accused from receiving a fair trial: section 10(3).

Primary prosecution disclosure, defence disclosure, secondary prosecution disclosure and the resolution of any disputes over disclosure must take place before the trial in summary cases.

In a Crown Court case, primary disclosure must be given shortly after committal and the government proposed that defence disclosure and secondary prosecution disclosure should, wherever possible, take place before the plea and directions hearing (PDH). A decision would then be taken at the PDH about whether a separate hearing was needed to resolve disputes over disclosure.

The government considered that the PDH itself was unlikely to be suitable for this, given that it is intended to be a very short hearing to deal with matters that may easily be determined. All stages of disclosure must be completed, and any disputes resolved, before the court begins to hear the prosecution case.

THE PROSECUTOR'S DUTY TO BE FAIR

When the Bill was before Parliament, the government referred to the prosecutor's duty to be fair as set out in the Bar's Code of Conduct and the Code for Crown Prosecutors. The Code places particular obligations on prosecuting counsel and states:

> *'Prosecuting counsel should not attempt to obtain a conviction by all means at his command. He should not regard himself as appearing for a party. He should lay before the court fairly and impartially the whole of the facts which comprise the case for the prosecution and should assist the court on all matters of law applicable to the case.'*

These obligations hold even though:

- the law might be against him or her;
- the court may be minded to proceed on the basis of the law which is more favourable to the
- Crown than that which the Crown understands to be the law.

The Code for Crown Prosecutors also contains provisions that ensure that proper ethical standards are followed by Crown prosecutors. The introduction states:

> *'Fair and effective prosecution is essential to the maintenance of law and order.'*

It further states:

> *'The duty of the CPS is to make sure ... that all relevant facts are given to the court ... Crown prosecutors must be fair.'*

The Solicitor-General has pointed out that: '*A body of law and a body of practice exists for all professionals involved in the prosecution to ensure that proper standards are followed.*'[3] The courts have described counsel for the Crown as a minister of justice whose prime concern is its fair and impartial administration.

What if the allegation is assault and the prosecutor has statements, which he or she believes to be untrue, from witnesses who were with the complainant earlier and heard him say that if he saw the accused he would 'teach him a lesson'? It is agreed that the prosecutor should give these as primary disclosure regardless of whether the accused had raised self-defence at the police station. The fact that the accused was advised, or chose, to remain silent and the solicitor neglected to give the prosecutor a defence statement does not affect the prosecutor's duty.

The CPS has said that a failure by the accused to disclose his case properly must not lead to the deliberate withholding of material which might enable him to achieve an acquittal.[4] At the time of writing, the Attorney General had issued draft guidelines on disclosure, for consultation, which stated that prosecutors should resolve any doubt they may have in favour of disclosure, unless the material is on the sensitive schedule and will be placed before the court for the issue of disclosure to be determined.[5]

In order to be fair, the prosecutor may give wider disclosure than is required by the Act. The prosecutor could, for example, invite the defence team to inspect all the non-sensitive unused material to help them to decide which material may assist their case. The Act merely set limits on what the accused is entitled to require the prosecutor to do.

A case does not have to be complex to highlight the extent to which the prosecution duty to be fair emerges as an extremely problematic personal and professional issue for the individual prosecutor.

THE METHOD OF DISCLOSURE

The prosecutor must disclose material either by giving a copy to the accused or allowing the accused to inspect the material.

Copying of material

Copies of material may be supplied to the accused either by the prosecutor or by the police, at the request of the prosecutor.

A copy may be made in such form as the prosecutor thinks fit and need not be in the same form as that in which the information has already been recorded (e.g. it may be scanned on to a computer and disclosed on computer disk).

Inspection of material

Home Office Minister David Maclean explained that: '*Inspection will include examination as of right by a legal representative, any forensic scientist or other expert instructed to assist an accused man in preparing his defence.*'[6]

An accused person is entitled to a copy of material that he or she has inspected unless the disclosure officer is of the opinion that it is not practicable or desirable to do so. The Code of Practice gives as examples of these situations:

- an object that cannot be copied;

- where the volume of material is too great;

- a statement by a child witness in a sexual offence if the officer believed that it was not desirable to pass it on: para. 10.3.

These are important provisions. You must liaise closely with an instructed expert on the matter of inspecting the material and particularly how to address the problem of a disclosure officer seeking to argue that material cannot be copied or should be withheld.

Object material

An object may well not be amenable to copying. This does not mean that it cannot be appropriately reproduced by other means, e.g. photographs, video recording, drawing, or other format by using any of the very large range of media now available to experts in particular fields.

Large amounts of material

It is accepted that the police service may not wish to devote valuable resources, particularly personnel, to photocopying large amounts of paperwork. The defence should assist with, and wherever possible relieve the police of, tasks that are notionally onerous and time-consuming.

There are simple rapid solutions.

Material held in HOLMES indexes

All the police have to do is download the material on to a floppy disk and hand over the disk. No photocopying is required. Even with a large number of computer files downloading takes minimal time, from a matter of seconds to two or three minutes. A Crown Court judge has already ordered the police to make such a disclosure.

Substantial documentary material

All you need to do is:

* take with you to the inspection session:
    - a portable computer;
    - an optical character recognition (OCR) scanner – which is available in two forms: handheld and, bulkier, flatbed – which can be bought or hired;
* scan the material you are given straight into the computer.

Material considered undesirable to release to the accused

The objection must be respected. However, there is no basis for a police objection to allowing the release of the material to an expert rather than the accused. This is well-established practice in cases involving children where experts are required to sign a declaration concerning security, and an undertaking not to copy or release the tape to third parties.

CONTINUING DUTY OF PROSECUTOR TO DISCLOSE

It is important to bear in mind that the prosecutor is under a continuing duty to disclose unused prosecution material: section 9.

The prosecutor must keep under review the question whether at any given time there is prosecution material that in his or her opinion might undermine the prosecution case against the accused or which might reasonably be expected to assist the accused's defence as disclosed by the defence statement given under section 5 or 6, and which has not been disclosed to the accused.

The prosecutor must disclose such material as soon as is reasonably practicable: section 9(2), (5). This obligation applies at all times:

- after the prosecutor makes primary prosecution disclosure under section 3 or secondary prosecution disclosure under section 7;

- before the accused is acquitted or convicted or the case is discontinued: section 9(1), (4).

The trial advocate has a key role to play: checking the brief to ensure that the MG forms are included and whether documents appear to be missing from the schedules, are insufficiently described or have not been disclosed when they should have been. If a schedule of unused material fails to describe the contents of documents adequately, they must be examined.

The prosecutor may come into possession of new material during the trial, which undermines its case in some respects, e.g. a witness statement suggesting that someone other than the accused had committed the crime. Also, as the trial develops, and the defence case becomes clearer, the prosecutor may find that previously undisclosed material may reasonably be expected to assist the accused's defence.

In relation to this continuing duty, the definition of prosecution material (section 9(6)), the treatment of sensitive material and the methods of disclosure are the same as they are for primary disclosure.

Circumstances for non-disclosure

Material must not be disclosed to the accused if the court, on application by the prosecutor, concludes it is not in the public interest to do so and orders accordingly: section 9(8).

At all stages of disclosure, material must not be disclosed:

- if it has been intercepted in compliance with a warrant issued under section 2 of the Interception of Communications Act 1985; or

- if it is indicated that such a warrant has been issued or that material has been intercepted in compliance with such a warrant: sections 7(6), 8(6) and 9(9).

PROSECUTOR PERFORMANCE IN RESPECT OF SECONDARY DISCLOSURE

The Law Society research on the operation of the CPIA indicated that:

- Six out of 10 respondents considered the prosecution response to requested disclosure of unused material to be either 'non-compliant' or 'highly non-compliant'.

- Eight out of 10 respondents considered prosecuting authorities' decisions on secondary disclosure to be either 'unreliable' or 'highly unreliable'.

- It was the experience of eight out of 10 respondents that items listed on the unused material schedule are not usually inspected before secondary-disclosure decisions are made, i.e. prosecuting authorities do not usually call for sight of items listed on unused material schedules, but rely on disclosure officers' judgements.

- Eight out of 10 respondents viewed the endeavours of prosecuting authorities (and police disclosure officers) to fulfil their continuing duty to ensure disclosure, e.g. providing the prosecuting trial advocate with copies of items of unused material, to be either 'inadequate' or 'highly inadequate'. A partner with 19 years' experience said: 'the CPS say that they will keep their disclosure obligations under continuing review, but the prosecution advocate does not have any documents other than those relied upon in evidence'.

APPLICATION TO THE COURT FOR DISCLOSURE

The justification for an application

As a general rule, courts expect that defence concerns about non-disclosure will be resolved outside the courtroom. However, under section 8(1) the accused can make an application to the court if:

- he or she has given a defence statement to the prosecutor under section 5 or 6; and

- the prosecutor has made secondary prosecution disclosure under section 7, or failed to do so; and

- the prosecutor refuses a request by your client for further prosecution disclosure.

The defence will have to justify its argument for disclosure. It must be shown that there is reasonable cause to believe that:

- there is prosecution material that has not been disclosed to your client;

- this material might reasonably be expected to assist your client's defence as disclosed by the defence statement given to the prosecutor under section 5 or 6: section 8(2).

The issue of justification is crucial and has been the subject of judicial commentary:

> 'Courts should certainly decline even to examine further documents unless the defendant can make out a clear prima facie case for supposing that despite the prosecutor's assertion to the contrary, the documents in question are indeed material.'

Simon Brown LJ in *R. v. Bromley Justices ex p. Smith and Wilkins* [1995] 2 Cr. App. R. 285

> 'Trial judges need to firmly discourage unnecessary and oppressive requests for discovery.'
>
> Steyn LJ in *R. v. Brown.* [1994] 1 W.L.R. 1599

It will be seen yet again why active defence rests upon investigation, particularly in analysing what has been disclosed throughout the course of your client's case from the moment of the call to attend the police station. As pointed out in Chapter 8, your fine-grain analyses will enable you to identify shortcomings and material that has been omitted, providing you with a sound prima facie basis for a request for disclosure.

The procedure

The applications procedure is laid down in the Magistrates' Court (Criminal Procedure and Investigations Act 1996) (Disclosure) Rules 1997 and the Crown Court (Criminal Procedure and Investigations Act 1996) (Disclosure) Rules 1997, which are reproduced in Appendix 11.

The application must:

- be in writing;
- be served on the court and the prosecutor at the same time;
- specify:
  - the material to which it relates;
  - that the material has not been disclosed;

- the date when the application was served on the prosecutor;
- the reason why the material might be expected to assist the accused's defence as disclosed by the defence statement given under section 5 or 6.

The prosecutor is required to give notice to the court, stating:

- either that he or she wishes to make representations concerning the material and what the substance of those representations are;

- or that he or she is willing to disclose the material.

The court's decision

The court can determine the application with or without a hearing. When a hearing takes place, it will be *inter partes* with the prosecutor. Your client is entitled to make representations, but the prosecutor may be given leave to make representations in the absence of you and your client.

A copy of an order made by the court will be served on the accused and the prosecutor.

Prosecution material for the purposes of section 8 has a wider meaning than for sections 3 and 7 as it includes material held by the police, which the prosecutor has not inspected: section 8(4).

In cases where the prosecution refused to disclose additional material because it thought the defence had not given sufficient particulars about the defence case, the court would grant the defence application if it considered that the defence had provided sufficient particulars. If the court refused the defence application, the defence would have to provide more particulars if it wished to obtain the disclosure of additional material in the possession of the prosecution.

If the prosecution refused to disclose specific unused material requested by the defence because it considered that the material could not assist the case disclosed by the defence, the court would grant the defence application only if it considered that the material which the prosecution wished to withhold could assist that case.

PREPARATORY HEARINGS

Part III of the CPIA creates a statutory scheme of preparatory hearings for long or complex cases tried in the Crown Court. Lord Mackay of Drumadoon, the Lord Advocate, told Parliament:

> *'Where a case is so complex that it requires a secondary document in order to steer and navigate it through the prosecution evidence, it would be likely to fall within the class of case where the judge may order a preparatory hearing.'[7]*

The scheme is modelled on that which applies in serious or complex fraud cases.

Part III applies in relation to offences where the accused is committed for trial, or proceedings are transferred the Crown Court, or where a bill of indictment is preferred on or after the day appointed by the Secretary of State. The provisions may be brought into force at different times in relation to different Crown Court centres: section 28.

A preparatory hearing may be ordered in response to an application by the prosecutor or the defence, or the judge's own motion, if he or she considers that such a hearing may help to (section 29):

- identify important issues for the jury;

- assist the jury's comprehension of those issues;

- expedite the proceedings before the jury;

- assist the judge's management of the trial.

The preparatory hearing takes place before the jury are sworn. It is technically the start of the trial and arraignment will take place if it has not already done so: section 30.

The judge may (section 31):

- make a ruling on any question as to the admissibility of evidence and any other question of law relating to the case;

- order the prosecution and then the defence to provide a detailed case statement;

- require the prosecution evidence and any explanatory material to be prepared in a form that

- the judge considers is likely to help the jury to understand it.

The Criminal Justice Act 1987 (Preparatory Hearings) Rules 1997 revoke and re-enact with amendments the existing rules governing the procedure for preparatory hearings in serious or complex fraud cases to take account of amendments to the 1987 Act made by the Criminal Procedure and Investigations Act 1996. They make provision for an application to be made for a preparatory hearing. This will be determined without a hearing unless a judge otherwise directs. They provide for the disclosure of the prosecution case (NB: no mention of case statement) and disclosure by the defence in response.

The Criminal Procedure and Investigations Act 1996 (Preparatory Hearings) Rules 1997 indicate the procedure to be followed in relation to preparatory hearings for long or complex cases. The scheme is modelled on that which applies to serious or complex fraud cases under the 1987 Act.

The Criminal Procedure and Investigations Act 1996 (Preparatory Hearings) (Interlocutory Appeals) Rules 1997 make provision for the practice and procedure of appealing to the Court of Appeal against rulings as to the admissibility of evidence and any other question of law made at a preparatory hearing in a long or complex case.

Notes

1. Attorney General. Draft Guidelines on Disclosure: A Consultation Document. 14 February 2000.

2. Home Secretary, House of Commons 2nd Reading. 27 February 1996, col. 740.

3. The Solicitor-General, House of Commons Committee. 21 May 1996, col. 135.

4. Calvert-Smith, D. (1999) Address to the British Academy of Forensic Sciences, 1 December 1999.

5. Attorney General. Draft Guidelines on Disclosure: A Consultation Document. 14 February 2000.

6. David Maclean, House of Commons Committee. 14 May 1996, col. 30.

7. Lord Mackay of Drumadoon, House of Lords Report Stage. 1 February 1996, col. 1588.

CHAPTER 13

Problematic disclosure: material subject to particular restrictions

'The question of discovery in criminal cases is not the sort of tactical tit for tat or a game of Happy Families played according to tactical rules such as if you do not say thank you for the card you lose your turn. It is a serious matter conducted in a court of law and, one piously hopes, in a court of justice as well.'

Lord Justice Steyn in *R. v. Livingstone* [1993] Crim. L.R. 597 CA

DECIDING PUBLIC INTEREST IMMUNITY ISSUES

The procedure

If the prosecutor wishes to apply to the court to order that it is not in the public interest to disclose certain sensitive material, the Magistrates' Courts (Criminal Procedure and Investigations Act 1996) (Disclosure) Rules 1997 and the Crown Court (Criminal Procedure and Investigations Act 1996) (Disclosure) Rules 1997 provide that this should be determined by the court in one of three ways (similar to the procedure established by the Court of Appeal: *R. v. Davis, Johnson and Rowe* (1993) 97 Cr. App. R. 110). The rules are set out in Appendix 11. A person claiming to have an interest in the material may apply to the court for an opportunity to be heard: section 16.

This procedure applies where the prosecutor is obliged to make primary disclosure of 'undermining' material (section 3(6)) or secondary disclosure of material that might be reasonably expected to assist the accused's defence (section 7(5)); where the accused applies to the court for an order requiring the prosecutor to disclose material that fits the tests for disclosure (section 8(5)); and where the prosecutor is under a continuing duty to disclose such material (section 9(8)).

In most cases, the prosecutor will give notice to the court and the accused that he or she is applying for a ruling by the court and specify to the accused the nature of the material to which the application relates. The hearing will be *inter partes* and the accused will have the opportunity to make representations to the court, although the prosecutor is entitled to apply to make representations in the absence of the accused and his or her legal representative. The court must examine the evidence in dispute.

The prosecutor need not specify the nature of the material if he or she has reason to believe that to reveal this to the accused would have the effect of disclosing what the prosecutor contends ought not to be disclosed. In this case, the prosecutor will give notice of the application to the court and the accused but the hearing will be *ex parte* when only the prosecutor will be entitled to make representations to the court and the accused will not be present. The judge will have a copy of the defence statement as this will have been sent to the court as well as to the prosecutor. The accused will be told of the order that is made. The court hearing the application may order that the normal procedure should be followed.

There is no need for the prosecutor to give notice of the application to the accused if the prosecutor has reason to believe that to reveal to the accused that an application is being made might 'let the cat out of the bag' and disclose the material concerned. The accused will then not be told that an order has been made. This procedure should be reserved for a highly exceptional case. If the court decides that notice should be given to the *accused or an inter partes* hearing should take place, it may so order.

The *ex parte* procedure which was established in R. v. *Davis, Johnson and Rowe*, and is preserved by the 1996 Act, is under review following a successful challenge in Strasbourg.[1] The applicants alleged that the *ex parte* procedure afforded the defence insufficient opportunity to make informed representations. Judgement was given on 16 February 2000.

If the court makes a non-disclosure order, it is required to state its reasons and, in the Crown Court, a record must be made of that statement.

The test

There is a presumption in favour of disclosure to the defence, and the Lord Chief Justice in *R.* v. *Keane* [1994] 2 All E.R. 484, set out guidance for trial judges about how to balance the competing interests of public interest immunity and fairness to the party claiming disclosure:

> *'If the disputed material may prove the defendant's innocence or avoid a miscarriage of justice, then the balance comes down resoundingly in favour of disclosing it.*

> *When the court is seized of the material, the judge has to perform the balancing exercise by having regard on the one hand to the weight of the public interest in non-disclosure. On the other hand, he must consider the importance of the documents to the issues of interest to the defence, present and potential, so far as they have been disclosed to him or he can foresee them. Accordingly, the more full and specific the indication the defendant's lawyers give of the defence issues they are likely to raise, the more accurately both prosecution and judge will be able to assess the value to the defence of the material.'*

If a court concludes that it is in the public interest that an item of sensitive material must be disclosed to the accused, this does not mean that sensitive documents must always be disclosed in their original form: for example, the court may agree that sensitive details still requiring protection should be blocked out, or that documents may be summarised, or that the prosecutor may make an admission about the substance of the material under section 10 of CJA: CPIA Code of Practice, para. 10.5.

Although the common law rules relating to whether disclosure is in the public interest have not been disapplied by CPIA, the prosecutor will only bring sensitive material before the court if he or she has decided that he or she would otherwise be under a duty to disclose it, i.e. it might undermine the case for the prosecution against the accused or might reasonably be expected to assist the accused's defence as disclosed by the defence statement.

If the accused is aware of the existence of sensitive material that the prosecutor does not consider he or she is obliged to disclose, and applies to the court for its disclosure, the application by the accused is limited to material that might reasonably be expected to assist the accused's defence as disclosed by the defence statement given under section 5 or 6: section 8(2).

NON-DISCLOSURE ORDER

In summary trials

In a case for summary trial, disclosure issues should be dealt with at a pre-trial hearing. Ideally, the same bench of magistrates should decide questions of disclosure as will conduct the subsequent trial. If that proves impossible, because the same lay bench cannot be reconvened, the trial bench should be told at the outset of any material that is the subject of a non-disclosure order: *R.* v. *Bromley JJ ex p. Smith and Wilkins* [1995] 2 Cr.

App. R. 285, DC, which will enable the magistrates to consider during the trial whether the order should continue.

When hearing a prosecution application for non-disclosure on PII grounds, the magistrates may receive information that makes it impossible for them to give the accused a fair trial. If the application was made *ex parte*, the accused will not know what the magistrates have been told about him or her or his or her case. The defence may apply to the court that the bench which heard the application should be disqualified from hearing the trial.

In *R.* v. *South Worcestershire JJ ex p. Lilley* [1995] Crim. L.R. 955, the justices considered the contents of an envelope and heard evidence from the investigating officer and submissions from the prosecutor in the absence of the defendant and his solicitors. The justices concluded that the sensitive material was immaterial but rejected the applicant's application that his summary trial should be conducted by a differently constituted bench. The Divisional Court held that even when justices have ruled evidence inadmissible, there may, in exceptional cases, be circumstances in which what has been ruled inadmissible is of so highly prejudicial a character that, as a matter of fairness and appearance of fairness, a differently constituted bench ought to conduct the trial.

If the magistrates make a non-disclosure order in a case for summary trial, there is no requirement in the Act for a continuous review of it by the court. If the prosecutor becomes aware of a change in circumstances such that the court should review a non-disclosure order, the prosecutor should raise this in an application to the court.

The only entitlement to a review is on application by the accused for a review of the question whether the court's decision is still in the public interest: section 14(2).

It may not be possible to reconvene the bench which made the original decision to hear this application. If a different bench hears the trial, to avoid prejudicing the accused, how can they keep any decisions about non-disclosure under review?

If the case is likely to be tried in the Crown Court, disputes between the parties about the disclosure of unused material should be resolved by the Crown Court only: *R.* v. *Crown Prosecution Service ex p. Warby* [1994] Crim. L.R. 281.

In the Crown Court

The Crown Court is required to keep a non-disclosure order under review (section 15(3)), whether or not the accused applies to the court for such a review: section 15(4).

Application by the accused to review a non-disclosure order

An accused person is entitled to apply to the court to review a non-disclosure order made by the court. The procedure is set out in the Magistrates' Courts (Criminal Procedure and Investigations Act 1996) (Disclosure) Rules 1997 and the Crown Court (Criminal Procedure and Investigations Act 1996) (Disclosure) Rules 1997, which are set out in Appendix 11.

The accused must:

- give notice in writing;

- specify the reasons why the accused believes that the court should review the order;

- serve the notice on the prosecutor and the court at the same time.

The court may decide to determine the application without a hearing.

A hearing must take place if it appears to the court that there are grounds on which it might conclude that it is in the public interest to disclose material to any extent. The hearing will usually be *inter partes*, with the accused and the prosecutor entitled to make representations, but after hearing the accused's representations the court may allow the prosecutor to make representations in the accused's absence.

If the accused was not given notice of the original hearing, when the non-disclosure order was made, a review hearing will be *ex parte* and only the prosecutor will be entitled to make representations.

INFORMANTS AND ABUSE OF PROCESS

Chapter 2 explains how the police service is placing increasing emphasis upon, intelligence-led, proactive investigation, i.e. based heavily upon information derived from maximum use of covert means, including informants. The Audit Commission has declared that informers are good value for money and extra money will be spent by police forces on paying informers.[2] Many more cases will be based, therefore, upon information derived from informants.

In Chapter 3 we describe the very wide range of risk in respect of informants, compounded by the pressure to recruit, the lack of police training, and the inadequacy or absence of effective control mechanisms: all well known to the service and highlighted by HMIC and official research.

It is worth reiterating that an official study on informants[3] found that:

- the typical registered informer is an unemployed male with a long history of criminality;

- most informers are under arrest or subject to police enquiries when they are recruited;

- without any supervisory oversight, officers arrange for charges to be reduced or dropped, shorten detention, expedite bail, do favours with the housing department, and do not investigate crimes committed or being committed by the informer;

- it is recognised by the police that informants are devious and the police 'con' them and are 'conned' by them;

- the most effective informers are those who are actively involved in the crime themselves – in the research, 36 per cent were participating informers;

- police handlers resort to secrecy and are unwilling to seek advice from supervisory officers whom they consider to be out of touch;

- police officers flout Home Office guidelines on the use of participating informers and the rules governing disclosure;

- one-third of officers are prepared to lie in court to protect their informers.

Finally, in **none** of the 31 cases that the researchers examined, and where the informer had been paid, had the fact of the informer's involvement been revealed to the CPS. This breaches the Code of Practice under CPIA.

These are also additional risks. During the passage of the Bill before Parliament, the government acknowledged that 'at times, it is difficult for the police to run informers properly and within the law without crossing the line and becoming *agents provocateurs*'.[4]

Under the Act, material relating to the identity or activities of an informer will only appear on the sensitive schedule. It is vital that you recognise the extent to which your client's defence would be assisted by this information. Points to consider include the following:

- when your client alleges that the informer or an associate of the informer tricked or pressurised your client or in some other way 'set him up'. This will need to be investigated, particularly the circumstances surrounding your client's arrest, e.g. by inspecting observation logs and other documents retained by the police. A jury which does not hear evidence about the information that led to your client's arrest may draw the conclusion that the accused was arrested because he was well known to the police;

- defendants in drug cases claim that the main player in trafficking operations is often acting on behalf of his or her police handler who is likely to encourage a much larger deal than would have taken place, or the use of a class-A rather than a class-B drug;[5]

- the informer is a non-police witness and he or she may be able to give evidence which contradicts that given by police officers and other prosecution witnesses.

Problems with disclosure concerning informants

The courts have held that the need to protect informers had to give way to the need to allow the defence to 'present a tenable case in its best light': *R.* v. *Agar* (1990) 90 Cr. App. R. 318, [1990] 2 All E.R. 442; *R.* v. *Reilly* [1994] Crim. L.R. 279 CA.

The behaviour of the informer and the prosecution may be so outrageous that to proceed with the prosecution would amount to a breach of process. Lord Griffiths said:

> *'The courts, of course, have no power to apply direct discipline to the police or the prosecution authorities, but they can refuse to allow them to take advantage of abuse of power by regarding their behaviour as an abuse of process and thus preventing a prosecution. It is an abuse of process for a prosecuting authority to invoke the jurisdiction of the court where its own behaviour has been obviously wrong.'*

> *R.* v. *Horseferry Road Magistrates' Court ex p. Bennett* [1994] 1 AC 42

Even if the accused can receive a fair trial, the courts should stay the process if the conduct of the prosecutor is an affront to the public conscience: *R.* v. *Latif* [1996] 1 W.L.R. 104; [1996] Crim. L.R. 414.

What is capable of being 'an affront to public conscience'? The commentator in the *Criminal Law Review* considered that the gravity of the offence to be prevented, relative to any wrong involved in the means used to procure a conviction, is very significant: the graver the offence to be prevented, the more the law enforcement authorities can get away with. It is a question of expediency.

Judges are advised to take a robust approach in declining to order disclosure of informants' names and roles. The Lord Chief Justice said in *R.* v. *Turner* [1995] 1 W.L.R. 264:

'There has been an increasing tendency for defendants to seek disclosure of informants' names and roles, alleging that those details are essential to the defence. Defences that the accused has been set up, and duress, which used one time to be rare, have multiplied. We wish to alert judges to the need to scrutinise applications for disclosure of details about informants with very great care. They will need to be astute to see that assertions of a need to know such details, because they are essential to the defence, are justified. If they are not so justified, then the judge will need to adopt a robust approach in declining to order disclosure. Clearly there is a distinction between cases in which the circumstances raise no reasonable possibility that information about the informant will bear upon the issues and cases where it will. Again, there will be cases where the informant is an informant and no more; other cases where he may have participated in the events constituting, surrounding, or following the crime. Even when the informant has participated, the judge will need to consider whether his role so impinges on an issue of interest to the defence, present or potential, as to make disclosure necessary.'

We cannot stress enough that active defence of a client in a case arising from, and relying upon, information derived from an informant must involve disclosure of information about the informant. Given what is known about informants and the risks arising from the shortcomings of police dealings with informants, we argue that in every case where an informant is involved the court has a right to know, if not the informant's identity or role, then at the very least:

- recruitment: how did the police come to recruit the informant;

- the motivation – particularly where an inducement or reward was involved:

    - what was asked of, or given, by the police;
    - whether the informant was on a 'retainer';

- the history of the informant – particularly spelling out:

    - the identity of the handler;
    - the duration of the relationship between the handler and the informant;
    - the relationship between payment and 'results';
    - the record of police assessments of:

        (a) the informer's motivation, reliability, and other factors bearing upon this, e.g. mental state, situational pressures;
        (b) the informer's performance, in terms of the validity and accuracy of the information provided, i.e. the extent to which he or she provided rubbish in return for a reward;

- the police's assessment of the informant – this is vital since the court will then know:

  – what the police really think of the informant and his or her information now;
  – what the police have thought of the informant and his or her information over a period of time.

All this information should be available, readily so given that many forces have IT in the form of a police informant management system (PIMS), and the ACPO and HM Customs and Excise Code of Practice on the use of informants.[6] Inability to produce this information raises fundamental doubts in respect of the relationship between the handler and the informant, of the integrity of the processes of control, tasking, and reward, and of the information upon which the police have relied.

The logic for allowing a court to know this information is straightforward. Proactive policing will increase the frequency of courts being invited to make decisions upon evidence arising from the actions and communications of people whom they will never see or hear in order to judge issues of credibility, validity and reliability. It is a fact of life that problems with openness and accountability within the police service, particularly in respect of informants, will endure. However, without any openness and accountability, a criminal justice system relying heavily upon individuals who are unseen, unheard and unreliable (even by the police account) will degenerate. Active defence is the only way to protect our system from this degeneration by pressing for the disclosure of key information about informants, which will enable a court to draw its own conclusions – even if it is denied knowledge of the informant's name or role.

DIFFERENT DUTIES OF DISCLOSURE

Different categories of individual have different duties of disclosure.

A prosecutor and a police officer

The disclosure duties set out in the CPIA and the Code of Practice apply to prosecutors, police officers and others who are charged with the duty of conducting an investigation. The duties under the Act and the Code replace the common law rules relating to disclosure by the 'prosecutor' (section 21(1)(b)), and police officers or other people charged with the duty of conducting an investigation: section 27(2)(a). The duty to disclose material to the prosecuting authority is limited to police officers and these other investigators: section 26. A prosecutor is defined in the Act as 'any person acting as prosecutor, whether an individual or body': section 2(3). The Code defines a prosecutor as 'the authority responsible for the conduct of criminal proceedings, on behalf of the Crown.'

So, for example, the duty to reveal material to the prosecutor, in accordance with the Code of Practice under the Act, does not extend to expert witnesses who are instructed by the police. The government assured Parliament that: 'It is not necessary to subject forensic scientists to detailed requirements relating to disclosure.'[7] Lord Mackay of Drumadoon added that:

> 'With the assurance that experts are members of professional bodies who strive to adhere to the highest possible standards, it is in my view correct for the government to take the view the Code of Practice is directed to those conducting the investigation and not to those who may be instructed to assist in one small part of it.'[8]

Duties under the Act and the Code are limited to material that the expert has communicated to the investigator and the prosecutor. The investigator is under a duty to retain, and the prosecutor to disclose in accordance with the provisions of the Act, communications between the police and experts, reports of work carried out by experts and schedules of scientific material prepared by the expert for the investigator: Code of Practice, para. 5.4. But the government acknowledged that statements of opinion prepared by expert witnesses:

> 'Tend to evolve when further information comes to light and earlier versions of such statements tend to be based on incomplete information and could be misleading (and would not be disclosed).'[9]

The prosecution team and the issue of confidential material

The duty of the prosecution to disclose has been extended by the courts to cover material produced by anyone who has assisted the prosecutor. Prosecution expert witnesses such as psychiatrists, forensic scientists and forensic medical examiners (police surgeons) have all been regarded as members of the 'prosecution team' and remain under a common law duty to disclose material to the prosecutor, which may assist the defence. In R. v. Bolton Justices ex p. Scally [1991] 2 All E.R. 619, [1991] 1 Q.B. 537, Glidewell LJ said:

> 'While the prosecuting authority as such may not have failed in its duty, the total apparatus of prosecution has failed to carry out its duty to bring before the court all the material evidence.'

In *R.* v. *Maguire* [1992] 2 All E.R. 433 CA, the court held that that the duty of disclosure is not confined to prosecution counsel but includes forensic scientists retained by the prosecution and accordingly failure by a forensic scientist to disclose material may be a material irregularity in the course of the trial providing grounds for an appeal against conviction to be allowed. Stuart-Smith LJ, giving the judgment, said:

> 'We are of the opinion that a forensic scientist who is an adviser to the prosecuting authority is under a duty to disclose material of which he knows and which may have some bearing on the offence charged and the surrounding circumstances of the case. The disclosure will be to the authority which retains him and which must in turn (subject to sensitivity) disclose the information to the defence.
>
> We can see no cause to distinguish between members of the prosecuting authority and those advising it in the capacity of a forensic scientist. Such a distinction could involve difficult and contested inquiries as to where knowledge stopped but, most importantly, would be entirely counter to the desirability of ameliorating the disparity of scientific resources as between the Crown and the subject.'

As explained in Chapter 2, the medical examiner provides the IO with a report immediately after his or her examination, but retains his or her detailed notes of the examination. However, notes will of necessity often contain information of a confidential nature.

Parliament had been concerned about the dual responsibility of the forensic medical examiner to report his or her examination to the police and, at the same time, respect the patient's wishes for details of his or her medical history and therapeutic information, given for treatment purposes, to remain confidential. The police and the CPS had been requiring a copy of the police surgeon's handwritten medical notes.

The Code does not apply to persons who are not charged with the duty of conducting an investigation as defined in the Act: para. 1.2. The government explained that forensic medical examiners:

> 'have no statutory position within police forces and they are under no statutory duty under PACE 1984 or elsewhere to conduct investigations of the kind described (in the Act) ... A police surgeon would be in the same position as any other third party who may have information which may be relevant to a criminal investigation and would be under no duty (arising from the Act) to retain material and reveal it to the prosecutor or investigator.'[10]

The police are unlikely to obtain a copy of the police surgeon's medical notes unless the patient has given consent or the court makes an order.

Third parties

Sometimes material will be in the possession of a third party. An example of this is records relating to children, which have been created and preserved by local authority social services departments. Third parties are not under a positive duty to disclose material that may assist the defence.

The third party may not even be aware that criminal proceedings are taking place. If the officer in charge of an investigation believes that a third party may be in possession of material that may be relevant to the investigation, he or she should ask the disclosure officer:

- to inform them of the existence of the investigation;

- to invite them to retain the material in case they receive a request for its disclosure.

The disclosure officer should inform the prosecutor that the third party may have such material: Code of Practice, para. 3.5.

Where the police and social services have worked together, the police may inspect this material and retain it in the form of a copy if the original is to be returned to its owner. If the material does not form part of the case against the accused, it must be listed on a schedule by the disclosure officer, which is then revealed to the prosecutor and disclosed to the accused if it is not sensitive and the prosecutor considers that it fits the tests for disclosure.

If the prosecutor applies to the court for a non-disclosure order, or the accused applies to the court to review an order, the court must give a person claiming an interest in the material an opportunity to be heard, providing that the person applies to be heard by the court and shows that he or she was involved in bringing the prosecutor's attention to the material: section 16. The government explained that:

> 'This new clause is designed for situations where a third party, such as a local authority social services department, is the originator of sensitive material which is put before a court for a decision on disclosure to the accused. The third party may well be more knowledgeable about the material and may be better placed to argue the issue of disclosure. The third party is able under this section to instruct separate counsel if necessary to make representations to the court instead of just the prosecutor.'[11]

Third parties, such as medical practices, banks or local authority social services departments, may have material that has not been inspected by the prosecution. The accused may attempt to obtain this material by applying for a witness summons requiring the third party to attend court and give evidence or produce their records.

OBTAINING A WITNESS SUMMONS

In the magistrates' court

The magistrates' court is obliged to consider whether issuing such a witness summons is justified. A justice of the peace must be satisfied that the third party is likely to be able to give material evidence (Magistrates' Courts Act 1980, s.97). There is a four-part test before a witness summons can be granted: *R.* v. *Reading JJ ex p. Berkshire County Council* [1996] Crim. L.R. 347 DC:

1. To be material evidence, documents must not only be relevant to the issues arising in the criminal proceedings, but also documents admissible in evidence.

2. Documents that are desired merely for the purpose of possible cross-examination are not admissible in evidence and thus are not material for the purposes of section 97.

3. Whoever seeks production of documents must satisfy the justices that the documents are 'likely to be material', in the sense indicated, 'likelihood' for this purpose involving a real possibility, although not necessarily a probability.

4. It is not sufficient that the applicant merely wants to find out whether or not the third party has such material documents. The procedure must not be used as a disguised attempt to obtain discovery.

The Crown Court

An accused has in the past been entitled to obtain a third-party witness summons. The accused would then in some cases wait for an application by the third party to set it aside. The third party has had the burden of persuading the court that the material was not likely to be material evidence. This had the advantage for the accused of requiring the third party to look at the material which they had in their possession, assess the likely relevance of any of it and to bring that material to court in order to argue that it should not be disclosed.

434

This can only be performed by the judge personally examining or viewing the evidence, so as to have the facts of what is contained in mind: *R.* v. *K.* (1993) 97 Cr. App. R. 342.

The defence will want the judge to read the material before deciding whether it should be disclosed. If the defence can persuade the judge to look at the relevant documents, having satisfied the tests of specificity and admissibility, the remaining consideration is whether or not disclosure of this type of material should be permitted.

Although the accused has had to satisfy the judge that the summons is not merely a 'fishing expedition', if the third party was represented, common sense and the interests of justice dictated that the third party's advocate assess the third-party material and flag up for the judge any papers that he or she should read before making a decision about their disclosure.

The government complained to the House of Commons that:

> 'the accused may request such material at a very late stage in the proceedings, without indicating its relevance to his or her defence. That places heavy burdens on third parties, who have to trawl through their records at the cost of considerable time and effort.'

The government introduced changes to align the procedures for issuing a witness summons in the Crown Court more closely with the magistrates' court:

> 'to create a more balanced and measured procedure for seeking third party evidence. The burden of proof will shift from third parties having to show why they should not disclose, to the applicant showing why they should. The greater detail required in applications will help all third parties to identify and assess material in their possession. That should benefit everyone by reducing the number of documents put before the courts.'[12]

Third-party disclosure

The Act makes it more difficult for an accused to obtain disclosure of third-party material. The burden is now on the accused instead, at the time of making the application for the summons, to satisfy the court that the third party is likely to be able to give evidence likely to be material evidence or is likely to be able to produce a document or thing likely to be material evidence.

Under the Act, an applicant seeking a witness summons for third-party disclosure in the Crown Court now has to justify the application and apply in good time. The issue should be raised by the defence at the same time as defence disclosure takes place.

The third party is given notice and is entitled to attend any hearing to put forward his or her views. The court may also order advance disclosure of third-party material and set aside the summons if it is no longer needed. The changes have been achieved by amending section 2 of the Criminal Procedure (Attendance of Witnesses) Act 1965 in section 66(2).

The Crown Court must be satisfied, when issuing a witness summons on application, that the person summonsed (section 2(1)):

- is likely to be able to give evidence likely to be material evidence; or

- is likely to be able to produce a document or thing likely to be material evidence; and

- that the person will not attend to give evidence or produce the document or thing voluntarily.

The application for a witness summons must be made as soon as is reasonably practicable after the person has been committed for trial or transferred or a bill of indictment has been preferred: section 2(4)–(6).

Crown Court summons for a witness to give oral evidence

The procedure is set out in Crown Court (Miscellaneous Amendment) Rules 1999, which came into force on 1 April 1999.

The application may be made orally to a judge or in writing specifying:

- the charge on which the proceedings concerned are based;

- a brief description of the evidence;

- the ground for believing that the potential witness is likely to be able to give the stipulated evidence; and

- the reasons why the applicant considers that the potential witness will not voluntarily attend.

Crown Court summons for a witness to produce documentary evidence

The procedure is set out in Crown Court (Miscellaneous Amendment) Rules 1999, which came into force on 1 April 1999.

The application should be made in writing to the appropriate officer of the Crown Court and should contain:

- a brief description of the required document or thing;
- reasons why the witness will not voluntarily produce it;
- reasons why the document or thing is likely to be material evidence;
- a supporting statement of truth setting out the charge and specifying:
  - the evidence in a way which will enable the potential witness to identify it;
  - grounds for believing that the witness is likely to be able to produce the evidence;
  - grounds for believing that it will be material evidence;
- where advance production is required, details of the time and place at which the witness is to produce it.

At the same time, the applicant should serve a copy of the application and supporting statement of truth on the potential witness. This should inform the potential witness that:

- it is his or her right to make representations in writing and at a hearing; and
- he or she has seven days to inform the court if he or she wishes to make representations.

Late applications in the Crown Court for documentary evidence

Under section 2 of the Criminal Procedure (Attendance of Witnesses) Act 1965 (as amended), the application for a witness summons must be made as soon as is reasonably practicable. The court may refuse to issue a summons if the requirements are not fulfilled.

If an application is made within seven days of the trial, the application should be completed in the manner described above, but should not be copied to the potential witness by the applicant. The appropriate officer should refer the application to the trial judge or other available judge to determine or give instructions, which may include copying to the witness.

If an application is made after the trial has begun, the application should be made orally to the judge to determine or give directions. The oral application should include:

- a brief description of the evidence;

- reasons why this is material evidence;

- reasons why the applicant considers that the witness will not voluntarily attend; and

- grounds for believing that the potential witness is likely to be able to produce the document or thing.

The court may direct that a witness summons shall be of no effect if the person to whom the summons is directed satisfies the court that he or she was not served with the notice of the application to issue the summons and that he or she was neither present nor represented at the hearing of the application and that he or she cannot give any evidence or produce any document or thing likely to be material evidence: section 2C.

The witness summons may also require the person to produce the document or thing for inspection at a place and time in advance of the Crown Court hearing: section 2A. Following inspection, the person who applied for the summons may apply to the court for a direction that the summons is no longer needed: section 2B.

While the defence must be sensitive to the needs of the complainant, it is the task of the defence to ensure that an innocent person is not convicted. There may be vital information in the possession of a third party, which could help the accused.

Wasted costs order

A wasted costs order can be made if the third party can show that the applicants were negligent in making their application in that they failed to act with the care, skill and competence reasonably to be expected of a solicitor.

The applicant must apply his or her mind to the law, and must have a justifiable belief that the documents demanded are likely to provide evidence material to the issues in the trial:

> 'In our view ... it is not proper to issue a witness summons for disclosure of a document or documents, still less for the whole contents of a file or files, for the speculative purpose that material might come to light which could discredit a complainant. We think the law is sufficiently clear to provide adequate guidance for the competent solicitor who directed his mind to it. In the present case there is no evidence to suggest that uncertainty in the law played any part in the appellants' decision to apply for disclosure of the contents of the social services files, nor that the appellants ever considered whether there were reasonable grounds for the application ... Accordingly we consider that the application made by

the appellants ... was made without reasonable cause and was one which no reasonably well informed and competent legal professional would have made in the circumstances.'

Beldam LJ in *Re A Solicitor (Wasted Costs Order)* [1996]
1 F.L.R. CA at p. 40

At the trial in Snaresbrook Crown Court, HH Judge Stable QC said in his judgment:

'I have been through each file and read each document. There is nothing in any document which could conceivably assist the defence. The documents are confidential and are not to be disclosed to the prosecution or the defence.

In my judgment the defence solicitors had no grounds for requiring the local authority to hand over their confidential documents. This was a speculative manoeuvre without any merit. I can only assume the solicitors thought there might be something in the files either showing some inconsistency between what is in the files and the written statement of the witness or something detrimental to the credit of the witness. If it is a proper thing to do in relation to a witness who has been in care, why is it not proper to conduct an inquiry into the background of every prosecution witness?'

In sexual offence cases, for example, you may wish to know whether the complainant has made previous and unsubstantiated allegations of abuse. What can you do? You can request but cannot require the police to make a speculative enquiry of a third party, such as a request to see confidential social services files or medical reports.

You could write to the local authority, setting out the allegation and the defence case, and ask:

* if the local authority has a file in relation to the complainant; and

* if the file contains information that might reasonably be expected to assist the defence case; and

* if the local authority is prepared to disclose that information without a court order.

A non-committal answer from the local authority may encourage you to probe further. A helpful answer by the local authority to the first two above questions may be sufficient to enable you to persuade the police to make further enquiries or, failing that, the judge to consider an application for a witness summons to look at the documents concerned.

You may be able to obtain certain information about the complainant from the accused or other witnesses. Armed with this information, you could invite the police, through the prosecutor, to reinterview the complainant to ascertain whether this information is correct and, if it is, disclose this fact to the defence.

The Act and the Code of Practice require the police, in conducting an investigation, to pursue all reasonable lines of enquiry, whether these point towards or away from the suspect. This is the spirit also of PEACE but Chapter 3 – in describing the pressures and problems within the police service, of defensive avoidance and the demand for results – gives substantial cause to question the police notion of what constitutes reasonable investigation.

According to the Act, what is reasonable in each case will depend upon the particular circumstances: section 23(1)(a) and Code of Practice, para. 3.4. The government explained that this provision:

> 'should help to ensure that relevant material is not overlooked. It also provides statutory backing for what is already regarded as good investigative practice.'[13]

Before the police are under a duty to make further investigations, they must have reason to believe that the third party may have relevant material, although that reason may come from information provided to the police by the accused or from other enquiries made or from other sources: Code of Practice, para. 3.5.

Material may be relevant to an investigation if it appears to an investigator, the officer in charge of an investigation or the disclosure officer, that it has some bearing on any offence under investigation or any person being investigated, or on the surrounding circumstances of the case, unless it is incapable of having any impact on the case: Code of Practice, para. 2.1. The police officer is required to make a record of any material that he or she has inspected and which is relevant to the inquiry.

This is all both fundamental and essential. It underlines why this text has sought to ensure that you are aware of what goes on and should go on in any police investigation. If you know what the service considers, claims and insists to be effective and ethical investigation and the requirement for supervision and quality controls, then anything short of this provides you with a substantial basis to press your case in actively defending your client.

APPEAL

Non-disclosure may be a ground for appeal. If the Court of Appeal considers that it may have made a difference to the outcome of the case and that the appellant's conviction, as a result of the non-disclosure, is unsafe, the court may allow the appeal and order a retrial or quash the conviction.

Notes

1. *Rowe and Davis* v. *United Kingdom*, Application no. 28910/95.

2. Association of Chief Police Officers/Her Majesty's Inspectorate of Constabulary/Audit Commission. (1996) *Tackling Crime Effectively: Management Handbook*. London: Audit Commission.

3. Dunningham, C. and Norris, C. (1996) *The Role of the Informer in the Criminal Justice System*. London: Economic and Social Research Council.

4. David Maclean, House of Commons Committee. 30 April 1996 col. 20.

5. Campbell, D. (1996) 'Put out to grass'. *The Guardian,* 30 April.

6. Association of Chief Police Officers and HM Customs and Excise. (1999) *Use of Informants: Code of Practice.*

7. Baroness Blatch, House of Lords Report Stage. 5 February 1996, col. 15.

8. Lord Mackay of Drumadoon, House of Lords 3rd Reading. 19 February 1996, col. 894.

9. Baroness Blatch, House of Lords Report Stage. 5 February 1996, col. 28.

10. Baroness Blatch, House of Lords Report Stage. 5 February 1996, col. 50.

11. Baroness Blatch, House of Lords. 26 June 1996, cols. 958, 959.

12. David Maclean, House of Commons Committee. 30 April 1996, col. 7.

13. Baroness Blatch, House of Lords. 26 June 1996, col. 963.

CHAPTER 14

Further defence investigations

The police and the prosecutor will inevitably seek to dismiss requests for information and access as 'fishing' and 'nit-picking'. Against these claims must be placed the proof that your active defence is well justified.

Across this text we have drawn to your attention, acknowledged, organisational, institutional, and individual shortcomings that are endemic, and endure, within the police service. Without solution or sanction, unmonitored and unchecked, they create the context for process corruption, much of it tacitly accepted: of the process of investigation, proactive and reactive, and the process of disclosure once a suspect has been charged.

There is the cumulative evidence that process corruption, whatever its causation, is commonplace. This evidence is found in daily experience of lawyers and the judiciary in the courts since the introduction of the CPIA, in the research by the Law Society and the Criminal Bar Association, and in the increasing incidence of reports in the media. There is an all too common picture of evidence withheld, of evidence mislaid, 'lost' or destroyed, of the inability of police and prosecutors to see something that even a lay person would instantly recognise as 'undermining', i.e. evidence that patently does not 'fit' the police and prosecution case, and, redolent of the case of Stephen Kisko, instances of prosecutions proceeding where both prosecution and police know that evidence exists, which not only points away from the accused, but could help to prove innocence beyond doubt.

There are no measures that the police service can hold up to the court to evidence real monitoring and real effort to minimise process corruption. The CPS can only look on since they are at a disadvantage, hostage to what police officers, unchecked and answerable to no one, choose to tell them. Your active defence, most particularly your investigation, your fine-grain analyses of evidence and your arguments for disclosure, predicated on a sound understanding of the operation and shortcomings of the processes of police investigation and disclosure, are the only safeguards against process corruption that currently exist within the criminal justice system.

Your commitment to investigation and systematic analysis begins from the time you are called to attend the police station. In this final chapter we give advice and information to enable you to investigate further: how to consult experts, how to interview witnesses and how to conduct an exhaustive examination and evaluation of the scene.

BASIC PRINCIPLES

You must observe some basic principles. They reflect the first – assess – stage of the ACCESS model of investigation and our suggestions for the management of case information (Chapter 7).

1. Your investigation must be focused. Assess the situation before you in order to establish:

    *   what you are looking for, i.e. your investigative *aim* – this can be spelled out as a simple statement: 'To ...';
    *   what you are hoping to do in practical terms, i.e. your investigative *goals* – put simply these are the actions, which, in fulfilling them, will mean you have achieved your declared aim.

2. There should be a reasonable chance of your investigation succeeding, i.e. it should be more likely than not that your investigation will produce something of significance in the case. Unlike the police and the prosecution, you are not able to call upon and to deploy resource, manpower and money, at will. You have to justify to the Legal Aid Board the logic of that upon which you are embarking.

3. You must keep full records. At the time when you make the decision to carry out the further investigation, as part of the assessment stage you should record:

    *   the information available to you at the time;
    *   the reason why you consider the investigation should be carried out.

You must observe these principles so that in hindsight you will be judged by the reasonableness of your decision to undertake a particular investigation at the time when you made that decision.

LEGAL AID

Obtaining prior authority

If a solicitor acting under a legal aid order considers it necessary for the proper conduct of proceedings in a magistrates' court or in a Crown Court to take steps that are unusual in their nature or involve unusually large expenditure, he or she may apply to the appropriate area committee for prior authority to do so: Legal Aid in Criminal and Care Proceedings (General) Regulations 1989, reg. 54(1).

The Board's application form APP 7 must be used.

Instructing an expert and obtaining an expert's report, or instructing an enquiry agent to carry our certain investigations on the solicitor's behalf, may fall within this category, depending on the work that is to be carried out.

The particular steps for which prior authority can be obtained include:

- obtaining a written report or opinion of one or more experts;
- employing a person to provide a written report or opinion (otherwise than as an expert);
- bespeaking transcripts of shorthand notes or of tape recordings of any proceedings, including police questioning of suspects;
- performing an act that is either unusual in its nature or involves unusually large expenditure.

Authority will be granted if the area committee is satisfied that the steps are necessary for the proper conduct of the proceedings and are reasonable in the circumstances. Applications must be made in good time and with sufficient information to allow the area office to make the decision.

The information which is required on APP 7 directly from you is:

- a brief summary of the prosecution case;
- the likely plea;
- a summary of the defence or mitigation;
- the name and address of the expert;
- whether there are other defendants, with whom there is no conflict of interest, who would benefit from the expenditure;

- whether alternative quotes have been obtained and, if so, the amounts quoted. The absence of alternative quotes will not, in itself, lead to refusal.

If the final fee is difficult to predict, an initial sum may be authorised to establish the benefit and costs involved in undertaking further work. There is no right of appeal against a refusal of authority, but the area director must give reasons for any refusal and the application can be renewed.

Authority is not needed if the solicitor is prepared to take his chance of being allowed the costs on assessment or taxation. Only in exceptional cases should a solicitor take such a risk. If an authority is obtained, then no question as to the propriety of the step taken or the amount authorised will be raised on the eventual determination of costs, unless the solicitor knew or ought reasonably to have known, before incurring the costs, that the purpose of the authority had failed or become unnecessary or irrelevant.

If authority is not obtained, or is applied for but refused, or the maximum amount allowed is exceeded, the solicitor is able to make a claim for the costs that still may be paid on determination. Alternatively, if authority is refused, the solicitor can pay for expert's fees or bespeaking transcripts out of private funds.

Reasonableness of undertaking work – solicitor's knowledge at the time

When considering whether or not an item in a bill is reasonable, the correct approach is to consider whether it was reasonable for the solicitor, in the light of his knowledge at the time when the work was done, to undertake the work: Legal Aid Board ref CRIMLA 38.

Payment of a disbursement on account

In Crown Court cases, where authority is granted for individual (rather than aggregated) expenditure of £100 or more and actual expenditure of £100 or more is incurred, the solicitor may apply to the Crown Court for a payment on account of the disbursement.

Use of enquiry agents for tracing witnesses

If it is necessary to employ an enquiry agent to trace a potential witness, then the fee for doing so, together with the fee for obtaining a statement from the witness when traced, may be allowable as a disbursement: Legal Aid Board ref CRIMLA 43.

INSTRUCTING AN EXPERT

The information that is required on APP 7 and needs to be obtained from the expert is:

- the type of expertise and qualifications;
- for medical reports, whether the expert is a consultant;
- the details of the charging rates (excluding VAT) per hour for preparation;
- the details of the charging rates (excluding VAT) per hour for travel time.

The authority will usually specify a maximum rate as well as a maximum amount.

When calculating a fee, the expert should take into account that where an area committee gives prior authority, it will authorise the maximum fee to be paid for any report, opinion, expert advice or transcript. This means that the expert should consider carefully how much time he or she is likely to spend on the case, which may include: reading documents, listening to tapes, watching videos and making any necessary transcriptions from them and analyses from them, examining the client, examining prosecution exhibits, research and preparing a report.

The expert should be told that court attendance fees of witnesses cannot be authorised. These are payable by the court out of central funds under regulations 16(1) and 20 of the Costs in Criminal Cases (General) Regulations 1986. A witness is defined in regulation 15 as: 'A person properly attending to give evidence, whether or not he or she gives evidence or is called at the insistence of one of the parties or of the court.' The solicitor should find out the court attendance fee that is likely to be allowed and tell the expert.

You should explain to the expert whom you consider instructing, in the fullest terms:

- the 'problem';
- the issues involved;
- what you intend should be questioned by the expert;
- critical time frames – there is no sense in going to great length if the expert is unable to do the work within the time frames applicable in your client's case.

You should ask the expert to specify the range of material that he or she will need to see in order to make a specification of the analyses he or she proposes to fulfil. A true expert should always be able to specify which documentation or exhibit material he or she will need to examine.

Items which you should always send to the expert at this early stage include:

- the charge sheet or indictment;

- the victim's statement;

- the video recordings of interviews with a child witness (these must be sent securely and the expert must undertake to keep them secure);[1]

- any tape recordings of a defendant's interviews with the police;

- all medical reports, statements and copies of original notes from which they were compiled;

- statements made by prosecution scientists;

- copies of prosecution photographs (not colour photocopies);

- the defendant's proof of evidence;

- any advice on evidence.

You should also:

- include a list of the other documents, used and unused material, which exist, indicating their length;

- depending upon the nature of the expert and the tasks you wish him or her to undertake, ensure that you give details of the whereabouts of:
  - your client;
  - any prosecution exhibits.

The expert should be asked to give a detailed breakdown of the tasks which he or she proposes to fulfil, such as:

- the amount and type of material to be processed;

- what the processing involves;

- the number, type, duration and location of interviews;

- the number, type, duration and location of assessments, analyses or other activities to be conducted;

- the use of support staff.

On the basis of this work specification, the expert must provide an estimate of:

- total hours for services at a specified rate;
- total hours' travelling time at a specified rate;
- travel costs;
- the report size.

The expert may be able to give a preliminary view on how the report can assist the defence case. This information and the expert's full CV can be attached to the application.

If there is a refusal of authority, the area director must give reasons.

These can be reported back to the expert and the application renewed with further information from the expert dealing with the points raised by the Board.

QUESTIONING EVIDENCE

Physical forensic evidence

The prosecution case will sometimes rely heavily upon physical forensic evidence. When this occurs, a jury will often find this scientific evidence compelling and place great trust in it.

Research for the RCCJ[2] found that, in three out of four cases, scientific evidence went unchallenged and that over a half of those challenges were by cross-examination only. Chapter 4 explained the substantial gap between theory and practice when it comes to the path of forensic evidence in terms of knowledge, skills, appropriate practice, and the application or even existence of quality controls and quality assurance. Similarly, Chapter 7 highlighted the fact that statements and reports by those involved in the forensic investigation are liable to have manifest shortcomings or to be characterised by omission.

To recapitulate, you need to remember the following facts about forensic evidence.

1. *It is highly selective in nature.* This is because of the way in which the police choose evidence to submit for examination and the way in which the prosecution scientist prepares the report for court.

448

2. *It can be wrong, for all manner of reasons*. The police may use laboratories to carry out work for them, which are not part of the Forensic Science Service (FSS) and where there is no proper control over the quality and reliability of the evidence that they produce and present to the court.

3. *It is open to interpretation*.

    •   *There may be another, innocent explanation for the match*. There is a risk that a jury, focusing entirely on the prosecution scientist's ability to match a sample to the defendant, may reach the wrong conclusion: that by proving the match the prosecution has, at the same time, proved the accused's guilt.

    •   *It may have been contaminated*. You will need to check the chain of custody of the exhibit from the moment when the police take custody of it until it is examined in the laboratory. Contamination can occur in very many ways, e.g.

        –   the placing of a hand or finger inside an exhibit bag;
        –   folding items containing wet semen or blood, so transferring it to other parts;
        –   folding items without separating the surfaces, so that the surfaces come into contact with each other;
        –   a suspect being placed in a cell used by another suspect and sharing the cell blanket;
        –   a police officer having contact with both the victim and a suspect;
        –   a suspect being placed in the same vehicle that had transported the victim.

4. *It may be totally irrelevant*.

5. *The absence of forensic evidence in a case may also be of significance*.

    •   Dr Angela Gallop of Forensic Access has provided us with an instance of this. A woman alleged that she had been raped by a taxi driver. He admitted getting into the back of the taxi cab with her and kissing her, but denied assaulting her. There were no semen traces and she said that he had not ejaculated. The defence forensic scientist was able to satisfy the court that it was inconceivable that he could have behaved as she alleged without fibres being transferred from her woolly skirt to his underclothes.

6. *Evidence may have been taken from the crime scene but not sent for analysis, or even if it has been sent, it may not be referred to in the prosecution scientist's report*.

449

Defence experts can have an important impact upon the production of prosecution forensic evidence, providing a corrective to the initial forensic investigations conducted by prosecution experts. An expert can ask about items that were submitted to the prosecution scientist as well as the items that were not submitted. An experienced forensic scientist may give evidence that, had the crime occurred in the manner alleged, certain evidence would have been found at the scene, or on the victim or the accused.

In some cases, the prosecution expert may be persuaded to revise his or her initial opinions, either because the defence expert provides new information or because he or she is able to spot the significance of some factor which the prosecution scientist has overlooked.

Similarly, the evidence of a medical examiner, a clinician who examined or attended the victim or your client, or a forensic pathologist are also open to question.

Where there are key documents offered in evidence, their veracity in terms of their genuineness and their contents need to be questioned, e.g. the custody record, as indicated in Chapter 7.

You must be sceptical about physical forensic evidence and find an expert to challenge it.

Behaviour that needs to be questioned by a specialist

The behaviour that accompanied the giving of testimony by witnesses and your client needs to be questioned, in terms of the 'what', 'how', and, by implication, the 'why' of the manner in which testimony emerged. Chapter 7 indicated that you should consider instructing an expert to question:

- audio and video recordings of interviews;
- language use, e.g. as recorded in contemporaneous notes or in a pocket book.

DIFFERENT AREAS OF EXPERTISE

The scope of forensic expertise

In a number of chapters we have underlined the fact that the term forensic science covers a very wide spectrum of investigative analytic techniques. The type of expert will necessarily be dictated by the nature of the offence with which your client is charged and the nature of the evidence in question.

Forensic science for the defence

The defence scientist is charged with investigating the soundness of the prosecution's scientific findings and the scope, if any, for some alternative innocent explanation for them. The scientist does this by:

- checking the analytical results emerging from the police and external scientist's work, and to undertake any such further tests as may be warranted;

- clarifying the nature of the police and external scientist's findings and the interpretation of them;

- assessing, and advising on, the significance of the scientific evidence overall in the light of the circumstances.

We provide below a necessarily brief, selective review of some areas of forensic expertise. Our selection reflects the commonest forms of evidence and other forensic factors that you will typically need to consider in respect of testimony derived from witnesses, complainants and clients. Annex 1 at the end of this chapter, gives a reading list of useful texts.

Forensic biology

Biological evidence is material that originates from a living source and is most relevant to the investigation of offences against the person. Examples are:

- hair and textile fibres;

- bloodstains on clothing and weapons;

- semen on underwear, bedding and swabs;

- saliva

- urine;

- clothing.

An experienced forensic biologist should be able to help the defence in a number of ways:

- whether material was cut or torn, how recently the damage was done and whether a particular knife could have caused it;

- the number of matching fibres found on your client's clothing, the number and type of each different fibre at the scene and how representative of them the fibres found on your client's clothing are (the absence of fibres might be significant);

- the distribution of blood and size of splashes will tell a forensic scientist a lot about what actually happened;

- human hair can be distinguished from animal hair. Dyes, colourings, rinses, sprays or lacquers help to identify the owner in comparison to a control sample. There is a two-way transfer of hair and fibres when woolly hats, balaclavas or masks are worn. Residue from the scene of the crime may be found in the offender's hair.

DNA evidence

We pointed out in Chapter 4 that there has been an exponential growth in DNA testing of suspects, particularly in the light of the creation of the National DNA database and awareness of the potential to conduct DNA analysis on minute, even single-cell, samples. This mentality is set to become even more widespread following the discovery of the ability to create profiles from DNA collected from surfaces that have been merely touched by an offender.

There has been a steady growth of a 'swab everything' mentality – swabbing of any surface and anyone that has been touched. This has paralleled the taking of DNA samples as a matter of routine from suspects, particularly by the use of mouth swab kits. This raises very important issues.

- The swabbing of a complete surface, such as a steering wheel, can produce a mixed profile and a situation where material is mixed with other material, the interpretation of which is extremely fraught: begging the question in such circumstances, when is a profile a profile?

- This constraint is particularly salient in respect of contamination of minute amounts of DNA. It is entirely possible for minute amounts of DNA to be transferred quite innocently:

  - from an individual to one or more people, e.g. by a sneeze, and for any one of these to transfer this DNA to a crime scene surface, be that an inanimate object or person;
  - from a suspect to a crime scene surface if measures have not been taken to ensure that contamination by the suspect does not occur *after the offence*.

The difficulties that the defence solicitor faces when the prosecution discloses the existence of DNA evidence, are similar to the problems that occur in relation to much forensic evidence. They were summarised in research conducted for the RCCJ:[3]

- lack of pre-trial notice of the existence of DNA evidence;
- it may take a considerable time for the defence to locate a suitable expert – DNA profiling is a highly specialised technique and there are relatively few experts outside the FSS who are experienced in this field;
- work is delayed while the defence apply for legal aid prior authority to instruct the expert;
- the number of experts is small and their workloads high; it may be several weeks before the defence expert is able to visit the prosecution laboratory to examine the results;
- there may be insufficient crime stain remaining for the defence expert to conduct an independent laboratory analysis.

The value of the defence forensic work is illustrated by the fact that, in the study, 38 per cent of defence lawyers who obtained an independent analysis of the evidence stated that their conclusions differed from those of the prosecution's expert.

The proper procedure for introducing DNA evidence in trials was established by the Court of Appeal in *R.* v. *Doheny and Adams* [1996] The Times, 14 August.

The court held that:

1. The scientist should adduce the evidence of the DNA comparisons together with his calculations of the random occurrence ratio.

   Once a scientist has found a match between the suspect and the profile of samples taken from a crime scene, a calculation will be made to estimate the rarity of that profile, a random occurrence ratio. This ratio is calculated by using information stored in a database of other DNA work done in the laboratory. The result is a statement:

   'it is estimated that the frequency with which the DNA characteristics in the profile is likely to be found in the population at large is one in ...'

2. Whenever such evidence was to be adduced, the Crown should serve upon the defence details of how the calculations were carried out, which were sufficient for the defence to scrutinise the basis of the calculations.

3. The Forensic Science Service should make available to a defence expert, if requested, the databases upon which the calculations were based.

The Crown's expert and the trial judge may fall into the trap of what has become known as the 'prosecutor's fallacy'. This involves an error of logic in legal reasoning involving probability. In criminal trials there are two questions to be asked:

- what is the probability that the defendant's DNA profile matches the crime sample, given that the defendant is innocent? (the match probability);

- what is the probability that the defendant is innocent given that the DNA profile matches the profile from the crime sample? (the guilt probability).

This error occurs when the answer to the first question is given as the answer to the second question. The match probability is the domain of the experts. The guilt probability is the question that is of direct relevance to the jury and which requires an assessment of all the evidence. It is, therefore, in the domain of the jury and not the expert. It is possible for the two questions to have different answers and, in particular, a very small probability in answer to the first question does not necessarily imply a very small probability in answer to the second question.[4]

Forensic chemistry

This is an area of expertise that is used in relation to offences against property, analysing and comparing material from a non-biological source. Below are some examples of situations in which forensic chemical analysis is applicable:

- where entry is forced, there may be contact traces on any wood, paint, or metal found on a person's clothes. The layer structure of paint, with different coats painted on top of each other, may be unique;

- oil stains on a person's clothing following a 'hit and run' can be compared with the oil on the underside of a car. The sequence of different oils put into the car's sump can produce an oil stain that is as individual as a fingerprint;

- glass fragments found on a person's clothing or shoes will be examined to determine the refractive index and composition and then matched with those from the scene of the crime. The distribution of the fragments and the surface on which they are found (they cling to different surfaces for different periods of time), may be significant;

- a footwear impression will show the size of the shoe, tread pattern and degree of wear. To tie it in with a particular shoe the scientist will look for a specific wear pattern (determined by the wearer's way of walking), random damage (a cut, for example), or a stone in between the tread;

- fire debris;
- tyre marks;
- purported drugs of abuse;
- blood, urine and breath alcohol specimens.

Fingerprints

The standard applied

Chapter 4 indicated that after 3 April 2000 there will not longer be a 'numerical standard'. Police fingerprint bureaux staff will no longer base their conclusions on a certain number of matching characteristics, but on their considered opinion, i.e. their judgement based upon experience.

Abandonment of the 16-point standard[5] will mean:

- the margin for error will be increased and wrong identifications will be made;
- there is potential for wide divergence of interpretation of prints with fewer points of agreement;
- fingerprint bureaux staff, who have been trained using the 16-point standard, will be essentially left to their own devices and their own persuasive powers in respect of making an interpretation on fewer points.

The ACPO accepts that the opinion of police fingerprint staff will be contested at court.

The Court of Appeal refused leave to appeal against the decision of a trial judge who refused to exclude fingerprint evidence falling below the 16-point standard. But the evidence was not relied upon solely to prove the guilt of the applicant, and the trial judge had pointed out to the jury that there was some benefit to be derived from the fingerprint evidence, and it was for them to give such weight to it as they considered appropriate: *R. v. Giles* (Case No: 97/5495/W2: February 13 1998); [1999] Archbold News February 5; [1999] Archbold News April 19. You can expect cases, therefore, when the prosecution will advance fingerprint evidence with significantly few characteristics, arguing that taken with other evidence, the combination is persuasive.

You should never be deterred from challenging fingerprint evidence, whether offered alone or in combination with other evidence. If fingerprint evidence is at issue in your client's case, follow the advice of Chapter 8 – analyse the statements of fingerprint bureau staff, noting the standard applied, whether eliminatory testing was conducted and the status of other prints found. Then instruct a fingerprint expert.

Unidentified prints

Chapter 2 indicated how the police should carry out eliminatory tests in order to exclude officers who attended the scene and others living at, or having access to, the scene. Chapter 4 pointed out that time and resource limitations in all too many cases mean that eliminatory testing does not take place. In one case, where the defence was that the evidence had been 'planted', a fingerprint found on the packaging was disclosed to the defence at trial as 'unidentified'. After conviction, the print was identified as belonging to a police officer who was part of the police operation but played no part in the arrest or detention of the suspect.

This makes it particularly important that you understand the terminology used in respect of prints that are 'unidentified'. As we pointed out in Chapter 2 and Chapter 4, in many cases, *'Outstanding'* marks from crime scenes, i.e. those not identified or eliminated to specific donors (the accused or persons with access) are often deemed to be of *'No value'* or of *'Insufficient detail for comparison purposes'*.

'No value' means that there are no ridge characteristics present to assist any comparison process. On the other hand, *'Insufficient detail'* means that there are characteristics present, but that in the opinion of the examiner not enough to arrive at any conclusion. This is one opinion. Another examiner might see sufficient detail to justify a positive result. A case of 'one person's "insufficient detail" is another person's "identification"'.

You must therefore be alert to critical, potentially disingenuous, use of these terms and others, e.g. 'no identifiable prints' or 'unusable partial prints'. In fact the prints may very well be capable of being identified but no match has been found that supports the police case, i.e. they are not the suspect's prints.

In addition, it is essential to know that elimination can take place on far fewer characteristics than one needs to make a positive identification. If as few as only one or two characteristics are present in a particular mark that are found not to be present on a suspect's prints, then he or she can be eliminated as being the donor of that mark. As we pointed out, this is particularly important if the position of a mark, or marks, at the crime scene takes on a similar degree of importance, i.e. marks on a murder weapon or at a point of entry.

Document examination

It will be recalled that forces are being encouraged to task their scientific support units with document analysis. Their findings, and those of an external forensic supplier, must be questioned.

Forensic document examiners have particular expertise in the following areas:

- disguised handwriting;

- ink analysis;

- typewriting analysis;

- photocopying analysis;

- electrostatic deposition analysis (ESDA) of indented handwriting.

Some examiners will conduct the whole range of analyses, others will specialise.

Psychological factors

Lawyers have typically limited themselves to requesting a 'psychologist's report' on their client or, in cases involving children and young persons, on the interview behaviour of the complainant or the 'specialist' interviewer.

Many lawyers continue to have difficulty differentiating between psychiatrists and psychologists. This is understandable since both professions involve study of, and applied and research work involving, psychology. Psychology is the science of human behaviour and experience. These are an interplay of *cognitive factors* (attention, perception, comprehension, memory, language, reasoning) and *non-cognitive factors* (emotion, disposition, motivation). The two professions focus on, and have specialists in, the development of these factors across the lifespan, particularly human learning, social behaviour, and the whole spectrum of task performance.

Psychiatrists and psychologists examine behaviour and experience from normal, abnormal and applied perspectives. In addition, because behaviour and experience are the result of mind, brain and body being interdependent and because they are affected by drugs, whether prescribed or recreational,

457

the professions take account of these, and have applied specialisms identified by key terms, e.g. 'neuro' and 'pharmaco' combined with 'psycho-', '-psychological' and '-psychiatric'. Another applied specialism is forensic work.

Psychiatrists are medically qualified doctors. Many, but not all, psychologists are 'doctors'. Their doctorates are usually for postgraduate research and practice over a number of years. In very broad terms, psychologists conduct assessments and analyses of individuals and their testimony. Hence a psychologist's report may contain detail on the results of:

- the administration of empirical tests (the validity and reliability of which have been demonstrated by research);
- the application of methods of analysis arising from postgraduate research and applied work within a specific area of psychology;
- formal experiments, e.g. to test whether individuals are able to perform in a manner corresponding to, or at all like, that asserted by a witness or your client.

However, in addition to psychologists and psychiatrists, other individuals with particular expert knowledge of psychological factors, such as physicians, pharmacologists and psychotherapists, have a potential to bring this to bear in assessing the validity and the reliability of testimony given by a witness, including the complainant, and your client.

The range of factors is very wide. It includes:

1. Vulnerabilities in the individual's psychological make-up:
    - personality traits, particularly disposition to suggestibility, compliance, acquiescence, extreme levels of anxiety, low self-esteem;
    - psychological disorders (diagnosed, or potentially diagnosable, clinical conditions), e.g. psychotic and neurotic states and illnesses, personality disorders, acute stress disorder and post-traumatic stress disorder;
    - intellectual disadvantage and limitations in social functioning;
    - specific learning difficulties and communication deficits, e.g. illiteracy.

2. Specific psychological stresses in the light of identified vulnerabilities:
    - being in detention;
    - the conduct and effects of interviewing by police officers and others, particularly:
        - inappropriate conversational and listening behaviour;
        - constraining, suggestive and 'shaping' questions;
        - inappropriate questioning behaviour, i.e. how questions are posed;

- pressuring behaviours, e.g. rejecting and disparaging commentary, hectoring, belittling;
- failure to follow recommended good practice, i.e. the PEACE model,[6-8] the *Memorandum of Good Practice on Video-Recorded Interviews with Child Witnesses for Criminal Proceedings;*[9]
- the mismatch between any advanced or specialist training received by the interviewer and the interviewer's performance;

- the psychological influence of inappropriate, pressurising and partial behaviours by appropriate adults, interpreters, and legal advisers.

3. The status of assertions made in witness conversations and statements, relative to what is known about:

- the psychological capabilities, limitations and vulnerabilities, particularly in terms of fallibility of memory and disclosure, of:

  - people in general;
  - individuals at a particular stage of development, under the influence of drugs (e.g. sleeping tablets, anti-depressants, tranquillisers, steroids and 'recreational' drugs), with a particular mental disorder, in a particular state of consciousness, or with a particular physical condition (e.g. epilepsy);

- the specific capabilities, limitations and vulnerabilities of the individual in question;
- the distortion and contamination of witness testimony that occurs through exposure to post-event information, particularly during the processes of investigation or counselling and treatment;
- points at which distortion and contamination actually or potentially occurred in respect of a particular individual.

4. Additional factors bearing upon the status of assertions made by suspects:[10]

- the risk of partially or completely false admissions;
- the likely nature of the confession – voluntary, coerced, compliant or internalised;
- potentially precipitating psychological factors.

We appreciate that this may appear a daunting list. However, active defence requires you to have a sound understanding of the basic psychological issues. This will enable you to identify potential factors so that you can instruct experts and respond appropriately to their reporting. Annex 1 at the end of this chapter recommends some introductory texts.

Forensic linguistics

Chapter 8 pointed out that you may need to enlist the expert services of a linguist or phonetician for a number of purposes. Linguistics is the academic discipline concerned with the analysis of language and speech. It embraces a number of sub-disciplines, including phonetics – the specialised study of speech and voice patterns. If your case involves written language alone, e.g. contested documents, allegedly dictated confession statements, then you would need to contact a general linguist. If it involves testimony concerning the ability of a 'lay-witness' to recognise a voice or any aspect of tape-recorded speech, then you would need to contact a forensic phonetician.

In summary, a general forensic linguist may be able to help by using lexico-grammatical and semantic methodologies to determine authorship of disputed texts. A specialist forensic phonetician may be able to help in:

- reliability of speaker recognition evidence provided by a witness;

- organisation of speaker identification parades and voice line-ups for witnesses – though see the Court of Criminal Appeal Ruling in the case *R. v. Hersey* (reference 96/8495/Y3, 1 December 1997, briefly reported in [1998] Crim. L.R. 281 with useful editorial commentary) to assess the degree to which an expert witness can assist a jury in determining the fairness of a voice line-up;

- use of auditory phonetic and acoustic analysis in determining the content of noisy and difficult audio recordings;

- speaker profiling – using phonetic, sociolinguistic and dialect data in determining the background, e.g. regional and social, of unknown speakers in criminal recordings.

Other experts who can help you

In many instances, you will need to consult:
- a clinical specialist who can advise on evidence in cases involving allegations of physical and sexual assault, child sex abuse and non-accidental injury;

- a pathologist who can advise upon evidence offered by the Crown in respect of time and cause of death, injuries and what caused these;

- the Meteorological Office to establish weather conditions and visibility at material times;

- a forensic accountant in fraud cases.

FINDING AN EXPERT

Particular problems with finding forensic scientists

Where can the defence go in order to test out or get an alternative interpretation of the evidence that a prosecution scientist would give the court, or to show how the defence case is supported by the presence or absence of other forensic evidence that may not have been touched upon by the prosecution?

Not everyone appreciates that forensic biology, forensic chemistry, firearms, document examination, fingerprints and photographs all require different training and skills. There are no minimum standards, no minimum qualifications and no set procedures that have to be followed. To remedy this, a Council for the Registration of Forensic Practitioners has been established, with support from the Home Office.

Furthermore, with very few exceptions, the FSS, which now includes the former Metropolitan Police Forensic Science Laboratories, is the sole repository of practical experience and expertise in the use of forensic science. There are very few other properly trained, experienced, competent forensic scientists, from whom the defence can seek advice.

The number of independent forensic scientists who are prepared to work for the defence when the defendant is legally aided is limited because of the low fees paid and the delays before payment. Forensic scientists are tempted to concentrate more on prosecution and civil than on criminal defence work because of the cash-flow problems that legal aid work brings.

Delays in serving prosecution forensic evidence on the defence, due to limited personnel and financial resources at the FSS, coupled with other delays in the system – the request by the police in the first place; the report being sent to the police and then on to the CPS; the report having to be shown to prosecuting counsel before it can be served on the defence – result in the defence expert sometimes being instructed at very short notice, making it difficult for the defence to find someone suitably qualified who is prepared and able to do the work. This was the conclusion of the RCCJ researcher[11] who predicted that defence solicitors could find their choice of independent expert becoming even more limited.

If you find a forensic scientist willing to take instructions, you must find out:

- on what basis he or she feels qualified to advise in your particular case;

- his or her recognised scientific qualifications;

- what practical experience he or she has:

461

- in investigating the sort of case that involves your client;
- in applying scientific techniques to assess the evidence at issue.

In the case of other areas of forensic expertise, e.g. medicine, psychology, psychiatry, linguistics, the problem is very much one of identifying an individual who is able to focus on critical matters within the circumstances of your client's case.

Tracking down an expert

There are a number of locations where you can track down an expert. The situation is far from straightforward. There are a number of different bodies, each claiming to represent expert witnesses. Many experts are members of more than one body.

Many experienced and much sought-after experts consider it unnecessary to be on anybody's 'list', preferring the process of personal recommendation, which keeps them more than fully employed.

Some argue that where an expert is not too busy you should ask why this is the case.

Annex 1 at the end of this chapter gives advice on tracking down an expert.

INTERVIEWING PROSECUTION WITNESSES: IN PRINCIPLE

There is no property in a prosecution witness. The Law Society advises that:

> 'It is permissible for a solicitor acting for any party to interview and take statements from any witness or prospective witness at any stage in the proceedings, whether or not that witness has been interviewed or called as a witness by another party.'[12]

Traditionally, defence solicitors have had a distinct disinclination to interview prosecution witnesses.

Clearly there are risks:

- rehearsing the witness for cross-examination. There is the risk of warning the witness in advance of the defence case that will later be put to the witness, so that you inadvertently rehearse him or her for cross-examination at trial. If a witness is not telling the truth, the jury should be able to see the witness respond to a challenging question for the first time;

- legal risks. If you interview a prosecution witness and subsequently his or her evidence is inconsistent with an earlier account that the witness gave to the police, you could find yourself accused of interference and perversion of the course of justice. Intentionally intimidating a witness is an offence punishable by five years' imprisonment: CJPOA, s.51.

Note for Guidance 3 to Principle 21.10 in *The Guide to the Professional Conduct of Solicitors* (1999) states:

> *'A solicitor should be aware that, in seeking to exercise the right to interview a witness who ... is likely to be called [by the other side], the solicitor may well be exposed to the suggestion that he or she has improperly tampered with the evidence. This may be so particularly where the witness subsequently changes his or her evidence.'*[13]

There are persuasive arguments for interviewing prosecution witnesses despite the risks.

An American law professor, studying the differences in the way in which criminal cases are prepared in England and Wales and the US,[14] indicated that there was a major reason for US lawyers being better prepared at trial than their English and Welsh counterparts: English and Welsh solicitors typically do not interview prosecution witnesses. He thought it remarkable that solicitors are restrained from interviewing prosecution witnesses for fear of being accused of influencing them.

He dismissed the argument that such an interview would be an unnecessary duplication of the work of the police by pointing to research in England and Wales, which suggests that police officers are selective in the written statements they take, to favour the prosecution. In his view:

> *'American lawyers would scoff at this reverence for the work of the police, worried that the police had either inadvertently failed to explore some area because they did not know the defence or deliberately chosen not to report information to the prosecution for disclosure to the defence.'*

He concluded that: *'Solicitors will need to overcome their hesitancy, and begin to interview the Crown's witnesses.'*

Chapter 3 indicated substantial shortcomings in the way in which police officers interview witnesses. Processes of distortion, shaping and non-compliance with guidelines such as the ADVOKATE checks mean that the contents of the statement are in many cases an inaccurate representation – reflecting errors of omission and commission. Chapter 8 pointed out how these can be detected by fine-grain analysis, such that you have the basis to request disclosure of the antecedents to a statement with manifest shortcomings. Analysis of the antecedents will provide confirmation of the processes of distortion, shaping and non-compliance.

At trial, a witness is under pressure to 'come up to proof', i.e. to stick with his or her account regardless. In interview, the witness is more likely to give an account that is at variance with that given in his or her statement. It is potentially helpful to identify in advance any differences between the account obtained by the police and the witness's own account when given the opportunity to have his or her say 'for real'.

With the abolition of live evidence ending the opportunity to cross-examine prosecution witnesses at committal, the need to interview certain types of prosecution witnesses becomes more pressing. The witness may have information that you cannot afford to leave until cross-examination at trial to obtain. It may by then be too late to follow up a lead that the witness provides.

We argue that:

- active defence demands that, where appropriate, you must interview prosecution witnesses, having weighed up the factors for and against and arrived at a reasoned decision for doing so – particularly one founded upon shortcomings you, and experts, have identified in the witness's statement;

- no prosecutor, police officer or court could object to your interviewing:
  - if you act appropriately – in a way which demonstrates best practices in which the police service should be engaged and to which no one could take exception; and
  - if you employ appropriate procedures to ensure the treatment of the witness is beyond reproach and there is a recording of this.

INTERVIEWING PROSECUTION WITNESSES: IN PRACTICE

You must be guided at all times by a fundamental basic rule:

> **ALWAYS think ahead and ALWAYS act in terms of the worst-case scenario: be prepared to withstand objections and accusations at every stage – by being above board, open and by recording everything.**

This section covers the practice of interviewing prosecution witnesses to ensure that you do not depart from this basic rule.

Identifying witnesses

There a number of ways of identifying witnesses.

From disclosed material

In many instances, the identity of witnesses will be manifest: their statements are included in the material disclosed to you.

However, Chapter 8 indicated that it is possible to identify missing witnesses whom you, at the time of analysing the material, do not know:

- have been interviewed but whose statements they have chosen to withhold;

- have been interviewed but from whom no statement was taken;

- have been questioned but have been deemed not to have been interviewed;

- have been not questioned at all.

If the prosecutor does not intend to call a witness as part of the prosecution case, the fact that the witness has been interviewed by the police, whether a statement was taken or not, is likely to be recorded in the sensitive schedule of unused material. The reason for doing this is the sensitivity of disclosing the name and address of the person to you. Therefore, it will not be apparent to you from the non-sensitive schedule whether house-to-house enquiries were conducted.

You will have to ask if house-to-house enquiries took place, and probe the response to this.

You will see why, in Chapter 9, we say it is essential to ask about house-to-house enquiries at the police station: this is just one instance of being able to gain disclosure of a vital piece of information early on, which will be denied to you later.

Advertising

The Law Society advises that a solicitor, on the client's instructions, may insert advertisements for witnesses to come forward as to a particular occurrence. However, care must be taken to draft the advertisement so that, as far as practicable, it does not suggest the detailed testimony sought.[15]

Weighing up the factors for and against interviewing

Factors in favour

There are a number of potential factors. Many, but by no means all, reflect what you know about shortcomings in the police investigative process:

- the witness's evidence is significant to the prosecution case against your client;
- you have reason to believe that the witness may be able to point you:
  - to missing witnesses (see Chapter 8);
  - towards lines of enquiry that may assist your client's defence;
- you need factual information from the witness to prepare for trial;
- you have reason to suspect the integrity of the police in the investigation;
- the statement points to the inherently invalid or unreliable nature of the witness's evidence given that:
  - it is internally inconsistent, i.e. does not agree in its details;
  - it is externally inconsistent, i.e. does not coincide:
    - (a) with other prosecution witness statements;
    - (b) with your client's instructions;
- the statement contains language use – vocabulary, verbal constructions and turns of phrase – that do not appear to be those of the witness;
- you have reason to believe that the witness's statement, taken by a police officer, may not reflect what he or she said or wished to say or is able to say;
- the witness has no objection to being interviewed by you.

Factors against

There are factors against:

- you have no reason to believe that interviewing the witness will significantly help the preparation or presentation of the defence case;
- the risk of the police or prosecutor making an allegation that you attempted to persuade the witness to change his or her evidence or to refuse to attend court outweighs the likely benefits of interviewing the witness;
- the witness does not agree to be interviewed by you.

Locating the witness

Locating a witness may not be a straightforward matter:

- the witness statement served on you by the prosecutor is unlikely to contain the witness's address;
- the current practice is not to put the witness's address on the face of the witness statement but on the reverse;
- precedents of the CJA, section 9 witness statement forms omit the address.

Ways of locating the witness's address include:

- other factual information given by the witness in the statement;
- consulting the telephone directory;
- consulting the electoral roll in the public library;
- asking your client;
- asking a defence witness;
- instructing an enquiry agent.

Alternatively, you can apply to the prosecution for this information. If you have to obtain the witness's address through the prosecutor, we recommend that your request should:

- be in writing;
- give the reasons why you wish to interview the witness;
- show a firm grasp of the prosecution case, the evidence and the police investigation, i.e. make it wholly 'one-off' relating to the detail of your client's particular case. You must never send a 'standard' letter: to do so invites rejection and obstruction.

The prosecutor's response

The prosecutor will consult with the police about your request and they, in turn, will consult the witness. Account will be taken of the witness's vulnerability. The prosecutor will advise the witness that:

- it is up to him or her to decide whether to be interviewed by you;
- he or she can refuse.

Given these circumstances, you can expect that many will not consent to be interviewed.

If the witness agrees to be interviewed by you, the prosecutor:

* will make the witness available for you;

* will advise that the witness can have his or her own legal representative present if he or she chooses;

* will arrange for a police officer to be present;

* may arrange for the interview to take place at the police station.

If you are told that the witness does not wish his or her address to be disclosed, refuses to be interviewed or there is some other objection to the disclosure, you must apply to the court if you wish to obtain the witness's address so that you can approach him or her directly.

You need to bear in mind a number of factors should you wish to proceed to this stage:

* you must make your application before the trial in order to avoid the case having to be adjourned while you follow up any lead that the witness may give you;

* the National Standards of Witness Care in the Criminal Justice System state that:

    'Unless it is necessary for evidential purposes, defence and prosecution witnesses should not be required to disclose their addresses in open court.'

* courts, increasingly reluctant to publicise a witness's address, often do not ask the witness to give an address in court.

Yet the law has not changed and it is the right of an accused at court to know the identity of a witness, including the witness's name and address: *R.* v. *Taylor* [1995] Crim. L.R. 253.

The Court of Appeal gave the following guidance for applications for anonymity:

* there must be real grounds for fear of the consequences if the identity of the witness were revealed. It might not be necessary for the witness himself to be fearful, or to be fearful for himself alone;

* the evidence must be sufficiently important to make it unfair to insist on the prosecution proceeding without it;

- the prosecution must satisfy the court that the creditworthiness of the witness has been fully investigated and disclosed;
- the court must be satisfied that there is no undue prejudice to the accused, although some prejudice is inevitable.

The prosecutor may ask a police officer to attend the hearing to give the reasons for the objection to disclosure of the address.

Approaching a witness whom you have located

If you find out the address of the witness yourself, your approach must be considered, considerate and observe the basic rule spelled out above.

What you decide will depend, to some extent, on:

- the importance of the witness's evidence to the prosecution;
- the risk of an accusation being made that you have interfered with the witness's evidence in some way.

The safest way to contact the witness is by letter.

Appropriate contents for the letter to a witness located without recourse to the prosecutor

You will have a personal preference as to how to phrase issues and what to include in the letter. You should, however:

1. explain the reason for the interview, i.e.
   - you represent the accused;
   - you wish to establish the truth of the allegation;
   - to that end you would like to interview him or her;
   - although you already have a copy of a statement made by the witness to the police, it is still necessary for you to speak to the witness;

2. explain the interview routines, i.e.
   - who will conduct the interview;
   - that you would prefer the witness to come to your office for the interview, so that:
     - there is more control over what takes place;
     - it is easier to arrange for the interview itself to be witnessed;
   - that the interview will be tape-recorded;

469

- the witness is free:
    - to take independent legal advice;
    - to have a friend or relative present;
    - to have a police officer present;

- you will take a statement from the witness, inviting him or her to sign it afterwards;
- you will give or send the witness a copy of the statement you have taken.

A standard letter to the witness is set out in Annex 2 at the end of this chapter.

Keeping the prosecutor in the picture

It is a matter of personal judgement whether you decide:

- to advise the prosecution of the interview arrangements – stressing that it will be tape-recorded;

- to send a copy of the statement to the prosecutor.

Dealing with a non-response to your letter

You have to find out why the witness did not reply to your letter. There are a range of possibilities:

- the witness may not have received it;

- the witness could not be bothered to contact you;

- the witness was unsure or did not understand what he or she was supposed to do.

In the event of a non-response you must make direct contact by telephone or, failing that, in person. You must observe the basic rule: record everything that is said between you and the witness. Equipment, which enables you to record telephone conversations, is now extremely inexpensive. Such telephone conversation recorders can be bought in electrical equipment stores found in any major high street.

If the witness declines to be interviewed by you, that is his or her right and you should not attempt to persuade the witness to do something against his or her will.

Interviewing the witness

In any interview you must take account of:

• the absolute requirement to produce tangible evidence of proper conduct;

• who should conduct the interview;

• who else should attend;

• the exact location of the interview;

• proof of identity and authority.

You must also be in a position to process the disclosures of the witness, capturing, working concurrently upon and responding appropriately to, the detail.

Tangible evidence of proper conduct

It cannot be stressed enough that you must:

• tape-record the interview;

• ensure you get the witness to sign a declaration that:

– he or she attended the interview of his or her own free will;
– he or she was not influenced or pressurised in any way whatsoever by you or others employed by you at any time prior to or during the interview.

Who should conduct the interview

There are two occasions when it is appropriate for someone other than yourself to interview the witness:

• when, notwithstanding the fact that the interview will be tape-recorded and a declaration signed, you consider there may be a problem of exercising appropriate control over the witness's behaviour – such that there is a possible risk of an allegation by the police or prosecutor that you attempted to pressurise the witness to change his or her evidence or not appear in court;

• when you instruct an individual, either a suitably trained member of staff or a psychologist, to conduct a cognitive interview of the witness (see p.474).

471

Who else should attend with you

Mindful of the basic rule you, or anyone interviewing on your behalf, should consider having another person to be in attendance at all times. This is another safeguard since the person can witness:

- what the witness says;

- that you conducted the interview properly;

- that there was no 'off-tape' interviewing;

- that you did not seek to influence or to pressurise the witness in any way whatsoever.

The other person may be a colleague or, if you wish to stress the independence of this person, a solicitor or a representative from another firm.

Proof of identity and authority

You, or whoever interviews on your behalf, should have a means of identification to show to the witness.

If the interview is to be conducted by a representative acting on your behalf, he or she should have a letter of authority from you.

The exact location of the interview

Wherever possible, interview the witness in the formal surroundings of your office, or any other formal location, since this will:

- make it easier for you set up the tape-recording equipment, laying out tapes, statement forms and the written declaration;

- make it easier for you to control any inappropriate behaviour by anyone who accompanies the witness, particularly a police officer;

- afford greater personal safety;

- enhance the formality of the contact and be conducive to keeping informal discussion ('small talk') to a minimum: an important factor because you must avoid any misunderstandings or misinterpretations of your actions by the witness.

Processing the witness's disclosures

Interviewers edit unconsciously the interviewee's disclosures, with the outcome of this editing being 'gist' understanding and compressed notes. *Analysing Witness Testimony* explains why and how people do this. (For publication details, see Annex 1 at the end of the chapter. You can overcome this by managing the conversation as a series of stages – enabling you to have more than one pass (or exposure) to the detail.

- At the outset, you need to tell the witness what you want to know and that you will want to get this detail in stages.

- For the first pass, ask the witness to tell you everything, in as much detail as possible, even the little bits, taking his or her time and letting the witness know that you will just listen intently. Set the witness going and concentrate on creating in your 'mind's eye' what the witness is saying rather than taking notes (since taking notes diverts some of your attention away from listening to writing). This result will be a very clear, overall, relatively detailed picture of what the witness has said.

- For the second pass, tell the witness that you want to go over it again but this time you will be taking down the details, so you will need to stop him or her to do this. Remind the witness that you want to hear everything, in as much detail as possible, even the little bits, and to take his or her time. Set the witness going and regulate the flow of detail as a continuous series of very small 'chunks', by stopping the witness to enable to write the 'chunk' as notes, as detail on an SE3R or as detail entered into your laptop, which has been loaded with *RealSense* (the computer version of SE3R). Where appropriate, invite the witness to make a drawing or sketch. (Of course, you may choose to capture detail by a combination of notes and SE3R or notes and *RealSense* on the computer.)

- For the third pass, review your notes, SE3R or your *RealSense* screens. Identify areas of anomaly, e.g. gaps, vagueness, ambiguity, jumps, inconsistency or episodes that you want the witness to go over again and to expand. Using appropriate questioning, systematically probe and expand the detail you have, recording the witness's disclosures in note form or as SE3R or *RealSense* entries.

- Finally, check back the detail you have, explaining to the witness that you wish him or her to confirm the accuracy of, or to alter or add to, the detail you have taken down. Then state exactly what you have written in your notes or is on the SE3R sheets or *RealSense* screens.

The fact that you have tape-recorded the interview provides additional opportunity to ensure comprehensive processing of the witness's disclosures:

- You can listen again to the first pass – during which you did not take notes but are now able to capture the detail in note, SE3R and **RealSense** form.

- You can compare this first pass with the witness's second and subsequent passes, enabling you to identify any anomalies.

- You can check the accuracy of the detail you registered on the second and subsequent passes.

Appendix 8 gives further advice on interviewing, spelling out a wide range of issues in respect of:

- planning and preparation;

- administrative preparations;

- conducting the interview.

Cognitive interviewing

Chapter 2 explains what constitutes cognitive (memory-enhancing) interviewing. It is an extremely effective method of facilitating maximum disclosure of detail. If properly carried out, the interviewer has minimal influence over the disclosure process. It requires a breadth of knowledge and skill that can only come from proper training.

As Chapter 3 points out, even though PEACE training devotes a significant amount of time to cognitive interviewing, police officers fail to put their training into practice on a continuous basis in order to develop basic skills and the requisite expertise.

Research shows that in the majority of cases, officers believe they are carrying out a cognitive interview when in fact all they are doing is:

- exercising better listening skills;

- asking more open-ended questions;

- deluding themselves into thinking that they are applying memory-enhancing techniques when in fact they are not.

A number of ex-police officers are offering training in cognitive interviewing to lawyers, purporting that cognitive interviewing can be imparted in as little as one day's training. This is nonsense. As Chapter 3 explains, the psychologists who developed cognitive interviewing are quite explicit as to what kind of programme of training and supervised practice is necessary to develop the basic skills of cognitive interviewing.[16]

We are particularly concerned that lawyers and individuals instructed by them should not set about conducting a cognitive interview, which results in an accusation by a prosecutor or the police that the interviewing was improperly conducted by a person who can be proven to be:

- technically incompetent;

- inadequately trained or experienced.

Cognitive interviewing should only be conducted by:

- a lawyer or representative who:
  - has reached the same level of expertise as police officers who have received PEACE training;
  - has had supervised practice;

- a psychologist who specialises in cognitive interviewing and has demonstrable practice in conducting this type of interviewing.

VISITING THE SCENE OF THE CRIME

You must consider visiting, or, less preferable, instructing others on your behalf to visit, the scene of the crime. The term scene here is used in the narrower sense, i.e. the physical location of the offence, its surroundings and routes to and from the location. Of course, it requires knowledge of the scene in the wider sense (used by the police service and forensic scientists), referring in addition to the location of the victim, the offender, and everything exchanged between them and found in the physical location.

Preparations

You should be fully conversant with relevant case material. Such material includes:

- descriptions, including visual representations, obtained in the consultation with the investigating officer prior to interviewing of your client;

475

- descriptions contained within statements and other documents disclosed by the prosecutor and your client (wherever possible converting the verbal description into a visual representation);

- disclosed drawings, sketches, photographs, annotated plans and maps;

- disclosed video recordings of the scene and other key locations.

You will need:

- copies of case material to be compared with the actual scene;

- relevant mapping, e.g. Ordnance Survey, plans produced by local government departments and a magnetic compass, e.g. one of the small, inexpensive types used by ramblers;

- measuring materials – a surveyor's tape is particularly useful;

- writing materials;

- materials to enable you to draw diagrams and sketches;

- a tape recorder – to record observations and commentary upon the comparison between what is contained in case material and the actual scene;

- camera with flash;

- a video recorder.

You should preferably visit the scene with at least one assistant. This not only facilitates the task of fully recording, but many of the tasks of examining, measuring, checking, testing out require two people.

At the scene

You need to approach your task systematically. This involves methodical physical inspection, triggered by awareness of the disclosed evidence and seeking answers to specific questions.

You must make a full record of your inspection and your review using the full range of means to do this: notes, drawings and sketches, photography, audio and video recording. Appendix 7 gives advice on making drawings of a scene.

This form of recorded material will:

- enable you and others instructed by you, e.g. counsel, experts, your client and witnesses interviewed by you to examine and to refer to the material;

- enable you to bring particular issues to the attention of the prosecutor, e.g. by producing copies of or extracts from the material.

By going to the crime scene you are able to 'reality' test:

- individuals' accounts of where they were positioned;

- what was (or was not) observed, heard or found, in terms of entry and exit routes, the vicinity of the scene, and the scene itself – compared with was is actually observable, able to be heard, the actual location, its physical properties, and where something was discovered or recovered.

The following are some points about human observational constraints.

- A significant proportion of the population has some form of visual impairment, requiring correction in the form of spectacles or contact lenses. Many do not know they are impaired. Of those that do, many for cosmetic reasons choose to limit the time and occasions, when they wear spectacles. The police rarely check whether a person has impaired vision or whether spectacles or contact lenses were being worn at the time of observation.

- Vision at night is markedly reduced. While movement continues to be detectable, actual detail is much harder to make out. The distance over which detail can be distinguished and people recognised reduces markedly. However, people are overconfident in their ability to see and to recognise despite these physical constraints.

- In terms of recognition of an individual:
  - at 30 feet/approximately 10 metres, a person is recognisable in bright moonlight;
  - at 100 feet/approximately 30 metres, in good illumination, a person who is not well known to an observer is recognisable;
  - at 150 feet/approximately 45 metres, in good illumination, a person who is well known to an observer is recognisable;
  - at 300 feet/approximately 90 metres, in good illumination, a person in distinctive clothing or with a distinctive manner, e.g. peculiar gait, is recognisable.

- Colour vision is progressively affected as illumination reduces such that at night, in the absence of a light source, colours cannot be distinguished: only shades of lightness and darkness can be discriminated. What people report in terms of colour is internally driven by expectation, e.g. pupils of eyes that are seen in very low light or near darkness are reported as being dark brown. They are erroneously extrapolating colour from brightness.

477

- Some 3 per cent of the population are colour blind. They are overwhelmingly male, because colour blindness is carried on the male chromosome.

We have already mentioned in Chapter 8 limitations in respect of CCTV. You should be aware that:

- CCTV is often of very poor quality and this is compounded since individuals are shown from a distance.
- The field of vision is often incomplete, e.g. trees and other obstacles are in the way.
- Continuous motion is frequently not recorded – with the camera recording only one frame every 2–3 seconds.
- The view is often from above, occasioning distortion and making identification difficult.
- Ordinary witnesses are surprisingly poor at identifying strangers from CCTV footage.
- Individuals are commonly able to identify someone they know from poor CCTV recording.

Entry/exit routes from the crime scene

1. Review the evidence derived from witnesses and inanimate surveillance indicating that:
   - the offender having entered or left the crime scene by a particular route;
   - the offender who entered or left by that route was your client.
2. Look for purported, and possible alternative, entry/exit routes. Review and check out:
   - Which routes were (or were likely to have been) taken?
   - What obstacles are there on an entry/exit route?
   - How were obstacles allegedly negotiated?
   - Is it possible to negotiate an obstacle?
   - How could an obstacle be negotiated?
3. Look for purported, and actual, forms of observation of entry/exit routes. Review and check out:
   - Was the entry/exit physically observable?
   - Was the entry/exit actually observed?
   - Is the area guarded by security personnel/dogs?

- Is the guard at a static duty point or a mobile patrol?
- What is the patrolling pattern, i.e. routes and times taken?
- How close was the guard to the entry/exit route?
- Is the entry/exit route covered by security surveillance CCTV?
- Does the system have all-weather (infrared) recording capability?
- What are the manning and monitoring arrangements of the system?
- Are the cameras and recording, automatically (intruder/time) activated or are they manually operated?
- If the camera rotates to scan a larger area, what arc does it traverse?
- What is the height of the camera above ground? (A likely source of distortion of images.)
- What is the distance from the camera to the nearest point on the entry/exit route? (A likely source of poor resolution of images.)
- Have the police taken possession of, and examined, the video recording for the material time frame?
- Was there static or mobile police surveillance?
- From observation logs, what surveillance locations/points were taken up?
- How proximate was the surveillance location/point to the entry/exit route?
- Was the entry/exit physically observable from the stated surveillance location/point?
- From photographs and video recordings taken by surveillance officers, does the position of the camera shot correspond to the surveillance location/point asserted by the police?

4. Consider the location, and assertions, of individual witnesses to entry/exit.

- Who were the potential witnesses to entry/exit of the offender?
- Who was spoken to by the police?
- To what outcome – in terms of supporting the police case or negative evidence?
- From whom were descriptions or accounts actually taken – recorded on the OIS/CAD system, in notes, in pocket books or in statements?
- What was the individual's purported location at the time of witnessing entry/exit?
- How proximate was the witness's location to the entry/exit route?
- Was the entry/exit physically observable from the location stated?
- Was there house-to-house questioning?
- Where were these visited locations relative to the entry/exit route?

- What were the results of the enquiries in terms of:

    - the emergence of witnesses who gave responses/statements supporting the police case?
    - negative evidence, i.e. not supportive of the police case?

5. Consider location, and assertions of witnesses, in respect of vehicles approaching or leaving the scene.

    - What reports were given of the movement or presence of the offender's vehicle?
    - By whom?
    - What reports were given of movement and presence of other vehicles?
    - By whom?

6. Consider the forensic evidence derived from the entry/exit route. Use your common sense, experience from other cases and knowledge of the present case, to review and to check the route to assess the significance of each type of forensic evidence, e.g. what CTM was found and where, which:

    - links the offender with entering and exiting by that route?
    - links the route with the offender?
    - links your client with the route?
    - links the route with your client?

The physical crime scene

1. Review the evidence:

    - of the offender having been at the actual crime scene;
    - that the offender was your client.

2. Look for purported observation of the crime scene. Review and check out:

    - Were the scene and the immediate vicinity observed?
    - Is the area guarded by security personnel?
    - Is the guard at a static duty point or a mobile patrol?
    - What is the patrolling pattern, i.e. routes and times taken?
    - How close was the guard to the crime scene?
    - Are the crime scene and the immediate vicinity covered by security CCTV?
    - Does the system have all-weather (infrared) recording capability?
    - What are the manning and monitoring arrangements of the system?
    - Are the cameras and recording, automatically (intruder/time) activated or are they manually operated?

- If the camera rotates to scan a larger area, what arc does it traverse?
- What is the height of the camera above ground? (A likely source of distortion of images.)
- What is distance from the camera to the scene? (A likely source of poor resolution of images.)
- Have the police taken possession of, and examined, the video recording for the material time frame?
- Was there static or mobile police surveillance?
- From observation logs, what surveillance locations/points were taken up?
- How proximate was the surveillance location/point to the scene?
- Was the scene physically observable from the stated surveillance location/point?
- From photographs and video recordings taken by surveillance officers, does the position of the camera shot correspond to the surveillance location/point asserted by the police?

3. Consider the location and assertions, of individual witnesses at the scene:

- Who were the potential witnesses to the offence?
- From whom were statements taken?
- Who was spoken to by the police?
- To what outcome – in terms of supporting the police case or negative evidence?
- From whom were descriptions or accounts actually taken – recorded on the OIS/CAD system, in notes, in pocket books or in statements?
- What was the individual's purported location at the time of witnessing?
- How proximate was the witness's location to the scene?
- Was the scene physically observable from the location stated?
- Was there house-to-house questioning?
- Where were these visited locations?
- What were the results of the enquiries in terms of:

    - emergence of witnesses who gave responses/statements supporting the police case?
    - negative evidence, i.e. not supportive of the police case?

- Who was at the scene, but made contact with the police later?
- To what outcome – in terms of supporting the police case or negative evidence?

4. Consider the forensic evidence derived from the scene and the immediate vicinity. Use your common sense, experience from other cases, and knowledge of the present case to review and to check the crime scene to assess the significance of each type of forensic evidence, e.g. what CTM was found and where, which links:

   • the offender with the scene?
   • the scene with the offender?
   • your client with the scene?
   • the scene with your client?

Assess the validity (accuracy) and credibility of assertions in witness evidence

For each eyewitness, consider:

1. *The asserted observation point and assertions as to what could be seen with what can actually be seen from that position*. Record, in as many forms as appropriate, what can actually be seen.

2. *Physical limitations*.

   • What was the distance between the witness and that which was purportedly observed?
   • Does the witness have poor vision requiring correction?
   • Was the witness wearing spectacles/contact lenses at the time of observation?

3. *Illumination and natural light at the time of observation*.

   • What were the sources of artificial light at the time?
   • What was the artificial and natural light like at the time (time of day/year)?
   • What were the weather conditions at the time (e.g. bad conditions, poor light)?

4. *Visibility and lines of sight*.

   • What were the weather conditions like at the time, e.g. rain?
   • Was the witness's visibility obstructed at that time by an object(s), e.g. traffic?

For each earwitness, consider:

1. The asserted observation point and assertions as to what could be heard with what can actually be heard from that position. Use audio and video recording, to make a permanent record of what can actually

be heard from a particular physical location (the video enables you to show visibly the location from which the sound is being heard).

2. The physical limitations:

- What was the distance between the witness and the witnessed sound?

- What obstacles/surfaces, e.g. walls, doors and windows, were there between the witness and the source of the sound?

- How audible are particular types of noise through the particular obstacle?

- What were background noises, and the levels of these, at the time of hearing the sound?

RECONSTRUCTING THE CRIME

In Chapter 8 we indicated that reconstruction of asserted detail is a potent test of reality. If the reconstruction shows something could not have happened in the way described, this permits argument that it did not happen. Furthermore, if events had occurred in the manner alleged, a reconstruction is able to reveal what witness and other evidence should be available, i.e. it is an aid to identifying gaps in the police investigation and the prosecution evidence.

Recreation can be assisted by a sketch and any other illustration or visual aid, which may or may not be contained in disclosed material. Conducting an experiment, or a re-enactment (role-play), is best done through physical role-play, visiting and going over the ground, and where necessary using (or improvising) props.

You must video-record the reconstruction and, where appropriate, take photographs.

PROSECUTION OBJECT EVIDENCE

If, in the course of making investigations into your client's defence, you come across evidence that is clearly material to the prosecution case, you must observe some common-sense rules:[17]

- Do not interfere with it in any way.

- Make a record of finding it.

- Leave it as you found it.

- Make a written record or draw a sketch or sketch plan of it, or take a photograph or make a video recording of it.

You are under no obligation to report the discovery of the evidence to the police.

If a client approaches you and asks you to keep something that you suspect may incriminate him or her, you should refuse to accept the item. Where the item is clearly indicative of guilt, you should advise the client appropriately on plea and if a conflict arises you should cease to act.

The position is more complicated if your client puts you in possession of such evidence either directly or through a friend. Occasionally, you may find that an item has been left in your office. Where the item is clearly of value to the police and the investigation of crime, you should arrange for it to be delivered to the police. You are not under an obligation to inform the police of how it came into your possession or of any other circumstances surrounding the delivery of it to you. You should tell your client what you are doing and consider whether a conflict of interest with your client has arisen.

If the police suspect you of committing a criminal offence because of the actions of your client, you may reveal confidential information concerning your client to the extent that it is reasonably necessary to establish a defence to a criminal charge.[18]

Notes

1. Annex 21D. (1999) *The Guide to the Professional Conduct of Solicitors.* (1999) London: Law Society Publishing.

2. Zander, M. and Henderson P. (1992) *The Crown Court Study, RCCJ Research Study No. 19.* London: HMSO.

3. Steventon, B. (1992) *The Ability to Challenge DNA Evidence, RCCJ Research Study No. 9.* London: HMSO.

4. Justice Annual Report. (1996) *Litigation and Casework – Court of Appeal.*

5. Graham, V. (1996) 'Points to prove'. *Police Review*, 9 August.

6. *A Guide to Interviewing.* (1992) Harrogate: Central Planning and Training Unit.

7. *A Guide to Interviewing.* (1996) Bramshill: Police Staff College.

8. *A Practical Guide to Investigative Interviewing.* (1998) Bramshill: National Crime Faculty

9. Home Office. (1992) *Memorandum of Good Practice on Video-Recorded Interviews with Child Witnesses for Criminal Proceedings.* London: HMSO.

10. Shepherd, E. (1996) *Becoming Skilled.* London: Law Society Publishing.

11. Roberts, P. and Willmore, C. (1992) *The Role of Forensic Science Evidence in Criminal Proceedings, RCCJ Research Study No. 11.* London: HMSO.

12. Principle 21.10. *The Guide to the Professional Conduct of Solicitors.* (1999) London: Law Society Publishing.

13. *Ibid.* Note for Guidance 3, Principle 21.10.

14. Tague, P. (1996) *Effective Advocacy for the Criminal Defendant: the Barrister v. the Lawyer.* Buffalo, New York: Hein.

15. Note for Guidance 8, Principle 21.10. *The Guide to the Professional Conduct of Solicitors.* (1999) London: Law Society Publishing.

16. Fisher, R. and Geiselman, R. (1992) *Memory-enhancing Techniques for Investigative Interviewing: the Cognitive Interview.* Springfield, ILL: Thomas.

17. Burleigh, D. (1994) 'Prosecution evidence – don't touch it'. *Criminal Practitioners Newsletter.* No. 20, October, 9.

18. Note for Guidance 12, Principle 16.02. *The Guide to the Professional Conduct of Solicitors.* (1999) London: Law Society Publishing.

ANNEX 1

USEFUL INFORMATION

- **Recommended reading** – to provide you with the necessary background knowledge to understand expert reports, to instruct and to work with experts.
- **Tracking down an expert** – details of those who have assisted us, and of databases on experts.
- **How to obtain RealSense** – the computer version of SE3R (the method for capturing, visually representing and analysing fine-grain detail), which can be applied in interviews (of any kind) and applied to one or more written texts of any form, e.g. statement, ROTI, IVRI or transcript.

RECOMMENDED READING

Forensic science

Ellen, D. (1997) *The Scientific Examination of Documents*. London: Taylor & Francis.

Grieve, M. (1999) *Forensic Investigation of Fibres*. London: Taylor & Francis.

Horswell, J. (2000) *The Practice of Crime Scene Investigation*. London: Taylor & Francis.

Robertson, J. (1999) *Forensic Examination of Hair*. London: Taylor & Francis.

White, P. (1999) *Crime Scene to Court: The Essentials of Forensic Science*. London: Royal Society of Chemistry.

Psychological factors

Gudjonsson. G. (1992) *The Psychology of Interrogations, Confessions and Testimony*. Chichester: Wiley.

Heaton-Armstrong, A., Shepherd, E. and Wolchover, D. (1999) *Analysing Witness Testimony: A Guide for Legal Practitioners and Other Professionals*. London: Blackstone.

Milne, R. and Bull, R. (1999) *Investigative Interviewing: Psychology and Practice*. Chichester: Wiley.

Forensic linguistics

Baldwin, J. and French, P. (1990) *Forensic Phonetics*. London: Pinter.

Hollien, H. (1991) *The Acoustics of Crime*. New York: Plenum.

General reference

Shepherd, E. (1996) *A Pocket Reference*. London: Law Society Publishing.

Shepherd, E. (1996) *Becoming Skilled*. London: Law Society Publishing.

TRACKING DOWN AN EXPERT

Sources of expertise and advice

The following have assisted us in this text, and are sources of expertise and advice:

- **Forensic Access** Provides forensic science services for solicitors and maintains a register of expert witnesses. If the enquiry is routine, no charge is made for referring a solicitor to an expert in the appropriate field. Enquiries to: Chequers Court, Station Road, Thatcham, Berkshire RG19 4PR. Tel: 01635 866877.

- **Investigative Science**. Provides forensic psychological services for solicitors and can help you to identify the particular psychological expertise you may require in your client's case. If the enquiry is routine, no charge is made for referring a solicitor to an appropriate psychologist or psychiatrist. Enquiries to: Wych End, The Spinney, Ford Lane, East Hendred, Oxfordshire OX12 8LS. Tel: 01235 833162.

- **Fingerprint Analysis**. Provides fingerprint analysis for solicitors. Enquires to: 35 Woodlands, Horbury, Wakefield, West Yorkshire WF4 5HH. Tel: 01924 290306.

- **J. P. French Associates**. Provides forensic linguistic services for solicitors and can help you to establish which particular area of expertise may be appropriate. If the enquiry is routine, no charge is made for referring a solicitor to an appropriate linguist. Enquiries to: 86 The Mount, York YO24 1AR. Tel: 01904 634821.

- **The Forensic Medicine Unit**, St George's Hospital Medical School (Head of Unit: Dr Richard Shepherd). Enquiries to: Jenner Wing, St George's Hospital Medical School, Cranmer Terrace, London SW17 0RE. Tel: 020 8725 0015.

Databases on experts

Large databases are held by:

- **The Law Society's *Directory of Expert Witnesses* and Helpline**. The Law Society and Sweet & Maxwell publish a *Directory of Expert Witnesses* and CD, with a supporting telephone enquiry service for subscribers provided by the Law Society. Enquiries to: Sweet & Maxwell – Tel: 020 7449 1111; or the Expert Witness Helpline, Tel: 020 7320 5710. Fax: 020 7831 1687.

- **The British Academy of Experts**. Provides the names and addresses of suitable members from its directory for a small charge. The Academy has some 2,000 members. Enquiries to: 116–18 Chancery Lane, London WC2A 1PP. Tel: 020 7637 0333.

- **The British Academy of Forensic Sciences**. Keeps a list of experts, including forensic pathologists. BAFS exists to 'encourage the study, improve the practice and advance the knowledge of legal, medical and forensic science'. BAFS publishes a quarterly journal, Medicine, Science and the Law, and holds an annual seminar on a controversial topic, sponsored by the Law Society and the Criminal Bar Association. Enquiries to: The Secretary, BAFS, Anaesthetic Unit, London Hospital Medical College, Turner Street, London E1 2AO. Tel: 020 7377 9201.

- **The Forensic Science Society**. This is an international body whose object is to advance the study of forensic science. It runs a directory of independent consultants. Enquiries to: Clarke House, 18a Mount Parade, Harrogate, North Yorkshire HG1 1BX. Tel: 01423 506068. Fax: 01423 530948.

- **The Forensic Science Service**. This is open to the defence as well as the prosecution. Solicitors can contact the Marketing Division to find out about the facilities the service offers and its charges. Enquiries to: Priory House, Gooch Street North, Birmingham B5 6QQ. Tel: 0121 666 6606. Fax: 0121 622 3536.

HOW TO OBTAIN *RealSense*

RealSense comes as a complete practitioner package, with a CD and a linked handbook, which gives instructions on:

- how best to interview in order to facilitate greater disclosure, increasing the potential of *RealSense* to capture large amounts of detail and to highlight the many forms of anomaly;

- how to apply *RealSense* to one or more written or recorded texts.

RealSense can be obtained from: **Forensic Solutions Limited**, Wych End, The Spinney, Ford Lane, East Hendred, Oxfordshire OX12 8LS. Tel: 01235 821205; Fax: 01235 821547.

ANNEX 2

STANDARD LETTER TO A PROSECUTION WITNESS WHOM YOU WISH TO INTERVIEW

Dear [name of witness],

[Accused's name]

[Court]

[Date of next hearing]

I am the solicitor who represents [name of accused], who is accused of [details of offence].

He/she denies [that he/she was involved/that he/she is to blame for what happened/that the events took place in the way described to the police]. I have to investigate this further and believe that you can help me.

I would like to interview you. [I know that you have already given a statement to the police, but there are still some questions that I need to ask you.]

Will you help me by allowing me to interview you?

I would like to conduct the interview at my office. I would tape-record everything that you say to me, make a full written record and let you have a copy of it afterwards.

I assure you that I will not pressurise you in any way. [You may bring a friend or relative along to the interview with you, if that will help put you at your ease.] [Being able to ask you questions now may mean that you do not have to attend court because I no longer need to question you at the trial.]

[I have sent a copy of this letter to the Crown Prosecution Service who will contact the officer in charge of the case. I will invite the police to send an officer along to sit in on the interview.][You may take independent legal advice before replying to me.]

Please telephone me to arrange a convenient day and time.

Yours sincerely

[Name of solicitor]

Appendices

Disclosure of unused material under the CPIA 1996 and its Code of Practice – an overview

A. The duty of the investigator to record and retain material

The investigator:

- investigates
- obtains
- records
- retains

} relevant material

Relevant material is:

- information and objects
- which may be relevant to the investigation
- which has some bearing on the offence/person being investigated/surrounding circumstances.

B. The duty of the investigator and the disclosure officer to reveal material to the prosecutor

Investigator	Disclosure Officer (DO)	Prosecutor (P)
Draws attention of DO to 'undermining' material	Lists material on (1) non-sensitive and (2) sensitive schedules and sends these to P	
Tells P of material too sensitive to include in sensitive schedule		
May ask P's advice about whether a particular item may be relevant to the investigation		

Investigator	Disclosure Officer (DO)	Prosecutor (P)
	Copies specified 'undermining' material to P and draws P's attention to other material which may fit the test for primary disclosure	May request to inspect any material or have it copied to P
		Inspects material too sensitive to have copied to P

C. The duty of the prosecutor to give primary disclosure to the accused

Trigger
- not-guilty plea in magistrates' court
- committal for trial/transfer

Time
- no time period at first – transitional provisions will apply: 'as soon as practicable'

Material
- previously undisclosed
- in the prosecutor's opinion
- might undermine the prosecution case

Transition
- applies to alleged offence into which no criminal investigation begun before the appointed day
- otherwise previous common law applies

Limited
- limited to material in the prosecutor's possession or which the prosecutor has inspected and which was obtained in relation to the present case

Schedule
- schedule of non-sensitive unused prosecution material

Undermining
- material which has an 'adverse effect' on the strength of the case
  - anything that tends to show a fact inconsistent with the case that must be proved by the prosecution

D. The obligation on the accused to give the prosecutor and the court a defence statement

When?	• After the prosecutor has given primary disclosure
	• Within 14 days, capable of extension
Why?	• To avoid an adverse inference being drawn in the Crown Court
	• To obtain secondary disclosure – material which assists the defence case disclosed
	• To persuade the prosecutor to discontinue the case or substitute alternative charges

Failure may lead to an adverse inference being drawn if:

- fail to give
- give late
- set out inconsistent defences
- at trial put forward a different defence
- at trial call alibi evidence

Musts

- not compulsory in the magistrates' court
- must be in writing
- must set out:
  - general nature of accused's defence
  - matters on which accused takes issue with the prosecution
  - reasons for taking issue
  - alibi and alibi witnesses

E. The duty of the disclosure officer to reveal material to the prosecutor for secondary disclosure

Prosecutor (P)	**Disclosure officer (DO)**
P sends the DO a copy of the defence statement	
	The DO looks at the retained material and draws P's attention to material which may fit the test for secondary disclosure
P discloses to the accused material which might reasonably be expected to assist the defence disclosed by the accused	

497

F. The duty of the prosecutor to give secondary disclosure to the accused

Trigger	• giving of defence statement by accused
Time	• no time period at first – transitional provisions will apply: 'as soon as practicable'
Material	• which might reasonably be expected
	• to assist the accused's defence as disclosed by the defence statement
	• limited to material in the prosecutor's possession or which the prosecutor has inspected and which was obtained in relation to the present case
Method	• the prosecutor copies material to the accused or requests the disclosure officer to do so
	• the accused is allowed to inspect it
Continuous review	• prosecutor's duty to disclose continues until conviction
If accused not satisfied	• can make application to the court
	• for any relevant material obtained by the police
	• must justify the application by showing that the material fits the test for disclosure

G. The treatment of sensitive material

Disclosure officer	• categorises it and includes it in a sensitive schedule
	– with reasons for having considered it to be sensitive
	• sends sensitive schedule to the prosecutor
Prosecutor	• decides if material on sensitive schedule is disclosable
	– might undermine the prosecution case
	– may be reasonably expected to assist the accused's defence as disclosed
	• if it does not fit either test for disclosure
	– takes no further action in relation to it
	• if it is disclosable
	– applies to the court for a non-disclosure order
Court	• has defence statement
	• hears application
	– with notice, *inter partes*, accused able to make representations

- – *ex parte*, accused not present but aware of application
- – *ex parte*, accused not informed that application being made

- • if non-disclosure order made
  - – Crown Court under a duty to continuously review
  - – magistrates' court under a duty to review if accused makes application.

APPENDIX 2

Giving a defence statement

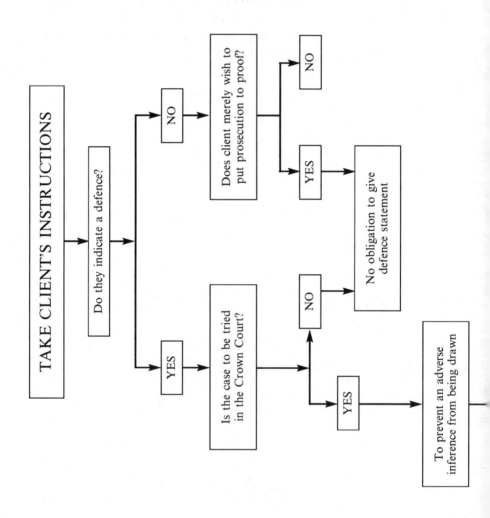

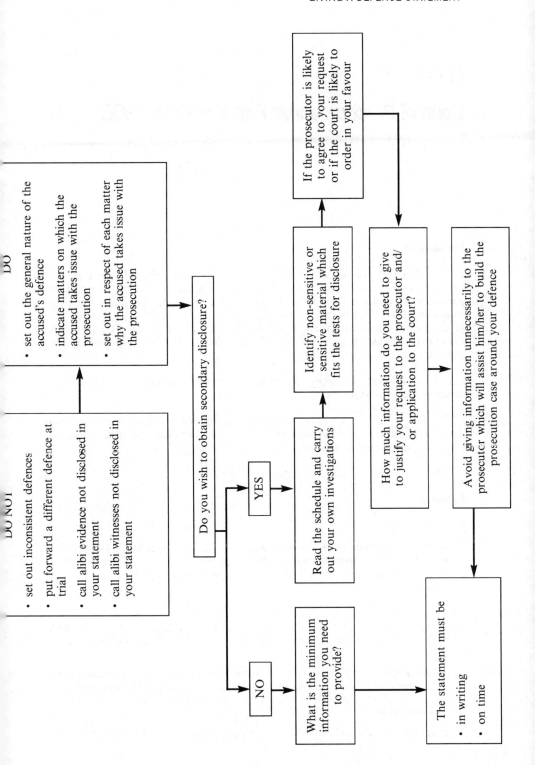

DO NOT

- set out inconsistent defences
- put forward a different defence at trial
- call alibi evidence not disclosed in your statement
- call alibi witnesses not disclosed in your statement

DO

- set out the general nature of the accused's defence
- indicate matters on which the accused takes issue with the prosecution
- set out in respect of each matter why the accused takes issue with the prosecution

Do you wish to obtain secondary disclosure?

YES

Read the schedule and carry out your own investigations

Identify non-sensitive or sensitive material which fits the tests for disclosure

If the prosecutor is likely to agree to your request or if the court is likely to order in your favour

How much information do you need to give to justify your request to the prosecutor and/or application to the court?

Avoid giving information unnecessarily to the prosecutor which will assist him/her to build the prosecution case around your defence

NO

What is the minimum information you need to provide?

The statement must be

- in writing
- on time

501

APPENDIX 3

Code of Practice under Part II of CPIA 1996

Introduction

1.1 This Code of Practice is issued under Part II of the Criminal Procedure and Investigations Act 1996 ('the Act'). It applies in respect of criminal investigations conducted by police officers which begin on or after the day on which this Code comes into effect. Persons other than police officers who are charged with the duty of conducting an investigation as defined in the Act are to have regard to the relevant provisions of the Code, and should take these into account in applying their own operating procedures.

1.2 This Code does not apply to persons who are not charged with the duty of conducting an investigation as defined in the Act.

1.3 Nothing in this Code applies to material intercepted in obedience to a warrant issued under section 2 of the Interception of Communications Act 1985, or to any copy of that material as defined in section 10 of that Act.

1.4 This Code extends only to England and Wales.

Definitions

2.1 In this Code:

- a *criminal investigation* is an investigation conducted by police officers with a view to it being ascertained whether a person should be charged with an offence, or whether a person charged with an offence is guilty of it. This will include:

  - investigations into crimes that have been committed;

  - investigations whose purpose is to ascertain whether a crime has been committed, with a view to the possible institution of criminal proceedings; and

  - investigations which begin in the belief that a crime may be committed, for example when the police keep premises or individuals under observation for a period of time, with a view to the possible institution of criminal proceedings;

- charging a person with an offence includes prosecution by way of summons;

- an *investigator* is any police officer involved in the conduct of a criminal investigation. All investigators have a responsibility for carrying out the duties imposed on them under this Code, including in particular recording information, and retaining records of information and other material;

- the *officer in charge of an investigation* is the police officer responsible for directing a criminal investigation. He is also responsible for ensuring that proper procedures are in place for recording information, and retaining records of information and other material, in the investigation;

- the *disclosure officer* is the person responsible for examining material retained by the police during the investigation; revealing material to the prosecutor during the investigation and any criminal proceedings resulting from it, and certifying that he has done this; and disclosing material to the accused at the request of the prosecutor;

- the *prosecutor* is the authority responsible for the conduct of criminal proceedings on behalf of the Crown. Particular duties may in practice fall to individuals acting on behalf of the prosecuting authority;

- *material* is material of any kind, including information and objects, which is obtained in the course of a criminal investigation and which may be relevant to the investigation;

- material may be *relevant to an investigation* if it appears to an investigator, or to the officer in charge of an investigation, or to the disclosure officer, that it has some bearing on any offence under investigation or any person being investigated, or on the surrounding circumstances of the case, unless it is incapable of having any impact on the case;

- *sensitive material* is material which the disclosure officer believes, after consulting the officer in charge of the investigation, it is not in the public interest to disclose;

- references to *primary prosecution disclosure* are to the duty of the prosecutor under section 3 of the Act to disclose material which is in his possession or which he has inspected in pursuance of this code, and which in his opinion might undermine the case against the accused;

- references to *secondary prosecution disclosure* are to the duty of the prosecutor under section 7 of the Act to disclose material which is in his possession or which he has inspected in pursuance of this Code, and which might reasonably be expected to assist the defence disclosed by the accused in a defence statement given under the Act;

- references to the disclosure of material to a person accused of an offence include references to the disclosure of material to his legal representative;

- references to police officers and to the chief officer of police include those employed in a police force as defined in section 3(3) of the Prosecution of Offences Act 1985.

General responsibilities

3.1 The functions of the investigator, the officer in charge of an investigation and the disclosure officer are separate. Whether they are undertaken by one, two or more persons will depend on the complexity of the case and the administrative arrangements within each police force. Where they are undertaken by more than one person, close consultation between them is essential to the effective performance of the duties imposed by this Code.

3.2 The chief officer of police for each police force is responsible for putting in place arrangements to ensure that in every investigation the identity of the officer in charge of an investigation and the disclosure officer is recorded.

3.3 The officer in charge of an investigation may delegate tasks to another investigator or to civilians employed by the police force, but he remains responsible for ensuring that these have been carried out and for accounting for any general policies followed in the investigation. In particular, it is an essential part of his duties to ensure that all material which may be relevant to an investigation is retained, and either made available to the disclosure officer or (in exceptional circumstances) revealed directly to the prosecutor.

3.4 In conducting an investigation, the investigator should pursue all reasonable lines of inquiry, whether these point towards or away from the suspect. What is reasonable in each case will depend on the particular circumstances.

3.5 If the officer in charge of an investigation believes that other persons may be in possession of material that may be relevant to the investigation, and if this has not been obtained under paragraph 3.4 above, he should ask the disclosure officer to inform them of the existence of the investigation and to invite them to retain the material in case they receive a request for its disclosure. The disclosure officer should inform the prosecutor that they may have such material. However, the officer in charge of an investigation is not required to make speculative enquiries of other persons: there must be some reason to believe that they may have relevant material. That reason may come from information provided to the police by the accused or from other enquiries made or from some other source.

3.6 If, during a criminal investigation, the officer in charge of an investigation or disclosure officer for any reason no longer has responsibility for the functions falling to him, either his supervisor or the police officer in charge of criminal investigations for the police force concerned must assign someone else to assume that responsibility. That person's identity must be recorded, as with those initially responsible for these functions in each investigation.

Recording of information

4.1 If material which may be relevant to the investigation consists of information which is not recorded in any form, the officer in charge of an investigation must ensure that it is recorded in a durable or retrievable form (whether in writing, on video or audio tape, or on computer disk).

4.2 Where it is not practicable to retain the initial record of information because it forms part of a larger record which is to be destroyed, its contents should be transferred as a true record to a durable and more easily-stored form before that happens.

4.3 Negative information is often relevant to an investigation. If it may be relevant it must be recorded. An example might be a number of people present in a particular place at a particular time who state that they saw nothing unusual.

4.4 Where information which may be relevant is obtained, it must be recorded at the time it is obtained or as soon as practicable after that time. This includes, for example, information obtained in house-to-house enquiries, although the requirement to record information promptly does not require an investigator to take a statement from a potential witness where it would not otherwise be taken.

Retention of material

(a) Duty to retain material

5.1 The investigator must retain material obtained in a criminal investigation which may be relevant to the investigation. This includes not only material coming into the possession of the investigator (such as documents seized in the course of searching premises) but also material generated by him (such as interview records). Material may be photographed, or retained in the form of a copy rather than the original, if the original is perishable, or was supplied to the investigator rather than generated by him and is to be returned to its owner.

5.2.Where material has been seized in the exercise of the powers of seizure conferred by the Police and Criminal Evidence Act 1984, the duty to retain it under this Code is subject to the provisions on the retention of seized material in section 22 of that Act.

5.3 If the officer in charge of an investigation becomes aware as a result of developments in the case that material previously examined but not retained (because it was not thought to be relevant) may now be relevant to the investigation, he should, wherever practicable, take steps to obtain it or ensure that it is retained for further inspection or for production in court if required.

5.4 The duty to retain material includes in particular the duty to retain material falling into the following categories, where it may be relevant to the investigation:

- crime reports (including crime report forms, relevant parts of incident report books or police officers' notebooks);
- custody records;
- records which are derived from tapes of telephone messages (e.g. 999 calls) containing descriptions of an alleged offence or offender;
- final versions of witness statements (and draft versions where their content differs from the final version), including any exhibits mentioned (unless these have been returned to their owner on the understanding that they will be produced in court if required);
- interview records (written records, or audio or video tapes, of interviews with actual or potential witnesses or suspects);
- communications between the police and experts such as forensic scientists, reports of work carried out by experts, and schedules of scientific material prepared by the expert for the investigator, for the purposes of criminal proceedings;
- any material casting doubt on the reliability of a confession;
- any material casting doubt on the reliability of a witness;

- any other material which may fall within the test for primary prosecution disclosure in the Act.

5.5 The duty to retain material falling into these categories does not extend to items which are purely ancillary to such material and possess no independent significance (for example, duplicate copies of records or reports).

(b) Length of time for which material is to be retained

5.6 All material which may be relevant to the investigation must be retained until a decision is taken whether to institute proceedings against a person for an offence.

5.7 If a criminal investigation results in proceedings being instituted, all material which may be relevant must be retained at least until the accused is acquitted or convicted or the prosecutor decides not to proceed with the case.

5.8 Where the accused is convicted, all material which may be relevant must be retained at least until:

- the convicted person is released from custody, or discharged from hospital, in cases where the court imposes a custodial sentence or a hospital order;
- six months from the date of conviction, in all other cases.

If the court imposes a custodial sentence or hospital order and the convicted person is released from custody or discharged from hospital earlier than six months from the date of conviction, all material which may be relevant must be retained at least until six months from the date of conviction.

5.9 If an appeal against conviction is in progress when the release or discharge occurs, or at the end of the period of six months specified in paragraph 5.8, all material which may be relevant must be retained until the appeal is determined. Similarly, if the Criminal Cases Review Commission is considering an application at that point in time, all material which may be relevant must be retained at least until the Commission decides not to refer the case to the Court of Appeal, or until the Court determines the appeal resulting from the reference by the Commission.

5.10 Material need not be retained by the police as required in paragraph 5.8 if it was seized and is to be returned to its owner.

Preparation of material for prosecutor

(a) Introduction

6.1 The officer in charge of the investigation, the disclosure officer or an investigator may seek advice from the prosecutor about whether any particular item of material may be relevant to the investigation.

6.2 Material which may be relevant to an investigation, which has been retained in accordance with this code, and which the disclosure officer believes will not form part of the prosecution case, must be listed on a schedule.

6.3 Material which the disclosure officer does not believe is sensitive must be listed on a schedule of non-sensitive material. The schedule must include a statement that the disclosure officer does not believe the material is sensitive.

6.4 Any material which is believed to be sensitive must be either listed on a schedule of sensitive material or, in exceptional circumstances, revealed to the prosecutor separately.

6.5 Paragraphs 6.6 to 6.11 below apply to both sensitive and non-sensitive material. Paragraphs 6.12 to 6.14 apply to sensitive material only.

(b) Circumstances in which a schedule is to be prepared

6.6 The disclosure officer must ensure that a schedule is prepared in the following circumstances:

- the accused is charged with an offence which is triable only on indictment;
- the accused is charged with an offence which is triable either way, and it is considered either that the case is likely to be tried on indictment or that the accused is likely to plead not guilty at a summary trial;
- the accused is charged with a summary offence, and it is considered that he is likely to plead not guilty.

6.7 In respect of either way and summary offences, a schedule may not be needed if a person has admitted the offence, or if a police officer witnessed the offence and that person has not denied it.

6.8 If it is believed that the accused is likely to plead guilty at a summary trial, it is not necessary to prepare a schedule in advance. If, contrary to this belief, the accused pleads not guilty at a summary trial, or the offence is to be tried on indictment, the disclosure officer must ensure that a schedule is prepared as soon as is reasonably practicable after that happens.

(c) Way in which material is to be listed on schedule

6.9 The disclosure officer should ensure that each item of material is listed separately on the schedule, and is numbered consecutively. The description of each item should make clear the nature of the item and should contain sufficient detail to enable the prosecutor to decide whether he needs to inspect the material before deciding whether or not it should be disclosed.

6.10 In some enquiries it may not be practicable to list each item of material separately. For example, there may be many items of a similar or repetitive nature. These may be listed in a block and described by quantity and generic title.

6.11 Even if some material is listed in a block, the disclosure officer must ensure that any items among that material which might meet the test for primary prosecution disclosure are listed and described individually.

(d) Treatment of sensitive material

6.12 Subject to paragraph 6.13 below, the disclosure officer must list on a sensitive schedule any material which he believes it is not in the public interest to disclose, and the reason for that belief. The schedule must include a statement that the disclosure officer believes the material is sensitive. Depending on the circumstances, examples of such material may include the following among others:

- material relating to national security;

- material received from the intelligence and security agencies;

- material relating to intelligence from foreign sources which reveals sensitive intelligence gathering methods;

- material given in confidence;

- material which relates to the use of a telephone system and which is supplied to an investigator for intelligence purposes only;

- material relating to the identity or activities of informants, or under-cover police officers, or other persons supplying information to the police who may be in danger if their identities are revealed;

- material revealing the location of any premises or other place used for police surveillance, or the identity of any person allowing a police officer to use them for surveillance;

- material revealing, either directly or indirectly, techniques and methods relied upon by a police officer in the course of a criminal investigation, for example covert surveillance techniques, or other methods of detecting crime;

- material whose disclosure might facilitate the commission of other offences or hinder the prevention and detection of crime;

- internal police communications such as management minutes;

- material upon the strength of which search warrants were obtained;

- material containing details of persons taking part in identification parades;

- material supplied to an investigator during a criminal investigation which has been generated by an official of a body concerned with the regulation or supervision of bodies corporate or of persons engaged in financial activities, or which has been generated by a person retained by such a body;

- material supplied to an investigator during a criminal investigation which relates to a child or young person and which has been generated by a local authority social services department, an Area Child Protection Committee or other party contacted by an investigator during the investigation.

6.13 In exceptional circumstances, where an investigator considers that material is so sensitive that its revelation to the prosecutor by means of an entry on the sensitive schedule is inappropriate, the existence of the material must be revealed to the prosecutor separately. This will apply where compromising the material would be likely to lead directly to the loss of life, or directly threaten national security.

6.14 In such circumstances, the responsibility for informing the prosecutor lies with the investigator who knows the detail of the sensitive material. The investigator should act as soon as is reasonably practicable after the file containing the prosecution case is sent to the prosecutor. The investigator must also ensure that the prosecutor is able to inspect the material so that he can assess whether it needs to be brought before a court for a ruling on disclosure.

Revelation of material to prosecutor

7.1 The disclosure officer must give the schedules to the prosecutor. Wherever practicable this should be at the same time as he gives him the file containing the material for the prosecution case (or as soon as is reasonably practicable after the decision on mode of trial or the plea, in cases to which paragraph 6.8 applies).

7.2 The disclosure officer should draw the attention of the prosecutor to any material an investigator has retained (whether or not listed on a schedule) which may fall within the test for primary prosecution disclosure in the Act, and should explain why he has come to that view.

7.3 At the same time as complying with the duties in paragraphs 7.1 and 7.2, the disclosure officer must give the prosecutor a copy of any material which falls into the following categories (unless such material has already been given to the prosecutor as part of the file containing the material for the prosecution case):

- records of the first description of a suspect given to the police by a potential witness, whether or not the description differs from that of the alleged offender;

- information provided by an accused person which indicates an explanation for the offence with which he has been charged;

- any material casting doubt on the reliability of a confession;

- any material casting doubt on reliability of a witness;

- any other material which the investigator believes may fall within the test for primary prosecution disclosure in the Act.

7.4 If the prosecutor asks to inspect material which has not already been copied to him, the disclosure officer must allow him to inspect it. If the prosecutor asks for a copy of material which has not already been copied to him, the disclosure officer must give him a copy. However, this does not apply where the disclosure officer believes, having consulted the officer in charge of the investigation, that the material is too sensitive to be copied and can only be inspected.

7.5 If material consists of information which is recorded other than in writing, whether it should be given to the prosecutor in its original form as a whole, or by way of relevant extracts recorded in the same form, or in the form of a transcript, is a matter for agreement between the disclosure officer and the prosecutor.

Subsequent action by disclosure officer

8.1 At the time a schedule of non-sensitive material is prepared, the disclosure officer may not know exactly what material will form the case against the accused, and the prosecutor may not have given advice about the likely relevance of particular items of material. Once these matters have been determined, the disclosure officer must give the prosecutor, where necessary, an amended schedule listing any additional material:

- which may be relevant to the investigation;

- which does not form part of the case against the accused;

- which is not already listed on the schedule; and

- which he believes is not sensitive;

unless he is informed in writing by the prosecutor that the prosecutor intends to disclose the material to the defence.

8.2 After a defence statement has been given, the disclosure officer must look again at the material which has been retained and must draw the attention of the prosecutor to any material which might reasonably be expected to assist the defence disclosed by the accused; and he must reveal it to him in accordance with paragraphs 7.4 and 7.5 above.

8.3 Section 9 of the Act imposes a continuing duty on the prosecutor, for the duration of criminal proceedings against the accused, to disclose material which meets the tests for disclosure (subject to public interest considerations). To enable him to do this, any new material coming to light should be treated in the same way as the earlier material.

Certification by disclosure officer

9.1 The disclosure officer must certify to the prosecutor that to the best of his knowledge and belief, all material which has been retained and made available to him has been revealed to the prosecutor in accordance with this Code. He must sign and date the certificate. It will be necessary to certify not only at the time when the schedule and accompanying material is submitted to the prosecutor, but also when material which has been retained is reconsidered after the accused has given a defence statement.

Disclosure of material to accused

10.1 If material has not already been copied to the prosecutor, and he requests its disclosure to the accused on the ground that:

- it falls within the test for primary or secondary prosecution disclosure; or

- the court has ordered its disclosure after considering an application from the accused,

the disclosure officer must disclose it to the accused.

10.2 If material has been copied to the prosecutor, and it is to be disclosed, whether it is disclosed by the prosecutor or the disclosure officer is a matter for agreement between the two of them.

10.3 The disclosure officer must disclose material to the accused either by giving him a copy or by allowing him to inspect it. If the accused person asks for a copy of any material which he has been allowed to inspect, the disclosure officer must give it to him, unless in the opinion of the disclosure officer that is either not practicable (e.g. because the material consists of an object which cannot be copied, or because the volume of material is so great), or not desirable (e.g. because the material is a statement by a child witness in relation to a sexual offence).

10.4 If material which the accused has been allowed to inspect consists of information which is recorded other than in writing, whether it should be given to the accused in its original form or in the form of a transcript is a matter for the discretion of the disclosure officer. If the material is transcribed, the disclosure officer must ensure that the transcript is certified to the accused as a true record of the material which has been transcribed.

10.5 If a court concludes that it is in the public interest that an item of sensitive material must be disclosed to the accused, it will be necessary to disclose the material if the case is to proceed. This does not mean that sensitive documents must always be disclosed in their original form: e.g. the court may agree that sensitive details still requiring protection should be blocked out, or that documents may be summarised, or that the prosecutor may make an admission about the substance of the material under section 10 of the Criminal Justice Act 1967.

Notice sent with primary disclosure: CPIA 1996, Part I: Disclosure – rights and duties of accused persons

1. The Criminal Procedure and Investigations Act 1996 makes important changes to the law on prosecution and defence disclosure in criminal cases. This notice sets out your rights and duties under the relevant provisions. Please read it carefully and show it to your solicitor if you have one.

2. Although this notice is sent to you by the prosecutor, he cannot advise you on its contents and you should not approach him for advice.

Disclosure by the accused

3. Before the trial begins, the prosecutor must disclose to you prosecution material which he thinks might undermine the case against you. If there is no such material, he must write to you to say so. In either case, he must also send you a schedule of non-sensitive material at the same time.

4. *If your case is to be tried in the Crown Court,* you must give the prosecutor and the court a 'defence statement' containing certain information about your defence. This must:

(a) set out in general terms the nature of your defence, i.e. the reasons for your intention to plead not guilty;

(b) state the matters on which you disagree with the prosecution; and

(c) state in each case the reason why you disagree.

5. If you have an alibi, you must give details of the alibi in the defence statement, including:

(a) if you know it, the name and address of any witness you believe is able to give evidence in support of the alibi; or

(b) any information you have which might be useful in finding any such witness.

'Evidence in support of an alibi' means 'evidence tending to show that by reason of the presence of the accused at a particular place or in a particular area at a particular time he was not, or was unlikely, to have been at the place where the offence is alleged to have been committed at the time of its alleged commission'.

6. You must give the defence statement within **14 days** of the prosecutor making disclosure to you. The 14-day period starts on the date when the prosecutor writes to you, not the date when you receive his letter. If you cannot give a defence statement within 14 days, you may ask the court for more time. The court will want to know why you cannot do so, and how much more time you need. If you apply for more time, you must:

(a) do so before the 14 days are up; and

(b) give the prosecutor a copy of your application.

7. Section 11 of the Act says that if you fail to comply with these requirements, certain consequences follow. You fail to comply with the requirements if you:

(a) do not give a defence statement; or

(b) give a defence statement after the end of the 14-day period, or after the end of any longer period of time allowed by the court; or

(c) set out inconsistent defences in the defence statement; or

(d) put forward a defence at trial which is different from any defence set out in the defence statement; or

(e) put forward evidence in support of an alibi at trial, without giving details of the alibi in the defence statement; or

(f) call a witness in support of an alibi at trial without giving details of the witness in the defence statement.

8. If you fail to comply with these requirements, the court (or, if the court allows, any other party) may comment on the failure to comply, and the jury may draw such inferences as appear proper in deciding whether you are guilty.

9. If you put forward a defence at trial which is different from any defence set out in the defence statement, then (when deciding whether to comment on the failure to comply) the court must consider the extent of the difference in the defences, and whether there is any justification for it.

10. You cannot be convicted solely on the basis of an inference drawn from a failure to comply with these requirements.

11. *If your case is to be tried in a magistrates' court,* you may give a defence statement if you wish (for example, to get further prosecution disclosure) but you are not required to do so. If you do not give a defence statement, no inference may be drawn. If you do give a defence statement, the same procedures apply as if your case was being tried in the Crown Court (paragraphs 4–10 above), except that there is no jury but the court may draw inferences from a failure to comply with the relevant requirements.

12. If you decide not to give a defence statement, your case may come to court more quickly if you tell the court and the prosecutor before the end of the 14-day period.

Right of accused person to apply for additional prosecution disclosure

13. If you give a defence statement, the prosecutor must then disclose to you any additional prosecution material which might reasonably be expected to assist the defence which you disclosed in your defence statement. If there is no such material, he must write to you to say so.

14. After this, if you have reason to believe that there is more prosecution material which has not been disclosed to you and which might reasonably be expected to assist the defence which you disclosed in your defence statement, you may apply to the court for an order to disclose it. You must:

(a) identify the material you need; and

(b) tell the court why you think it might assist your defence.

If you apply to the court, you must give the prosecutor a copy of your application. If you contact the prosecutor first, you may be able to obtain the material you need without having to apply to the court.

Right of accused person to apply for review of a non-disclosure ruling

15. If the prosecutor has material which he ought to disclose to you, but which is sensitive for some reason, he may apply to the court for a ruling that on balance it is not in the public interest to disclose it.

16. If the court rules against disclosure, you may ask the court to review its ruling. If you do so, you must:

(a) say why you think the ruling should be reviewed; and

(b) give the prosecutor a copy of your application.

Duty to treat disclosed material in confidence

17. You may use material disclosed to you for the purpose of your trial, or (if you are convicted) in connection with any appeal. If you want to use the material for any other purpose, you must first apply to the court for permission to do so, and say why you want to use it. You must also give a copy of your application to the prosecutor.

18. If you use the material for any other purpose without getting the permission of the court, you may be liable to proceedings for contempt of court. If the court finds you guilty of contempt, it may commit you to custody for a specified period or fine you or both.

APPENDIX 5

The content of police files

Up-date October 1999		File type		
Form No.	**Description**	**Remand**	**Expedited**	**Full**
MG1	File front sheet	o	o	o
MG4	Charge(s)	o	o	o
MG4A	Police grant of conditional bail	•	•	•
MG4B	Variation of police conditional bail	•	•	•
MG4C	Police conditional bail surety/security	•	•	•
MG5	Case summary	o		
MG6	Confidential information	•	•	•
MG6B	Police officer's disciplinary record			•
MG6C	Police schedule of non-sensitive unused material			•
MG6D	Police schedule of sensitive material			•
MG6E	Disclosure officer's report			•
MG7	Remand application form	o		
MG8	Breach of court bail conditions form	•		
MG9	Witness list			o
MG10	Witness non-availability			o
MG11	Copies of statements from witnesses			
	Key witnesses	o	o	
	All witnesses			o
MG12	Exhibit list			o
MG14	Written statement under caution		•	•
MG15	Record of taped interview	•		•
	Short descriptive note		o	
MG16	Previous convictions defendant	•	•	•
MG16A	Previous convictions witnesses			•
MG17	Previous cautions defendant	•	•	•
MG18	TIC forms		•	•
MG19	Compensation form		•	•
MG20	Further evidence/information report			
MG21	Custody remand update			
MG21A	Bail enquiry form			

Legend: o Core documents that must be included in the file
     • Documents that should be included where available and applicable

The Code for Crown Prosecutors (June 1994)

1 INTRODUCTION

1.1 The decision to prosecute an individual is a serious step. Fair and effective prosecution is essential to the maintenance of law and order. But even in a small case, a prosecution has serious implications for all involved – the victim, a witness and a defendant. The Crown Prosecution Service applies the Code for Crown Prosecutors so that it can make fair and consistent decisions about prosecutions.

1.2 The Code contains information that is important to police officers, to others who work in the criminal justice system and to the general public. It helps the Crown Prosecution Service to play its part in making sure that justice is done.

2 GENERAL PRINCIPLES

2.1 Each case is unique and must be considered on its own, but there are general principles that apply in all cases.

2.2 The duty of the Crown prosecution Service is to make sure that the right person is prosecuted for the right offence and that all relevant facts are given to the court.

2.3 Crown prosecutors must be fair, independent and objective. They must not let their personal views of the ethnic or national origin, sex, religious beliefs, political views or sexual preference of the offender, victim or witness influence their decisions. They must also not be affected by improper or undue pressure from any source.

3 REVIEW

3.1 Proceedings are usually started by the police. Sometimes they may consult the Crown Prosecution Service before charging a defendant. Each case that the police send to the Crown Prosecution Service is reviewed by a Crown prosecutor to make sure that it meets the tests set out in this Code. Crown prosecutors may decide to continue with the original charges, to change the charges or sometimes to stop the proceedings.

3.2 Review, however, is a continuing process so that Crown prosecutors can take into account any change in circumstances. Wherever possible, they talk to the police first if they are thinking about changing the charges or stopping the proceedings. This gives the police the chance to provide more information that may affect the decision. The Crown Prosecution Service and the police work closely together to reach the right decision, but the final responsibility for the decision rests with the Crown Prosecution Service.

4 THE CODE TESTS

4.1 There are two stages in the decision to prosecute. The first stage is **the evidential test**. If the case does not pass the evidential test, it must not go ahead, no matter how important or serious it may be. If the case does pass the evidential test, Crown prosecutors must decide if a prosecution is needed in the public interest.

4.2 The second stage is **the public interest test**. The Crown Prosecution Service will only start or continue a prosecution when the case has passed both tests. The evidential test is explained in section 5 and the public interest test is explained in section 6.

5 THE EVIDENTIAL TEST

5.1 Crown prosecutors must be satisfied that there is enough evidence to provide a 'realistic prospect of conviction' against each defendant on each charge. They must consider what the defence case may be and how that is likely to affect the prosecution case.

5.2 A realistic prospect of conviction is an objective test. It means that a jury or bench of magistrates, properly directed in accordance with the law, is more likely than not to convict the defendant of the charge alleged.

5.3 When deciding whether there is enough evidence to prosecute, Crown prosecutors must consider whether the evidence can be used and is reliable. There will be many cases in which the evidence does not give any cause for concern. But there will also be cases in which the evidence may not be as strong as it first appears. Crown prosecutors must ask themselves the following questions.

Can the evidence be used in court?

a Is it likely that the evidence will be excluded by the court? There are certain legal rules which might mean that evidence which seems relevant cannot be given at a trial. For example, is it likely that the evidence will be excluded because of the way in which it was gathered or because of the rule against using hearsay as evidence? If so, is there enough other evidence for a realistic prospect of conviction?

Is the evidence reliable?

b Is it likely that a confession is unreliable, for example, because of the defendant's age, intelligence or lack of understanding?

c Is the witness's background likely to weaken the prosecution case? For example, does the witness have any dubious motive that may affect his or her attitude to the case or a relevant previous conviction?

d If the identity of the defendant is likely to be questioned, is the evidence about this strong enough?

5.4 Crown prosecutors should not ignore evidence because they are not sure that it can be used or is reliable. But they should look closely at it when deciding if there is a realistic prospect of conviction.

517

6   THE PUBLIC INTEREST TEST

6.1 In 1951, Lord Shawcross, who was Attorney-General, made the classic statement on public interest, which has been supported by Attorneys-General ever since: 'It has never been the rule in this country – I hope it never will be – that suspected criminal offences must automatically be the subject of prosecution' (House of Commons Debates, volume 483, column 681, 29 January 1951).

6.2 The public interest must be considered in each case where there is enough evidence to provide a realistic prospect of conviction. In cases of any seriousness, a prosecution will usually take place unless there are public interest factors tending against prosecution which clearly outweigh those tending in favour. Although there may be public interest factors against prosecution in a particular case, often the prosecution should go ahead and those factors should be put to the court for consideration when sentence is being passed.

6.3 Crown prosecutors must balance factors for and against prosecution carefully and fairly. Public interest factors that can affect the decision to prosecute usually depend on the seriousness of the offence or the circumstances of the offender. Some factors may increase the need to prosecute but others may suggest that another course of action would be better.

The following lists of some common public interest factors, both for and against prosecution, are not exhaustive. The factors that apply will depend on the facts in each case.

Some common public interest factors in favour of prosecution

6.4 The more serious the offence, the more likely it is that a prosecution will be needed in the public interest. A prosecution is likely to be needed if:

a   a conviction is likely to result in a significant sentence;

b   a weapon was used or violence was threatened during the commission of the offence;

c   the offence was committed against a person serving the public (e.g. a police or prison officer, or a nurse);

d   the defendant was in a position of authority or trust;

e   the evidence shows that the defendant was a ringleader or an organiser of the offence;

f   there is evidence that the offence was premeditated;

g   there is evidence that the offence was carried out by a group;

h   the victim of the offence was vulnerable, has been put in considerable fear, or suffered personal attack, damage or disturbance;

i   the offence was motivated by any form of discrimination against the victim's ethnic or national origin, sex, religious beliefs, political views or sexual preference;

j   there is a marked difference between the actual or mental ages of the defendant and the victim, or if there is any element of corruption;

k   the defendant's previous convictions or cautions are relevant to the present offence;

l   the defendant is alleged to have committed the offence whilst under an order of the court;

m   there are grounds for believing that the offence is likely to be continued or repeated, e.g. by a history of recurring conduct; or

n   the offence, although not serious in itself, is widespread in the area where it was committed.

Some common public interest factors against prosecution

6.5 A prosecution is less likely to be needed if:

a   the court is likely to impose a very small or nominal penalty;

b   the offence was committed as a result of a genuine mistake or misunderstanding (these factors must be balanced against the seriousness of the offence);

c   the loss or harm can be described as minor and was the result of a single incident, particularly if it was caused by a misjudgement;

d   there has been a long delay between the offence taking place and the date of the trial, unless:

- the offence is serious;
- the delay has been caused in part by the defendant;
- the offence has only recently come to light; or
- the complexity of the offence has meant that there has been a long investigation;

e   a prosecution is likely to have a very bad effect on the victim's physical or mental health, always bearing in mind the seriousness of the offence;

f   the defendant is elderly or is, or was at the time of the offence, suffering from significant mental or physical ill health, unless the offence is serious or there is a real possibility that it may be repeated. The Crown Prosecution Service, where necessary, applies Home Office guidelines about how to deal with mentally disordered offenders. Crown prosecutors must balance the desirability of diverting a defendant who is suffering from significant mental or physical ill health with the need to safeguard the general public;

g   the defendant has put right the loss or harm that was caused (but defendants must not avoid prosecution simply because they can pay compensation); or

h   details may be made public that could harm sources of information, international relations or national security.

6.6 Deciding on the public interest is not simply a matter of adding up the number of factors on each side. Crown prosecutors must decide how important each factor is in the circumstances of each case and go on to make an overall assessment.

The relationship between the victim and the public interest

6.7 The Crown Prosecution Service acts in the public interest, not just in the interests of any one individual. But Crown prosecutors must always think very carefully about the interests of the victim, which are an important factor, when deciding where the public interest lies.

Youth offenders

6.8 Crown prosecutors must consider the interests of a youth when deciding whether it is in the public interest to prosecute. The stigma of a conviction can cause very serious harm to the prospects of a youth offender or a young adult. Young offenders can sometimes be dealt with without going to court. But Crown prosecutors should not avoid prosecuting simply because of the defendant's age. The seriousness of the offence or the offender's past behaviour may make prosecution necessary.

Police cautions

6.9 The police make the decision to caution an offender in accordance with Home Office guidelines. If the defendant admits the offence, cautioning is the most common alternative to a court appearance. Crown prosecutors, where necessary, apply the same guidelines and should look at the alternatives to prosecution when they consider the public interest. Crown prosecutors should tell the police if they think that a caution would be more suitable than a prosecution.

7 CHARGES

7.1 Crown prosecutors should select charges which:

a reflect the seriousness of the offending;

b give the court adequate sentencing powers; and

c enable the case to be presented in a clear and simple way.

This means that Crown prosecutors may not always continue with the most serious charge where there is a choice. Further, Crown prosecutors should not continue with more charges than are necessary.

7.2 Crown prosecutors should never go ahead with more charges than are necessary just to encourage a defendant to plead guilty to a few. In the same way, they should never go ahead with a more serious charge just to encourage a defendant to plead guilty to a less serious one.

7.3 Crown prosecutors should not change the charge simply because of the decision made by the court or the defendant about where the case will be heard.

8 MODE OF TRIAL

8.1 The Crown Prosecution Service applies the current guidelines for magistrates who have to decide whether cases should be tried in the Crown Court when the offence gives the option. (See the 'National Mode of Trial Guidelines' issued by the Lord Chief Justice.) Crown prosecutors should recommend Crown Court trial when they are satisfied that the guidelines require them to do so.

8.2 Speed must never be the only reason for asking for a case to stay in the magistrates' courts. But Crown prosecutors should consider the effect of any likely delay if they send a case to the Crown Court, and any possible stress on victims and witnesses if the case is delayed.

9 ACCEPTING GUILTY PLEAS

9.1 Defendants may want to plead guilty to some, but not all, of the charges. Or they may want to plead guilty to a different, possibly less serious, charge because they are admitting only part of the crime. Crown prosecutors should only accept the defendant's plea if they think the court is able to pass a sentence that matches the seriousness of the offending. Crown prosecutors must never accept a guilty plea just because it is convenient.

10 RE-STARTING A PROSECUTION

10.1 People should be able to rely on decisions taken by the Crown Prosecution Service. Normally, if the Crown Prosecution Service tells a suspect or defendant that there will not be a Prosecution, or that the prosecution has been stopped, that is the end of the matter and the case will not start again. But occasionally there are special reasons why the Crown prosecution Service will re-start the prosecution, particularly if the case is serious.

10.2 These reasons include:

a rare cases where a new look at the original decision shows that it was clearly wrong and should not be allowed to stand;

b cases which are stopped so that more evidence which is likely to become available in the fairly near future can be collected and prepared. In these cases, the Crown prosecutors will tell the defendant that the prosecution may well start again;

c cases which are stopped because of a lack of evidence but where more significant evidence is discovered later.

11 CONCLUSION

11.1 The Crown Prosecution Service is a public service headed by the Director of Public Prosecutions. It is answerable to Parliament through the Attorney General. The Code for Crown Prosecutors is issued under section 10 of the Prosecution of Offences Act 1985 and is a public document. This is the third edition and it replaces all earlier versions. Changes to the Code are made from time to time and these are also published.

11.2 The Code is designed to make sure that everyone knows the principles that the Crown Prosecution Service applies when carrying out its work. Police officers should take account of the principles of the Code when they are deciding whether to charge a defendant with an offence. By applying the same principles, everyone involved in the criminal justice system is helping the system to treat victims fairly, and to prosecute defendants fairly but effectively.

11.3 The Code is available from:

Crown Prosecution Service
Information Branch
50 Ludgate Hill
London
EC4M 7EX
Telephone: 0171-273 8078
Facsimile: 0171-329 8377

Information-processing methods

This Appendix describes methods for:

* constructing a case chronology;
* fine-grain analysis of documents and recordings;
* drawing locations.

CONSTRUCTING A CASE CHRONOLOGY

Throughout this text, we have argued that you must create a case chronology in order:

* to gain a clear, crisp, comprehensive understanding of the course of events in your client's case, i.e. events prior to the offence, the offence, police investigation;
* to identify:

    – gaps and other anomalies within the actions and decisions by the police, the prosecution and key individuals within the case;

    – areas that require a managed defence response, e.g. representations to the CPS, the police or the court; consultations with the client, trial advocate, colleagues or other key individuals; issuing instructions for work to be done by the client, colleagues, expert witnesses, investigators.

Once started, the case chronology becomes the ever-growing record of the course of events in respect of your client's case and which are either personally garnered by you or your colleagues or brought to your attention.

A major source of information will be documents and recordings disclosed by the CPS. However, other vital sources will be:

* information that you or another obtained at the police station when attending your client: in consultation with the custody officer, the IO, your client, and, where applicable the appropriate adult; during the police interview; from the identification officer and others briefed on the case and who had contact with your client, e.g. the police surgeon/medical examiner;

- information from your client at court;
- briefings and disclosures by the CPS and police at various stages in the court process;
- expert witnesses.

In effect, a case chronology is a very uncomplicated record – a 'diary' – of occurrences, stages, steps and decisions within the course of your client's case. For each of these you need to log:

- when it happened – as *Date/Time*;
- what happened – as *Item/Event*, no more than two or three lines at most, you must avoid reams of detail;
- its origin – as *Reference/Source* – enabling you to use a discrete referencing system to record where you read or heard it, or to note how you acquired the detail;
- your immediate response – as *Comments/Action*.

Figure 7.1 on page 253 is an illustration of a case chronology.

The *Post-It* method

This is an extremely simple method that can be applied to documents and recordings.

The materials you need

You need:

- a supply of *Post-Its*. These are pads of notelets ('stickies'), which are adhesive on the top reverse edge and can be affixed to, and removed easily from, any surface. They are obtainable in all colours – the commonest being yellow – and in a range of sizes. An appropriate size is 76 mm x 76 mm;
- four A4 plain manila folders, sometimes called plain 'file covers'. As you become more adept at the system and in straightforward cases with relatively little material you will find you probably need fewer. However, you will find it helpful when you are gaining confidence in the system to use five;
- a notebook.

Preparation

Mark three file covers with the part of the case chronology whose details will be posted within:

- *Pre-offence;*
- *The offence;*
- *The police investigation.*

However, you will be working first of all with the fourth cover – your *working file*.

Post-It applied to documents

Take the first document you have to process.

1. On the top right corner of the top *Post-It* on the pad write the *discrete reference* for the document, e.g. *CB 3* this being the Committal Bundle page 3; *AI 4* this being Advance Information page 4.

2. On the top left put the *source of the information*, e.g. the witness's name; the officer preparing the ROTI; the officer from whose pocket book it is copied. Put this individual's initials in brackets. Enter the individual's details in your notebook with his or her initials. In this way, you will gradually accumulate a list of people involved in the case and, as you add detail, the particular role each person occupies or occupied.

3. Below the source, *put the date of the document*, e.g. the date of the statement; the date of the ROTI's production.

4. In the 'white space' of the *Post-It* summarise the nature of the document, e.g. *Statement by AB to WDC S.*

5. Open up your working file, remove the completed *Post-It* from the pad and place it in the top left corner of the opened file.

6. Now you must get the overall gist of the document. Do this by skim-reading the document in its entirety, i.e. read it through completely at an even, steady pace, rather quicker than your normal reading speed.

   Resist the following temptations:

   • to glance forward;

   • to stop your flow to dwell on some details rather than others;

   • to look back to check what you have just read or something earlier in the document.

   Equipped with your overall grasp you are now in a position to extract:

   • key occurrences, steps, stages or decisions recorded within the document;

   • detail on key individuals, locations and objects, e.g. vehicles.

7. Go back to the beginning of the document, and reread the text:

   • systematically reduce the document to a series of *topic summaries*, i.e. each key occurrence, step, stage or decision – summarised as a topic heading;

   [Note: resist going into minute detail by bearing in mind that your aim is to produce a chronology of 'bullet points' – each being a minor 'landmark' in the unfolding saga that is your client's case and your management of this.]

   • for each occurrence create a continuation *Post-It*, i.e.

   – put the discrete reference number in the top right;

   – put the source's initials on the left and the abbreviation *Ctd*;

   – write the actual or purported date of the occurrence, step, stage or decision;

   [Note: it is important that you record the date the event actually or purportedly happened, not the date of the document you are processing.]

- write a topic summary which captures the essence of what you have just read;

- remove the continuation *Post-It* and place it in your working file beneath the previous *Post-It*;

- for each identity, location or object mentioned make a note in your notepad – assigning initials where applicable or noting other identifying detail, e.g. registration, colour.

8. Gradually, you will be creating a column of *Post-Its* in your working file. When a column reaches the bottom of the folder, start a new column at the top adjacent to the previous column. If the case is particularly complicated or the document is lengthy you may find you need to open up another working file. This will be a rare occurrence.

9. When you have finished processing the document methodically transfer the *Post-Its* from your working file into the appropriate file, i.e. those referring to the events prior to the offence in the **Pre-offence** file, to the offence in the **Offence** file, to the investigation in the **Police Investigation** file, and to events since charge in the **Following charge** file.

10. Proceed to the next document and repeat steps 1–9.

11. When you have processed all documents, each of the three files (**Pre-offence, Offence** and **Police investigation**) will contain the accumulated key 'diary' detail you have extracted.

Rearrange the *Post-Its* in each file into chronological order, once again ordering these in columns, from left to right across the inside surfaces of the file. This is a very easy and rapid jigsaw type task because *Post-Its* can be removed and stuck on any surface, e.g. the desk area around the file you are working on!

There will be instances when there are two or more Post-Its giving different versions of a key occurrence, step, stage or decision:

- sort the versions in chronological order – earliest to latest;

- label the versions, i.e. *V1*, *V2*, *V3* and so on;

- place *V1* in the column, *V2* to the right of this, *V3* to the right of this, and so on – in effect a branch extending outwards to the right of the column.

12. Once you have reordered the files, their contents can be entered into a word-processed document, e.g. using a program such as Word, which enables you to create a table with four columns – headed **Date/Time**, **Item/Event**, **Reference/Source**, **Comment/Action** and a requisite number of rows.

At the head of the document it is important to record two dates:

- the date of compilation;

- the date of inputting into the word processor (which may be after some delay).

- You can open a separate document (table) for each stage: **Pre-offence**, **Offence** and **Police Investigation**.

13. As an alternative to 11, if you or a colleague are able to proceed immediately to word processing, you can work directly from your files:

- create a four-column table with headings;

525

- taking one *Post-It* at a time, enter the detail directly into the table;
- use the facility in the word-processing package to reorder the rows into chronological order;

  [Note: reordering can only occur if you enter the date of the occurrence, step, stage or decision on each Post-It. It will not be able to classify those that do not have a date in the first cell in the row.

  When more than one version occurs and a *Post-It* for an earlier version arises after a later version, this simply create a new row ahead of the existing row.]

- record the two key dates:
  - the date of compilation;
  - the date of inputting into the word processor.

14. Once the case chronology has been converted into a document, it is advisable to read it. This ensures you obtain a coherent, overall grasp of the occurrences, steps, stages and decisions from the earliest point up to the latest point referred to in the material available to you.

Post-It applied to recordings

Recordings should be treated like documents, the routine being slightly modified to account for the difference in the medium being processed and the manner in which it is referenced by the police and the CPS.

1. On the top right corner of the top *Post-It* on the pad write the *discrete reference* of the tape recording, which will be the officer who tenders it as an exhibit collected by him or her and identified by his or her initials.

2. On the top left put the *source of the information*, e.g. the interviewee (who may or may not be your client).

3. On the top left below the source, put the *date of the interview*.

4. In the 'white space' of the *Post-It* summarise the nature of the document, e.g. *Interview of AB by WDC S – Grimley Police Station – KL present.*

5. Open up your working file, remove the completed *Post-It* from the pad and place it in the top left corner of the opened file.

6. Listen to the tape in its entirety – akin to getting an overall grasp of the content of a document.

7. Rewind the tape and systematically reduce the verbal exchanges to a series of *topic summaries*, i.e. each key occurrence, step, stage or decision – summarised as a topic heading:

   - listen to a section of tape;
   - when the topic changes, pause the tape;
   - for this topic create a continuation *Post-It*, i.e.
     - put the exhibit number in the top right;
     - put the source's initials on the left and the abbreviation *Ctd*;
     - write the actual or purported date of the occurrence, step, stage or decision;

[Note: it is important that you record the date the event actually or purportedly happened, not the date of the interview you are processing.]

- write a topic summary that captures the essence of what you have just listened to;

• remove the continuation *Post-It* and place it in your working file beneath the previous *Post-It*.

Identities

The identities – persons, locations, objects – that you have abstracted from documents and recordings into your notebook should be converted in to a wordprocessed file as a *master identity list*. This should be attached to the case chronology.

Processing subsequent information

When you receive more information, e.g. additional documents at the primary-disclosure stage, all you need to do is to follow the same *Post-It* system and to update the word-processed files. You will need to ensure that the key dates – date of compilation and date of inputting – are amended to reflect the updating.

The optimum location for the case chronology and master identity list

This is a matter of personal preference. At a very minimum, there should be a printed-out copy of these in the case file.

They can be effectively filed in a clear plastic/Nyrex gusset folder that has a hole at the top left or along the sides to allow it to be attached such that it is always the top 'folio' on the file. When new documentation is added to the file, the folder is removed, the additional items filed, and the folder reattached.

This routine leaves the left inside cover free for you to attach the case management record in its own clear plastic/Nyrex folder.

With this arrangement whoever picks up the file has immediate access to the two critical case documents and can quickly translate initials into names.

FINE-GRAIN ANALYSIS OF A RECORDING OR A DOCUMENT

The need to grasp detail and to detect anomaly

When you listen to or read an account – a description or a narrative – your fundamental concerns are the *validity* and *reliability* of what is being asserted.

Validity refers to the extent to which the representation of detail maps on to physical or psychological reality. Validity is often confused with reliability.

Reliability is used in two ways:

• relative consistency of detail;

• the extent to which this account, or any account by this individual, can be trusted.

Contradictory detail within a recorded interview or a document, e.g. a statement, raises doubt as to the internal consistency of the individual's account. External consistency is threatened by detail that contradicts earlier disclosures by the individual or others.

Ability to assess the validity and reliability of a recorded or written account rests upon systematic processing of the text in order:

• to gain a secure grasp – comprehension and memory – of the detail;

• to detect anomaly within the detail.

Fine-grain analysis of text

Processing any text – spoken or written – is a challenging task. As text unfolds, we are exposed to a sequence of topics, each containing detail of situations and sets of circumstances, in which events, verbal exchanges and transactions take place, involving people and objects.

This creates two tasks:

• as you seek to make sense of what has just been asserted, more information is arriving (the current assertion);

• it is necessary to bear in mind what was asserted earlier in order to make sense of what has just been or is currently being asserted.

These two tasks make substantial demands upon what psychologists term *working memory*. In working memory, we keep track of, marshal and work upon emergent, accumulating fragments of information. The result is a representation in our mind's eye of what is being asserted, together with inferences and conclusions we have drawn about the account and the giver of the account in the context of what we know, have heard or read about in respect of the police case, other evidence and the police investigation.

Generally, we cope by being highly selective in order to generate in our mind's eye a stripped-down, gist-like representation of what the person is asserting in the spoken or written words. The risks are obvious. As more and more information comes to our attention, working memory becomes stretched as we take up, hold and work simultaneously upon current and previous detail. The manifest readily grabs our attention. Gaps are unwittingly glossed over, as we fill in what has *not* been said with the substance of our assumptions and our knowledge of 'reality' – our view and experience of the world and the way things happen and work. We are at great risk of failing to detect subtle anomalies and the unstated.

Many, but not all, legal professionals have good working memories enabling them to retain a large number of information fragments, linking detail and spotting anomalies across an entire recorded interview or document. However, even those with an excellent working memory are unable to identify, let alone to register the breadth or the complexity of, the fragments and the detail therein. It gets even harder when it is not one recording or document but the latest in a run of such texts, e.g. a committal bundle. Given the detailed, diverse and demanding material that you have to handle, the risks are very great that you will fail to secure a firm grasp on the detail and will not detect subtle anomalies and the unstated.

Arguably, when you have a record of text – a tape recording or written document – you can backtrack, to listen to or to read something as many times as you wish. However, while this may improve your ability to hold the material in memory, it does not fundamentally reduce the likelihood of you being seduced by the salient, of the potentially significant being lost in the stream of detail, and of the paradoxical – the missing, the ambiguous, the vague and the contradictory – going unnoticed. You have to be systematic in your approach to the stream of detail. However, being systematic is only half the issue. You need systems – methods – to capture and to represent detail in order to work upon it and to make decisions.

The methods you need

One universal system is note-taking. Nearly all notes reflect an attempt to compress time and detail, i.e. rapidly derived gist. Detail is lost, including crucial anomalies. For those who capture the stream virtually verbatim, there is more detail but the problem of making sense is paradoxically still there.

Suitable systems enable you:

- to abstract quickly as many fragments of information as possible;

- to produce a representation that you can analyse, draw conclusions about and, importantly, do – or get others to do – something about.

Three methods are described below:

- *SE3R:* a manual method for representing narrative detail, and its computer software equivalent, *RealSense*;

- *genograms:* a method for representing relationships between individuals;

- *tabulation*.

SE3R: A METHOD FOR REPRESENTING NARRATIVE DETAIL

SE3R (S – E – Three R) is an acronym, specifying the steps of the method: survey, extract, read, review, recall. The method is used by police officers and by investigators in the public and private sectors, as well as in academic and clinical contexts. It represents narrative detail visually, facilitating rapid analysis and assisting storage of this detail in memory. It is applicable to written or recorded texts from one or more individuals. It can also be applied in live interviews conducted face to face or on the telephone.

At the heart of the method is the recognition that visual images of narrative and collated detail do something that your mind's eye never can: communicate detail coherently and clearly, conduct assessments of content systematically, and commit detail to memory more effectively.

Key features are:

- the separation of event information from narrative supporting information;

- visual representation in the form of:

    - an *event line*: linear representation of the 'passage of time', enabling events both to be grasped as an unfolding chronological sequence and to be located relative to one another;

- *identity bins*: 'index card'-like representations of detail, verbal and visual, concerning people, entities, locations;

- it converts the text of statements into the present tense and direct speech, making the narrative real and revealing anomalies that would otherwise not have been detected;

- when applied to what one person says across the course of one or more narratives, or what more than one person say across a number of narratives, it enables the easy detection of similarities and differences.

Most people find it best to learn the method, and to gain practice and confidence, by applying it to documents before proceeding to use it with interview text.

The outcome

The outcome of applying the method is called an SE3R, comprising one or more sheets of information extracted from the narrative using the SE3R method. This representation enables identification of a wide range of anomaly, e.g. deficiencies in detail, vagueness, ambiguity, incongruous use of language, variation and contradiction.

An example of an SE3R is at Annex A to this Appendix.

The materials you need

You need:

- a notepad – at least A4 size. Many experienced users of SE3R use A3 pads. However, any size of notepad can be used, e.g. the author uses a spiral-bound shorthand pad when applying SE3R to spoken narrative;

- a small pad – to note any questions or queries raised by your SE3R analysis;

- pencils with an eraser head. Pencil notes are easier to amend than notes taken in biro, pen or felt-tip. The eraser head is for convenience, but a separate eraser can be used if preferred. Similarly, if you prefer using ballpoint, pen or felt-tip, please do;

- coloured felt-tip and fluorescent highlighter pens. These are to highlight particular areas of detail, absence of detail or inconsistency. They are not essential, but if you have them you will be able to manage and to refer to your material much more efficiently and rapidly.

Applying the method to a single document

In the top right or left corner of the SE3R sheet, record core reference information:

- today's date and time;

- details of the document (e.g. written statement, pocket book entry, custody record) including:

  - number of pages;

  - its position in terms of sequence of production if it is a second or subsequent document from the narrative giver;

- date, time and place the document was produced, e.g. the date on the statement form;
- details of the narrative giver, e.g. the person making the statement, the officer making the pocket book entry or the entry in the custody record;
- where applicable details of the amanuensis, i.e. the person who wrote down the document on behalf of the narrative giver.

S – Survey

Skim-read the document through completely at an even, steady pace, rather quicker than your normal reading speed.

Resist the following temptations:

- to glance forward;
- to stop your flow to dwell on some details rather than others;
- to look back to check what you have just read or something earlier in the document.

E – Extract

Conventions in notation

There are a number of conventions in notation that ensure critical detail and important aspects of detail are recorded appropriately. Qualifying utterances must always be noted. If the narrative giver:

- says 'about' write 'about', e.g. *about 2 pm*;
- uses a form of words locating the event in time write the words verbatim, e.g. *soon after*; *as he was leaving*;
- qualifies a detail, i.e. saying he or she is 'not sure' or words to this effect, put the letters *NS* after the qualified detail;
- says he or she 'does not know' or words to this effect, use the letters *NK* by the category of detail, e.g. *date NK*; *loc NK*; *speaker NK*.

Missing or anomalous detail needs to be noted:

- omitted detail – use a question mark, ?, indicating this as a point to be queried;
- anomalous or doubtful detail – use an exclamation mark in brackets (!), indicating this as a point to be queried.

Improving your ability to note down information

Many journalists use speed-writing systems, which commonly drop out the vowels (a – e – i – o – u) in words. Experiment with abbreviating words in this manner. Remember your SE3R must be comprehensible to others so ensure the abbreviated word is recognisable and unambiguous.

You will find it particularly useful if:

- you use abbreviations for high-frequency words – there is nothing to stop you devising your own (but remember to be consistent!). Examples of useful abbreviations are:

stat	statement	st; sb	something; somebody
pb	pocket book	w	with
offr	officer	fwd	forward
AA	appropriate adult	l; r	left; right
wit	witness	s/o; d/o	son of; daughter of
vm	victim	aka	also known as
sa	sexual assault	Nport	Newport

- you abbreviate the names of key people in the narrative, e.g.

  Beth   B
  Gary   G
  Chalky C

Be careful that you do not use the same letter for two people whose names start with that letter. In such a case use two letters, e.g. first and second name;

- you use symbols to replace words, e.g.

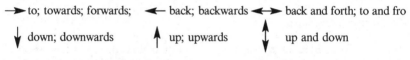

Layout

As with all note-taking, how you lay out information in the space available to you affects your ability to grasp detail, and to commit this to – and to retrieve it from – memory. There are many ways in which to make detail clear and memorable:

- underline surnames;

- try not to squash in detail;

- be as neat as possible;

- use white space, i.e. try to separate out information.

Extracting information

Go through the document systematically.

Turn your pad on its side, i.e. so it forms a long rectangular tablet.

Draw a line about two-thirds up the page, extending all the way from left to right across its entire width (Figure 1). This is your ***event line***.

Now work your way through the document:

- identifying each event as it appears in the narrative;

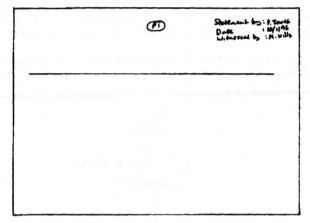

Figure 1 Relative location of event line on notepad

• mapping each event chronologically on to your event line;

• recording supporting detail connected with the event, e.g. detail on people, entities and locations.

Mapping events

When you identify an event draw a North–South line that cuts the event line (Figure 2).

Each cutting line is an event. You need to create some space between one cut and the next. Practice will enable you to find what spacing suits you but in the initial stages experiment with a gap of just over an inch (or about three centimetres).

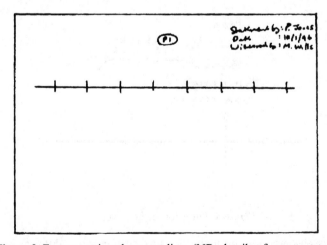

Figure 2 Events cutting the event line. (NB: details of events not shown)

533

Temporal and location detail

Write temporal and location details above the North point of the event line. Imagine you are writing the detail in a column or block of white space.

Be consistent in the order of detail. The most sensible order is descending: day, date, time, geographical location, more specific location (e.g. room) (Figure 3).

Figure 3 Temporal and location detail

You do not need to replicate day and date for subsequent events occurring on the same day (date). Simply omit this detail but remember to indicate when the day (date) changes.

Time phrases (e.g. *about 11*) are entered verbatim.

Indicate duration by a bracket extending eastwards towards the next event. Write above the bracket the duration (Figure 4).

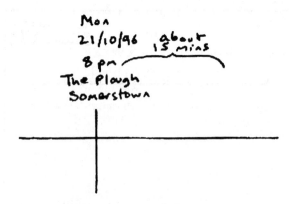

Figure 4 Duration of an event

Indicate successive events occurring in the same location with a ditto symbol.

Episodic detail

Enter episodic detail on **actors, entities, actions** and **reactions** below the South point of the event line. Again imagine you are writing the detail in a column or block of white space (Figure 5).

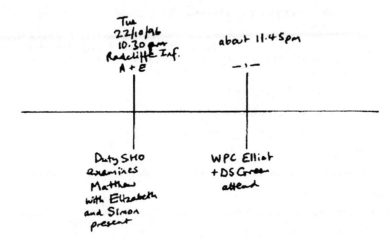

Figure 5 Episodic detail

There are three important **conversion rules** that you help you extract episodic detail in respect of tense, voice and reported speech.

1. **Past tense into present tense.**

   Convert text in the past tense into the present tense, e.g. in a statement by Trevor:

   Text in statement

   I saw Tracy sitting on Ian's lap.

   SE3R entry

   Trevor sees Tracy sitting on Ian's lap.

This conversion from past into present is crucial:

- it coincides with our underlying mental processes, i.e. transforming a verbal image of a past occurrence into a current – visual – image (though some people may not be conscious of doing this);

- it makes the narrative more real and more memorable, i.e. an account of actions in the present time is easier to picture and therefore easier to remember;

- it highlights earlier events that should be mapped on to the event line in the appropriate chronological position, e.g.

   Text in statement

   George decided to do something about it after what we found out a couple of days earlier.

535

SE3R isolates two events:

an earlier event:

a couple of days earlier – we (?) find out (?)

this event:

George decides to do something having found out (?) (a couple of days earlier).

You will note that SE3R has highlighted a range of questions raised by the statement which may not have been noticed by someone reading the text in the usual manner.

To whom does *we* refer?

What was found out?

How? From where or from whom?

When?

What was it exactly that led George to decide to do something?

2. *Passive into active*.

Convert the passive voice into active voice, e.g. in a statement by Peggy:

Text in statement

Lucy was comforted by me and my mum.

SE3R entry

Peggy and her mother comfort Lucy.

This conversion from passive to active is crucial:

- it coincides with our underlying mental processes, i.e. we rearrange the passive into an active construction (though some people may not be conscious of doing this);

- it makes the narrative more real and more memorable, i.e. an account of actions in the present time is easier to picture and therefore easier to remember;

- as pointed out earlier, the passive voice can obscure wittingly or unwittingly detail of forensic significance, e.g. in a statement by Sean:

Text in statement

They were all standing round the bed. He was being assaulted. Then I was pulled forward. I had to do the same as what was done to him. They threatened to kill me.

SE3R reveals

They are all standing round the bed.

? is/are assaulting (?) him.

? puls/pull Sean forward.

Sean has to do the same (?) as ? did to him.

? threatens/threaten to kill Sean.

- you will note that yet again SE3R highlights a range of questions that may have eluded a reader unaware of this obscuring property of the passive:
  - The identity of the person/persons carrying out the assault.
  - The nature of the assault.
  - The identity of the person/persons pulling Sean forward.
  - The actions which Sean describes as 'the same'.
  - The identity of the person/persons threatening to kill Sean.

Remember: Always use a question mark *?* to highlight instances of omitted detail, ambiguities and anomalies;

- you must constantly be on the look-out for the passive voice. It is frequently used by those in the role of an amanuensis (a person writing a document for another, e.g. a police officer writing a statement for an individual), who wittingly or unwittingly change the phraseology and words used by the person giving the account. When writing down statements, police officers in particular have a penchant for rephrasing what the interviewee actually said and for using more ponderous vocabulary and verbal constructions, most particularly the passive voice. In all too many cases the interviewee using the (more commonly occurring) active voice gave the requisite detail but this was lost when the police officer rearranged the active into the passive. The net effect is both to obscure and to refine what the narrative giver actually said.

3. *Indirect reported speech into direct reported speech.*

   Turn indirect reported speech into direct reported speech and put quotation marks around the utterance, e.g. in Trevor's statement:

   Text in statement

   > *Tracy was very upset and said to me Uncle Ian had done something awful to her.*

   SE3R entry

   > **Tracy is very upset and says to Trevor: 'Uncle Ian has done something awful to me.'**

   This conversion is important:

   - as pointed out above, police officers in particular have a tendency to use much more complex verbal constructions, ponderous phraseology, 'high faluting', 'difficult' or 'long' (polysyllabic) words, as well as technical words (particularly describing the action in legal terms). Again, the officer effectively obscures and refines what was actually said. This is particularly damaging to reported speech;
   - some tellers use ponderous words and phraseology that they would not use in everyday conversation. Their reasons for doing this differ. They may be overwhelmed by the process of giving a statement. They may see the statement rather like doing a piece of assessed 'school' work. They may want to avoid giving detail (for any number of innocent or guilty reasons).

   Many investigators accept unquestioningly the utterances deemed to have been said by the person in question. They need to be aware of phraseology and words whose choice, precision and refinement appear potentially 'out of character' with the origin, personality and development of the person who purportedly uttered them.

The following example illustrates how the SE3R requirement to convert indirect into direct speech raises awareness, in a statement by Kylie concerning what Jennifer, a fellow student, said to her:

Text in statement

> *Jennifer told me she had been sexually assaulted by Mr Piggot in his room. She said Mr Piggot fondled her repeatedly about her private parts and then asked her to fellate him.*

SE3R entry

> **Jennifer tells Kylie: 'I have been sexually assaulted (?) by Mr Piggot in his room.'**

> **Jennifer says: 'Mr Piggot fondled me repeatedly about my private parts (?) and then asked me to fellate (?) him.'**

SE3R thus brings to the fore the necessity to check exactly what Jennifer said to Kylie.

You need to use specific types of notation to capture particular forms of episodic detail:

• Simultaneous events, actions and reactions.

List each simultaneous action, each action being preceded by a hyphen (Figure 6).

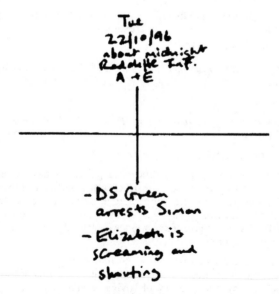

Figure 6 Simultaneous events

If the narrative describes two (or more) events as happening in different locations, simply create a second event line and enter detail in exactly the same manner on this second line. If more lines are needed just create these in parallel. These parallel lines only need to be as long as is necessary to include the simultaneous activity (Figure 7).

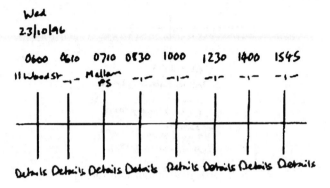

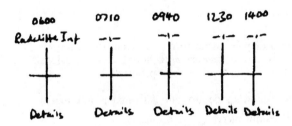

Figure 7 Events occurring in different locations. (NB: for the sake of simplicity, actual details are omitted)

- Dialogue.
  - Dialogue occurring without other intervening actions taking place.
  - A reported verbal exchange is represented as a continuous event, i.e. list the utterances below the South line (Figure 8).

539

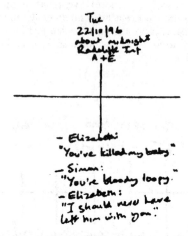

Figure 8 Dialogue without intervening actions

- Actions with intervening utterances.

  The actions and the utterances constitute separate events on the event line.

Identity bins

Use the lower third of your paper to record detail that supports the narrative, in shapes akin to index cards – *identity bins*. Initial detail occasions the creation of a bin. Subsequent detail is entered in the appropriate bin.

Always draw lines round an identity bin. This makes sure that:

- information does not merge between bins;
- the material in the bin is eye-catching and can be easily referred to later, e.g. in a consultation or in the police interview;
- gaps or inconsistencies are readily noted in the collated material.

Bins should be opened to collate details of:

- each individual mentioned in the text, e.g.
  - names – first name(s), second name, nickname, alias;
  - date and place of birth plus current age (always useful – put it in brackets if you wish)
  - employment status; work details if employed;
  - address(es) – residential; work;
  - ownership of property (e.g. vehicle);
  - living with; married to; son of; daughter of; friend of;
  - associates with, etc.;
- entities – objects, vehicles, documents, property, etc.;

- routine or repeated activities (e.g. cashing up the till at the end of the working day), giving this a label (in this case, 'cashing-up'), which you can use, and refer to, in your event line detail.

A bin can be used to collate a visual image, e.g.

- a sketch of an entity – such as an object, feature, clothing, etc.;
- a layout described in the narrative, e.g. a room, house, intersection of routes;
- relative positioning and orientation of people – this enables illustration of what or who was reportedly (and was actually) visible from where and by whom.

This use of an identity bin is very useful:

- attempting to turn words into images often reveals that what is reported is an invalid (unreal) representation of reality;
- it provides the basis for comparison with:
  - any subsequent diagram requested from the individual;
  - the real entity, e.g. the actual location.

Examples of identity bins are given in Figure 9 below. Note the use of abbreviations, including use of single initials to reduce text in the episode detail.

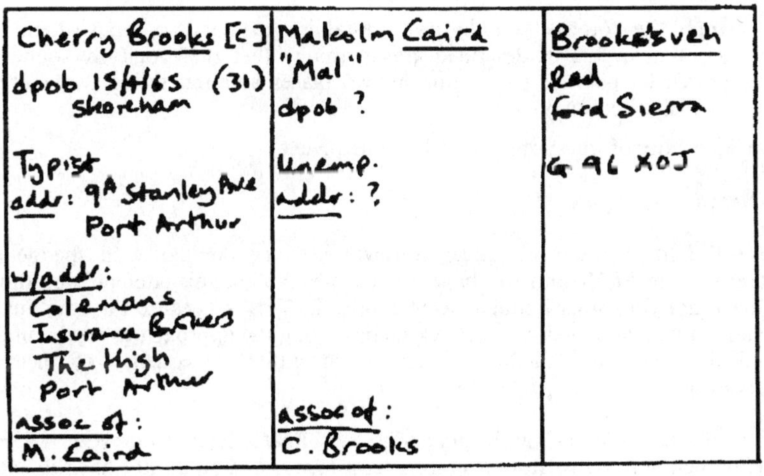

Figure 9 Examples of identity bins

An example of an SE3R illustrating the extraction of detail from a statement is set out in Annex A to this Appendix (p. 564).

R – Read

Read through the document at your normal reading speed:

- check the material in the text with the entries in your SE3R;

- correct any errors of omission (i.e. entering detail which was missed) or commission (i.e. inaccuracy).

R – Review

Put the document to one side.

Reviewing involves methodical examination and evaluation of your SE3R.

Be systematic in your reviewing:

- make noteworthy detail just by using fluorescent highlighter pens, felt-tips, different coloured pens or ballpoints;

- scan the event line. Look for breaks in narrative continuity, i.e. unaccountable gaps between one event and the next;

- examine each event and discrete sequences of events (episodes) that are, or are purportedly, linked:

  - note any consistencies (repetitions of disclosed detail), gaps, ambiguities, vagueness, inconsistencies, contradictions and any other forms of anomaly;

  - apply the 'forensic twaddle test' – establish in your own mind whether the event or events as described are anything other than logically sound and physically possible (e.g. being in two places at once; doing two mutually exclusive actions);

- make a note of questions raised by your review.

R – Recall

You will find that by this stage you will be very familiar with the detailed content of your SE3R and will have a good memory for this content even though you have not consciously sought to memorise it. This is because the combination of skim-reading, systematic, critical extraction using the approach to representation described above, and methodical review constitute a sequence of memorial processes.

The recall step is aimed at helping you consolidate detail from your SE3R in working memory and to store it in long-term memory. You do not have to engage in this stage unless you feel it necessary.

If you decide to memorise material, be systematic:

- do it in stages – identity bin detail first, then events;

- break down the task, i.e. within each stage memorise in 'chunks' Do not try to remember everything in one go.

Memorising identity information

Isolate the identity bins that you want to memorise.

Take one bin at a time:
- look at the bin;
- scan its contents;
- study – look at each detail in turn;
- close your eyes;
- visualise the bin, then its individual contents;
- open your eyes;
- check – scan and study;
- close your eyes, visualise and so on.

Memorising event line information

Look at the event line. Memorise it in terms of gist:
- identify key events;
- isolate discrete episodes;
- note the number of steps (events) within an episode.

Adopt the same approach as for memorising the content of identity bins.

Checking your recall

A good method of checking your recall is·
- turn your SE3R sheet over so that it is face down;
- reproduce on another sheet the detail of your SE3R from memory. Put in the key event and identity details in exactly the same location.

Applying SE3R to multiple written texts

To represent more than one account there are three options:
- ***Representing two accounts***. The second text can be treated in the same way as a simultaneous event or two versions of the same text (see above). The event line of the second account is drawn under that of the first, with coinciding events reflected as being in the same relative position on the event line. Where there are more than two accounts, this is not recommended since the amount of information becomes too great.

- ***Representing two or more accounts***. Use a common event line and identity bins but differentiate the sources by using a different-coloured pen for each account. If you are using one colour for two or more accounts you can give precision referencing by:
  - using the four areas of white space created by an event bisecting the event line, entering such detail as the initials of the witness, the statement page number and even the line number where the text detail is located;

- putting the source of the detail in brackets, e.g. beside the detail in the identity bins or opposite temporal and location details above the event line.

- **Convert the SE3R representation of two or more accounts into a grid** (see the section on tabulation, p. 548). The event detail of the first account or statement is entered into the first column, that of the second statement or account into the second column, and so on.

Applying SE3R to recorded text

S – Survey

Listen to, and, in the case of video, observe, intently the recording only stopping to resolve indistinct utterances or difficult to differentiate detail on the video recording.

E – Extract

Interviews underline the fact that the narrative sequence, i.e. the order in which an individual describes the occurrence of events, very often does not correspond to the order of actual events. This is complicated by the fact that police officers tend to change the topic rapidly and without apparent logic, and return to the topic across the course of the interview – sometimes repeatedly and endlessly.

When an event pops up out of sequence, all that is necessary is to exercise a degree of decision-making. If it antedates an earlier event on the event line, place the event in the appropriate place.

If an event pops up only to be deferred to a later time in the interview for disclosure, exercise judgement and place the event some distance ahead on the yet-to-be-completed event line. If you overestimated the situation this is easily resolved: bring the detail back into line, at the right chronological point.

If you underestimated, leaving yourself with too little space between events, simply write the word INSERT above the space and open up a separate SE3R sheet to represent the events which occurred. Remember to number insert sheets, e.g. INSERT 1, INSERT 2, and so on, should you need more than one insert sheet.

Everything else is as for conducting an SE3R on a written text.

Applying SE3R to a live interview

This is very simple. You create an SE3R from the interviewee's narrative. Using a different colour, you reflect the outcome of probing, entering detail on the SE3R and, where necessary, opening up INSERT sheets.

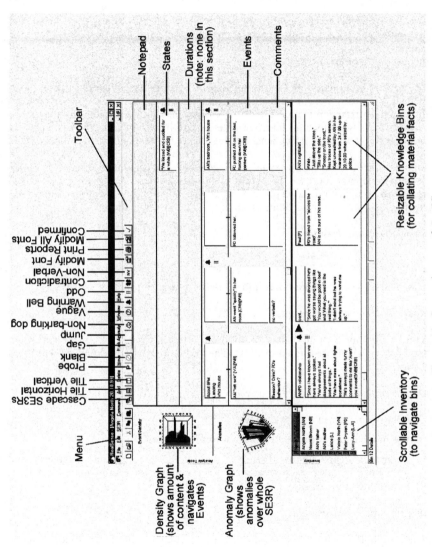

Figure 10 Screen layout of *RealSense*

RealSense: THE COMPUTER VERSION OF SE3R

The design of *RealSense* harnesses the power of information technology to enable you to create, and to work with, one or more SE3Rs – flexibly, with ease, efficiency and rapidity.

RealSense can be applied to any form of written text and to any form of spoken text, either a recording or in a real-time exchange, e.g. an interview. Information is instantly stored in an immediately accessible database. Your SE3Rs can be stored on disk and communicated via e-mail.

The functional design of *RealSense* includes the conventional range of drop-down menus. You can resize or extend any area or component, and switch between different formats, fonts and colours. *RealSense* has unique keyboard commands, function keys for impactful marking. Even if you have limited keyboard skills you can operate at speed, comprehensively capturing and responding to critical detail.

Figure 10 shows the screen layout of *RealSense*. The on-screen, scrollable display means that one or more SE3Rs can be referred to at any time for any purpose, e.g. an aid to comparing (and capturing) what the individual is saying in evidence-in-chief against an earlier account; as an aid to cross-examination.

Some *RealSense* features

Notepad facility

This enables you to make notes immediately for any purpose.

Abbreviation/expansion facility

You create your own dictionary of abbreviations, enabling you to make maximum use of these when creating your SE3R. They are automatically expanded when you want.

On-screen analyses of the entire account

Cumulative on-screen displays show:

* the number of narrative steps and amount of detail.
* anomalies – gaps, jumps, absence of reasonably expected detail, vagueness and ambiguity, contradiction, odd behaviour counter to reasonable expectations across the entire SE3R.

Inventory of knowledge bins

The scrollable inventory locates quickly a particular person, place, object, routine or other area of knowledge. The bin with this information is immediately placed before you.

Immediate marking of anomalies

Using the function keys you can rapidly mark anomalies, using visually impactful symbols: done when you detect them or during a systematic review.

Immediate annotation

Text can be instantly annotated, e.g. detail for action – probing, validating, researching; cross-references; commentary or observations; points of probing questioning, their content, the replies given and observed reactions.

Immediate marking of significant material

Preparation and planning is aided by immediate marking of material facts, i.e. significant detail, and material time frames, i.e. key episodes, with a key bearing upon the case.

Editing and layering facilities

You edit with cut, copy and paste facilities. Layering enables work on more than one SE3R simultaneously: different versions of the same SE3R, or with completely different SE3Rs. You can switch between SE3Rs to compare, analyse and annotate their content.

You can create a 'composite' SE3R from two or more SE3Rs. A composite SE3R can show:

- the 'evolving' narrative given by an individual in accounts given at different times – with the detail from each account in a distinctive colour;
- a 'master narrative', again using different colours, bringing together the different accounts given by more than one individual about the same event or time frame.

Print facility

You can print the complete or selected contents of any SE3R, and your notepad entries. The output can be an aid to proofing, interviewing or cross-examination, tasking, briefing and case discussions. It can be converted into any other medium, e.g. overhead transparency, projection slide or PowerPoint slide.

Further details about **RealSense** can be obtained from: *Forensic Solutions Limited*, Wych End, The Spinney, Ford Lane, East Hendred, Oxfordshire OX12 8LS (01235 821205; FAX 01235 821547) or via http/www.forensicsolutions.co.uk.

TABULATION

Systematic extraction of detail from accounts – descriptions and narratives – in order to compare these is essential. This is because across written and recorded material derived from police interviews of one or more individuals there is always a very high likelihood of anomalies occurring. These include:

- *contradictions*;
- *gaps*;
- *contrast*: variations in amount of information or detail within and between accounts;
- *evolving accounts*: how an individual's accounts change over time:
  - *across a number of interviews*: from the first description to the formal statement variations may occur in what is asserted. This is why:
    - (a) PEACE guides officers to apply the criteria of the ADVOKATE mnemonic;
    - (b) many officers do not apply the ADVOKATE mnemonic;
  - *within the same interview*: the individual gives more than one version across the course of the interview. The existence of more than one version is obscured by:
    - (a) officers concentrating on one version and ignoring or downplaying detail indicative of other versions, e.g. when preparing a summary ROTI (record of tape-recorded interview) or IVRI (index of video-recorded interview);
    - (b) lawyers not listening to, or viewing the recording, in a systematic way that enables the detection of different versions;
- *migration of detail*: detail that first appears in one individual's account pops up in another taken later in time – a strong clue that:
  - the officer taking the second person's account was aware of the detail in the first person's account (and may even have taken it). The officer then interviewed the second person in a manner that influenced that person to make assertions incorporating this detail known to the officer. This is precisely why:
    - (a) officers interviewing witnesses should produce comprehensive notes and recordings of earlier police interviews of witnesses;
    - (b) there is a widespread disinclination among officers to make comprehensive notes and recordings;
  - the first person spoke to the second such that the second person was 'primed' to give particular detail to the interviewing officer or the officer taking the account. This is precisely why FOAs should specifically instruct witnesses not to talk to each other about the offender and 'what happened'.

Tabulating key detail is the simplest, most efficient way of comparing accounts in order to detect anomaly within accounts (descriptions or narratives) emanating from:

- one individual on a number of occasions;
- more than one individual.

If you have produced SE3Rs for key accounts you will be in a better position to extract information since this will be located within the identity bins or the event line.

However, you can extract information into a table without necessarily producing an SE3R for the document. Whether you produce an SE3R first or work straight from the document is a matter of preference: the important thing is that you construct tables as a matter of course. The logic for doing so is the same as that for constructing an SE3R:

- you can systematically and critically analyse and assess the material before you;
- you can communicate your findings to others – your client, colleagues and, very significantly, to the court, the CPS and the police.

Tables are effective because they bring anomalies to immediate attention. If you are able to demonstrate anomalies, the CPS or a judge is more likely to be persuaded by your arguments, e.g. for further disclosure; casting doubt upon the nature of the police case, the status of the prosecution evidence and the quality of the police investigation.

The basic format

The basic format of a table is a grid:

- an *index column* – comprising a number of *datum cells* each specifying a particular item of detail or area of information to be sought in each description or account;
- a column for each description or account examined;
- rows extending from each datum cell across the columns, with cells showing what each description or account said – or did not say – in respect of that particular item of detail or area of information.

Drawing up a grid

Arrange the accounts (documents and recordings) to be processed in chronological order – earliest first, most recent last.

Process one account at a time.

549

Creating your index column

You can draw up an index column before you start processing. This can be the product of:

- ***applying common sense***, e.g. age, height, features, build, clothing, shoes, voice, unusual characteristics, or bringing to bear what you know about the particular circumstances of the case;

- ***taking a 'slice' out of the event line, e.g. for the offence***: this may be drawn from the case chronology (if you draw these up in some detail) or from the SE3R you have made of the account of the victim or a key witness.

  Each episode in the slice may constitute a datum cell or you may break each episode down into smaller pieces, each with a datum cell, e.g. actions before attack; words said before attack; actions when attacking; words said during attack; actions after attack; words said after attack;

- ***adding datum cells as you go along***: whether or not you have drawn up an initial index column, as you progress through the documents or recordings and another item of detail or area of information emerges, all you need to do is to create a datum cell for this. When you do it, this will create empty cells for this item/area in accounts that you have already processed. Put a small c in the empty cells in question as a simple error-trap – a reminder to go back and to check for this item/detail in the accounts already processed.

The great thing about tables is that they allow you to be flexible: as they grow, so you will find the detail of the case – and the anomalies – will be revealed.

After a measure of practice, you will become very adept at producing tables with sufficient cells and space within these for detail.

Creating a table manually

If you are creating the table manually, it helps to think ahead:

- use sufficiently wide paper to accommodate the index row and a row for each account to be processed – optimally this should be at least A4 on its side, A3 is better, and A1 (flip-chart size) if you have a complex case with many accounts and a likelihood of large numbers of datum cells;

- draw columns down the page – if you are using lined A4 this is that bit easier;

- draw rows across – leaving sufficient space for the material to be inserted in the cells;

- label the first datum cell ***Source*** – then move across the row and enter this detail for each account;

- work progressively down the index column – entering the specification of each datum cell, if these have been established, by forethought or from a slice of the case chronology/key SE3R;

- when you reach the end of the sheet, attach another sheet to the bottom. The best material for attaching sheets is paper masking tape since this allows you to separate pages to insert another should this be necessary. You will not be able to insert pages easily if you use Sellotape or have stuck sheets together with an adhesive such as Pritt Stick. However, the choice is yours.

Source	CD (AB's friend)	E* (AB's best friend)	GH (Tutor: AB's school)	IJ (Deputy Head: AB's school)	KL (General practitioner)	MN (AB's friend)	OP (Tutor: AB's school)	WPC Q and PC R (FOAs) Log	Progress sheet [signature illegible]	video of int of AB by WDC S [VRI]	DC 1 (Arresting officer + IO) Pocket book
Date [ref]	Wed 15 July [UniUM-p5]	Wed 15 July [UniUM-p3]	Thurs 16 July [UniUM-p3]	Thurs 16 July [UniUM-p2]	Thurs 16 July [UniUM-p1]	Sun 19 July [UniUM-p2]	Thurs 16 July [UniUM-p4-5]	Tues 14 July [UniUM-p8]	Tues 14 July [UniUM-p10]	Wed 15 July (CB-p11-38)	Sat 18 July [UniUM-p11]
When AB spoke to witness	Sat 11 July 1630	Mon 13 July 0900	Mon 13 July 1050	Mon 13 July 1100-1200	Mon 13 July 13 5	Tues 14 July after break	Tues 14 July afternoon	Tues 14 July about 2200	Tues 14 July	N/A	N/A
Age	Male, 19 to 25	Man	Lad about 17-18	Youth	Man	Man	Lad	No description taken!!	Youth about 17	17/18	Boy, 14
Height	5'7"-5'8"									5'6"	5'9"-5'10"
Build	well built						strong			skinny	skinny
Colour									white	white	
Hair	• light brown/ blonde • short						• blonde • short		blonde	• 'light – like blonde' • quite short	• dark brown • normal length
Eyes										• light • 'maybe blue'	brown
Accent	• London accent • 'definitely not local' (West country)									• Northern • London cockney accent • 'not strong'	Strong local (West country)
Hat	• black hat • with 'logo on the front'						hat		baseball hat	• black hat • tight fitted to the head with a band turned up • with a person on it (with a red top on and wearing a hat)	No hat on arrest – search found: • black wool hat with motif (man lying down) • black wool hat with motif of man sitting up
Coat/jacket	• brown-coloured, waist-length jacket • waterproof in places • 'brown patches' • writing/pattern on back									• tawny/fawny coloured 'coat', quite short • poss. half leather/half material, normal coat material, poss. padded cotton on arm/back • 'bomber type jacket'	• plain fawn bomber type jacket, single material [when arrested] • no other jacket [established from search]
Shirt	white									• blue checked • blue and white checked, poss. quite thick material	• beige [when arrested] • green shirt (from search)
Trousers	black 'trousers'								• blue jeans	• black 'trousers' • quite baggy	• black jeans [when arrested] • black trousers (from search)
Footwear	shoes									poss. trainers -dark	• black trainers [when arrested] • pair of LA bear black boots (from search)
Ability to recognise attacker again				AB says she cannot remember enough about the youth to report it to the police			AB says: • she does not know the lad • she would recognise him again		• AB cannot provide any further description of the youth • AB 'might only' be able to recognise him again	AB says she has never seen him before	

Table 1 Example of table comparing details from different accounts

As you work your way through each account:

- simply enter the detail that emerges in respect of the datum cell;
- if nothing is stated in the account, then leave the cell blank.

Creating a table using information technology

All current word-processing packages, e.g. Word, enable you to create tables.

If you have a large number of accounts to process, you may find that the table exceeds the width of your screen. This problem is easily resolved. When you have completed the column on the extreme right of your screen:

- save the document;
- create a copy of the document with the same title with an identifier that it is the second in the series, e.g. *Accts 2*;
- open up the new document;
- leave the index column intact;
- delete all details in the remaining columns;
- continue opening up columns for each subsequent account you are working on;
- when you reach the extreme right of the screen, repeat the routine – save, create new document, open the new document, strip account cells, carry on processing.

When you have completed processing all accounts, print off the documents and affix these to each other vertically and horizontally, like a patchwork quilt.

Two examples of tabulation

Table 1 on page 551 is an example of a table created in a real case in which dates and identities have been changed. A 14-year-old girl had run away from home and once she had been found and taken home, told her friend but not her parents that she had been sexually assaulted/raped. During the next week, she gave accounts to friends, teachers, a general practitioner, FOAs and a detective in a child protection unit. A week after the alleged offence, a detective arrested a 14-year-old boy who attended the same school as the girl.

The telling aspect of this example is that it shows how the police did not make any attempt to examine her accounts systematically. The IO who arrested the boy clearly did not apply any of the ADVOKATE criteria. All of the anomalies were to be found in the unused material with the exception of the video-recorded interview. It is an object lesson of how the CPS, the defence and the courts must appreciate the pervasive disposition within the police service to ignore anomalies.

Table 2 on page 553 is an example of how a suitably constructed grid can capture a very large amount of detail. Here it is able to collate detail from the accounts of seven witnesses concerning the descriptions and actions of three men – a driver, front passenger and a rear passenger – involved in a case of murder.

Analysing Witness Testimony gives more detail on grids and more examples of their application. It also describes THEMA (thematic emergence of anomaly), the application of grid method to the identification of anomaly in audio- and video-recorded text.

	WITNESS 1	WITNESS 2	WITNESS 3	WITNESS 4	WITNESS 5	WITNESS 6	WITNESS 7
DRIVER							
Description							
Actions							
FRONT PASSENGER							
Description							
Actions							
REAR PASSENGER							
Description							
Actions							

Table 2 Tabulation of the descriptions and actions
of three men given by seven witnesses

GENOGRAMS: A METHOD FOR REPRESENTING RELATIONSHIPS BETWEEN INDIVIDUALS

Genograms are visual representation of links between people, particularly family membership, structure, history, quality of relationship and current arrangements. They are widely used in social services and child protection team contexts. However, they are applicable to any investigative context where there is a large amount of detail involving one or more generations within one or more families or households.

There are a number of basic symbols for people, relationships, children and individuals living together.

The basic symbols: people

Male	Female	Gender unknown	Dead
□	○	△	✕

Your client in double lines e.g.

▢

Relationships

Married

Living together

Close relationship

Conflictual relationship

Distant relationship

Separated

Divorced

Children

Natural children

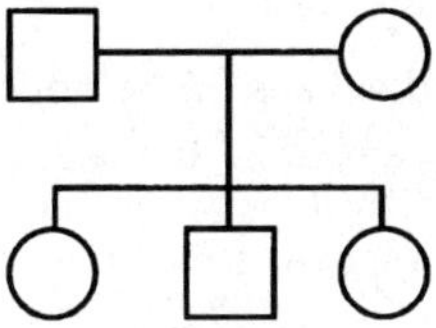

Adopted child

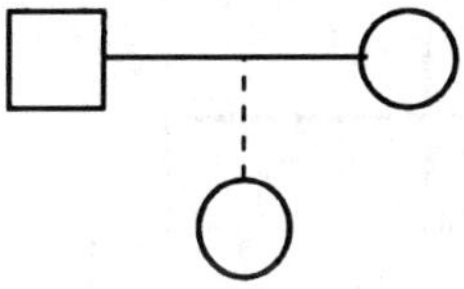

Fraternal twins

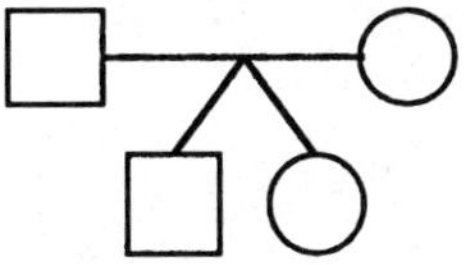

Identical twins

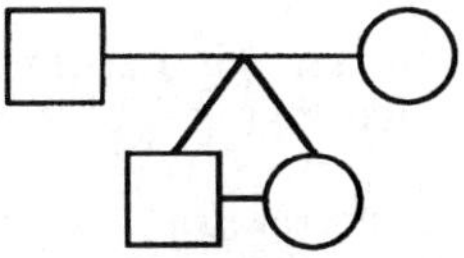

Pregnancy

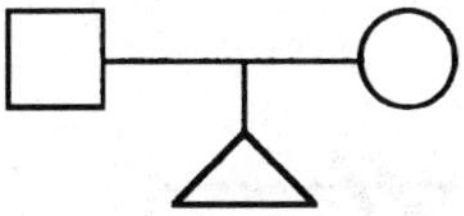

Miscarriage

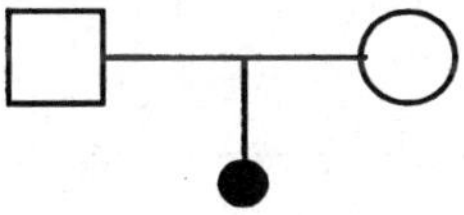

Abortion

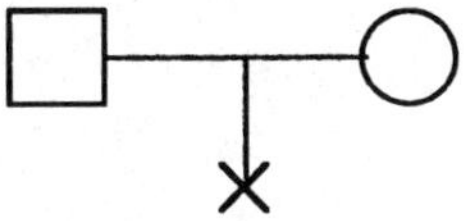

Stillbirth

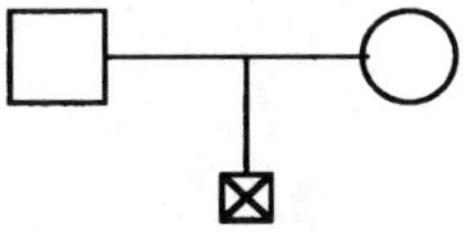

Individuals living together

Use a broken line to encircle the individuals in the household.

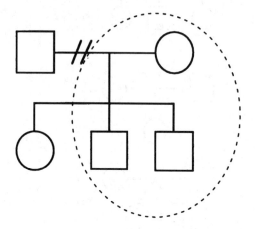

Adding detail

Write in text within or adjacent to the symbol. Lapsed time (e.g. age now; age at death; stage in pregnancy; time in a location or job) is placed in brackets.

The Browns

Living in Bath?   Living in Bristol

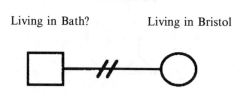

An example of a genogram

Figure 11 on page 557 shows an example of a simple genogram.

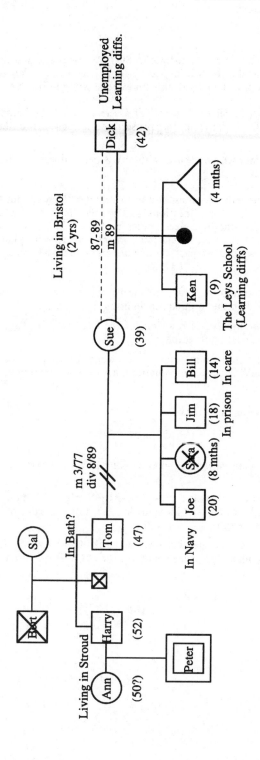

Figure 11 An example of a genogram

Drawing locations

It is of vital importance that you demonstrate to the CPS, the police and the courts that you have sought to make yourself intimately acquainted with the key locations involved in your client's case. Only with this knowledge will you be able:

- to assess the validity (the physical reality) of assertions made by individuals in the police case and, crucially, in the prosecution evidence and the police investigation;

- to brief colleagues, counsel, your client and any expert witnesses instructed by you.

You cannot rely upon the police to assist you in this matter. They cannot be relied upon to provide drawings of key locations and scenes. This is assuming that drawings were generated in the first place, either by the FOA, SOCO or another officer assigned with this task. You should not content yourself with photography or video recordings forwarded as part of the disclosed material. You must be prepared:

- to visit any key location in order to 'walk the ground', i.e. physically acquainting yourself with the 'ground', including routes taken;

- to produce a requisite number of drawings of the location – backing these up with video recordings and photography;

- to visit a location at a time comparable to that when the offence occurred – in order to check out such issues as illumination and visibility, marking this detail on any appropriate drawings.

Simple guidelines for drawing a location

Buildings

1. Make a drawing in plan elevation ('view looking down from above') of each floor level/storey.

2. For significant rooms or areas, draw a separate plan elevation showing dimensions with walls from each side laid flat, e.g. like the sides of flat-pack furniture (see Figure 12 below).

3. On the flattened walls, indicate the location and relative size of doors and windows, as well as other significant detail, e.g. height of fitted furniture, wall-mounted lights, radiators, furnishings.

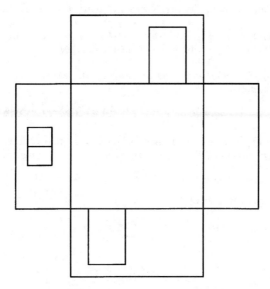

Figure 12   Flat-pack method of showing walls

4. On the plan elevation, show type and direction of opening of each door and window.

5. Use graphic symbols (see Figure 13 on pages 560–3) showing dimensions.

6. Using a pocket compass identify North and mark this on the sketch.

Exterior locations

1. Make a plan drawing, attempting to keep this to scale, and showing the location of key objects using graphic symbols for:

   • buildings, out-buildings, yards;

   • walls, hedges, fences, gates and gaps;

   • roads, driveways, tracks, footpaths, walkways;

   • railway lines, rivers, watercourses;

   • trees.

2. Using a pocket compass identify North and mark this on the sketch.

It is always helpful to obtain local mapping which shows areas in small scale, e.g. the Land Registry; the Council Works department:

- such mapping can be enlarged on a photocopier, making the task of drawing plans much easier;
- *Tippex* can be used to mask out unwanted or irrelevant details on the 'blown up' plan;
- the 'cleaned up' mapping can then be copied as many times as you wish, providing you with outlines that you can draw upon, making any markings you wish.

Graphic symbols used in drawings

Camera (position of shot)

Stairs (arrow indicates up)

Door — (indicating direction of opening)

Double doors

Sliding doors

Folding door — Hinge

Chair

Sofa, couch, day bed

Table (show legs)

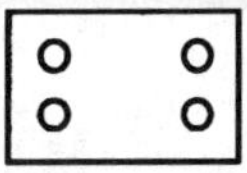

Table (round)

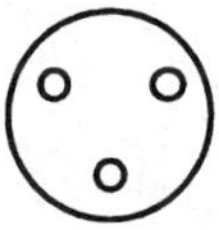

Television

Lamp

Cooker (indicate burners)

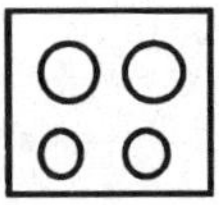

Refrigerator

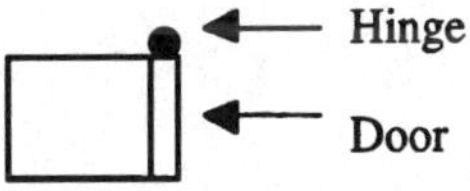

Hinge

Door

Sink

One bowl

Two bowls

Fitted units

Island in kitchen, also
counter in shop

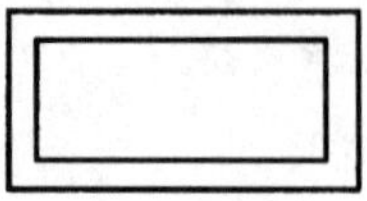

Bed

Dresser

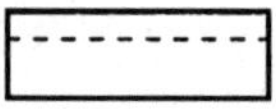

Bath

Shower

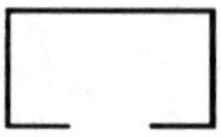

WC (toilet bowl)

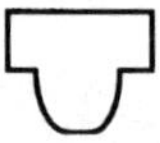

Vehicle    Front

Bicycle/Motorcycle   Front

Road or driveway

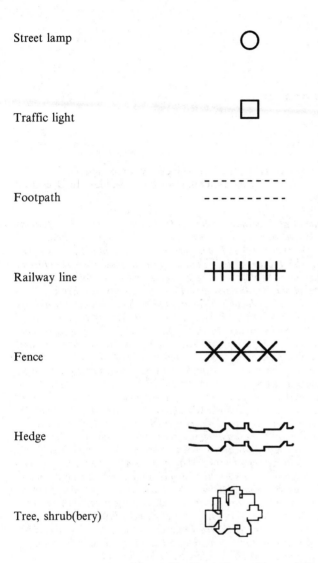

Street lamp

Traffic light

Footpath

Railway line

Fence

Hedge

Tree, shrub(bery)

Figure 13 Typical graphic symbols

ANNEX A

A WORKED EXAMPLE OF SE3R

The material for this example is a statement given by Frederick Ussher. The statement was taken down by PC 256 James Goldsworthy on Sunday, 16 December 1996. The statement says:

> *I am a final year student at Trentham College. At weekends I work part-time as a barman in the Feathers public house in George Street, Purleigh. At about 10.30 pm on Saturday, 15 December 1996, I was serving in the public bar. Two men who are regulars and who I know to be called Jason and Ernie were standing at the left end of the bar near the doors to the women's and men's toilets. Jason is about 20 and Ernie is about 30. Jason was nearest the toilets and Ernie was to his right. They were celebrating Jason's birthday and he had been bought a drink by someone at the bar to Ernie's right. Behind them and in front of the large round pillar by the door to the men's toilets stood a group of three men and a woman. The man nearest the men's toilets was fair-haired. He was in his early twenties and was wearing a combat jacket. Facing him, that is towards the toilets, stood a balding man in his forties with a Frank Zappa moustache wearing a green Army jumper. Between them with his back to Jason and Ernie was a stocky dark-haired man. I think he was wearing a dark green top. I think it was a roll-neck jumper but I am not sure. He had a strong Newcastle accent. The woman was about 18-19. She wore a fur bolero jacket and a black mini-skirt. She went to the toilet. When she came out of the toilet she was tugging her mini-skirt down as she walked back to her group. Jason pointed towards her with his pint glass which was nearly empty. He said very loudly in her direction that if she needed help she only had to ask. Someone in the group said something about people need to be taught to keep their eyes to themselves. The man with his back to the bar was given an empty glass and swung round towards Jason. He hit Jason's glass with his glass and jabbed the broken rim towards Jason's face. I rushed through to the saloon bar to get Mr Fyfe the manager. When we returned to the public bar the group had gone. Jason was leaning on the bar holding a bar towel to his eyes. I looked over the bar. Ernie was laying motionless face down on the floor.*

The SE3R representation of this statement is on the next two pages.

When you read the SE3R note:

- the use of abbreviations and symbols;
- conversion of past tense into present;
- conversion of reported speech into direct speech;
- conversion of passive into active – revealing the need to investigate the identities involved;
- the simple diagram derived from Ussher's verbal descriptions.

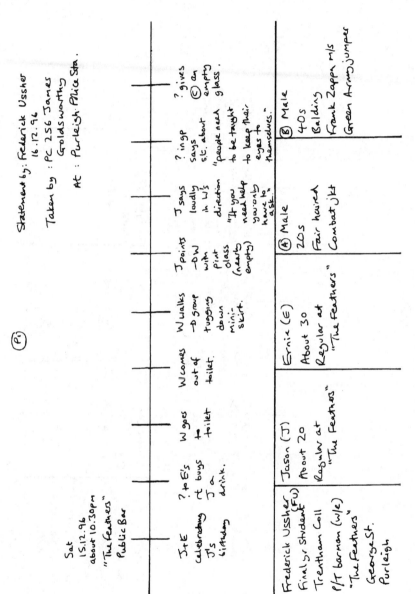

Figure 14 A worked example of SE3R

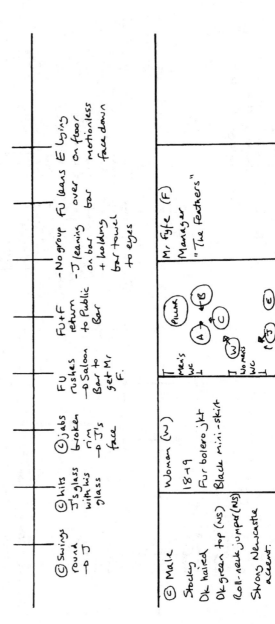

Figure 14 (continued) A worked example of SE3R

Investigative interviewing

Interviewing is a fundamental activity in the defence of a client to obtain statements from potential witnesses for the defence. The active defence of a client extends the range of potential interviewing. You, or an employee or an investigator upon your instructions, will, as part of your investigation, seek to obtain accounts from diverse individuals. This could be someone – identified in the material disclosed by the CPS, or uncovered through your systematic analysis of case material disclosed by the CPS or through your own investigation – who may have been at or near the location of the offence at the material time, who may or may not have been interviewed by the police or another agency (e.g. social services, Customs and Excise), or who has been involved as an expert and may or may not give a statement or report but is, in effect, a neutral party (e.g. a fire brigade investigation officer, an ambulance officer who attended the scene).

PLANNING AND PREPARATION

Many interviews are lost before they begin because of a failure to plan and to prepare. Planning and preparation require forethought. Methodical examination of relevant material, any necessary prior investigation, and systematic work upon the material prior to the interview are essential.

Identify your interview aim

You must be in no doubt about the purpose of interviewing this person. Two common aims are:

* to obtain the fullest possible, detailed account from an individual who is a potential source of testimony but who has not given this testimony.

  Such individuals are identified as you map out the case chronology and conduct a fine-grain analysis of disclosed accounts and other material, or visit, assess and record the scene or the vicinity of the offence. For whatever reason, in the course of the police investigation such individuals despite being potential witnesses:

  - were not interviewed;
  - if interviewed, gave an account that was not written down as notes or as a statement;
  - were not asked to render a report;

- to obtain another, as full as possible, detailed account from an individual who during, or as a result of, the police investigation gave an account or statement or rendered a report.

You will have identified the necessity to obtain another account as you engage in the continuous process of collection, collation and analysis of case information, i.e.

- the cumulative construction of the case chronology;
- the fine-grain analysis of accounts by these individuals and others;
- a detailed understanding of other material;
- first-hand knowledge of the details of the scene or the vicinity of the offence.

Specify your objectives

Your objectives are the specific areas and items of information you require to obtain or to put to the test by the end of the interview.

Shortcomings, gaps, ambiguity, vagueness, contradiction and other anomalies within the case chronology, the detail of accounts and other material disclosed by the police and the CPS, and your knowledge of the 'ground' and other factors (e.g. background information, objective technical data, or expert assessments) raise doubts as to the validity or reliability of asserted facts.

Identifying objectives

This is where the case chronology and manual SE3R or *RealSense* (on the computer) analyses of accounts prove their worth (see Appendix 7). Working your way through these will enable you to identify rapidly and systematically the objectives for your interview.

Spelling out your objectives

You must list your objectives. It does not matter if you phrase them as simple points or as questions; the important issue is that you explicitly state them. This will enable you:

- to prepare an interview plan that includes these objectives;
- to ensure that all objectives will be covered by following your plan during the interview.

Prepare an interview plan

You must think ahead, to ensure that you are able to manage the exchange of information, i.e. the topics covered, the focus, breadth and depth of detail requested and disclosed.

Preparing to manage the exchange of information

In any interview you will be seeking *either* to obtain the fullest possible account of 'what happened' or what the person knows or believes to be the case, *or* to obtain the fullest possible responses to focused questioning on a number of discrete issues, *or* a combination of a full account and answers to questions on topics other than those raised in the account.

In all cases, it will be a process of obtaining the fullest possible response to a question and then systematically probing the response. To prepare for this:

- ***Identify the topics you wish to cover***

  Look at the list of areas or details you have identified through your analyses and fuller understanding of the police case, the evidence and the police investigation. Aided by the visual case chronology and SE3R sheets (or ***RealSense*** screen print-outs) you will be in a position to pull these together under separate topic headings. Taking a specific example: e.g. discovery of the theft of high-value items; actions following discovery of the theft; responses by depot staff; interviewing of the witness at the depot – initial version written in the police officer's notebook; first formal statement; second formal statement; accounting for attractive, high-value items; the witness's relationship with Tom the storeman (your client); accounting procedures for stores; the witness's job in the stores.

  Now reorder the topics to generate a *line of questioning*, i.e. a logical sequence of topics that you wish to investigate through questioning. Wherever possible you should try to funnel topics. This can be done in two ways: from the general – everyday, routine or wider issues or detail – to the specific – the one-off instance, occurrence or detail; from the specific to the general. Moving from the general to the specific is the easiest line of questioning to control. There is always a risk with going from the specific, that the topics unfold in a way that makes it difficult to bring the line of questioning smoothly, if at all, round to those matters you wish to cover.

  Using the example above, a general to specific line of questioning could be:

  (1) The witness's job in the stores.

  (2) The witness's relationship with Tom the storeman (your client).

  (3) Accounting procedures for stores. Accounting for attractive, high-value items.

  (4) Discovery of the theft, actions following discovery of the theft.

  (5) Responses by depot staff.

  (6) Interviewing of the witness at the depot – initial version written in the police officer's note book.

  (7) First formal statement.

  (8) Second formal statement.

  Of course, in the case of someone who has never given an account of 'what happened' you may decide it appropriate to set this as the first topic, and then to follow this by specific topics.

  However, there is a simple reason for specifying your line of questioning before the interview. It enables you to inform the individual at the outset of the interview of the topics you wish to cover, as part of your explicit *route map* – your agenda for the interview. This not only puts your intentions on the record and puts the person clearly in the picture, it gives you a framework for the management of information. For example, if the individual digresses or drifts

569

off you can bring him or her back to the topic. Similarly, you can indicate that you have noted what has been said but remind the individual that, as you indicated at the outset of the interview, that specific topic will be covered in due course.

- *List your questioning objectives under each topic*

Simply note down the areas or details you wish to ask about. These specific points you need to keep to yourself, i.e. they are not incorporated into your declared route map.

- *Decide how you will open a topic and consider possible blocks*

There are three distinct ways of opening a topic: an antecedent, a parameter, or a trailer:

- *Antecedent*

This term comes from the Latin meaning falling before. Here you focus the individual on a specific circumstance prior to the offence or the interview, e.g.

Tell me about the job you do with BT.

How did you get on with Tanya before this all happened?

What's the routine for cashing-up at the end of each day?

Over the years, interviewers have devalued antecedent questions – many thinking they are just 'background' questions to build rapport before moving on to the 'real' issues. If you engage in such questions to break the ice you will be quickly found out – most particularly by a failure to probe these appropriately or by a far from smooth change to the next topic.

Prepare your use of the antecedent:

(a) think through how you will move smoothly from questioning on one antecedent to another or to another topic altogether;

(b) anticipate blocking responses from the individual, e.g. *Why do you want to know that?* – and consider an appropriate answer.

- *Parameter*

This is an opener that invites information on events occurring between one point (parameter) and another. Parameters may be points in time – *Tell me everything that happened between when you left the bank on Friday afternoon with Ted White and the time you gave your statement to WPC Green early on Sunday morning* – or points in space – *Tell me where you went from turning off at Exit 26 until you arrived at Southport.*

Prepare your use of the parameter:

(a) identify points that are an appropriate distance apart in terms of time and space. If you set them too far apart you will be faced with a large amount of information that may be potentially useless; if too narrow you may never learn vital information;

(b) wherever possible, link your parameter to the visual representation you have constructed from the material disclosed to you by the police and the CPS. Your SE3R sheets (or *RealSense* screen print-outs) of key disclosure will be invaluable here since areas of correspondence and difference will be immediately obvious. You will be in a position to map what the individual asserts against what you have in front of your eyes;

(c) forbid yourself interrupting and probing until the individual has completed his or her answer to the parameter question. Remind yourself that interviewers destroy the value of a parameter by jumping in, interrupting and engaging in premature, inappropriate probing of what the individual has just said. This disrupts the flow of the individual's account and also your memory for this;

(d) anticipate blocking responses from the individual, e.g. *Why do you want to know that?* – and consider an appropriate answer.

– *Trailer*

A trailer is a series of assertions – presenting the individual with a connected sequence of incontrovertible details which constitute a puzzle, a paradox (logical contradiction) or an inescapable situation – followed by an invitation to the individual to give an explanation, e.g.

> *You first told the police you saw a small man in a combat jacket hit Wayne from behind with a baseball bat.*
>
> *You said you recognised the smaller man as Jim.*
>
> *You have known Jim for years.*
>
> *You said you saw Jim that night in The Swan, wearing a combat jacket.*
>
> *You then told the police you were not sure if it was a smaller man, if he wore a combat jacket, or if it was Jim.*
>
> *How do you account for that change?*

A trailer works if you are absolutely sure of the detail. There are a number of critical factors in framing and delivering a trailer:

(a) each of the assertions must be incontrovertible. If any one assertion is open to valid challenge the investigative potential of the trailer is destroyed;

(b) the assertions must be direct, precise and not too long;

(c) too few assertions create no impact. Too many reduce impact because the individual is overwhelmed with information. A good yardstick is around four or five assertions;

(d) there must be a definite pause between each assertion, and before the invitational question. This enables each element to register and the trailer to have a cumulative impact;

(e) the question seeking an explanation must be either open-ended – *How do you account for that?* – or invitational – *Could you explain that change?*

Prepare your use of the trailer:

(a) the best way to put a trailer together is to write out the assertions and the question on a piece of paper with 'white space' between each element;

(b) rehearse your trailer aloud, delivering each element at a considered pace, with pauses;

571

(c) be prepared for blocking. Trailers are difficult to block. Individuals usually attempt to bluster or interrupt the staged delivery of your assertions. Mentally prepare yourself for disruptive talk, i.e. remind yourself that:

(i) you need to stop the assertion, let the individual stop talking, then finish the assertion;

(ii) you must not start the sequence or the interrupted assertion from scratch – just carry on.

Administrative preparations

Setting up the interview

Put yourself in the person's shoes. If you turn up out of the blue you must expect that the person has other commitments so that interviewing him or her straight away will be inappropriate. Even if the person agrees to be interviewed, it is important to establish if the person has any commitments or concerns that might divert attention away from the interview or distract him or her, e.g. children to collect from school, an appointment to be kept.

However, too great a warning may lead the person to decide not to be interviewed at all. You need to strike a fine balance. Sound the person out. Then make arrangements to conduct the interview as soon as possible.

Location

Wherever possible, interview a person on your 'ground' not theirs.

Whether the location is chosen by you, or you decide to accept an offer from the individual to find a location, try to get a room that is quiet, comfortable, well-lit, and is likely to be relatively free from interruption by others.

Be prepared to request other individuals:

- to keep noise to a minimum;
- not to interrupt you during the interview except in the case of an emergency.

Persons present

In some cases the individual may want to be accompanied by a friend or relative. If that person is involved in the case, you must arrange for someone 'neutral' to be present instead.

You must be prepared to advise the friend or relative about:

- confidentiality – an assurance must be given that he or she will not disclose the content of the interview to others;
- remembering his or her role – he or she should not take part in the interview, should not assume your role of asking questions, should not answer for the individual, and should not attempt to influence in any way the individual's responses.

Recording the interview

It is vital that any interview conducted by you (or by any employee or investigator instructed by you) must be above reproach, i.e. what you did and how must be manifestly accountable and open to scrutiny. You must be in a position to demonstrate to the court that:

* the interview was conducted properly – without pressure of any kind;
* the individual was participating of his or her own free will.

To ensure this, you, or those instructed by you, should carry out a set of simple procedures that provide safeguards akin to those provided in police interviews conducted under PACE.

Always record the interview

As obvious as it sounds, it is essential that you have a record of the interview:

* you should make a *full* documentary record;
* when it is practicable to do so, tape-record the interview. Inexpensive handheld or small book-size tape recorders with built-in condenser microphones are widely available and both run on batteries and have small mains adaptors. You should get a machine with the best microphone quality. This will require shopping around and comparison-testing. Use mains supply wherever possible since this avoids the risk of battery failure.

Give an assurance and obtain a declaration

You must explain to the person you wish to interview that for your joint protection:

* you wish to record the conversation between the two of you;
* you will undertake to provide the individual with a copy of the tape if he or she wishes – within a specified time frame;
* you will ask the individual at the end of the interview to sign a written declaration (which you have prepared in advance) to the effect that the interview was conducted properly without any pressure and that participation was totally voluntary.

Notes and tapes

You may have to produce the record of the interview in evidence.

So that your record will appear to be professional and carry weight in court, in the case of tape recording the interview, always use new cassette tapes wrapped and sealed in cellophane. This way you will not risk using a damaged tape or a tape with other material recorded on it.

Only ever use one side of a tape. This is an efficiency measure. When working on tapes and scanning for specific material, it is easier if the material is on one side rather than on both.

Prepare your interview 'kit'

Your interview 'kit' comprises the necessary equipment, items and materials for you to conduct the interview:

- a prompt sheet that sets out what needs to be covered at each phase of the interview;

- a prompt sheet that spells out:

  - the topics – that you will disclose as part of your explanation;

  - the objectives – the detailed subject-matter that you wish to cover under each topic and which, at the appropriate time in the interview, you may raise or perhaps even choose not to raise;

- a copy of your case chronology;

- SE3R sheets (or *RealSense* screen print-outs) for any key item, e.g. previous statement(s) made by the individual to be interviewed;

- photocopies of key items to which you intend to refer, e.g. statements, reports, extracts from pocket books, diagrams, maps, photography or a relevant video recording (for example taken by you of a location). For obvious reasons, you must never play recordings of interviews subject to disclosure caveats. Similarly, you must judge when it is appropriate to play a copy of a PACE tape;

- a full range of writing materials;

- cassette recorder, mains adaptor, spare batteries.

Arrange your paperwork

Shuffling through assorted papers in the interview in order to find a specific item to be referred to, creates an unprofessional impression and anxiety if you struggle or fail to find the item you require.

You must sort out your paperwork into the sequence in which you intend to use it.

Once sorted, place each item in a form of file that allows you to go straight to the item in order to present it for view either by showing, pointing to or removing it.

The best form of file is a Nyrex 'see through' folder, with plastic envelopes into which sheets, documents, diagrams, maps and the like can be slipped.

Use separate folders for documents, diagrams, photographs and maps. Simply mark the outside with a key word or words indicating the contents.

You can index and highlight the items within the folders with Post-it stickers.

Personal preparation

Mentally

Make sure you have a sound grasp of:

- your aim and your objectives;

- the case chronology;

- those aspects of the police case, the prosecution evidence and the police investigation that bear upon this individual and this interview;

- items to which you will be referring;

- your SE3R sheets (or **RealSense** printouts).

Read your prompt sheets, reminding yourself and rehearsing the taping preamble and how you will manage each phase of the interview.

Preparation of others

You need to be entirely clear as to what you expect of others who will be present and brief them accordingly.

It is a personal decision whether you wish to involve a colleague in the actual process of questioning. As a rule of thumb only one person should conduct an interview. The reasons for this are psychological and practical:

- *potential allegations of oppression.* Two people interviewing by continuously or rapidly switching the questioning role from one to the other could be construed as oppressive, particularly if there is no other person present to support the individual;

- *maintaining control.* It is hard enough to keep track of the individual's and your own thinking processes and to control your own pressures. You can do without additional sources of pressure, i.e. trying to second-guess what a colleague has in mind and to cope when he or she interrupts, breaks a pause you have created or talks at the same time as you; trying to regain the interviewing role if the colleague gets carried away; trying to put things right if the colleague makes inaccurate, inappropriate or alienating assertions.

If a colleague is to be present, your briefing should include:

- if he or she has not been involved thus far, a short background orientation to the case, the individual and any other person you expect to be present;

- your interview aim and objectives;

- your respective roles;

- what specific tasks you wish him or her to perform, e.g. taking notes;

Setting up the interview location

There is a practical as well as a psychological reason for carrying out an interview on your territory rather than in a residence or at the individual's place of work. You can set up the interview location with seating to achieve maximum rapport and working surfaces and materials to reduce distraction to a minimum.

Seating

Wherever possible place seats in a 10-to-2 orientation, with your seat either facing into the table or side on to the table. If you are right-handed, occupy the 2 o'clock position, with the person to your left at 10 o'clock, away from the table, sitting obliquely but looking towards you. If you are left-handed, you occupy the 10 o'clock position, the person the 2 o'clock.

This positioning allows you to operate the tape recorder, to write and to access materials (which will be either in front of you, or to your right – if you are right-handed, or to your left – if you are left-handed). It is also psychologically appropriate. Research has shown that people perceive oblique orientation to be collaborative and non-threatening. Face-to-face is felt to be confrontational and threatening. Side by side is very difficult to control, since the person is able to look at what you are doing or referring to.

Working surface

Make sure that the working surface is free of distractions, i.e. there is nothing other than the tape recorder, your files, and the materials you wish to use and refer to.

CONDUCTING THE INTERVIEW

You need a structure that enables you to manage the exchange, i.e. the process or conduct of the interview and ensures you communicate empathy and confidence, and do not miss out anything. A simple five-stage structure is: greeting, explanation, monitor/assert; close.

Explanation

Reason

Give an explicit, straightforward, relatively short reason for the interview. This will necessarily reflect your aim, e.g.

> *I'd like to interview you to find out what you know about the incident which happened in the White Hart on Friday evening.*

Route map

The route map is your 'agenda' for the interview. State this simply and explicitly, pausing after each topic, e.g.

> *In this interview I'd like to ask you for your version of what happened, (pause) then about how you came to give a statement on the Saturday, (pause) and to give a second statement on the following Monday. (pause)*

As you spell out each topic and pause, look closely at the person's non-verbal response. Be on the look-out for changes in behaviour, for signs of stress when a particular topic is mentioned.

If the person interrupts, stop talking, wait for the interruption to cease, acknowledge the interruption, request that you be allowed to finish, and state you will ask for the person's views later on, e.g.

> *I can see you have strong views on that matter. Please let me finish what I want to say. You will have the chance to have your say then.*

Spelling out the route map is a fundamental aid to both the management of the interview and the management of exchange of information across the interview. If, during the course of the interview, the person digresses or seeks to change the topic that you intend to cover somewhat later, you need only acknowledge the disclosure and use your route map to bring him or her on course, e.g.

> *I see that. What you say fits in with what I want to cover later on. You remember that at the beginning of this interview I explained what I want to ask you about. Can I ask you to hang on to what you want to say on that matter at the moment. Let's 'put it on the back burner' as they say. Returning to what I was asking about...*

Routines

The individual needs to know:

- that you (or any colleague with you) will be:
  - taking notes (entering detail on your computer) and referring to what are in effect exhibit items, e.g. SE3R sheets or **RealSense** screen print-outs, documents, diagrams, photographs;
  - (where practicable) tape recording the interview – giving the individual a copy of the tape;
- how you will be requesting detail. (The individual may be anticipating a 'question–answer' session (rather like the kind of performances seen on television dramas. This is not professional interviewing. The individual needs to be told how the process will unfold.)
- the role of others present, e.g. a friend accompanying the person;

Simply explain what actions will be carried out by yourself and others present, e.g.

> *During the interview I'll need to take notes (put details on my computer) at some time. I might have to refer to some information and other items I have here (points to notes and exhibit items). You will see I have a tape recorder here in order to record the interview. Please don't worry. I will give you a copy of the tape.*

> *It will help both of us if you give me information in stages. First of all, I'll ask you to tell me your version of things and when you are doing this I'll just listen – I won't take notes at that stage. When you've finished, I'll ask you to go over it again, and when you do, I'll take down the detail.*

> *Your friend who you've asked to be present is here to support you but she knows she must not answer for you or put words in your mouth.*

Expectations

It is essential to spell out expectations, i.e. what the individual can expect of you and what you expect of the individual, e.g.

> *During this interview I will give you plenty of time to think about my questions and about your answers. Please do not rush to answer. Take your time.*

> *For my part I will not interrupt you when you are talking except if I miss or I don't understand something. I might also interrupt to ask you to draw something if I think that might help. I would appreciate it if you would not interrupt me*

577

when I am talking except please let me know if you don't understand anything I say or ask.

Thus the individual is aware of the ground rules. There will be no pressure to reply rapidly. He or she will get a fair hearing and can let on when he or she wishes to make a point or make a request.

Two expectations are a fundamental aid to managing the exchange of information across the interview: except for purposes of clarification, neither should interrupt when the other is speaking; and silence will occur – it is not a source of pressure, rather it is to think about what has been said and what will be said.

Check comprehension

In your explanation you will have covered a lot of ground. It is sensible and ethical to check back if the person has any queries, doubts or anxieties. Always invite feedback, e.g.

> *That's quite a lot I've covered. Do you have any questions about why I'm here, (pause) what I want to cover, (pause) what I'll be doing (pause) and what we can expect of each other? (pause).*

Always answer questions. You will, of course, have to adjust your reply to the circumstances. Don't get bogged down in detail on topics to be covered in the interview. If the person asks about the topics, simply repeat these and explain that you will cover them in detail when you come to them.

Monitor and assert phase

This phase is the 'heart' of your investigative interview. Here, you seek to achieve your objectives by a dual process of:

*   ***monitoring***: listening to and observing closely the individual's spontaneous and considered communication – verbal and non-verbal – particularly in response to assertions by you;
*   ***assertions by you***: your questions, comments, observations and disclosures concerning critical detail.

The process of tape recording reinforces the fact that you accept your interviewing practice is open to assessment and must observe good interviewing practices. This means being a reflective practitioner – thinking consciously about what you are doing and how you are doing it. You need to be aware of ***appropriate questions*** and ***appropriate questioning behaviour*** – how best to elicit, and to work with, information.

Appropriate questions: the qualities of a good question

Good questions reflect awareness of the necessity to bear in mind moral, legal and practical issues when asking a given individual of a recognisable make-up and state of mind about a particular set of material circumstances with a bearing upon the police case, the prosecution evidence and the police investigation. Table 1 summarises the qualities of a good question.

Ethical	Respectful; not oppressive, hectoring, threatening, insulting, embarrassing, belittling or demeaning.
Truthful	Not mendacious; not attributing to the person something he or she has not said or done.
Purposeful	Directed towards a specific purpose.
Truly inquiring	Seeking new information; testing earlier or other information; checking on comprehension and how the person is coping with, and feels about, the questioning process.
Relevant	Bearing upon the issue.
Empathetic	Sensibly and sensitively pitched choice of words and length and construction of sentences mindful of the person's: • emotional, mental and motivational state; • level of intellect and development; • language use (= clue to expressive ability).
Comprehensible	Clear, unambiguous, not 'all over the place'.
Brief	Concise, straightforward, to the point, not long-winded or rambling, not multiple (i.e. not several questions rolled into one).

Table 1   Qualities of a good question

Productive, risky and counter-productive questions

All questions contain information – what is in the questioner's mind. Questions differ as to the extent to which they communicate the questioner's underlying beliefs, attitudes, motivation and even feelings. The more a question indicates these, the less productive it is as a means of finding out objective information:

- *productive questions* are objective, neutral and not at all suggestive. They increase the likelihood of disclosure of new and spontaneous information;

- *risky questions* invite confirmation: a yes or no reply. They drastically narrow the response options of the individual. Although the questioner does not intend them to be suggestive, they are nonetheless suggestive. People do not like to disagree and will go to great lengths to please, to keep on the right side of, or to be 'helpful' by agreeing unquestioningly with what is put to them. Research has shown that people are more disposed to say 'yes' rather than 'no'. People who lack assertion skills, people who are particularly prone to acquiesce (females, ethnic minorities and the range of vulnerable people as defined by PACE), people who are compliant by nature and people who distrust their memories, are particularly disposed to agree rather than disagree. In sum, whether the person knows his or her answer to be untrue or does not know either way, the risk is the same: creating false testimony;

- **counter-productive questions** are far from neutral. Their content is overtly biased, directive and markedly suggestive. Often there is a clear emotional appeal or pressure. They not only point, they apply pressure on the person to accept and go along with what the questioner is proposing. The same vulnerabilities that apply with risky questions apply with counter-productive questions but very much more so. Those who lack assertion skills, are prone to acquiesce, are compliant by nature, and who distrust their memories are particularly at risk of creating false testimony.

Table 2 lists productive, risky and counter-productive question forms.

Appropriate questioning behaviour

Appropriate questioning behaviour implies following a number of simple, basic ground rules for eliciting as much information as possible and processing disclosed detail.

1. **Pacing**. Listen to any reasonably extended question-answer sequence and the questioner's pacing – the rate at which questions are posed and replies are responded to – and variations to this are readily detected. The questioner creates the tempo of the conversation.

   Everyday conversation is a remarkably quick-fire exchange. In contrast, conversation in an interview should be significantly slower, to afford respect for the individual involved, to be considerate to what he or she has in, and on, his or her mind, and to facilitate the tasks of collecting thoughts, recall and disclosure, which may be extremely difficult or painful.

   Appropriate interview pacing:

   - creates an unpressured atmosphere – for the questioner and the individual;
   - motivates the individual because the questioner is manifestly respectful and attending;
   - produces more information, in more detail;
   - gives the questioner more time to observe the individual and the effects of a given question or cumulative questions.

	Question form	Examples
Productive	Open-ended opener	*So what happened?; What did you do between ... and...?*
	Open-ended probe	*What makes you say that?*
	Invitation	*Could you tell me...?*
	Statement, observation, comment + pause	*I've read the statement you made to the police. (pause); A number of people say they saw the incident. (pause); It's a long time since you spoke to the police. (pause)*
	Simple interrogative	Identification: *What?; Who?; When?;* Explanation/justification: *How?; Why?; Why not?*
	Echo probe (= repetition of key words in the person's reply) (Encourages continued disclosure.)	Reply: *I didn't know what to do. The man kept on hitting him.* Echo: *Hitting him?* Reply: *Mm. First with his fist then with ... a block of wood, I think.*
	Mirror (= repetition of the person's reply) (Encourages continued disclosure.)	Reply: *Blood everywhere. I checked he was still alive.* Mirror: *You checked he was still alive?* Reply: *Yes. I felt the pulse in his neck.*
	Reflection	*It seems that...*
	Summary	*So according to you...*
	Supportive statement	*That's interesting.; I see.;*
	Non-verbal noise	*Uh-huh. Mm.*
	Non-verbal movement	Nodding (= sign of following); expression of concern
	Pause	
Risky	Closed yes/no (Invites confirmation.)	*Did you...? Has she...?*
Counter-productive	Suggestive (Provides information which does not come from the person.)	*Where was the **red** van when all this happened?; What about the **black** one – what did he do?*
	Option	*Was she at home or at work?*
	Leading	*Didn't he...? Isn't it the case that...? Did he **really**...?*
	Multiple (= successive questions without a pause)	*You went to the farm? Did you go upstairs? Or did they stay downstairs? Where was the car parked?*
	Question – provide answer	*Where were you last night? You were seen at the Red Lion and then at Bubbles Disco.*

Table 2 Productive, risky and counter-productive question forms

Inappropriate interview pacing:

- generates rapid fire questioning – which quickly degenerates into a stream of risky or counter-productive questions;

- puts pressure on the individual – who more often than not 'closes down', alienated and silenced by the stream of questions;

- assists the individual who was already unmotivated to disclose – given little time to say anything enables him or her to say little or nothing;

- puts pressure on the questioner – creating the real risk of gabbling and rapid and cumulative exhaustion.

2. **Pausing**. In the *explanation* phase, you pointed out that you would give the individual plenty of time to think about your questions and plenty of time to think about his or her answers.

You promised to 'pose and pause' and to 'listen and pause'. If you keep in mind the following points, it will help you to keep this promise:

- when you ask a question you pass the talking turn to the other person;

- you are likely to be under some pressure, e.g. anxiety, a desire to get things right, to find out as much as possible, time constraints. Such pressures are the most common cause for a questioner taking back the talking turn when the person has not replied immediately or is taking time to think before replying. Questioners frequently misjudge lapsed time, such that they think the silence to be much longer than is really the case. When a questioner poses a question, fails to wait for a reply and starts talking again this is called 'filling the pause';

- a common form of filling the pause is the open–closed question sequence, e.g.

    What did you do on Friday night? (Little or no pause) Did you go to the cinema?

Open–closed sequences are very common – particularly when adults are talking to children;

- multiple questions are the counter-productive outcome of successively filling the pause. In effect, the questioner is not posing questions to be answered. Rather he or she is 'thinking out loud', verbalising his or her remembrance of the sequence of events;

- the response to a question is in two parts. The first part is the time taken by the person to register and to think about the question, and any accompanying non-verbal behaviour. The second part is the reply – the verbal utterance and any non-verbal behaviour;

- you need to make a careful note of the first part and then the second part;

- in effect, any question 'buys' time to pause: for the person to think, and for you to listen, to look and to think. The amount of time bought is linked to the amount of information likely to be generated by the question.

If you pose a productive form of question much more pausing time is bought because the reply will be notionally of some length. Any productive question merits some three to five, if not more, seconds' pause according to the amount of information you aspire to in the reply. For instance, if you pose a parameter question – *What did you do between the time you went into the Halifax until you gave a statement to the police?* – the period covered will be far from short. Similarly, an explanation or justification implies a fair degree of antecedent thought before the person starts talking.

If you ask a risky closed confirmatory (yes/no) question you buy very little pausing time.

Counter-productive and leading questions are pre-emptive and pressuring. They are alien to pausing. Another reason for not using them!

- when a person stops talking it does not mean that he or she has decided to pass back to you. It may be that he or she is pausing for thought, taking breath, or both. The only way you will ever know is to say nothing. So say nothing, just pause;

- even if the person has decided to stop talking for the moment and looks straight at you indicating he or she is passing the talking turn back to you, you do not have to take the talking turn. Give the talking turn straight back. Look the person in the eyes – *don't stare* – and pause. This is why a pause is a productive form of question;

- questioners who are under some pressure feel they are neither ready, willing or able to sit it out and give the talking turn back, experiencing the silence to be increasingly stressful. Just hold on. Nine times out of 10 the person will start talking again.

3. ***Referring to notes and other material.*** Never look down at notes or other material when speaking. Look at the individual.

If you need to refer to notes or other material stop speaking and give your full attention to studying the material.

4. ***Obtaining a first account.*** Use a productive opener question to generate the fullest possible first account. This account will be either a ***narrative*** – rather like a saga – ***or disclosures on the topic*** raised in your question, e.g. a state of affairs, a relationship, a routine, a description.

> *I'd like you to tell me everything you can remember about what happened from the time you went into the Halifax up until the police arrived. Please include as much detail as you can possibly remember, even the tiny bits you may not think are important – they may be. Take your time. There is no rush. If you slow down, or stop from time to time, this will help you to remember.*

> *As I said earlier, I won't take notes while you tell me what you remember. I'll just listen. I promise I won't interrupt unless it is absolutely necessary.*

As the person gives this account your task is to concentrate on capturing what he or she is saying. We strongly recommend that you do not attempt to take notes. The aim is for you to image what he or she is saying. You will have an opportunity later to take notes and, given that you are tape-recording you can always check out later what the person has said in this first pass.

The result will be a coherent understanding and a good recall of what has been said.

The first account is bound to include:

- new detail about identities (people, places, things, settings) and episodes (actions, reactions) about which you know little or nothing;

- anomalous detail – gaps, ambiguities, vagueness and contradictions with other accounts by this individual, another or others.

There is a strong pressure to stop the account in order to probe new and anomalous detail. You must resist this.

Interrupting and over-talking (talking at the same time) is ill-mannered and the mark of a poor listener. However, there are sound psychological and practical reasons for not interrupting to probe new or anomalous detail across an account:

- it sidetracks the individual and you;
- it disrupts the process of telling, as the individual stops and starts;
- it renders the account incoherent as you hop from one topic to another;
- it frustrates and demotivates the individual, who struggles to keep track, to pick up where he or she left off. With each interruption, he or she will be disposed to say less and less.

Interrupting thus becomes self-defeating for you. You will not get the fullest possible account you were seeking and you will have bogged yourself down in detail, such that you emerge with a poor overall grasp and will remember much less.

There are only four circumstances when interruption is constructive. All of them you will have covered in your *explanation*:

- when you have not heard something;
- when something is ambiguous and needs explanation, e.g. a word, name or action that needs to be expanded. An example of the latter would be:

  (Witness) and then it looked like the man raped her...

  (You) Raped her... (echo probe)

  (Witness) Yeah, he pushed her down on the ground, tore her skirt away and laid on top of her.

- when the individual starts to give a verbal description of a location, individual or object. This is the appropriate time to get the best form of description – a diagram or drawing – since this can be referred to, modified, elaborated and used evidentially at some time in the future.

Thank the individual when he or she has finished giving his or her account and explain that you need a few moments to think about what he or she has said.

5. *Obtaining a second account*. This constitutes your second pass at processing the detail of the individual's account.

   As I said earlier, I'd like you to go over things for a second time. This time I will be taking notes (putting detail into my computer). As I am taking down detail, I will need to slow you down and to stop you from time to time – that's because people speak hundreds of words a minute but can only write fifteen or so words a minute. Please be patient.

   So, please tell me again everything you can remember about what happened from the time you went into the Halifax up until the police arrived. As I said before, include as much detail as you can possibly remember, even the tiny bits you may not think are important – they may be. Take your time. There is no rush. If you slow down, or stop from time to time, this will help you to remember.

As the person gives this account, your task is to regulate the rate of disclosure. This comes with practice. You will recall that the SE3R method (applied manually or using *RealSense* on the computer) captures the narrative as episodes, each a stem on the line, describing a single step or event. It is not a bad idea to stop the individual after he or she has described a single step, e.g.

> *Can I stop you there a moment ... (make a note, or enter the detail on your SE3R, or enter the detail into your RealSense screen on your computer).*

People very quickly get the idea and actually pace themselves. You will find that they describe a step – a 'chunk' of information – and then stop automatically to allow you to take the detail down. You merely have to set them going again with a minimal prompt, e.g.

> *You were saying...*

Of course, you will need to stop the individual at any point where it is necessary to obtain a sketch or drawing. The result will be an extremely full record of what the individual has said.

Thank the individual when this second pass is completed.

6. ***Probing***. Prepare for probing by systematically reviewing the detail that you have written down, entered on the SE3R or entered into the *RealSense* screens on your computer.

- compare what is there, and any diagrams or drawings with:
  - the detail of the image you created in working memory when you listened to the individual's first account;
  - the relevant parts of the case chronology;
  - the SE3R sheets or *RealSense* print-out you have prepared from any previous accounts given by this individual;
  - if he or she has given no previous account, the SE3R sheets or *RealSense* print-out you have prepared of accounts by one or more key witnesses;
- annotate your notes and SE3R – ticking points of correspondence and using your own form of shorthand, abbreviations or symbols to highlight gaps, anomalies, contradictions and significant new material; if you are using *RealSense* use the assigned letters on the keyboard to do this annotation;
- review your annotations. Note areas that require probing in detail. These are new objectives;
- scan your interview objectives. See that of these have been covered. Note which have and have not.

Probing can take the form of requests for repetition or expansion, or focused questioning:

- ***Repetition***

Requesting a repetition is a particularly useful form of probing, e.g.

> *That's a lot of detail. It would be a great help if you could go over that again. This time, can I ask you to take things a little more slowly so that I can take some notes.*

For a narrative: use a different-coloured pen or pencil. Tick detail that corresponds, insert new and anomalous detail.

For disclosure of detail on a topic: use the second column of your note book, wherever possible aligning notes on corresponding subject-matter.

Compare the two accounts and engage in further probing.

- **Expansion**

After the first or the second account, expansion is necessary. If it is a narrative or a substantial amount of disclosure on a topic it is sensible to break this down into smaller chunks for expansion, e.g.

> *It would be helpful if we could concentrate on the time between the men running in (pause) and the time when you heard the shotgun go off. (Pause) Could you go over that in as much detail as possible? (Pause) Again take your time. (Pause) There's no rush.*

Make notes of the expansion in the same way as for repetition. Compare the accounts and engage in focused probing.

- **Focused questioning**

With focused questioning, you focus on the detail of a reply, concentrating upon and using the detail to form the content of your question. It can be a question aimed at uncovering more detail or securing an explanation or justification.

Focused questioning underlines a fact of life in respect of investigative interviewing: wherever possible questions should be born of answers. Too many questioners fail to listen to answers. They are too busy – anxiously dreaming up the next question. This behaviour gives rise to topic-hopping, moving rapidly and unaccountably from one issue to another. This can be extremely disruptive and disconcerting for an individual who fails to follow the questioner's logic.

The additional benefit of using the detail of answers to frame questions is that probing becomes a coherent, searching activity as events or disclosures on a topic are systematically examined.

Guides to focused probing will be: your notes, SE3R sheets or **RealSense** screens, diagrams, photography and outstanding items on your list of interviewing objectives.

7. **Summarising**. Summarising has a number of benefits:

- it allows the individual to confirm, modify and add detail;
- it signals to the individual that you are really listening;
- it helps to consolidate your memory, and overall comprehension, of what the individual has said.

Summarising occurs in two forms: stage summarising and making a final summary:

- *Stage summarising*: after a run of focused probing – and certainly when you feel you have reached the limits of your ability to remember the sum of replies to a series of focused questions – you must summarise. Let the person know you are about to do this and that you want feedback, e.g.

> *Right. Let's check out what you've said so far. Come back at me if you want to add or to change something. You said...*

Your summary must be accurate and inclusive. Wherever possible, use the words and phraseology used by the individual.

Stage summarising is a very professional way of moving the interviewee from one topic on your 'route map' to the next. This process is called the *interview spiral*:

- *open up a topic* – using a productive opener question;
- *probe* the topic – repetition, expansion, focused probing;
- *summarise* – to confirm, modify or add disclosures;
- *link* to the next topic – using a suitable bridging assertion;
- *open* up the next topic.

- *Final summary*: reading from your notes, or your SE3R sheets, or your *RealSense* screens, you take the individual through the entire run of detail he or she has disclosed. When you reach a point where, say the individual has given two versions, do not confront him or her baldly with the fact that this has happened. Be subtle, e.g.

  You got to the counter ... I'm not clear what happened then ... Could you take me over that again?

  Note down the detail of this reply. This is the version that the individual is committing himself or herself to. If it is at variance to an earlier or earlier versions, this is evidentially significant.

  As with stage summaries, your final summary must be accurate and try to use the words and phraseology used by the individual.

Close

Forward focus

Explain to the individual that you will use the tape recording and your notes to prepare a statement. You will give this to him or her for approval, amendments or additions. After any amendments and additions have been made, he or she will be asked to sign the statement.

Copy of the recording

If you have tape-recorded the interview, point out that the individual can have a copy of the recording if he or she wishes.

Declaration

Give the individual the declaration. The wording of the declaration is a matter of personal and professional preference within your practice. The important point is that it should *minimally* state:

- the name, address and contact details of your practice;
- who conducted the interview;
- who was interviewed;
- who else was present;
- where the interview took place;
- the date of the interview;

- that the interview was conducted properly without any pressure, or words to this effect;
- that the individual's participation was totally voluntary, or words to this effect;
- the interview started at (time entered in blank);
- the declaration was signed at (time entered in blank).

The declaration must be signed by the individual and must be counter-signed by you and by all other persons present.

Final actions

Thank the individual and, if you are tape-recording, turn off the tape at the end of your discussions.

Use one of the self-adhesive labels that are contained in all tape cassettes. Stick this to the side which you have just recorded.

Changing tape

Optimally, you should note the time as the interview progresses such that you stop the tape shortly before it comes to the end of the spool. If you do this you simply need to state that the tape is almost ended, that you need to change tapes, say the time aloud and stop the tape.

If the tape runs out:

- make a note of the time;
- rewind the tape for a short section;
- make a note in your notebook of the last utterance or a suitable number of words (e.g. some 5–10) leading up to the cessation of taping.

AFTER THE INTERVIEW

If you tape-recorded the interview, remove the safety lugs from the tape cassettes.

When the interviewee has gone, when you are back at your own location, process the tape:

- make notes, or an SE3R, or **RealSense** screens of the first individual's first account, i.e. the first pass to which you listened but during which you did not take down details;
- compare this version with the second pass, the probing pass and the final-summary pass – annotating any anomalies;
- have the tape recording transcribed;
- make a copy of the tape to give to the individual (as you promised you would).

Analyse the interview using the methods described in Chapter 8.

Produce a statement by:

- drafting a text incorporating the detail of your notes, the SE3R sheets or the *RealSense* screens;
- have the draft typed up or word-processed;
- check the accuracy of the statement.

ACCEPTANCE OF THE STATEMENT

Give the individual the statement, asking him or her to check its contents in detail, to amend as necessary (initialling any amendments) and then sign and date the document. You (or whoever is presenting the draft statement for checking, amendment and signature) must witness the individual's signature.

You should also give the individual his or her copy of the tape.

APPENDIX 9

Forensic glossary

Prepared by Dr Richard Shepherd

The aim of this glossary is to provide you with ready access to simple definitions of common terms you may find in forensic reports.

If you need further information or a term is missing you will need to consult a good medical dictionary.

Abdomen	Area of body below the ribs and above the pelvis. Contains abdominal organs – liver, bowel, etc.
Abortion	Expulsion of a foetus; can be spontaneous (miscarriage), therapeutic or criminal.
Abrasion	An injury to the skin involving the outer surface (epidermis) only. Commonly termed a scratch or a graze. Abrasions are caused by contact by or against a blunt object and are one of the triad of injuries caused by blunt force. (See contusion and laceration.)
Abscess	Collection of pus.
Acetaminophen	American name for paracetamol.
Acidosis	Raised level of acidity in the blood. Can be caused by many diseases including diabetes. Raised acidity is reflected in a low pH value. Normal blood pH is 7.4.
Acquired Immunodeficiency Syndrome (AIDS)	A disease complex developing as a result of infection with the HIV virus. AIDS is the terminal phase of HIV infection and is almost universally fatal although a few cases survive for many years.
Acute Tubular Necrosis	Damage to the kidneys usually caused as a result of a period of low blood pressure. Many cases are treatable with medical support (dialysis).

Adipocere	An unusual type of change seen in the fat of decomposing bodies that have been lying in wet conditions. The fat instead of degenerating forms a hard greasy substance.
Adipose tissue	Fat.
Adrenal	Glands lying above each kidney which are responsible for the production of adrenalin and a group of chemicals known as steroids which have profound effects on the normal metabolism of the body.
Adrenalin	Hormone produced by the medulla of the adrenal glands. The effects of adrenalin are to prepare the body for strenuous exercise. This hormone results in an increase in heart rate and blood pressure. Sometimes called 'Fight or Flight' hormone.
Adult Respiratory Distress Syndrome (ARDS)	Syndrome causing failure of the exchange of oxygen in the lungs. Can be caused by many severe infections, inhalation of irritant gases, etc. Treated by ventilation at high pressure.
Afferent	Going towards a central part or area.
AIDS	See Acquired Immunodeficiency Syndrome.
AIDS-related complex	Group of symptoms and signs in individuals with HIV infection. A precursor of true AIDS.
Air embolism	Blockage of arteries (usually of the brain) by bubbles of air. Most often caused by injury to the veins of the neck. Bubbles of air may also be found in the right ventricle of the heart.
Alveoli	Smallest component of the lung; site of exchange of gases between inspired air and the blood.
Amino acid	Basic building blocks of proteins. There are 20 different amino acids only in the human body. Some can be manufactured by the body, others (the essential amino acids) have to be ingested in protein in the diet.
Amitriptyline	Antidepressant drug.
Amnesia	Loss of memory. May be permanent or temporary. Caused by disease or trauma.
Amniotic fluid	Fluid which surrounds the growing foetus/baby.
Anaemia	Reduced level of haemoglobin in the blood, can be caused by many diseases or by lack of specific vitamins.

Anaesthetic	Drugs used to induce states of unconsciousness.
Analgesic	Drugs used to suppress the sensation of pain.
Aneurysm	A weakness in the wall of a blood vessel, usually an artery. May be congenital or the result of disease or trauma. May rupture and cause sudden death.
Angiography	The examination of blood vessels, usually arteries, using imaging techniques (X Ray, MRI, Ultrasound etc). May involve the injection of a substance that can be easily seen with the imaging technique employed.
Anoxia	Complete lack of oxygen. This may be applied to the body as a whole or to a group of cells within the body.
Anterior	The front of the body, limb, organ, etc.
Anuria	Failure to produce any urine.
Anus	Terminal portion of the intestines. Contains a complex group of muscles to control defecation.
Aorta	Main artery of the body. Originates from the left ventricle of the heart, passes over the left lung and then descends on the back wall of the body in front of the spine. Other arteries of the body originate from the aorta to supply the organs and tissues.
Apnoea	Cessation of breathing.
Arachnoid	The middle of the three coverings of the brain (meninges).
ARC	See AIDS-related complex.
Arcus senilis	Curved whitish discolouration of the margin of the pupil of the eye, most commonly seen in the upper and lower sections. Associated with old age or high cholesterol levels.
ARDS	See Adult Respiratory Distress Syndrome.
Arrhythmia	Absence of cardiac rhythm.
Asphyxia	Lack of oxygen to the cells of the body caused by lack of oxygen in the inspired air, obstruction of the external or internal airways, inability of the blood to carry or of the cells to utilise oxygen. Forensically equated with strangulation, etc.
Asphyxiation	The act of inducing asphyxia.

Aspiration

1. To remove abnormal collection of fluid from an area of the body.
2. The entry of foreign bodies or material (esp. vomit) into the airways.

Asthma

Allergic response of the air passages to specific substances or materials which results in constriction of the air passages and the production of thick mucus leading to a decreased ability to breathe.

Atheroma

The fatty material deposited into the walls of arteries leading to blockage and weakness of the arterial wall. Associated with thrombosis, myocardial infarction and development of aneurysms.

Atlanto-occipital

Junction of the bones of the neck and the base of the skull.

Atlas

Uppermost bone of the neck, lies immediately below the skull.

ATN

See Acute Tubular Necrosis.

Atrium

The upper, smaller chambers of each side of the heart which receive blood from the veins and, at the correct time, force it into the ventricles of the heart ready to be pumped into the lungs (right ventricle) or around the body (left ventricle).

Atrophy

Grow smaller usually through disuse or lack of blood supply.

Autoerotic

Solitary sexual practices, may be associated with deliberately induced partial asphyxia.

Autolysis

Breakdown of cells usually as a result of cell death, may involve the whole body or a single part.

Autonomic nervous system

The nervous system of the body that is not in conscious control; it has two opposing parts – the sympathetic and parasympathetic systems.

Autopsy

Post mortem examination.

Axon

The part of a nerve cell that extends to connect and carry messages to another nerve cell or a muscle cell.

Back

Area of body below neck and above buttocks.

Bacteraemia

Bacteria present in the blood stream.

593

Bacteria Micro-organisms, usually single cells, which have their own metabolism. Some are associated with diseases, others are present in the human body without causing disease (commensal).

Barbiturates Group of sedative drugs. Now seldom used because of the risk of addiction.

Barotrauma Injury to internal organs caused by sudden and rapid changes in environmental pressure, e.g. explosions.

Basal ganglia Part of the brain.

Basilar artery Artery on the base of the brain formed from the junction of the two vertebral arteries and leading to the arteries forming the Circle of Willis.

Battered baby Deliberately injured child (child abuse).

Benign Usually used in reference to tumours to indicate a lack of malignant potential.

Benzodiazepines Group of sedative drugs, the most common of which are Valium (diazepam), Temazepam and Mogadon (nitrazepam). Some are now associated with addiction and abuse.

Berry aneurysm Weakness in the wall of an artery at the base of the brain believed to be caused by a congenital defect. Can rupture spontaneously causing a subarachnoid haemorrhage which may be fatal.

Bile Yellow/green fluid produced by the liver. Contains chemical to aid digestion of fat in the bowel. Also contains some of the degraded toxic chemicals that have been removed from the blood by the liver.

Bite Injury caused by the mouth and/or teeth of an assailant. Often has a crescent or curved appearance and may contain indentations or bruises caused by the teeth which can be used to compare with the dental chart of the suspect.

Black eye Bruising around some or all of the circumference of an eye socket. Commonly associated with direct blunt trauma to the eye but can also be associated with trauma to the bridge of the nose or fractures of the base of the skull.

Bladder A hollow organ used for the storage of fluid. Two types are present in humans: the urinary bladder for the storage of urine and the gall bladder which is for the storage of bile.

Blast

A short episode of high pressure usually caused by an explosion, commonly followed by a shorter period of lowered pressure. Can cause barotrauma.

Bleeding

Leakage of blood caused by damage to blood vessels by trauma, disease, etc.

Blisters

Collection of fluid derived from blood which lies below the outermost layer of the skin (epidermis). Caused by diseases and many types of trauma, particularly heat and electrical. Also associated with hypothermia and barbiturate poisoning.

Blood

A complex mixture of fluid, chemicals, nutrients and cells required to sustain life.

Blowflies

Bluebottles, greenbottles and other sarcophageous flies. Their maggots and pupae can be used to assist in the determination of the time of death in cases of advanced decomposition.

Blunt force

See Blunt injuries.

Blunt injuries

Term used to describe the group of three types of injury caused by blunt objects: abrasions (grazes), contusions (bruises) and lacerations. Many objects may act as blunt weapons. The largest is the ground, the most common is the fist.

Bondage

The use of restraints as part of sexual behaviour.

Bone

A solid structure in the body which forms part of the skeleton and which provides points of attachment for muscles. Formed from a complex matrix of calcium. Despite its hard structure it is being continually remodelled.

Bradycardia

Slow heart rate.

Brain

Major part of the central nervous system (CNS). Contained within the skull and covered by meninges. Divided into two main parts: cerebrum and cerebellum. Connected to the spinal cord by the brain stem.

Brain death

Complete absence of any functional activity in the brain. Diagnosed after a specified series of neurological tests have been performed at least twice and the effects of drugs, alcohol, hypothermia, etc. have been excluded.

Brain stem	Part of the brain which connects the main neurological areas with the spinal cord. Also contains the controlling centres for respiration and heart rate (vital centres).
Brittle Bone Disease	A group of congenital abnormalities that each result in abnormally fragile bones leading to multiple fractures in children. May lead to the erroneous suggestion of child abuse.
Bronchopneumonia	Infection of the lungs which commonly results in the production of purulent sputum. Common in elderly or unconscious patients. May cause death but is also a common terminal event in individuals with other serious diseases.
Bruise	See Contusion.
Bullets	Projectiles fired singly from rifled weapons.
Burns	Injury caused by either wet or dry heat. Three degrees of severity: First = outer surface of skin only; Second = full thickness of skin; Third = deeper tissues as well. Surface area of body affected calculated by Rule of Nines.
Cachexia	Emaciation due to lack of sufficient nutrition for a prolonged period. Can also be seen in individuals with malignancy or other serious diseases even when receiving adequate nutrition.
Cadaveric spasm	Extremely rare form of *rigor mortis* which is of instantaneous onset, said to be associated with traumatic death following exertion.
Café coronary	Type of sudden death due to impaction of a mass (bolus) of food, commonly poorly chewed meat, in the throat. Associated with alcohol intoxication.
Caffey's Syndrome	Syndrome first described by Dr Caffey, a radiologist, who noted multiple fractures of varying age in children. Initially thought to be due to disease, now known to be a feature of child abuse.
Calcification	Deposition of calcium in the tissues of the body.
Callus	A band of cartilage and new bone which forms around the site of a fracture during healing. Can be aged (within broad time bands) by X-Ray.
Calvarium	Top of the skull.

Capillary	Smallest type of blood vessel in the body, only visible under a microscope. Walls are one cell thick and allow for exchange of oxygen, nutrients and waste products with the tissues.
Carbon dioxide	Normal constituent of air, also produced by the body as a result of metabolism.
Carbon monoxide	Poisonous gas without smell or taste. Attaches very firmly to haemoglobin in the red blood cells and prevents the carriage of oxygen causing hypoxia of the tissues (especially the brain) which may lead to death.
Carboxyhaemoglobin	Haemoglobin which is linked to carbon monoxide, often written as HbCO.
Cardiac arrest	Cessation of detectable heart beat.
Cardiac massage	Manual compression of the chest to maintain blood circulation. Sometimes called external cardiac massage (ECM).
Cardiac tamponade	A condition where the sac which surrounds the heart (pericardium) is filled with fluid or blood which restricts the movement of the heart and causes decreased cardiac function.
Cardiomyopathy	A group of diseases of the muscle of the heart other than those caused by the blockage of the coronary arteries. Some cardiomyopathies are inherited, others are acquired as a result of viral infection, alcohol abuse or other causes. Can cause sudden death.
Carotid arteries	Main arteries supplying blood to the head and neck. One on each side of the neck just to the side of the throat and trachea.
Carotid sinus	Specialised area of the carotid arteries that are sensitive to and involved in the control of blood pressure.
Catecholamines	A group of chemicals which have an effect similar to adrenalin and cause an increase in heart rate and blood pressure.
Cerebral	Relating to the brain.
Cerebral hemispheres	The two halves of the cerebrum.
Cerebrospinal fluid (CSF)	A clear fluid produced in specialised cells in the ventricles of the brain and which circulates through the ventricles and over the surface of the brain. CSF is involved in the protection of the brain and meninges from infection.

Cervical	1. Relating to the neck. 2. Relating to the cervix.
Cervix	The neck of the uterus (womb). Lies at the junction of the uterus and the top of the vagina.
Chest	Area of the body below the neck and above the abdomen, contains heart and lungs in a rigid cage formed by the ribs.
Child abuse	Infliction of injury, usually over a period of time, on a child or infant. May be physical, sexual or psychological.
Choking	Accidental or deliberate obstruction of the upper airways leading to asphyxiation.
Chromosome	Specific groupings of the DNA of the individual which are organised into 23 pairs of chromosomes, one of each pair being inherited from the mother and one from the father. There are tens of thousands of individual genes on each chromosome.
Chronic bronchitis	Repetitive infections of the bronchi associated with production of large quantities of sputum.
Chronic obstructive airway disease	A complex group of chronic inflammatory and infective diseases of the lungs which includes chronic bronchitis and emphysema. Often called COAD.
Circle of Willis	A group of linked arteries at the base of the brain.
Circumcision	In the male – removal of the foreskin of the penis. In the female – surgical removal of the clitoris with or without the labia minora.
Cirrhosis	Disease of the liver associated with increasing fibrosis (scarring) leading eventually to liver failure. Commonest cause is long term alcohol abuse but cirrhosis may also develop following viral infections of the liver (viral hepatitis).
Clavicle	Collar bone.
Clotting	See Coagulation.
Clubbing	Change in shape of the tips of the fingers associated with long term respiratory diseases.
COAD	See Chronic obstructive airways disease.

Coagulation   Clotting of the blood. Controlled by a complex series of reactions by specific chemicals in the blood (factors) which lead to the formation of blood clots at the site of damage to the blood vessels. Fragments of specialised cells (platelets) also involved.

Coagulopathy   Disorder of coagulation of the blood may be due to congenital defects (e.g. haemophilia), diseases (e.g. DIC) or excessive use drugs used to reduce coagulation (e.g. warfarin).

Collagen   Strands of fibrous tissue which form a firm 'skeleton' to the organs and tissues of the body.

Colon   Large bowel.

Commensal   Bacterium present in or on the body without causing a disease. Some bacteria (e.g. those in the bowel) serve useful functions.

Concussion   Lay term for the effects of a head injury. No generally agreed medical definition exists. However, a group of symptoms including amnesia, confusion and altered consciousness are referred to as Post Concussional Syndrome.

Congenital   Defect present at birth, the effects may be immediately apparent or may not become apparent until later life.

Congestion   Distension of blood vessels, particularly capillaries, caused by blockage of the outflow of blood which causes a reddened appearance to the skin.

Conjunctiva   Transparent covering of the eye and inner surface of the eyelids.

Contrecoup   Injury to the brain on the opposite side to the site of an injury to the head. Some accept that contrecoup injuries indicate that the head was free to move when struck, others dispute this.

Contusion   Leakage of blood from a damaged blood vessel, most commonly the smallest vessels – capillaries. One of the triad of blunt injuries. Colour, shape, appearance and resolution almost infinitely variable. Ageing extremely difficult and very unreliable.

Coronary   Relating to the heart.

Coronary atheroma   Narrowing caused by atheroma (furring up) of one of the coronary arteries. Site of atheroma is associated with a greatly increased risk of blood clot formation (thrombosis) which causes complete blockage and death of part of the heart muscle.

Coronary thrombosis	Complete blockage of one of the coronary arteries by blood clot (thrombosis), usually associated with pre-existing atheroma of the artery.
Corpus callosum	Part of the brain. A thin sheet of nervous tissue which joins the two cerebral hemispheres together.
Cortex	Outer region of organs that have two distinct zones, e.g. kidney and adrenal.
Corticosteroids	See Steroids.
Costal cartilage	The ends of the ribs nearest to the sternum (breast bone) which are composed of cartilage rather than bone. In mid to old age these areas calcify.
Cot death	Sudden Infant Death Syndrome (SIDS), also called crib death in the USA.
Cranium	Skull.
Crepitations	Crackling sound heard in lungs when they contain excess fluid.
Crepitus	Sensation and sound of the broken ends of bone moving against each other.
Cribriform plate	Area of the base of the front of the skull through which pass the nerves to the nose.
Cricoid cartilage	A ring shaped piece of cartilage which is the lowest of the three main structural cartilages of the larynx. May be broken during strangulation.
CSF	See Cerebro-spinal fluid.
Cut	Popular terminology for a break in the surface of the skin. Correct forensic terminology depends on the cause of the skin injury: blunt trauma causes lacerations, sharp trauma causes incisions.
Cutis anserina	'Goose flesh', may be seen as a post mortem change.
CVA	See Cerebrovascular accident.
Cyanosis	Blueness of the skin caused by lack of oxygen in the blood.
DAI	See Diffuse axonal injury.
Dartos	Muscle attached to the testicle.

Death	The cessation of life diagnosed by the absence of heart beat and respiration. The timing of death is extremely unreliable although temperature measurements can be used in the first 24 hours to get some estimate of the time since death.
Decalcify	Removal of calcium.
Decapitation	Removal of head.
Deceleration	Reducing speed.
Decomposition	Decay of body after death. Very variable and exact type and speed of decomposition will depend on body type, environmental temperature, availability of water, etc.
Decompression	Exposure to low pressure.
Deep vein thrombosis (DVT)	Blockage of veins in leg by blood clot (thrombosis). Sometimes causes pain and swelling in leg but may be symptomless. Development of DVT associated with immobility. Small increased risk with use of oral contraceptive.
Defence wounds	Injuries received by victim, while defending themselves. Most commonly seen with attacks involving a sharp weapon but any object can be the cause of defence wounds. Injuries are typically on the palm of the hand and/or outer border of the forearm.
Defibrillation	Part of modern resuscitative techniques used to try to correct an abnormal rhythm of the heart by passing an electrical current across the chest.
Dehydration	Lack of water in the body. Can occur in starvation, neglect, hyperthermia, etc.
Dermis	Part of the skin which lies below the outer hard layer (epidermis). The dermis contains blood vessels and nerves.
Diabetes mellitus	Illness caused by the lack of insulin as a result of disease of the pancreas. Lack of insulin causes hyperglycaemia which results in polyuria and polydipsia. Treated by insulin injections, tablets or diet depending on severity.
Dialysis	Medical treatment to assist or replace failing kidneys by filtering the blood by machine.
Diamorphine	Drug composed of two molecules of morphine. Highly addictive, commonly abused.

Diatoms Tiny, unicellular organisms that are found in some types of water. Some believe that their identification in the organs of a body can be used to determine if death was due to drowning, others strongly disagree.

Diazepam Valium, one of the Benzodiazepine group of sedative drugs.

DIC See Disseminated intravascular coagulation.

Diffuse axonal injury (DAI) Severe brain injury associated with rapid acceleration and deceleration of the brain causing tearing of the axons of the nerves. Does not have to be associated with a skull fracture.

Digestion Process of breaking down ingested food into smaller chemicals that can be absorbed by the bowel and used by the body.

Diploe Bone formed from the close apposition of two thin sheets of bone separated by a narrow space. The skull is the best example.

Disseminated intravascular coagulation A complex disease process in which there is uncontrolled clotting of the blood inside blood vessels. It can be triggered by many factors including septicaemia, severe trauma, etc. Results in damage to many organs and is commonly fatal.

DNA The molecule that forms the genetic code in the cells of the body. The DNA is found in the nucleus of cells and during cell replication it is arranged into groups known as chromosomes.

Down's Syndrome A group of abnormalities associated with the presence of an extra chromosome in the cells of the body. Also called Trisomy 2, used to be called Mongolism.

Drowning Death caused by immersion in a fluid, usually water. Pathological features may be absent if death was rapid and they differ for fresh and salt water drowning.

Duodenum First part of the small intestine. Other parts are jejunum and ileum.

Dura See Dura Mater.

Dura Mater Membrane of firm white tissue that surrounds the brain. Outermost, and thickest, of the three layers of the meninges.

Dyspnoea Breathlessness caused by disease.

Dysrhythmia Abnormal rhythm of the heart.

Ecchymosis	Sometimes used instead of contusion. A few authors suggest that the term ecchymosis should be used to indicate a large bruise. Now generally redundant.
ECG	Electrocardiogram, measurement of the electrical activity of the heart. Can be used to detect evidence of heart attack, abnormal rhythms, etc.
Ecstasy	Hallucinogenic drug derived from amphetamine, associated with some fatalities
EEG	Electroencephalogram. Measurement of the electrical activity of the brain.
Ejaculation	Projection of semen from the penis.
Electrocution	Death or injury caused by the passage of an electrical charge. Effects depend on both the voltage, amps and the time for which the current flows. High voltages can result in great tissue damage while low voltages may leave only minimal marks.
Electrolytes	In a medical context electrolytes are the important chemicals within the blood. The most commonly measured electrolytes are sodium, potassium, chloride, bicarbonate.
Emboli	Portions of extraneous material, blood clot, fat, air, etc., in the blood stream. May block an artery and cause damage to organs.
Embolism	Blockage of a blood vessel, usually an artery, by an extraneous object or material. Commonest form is the blockage of the arteries of the lungs by fragments of blood clot which have become detached from areas of deep venous thrombosis (DVT) in the legs.
Emphysema	Progressive disease of the lungs which results in the destruction of the tiny lung spaces (alveoli). Part of a chronic obstructive airways disease (COAD) complex.
Endocardium	Lining of the chambers of the heart.
Endothelium	Single celled lining of blood vessels.
Endotracheal tube	Tube passed through the mouth and into the airways to assist breathing.
Entomology	Study of insects. Can be useful in forensic medicine for the estimation of the time of death from the blowflies, etc., present on the body.

Enzyme A chemical which acts to speed up and assist in a chemical reaction in the body without being used up itself. The biological equivalent of a catalyst.

Epidermis Hard outer layer of the skin.

Epidural Space between the sheet of tissue covering the spinal cord (meninges) and the inner surface of the spinal canal. Site of pain-killing injections during delivery, surgery and intractable pain.

Epiglottis Flap of cartilaginous tissue at the back of the throat which folds across the entrance to the airways (larynx) during swallowing to prevent the entry of food or fluid.

Epilepsy Episodes of decreased consciousness or loss of consciousness (fits) precipitated by abnormal electrical activity of a localised area of the brain. These episodes may be associated with abnormal movements.

ET tube See Endotracheal tube.

Exhumation Recovery of a body from an official or unofficial grave.

Exit wound Site where a weapon, most commonly a bullet, leaves the body.

Explosion Sudden generation of vast quantities of gas. Commonly associated with heat and noise.

Exposure Lowering of body temperature (hypothermia) due to insufficient clothing for the environmental temperature and conditions. The environmental conditions do not have to be extreme for this to occur.

Extradural haemorrhage Bleeding into the extradural space. Associated with skull fractures, particularly of the temporal regions where the middle meningeal artery lies in or on the inner surface of the skull.

Extradural space Potential space between the dura and the skull. Called the epidural space in the spinal canal.

Factors A group of specialised chemicals in the blood that are responsible for coagulation.

Falx Fold of meninges that lies between the two cerebral hemispheres.

Fat Adipose tissue.

Fat embolism	Blockage of blood vessels, particularly of the lungs and kidneys, by portions of fat. Seen following trauma, particularly fractures.
Febrile	Having a raised temperature.
Femur	Bone of the upper leg.
Fetus (Foetus)	Unborn baby before 24 weeks of gestation.
Fibrillation	A highly abnormal rhythm of the heart that is so disorganised that blood is not pumped. It has been described as looking like 'a can of worms'.
Fibrin	Compound produced by the clotting process which forms the seal in the blood vessel wall.
Fibrinolysis	Process of breaking down and removing fibrin from blood clots.
Fibroblasts	Cells which produce collagen.
Fibrosis	An increase of fibrous tissue, usually an abnormal feature.
Fibula	Bone of the lower leg.
Finger tip bruises	Specific oval areas of bruising, often in groups, caused by the finger tips during forceful gripping. Often found on the upper arm of adults but may be seen anywhere in children. May be seen on the neck in manual strangulation.
Fixation	Process of preserving body organs, usually by placing them in a solution of formalin.
Flail chest	Destruction of the rigid structure of some or all of the chest wall caused by multiple rib fractures. Renders breathing difficult.
Flotation test	Discredited test used to determine if a baby was born alive by placing the lungs in water. It was thought that if the child had breathed the lungs floated, if not they sank.
Fontanelles	'Soft spots' on a baby's skull covered only by soft fibrous tissue. Formed in the areas where the skull bones have not yet joined completely. Two are present, one at the front (anterior) and one at the back (posterior).
Foramen magnum	Hole in the base of the skull through which passes the brain stem and spinal cord.

Foreign body	Any object that is not normally found at that site.
Formalin	Fixative solution used to preserve organs.
Fracture	Break in a bone or cartilage.
Frenulum	Thin band of loose tissue that joins the central regions of the upper and lower gums to the back of the lip. Tearing of the frenulum is one of the injuries that is highly suggestive of child abuse but is not specific for it.
Frontal lobe	Part of the brain lying at the front of the head.
Frontal sinuses	Air spaces in the skull of the forehead.
Frostbite	Severe cold injury commonly to the feet and hands due to exposure to low environmental temperatures.
Gagging	Placing of an obstruction across or in the mouth.
Gall bladder	Small sac-like organ on the under surface of the liver which stores bile.
Garrotting	A form of ligature strangulation.
Gastric	Relating to the stomach.
Gastrointestinal	Relating to the digestive system.
Gene	A length of DNA which codes for specific part of the individual.
Genital	Relating to the genitalia.
Glasgow Coma Scale	A numerical method of assessing the level of unconsciousness of an individual by testing three neurological features: eye opening, verbal response and movement. Lowest score = 3, highest = 15.
Glottis	Throat.
Glucose	One type of sugar, commonest form used in human metabolism.
Glycogen	Complex molecule formed from glucose used for storage of carbohydrates in humans.
Granulation tissue	Type of tissue produced during repair of skin wounds.
Graze	See Abrasion.
Gynaecology	Branch of medicine that specialises in the female genital tract.

Haematoma

Used to describe a significant collection of blood outside blood vessels and in the tissues of the body.

Haematoxylin

Chemical used in the staining of tissue on microscope slides for routine examination, usually combined with Eosin. Often written as 'H & E'.

Haemodialysis

See Dialysis.

Haemoglobin

Complex molecule in red blood cells that is responsible for carrying oxygen. Contains four strands of protein that normally consist of two sets of pairs. Congenital defects occur which cause abnormalities of red cell function.

Haemopericardium

Presence of blood in the sac (pericardium) surrounding the heart.

Haemophilia

A disease of male children associated with excessive bleeding. Caused by a genetic defect on the X chromosome which results in the decreased production of one of the factors (VIII) essential for normal blood clotting.

Haemoptysis

Coughing up blood or blood stained sputum.

Haemorrhage

Bleeding.

Haemosiderin

Chemical form of iron stored in the body.

Haemostasis

The process of blood clotting or the act of preventing bleeding by pressure, etc.

Haemothorax

Blood within the chest cavity.

Hanging

Form of ligature strangulation where the pressure on the neck is produced by the weight of the body.

Heart

Organ which pumps blood around the body. Composed of two pumping chambers (ventricles) and two storage chambers (atria). Blood flow through the heart is controlled by a set of valves.

Heparin

Drug used to control coagulation, only given by injection.

Hepatitis

Inflammation of the liver caused by one of a group of viruses. Several types of hepatitis occur (A, B, C, etc.); some are relatively minor illnesses while others may be fatal or lead to long term liver damage.

Heroin

See Diamorphine

Hide & Die Syndrome	Variant of death from hypothermia where the individual hides away in small space, e.g. a cupboard either in an attempt to keep warm or through confusion induced by the low body temperature.
Histochemistry	Special type of microscopic examination where staining techniques are used to identify specific chemicals in the tissues.
Histology	Examination of tissues under the microscope.
HIV	See Human Immunodeficiency Virus.
Homicide	Murder.
Human Immunodeficiency Virus (HIV)	Virus associated with the development of AIDS.
Humerus	Bone of upper arm.
Hydrogen cyanide	Extremely poisonous gas produced in fires, causes rapid death.
Hymen	Thin sheet of tissue usually present in the lower vagina of female children. If present this tissue may be damaged during penetration of the vagina by an object or by a penis during intercourse.
Hyoid	One of the cartilaginous components of the larynx. May be broken during strangulation.
Hyper-	Prefix which denotes an abnormally increased level or value.
Hyperglycaemia	Raised blood sugar, usually caused by lack of insulin.
Hypertension	Raised blood pressure.
Hyperthermia	Raised body temperature. May be caused by exercise, fever or other illnesses.
Hyperthyroidism	The effects of an overactive thyroid gland.
Hypo-	Prefix which denotes the presence of an abnormally low level or value.
Hypoglycaemia	Low blood sugar, usually caused by the presence of excess insulin.
Hypostasis	The red staining of the skin of a corpse caused by the settling of red blood cells under the influence of gravity. Areas of the body that are in contact with surfaces will be unaffected and will remain white. Of no value in assessing time of death.

Hypotension	Low blood pressure.
Hypothermia	Body temperature of less than 30 degrees Centigrade. Can be fatal.
Hypoxia	Low levels of oxygen in the blood and tissues.
Idiopathic	From unknown or uncertain cause.
IHD	See Ischaemic Heart Disease.
Ileum	Final part of the small bowel.
Immersion	Placing in a fluid.
Immunological response	Relating to the body's reaction to extraneous material, whether a bacterium, virus or inanimate object.
Incision	Break in the continuity of the skin caused by an object with a sharp edge.
Infanticide	Killing of a baby or child by its mother.
Infarction	Death of a cell or group of cells as a result of lack of an adequate blood supply. The dead cells are usually surrounded by other living cells with a good blood supply.
Infection	Infiltration of the body tissues or spaces by an organism whether bacterium or virus.
Inferior	The lower part of the body, limb, organ, etc.
Inferior vena cava (IVC)	Main vein returning blood from below the diaphragm to the heart, drains blood into the right atrium.
Inflammation	Body's response to infection or a foreign body. The inflammatory response results in movement of fluid and specialised cells from the blood stream into the tissues. The fluid causes swelling and the cells are the major constituent of pus.
Injection	Delivery of a fluid into a blood vessel. May be therapeutic or due to drug abuse.
Insulin	Hormone produced by specialised cells in the pancreas which is essential for maintaining the correct level of sugar (glucose) in the blood stream.
Intercostal muscles	Thin sheets of muscle lying between the ribs.
Interventricular septum	Sheet of muscle separating the two ventricles of the heart.

Intestine	Bowel. Composed of two parts: small and large.
Intracerebral	Within the brain.
Intracranial	Within the skull.
Intrapulmonary	Within the lung.
Intrauterine	Within the uterus.
Ischaemic	Lack of blood.
Ischaemic Heart Disease (IHD)	Heart disease caused by narrowing of the coronary arteries by atheroma which leads to areas of damage to the myocardium.
IVC	See Inferior vena cava.
Jejunum	Middle part of the small bowel.
Joule burn	Burn caused by passage of an electrical current.
Jugular vein	Main vein draining the head and neck.
Keloid	Unusual type of excessive scar formation most commonly seen in Afrocaribbeans.
Keratin	Hard layer on the surface of the skin. Keratin is also a constituent of nails and hair.
Kick	Blow caused by a foot.
Kidney	Organ responsible for filtering the blood and the removal of soluble waste products and excess fluid. Urine produced passes through the ureters to the urinary bladder.
Kinetic energy	Potential energy of a moving object.
Knife	Sharp object with at least one cutting edge.
Laceration	Break in the continuity of the skin or organ caused by application of blunt force. One of the triad of injuries associated with this type of force. Lacerations are not caused by sharp objects, which cause incisions.
Lactic acid	Chemical produced by the metabolic processes of cells when sufficient oxygen is lacking.
Larynx	Upper part of the airways. It is given a rigid structure by the presence of three cartilaginous structures, the hyoid, thyroid and cricoid cartilages, which may be injured in strangulation. In lay terms can be seen in the neck as the 'Adam's Apple'.

Lateral	The outer part of the body, limb, organ, etc
Leucocyte	General term for all types of white blood cells which are involved in fighting infection.
Ligature	Band of material used to apply pressure to part of the body, most commonly used in terms of pressure to the neck.
Lines of Zahn	Pattern visible in the structure of deep venous thromboses and pulmonary emboli. Of pathological interest only.
Liver	Large organ situated in the upper right abdomen. Responsible for many metabolic processes including removal and degradation of toxic chemicals from the blood, storage of glucose, etc.
Lividity	See Hypostasis.
Local anaesthetic	Drug used to induce a small area of lack of sensation.
Lung	Organ in the chest. Site of gas exchange between blood and inspired air.
Lymphocyte	Type of white blood cell.
Lysergic Acid Diethylamide (LSD)	One type of consciousness altering drug. Use may lead to long term psychological complications.
Maceration	Destruction of tissues or a body caused by a combination of trauma and decomposition.
Maggot	Developing stage of many insects.
Malignant	Commonly used to describe cancers but may also be used to describe other severe, rapidly progressing diseases.
Mandible	Lower jaw.
MAOI	See Monoamine oxidase inhibitors.
Marasmus	See Cachexia.
Maxilla	Upper jaw.
MDMA	See Ecstasy.
Medial	The inner part of the body, limb, organ, etc.
Mediastinum	Area in the centre of the chest between the lungs containing the oesophagus, trachea, descending aorta, etc.

Medulla	Central region of organs that have two distinct zones, e.g. kidney and adrenal.
Meninges	Coverings of brain. Three layers are present: dura mater, arachnoid and the pia mater.
Meningococcus	A type of bactrium associated with meningitis and septicaemia.
Mesentery	Sheet of fatty tissue that supports the small intestines.
Metabolism	A group of interlinked chemical processes involved in sustaining life.
Metaphysis	Area of bone growth, found in the long bones of children.
Methadone	Drug used in the treatment of heroin addiction. Methadone is given as a fluid which is taken orally. Often abused.
Methylenedioxymeth-amphetamine (MDMA)	See Ecstacy.
Microbiology	Study of bacteria, viruses, etc.
Midbrain	Part of the brain stem.
Middle meningeal artery	Artery which runs in or on the inner surface of the temporal region of the skull. May be damaged by fractures in that area causing extradural haemorrhage.
Miscarriage	Spontaneous abortion.
Mitral valve	The valve between the left atrium and the left ventricle of the heart.
Monoamine oxidase inhibitors	Group of antidepressant drugs. May be associated with severe side effects if foods, etc. with a high tyramine content (cheese, yeast, red wine, etc.) are eaten.
Morphine	Powerful analgesic drug. Known to have addictive properties and to be abused. The linking of two molecules of morphine produces heroin (diamorphine).
Mummification	Type of decomposition associated with warm dry conditions where the body dehydrates. Often results in remarkably good preservation. Usually involves the whole body but may involve only part, most commonly the extremities.

Munchausen Syndrome   A complex psychiatric syndrome associated with a desire to obtain medical treatment (often invasive) by complaining of fictitious illnesses. May also involve the children of the individual, when it is called Munchausen Syndrome By Proxy.

Muscle   Tissue with a capability to contract or shorten. Control of muscle contraction is either by voluntary control (e.g. movement of a limb) or involuntary and under the control of the autonomic nervous system (e.g. movement of the bowel).

Myocardial   Relating to the muscle of the heart. Often used in a broader sense to mean relating to the heart generally.

Myocardial infarction   Death of part of the heart muscle due to blockage of one of the coronary arteries. Commonly called 'heart attack'.

Myocarditis   Infection of the myocardium, usually viral.

Myocardium   Muscle of the heart.

Myxoedema   Disease associated with lack of hormone produced by the thyroid gland.

Myxoma   Rare type of tumour, may involve the atria of the heart and lead to sudden death.

Necropsy   Autopsy, post mortem examination.

Necrosis   Death of a group of cells from whatever cause.

Neurones   Nerve cells.

Nitrazepam   One of the benzodiazepine group of drugs.

Nitrogen   Most abundant gas in the atmosphere.

Noradrenalin   Hormone produced by the adrenal medulla, has very similar effects to adrenalin.

Nortryptyline   Breakdown product of amitryptyline.

Nucleus   Defined area within a cell that contains the genetic code (DNA).

Obesity   Excess weight.

Obstetric   Relating to pregnancy and birth.

Occipital   Area at the back of the head.

Odontology   Study of teeth.

613

Oedema	Waterlogging of the tissues caused by the movement of fluid out of the blood stream.
Oesophagus	Muscular tube which passes from the back of the throat (pharynx) to the stomach. Entry of food or fluid into the upper oesophagus initiates a series of co-ordinated muscular contractions to move the material into the stomach.
Omentum	A sheet of fatty tissue in the abdomen.
Opioid	Drugs derived from opium: morphine, heroin, etc.
Orbit	Group of bones which surround and protect the eye.
Organic	1. Relating to an organ. 2. A disease that is not of psychological origin. 3. Relating to carbon based compounds.
Organophosphorus	Type of chemical commonly used in agriculture as pesticide. May cause damage to the nervous system.
Ossification	Process of changing cartilage into bone as part of normal development and growth. In children ossification occurs at specific sites in bones known as ossification centres.
Osteogenesis Imperfecta	Rare type of bone disease which in its most severe form results in multiple fractures which are present from birth. Less severe forms can lead to an increased susceptibility to fractures in infancy which may be confused with child abuse.
Osteoporosis	Loss of calcium from bones leading to increased weakness of the bones and increased risk of fractures. Can occur for many reasons but is common in post menopausal women.
Overlaying	Said to occur when an adult 'lies over' a child while asleep. Once believed to be the cause of SIDS.
Oxygen	Gas essential for life.
Pachymeninges	A general term used to describe the three meningeal layers.
Pancreas	Abdominal organ that produces chemicals (enzymes) to aid in the digestion of food in the small bowel. Also contains specialised cells (Islets of Langerhan) that produce insulin.
Pancreatitis	Inflammation or infection of the pancreas.

Paracetamol	Common analgesic. May cause liver failure if taken to excess.
Paraquat	Herbicide. Causes lung damage if ingested.
Pelvis	Bones of the pelvic girdle.
Penetrating injuries	Injuries which pass through the skin.
Peptic ulcer	Ulcer of the stomach and duodenum initially thought to be caused by the action of gastric acid, etc. Now thought to be associated with infection by a bacterium called Helicobater Pylori.
Pericarditis	Infection or inflammation of the pericardium.
Pericardium	Thin sac which surrounds the heart.
Perineum	Area of the pelvis that lies between the upper legs. In the female contains the vulva.
Periorbital haematoma	See Black eye.
Periosteum	Thin sheet of tissue which covers bones.
Peritoneum	Thin lining of the abdominal cavity.
Peritonitis	Inflammation or infection of the abdominal cavity.
Perivascular	Adjacent to blood vessels.
Petechial haemorrhages	Tiny, 'pin point' areas of bleeding in the skin. They are one of the features of asphyxiation but may be caused by many other events including sneezing, coughing and resuscitation.
Pethidine	Strong analgesic.
Pharynx	Area at the back of the throat which is the common route to both the larynx and oesophagus.
Pia	The thinnest and innermost lining of the brain (meninges), the pia mater is closely attached to the surface of the brain.
Placenta	Organ developed from foetal tissue to allow exchange of food and oxygen between foetus and mother.
Platelets	Small portions of specialised cells in the bone marrow that break off and circulate in the blood stream. Essential for proper coagulation.

Pleura   Thin sheets of tissue that cover the lungs and line the inner wall of the chest cavity. A potential space exists between these two sheets which may be opened if fluid, blood or gas enters the space.

Pleural   Relating to the pleura.

Pneumonia   Infection of the lung.

Pneumothorax   Abnormal presence of gas (usually air) between the two sheets of pleura.

Poison   Any substance that causes damage to the cells or metabolic processes of the body.

Polydipsia   Excessive drinking of water.

Polymorphonuclear leucocytes   One type of white blood cell. Often called just 'Polymorphs'.

Polymorphs   See Polymorphonuclear leucocytes.

Polyuria   Excessive, frequent urination.

Pons   Area of brain stem.

Pontine   Relating to the pons.

Post concussional syndrome   Complex group of neurological symptoms that may be associated with a head injury.

Post mortem   1. After death.
                         2. Examination of a body after death.

Posterior   The back of the body, limb, organ, etc.

Potassium   One of the most important chemicals in the body, abnormally high or low levels may cause death.

Protein   Complex molecules built from amino acids. The sequence of amino acids in each protein is coded for in the DNA.

Pubic symphysis   Junction of the two pelvic bones at the front of the pelvis.

Pugilistic attitude Term used to describe the position of the arms in a body that has been severely affected by heat where the contraction of the muscles caused by the heat results in the positioning of the arms in a way thought to look like the stance of a boxer.

Pulmonary   Relating to the lungs.

Pulmonary embolism	Blockage of the arteries to the lungs by a blood clot from the legs. May cause sudden death.
Putrefaction	Decomposition.
Quinsy	Severe infection of the tonsils.
Radius	One of the bones of the forearm.
Rape	Illegal sexual intercourse.
RDS	See Respiratory Distress Syndrome.
Rectal	Relating to the rectum.
Rectum	Portion of bowel immediately before the anus.
Reflex	Automatic response to a stimulus or event.
Renal	Relating to the kidney.
Respiration	1. Breathing. 2. The complex series of chemical events at a cellular level that use oxygen and sugar to produce energy.
Respiratory Distress Syndrome (RDS)	Syndrome causing failure of the exchange of oxygen in the lungs, in premature infants caused by failure of the lungs to inflate after birth and/or lack of a specific fluid (surfactant) which assists expansion. Similar syndrome in adults (ARDS).
Resuscitation	Attempts to revive a seriously ill individual. This term may indicate cardiac massage alone or it may be used to indicate extensive surgical and medical treatment over a period of time.
Retina	Sheet of light sensitive cells at the back of the eye.
Retroperitoneal space	Potential space between the peritoneum and the back wall of the abdomen.
Rib	A thin flat bone that forms part of the chest wall.
Rifled weapon	Weapon with grooves in the barrel that impart rotation to the bullets fired.
Rigor mortis	Stiffening of the muscles after death. Very variable process which is affected by many factors and cannot be used to give an accurate time of death.
Rule of Nines	Method of estimating the extent of burns on an individual.

Sacrum   Part of the lower spine, forms the back of the pelvic ring.

Salicylate   Analgesic commonly known as aspirin. Can be fatal if taken in excess. Also causes changes in blood clotting and can be used to treat or prevent thrombosis.

Scald   Heat trauma caused by fluid.

Scalp   Skin covering skull.

Scapula   Shoulder blade, wing shaped flat bone which lies over the upper back but which is part of the shoulder joint.

Scar   Area of repair of damaged tissue which results in formation of fibrous tissue.

Sclera   White of the eye.

Scratch   Linear abrasion.

Serology   Tests of the blood to determine blood groups, etc.

Shock
1. Lay – effects of sudden surprise or event.
2. Medically – used to describe a combination of symptoms including raised pulse rate and low blood pressure that are a response to severe trauma, disease, etc.

Shotgun   Weapon without rifling in the barrel (smooth bore) which usually fires multiple small projectiles.

SIDS   See Sudden Infant Death Syndrome.

Skeletal   Relating to the skeleton.

Skin   Covering of the body. Composed of several layers.

Skull   A group of bones which together from a solid container for the brain. The bones of the skull are composed of two layers – the inner and outer tables.

Slash   Lay term indicating an injury caused by the undirected action of a sharp weapon.

Smoke   Complex substance containing hot gases and particulate matter produced by combustion. The exact composition depends on the substance being burnt.

Smothering   Obstruction of the external air passages.

Sodium   One of the most important chemicals in the body. Abnormally high or low levels may cause death.

Solvent	A wide range of substances, usually liquids, that can be used to dissolve dirt, oil, etc. May be abused by inhalation.
Solvent abuse	Deliberate inhalation of solvents. May be fatal.
Spleen	Organ in the abdomen. Functions include removal of old, damaged red blood cells and maturation of lymphocytes. May be injured in blunt abdominal trauma causing life-threatening haemorrhage.
Stab	A penetrating injury caused by a sharp object which is deeper than it is wide.
Stamping	Forceful downward action of a foot.
Starvation	Lack of food.
Stenosis	Narrowing.
Sternomastoid	Muscle of the neck.
Sternum	Breast bone. Point of attachment of the ribs at the front of the chest.
Steroid	1. Broad description of a wide category of hormones produced by the adrenal cortex which have very significant effects on the body's metabolism. 2. A type of drug commonly used to suppress inflammation or allergic responses.
Stillbirth	Birth of a dead baby after 24 weeks gestation.
Stomach	First organ in the digestive system. Contains numerous enzymes and acid to initiate digestion of food.
Strangulation	Application of pressure to the neck resulting in obstruction of the airways with or without obstruction of the blood vessels.
Stroke	Lay term for brain injury caused by either haemorrhage into the brain (rupture of an aneurysm) or death of brain tissue (blockage of an artery). Sometimes referred to medically as a cerebrovascular accident (CVA).
Subarachnoid	Potential space beneath the arachnoid membrane covering the brain.
Subarachnoid haemorrhagea	Bleeding into the subarachnoid space. Commonly cause by rupture of Berry aneurysm but may also be caused by trauma.

619

Subclavian vein	Main vein draining the arm which lies beneath the clavicle. Common site of intravenous therapy.
Subdural haemorrhage	Haemorrhage into the subdural space, associated with trauma to the head. May or may not be associated with a skull fracture. Commonly the individual has a period of relative normality after a head injury (lucid period) and then deteriorates.
Subdural space	Potential space between the dura and the arachnoid membrane.
Sudden death	No specific definition of sudden death exists. Some state that the time period should be less than a few minutes, others include periods of up to a day.
Sudden Infant Death Syndrome	Sudden unexpected death of a child of less than two years which is unexplained despite extensive tests.
Suffocation	Asphyxiation caused by obstruction of the external airways or lack of oxygen in the inspired air.
Suicide	Deliberate act causing the death of the individual committing it.
Superior	The upper part of the body, limb, organ, etc.
Superior vena cava	Main vein that returns blood from above the diaphragm to the right atrium.
Suppuration	Production of pus.
Suspension	See hanging.
SVC	See Superior vena cava.
Tache noire	Dark staining in the sclera of eye after death. An interesting finding but of no forensic relevance.
Tachycardia	Raised heart rate.
Tardieu spots	Petechial haemorrhages seen beneath the pleura, sometimes more widely used to mean petechial haemorrhages generally.
Temazepam	One of the benzodiazepine group of drugs.
Temperature	Measurement of the body temperature after death can provide some information as to the time of death but it is inexact and, on its own, it only accurate to plus or minus approximately three hours.
Temporal bone	Thin bone of the side of the skull.

Tentorium	Sheet of dura that partially subdivides the cranial cavity with the cerebrum above and the cerebellum below.
Thallium	Heavy metal poison which causes loss of hair and damage to the nervous system. Commonly fatal.
Thoracic cage	General term used to describe the thorax.
Thorax	Chest and chest cavity.
Throat	Lay term which includes the pharynx, larynx and the associated structures in the neck.
Thrombosis	Blood clot formed inside a blood vessel.
Throttling	See Strangulation.
Thymus	Organ present in the chest of children and young adults associated with the maturation of lymphocytes.
Thyroid	Gland in the neck which produces a number of hormones which are responsible for regulating the speed of the body's metabolism.
Thyroid cartilage	Cartilage in the neck which can be seen externally as the 'Adam's Apple'. May be injured in strangulation especially in the elderly when it has partially calcified.
Tibia	Bone of the lower leg.
Toluene	A type of solvent commonly associated with solvent abuse.
Toxicology	Tests performed to determine the presence of drugs.
Trachea	Main airway which runs from the larynx to the bronchi.
Trauma	Injury.
Traumatic asphyxia	Asphyxiation caused by restriction of the movements of the chest wall. e.g. crushing. Asphyxial changes are often florid and extend on to the upper chest.
Tricyclics	A group of antidepressant drugs.
Ulna	One of the bones of the forearm.
Ultraviolet light	Light at the blue end of the spectrum, can be used to identify old injuries. Most commonly used in the identification of old bite marks which may be several weeks old.

Umbilical cord	Cord containing blood vessels that links a baby to the placenta.
Uraemia	High levels of urea in the blood, associated with kidney failure.
Urine	Fluid produced by the kidneys containing excess water and soluble waste products.
Uterus	Womb.
Vagal inhibition	Slowing or stoppage of the heart caused by stimulation of the vagus nerve, can be caused by pressure on the neck.
Vagina	Part of female sexual anatomy. Extends from the vulva to the neck of the womb (cervix).
Vagus	Nerve which passes from the brain to the chest through the neck. Involved in the regulation of heart rate. Pressure on the neck may injure the nerve and cause cardiac arrest.
Valium	One of the benzodiazepine group of drugs.
Vasectomy	Form of contraception that involves the surgical division of the tubes (vasa) that connect the testes to the penis.
Vaso-vagal shock	See Vagal inhibition.
Venepuncture	Removal of blood from a vein.
Ventricle	Cavity in the brain or heart. In the heart the ventricles are the main pumping areas.
Ventricular fibrillation	Abnormal, unco-ordinated and irregular contraction of the heart muscle which does not result in movement of blood.
Vertebra	One of the bones of the spine.
Vertebral arteries	Two small arteries that supply blood to the brain. These arteries run alongside the cervical spine and pass into the skull through the foramen magnum where they join together to form the basilar artery.
Vertebral bodies	Main part of the vertebrae.
Virus	A small lifeless package of DNA that can enter a cell and take over the running of that cell using its DNA. Sole purpose is to make more copies of the DNA and hence more viruses.

Viscera	Organs of the body.
Vitreous humour	Fluid in the eye.
Vomit	Material expelled from the stomach. Usually very acidic.
Vulva	External sexual organs of the female. Consist of the labia majora on the outside and smaller labia minora on the inside.
Warfarin	Drug used to (partially) inhibit coagulation and prevent the formation of blood clots. Dosage has to be controlled with care as too much may lead to uncontrolled haemorrhage.
Washer-woman changes	The water-logging and puckering of the skin of the hands and feet caused by immersion in fluid.
WBC	White blood cell – general term for all of the many different types of white blood cells.
Whiplash	Type of injury to the neck usually caused by sudden backwards and forwards movement(s).
Wound	Injury.
Zygoma	Arch of bone which forms the cheek bone.

APPENDIX 10

Extract from the Criminal Procedure and Investigations Act 1996

1996 CHAPTER 25

An Act to make provision about criminal procedure and criminal investigations. [4th July 1996]

B E IT ENACTED by the Queen's most Excellent Majesty, by and with the advice and consent of the Lords Spiritual and Temporal, and Commons, in this present Parliament assembled, and by the authority of the same, as follows:—

PART I

DISCLOSURE

Introduction

1.—(1) This Part applies where—

(a) a person is charged with a summary offence in respect of which a court proceeds to summary trial and in respect of which he pleads not guilty,

(b) a person who has attained the age of 18 is charged with an offence which is triable either way, in respect of which a court proceeds to summary trial and in respect of which he pleads not guilty, or

(c) a person under the age of 18 is charged with an indictable offence in respect of which a court proceeds to summary trial and in respect of which he pleads not guilty.

(2) This Part also applies where—

(a) a person is charged with an indictable offence and he is committed for trial for the offence concerned,

(b) a person is charged with an indictable offence and proceedings for the trial of the person on the charge concerned are transferred to the Crown Court by virtue of a notice of transfer given under section 4 of the Criminal Justice Act 1987 (serious or complex fraud),

Application of this Part.

1987 c. 38.

(c) a person is charged with an indictable offence and proceedings for the trial of the person on the charge concerned are transferred to the Crown Court by virtue of a notice of transfer served on a magistrates' court under section 53 of the Criminal Justice Act 1991 (certain cases involving children),

(d) a count charging a person with a summary offence is included in an indictment under the authority of section 40 of the Criminal Justice Act 1988 (common assault etc.), or

(e) a bill of indictment charging a person with an indictable offence is preferred under the authority of section 2(2)(b) of the Administration of Justice (Miscellaneous Provisions) Act 1933 (bill preferred by direction of Court of Appeal, or by direction or with consent of a judge).

(3) This Part applies in relation to alleged offences into which no criminal investigation has begun before the appointed day.

(4) For the purposes of this section a criminal investigation is an investigation which police officers or other persons have a duty to conduct with a view to it being ascertained—

(a) whether a person should be charged with an offence, or

(b) whether a person charged with an offence is guilty of it.

(5) The reference in subsection (3) to the appointed day is to such day as is appointed for the purposes of this Part by the Secretary of State by order.

General interpretation.

2.—(1) References to the accused are to the person mentioned in section 1(1) or (2).

(2) Where there is more than one accused in any proceedings this Part applies separately in relation to each of the accused.

(3) References to the prosecutor are to any person acting as prosecutor, whether an individual or a body.

(4) References to material are to material of all kinds, and in particular include references to—

(a) information, and

(b) objects of all descriptions.

(5) References to recording information are to putting it in a durable or retrievable form (such as writing or tape).

(6) This section applies for the purposes of this Part.

The main provisions

Primary disclosure by prosecutor.

3.—(1) The prosecutor must—

(a) disclose to the accused any prosecution material which has not previously been disclosed to the accused and which in the prosecutor's opinion might undermine the case for the prosecution against the accused, or

(b) give to the accused a written statement that there is no material of a description mentioned in paragraph (a).

(2) For the purposes of this section prosecution material is material—

(a) which is in the prosecutor's possession, and came into his possession in connection with the case for the prosecution against the accused, or

(b) which, in pursuance of a code operative under Part II, he has inspected in connection with the case for the prosecution against the accused.

(3) Where material consists of information which has been recorded in any form the prosecutor discloses it for the purposes of this section—

(a) by securing that a copy is made of it and that the copy is given to the accused, or

(b) if in the prosecutor's opinion that is not practicable or not desirable, by allowing the accused to inspect it at a reasonable time and a reasonable place or by taking steps to secure that he is allowed to do so;

and a copy may be in such form as the prosecutor thinks fit and need not be in the same form as that in which the information has already been recorded.

(4) Where material consists of information which has not been recorded the prosecutor discloses it for the purposes of this section by securing that it is recorded in such form as he thinks fit and—

(a) by securing that a copy is made of it and that the copy is given to the accused, or

(b) if in the prosecutor's opinion that is not practicable or not desirable, by allowing the accused to inspect it at a reasonable time and a reasonable place or by taking steps to secure that he is allowed to do so.

(5) Where material does not consist of information the prosecutor discloses it for the purposes of this section by allowing the accused to inspect it at a reasonable time and a reasonable place or by taking steps to secure that he is allowed to do so.

(6) Material must not be disclosed under this section to the extent that the court, on an application by the prosecutor, concludes it is not in the public interest to disclose it and orders accordingly.

(7) Material must not be disclosed under this section to the extent that—

(a) it has been intercepted in obedience to a warrant issued under section 2 of the Interception of Communications Act 1985, or

(b) it indicates that such a warrant has been issued or that material has been intercepted in obedience to such a warrant.

(8) The prosecutor must act under this section during the period which, by virtue of section 12, is the relevant period for this section.

4.—(1) This section applies where—

Primary disclosure: further provisions.

(a) the prosecutor acts under section 3, and

(b) before so doing he was given a document in pursuance of provision included, by virtue of section 24(3), in a code operative under Part II.

(2) In such a case the prosecutor must give the document to the accused at the same time as the prosecutor acts under section 3.

5.—(1) Subject to subsections (2) to (4), this section applies where—

    (a) this Part applies by virtue of section 1(2), and

    (b) the prosecutor complies with section 3 or purports to comply with it.

(2) Where this Part applies by virtue of section 1(2)(b), this section does not apply unless—

    (a) a copy of the notice of transfer, and

    (b) copies of the documents containing the evidence,

1987 c. 38.

have been given to the accused under regulations made under section 5(9) of the Criminal Justice Act 1987.

(3) Where this Part applies by virtue of section 1(2)(c), this section does not apply unless—

    (a) a copy of the notice of transfer, and

    (b) copies of the documents containing the evidence,

1991 c. 53.

have been given to the accused under regulations made under paragraph 4 of Schedule 6 to the Criminal Justice Act 1991.

(4) Where this Part applies by virtue of section 1(2)(e), this section does not apply unless the prosecutor has served on the accused a copy of the indictment and a copy of the set of documents containing the evidence which is the basis of the charge.

(5) Where this section applies, the accused must give a defence statement to the court and the prosecutor.

(6) For the purposes of this section a defence statement is a written statement—

    (a) setting out in general terms the nature of the accused's defence,

    (b) indicating the matters on which he takes issue with the prosecution, and

    (c) setting out, in the case of each such matter, the reason why he takes issue with the prosecution.

(7) If the defence statement discloses an alibi the accused must give particulars of the alibi in the statement, including—

    (a) the name and address of any witness the accused believes is able to give evidence in support of the alibi, if the name and address are known to the accused when the statement is given;

    (b) any information in the accused's possession which might be of material assistance in finding any such witness, if his name or address is not known to the accused when the statement is given.

(8) For the purposes of this section evidence in support of an alibi is evidence tending to show that by reason of the presence of the accused at a particular place or in a particular area at a particular time he was not, or was unlikely to have been, at the place where the offence is alleged to have been committed at the time of its alleged commission.

(9) The accused must give a defence statement under this section during the period which, by virtue of section 12, is the relevant period for this section.

627

PART I
Voluntary
disclosure by
accused.

6.—(1) This section applies where—

  (a) this Part applies by virtue of section 1(1), and

  (b) the prosecutor complies with section 3 or purports to comply with it.

(2) The accused—

  (a) may give a defence statement to the prosecutor, and

  (b) if he does so, must also give such a statement to the court.

(3) Subsections (6) to (8) of section 5 apply for the purposes of this section as they apply for the purposes of that.

(4) If the accused gives a defence statement under this section he must give it during the period which, by virtue of section 12, is the relevant period for this section.

Secondary
disclosure by
prosecutor.

7.—(1) This section applies where the accused gives a defence statement under section 5 or 6.

(2) The prosecutor must—

  (a) disclose to the accused any prosecution material which has not previously been disclosed to the accused and which might be reasonably expected to assist the accused's defence as disclosed by the defence statement given under section 5 or 6, or

  (b) give to the accused a written statement that there is no material of a description mentioned in paragraph (a).

(3) For the purposes of this section prosecution material is material—

  (a) which is in the prosecutor's possession and came into his possession in connection with the case for the prosecution against the accused, or

  (b) which, in pursuance of a code operative under Part II, he has inspected in connection with the case for the prosecution against the accused.

(4) Subsections (3) to (5) of section 3 (method by which prosecutor discloses) apply for the purposes of this section as they apply for the purposes of that.

(5) Material must not be disclosed under this section to the extent that the court, on an application by the prosecutor, concludes it is not in the public interest to disclose it and orders accordingly.

(6) Material must not be disclosed under this section to the extent that—

  (a) it has been intercepted in obedience to a warrant issued under section 2 of the Interception of Communications Act 1985, or

  (b) it indicates that such a warrant has been issued or that material has been intercepted in obedience to such a warrant.

1985 c. 56.

(7) The prosecutor must act under this section during the period which, by virtue of section 12, is the relevant period for this section.

Application by
accused for
disclosure.

8.—(1) This section applies where the accused gives a defence statement under section 5 or 6 and the prosecutor complies with section 7 or purports to comply with it or fails to comply with it.

PART I

(2) If the accused has at any time reasonable cause to believe that—

   (a) there is prosecution material which might be reasonably expected to assist the accused's defence as disclosed by the defence statement given under section 5 or 6, and

   (b) the material has not been disclosed to the accused,

the accused may apply to the court for an order requiring the prosecutor to disclose such material to the accused.

(3) For the purposes of this section prosecution material is material—

   (a) which is in the prosecutor's possession and came into his possession in connection with the case for the prosecution against the accused,

   (b) which, in pursuance of a code operative under Part II, he has inspected in connection with the case for the prosecution against the accused, or

   (c) which falls within subsection (4).

(4) Material falls within this subsection if in pursuance of a code operative under Part II the prosecutor must, if he asks for the material, be given a copy of it or be allowed to inspect it in connection with the case for the prosecution against the accused.

(5) Material must not be disclosed under this section to the extent that the court, on an application by the prosecutor, concludes it is not in the public interest to disclose it and orders accordingly.

(6) Material must not be disclosed under this section to the extent that—

   (a) it has been intercepted in obedience to a warrant issued under section 2 of the Interception of Communications Act 1985, or

1985 c. 56.

   (b) it indicates that such a warrant has been issued or that material has been intercepted in obedience to such a warrant.

Continuing duty of prosecutor to disclose.

9.—(1) Subsection (2) applies at all times—

   (a) after the prosecutor complies with section 3 or purports to comply with it, and

   (b) before the accused is acquitted or convicted or the prosecutor decides not to proceed with the case concerned.

(2) The prosecutor must keep under review the question whether at any given time there is prosecution material which—

   (a) in his opinion might undermine the case for the prosecution against the accused, and

   (b) has not been disclosed to the accused;

and if there is such material at any time the prosecutor must disclose it to the accused as soon as is reasonably practicable.

(3) In applying subsection (2) by reference to any given time the state of affairs at that time (including the case for the prosecution as it stands at that time) must be taken into account.

(4) Subsection (5) applies at all times—

   (a) after the prosecutor complies with section 7 or purports to comply with it, and

(b) before the accused is acquitted or convicted or the prosecutor decides not to proceed with the case concerned.

(5) The prosecutor must keep under review the question whether at any given time there is prosecution material which—

    (a) might be reasonably expected to assist the accused's defence as disclosed by the defence statement given under section 5 or 6, and

    (b) has not been disclosed to the accused;

and if there is such material at any time the prosecutor must disclose it to the accused as soon as is reasonably practicable.

(6) For the purposes of this section prosecution material is material—

    (a) which is in the prosecutor's possession and came into his possession in connection with the case for the prosecution against the accused, or

    (b) which, in pursuance of a code operative under Part II, he has inspected in connection with the case for the prosecution against the accused.

(7) Subsections (3) to (5) of section 3 (method by which prosecutor discloses) apply for the purposes of this section as they apply for the purposes of that.

(8) Material must not be disclosed under this section to the extent that the court, on an application by the prosecutor, concludes it is not in the public interest to disclose it and orders accordingly.

(9) Material must not be disclosed under this section to the extent that—

    (a) it has been intercepted in obedience to a warrant issued under section 2 of the Interception of Communications Act 1985, or   1985 c. 56.

    (b) it indicates that such a warrant has been issued or that material has been intercepted in obedience to such a warrant.

10.—(1) This section applies if the prosecutor—   Prosecutor's failure to observe time limits.

    (a) purports to act under section 3 after the end of the period which, by virtue of section 12, is the relevant period for section 3, or

    (b) purports to act under section 7 after the end of the period which, by virtue of section 12, is the relevant period for section 7.

(2) Subject to subsection (3), the failure to act during the period concerned does not on its own constitute grounds for staying the proceedings for abuse of process.

(3) Subsection (2) does not prevent the failure constituting such grounds if it involves such delay by the prosecutor that the accused is denied a fair trial.

11.—(1) This section applies where section 5 applies and the accused—   Faults in disclosure by accused.

    (a) fails to give a defence statement under that section,

    (b) gives a defence statement under that section but does so after the end of the period which, by virtue of section 12, is the relevant period for section 5,

(c) sets out inconsistent defences in a defence statement given under section 5,

(d) at his trial puts forward a defence which is different from any defence set out in a defence statement given under section 5,

(e) at his trial adduces evidence in support of an alibi without having given particulars of the alibi in a defence statement given under section 5, or

(f) at his trial calls a witness to give evidence in support of an alibi without having complied with subsection (7)(a) or (b) of section 5 as regards the witness in giving a defence statement under that section.

(2) This section also applies where section 6 applies, the accused gives a defence statement under that section, and the accused—

(a) gives the statement after the end of the period which, by virtue of section 12, is the relevant period for section 6,

(b) sets out inconsistent defences in the statement,

(c) at his trial puts forward a defence which is different from any defence set out in the statement,

(d) at his trial adduces evidence in support of an alibi without having given particulars of the alibi in the statement, or

(e) at his trial calls a witness to give evidence in support of an alibi without having complied with subsection (7)(a) or (b) of section 5 (as applied by section 6) as regards the witness in giving the statement.

(3) Where this section applies—

(a) the court or, with the leave of the court, any other party may make such comment as appears appropriate;

(b) the court or jury may draw such inferences as appear proper in deciding whether the accused is guilty of the offence concerned.

(4) Where the accused puts forward a defence which is different from any defence set out in a defence statement given under section 5 or 6, in doing anything under subsection (3) or in deciding whether to do anything under it the court shall have regard—

(a) to the extent of the difference in the defences, and

(b) to whether there is any justification for it.

(5) A person shall not be convicted of an offence solely on an inference drawn under subsection (3).

(6) Any reference in this section to evidence in support of an alibi shall be construed in accordance with section 5.

Time limits

Time limits.

12.—(1) This section has effect for the purpose of determining the relevant period for sections 3, 5, 6 and 7.

(2) Subject to subsection (3), the relevant period is a period beginning and ending with such days as the Secretary of State prescribes by regulations for the purposes of the section concerned.

(3) The regulations may do one or more of the following—

(a) provide that the relevant period for any section shall if the court so orders be extended (or further extended) by so many days as the court specifies;

(b) provide that the court may only make such an order if an application is made by a prescribed person and if any other prescribed conditions are fulfilled;

(c) provide that an application may only be made if prescribed conditions are fulfilled;

(d) provide that the number of days by which a period may be extended shall be entirely at the court's discretion;

(e) provide that the number of days by which a period may be extended shall not exceed a prescribed number;

(f) provide that there shall be no limit on the number of applications that may be made to extend a period;

(g) provide that no more than a prescribed number of applications may be made to extend a period;

and references to the relevant period for a section shall be construed accordingly.

(4) Conditions mentioned in subsection (3) may be framed by reference to such factors as the Secretary of State thinks fit.

(5) Without prejudice to the generality of subsection (4), so far as the relevant period for section 3 or 7 is concerned—

(a) conditions may be framed by reference to the nature or volume of the material concerned;

(b) the nature of material may be defined by reference to the prosecutor's belief that the question of non-disclosure on grounds of public interest may arise.

(6) In subsection (3) "prescribed" means prescribed by regulations under this section.

13.—(1) As regards a case in relation to which no regulations under section 12 have come into force for the purposes of section 3, section 3(8) shall have effect as if it read— *Time limits: transitional.*

"(8) The prosecutor must act under this section as soon as is reasonably practicable after—

(a) the accused pleads not guilty (where this Part applies by virtue of section 1(1)),

(b) the accused is committed for trial (where this Part applies by virtue of section 1(2)(a)),

(c) the proceedings are transferred (where this Part applies by virtue of section 1(2)(b) or (c)),

(d) the count is included in the indictment (where this Part applies by virtue of section 1(2)(d)), or

(e) the bill of indictment is preferred (where this Part applies by virtue of section 1(2)(e))."

(2) As regards a case in relation to which no regulations under section 12 have come into force for the purposes of section 7, section 7(7) shall have effect as if it read—

"(7) The prosecutor must act under this section as soon as is reasonably practicable after the accused gives a defence statement under section 5 or 6."

Public interest

Public interest: review for summary trials.

14.—(1) This section applies where this Part applies by virtue of section 1(1).

(2) At any time—

  (a) after a court makes an order under section 3(6), 7(5), 8(5) or 9(8), and

  (b) before the accused is acquitted or convicted or the prosecutor decides not to proceed with the case concerned,

the accused may apply to the court for a review of the question whether it is still not in the public interest to disclose material affected by its order.

(3) In such a case the court must review that question, and if it concludes that it is in the public interest to disclose material to any extent—

  (a) it shall so order, and

  (b) it shall take such steps as are reasonable to inform the prosecutor of its order.

(4) Where the prosecutor is informed of an order made under subsection (3) he must act accordingly having regard to the provisions of this Part (unless he decides not to proceed with the case concerned).

Public interest: review in other cases.

15.—(1) This section applies where this Part applies by virtue of section 1(2).

(2) This section applies at all times—

  (a) after a court makes an order under section 3(6), 7(5), 8(5) or 9(8), and

  (b) before the accused is acquitted or convicted or the prosecutor decides not to proceed with the case concerned.

(3) The court must keep under review the question whether at any given time it is still not in the public interest to disclose material affected by its order.

(4) The court must keep the question mentioned in subsection (3) under review without the need for an application; but the accused may apply to the court for a review of that question.

(5) If the court at any time concludes that it is in the public interest to disclose material to any extent—

  (a) it shall so order, and

  (b) it shall take such steps as are reasonable to inform the prosecutor of its order.

(6) Where the prosecutor is informed of an order made under subsection (5) he must act accordingly having regard to the provisions of this Part (unless he decides not to proceed with the case concerned).

16. Where—

(a) an application is made under section 3(6), 7(5), 8(5), 9(8), 14(2) or 15(4),

(b) a person claiming to have an interest in the material applies to be heard by the court, and

(c) he shows that he was involved (whether alone or with others and whether directly or indirectly) in the prosecutor's attention being brought to the material,

the court must not make an order under section 3(6), 7(5), 8(5), 9(8), 14(3) or 15(5) (as the case may be) unless the person applying under paragraph (b) has been given an opportunity to be heard.

Confidentiality

17.—(1) If the accused is given or allowed to inspect a document or other object under—

(a) section 3, 4, 7, 9, 14 or 15, or

(b) an order under section 8,

then, subject to subsections (2) to (4), he must not use or disclose it or any information recorded in it.

(2) The accused may use or disclose the object or information—

(a) in connection with the proceedings for whose purposes he was given the object or allowed to inspect it,

(b) with a view to the taking of further criminal proceedings (for instance, by way of appeal) with regard to the matter giving rise to the proceedings mentioned in paragraph (a), or

(c) in connection with the proceedings first mentioned in paragraph (b).

(3) The accused may use or disclose—

(a) the object to the extent that it has been displayed to the public in open court, or

(b) the information to the extent that it has been communicated to the public in open court;

but the preceding provisions of this subsection do not apply if the object is displayed or the information is communicated in proceedings to deal with a contempt of court under section 18.

(4) If—

(a) the accused applies to the court for an order granting permission to use or disclose the object or information, and

(b) the court makes such an order,

the accused may use or disclose the object or information for the purpose and to the extent specified by the court.

(5) An application under subsection (4) may be made and dealt with at any time, and in particular after the accused has been acquitted or convicted or the prosecutor has decided not to proceed with the case concerned; but this is subject to rules made by virtue of section 19(2).

(6) Where—

(a) an application is made under subsection (4), and

(b) the prosecutor or a person claiming to have an interest in the object or information applies to be heard by the court,

the court must not make an order granting permission unless the person applying under paragraph (b) has been given an opportunity to be heard.

(7) References in this section to the court are to—

(a) a magistrates' court, where this Part applies by virtue of section 1(1);

(b) the Crown Court, where this Part applies by virtue of section 1(2).

(8) Nothing in this section affects any other restriction or prohibition on the use or disclosure of an object or information, whether the restriction or prohibition arises under an enactment (whenever passed) or otherwise.

Confidentiality: contravention.

18.—(1) It is a contempt of court for a person knowingly to use or disclose an object or information recorded in it if the use or disclosure is in contravention of section 17.

(2) The following courts have jurisdiction to deal with a person who is guilty of a contempt under this section—

(a) a magistrates' court, where this Part applies by virtue of section 1(1);

(b) the Crown Court, where this Part applies by virtue of section 1(2).

(3) A person who is guilty of a contempt under this section may be dealt with as follows—

(a) a magistrates' court may commit him to custody for a specified period not exceeding six months or impose on him a fine not exceeding £5,000 or both;

(b) the Crown Court may commit him to custody for a specified period not exceeding two years or impose a fine on him or both.

(4) If—

(a) a person is guilty of a contempt under this section, and

(b) the object concerned is in his possession,

the court finding him guilty may order that the object shall be forfeited and dealt with in such manner as the court may order.

(5) The power of the court under subsection (4) includes power to order the object to be destroyed or to be given to the prosecutor or to be placed in his custody for such period as the court may specify.

(6) If—

(a) the court proposes to make an order under subsection (4), and

(b) the person found guilty, or any other person claiming to have an interest in the object, applies to be heard by the court,

the court must not make the order unless the applicant has been given an opportunity to be heard.

(7) If—

(a) a person is guilty of a contempt under this section, and

(b) a copy of the object concerned is in his possession,

the court finding him guilty may order that the copy shall be forfeited and dealt with in such manner as the court may order.

(8) Subsections (5) and (6) apply for the purposes of subsection (7) as they apply for the purposes of subsection (4), but as if references to the object were references to the copy.

(9) An object or information shall be inadmissible as evidence in civil proceedings if to adduce it would in the opinion of the court be likely to constitute a contempt under this section; and "the court" here means the court before which the civil proceedings are being taken.

(10) The powers of a magistrates' court under this section may be exercised either of the court's own motion or by order on complaint.

Other provisions

19.—(1) Without prejudice to the generality of subsection (1) of—   Rules of court.

    (a) section 144 of the Magistrates' Courts Act 1980 (magistrates'   1980 c. 43.
        court rules), and

    (b) section 84 of the Supreme Court Act 1981 (rules of court),   1981 c. 54.

the power to make rules under each of those sections includes power to make provision mentioned in subsection (2).

(2) The provision is provision as to the practice and procedure to be followed in relation to—

    (a) proceedings to deal with a contempt of court under section 18;

    (b) an application under section 3(6), 7(5), 8(2) or (5), 9(8), 14(2) , 15(4), 16(b), 17(4) or (6)(b) or 18(6);

    (c) an application under regulations made under section 12;

    (d) an order under section 3(6), 7(5), 8(2) or (5), 9(8), 14(3), 17(4) or 18(4) or (7);

    (e) an order under section 15(5) (whether or not an application is made under section 15(4));

    (f) an order under regulations made under section 12.

(3) Rules made under section 144 of the Magistrates' Courts Act 1980 by virtue of subsection (2)(a) above may contain or include provision equivalent to Schedule 3 to the Contempt of Court Act 1981 (proceedings   1981 c. 49. for disobeying magistrates' court order) with any modifications which the Lord Chancellor considers appropriate on the advice of or after consultation with the rule committee for magistrates' courts.

(4) Rules made by virtue of subsection (2)(b) in relation to an application under section 17(4) may include provision—

    (a) that an application to a magistrates' court must be made to a particular magistrates' court;

    (b) that an application to the Crown Court must be made to the Crown Court sitting at a particular place;

    (c) requiring persons to be notified of an application.

(5) Rules made by virtue of this section may make different provision for different cases or classes of case.

20.—(1) A duty under any of the disclosure provisions shall not affect or be affected by any duty arising under any other enactment with regard to material to be provided to or by the accused or a person representing him; but this is subject to subsection (2).

(2) In making an order under section 9 of the Criminal Justice Act 1987 or section 31 of this Act (preparatory hearings) the judge may take account of anything which—

(a) has been done,

(b) has been required to be done, or

(c) will be required to be done,

in pursuance of any of the disclosure provisions.

(3) Without prejudice to the generality of section 144(1) of the Magistrates' Courts Act 1980 (magistrates' court rules) the power to make rules under that section includes power to make, with regard to any proceedings before a magistrates' court which relate to an alleged offence, provision for—

(a) requiring any party to the proceedings to disclose to the other party or parties any expert evidence which he proposes to adduce in the proceedings;

(b) prohibiting a party who fails to comply in respect of any evidence with any requirement imposed by virtue of paragraph (a) from adducing that evidence without the leave of the court.

(4) Rules made by virtue of subsection (3)—

(a) may specify the kinds of expert evidence to which they apply;

(b) may exempt facts or matters of any description specified in the rules.

(5) For the purposes of this section—

(a) the disclosure provisions are sections 3 to 9;

(b) "enactment" includes an enactment comprised in subordinate legislation (which here has the same meaning as in the Interpretation Act 1978).

21.—(1) Where this Part applies as regards things falling to be done after the relevant time in relation to an alleged offence, the rules of common law which—

(a) were effective immediately before the appointed day, and

(b) relate to the disclosure of material by the prosecutor,

do not apply as regards things falling to be done after that time in relation to the alleged offence.

(2) Subsection (1) does not affect the rules of common law as to whether disclosure is in the public interest.

(3) References in subsection (1) to the relevant time are to the time when—

(a) the accused pleads not guilty (where this Part applies by virtue of section 1(1)),

(b) the accused is committed for trial (where this Part applies by virtue of section 1(2)(a))

(c) the proceedings are transferred (where this Part applies by virtue of section 1(2)(b) or (c)),

(d) the count is included in the indictment (where this Part applies by virtue of section 1(2)(d)), or

(e) the bill of indictment is preferred (where this Part applies by virtue of section 1(2)(e)).

(4) The reference in subsection (1) to the appointed day is to the day appointed under section 1(5).

PART II

CRIMINAL INVESTIGATIONS

22.—(1) For the purposes of this Part a criminal investigation is an investigation conducted by police officers with a view to it being ascertained— Introduction.

(a) whether a person should be charged with an offence, or

(b) whether a person charged with an offence is guilty of it.

(2) In this Part references to material are to material of all kinds, and in particular include references to—

(a) information, and

(b) objects of all descriptions.

(3) In this Part references to recording information are to putting it in a durable or retrievable form (such as writing or tape).

23.—(1) The Secretary of State shall prepare a code of practice containing provisions designed to secure— Code of practice.

(a) that where a criminal investigation is conducted all reasonable steps are taken for the purposes of the investigation and, in particular, all reasonable lines of inquiry are pursued;

(b) that information which is obtained in the course of a criminal investigation and may be relevant to the investigation is recorded;

(c) that any record of such information is retained;

(d) that any other material which is obtained in the course of a criminal investigation and may be relevant to the investigation is retained;

(e) that information falling within paragraph (b) and material falling within paragraph (d) is revealed to a person who is involved in the prosecution of criminal proceedings arising out of or relating to the investigation and who is identified in accordance with prescribed provisions;

(f) that where such a person inspects information or other material in pursuance of a requirement that it be revealed to him, and he requests that it be disclosed to the accused, the accused is allowed to inspect it or is given a copy of it;

(g) that where such a person is given a document indicating the nature of information or other material in pursuance of a requirement that it be revealed to him, and he requests that it be disclosed to the accused, the accused is allowed to inspect it or is given a copy of it;

(h) that the person who is to allow the accused to inspect information or other material or to give him a copy of it shall decide which of those (inspecting or giving a copy) is appropriate;

(i) that where the accused is allowed to inspect material as mentioned in paragraph (f) or (g) and he requests a copy, he is given one unless the person allowing the inspection is of opinion that it is not practicable or not desirable to give him one;

(j) that a person mentioned in paragraph (e) is given a written statement that prescribed activities which the code requires have been carried out.

(2) The code may include provision—

(a) that a police officer identified in accordance with prescribed provisions must carry out a prescribed activity which the code requires;

(b) that a police officer so identified must take steps to secure the carrying out by a person (whether or not a police officer) of a prescribed activity which the code requires;

(c) that a duty must be discharged by different people in succession in prescribed circumstances (as where a person dies or retires).

(3) The code may include provision about the form in which information is to be recorded.

(4) The code may include provision about the manner in which and the period for which—

(a) a record of information is to be retained, and

(b) any other material is to be retained;

and if a person is charged with an offence the period may extend beyond a conviction or an acquittal.

(5) The code may include provision about the time when, the form in which, the way in which, and the extent to which, information or any other material is to be revealed to the person mentioned in subsection (1)(e).

(6) The code must be so framed that it does not apply to material intercepted in obedience to a warrant issued under section 2 of the Interception of Communications Act 1985.

1985 c. 56.

(7) The code may—

(a) make different provision in relation to different cases or descriptions of case;

(b) contain exceptions as regards prescribed cases or descriptions of case.

(8) In this section "prescribed" means prescribed by the code.

Examples of disclosure provisions.

24.—(1) This section gives examples of the kinds of provision that may be included in the code by virtue of section 23(5).

(2) The code may provide that if the person required to reveal material has possession of material which he believes is sensitive he must give a document which—

(a) indicates the nature of that material, and

(b) states that he so believes.

(3) The code may provide that if the person required to reveal material has possession of material which is of a description prescribed under this subsection and which he does not believe is sensitive he must give a document which—

    (a) indicates the nature of that material, and

    (b) states that he does not so believe.

(4) The code may provide that if—

    (a) a document is given in pursuance of provision contained in the code by virtue of subsection (2), and

    (b) a person identified in accordance with prescribed provisions asks for any of the material,

the person giving the document must give a copy of the material asked for to the person asking for it or (depending on the circumstances) must allow him to inspect it.

(5) The code may provide that if—

    (a) a document is given in pursuance of provision contained in the code by virtue of subsection (3),

    (b) all or any of the material is of a description prescribed under this subsection, and

    (c) a person is identified in accordance with prescribed provisions as entitled to material of that description,

the person giving the document must give a copy of the material of that description to the person so identified or (depending on the circumstances) must allow him to inspect it.

(6) The code may provide that if—

    (a) a document is given in pursuance of provision contained in the code by virtue of subsection (3),

    (b) all or any of the material is not of a description prescribed under subsection (5), and

    (c) a person identified in accordance with prescribed provisions asks for any of the material not of that description,

the person giving the document must give a copy of the material asked for to the person asking for it or (depending on the circumstances) must allow him to inspect it.

(7) The code may provide that if the person required to reveal material has possession of material which he believes is sensitive and of such a nature that provision contained in the code by virtue of subsection (2) should not apply with regard to it—

    (a) that provision shall not apply with regard to the material,

    (b) he must notify a person identified in accordance with prescribed provisions of the existence of the material, and

    (c) he must allow the person so notified to inspect the material.

(8) For the purposes of this section material is sensitive to the extent that its disclosure under Part I would be contrary to the public interest.

(9) In this section "prescribed" means prescribed by the code.

PART II
Operation and
revision of code.

25.—(1) When the Secretary of State has prepared a code under section 23—

(a) he shall publish it in the form of a draft,

(b) he shall consider any representations made to him about the draft, and

(c) he may modify the draft accordingly.

(2) When the Secretary of State has acted under subsection (1) he shall lay the code before each House of Parliament, and when he has done so he may bring it into operation on such day as he may appoint by order.

(3) A code brought into operation under this section shall apply in relation to suspected or alleged offences into which no criminal investigation has begun before the day so appointed.

(4) The Secretary of State may from time to time revise a code previously brought into operation under this section; and the preceding provisions of this section shall apply to a revised code as they apply to the code as first prepared.

Effect of code.

26.—(1) A person other than a police officer who is charged with the duty of conducting an investigation with a view to it being ascertained—

(a) whether a person should be charged with an offence, or

(b) whether a person charged with an offence is guilty of it,

shall in discharging that duty have regard to any relevant provision of a code which would apply if the investigation were conducted by police officers.

(2) A failure—

(a) by a police officer to comply with any provision of a code for the time being in operation by virtue of an order under section 25, or

(b) by a person to comply with subsection (1),

shall not in itself render him liable to any criminal or civil proceedings.

(3) In all criminal and civil proceedings a code in operation at any time by virtue of an order under section 25 shall be admissible in evidence.

(4) If it appears to a court or tribunal conducting criminal or civil proceedings that—

(a) any provision of a code in operation at any time by virtue of an order under section 25, or

(b) any failure mentioned in subsection (2)(a) or (b),

is relevant to any question arising in the proceedings, the provision or failure shall be taken into account in deciding the question.

Common law
rules as to
criminal
investigations.

27.—(1) Where a code prepared under section 23 and brought into operation under section 25 applies in relation to a suspected or alleged offence, the rules of common law which—

(a) were effective immediately before the appointed day, and

(b) relate to the matter mentioned in subsection (2),

shall not apply in relation to the suspected or alleged offence.

(2) The matter is the revealing of material—

(a) by a police officer or other person charged with the duty of conducting an investigation with a view to it being ascertained whether a person should be charged with an offence or whether a person charged with an offence is guilty of it;

(b) to a person involved in the prosecution of criminal proceedings.

(3) In subsection (1) "the appointed day" means the day appointed under section 25 with regard to the code as first prepared.

PART III

PREPARATORY HEARINGS

Introduction

28.—(1) This Part applies in relation to an offence if—

Introduction.

(a) on or after the appointed day the accused is committed for trial for the offence concerned,

(b) proceedings for the trial on the charge concerned are transferred to the Crown Court on or after the appointed day, or

(c) a bill of indictment relating to the offence is preferred on or after the appointed day under the authority of section 2(2)(b) of the Administration of Justice (Miscellaneous Provisions) Act 1933 (bill preferred by direction of Court of Appeal, or by direction or with consent of a judge).

1933 c. 36.

(2) References in subsection (1) to the appointed day are to such day as is appointed for the purposes of this section by the Secretary of State by order.

(3) If an order under this section so provides, this Part applies only in relation to the Crown Court sitting at a place or places specified in the order.

(4) References in this Part to the prosecutor are to any person acting as prosecutor, whether an individual or a body.

Preparatory hearings

29.—(1) Where it appears to a judge of the Crown Court that an indictment reveals a case of such complexity, or a case whose trial is likely to be of such length, that substantial benefits are likely to accrue from a hearing—

Power to order preparatory hearing.

(a) before the jury are sworn, and

(b) for any of the purposes mentioned in subsection (2),

he may order that such a hearing (in this Part referred to as a preparatory hearing) shall be held.

(2) The purposes are those of—

(a) identifying issues which are likely to be material to the verdict of the jury;

(b) assisting their comprehension of any such issues;

(c) expediting the proceedings before the jury;

(d) assisting the judge's management of the trial.

(3) No order may be made under subsection (1) where it appears to a judge of the Crown Court that the evidence on an indictment reveals a

case of fraud of such seriousness or complexity as is mentioned in section 7(1) of the Criminal Justice Act 1987 (preparatory hearings in cases of serious or complex fraud).

(4) A judge may make an order under subsection (1)—

    (a) on the application of the prosecutor,

    (b) on the application of the accused or, if there is more than one, any of them, or

    (c) of the judge's own motion.

30. If a judge orders a preparatory hearing—

    (a) the trial shall start with that hearing, and

    (b) arraignment shall take place at the start of that hearing, unless it has taken place before then.

31.—(1) At the preparatory hearing the judge may exercise any of the powers specified in this section.

(2) The judge may adjourn a preparatory hearing from time to time.

(3) He may make a ruling as to—

    (a) any question as to the admissibility of evidence;

    (b) any other question of law relating to the case.

(4) He may order the prosecutor—

    (a) to give the court and the accused or, if there is more than one, each of them a written statement (a case statement) of the matters falling within subsection (5);

    (b) to prepare the prosecution evidence and any explanatory material in such a form as appears to the judge to be likely to aid comprehension by the jury and to give it in that form to the court and to the accused or, if there is more than one, to each of them;

    (c) to give the court and the accused or, if there is more than one, each of them written notice of documents the truth of the contents of which ought in the prosecutor's view to be admitted and of any other matters which in his view ought to be agreed;

    (d) to make any amendments of any case statement given in pursuance of an order under paragraph (a) that appear to the judge to be appropriate, having regard to objections made by the accused or, if there is more than one, by any of them.

(5) The matters referred to in subsection (4)(a) are—

    (a) the principal facts of the case for the prosecution;

    (b) the witnesses who will speak to those facts;

    (c) any exhibits relevant to those facts;

    (d) any proposition of law on which the prosecutor proposes to rely;

    (e) the consequences in relation to any of the counts in the indictment that appear to the prosecutor to flow from the matters falling within paragraphs (a) to (d).

(6) Where a judge has ordered the prosecutor to give a case statement and the prosecutor has complied with the order, the judge may order the accused or, if there is more than one, each of them—

    (a) to give the court and the prosecutor a written statement setting out in general terms the nature of his defence and indicating the principal matters on which he takes issue with the prosecution;

    (b) to give the court and the prosecutor written notice of any objections that he has to the case statement;

    (c) to give the court and the prosecutor written notice of any point of law (including any point as to the admissibility of evidence) which he wishes to take, and any authority on which he intends to rely for that purpose.

(7) Where a judge has ordered the prosecutor to give notice under subsection (4)(c) and the prosecutor has complied with the order, the judge may order the accused or, if there is more than one, each of them to give the court and the prosecutor a written notice stating—

    (a) the extent to which he agrees with the prosecutor as to documents and other matters to which the notice under subsection (4)(c) relates, and

    (b) the reason for any disagreement.

(8) A judge making an order under subsection (6) or (7) shall warn the accused or, if there is more than one, each of them of the possible consequence under section 34 of not complying with it.

(9) If it appears to a judge that reasons given in pursuance of subsection (7) are inadequate, he shall so inform the person giving them and may require him to give further or better reasons.

(10) An order under this section may specify the time within which any specified requirement contained in it is to be complied with.

(11) An order or ruling made under this section shall have effect throughout the trial, unless it appears to the judge on application made to him that the interests of justice require him to vary or discharge it.

32.—(1) This section applies where—   *Orders before preparatory hearing.*

    (a) a judge orders a preparatory hearing, and

    (b) he decides that any order which could be made under section 31(4) to (7) at the hearing should be made before the hearing.

(2) In such a case—

    (a) he may make any such order before the hearing (or at the hearing), and

    (b) section 31(4) to (11) shall apply accordingly.

33.—(1) Crown Court Rules may provide that except to the extent that   *Crown Court Rules.* disclosure is required—

    (a) by rules under section 81 of the Police and Criminal Evidence   *1984 c. 60.* Act 1984 (expert evidence), or

(b) by section 5(7) of this Act,

anything required to be given by an accused in pursuance of a requirement imposed under section 31 need not disclose who will give evidence.

(2) Crown Court Rules may make provision as to the minimum or maximum time that may be specified under section 31(10).

Later stages of trial.

34.—(1) Any party may depart from the case he disclosed in pursuance of a requirement imposed under section 31.

(2) Where—

(a) a party departs from the case he disclosed in pursuance of a requirement imposed under section 31, or

(b) a party fails to comply with such a requirement,

the judge or, with the leave of the judge, any other party may make such comment as appears to the judge or the other party (as the case may be) to be appropriate and the jury may draw such inference as appears proper.

(3) In deciding whether to give leave the judge shall have regard—

(a) to the extent of the departure or failure, and

(b) to whether there is any justification for it.

(4) Except as provided by this section no part—

(a) of a statement given under section 31(6)(a), or

(b) of any other information relating to the case for the accused or, if there is more than one, the case for any of them, which was given in pursuance of a requirement imposed under section 31,

may be disclosed at a stage in the trial after the jury have been sworn without the consent of the accused concerned.

Appeals

Appeals to Court of Appeal.

35.—(1) An appeal shall lie to the Court of Appeal from any ruling of a judge under section 31(3), but only with the leave of the judge or of the Court of Appeal.

(2) The judge may continue a preparatory hearing notwithstanding that leave to appeal has been granted under subsection (1), but no jury shall be sworn until after the appeal has been determined or abandoned.

(3) On the termination of the hearing of an appeal, the Court of Appeal may confirm, reverse or vary the decision appealed against.

1981 c. 54.

(4) Subject to rules of court made under section 53(1) of the Supreme Court Act 1981 (power by rules to distribute business of Court of Appeal between its civil and criminal divisions)—

(a) the jurisdiction of the Court of Appeal under subsection (1) above shall be exercised by the criminal division of the court;

(b) references in this Part to the Court of Appeal shall be construed as references to that division.

Appeals to House of Lords.
1968 c. 19.

36.—(1) In the Criminal Appeal Act 1968, in—

(a) section 33(1) (right of appeal to House of Lords), and

    (b) section 36 (bail),

after "1987" there shall be inserted "or section 35 of the Criminal Procedure and Investigations Act 1996".

(2) The judge may continue a preparatory hearing notwithstanding that leave to appeal has been granted under Part II of the Criminal Appeal Act 1968, but no jury shall be sworn until after the appeal has been determined or abandoned.

APPENDIX 11

The rules of court

STATUTORY INSTRUMENTS

1997 No. 705 (L.11)

MAGISTRATES' COURTS

The Magistrates' Courts (Advance Notice of
Expert Evidence) Rules 1997

Made   *10th March 1997*

Laid before Parliament   *11th March 1997*

Coming into force   *1st April 1997*

The Lord Chancellor, in exercise of the powers conferred on him by section 144 of the Magistrates' Courts Act 1980(**a**) and section 20(3) and (4) of the Criminal Procedure and Investigations Act 1996(**b**), and after consultation with the Rule Committee appointed under the said section 144, hereby makes the following Rules:

1. These Rules may be cited as the Magistrates' Courts (Advance Notice of Expert Evidence) Rules 1997 and shall come into force on 1st April 1997.

2. These Rules shall not have effect in relation to any proceedings which relate to an alleged offence into which a criminal investigation has begun before 1st April 1997.

3.— (1)   Where a magistrates' court proceeds to summary trial in respect of an alleged offence and the person charged with that offence pleads not guilty in respect of it, if any party to the proceedings proposes to adduce expert evidence (whether of fact or opinion) in the proceedings (otherwise than in relation to sentence) he shall as soon as practicable after the person charged has so pleaded, unless in relation to the evidence in question he has already done so—

> (a)   furnish the other party or parties with a statement in writing of any finding or opinion which he proposes to adduce by way of such evidence; and

> (b)   where a request in writing is made to him in that behalf by any other party, provide that party also with a copy of (or if it appears to the party proposing to adduce the evidence to be more practicable, a reasonable opportunity to examine) the record of any observation, test, calculation or other procedure on which such finding or opinion is based and any document or other thing or substance in respect of which any such procedure has been carried out.

(**a**) 1980 c.43.
(**b**) 1996 c.25

(2)   A party may by notice in writing waive his right to be furnished with any of the matters mentioned in paragraph (1) above and, in particular, may agree that the statement mentioned in sub-paragraph (a) thereof may be furnished to him orally and not in writing.

(3)   In paragraph (1) above, 'document' means anything in which information of any description is recorded.

4.—   (1)   If a party has reasonable grounds for believing that the disclosure of any evidence in compliance with the requirements imposed by rule 3 above might lead to the intimidation, or attempted intimidation, of any person on whose evidence he intends to rely in the proceedings, or otherwise to the course of justice being interfered with, he shall not be obliged to comply with those requirements in relation to that evidence.

(2) Where, in accordance with paragraph (1) above, a party considers that he is not obliged to comply with the requirements imposed by rule 3 above with regard to any evidence in relation to any other party, he shall give notice in writing to that party to the effect that the evidence is being withheld and the grounds therefor.

5. A party who seeks to adduce expert evidence in any proceedings and who fails to comply with rule 3 above shall not adduce that evidence in those proceedings without the leave of the court.

Dated 10th March 1997   Mackay of Clashfern   C

EXPLANATORY NOTE

(This note is not part of the Rules)

These Rules provide for mutual disclosure of expert evidence between parties to proceedings for the summary trial of an offence where the person charged with the offence pleads not guilty.

Rule 3 requires a party to disclose any expert evidence which he proposes to adduce as soon as practicable after the plea is taken. Rule 3(1)(b) enables a party to examine the basis of any findings or opinions proposed to be adduced by way of expert evidence by another party. Rule 4 provides for a party to withhold any matter where he has reasonable grounds for suspecting that its disclosure might lead to intimidation or the course of justice being interfered with. In such a case the party is required to give to the other party notice in writing, which must include the grounds on which disclosure is being withheld. By Rule 5 a party who fails to comply with rule 3 in respect of any evidence may not adduce that evidence without the leave of the court.

The Rules, by virtue of rule 1, come into force on 1st April 1997 and, by virtue of rule 2, have effect in relation to proceedings for an offence into which no criminal investigation has begun before that date.

STATUTORY INSTRUMENTS

1997 No. 684

CRIMINAL LAW, ENGLAND AND WALES

The Criminal Procedure and Investigations Act 1996
(Defence Disclosure Time Limits) Regulations 1997

Made   *8th March 1997*

Laid before Parliament   *11th March 1997*

Coming into force   *1st April 1997*

The Secretary of State, in pursuance of sections 12 and 77(2) and (4) of the Criminal Procedure and Investigations Act 1996(**a**), hereby makes the following Regulations:

1.— (1)   These Regulations may be cited as the Criminal Procedure and Investigations Act 1996 (Defence Disclosure Time Limits) Regulations 1997 and shall come into force on 1st April 1997.

(2)   These Regulations extend to England and Wales only.

(3)   In these Regulations, the expression 'the Act' means the Criminal Procedure and investigations Act 1996.

2. Subject to regulations 3, 4 and 5, the relevant period for sections 5 and 6 of the Act 3 (disclosure by the accused) is a period beginning with the day on which the prosecutor complies, or purports to comply, with section 3 of that Act and ending with the expiration of 14 days from that day.

3.— (1)   The period referred to in regulation 2 shall, if the court so orders, be extended by so many days as the court specifies.

(2)   The court may only make such an order if an application which complies with paragraph (3) below is made by the accused before the expiration of the period referred to in regulation 2.

(3)   An application under paragraph (2) above shall—

(a)   state that the accused believes, on reasonable grounds, that it is not possible for him to give a defence statement under section 5 or, as the case may be, 6 of the Act during the period referred to in regulation 2;

(b)   specify the grounds for so believing; and

(**a**) 1996 c.25.

(c)   specify the number of days by which the accused wishes that period to be extended.

(4)   The court shall not make an order under paragraph (1) above unless it is satisfied that the accused cannot reasonably give or, as the case may be, could not reasonably have given a defence statement under section 5 or, as the case may be, 6 of the Act during the period referred to in regulation 2.

(5)   The number of days by which the period referred to in regulation 2 may be extended shall be entirely at the court's discretion.

4.— (1)   Where the court has made an order under regulation 3(1), the period referred to in regulation 2 as extended in accordance with that order shall, if the court so orders, be further extended by so many days as the court specifies.

(2)   Paragraphs (2) to (5) of regulation 3 shall, subject to paragraph (4) below, apply for the purposes of an order under paragraph (1) above as they apply for the purposes of an order under regulation 3(1).

(3)   There shall be no limit on the number of applications that may be made under regulation 3(2) as applied by paragraph (2) above; and on a second or subsequent such application the court shall have the like powers under paragraph (1) above as on the first such application.

(4)   In the application of regulation 3(2) to (5) in accordance with paragraph (2) above, any reference to the period referred to in regulation 2 shall be construed as a reference to that period as extended or, as the case may be, further extended by an order of the court under regulation 3(1) or paragraph (1) or (3) above.

5.— (1)   Where the period referred to in regulation 2 or that period as extended or, as the case may be, further extended by an order of the court under regulation 3(1) or 4(1) or (3) would, apart from this regulation, expire on any of the days specified in paragraph (2) below, that period shall be treated as expiring on the next following day which is not one of those days.

(2)   The days referred to in paragraph (1) above are Saturday, Sunday, Christmas Day, Good Friday and any day which under the Banking and Financial Dealings Act 1971(**a**) is a bank holiday in England and Wales.

Home Office   Michael Howard
                     One of Her Majesty's Principal Secretaries of State
8th March 1997

(**a**) 1971 c.80.

EXPLANATORY NOTE

(This note is not part of the Regulations)

These Regulations which extend to England and Wales only, prescribe the relevant period for sections 5 and 6 of the Criminal Procedure and Investigations Act 1996 ('the 1996 Act') (which relate respectively to compulsory and voluntary disclosure by the accused in criminal proceedings).

Regulation 2 prescribes the day when the prosecutor complies with section 3 of the 1996 Act (primary disclosure by prosecutor) as the beginning, and the expiration of 14 days after that day as the end, of the relevant period for disclosure by the accused, whether compulsory or voluntary.

Regulation 3 provides for the extension of that period by the court, on application by the accused, if the court is satisfied that the accused could not reasonably have acted within the period prescribed by regulation 2. There is no limit on the number of days by which the period may be extended.

Regulation 4 provides for further extensions of that period subject to similar conditions.

Regulation 5 provides for periods which end on specified days such as bank holidays and weekends to be extended so as to expire on the next day which is not one of those specified days.

No period is prescribed in these Regulations for section 3 or 7 of the 1996 Act (which relate to prosecution disclosure); the relevant periods for those sections are therefore governed by section 13 of the 1996 Act (transitional provisions).

STATUTORY INSTRUMENTS

1997 No. 703 (L.9)

MAGISTRATES' COURTS

The Magistrates' Courts (Criminal Procedure and Investigations Act 1996) (Disclosure) Rules 1997

Made	*10th March 1997*
Laid before Parliament	*11th March 1997*
Coming into force	*1st April 1997*

The Lord Chancellor, in exercise of the powers conferred upon him by section 144 of the Magistrates' Courts Act 1980(**a**) and section 19 of the Criminal Procedure and Investigations Act 1996(**b**), and after consultation with the Rule Committee appointed under the said section 144, hereby makes the following Rules:

Commencement, citation and interpretation

1.— (1) These Rules may be cited as the Magistrates' Courts (Criminal Procedure and Investigations Act 1996) (Disclosure) Rules 1997 and shall come into force on 1st April 1997.

(2) In these Rules any reference to a numbered section or Part is a reference to the section or Part so numbered in the Criminal Procedure and Investigations Act 1996.

Public interest: application by prosecutor

2.— (1) This rule applies to the making of an application by the prosecutor under section 3(6), 7(5), 8(5) or 9(8) where Part I applies by virtue of section 1(1) (summary trial).

(2) Notice of an application to which this rule applies shall be served on the clerk of the magistrates' court trying the offence referred to in section 1(1) and shall specify the nature of the material to which the application relates.

(3) Subject to paragraphs (4) and (5) below, a copy of the notice of application shall be served on the accused by the prosecutor.

(4) Where the prosecutor has reason to believe that to reveal to the accused the nature of the material to which the application relates would have the effect of disclosing that which the prosecutor contends should not in the public interest be disclosed, paragraph (3) above shall not apply but the prosecutor shall notify the accused that an application to which this rule applies has been made.

(a) 1980 c.43.
(b) 1996 c.25.

(5)   Where the prosecutor has reason to believe that to reveal to the accused the fact that an application is being made would have the effect of disclosing that which the prosecutor contends should not in the public interest be disclosed, paragraph (3) above shall not apply.

Public interest: hearing of application by prosecutor

3.— (1)   This rule applies to the hearing of an application by the prosecutor under section 3(6), 7(5), 8(5) or 9(8) where Part I applies by virtue of section 1(1).

(2)   Subject to paragraph (3) below and to rule 6(4), where a copy of the notice of application has been served on the accused in accordance with rule 2(3)-

> (a)   the clerk of the court shall give notice to—
>
> > (i)   the prosecutor;
> >
> > (ii)   the accused; and
> >
> > (iii) any person claiming to have an interest in the material to which the application relates who has applied under section 16(b) to be heard by the court,
>
> of the date and time when and the place where the hearing will take place and, unless the court orders otherwise, such notice shall be given in writing;
>
> (b)   the hearing shall be *inter partes*; and
>
> (c)   the prosecutor and the accused shall be entitled to make representations to the court.

(3)   Where the prosecutor applies to the court for leave to make representations in the absence of the accused, the court may for that purpose sit in the absence of the accused and any legal representative of his.

(4)   Subject to rule 6(4), where a copy of the notice of application has not been served on the accused in accordance with rule 2(3)-

> (a)   the hearing shall be *ex parte*;
>
> (b)   only the prosecutor shall be entitled to make representations to the court; and
>
> (c)   the accused shall not be given notice as specified in paragraph (2) above.

Public interest: non-disclosure order

4.— (1)   This rule applies to an order under section 3(6), 7(5), 8(5) or 9(8).

(2)   On making an order to which this rule applies, the court shall state its reasons for doing so.

(3)   In a case where such an order is made following—

(a)   an application to which rule 2(4) applies, or

(b)   an application notice of which has been served on the accused in accordance with rule 2(3) but the accused has not appeared or been represented at the hearing of that application,

the clerk of the court shall notify the accused that an order has been made.

Review of non-disclosure order: application by accused

5.— (1)   This rule applies to an application by the accused under section 14(2).

(2)   An application to which this rule applies shall be made by notice in writing to the clerk of the magistrates' court trying the offence referred to in section 1(1) and shall specify the reason why the accused believes the court should review the question mentioned in section 14(2).

(3)   A copy of the notice referred to in paragraph (2) above shall be served on the prosecutor at the same time as it is sent to the clerk of the court.

(4)   On receipt of an application to which this rule applies the clerk of the court shall take such steps as he thinks fit to ensure that the court determining the application has before it any document or other material which was available to the court which made the order mentioned in section 14(2).

(5)   Subject to paragraphs (6) to (8) below and to rule 6(4), the hearing of an application to which this rule applies shall be *inter partes* and the accused and the prosecutor shall be entitled to make representations to the court.

(6)   Where the court considers that there are no grounds on which it might conclude that it is in the public interest to disclose material to any extent it may determine the application without hearing representations from the accused, the prosecutor or any person claiming to have an interest in the material to which the application relates.

(7)   Where after hearing the accused's representations the prosecutor applies to the court for leave to make representations in the absence of the accused, the court may for that purpose sit in the absence of the accused and any legal representative of his.

(8)   Subject to rule 6(4), where the order to which the application relates was made following an application of which the accused was not notified under rule

655

2(3) or (4), the hearing shall be *ex parte* and only the prosecutor shall be entitled to make representations to the court.

    (9)   The clerk of the court shall give notice in writing to—

        (a)   the prosecutor;

        (b)   except where a hearing takes place in accordance with paragraph (8) above, the accused; and

        (c)   any person claiming to have an interest in the material to which the application relates who has applied under section 16(b) to be heard by the court,

of the date and time when and the place where the hearing of an application to which this rule applies will take place and of any order which is made by the court following its determination of the application.

Applications: interested persons

    6.—   (1)   Where the prosecutor has reason to believe that a person who was involved (whether alone or with others and whether directly or indirectly) in the prosecutor's attention being brought to any material to which an application under section 3(6), 7(5), 8(5), 9(8) or 14(2) relates may claim to have an interest in that material, the prosecutor shall—

        (a)   in the case of an application under section 3(6), 7(5), 8(5) or 9(8), at the same time as notice of the application is served under rule 2(2),

        (b)   in the case of an application under section 14(2), when he receives a copy of the notice referred to in rule 5(2),

give notice in writing to—

        (i)   the person concerned of the application, and

        (ii)   the clerk of the court of his belief and the grounds for it.

    (2)   An application under section 16(b) shall be made by notice in writing to the clerk of the court as soon as is reasonably practicable after receipt of notice under paragraph (1)(i) above or, if no such notice is received, after the person concerned becomes aware of the application referred to in that sub-paragraph and shall specify the nature of the applicant's interest in the material and his involvement in bringing the material to the prosecutor's attention.

    (3)   A copy of the notice referred to in paragraph (2) above shall be served on the prosecutor at the same time as it is sent to the clerk of the court.

    (4)   At the hearing of an application under section 3(6), 7(5), 8(5), 9(8) or 14(2) a person who has made an application under section 16(b) in accordance with paragraph (2) above shall be entitled to make representations to the court.

Disclosure: application by accused and order of court

7.— (1)   This rule applies to an application by the accused under section 8(2).

(2)   An application to which this rule applies shall be made by notice in writing to the clerk of the court and shall specify—

    (a)   the material to which the application relates;

    (b)   that the material has not been disclosed to the accused;

    (c)   the reason why the material might be expected to assist the applicant's defence as disclosed by the defence statement given under section 6; and

    (d)   the date of service of a copy of the notice on the prosecutor in accordance with paragraph (3) below.

(3)   A copy of the notice referred to in paragraph (2) above shall be served on the prosecutor at the same time as it is sent to the clerk of the court.

(4)   The prosecutor shall give notice in writing to the clerk of the court within 14 days of service of a notice under paragraph (3) above that—

    (a)   he wishes to make representations to the court concerning the material to which the application relates; or

    (b)   if he does not so wish, that he is willing to disclose that material;

and a notice under sub-paragraph (a) above shall specify the substance of the representations he wishes to make.

(5)   Subject to paragraphs (6) and (7) below—

    (a)   the clerk of the court shall give notice in writing to the prosecutor and the applicant of the date and time when and the place where the hearing will take place;

    (b)   the hearing shall be *inter partes*; and

    (c)   the prosecutor and the applicant shall be entitled to make representations to the court.

(6)   The court may determine the application without hearing representations from the applicant or the prosecutor unless—

    (a)   the prosecutor has given notice under paragraph (4)(a) above and the court considers that the representations should be made at a hearing; or

(b)   the court considers it necessary to hear representations from the applicant or the prosecutor in the interests of justice for the purposes of determining the application.

(7)   Where the prosecutor applies to the court for leave to make representations in the absence of the accused, the court may for that purpose sit in the absence of the accused and any legal representative of his.

(8)   A copy of any order under section 8(2) shall be served on the prosecutor and the applicant.

Disclosure: application for extension of time limit and order of the court

8.— (1)   This rule applies to an application under paragraph (2) of regulation 3 of the Criminal Procedure and Investigations Act 1996 (Defence Disclosure Time Limits) Regulations 1997(**a**) ('the 1997 Regulations'), including that paragraph as applied by regulation 4(2) of the 1997 Regulations.

(2)   An application to which this rule applies shall be made by notice in writing to the clerk of the court and shall, in addition to the matters referred to in paragraphs (a) to (c) of regulation 3(3) of the 1997 Regulations, specify the date of service of a copy of the notice on the prosecutor in accordance with paragraph (3) below.

(3)   A copy of the notice referred to in paragraph (2) above shall be served on the prosecutor at the same time as it is sent to the clerk of the court.

(4)   The prosecutor may make representations to the court concerning the application and if he wishes to do so he shall do so in writing within 14 days of service of a notice under paragraph (3) above.

(5)   On receipt of representations under paragraph (4) above, or on the expiration of the period specified in that paragraph if no such representations are received within that period, the court shall consider the application and may, if it wishes, do so at a hearing.

(6)   Where a hearing is held in pursuance of this rule—

(a)   the clerk of the court shall give notice in writing to the prosecutor and the applicant of the date and time when and the place where the hearing will take place;

(b)   the hearing shall be *inter partes*; and

(c)   the prosecutor and the applicant shall be entitled to make representations to the court.

(7)   A copy of any order under regulation 3(1) or 4(1) of the 1997 Regulations shall be served on the prosecutor and the applicant.

(**a**) S.I. 1997 No. 684.

General

9.— (1)   Any hearing held in pursuance of or in accordance with these Rules may be adjourned from time to time.

(2)   Any hearing referred to in paragraph (1) above other than one held in pursuance of rule 8 may be held in private.

Dated 10th March 1997   Mackay of Clashfern   C

EXPLANATORY NOTE

(This note is not part of the Rules)

These Rules provide for the practice and procedure to be followed in magistrates' courts in relation to—

(a)   applications under sections 3(6), 7(5), 8(2) and (5), 9(8), 14(2) and 16(b) of the Criminal Procedure and Investigations Act 1996 ('the 1996 Act');

(b)   applications under the Criminal Procedure and investigations Act 1996 (Defence Disclosure Time Limits) Regulations 1997 ('the 1997 Regulations');

(c)   orders under sections 3(6), 7(5), 8(2) and (5) and 9(8) of the 1996 Act;

(d)   orders under section 14(3) of the 1996 Act; and

(e)   orders under the 1997 Regulations.

STATUTORY INSTRUMENTS

1997 No. 698 (L.4)

SUPREME COURT OF ENGLAND AND WALES

The Crown Court (Criminal Procedure and Investigation Act 1996)
(Disclosure) Rules 1997

Made   *10th March 1997*

Laid before Parliament   *11th March 1997*

Coming into force   *1st April 1997*

We, the Crown Court Rule Committee, in exercise of the powers conferred upon us by sections 84(1) and 86 of the Supreme Court Act 1981(**a**) and section 19 of the Criminal Procedure and Investigations Act 1996(**b**), hereby make the following Rules:

Commencement, citation and interpretation

    1.— (1)   These Rules may be cited as the Crown Court (Criminal Procedure and Investigations Act 1996) (Disclosure) Rules 1997 and shall come into force on 1st April 1997.

    (2)   In these Rules—

        'the Act of 1996' means the Criminal Procedure and Investigations Act 1996;

        and

        'the start of the trial' and cognate expressions shall be construed in accordance with section 39(3) of the Act of 1996;

and any reference to a numbered section or Part is a reference to the section or Part so numbered in the Act of 1996.

Public interest: application by prosecutor

    2.— (1)   This rule applies to the making of an application by the prosecutor under section 3(6), 7(5), 8(5) or 9(8) where Part I applies by virtue of section 1(2) (trial on indictment).

(**a**) 1981 c.54; section 86 was amended by paragraph 36(2) of Schedule 18 to the Courts and Legal Services Act 1990 (c.41).
(**b**) 1996 c.25.

(2)   Subject to paragraphs (3) to (5) below, notice of an application to which this rule applies shall be served on the appropriate officer of the Crown Court and on the accused and shall specify the nature of the material to which the application relates.

(3)   Where the prosecutor has reason to believe that to reveal to the accused the nature of the material to which the application relates would have the effect of disclosing that which the prosecutor contends should not in the public interest be disclosed, paragraph (2) above shall have effect as if the words from 'and shall specify' to the end were omitted.

(4) Where the prosecutor has reason to believe that to reveal to the accused the fact that an application is being made would have the effect of disclosing that which the prosecutor contends should not in the public interest be disclosed, paragraph (2) above shall have effect as if the words from 'and on the accused' to the end were omitted.

(5) Where an application to which this rule applies is made under paragraph (2) above as it has effect in accordance with paragraph (4) above, notice of the application may be served on the trial judge or, if the application is made before the start of the trial, on the judge, if any, who has been designated to conduct the trial instead of on the appropriate officer of the court.

Public interest: hearing of application by prosecutor

3.—   (1)   This rule applies to the hearing of an application by the prosecutor under section 3(6), 7(5), 8(5) or 9(8) where Part I applies by virtue of section 1(2).

(2)   On receipt of an application to which this rule applies the appropriate officer of the Crown Court shall refer it—

    (a)   if the trial has started, to the trial judge, or

    (b)   if the application is received before the start of the trial either—

        (i)   to the judge who has been designated to conduct the trial, or

        (ii)   if no judge has been designated for that purpose, to such judge as may be designated for the purposes of hearing the application.

(3)   Subject to paragraphs (4) and (5) below and to rule 6(4), where the application is made in accordance with rule 2(2)—

    (a)   the appropriate officer of the Crown Court shall give notice to—

        (i)   the prosecutor;

        (ii)   the accused; and

(iii) any person claiming to have an interest in the material to which the application relates who has applied under section 16(b) to be heard by the court,

of the date and time when and the place where the hearing will take place and, unless the court orders otherwise, such notice shall be given in writing;

(b) the hearing shall be *inter partes*; and

(c) the prosecutor and the accused shall be entitled to make representations to the court.

(4)   Where the prosecutor applies to the court for leave to make representations in the absence of the accused, the court may for that purpose sit in the absence of the accused and any legal representative of his.

(5)   Subject to rule 6(4), where the application is made under rule 2(2) as it has effect in accordance with rule 2(3) or (4)—

(a) the hearing shall be *ex parte*;

(b) only the prosecutor shall be entitled to make representations to the court; and

(c) the accused shall not be given notice as specified in paragraph (3) above;

and, where notice of the application has been served in pursuance of rule 2(5), the judge on whom it is served shall take such steps as he considers appropriate to ensure that notice is given as required by paragraph (3)(a)(i) and (iii) above.

Public interest: non-disclosure order

4.— (1)   This rule applies to an order under section 3(6), 7(5), 8(5) or 9(8).

(2)   On making an order to which this rule applies, the court shall state its reasons for doing so and a record shall be made of that statement.

(3)   In a case where such an order is made following—

(a) an application which has been made under rule 2(2) as it has effect in accordance with rule 2(3), or

(b) an application which has been made in accordance with rule 2(2) but the accused has not appeared or been represented at the hearing of that application,

the appropriate officer of the Crown Court shall notify the accused that an order has been made:

Provided that no notification shall be given under this paragraph in a case where an order is made following an application which has been made under rule 2(2) as it has effect in accordance with rule 2(4).

Review of non-disclosure order: application by accused

5.— (1) This rule applies to an application by the accused under section 15(4).

(2) An application to which this rule applies shall be made by notice in writing to the appropriate officer of the Crown Court and shall specify the reason why the accused believes the court should review the question mentioned in section 15(3).

(3) A copy of the notice referred to in paragraph (2) above shall be served on the prosecutor at the same time as it is sent to the appropriate officer of the court.

(4) On receipt of an application to which this rule applies the appropriate officer of the Crown Court shall refer it—

  (a) if the trial has started, to the trial judge, or

  (b) if the application is received before the start of the trial either—

   (i) to the judge who has been designated to conduct the trial, or

   (ii) if no judge has been designated for that purpose, to the judge who made the order to which the application relates.

(5) The judge to whom an application to which this rule applies has been referred under paragraph (4) above shall consider whether the application may be determined without a hearing and, subject to paragraph (6) below, may so determine it if he thinks fit.

(6) No application to which this rule applies shall be determined without a hearing if it appears to the judge that there are grounds on which the court might conclude that it is in the public interest to disclose material to any extent.

(7) Subject to paragraphs (8) and (9) below and to rule 6(4), the hearing of an application to which this rule applies shall be *inter partes* and the accused and the prosecutor shall be entitled to make representations to the court.

(8) Where after hearing the accused's representations the prosecutor applies to the court for leave to make representations in the absence of the accused, the court may for that purpose sit in the absence of the accused and any legal representative of his.

(9) Subject to rule 6(4), where the order to which the application relates was made following an application which was made under rule 2(2) as it has effect in

accordance with rule 2(4), the hearing shall be *ex parte* and only the prosecutor shall be entitled to make representations to the court.

    (10)   The appropriate officer of the court shall give notice in writing to—

        (a)   the prosecutor;

        (b)   except where a hearing takes place in accordance with paragraph (9) above, the accused; and

        (c)   any person claiming to have an interest in the material to which the application relates who has applied under section 16(b) to be heard by the court,

of the date and time when and the place where the hearing of an application to which this rule applies will take place and of any order which is made by the court following its determination of the application.

    (11)   Where an application to which this rule applies is determined without a hearing in pursuance of paragraph (5) above, the appropriate officer of the court shall give notice in writing in accordance with paragraph (10) above of any order which is made by the judge following his determination of the application.

Applications: interested persons

    6.—   (1)   Where the prosecutor has reason to believe that a person who was involved (whether alone or with others and whether directly or indirectly) in the prosecutor's attention being brought to any material to which an application under section 3(6), 7(5), 8(5), 9(8) or 15(4) relates may claim to have an interest in that material, the prosecutor shall—

        (a)   in the case of an application under section 3(6), 7(5), 8(5) or 9(8), at the same time as notice of the application is served under rule 2(2) or (5),

        (b)   in the case of an application under section 15(4), when he receives a copy of the notice referred to in rule 5(2),

give notice in writing to—

        (i)   the person concerned of the application, and

        (ii)   the appropriate officer of the Crown Court or, as the case may require, the judge of his belief and the grounds for it.

    (2)   An application under section 16(b) shall be made by notice in writing to the appropriate officer of the Crown Court or, as the case may require, the judge as soon as is reasonably practicable after receipt of notice under paragraph (1)(i) above or, if no such notice is received, after the person concerned becomes aware of the application referred to in that sub-paragraph and shall specify the nature of the applicant's interest in the material and his involvement in bringing the material to the prosecutor's attention.

(3)   A copy of the notice referred to in paragraph (2) above shall be served on the prosecutor at the same time as it is sent to the appropriate officer of the court or the judge.

(4)   At the hearing of an application under section 3(6), 7(5), 8(5), 9(8) or 15(4) a person who has made an application under section 16(b) in accordance with paragraph (2) above shall be entitled to make representations to the court.

Disclosure: application by accused and order of court

7.— (1)   This rule applies to an application by the accused under section 8(2).

(2)   An application to which this rule applies shall be made by notice in writing to the appropriate officer of the Crown Court and shall specify—

(a)   the material to which the application relates;

(b)   that the material has not been disclosed to the accused;

(c)   the reason why the material might be expected to assist the applicant's defence as disclosed by the defence statement given under section 5; and

(d)   the date of service of a copy of the notice on the prosecutor in accordance with paragraph (3) below.

(3)   A copy of the notice referred to in paragraph (2) above shall be served on the prosecutor at the same time as it is sent to the appropriate officer of the court.

(4)   On receipt of an application to which this rule applies, the appropriate officer of the Crown Court shall refer it—

(a)   if the trial has started, to the trial judge, or

(b)   if the application is received before the start of the trial—

(i)   to the judge who has been designated to conduct the trial, or

(ii)   if no judge has been designated for that purpose, to such judge as may be designated for the purposes of determining the application.

(5)   The judge to whom an application to which this rule applies has been referred under paragraph (4) above shall consider whether the application may be determined without a hearing and, subject to paragraph (7) below, may so determine it if he thinks fit.

(6)   The prosecutor shall give notice in writing to the appropriate officer of the court within 14 days of service of a notice under paragraph (3) above that—

665

(a)   he wishes to make representations to the court concerning the material to which the application relates; or

(b)   if he does not so wish, that he is willing to disclose that material;

and a notice under sub-paragraph (a) above shall specify the substance of the representations he wishes to make.

(7)   No application to which this rule applies shall be determined without a hearing if—

(a)   the prosecutor has given notice under paragraph (6)(a) above and the judge to whom the application has been referred considers that the representations should be made at a hearing; or

(b)   that judge considers a hearing to be necessary in the interests of justice for the purposes of determining the application.

(8)   Subject to paragraph (9) below, where a hearing is held in pursuance of this rule—

(a)   the appropriate officer of the court shall give notice in writing to the prosecutor and the applicant of the date and time when and the place where the hearing will take place;

(b)   the hearing shall be *inter partes*; and

(c)   the prosecutor and the applicant shall be entitled to make representations to the court.

(9)   Where the prosecutor applies to the court for leave to make representations in the absence of the accused, the court may for that purpose sit in the absence of the accused and any legal representative of his.

(10)   A copy of any order under section 8(2) shall be served on the prosecutor and the applicant.

Disclosure: application for extension of time limit and order of the court

8.—   (1)   This rule applies to an application under paragraph (2) of regulation 3 of the Criminal Procedure and Investigations Act 1996 (Defence Disclosure Time Limits) Regulations 1997**(a)** ('the 1997 Regulations'), including that paragraph as applied by regulation 4(2) of the 1997 Regulations.

(2)   An application to which this rule applies shall be made by notice in writing to the appropriate officer of the Crown Court and shall, in addition to the matters referred to in paragraphs (a) to (c) of regulation 3(3) of the 1997 Regulations, specify the date of service of a copy of the notice on the prosecutor in accordance with paragraph (3) below.

(a) S.I. 1997

(3)   A copy of the notice referred to in paragraph (2) above shall be served on the prosecutor at the same time as it is sent to the appropriate officer of the court.

(4)   The prosecutor may make representations to the court concerning the application and if he wishes to do so he shall do so in writing within 14 days of service of a notice under paragraph (3) above.

(5)   On receipt of representations under paragraph (4) above, or on the expiration of the period specified in that paragraph if no such representations are received within that period, the court shall consider the application and may, if it wishes, do so at a hearing.

(6)   Where a hearing is held in pursuance of this rule—

   (a)   the appropriate officer of the court shall give notice in writing to the prosecutor and the applicant of the date and time when and the place where the hearing will take place;

   (b)   the hearing shall be *inter partes*; and

   (c)   the prosecutor and the applicant shall be entitled to make representations to the court.

(7)   A copy of any order under regulation 3(1) or 4(1) of the 1997 Regulations shall be served on the prosecutor and the applicant.

General

9.—   (1)   Any hearing held in pursuance of or in accordance with these Rules may be adjourned from time to time.

(2)   Any hearing referred to in paragraph (1) above other than one held in pursuance of rule 8 may be held in private.

(3)   Where a hearing, or any part thereof, is held in private in pursuance of paragraph (2) above, the court may specify conditions subject to which the record of its statement of reasons made in pursuance of rule 4(2) is to be kept.

(4)   Where an application or order to which any provision of these Rules applies is made after the start of the trial, the trial judge may direct that any provision of these Rules requiring notice of the application or order to be given to any person shall not have effect and may give such directions as to the giving of notice in relation to that application or order as he thinks fit.

Dated 10th March 1997

Mackay of Clashfern C
Bingham of Cornhill C.J.

EXPLANATORY NOTE

(This note is not part of the Rules)

These Rules provide for the practice and procedure to be followed in the Crown Court in relation to—

(a) applications under sections 3(6), 7(5), 8(2) and (5), 9(8), 15(4) and 16(b) of the Criminal Procedure and Investigations Act 1996 ('the 1996 Act');

(b) applications under the Criminal Procedure and investigations Act 1996 (Defence Disclosure Time Limits) Regulations 1997 ('the 1997 Regulations');

(c) orders under sections 3(6), 7(5), 8(2) and (5) and 9(8) of the 1996 Act;

(d) orders under section 15(5) of the 1996 Act; and

(e) orders under the 1997 Regulations.

APPENDIX 12

Preparation of defence case statements – guidance on the duties of counsel

General Council of the Bar
Professional Conduct and Complaints Committee

The Preparation of Defence Case Statements Pursuant to the
Criminal Procedure and Investigations Act 1996

Guidance on the Duties of Counsel
(As approved by the PCCC on 24th September 1997)

1. It is becoming increasingly common for solicitors to instruct counsel to draft or settle defence case statements, required under section 5 of the Criminal Procedure and Investigations Act 1996. Often these instructions are given to counsel with no or little previous involvement in the case shortly before the expiry of the time limit.

2. The relevant legislation is set out at § 12–82 *et seq.* of the 1997 edition of Archbold. In summary, however:

(i) the time limit for compliance is short – 14 days from service of prosecution material or a statement that there is none. The permitted grounds for an extension of time are limited[1];

(ii) the contents of the defence case statement are obviously of great importance to the defendant. An inaccurate or inadequate statement of the defence could have serious repercussions for the defendant, if the trial judge permits 'appropriate' comment;

(iii) whilst it will be the natural instinct of most defence counsel to keep the defence case statement short, a short and anodyne statement may be insufficient to trigger any obligation on the prosecution to give secondary disclosure of prosecution material.

3. Normally it will be more appropriate for instructing solicitors to draft the defence case statement, since typically counsel will have had little involvement at this stage.

---

[1]See the Defence Disclosure Time Limit Regulations 1997 made pursuant to the Act: Archbold Supplement § 12-93.

4. However, there is nothing unprofessional about counsel drafting or settling a defence case statement, although it must be appreciated that there is no provision in the current regulations for graduated fees allowing for counsel to be paid a separate fee for this work. This most unsatisfactory situation (which has arisen, as a result of the 1996 Act, since the graduated fees regulations were negotiated) is being addressed urgently by the Fees and Legal Aid Committee. A barrister has no obligation to accept work for which he will not be paid. The absence of a fee will justify refusal of the instructions by counsel who are not to be retained for the trial and are simply asked to do no more than draft or settle the defence case statement. Where counsel is retained for the trial, Rule 502(b) of the Code of Conduct deems instructions in a legally aided matter to be at a proper fee and counsel would not be justified in refusing to draft or settle a defence case statement on the sole ground that there is no separate fee payable for this work.

5. Many members of the Bar will nevertheless feel that, in the interests of their lay client and/or of good relations with instructing solicitors, they cannot refuse the work, even where they would otherwise be entitled to do so. Those who do so need to recognise the crucial importance of:

(i) obtaining all prosecution statements and documentary exhibits;

(ii) getting instructions from the lay client, from a properly signed proof and preferably a conference. Those instructions need to explain the general nature of the defence, to indicate the matters on which issue is taken with the prosecution and to give an explanation of the reason for taking issue. They must also give details of any alibi defence, sufficient to give the information required by section 5(7) of the 1996 Act;

(iii) getting statements from other material witnesses;

(iv) ensuring that the client realises the importance of the defence case statement and the potential adverse consequences of an inaccurate or inadequate statement;

(v) getting proper *informed* approval for the draft from the client. This is particularly important, given the risks of professional embarrassment if the client seeks to disown the statement during the course of the trial, perhaps when the trial is not going well or when under severe pressure in cross-examination. Counsel ought to insist on getting written acknowledgement from the lay client that:

(a) he understands the importance of the accuracy and adequacy of the defence case statement for his case;

(b) he has had the opportunity of considering the contents of the statement carefully and approves it.

This may often mean having a conference with the lay client to explain the defence case statement and to get informed approval, although in straightforward cases where counsel has confidence in the instructing solicitor, this could be left to the solicitor. Where this latter course is taken, a short written advice (which can be in a standard form) as to the importance of obtaining the written acknowledgement *before* service of the statement should accompany the draft defence case statement. A careful record should be kept of work done and advice given;

(vi) if there is inadequate time, counsel should ask the instructing solicitor to apply for an extension of time. This needs to be considered at a very early stage, since the application must be made *before* the expiry of the time limit.

6. It follows that counsel ought not to accept any instructions to draft or settle a defence case statement unless given the opportunity and adequate time to gain proper familiarity with the case and to comply with the fundamental requirements set out above. In short, there is no halfway house. If instructions are accepted, then the professional obligations on counsel are considerable.

Index